# THE
# ANATOMY
## OF THE
# NUREMBERG
# TRIALS

*A Personal Memoir*

## TELFORD TAYLOR

Skyhorse Publishing

The International Military Tribunal in session, summer 1946. *National Archives*

Skyhorse Publishing books may be purchased in bulk at special
discounts for sales promotion, corporate gifts, fund-raising, or
educational purposes. Special editions can also be created to
specifications. For details, contact the Special Sales Department,
Skyhorse Publishing, 307 West 36th Street, 11th Floor, New York, NY
10018 or info@skyhorsepublishing.com.

Skyhorse® and Skyhorse Publishing® are registered trademarks of
Skyhorse Publishing, Inc.®, a Delaware corporation.

Visit our website at www.skyhorsepublishing.com.

10 9

Library of Congress Cataloging-in-Publication Data is available on file.

ISBN: 978-1-62087-788-3

Printed in China

*To Toby Golick*

# Contents

Introduction      *ix*

*Chapter 1*    Nuremberg and the Laws of War     3

*Chapter 2*    The Nuremberg Ideas     21

*Chapter 3*    Justice Jackson Takes Over     43

*Chapter 4*    Establishing the Court: The London Charter     56

*Chapter 5*    The Defendants and the Charges: Krupp and the German General Staff     78

*Chapter 6*    Berlin to Nuremberg     116

*Chapter 7*    Nuremberg: Pretrial Pains and Problems     129

*Chapter 8*    On Trial     165

*Chapter 9*    The Nuremberg War Crimes Community     208

*Chapter 10*    The SS and the General Staff–High Command     236

*Chapter 11*    Individual Defendants, Future Trials, and Criminal Organizations     262

*Chapter 12*    The French and Soviet Prosecutions     293

*Chapter 13*    The Defendants: Goering and Hess     319

# Contents

| | | |
|---|---|---|
| Chapter 14 | The Defendants: "Murderers' Row" | 351 |
| Chapter 15 | The Defendants: Bankers and Admirals | 381 |
| Chapter 16 | The Defendants: The Last Nine | 417 |
| Chapter 17 | The Closing Arguments | 473 |
| Chapter 18 | The Indicted Organizations | 501 |
| Chapter 19 | The Defendants' Last Words | 534 |
| Chapter 20 | The Judgments of Solomons | 546 |
| Chapter 21 | Judgment: Law, Crime, and Punishment | 571 |
| Chapter 22 | Epilogue and Assessment | 612 |
| | Appendices | 643 |
| | Source Notes | 655 |
| | Bibliography | 677 |
| | Index | 683 |

Photographs follow pages 130 and 354.

# Introduction

In the spring of 1945, I was a reserve colonel in the intelligence branch of the United States Army. My duties had to do with information derived from the deciphering of enemy messages, the product of which in recent years has become publicly known as "Ultra" or "Magic." My base of operations was in southern England, but I had been given general responsibility for the security of Ultra and its distribution to the principal American army and air headquarters in Western Europe, and this required frequent trips to the Continent.

By April, it had become apparent that the Third Reich was in its death throes and that a total Allied military victory in Europe was imminent. Accordingly, early that month I embarked on what I expected to be, and was, the last of my circuits around the commands that we were servicing. On about April 20, en route to General Patton's headquarters at Erlangen in northern Bavaria, I drove through nearby Nuremberg, where I had never been before.

Little of its famed beauty was to be seen. The city had been heavily bombed by the Royal Air Force in January and March and taken, only after heavy fighting during the past few days, by General Wade Haislip's XV Corps. Most of the city lay in ruins, parts were still burning, and the streets were so choked with rubble that I could hardly get through.

Returning to England a week later, I was met at the airfield by my colleague Lieutenant Colonel Ted Hilles (in peacetime a distinguished professor of English literature at Yale), bringing a message to me from my superiors at the War Department in Washington. Its burden was that Robert H. Jackson, Associate Justice of the Supreme Court of the United States, had been appointed by President Truman to represent the United States as chief prosecutor at a projected international trial of "war criminals," to be held as soon as possible after the victorious end of hostilities. The message went on to say that Justice Jackson was assembling a legal staff to assist him and had asked that the War Department make me available for that purpose.

The tone of the message suggested that the departmental authorities would be pleased if I acceded to the Justice's request, but it was made clear that the decision was up to me. The proposition gave me plenty to think about, both professionally and personally.

I had graduated from Harvard Law School in 1932 and during the next ten years had held a succession of federal government legal positions. In 1939 and 1940 I had served briefly as a Special Assistant to the Attorney General. During those years Jackson had been Attorney General until his appointment to the Supreme Court. I had met him a few times, heard him argue several cases, and had myself argued one case before the Supreme Court after Jackson had become a member. I was well aware of and shared the high opinion of his character and ability which was generally held. He was a man under whom I would be proud to serve, and I had no doubt that his mission would be a unique and challenging one.

On the other hand, nothing in my legal education or experience had involved international law in general or war crimes in particular; to me it was unknown territory. Furthermore, I had not given "law" a thought since going into the army in 1942, and my military duties had taken me far afield from cases and courts. I had never been in private practice and had intended, upon leaving the army, to return to New York to get some badly needed experience in the private sector and develop an independent footing as a lawyer. At the age of thrity-seven, this was a step which should not be long postponed.

As for the military side of the matter, it was plain that the Germans would surrender in a few days and that my own mission in Europe was as good as finished. But the war against Japan was not, and it was feared that a massive invasion of the Japanese mainland might be necessary to bring about a surrender. Many of the senior American officers, particularly the regulars, were anticipating reassignment to the Pacific theater. I myself had expected that I would soon be recalled to the Pentagon building and perhaps sent to the "other war." I had no idea how near Japan was to defeat or whether there was a place for me in the Pacific intelligence structure. But I was somewhat reluctant to get out of uniform until the war as a whole was over, and therefore I decided to ask permission to return to Washington before making a final decision about Jackson's invitation.

Personal feelings and problems moved me in the same direction. My marital situation was in disarray in consequence of an intense relationship with a young Englishwoman who was married to a British officer of my acquaintance. Returning to my home in Washington might at least ease immediate tensions and allow time to try to sort things out.

The Pentagon readily approved my request, so I said my farewells in England and flew to Washington, arriving home about May 22. During the next few days I visited Jackson's staff headquarters and discussed the situation in the Pacific theater with my superiors in the intelligence division, particularly with Colonel Alfred McCormack, in peacetime a law partner of John J. McCloy, the Assistant Secretary of War. I knew that McCormack was as well informed and otherwise equipped as anyone to assess the prospects of the war against Japan. Whether or not he was in on the secret of the atom bomb I do not know, but he told me categorically that the Japanese military situation was hopeless, that the Emperor's advisers knew it, and that intercepted Japanese diplomatic messages revealed their anxiety to make peace. He thought it highly unlikely that an invasion of the Japanese mainland would be necessary or that the war would last much longer.

As for me, McCormack said that if I wanted an assignment in the Pacific, no doubt that could be arranged, but that there was no real necessity for it. I should feel entirely free to leave the intelligence division and go with Jackson, or (since I had been on overseas duty for two years and was eligible for immediate discharge) to private law practice, as I saw fit.

I had been home less than a week and already felt restless. The war had not subjected me to much danger, but the exposure to a rapidly changing succession of new places, people, and problems had been exhilarating and, in many ways, rewarding. Europe was obviously on the verge of enormous change, and it would be interesting to be at the scene. I knew that before long I ought to repatriate myself and settle down to a more stable and less peripatetic life, but I simply did not feel ready for it.

And so I decided to accept Justice Jackson's invitation and went back to his staff offices in the Pentagon and signed on. The unforeseen consequence was that I spent nearly four years in Nuremberg, the ravaged city that I had passed through five weeks earlier.

My decision to join Jackson's staff was not influenced by any expertise or special interest in the laws of war or international law, none of which I possessed. Nor was it governed by expectations of professional advancement, although I knew that the projected trial would be a major and unique affair which might bring me some publicity. But the wiser course professionally would have been to get out of uniform and into traditional legal work as soon as possible.

Certainly I was not moved by vengeful or anti-German feelings. To be sure, I detested Nazism and had been in Germany a few weeks earlier when the Dachau and Buchenwald concentration camps were captured and the inmates liberated by American troops. But like so many others, I remained ignorant of the mass extermination camps in Poland, and the full scope of the Holocaust did not dawn on me until several months later, at Nuremberg. I am not Jewish and had, as far as I knew, no relations or close friends on the European continent. In pre-Nazi times, I had greatly enjoyed travel in Germany and Austria.

Accordingly, I think it would be fair to say that my decision had virtually nothing to do with the subject matter of Jackson's mission and that I would probably have joined any other attractive American undertaking in postwar Europe. My motivation was derived from my personal circumstances and was, in a word, selfish.

It follows that my initial adherence to the Jackson mission was not a passionate commitment. This was, indeed, a limiting factor on my effectiveness, at least during the first year of my Nuremberg tenure. But now I may at least hope that this aloofness, if so it may be called, has fostered balance and accuracy in the description and judgments presented in this memoir.

In the course of the first Nuremberg trial it became apparent that the evidence had disclosed numerous important Nazis, military leaders, and others who could best be tried by civilian tribunals. In the autumn of 1945 it was decided that later trials of such defendants would also be held at Nuremberg, and eventually twelve such trials, presided over by American judges applying international laws of war, were held during the years 1946–1949.

I was appointed Chief of Counsel for War Crimes to serve as chief prosecutor of these cases, and I hope later to write a description of these subsequent trials, which involved many defendants, problems, and decisions quite different from those of the first Nuremberg trial.

In the preparation of the present account of the first Nuremberg trial, I am deeply indebted to the Columbia Law School; to Jonathan Segal, my editor at Alfred A. Knopf; to Robert Wolfe, of the National Archives; to Nancy Demmon, of the Columbia Law School, for excellent secretarial assistance; and for helpful counsel to Peter Calvocoressi, Herbert Wechsler, and my wife, Toby Golick.

*The*
*Anatomy*
*of the*
*Nuremberg*
*Trials*

# Chapter 1

# NUREMBERG AND
# THE LAWS OF WAR

The plan of this book is to record a personal memoir of the creation of the International Military Tribunal (IMT) and of war crimes trials held in Nuremberg from 1945 to 1946. I might have written about Nuremberg twenty-five or more years ago, when my own and others' memories were sharper. I had found time to write other books, so I can hardly plead lack of time or opportunity. My disinclination was partly a desire to put my mind at a distance from the subject that had engrossed me for four years and to turn my energies in other directions. More influential, however, was a belief that my sense and assessment of Nuremberg as a whole would benefit from the passage of time, opportunity for reflection, and the illumination that subsequent events might shed upon the past of which Nuremberg was a part.

The delay has in one respect complicated my task. In 1945 and for fifteen to twenty years thereafter, the reading public in the Western world knew a good deal about the structure and record of the Third Reich and the names of its leading personalities—Hitler, Goering, Goebbels, Ribbentrop, Himmler, among others—were household words. Today that is no longer the case; much more by way of historical context is necessary to make such a narrative meaningful for the new generations. The events of the Nazi era were the stuff of the Nuremberg trials. Indeed, one recent and competent book about Nuremberg devotes as much space to what happened in those years as to the course of events in the Nuremberg courtroom. Since my main purpose is to tell the story of Nuremberg, I have struck a different balance, in which the history of Hitler's Reich is in the background and the focus is on the trials and their legal and political underpinnings.

I have described this book as a "personal memoir" because it will portray Nuremberg as I saw, heard, and otherwise sensed it at the time and not as a detached historian working from the documents might picture it. And apart from the legal and moral questions stirred by the Nuremberg ideas and judgments, I have sought to convey an impression of the Nuremberg participants as a community—an enclave geographically and socially—of the many and varied people crowded into the enclave and following a semicolonial life-style while they wrestled with the professional and personal problems that pressed upon them.

I have titled my book *The Anatomy of the Nuremberg Trials* because it will embrace much more than the events which took place in open court. This was a complex trial which sought to break new legal ground on major issues of international law.

To be sure, at the time of the trials the defendants were the main focus of public attention, and the press was full of commentary on their personalities, their comparative degrees of guilt, and the fairness of the tribunals' judgments. But the defendants and their fates were not the reason why Nuremberg has remained a bench mark in international law and the lodestar of thought and debate on the great moral and legal questions of war and peace.

Some twenty-five years ago, widespread controversy arose over the meaning of Nuremberg vis-à-vis the Vietnam War. Secretary of State Dean Rusk invoked Nuremberg to justify American military intervention, but thousands of young men contended, to the contrary, that under the Nuremberg principles they were legally bound not to participate in what they regarded as the United States' aggressive war.

The Nuremberg which is remembered and invoked today is Nuremberg as a source and test of the international law of war. While there are many who deny Nuremberg's validity as a source, they are far outweighed by the nations, international institutions, and people who have accepted Nuremberg's validity or at least look to it for precedent and guidance. There are no permanently established means of enforcing the Nuremberg principles, and they are often flouted, but as a moral and legal statement, clothed with judicial precedent and United Nations recognition, the Nuremberg principles are an international legal force to be reckoned with.

The ideas which led to the expanded principles of the Nuremberg trials were largely developed by a group of New York lawyers during the autumn and winter of 1944–45, most notably by Henry L. Stimson, John J. McCloy, Murray Bernays, William C. Chanler, Samuel Rosenman, Robert H. Jackson, and (though we do not usually think of him as a lawyer) President Franklin Delano Roosevelt.

Initially and, in my view most important, was the decision of Stimson, then Secretary of War, to pass over the military courts-martial generally used for the trial of military crimes and establish an international court. On September 9, 1944, he wrote to the President: "I am disposed to believe that at least as to the chief Nazi officials, we should participate in an international tribunal constituted to try them." The result was the unprecedented creation of the International Military Tribunal, the most important and, I believe, successful new entity in the enforcement of the laws of war.

The trial, and the judgment of the Tribunal, were of course the public capstone of the Nuremberg enterprise. The subject matter, the notoriety of the defendants, and the caliber of some of the witnesses brought about many sensational and shocking revelations. I remember the stunned silence of the audience that followed the SS officer Otto Ohlendorf's cold, impassive statement that, in southern Russia, his troops had rounded up and killed some 90,000 Jews. And I remember the sheer panic of the defendant Walter Funk, formerly President of the Reichsbank (German State Bank), when prosecutor Thomas Dodd, cross-examining, suddenly produced, and put into evidence, documents showing that Funk well knew that the Reichsbank was receiving jewels and other valuables, including gold teeth, which had been taken from the bodies of Jews and other inmates of concentration camps.

But what law was the International Military Tribunal enforcing? Ordinary courts and trials are based on the statutes of sovereign nations. However, the IMT was no ordinary court. It was established by the United States and three major European nations, and the laws by which the IMT was bound were not the laws of any of those or of any other nations. For its rules on crime the IMT looked primarily to the international "laws of war," violations of which are called "war crimes."

Ask the passerby what the words "war crimes" bring to his mind, and the chances are that the reply will be "Nuremberg." This may be a deserved acknowledgment of the seat of the most famous war crimes trials, but it also fosters the wholly mistaken notion that the Nuremberg trials were the original source of the "laws of war." And in order to understand the anatomy of the Nuremberg trials, it is necessary, first, to know something of the nature and scope of the laws of war before and during World War II and, second, to see what additions to the already existing laws of war those who were building the IMT sought to make.

The root circumstances which gave rise to the laws of war as we know them today are part of the great waves of change that swept Western civilization in the eighteenth and nineteenth centuries, including the decline of the Church and the Holy Roman Empire and the rise of nation-states as the main repositories of temporal power, the Industrial Revolution, and the Age of Enlightenment. Humanitarianism played a part in the development of these laws, but the prime motivations were commercial and military. They were, in fact, very largely the product of what Dwight Eisenhower, when retiring from the presidency, called the "military-industrial complex."

Changes in the "art" of war were the most immediate cause for the customs and practices, limiting the means and manners of warfare, which later turned into rules and then laws. From feudal times until well into the seventeenth century, "armies" were composed largely of mercenaries, whose pay was intermittent and who, for lack of a regular supply service, had to "live off the country." This was devastating both to the effectiveness of the armies and to the economy of nearby farms and towns. Soldiers were brutalized and undisciplined. The Thirty Years War (1618–1648) left much of Europe a shambles; it is estimated that over half the German-speaking population was wiped out, and famine and pestilence were widespread.

From these disastrous years, military lessons were learned. Soldiers who were regularly fed and paid, and who did not have to forage for food and shelter, could be disciplined and trained to a pitch of efficiency that greatly raised the tactical level of operations. Troops were organized under a regular chain of command, in battalions, regiments, and other standard units. Administrative staffs handled supplies, pay, and other logistical necessities. Military police helped enforce discipline, and procedures something like courts-martial were established to punish offenders.°

Thus soldiering became a profession, and the distinction between soldier and civilian was stabilized. And so were born the customs and rules governing the conduct of occupying troops, requiring respect for the lives and livelihoods of the civilian inhabitants, as long as they remained non-combatants.

These rules form a major segment of the laws of war today, but of course at the time of their origin they were not thought of as "international law,"† but merely as sensible military regulations. Their consequences in practical application were humane and fitted well with the libertarian and humanitarian ideas of the philosophers and publicists of the eighteenth-century Enlightenment—the era of thinkers such as Bentham in England, and in France Voltaire and in particular Jean-Jacques Rousseau. In Rousseau's opinion, warfare was legitimate only in defense against an aggressor's attack—a principle very close to those embodied today in the Charter of the United Nations. In his most famous writing, *The Social Contract* (1762), Rousseau put forward the proposition that war was a relation only between states and not between individuals:

°Execution was the usual punishment for troops who pillaged or otherwise molested the citizenry. It is reported that General Thomas Gage, commander of British troops in Boston in 1774–1775, had two of his soldiers hanged for breaking into a colonist's store.

†Jeremy Bentham (1748–1832) is generally credited with coining the phrase "international law" in his *Introduction to the Principles of Morals and Legislation* (1789). Before that the accepted expression had been "law of nations," which Bentham regarded as insufficiently explicit since it seemed "to refer to internal jurisprudence."

War, then, is not a relation of man to man, but of State to State, in which individuals are enemies only accidentally, and not as men, nor even as citizens, but as soldiers; not as members of their country, but as its defenders.

The temper of the times, embodying both mercantile and philosophic values, is strikingly reflected in a letter dated November 20, 1806, to Napoleon from his foreign minister, Prince de Talleyrand:

> Three centuries of civilization have given Europe a law of nations, for which . . . human nature cannot be sufficiently grateful.
> According to the maxim that war is not a relation between one man and another, but between state and state, in which private persons are only accidental enemies, not as men, nor even as members or subjects of the state, but simply as its defenders, the law of nations does not permit that the rights of war, and of conquest thence derived, should be applied to peaceable, unarmed citizens, to private properties and dwellings, to the merchandise of commerce, to the magazines which contain it, to the vehicles which transport it, to unarmed ships which carry it on streams and seas, in one word, to the person and the goods of private individuals.
> The law of war, born of civilization, has favored its progress. It is to this that Europe must ascribe the maintenance and increase of her prosperity, in the midst of the frequent wars that have divided her.

Odd it is to find Talleyrand cribbing from Rousseau to educate Napoleon. But Talleyrand was only one of many who tapped that source to the same purpose; in 1871 the King of Prussia, marching his men into France, declared that he was fighting French soldiers but not the French people. And this distinction between soldier and civilian, together with the soldier's obligation to respect the rights of noncombatant civilians of enemy countries, remains to this day, despite Hamburg, Dresden, Hiroshima, Tokyo, and Nagasaki, a vital part of the structure and content of the laws of war.

During these same years, customs and rules for the taking and protection of prisoners of war were also developing. The wasteful stupidity of mass killings led increasingly to exchanges of prisoners. Often such exchanges were provided for in advance of hostilities; our own 1785 treaty with Prussia provided, in the event of war, for the humane care of prisoners taken on either side.

Still it remained doubtful whether surrender into captivity was a matter of right or of grace, and whether "no quarter" could not be declared, at least in some circumstances. Napoleon Bonaparte, for one, took a very "practical" view of the matter in 1799, at the unsuccessful end of his campaign in Egypt and Palestine. In March 1799 he captured the fortress of Jaffa, where the Mameluke garrison surrendered on the promise that their lives would be spared. But the promise was not kept, and as Napoleon sailed away, Mamelukes to the number of 1,200 (as he reported) or 3,500 (as eyewitnesses testified) were slaughtered on the beaches of the Mediterranean.°

A few old rules of exception to the obligation to take prisoners lingered on, one of which is still alive today: capital punishment for spies. Well settled as it is on the basis that spies do not wear uniforms, this is an odd doctrine, as no moral obloquy now attaches to espionage. Witness the case of Nathan Hale, honored by a statue on the old campus at Yale and a plaque on the wall of the Yale Club in New York City, near his place of execution. The sporting aspect of espionage is underlined by the rule that if a spy succeeds in returning from behind the enemy lines to his own army, his responsibility for espionage is erased and if subsequently captured he must be treated as a prisoner of war—just as the base runner, surprised by an improbable catch, will be safe if he can beat the ball back to base.

Today the value of prisoner interrogation for intelligence purposes and the fear of reprisals have ensured among the major powers (though by no means universally) observance of the obligation to accept surrender and grant humane treatment to prisoners of war.

## 2

Although the foregoing core elements of the laws of war were in place by the middle of the nineteenth century, they remained uncodified. Largely unwritten in any official sense, they were known as "customary law." It was the United States, during the War Between the States, that took the lead in having them systematized and embodied in an officially adopted code.

The principal draftsman of this first codification of the law of war was Francis Lieber, a German who, as a young man, had fought under Field Marshal von Blücher against Napoleon. A well-educated political dissident, he emigrated to the United States and took citizenship in 1832. His talents won him a professorship at South Carolina College, but he detested slavery and in 1857 he moved to New York and became a professor at Columbia College and subsequently at the newly established Columbia Law School.

The War Between the States, in Lieber's words, "knocked rudely at my door," for his eldest son was mortally wounded fighting for the Confederacy, whose cause Lieber abominated, while his two younger sons were in the Union Army. When one of them lost an arm in Tennessee at Fort

°Napoleon's action was criticized at the time. The episode remained a subject of controversy for many years; see the discussion in Thomas Mann, *Buddenbrooks*, chapter 5 (1901).

Donelson, Lieber went west to visit him, and while there met General Henry W. Halleck, at that time commander of the Union forces in the West. In July 1862, Halleck was appointed military adviser to President Lincoln with the title General in Chief.

Halleck, himself the author of a treatise on international law, had been impressed by Lieber's combination of military, legal, and political pursuits, and in December 1862 he appointed Lieber to propose "a code of regulations for the government of Armies in the field of battle authorized by the laws and usages of war." Early in 1863 Lieber submitted a draft which was promulgated in May 1863 as General Orders No. 100, entitled "Instructions for the Government of Armies of the United States in the Field." It remained for over half a century the official army pronouncement on the laws of land warfare.

The Lieber Code contains 157 brief "articles," some of which read more like moral maxims than legal rules. The greater part of the code, however, reflects the history we have traced and deals with prisoners, the rights of noncombatants, partisans, and spies. In a few instances it prohibits particular means of warfare, such as the use of poisons. The code is humanitarian in its condemnation of cruelty and unnecessary violence and destruction, but the concept of "military necessity" is broad; for example, it authorizes a commander to direct his troops to give no quarter "in great straits, when his own salvation makes it *impossible* to cumber himself with prisoners."

In its specific content, therefore, the Lieber Code did not constitute a great leap forward in a reformist sense. Its great importance was recognition of the necessity of systematizing and articulating the accumulated experience and practices of the previous century. It thus laid the basis for instruction and training of the officers and men of large wartime armies, composed chiefly of drafted civilians unfamiliar with military affairs, and established standards for compliance with the rules and for their enforcement by courts-martial and other disciplinary measures.

### 3

The provisions of General Orders No. 100 were derived from international usage, but the Orders did not purport to be international law; it was a domestic regulation of the United States Army. However, it was promulgated at a time when events in Europe, especially the Crimean (1853–1856) and Franco-Austrian (1859) wars, had raised problems which were moving the major powers toward international agreement as a means of mitigating war's ravages.

Despite the progress of medical science, the warring powers in Europe had failed to make adequate provision for hospitals, doctors, and medical equipment at the scene of hostilities. In the Crimea, Florence Nightingale's administrative reforms and personal dedication to care for the wounded aroused popular feelings which were intensified in 1862 by the Swiss philanthropist Henri Dunant's widely read writings which gave a shocking account of the neglect suffered by the wounded at the Franco-Austrian battle at Solferino in Italy in 1859. At Geneva in 1864, twelve European nations signed a "Convention for the Amelioration of the Condition of the Wounded in Armies in the Field," the first of a series of international Red Cross conventions for this purpose.°

In the field of war crimes, however, the international breakthrough occurred at The Hague in 1899, when a "Convention with Respect to the Laws and Customs of War on Land" was signed by the United States, Mexico, Japan, Persia, Siam, and nineteen European nations, including all the major European powers. In both organization and content, the Convention leaned heavily on the Lieber Code and accordingly dealt chiefly with prisoners of war and the relations between occupation troops and noncombatant civilian inhabitants. Unlike the Lieber Code, however, the Convention included an unqualified prohibition of declaring "no quarter" or attacking enemy soldiers who have surrendered.

Other conventions signed at The Hague in 1899 forbade the use of expanding (dum-dum) bullets, the use of projectiles containing "deleterious gases," and "the launching of projectiles and explosives from balloons, or by other new methods of similar nature." In 1907 a second Hague Convention on the laws of land warfare, differing in no major respect from the 1899 Convention, was signed by over forty nations.

In all of these treaties, the laws of war are stated as general principles of conduct, and neither the means of enforcement nor the penalties for violation are specified. However, the substance of many of their provisions was soon incorporated into the military law of the major powers and many other nations.

In the United States, General Orders No. 100 was replaced in 1914 by an army field manual entitled "The Law of Land Warfare" which, updated, is still in force. It sets forth that the laws of war are part of the law of the United States and that they may be enforced against both soldiers and civilians, including enemy personnel, by military or international tribunals.

Such was the state of the laws of war in 1914, when World War I began. Up to this time the laws of war contained virtually nothing dealing with aerial warfare. The Hague Convention in 1899 antedated the Wright brothers' famous flight at Kitty Hawk in 1903, and the 1907 Convention

---

°The United States adhered to the 1864 Convention in 1882. The Red Cross Convention of 1906, also signed at Geneva, greatly expanded the terms of the 1864 Convention and was signed by thirty-six nations.

came only a few years later. Military aviation was still in its infancy in 1914 when major-power warfare was renewed.

The naval situation was wholly different. Over the past centuries of maritime warfare, many customs and rules, sometimes embodied in treaties, had been adopted dealing with such matters as false flags and other ruses, blockade, privateers, and the treatment of neutral shipping.

The Hague meetings produced a number of agreements to internationalize both preexistent and some new naval rules. In 1907, no less than eight naval conventions were adopted, covering such matters as the status of enemy ships at the outbreak of hostilities, the converting of merchant ships into warships, minelaying, and coastal bombardment.

Most of these rules were of such a nature that their violation would lead to reprisals, or claims for compensation, rather than criminal prosecutions. Navies do not ordinarily occupy enemy territory nor take large quantities of prisoners. These factual differences no doubt explain why there was no general naval code comparable to the Hague Conventions on land warfare.

None of the Hague Conventions, nor the predecessor concepts on which they were based, imposed any limitation on the sovereign right to make war. Wars had played a large part in the rise and proliferation of nation-states, whose leaders generally scorned as sentimental rubbish the "just and unjust war" concept of earlier centuries. To be sure, governments might still give reasons for resorting to war that stressed the righteousness of their cause, but none of this was of any legal significance.

Lieber, progressive as he was with regard to the conduct of warfare, had no doubts about its intrinsic validity, and accordingly General Orders No. 100 declared that "war has come to be acknowledged not to be its own end, but the means to obtain great ends of state. . . ." Therefore "The law of nations allows every sovereign government to make war upon another sovereign state . . . ," and the nation attacked is bound to abide by the laws of war even though it regards the enemy "as a wanton and unjust assailant."

And so in 1914 when the "Guns of August" thundered, there was nothing in the acknowledged content of international law that made any state or individual liable to criminal charges for declaring and engaging in war. But the Hague Conventions, and other treaties and conclaves in the preceding half century, had internationalized the whole subject of limits on warfare and laid the basis for an extraordinary expansion of public and political concern with "war crimes" throughout the course and aftermath of World War I.

*4*

From the very beginning of that war, Kaiser Wilhelm II and his general staff contrived to conduct German war operations in such a way as to raise a worldwide storm of hate and fear, almost comparable to that achieved by Adolf Hitler a quarter of a century later. I use the word "contrived" advisedly, for whereas the Hitlerian atrocities reflected fundamental Nazi doctrine, the crimes and errors of Imperial Germany appear to have been the result of clumsiness, arrogance, and sheer brutality.

Historians still debate the apportionment of responsibility for the onset of World War I, but no one contends that Belgium started it by attacking Germany. The German High Command conceived that their forces needed the deployment space of Belgium for a speedy victory over France, and as soon as there was a state of war between Germany and France, the German government sent Belgium a demand to allow the transit of German troops. When the Belgians declined, the German Army attacked across the Belgian frontier, in violation of the multinational Belgian neutrality treaty of 1839, which the German Chancellor Theobald von Bethmann-Hollweg publicly scorned as a "scrap of paper." A few hours later Britain, invoking the 1839 treaty, declared war on Germany.

The Germans' ruthless attack on a small neutral country not only ensured British hostility but also scandalized world opinion. With the invasion came reports of wanton destruction and brutalities by the Germans: the ancient city of Louvain was sacked and its world-famous library destroyed by fire; innocent civilians were taken hostage and often shot; in some places the invading soldiers were said to have raped women and killed adults and children alike. Soon there were comparable reports from German-occupied areas in France, where the troops of a brigade commanded by General Karl Stenger had denied quarter to French soldiers, including the wounded.

During 1915 the pitch of public indignation climbed even higher. In January the huge German lighter-than-air ships known (after their designer) as zeppelins started bombing raids over England; their military value was slight, but by the end of the year over 200 civilians had been killed and many were terrorized. The following month the German government proclaimed a "war zone" around the British Isles, in which their submarines would sink enemy merchant ships without warning. In April the huge Cunard liner *Lusitania* was sunk by a U-boat off the Irish coast with the loss of some 1,200 lives. That same month the Germans first employed poison gas as a weapon during the battle of Ypres. At about the same time the "Young Turk" government of the Ottoman Empire (which had entered the war as an ally of Germany in November 1914) began the deportation of Armenians to the Syrian desert, where they were massacred by the thousands. In October the British public was enraged by the Germans' execution of Edith Cavell, the director of a nurses' training school in Brussels. The following night a zeppelin raid over London killed 127 inhabitants.

This list (far from complete) of German and Turkish actions is certainly adequate to explain why, in both Allied and neutral nations, the Germans came to be referred to as "Huns" and their military policies as "frightfulness." But in nearly every case, there were serious evidentiary or legal questions whether these acts could rightly be labeled "war crimes."

The neutrality treaty violated by the German invasion of Belgium did not embody criminal sanctions, and as soon as Belgium resisted she ceased to be neutral. As for the conduct of German troops in Belgium, most of the stories of indiscriminate murder, rape, and infanticide were later exposed as the fabrications of propagandists. The destruction in Louvain, to be sure, was plainly contrary to several clauses of the Hague Convention, but the taking and even killing of hostages was not so covered, and as late as 1948 was held permissible under the laws of war by one of the Nuremberg tribunals. Edith Cavell publicly acknowledged that in the autumn of 1914 she had been part of an "underground railway" to assist Allied soldiers trapped behind the German lines to escape capture and rejoin their compatriots. Her execution was draconian, and from a public relations standpoint stupid, but it was no war crime.

The zeppelin raids ushered in the era of urban bombardment from the air, but violated no law of war—the Hague Conventions on land warfare forbade the bombardment of *undefended* cities, but London was not undefended; the separate 1907 Hague Convention prohibiting the discharge of explosives from "balloons, or by other new methods of a similar nature" was not in force, as neither Germany nor France had signed it. No international agreement governing submarine operations had been adopted, and, except for hospital ships, German U-boat attacks on enemy shipping violated no international law, save in the few cases in which survivors of a sinking ship were attacked. However, the use of poison gas was much less defensible, as the Hague Convention on land warfare explicitly forbade the use of "poison or poisoned arms." But even here, questions might be raised under the Hague Convention on "asphyxiating or deleterious gases," which was limited to their diffusion by "the use of projectiles." The Armenians were citizens of the Ottoman Empire; there was no formal state of war between Armenians and Turks, and so the Hague Conventions were wholly inapplicable. In May 1915 a joint Allied declaration denounced the Turkish actions as "crimes against humanity and civilization," but that was a concept quite outside the scope of any treaties or recognized doctrine.

5

Such negative arguments were overwhelmed by the tide of anger against Imperial Germany which engulfed the Allied and many neutral peoples. Initially, public rage focused on the Kaiser; before the war was a month old there were published demands for his exile to St. Helena, Devil's Island, or some other suitable place. Almost as soon, however, voices were raised insisting upon trial and punishment by law, preferably before an international tribunal.

Pressure for punitive action against the Kaiser and other German war criminals was strongest in Britain, which was bearing the brunt of the U-boat and zeppelin operations. In 1916, Prime Minister Herbert Asquith told the House of Commons that his government was "determined to bring to justice the criminals, whoever they may be and whatever their station."

In February 1917 the German government declared a new zone around the British Isles in which U-boats would sink enemy *and neutral* shipping alike, without warning or regard for the safety of crews or passengers. This was so contrary to maritime practice, and so hazardous to American lives and property, that two months later the United States declared war against Germany. A year later over a million American soldiers had joined the Allied forces in France.

Since American sympathies had lain with the Allies from the beginning of the war, it is not surprising that in the United States there had been almost as much discussion of war crimes trials as in Britain. In both countries the general public's wrath was directed at the Kaiser, but in legal and academic circles there was a strong current of opinion that judicial trials would promote the development of international law as an instrument of peace. This fitted well with Wilsonian internationalism and the President's insistence that the war was a crusade: a war "to end war" and "to make the world safe for democracy."

When victory came via the Armistice in November 1918, it was accompanied by the Kaiser's flight to Holland, a country with a long tradition as a haven for political refugees. This was a complicating factor, but did nothing to quell the public demand for his punishment. In Britain, Prime Minister David Lloyd George and his Cabinet pledged support for a trial of the Kaiser as part of their successful parliamentary election campaign in December 1918.

In France, the public appetite for war crimes trials had increased, partly because the Germans had carried out what amounted to a "scorched earth" policy in their final retreat through northern France. The practical French were, however, much more concerned about reparations and future national security than international justice. As for the Kaiser, he was one of the guilty, but there was opposition to his exile to St. Helena—a proposal which was condemned as an insult to Napoleon and the French nation!

There was no unity of viewpoint about war crimes among the three major powers when the delegates assembled, on January 18, 1919, at the opening session of the Paris Peace Conference—a conclave dominated by Lloyd George, Georges Clemenceau, and Woodrow Wilson. For the first-named, the establishment of an international tribunal to try the Kaiser, and provisions for the trial and punishment of other war criminals, was both a political necessity and a program which reflected his own and a majority of his countrymen's strong desires. But for both Clemenceau and Wilson, war crimes were collateral to their larger aims: for Clemenceau, reparations and security; for Wilson, a moderate peace, a viable democratic government for Germany, and, most of all, a League of Nations to secure future peace.

The war crimes issue was the first item on the conference's agenda, and a Commission on the Responsibility of the Authors of the War and the Enforcement of Penalties was established to study and report back on the matter. The chairman and dominant figure was the American Secretary of State, Robert Lansing, whose views on war crimes issues were fiercely conservative; he did not really believe in any supranational law and op-posed any international punitive action against the Kaiser or the establish-ment of international courts for war crimes trials.

The commission's report, submitted in March 1919, charged Germany and her allies (the Central Powers) with extensive violations of the laws of war. Some offenders could be tried before national tribunals, but those in high authority and responsible for crimes on a large scale would be brought before a twenty-two-member international High Tribunal. The commission also found that the Central Powers had, with premeditation, launched a "war of aggression" in violation of treaties, but that this conduct did not provide the basis for a criminal charge under existing international law; it should, however, be strongly condemned and made a penal offense for the future. As for the Kaiser, the commission recommended his trial before an international tribunal on the charge that he was responsible for German violations of the laws of war.

The report was nominally unanimous, but the American "reserva-tions" were so fundamental that they amounted to a dissent. President Wilson was not as rigid as Lansing on these issues, but he was worried about "victors' justice" and had told Lansing that he wanted "a minority report rejecting High Tribunal and opposing trial of the Kaiser." Lloyd George, however, made it clear that he could not sign a treaty that failed to provide for the Kaiser's punishment. Confrontation then gave way to compromise, embodied in Articles 227 and 230 of the Treaty of Versailles, signed in June 1919.

Under Article 227 the Kaiser was to be tried before a "special tribunal" of five judges, one each from the United States, Great Britain, France, Italy, and Japan. He was not to be charged with responsibility for war crimes, but with "a supreme offence against international morality and the sanctity of treaties." The three ensuing articles called for trials of "persons accused of having committed acts in violation of the laws and customs of war" before "military tribunals" of the aggrieved nations, and required the German government to "hand over" the individuals so accused to any of the "Allied and Associated Powers" so requesting. Provisions comparable to Articles 228–230 were included in the later peace treaties with Austria, Hungary, and Bulgaria.

Thus the hopes of Lloyd George and other European statesmen to use the victorious peace as an occasion for confirming and expanding the international law of war foundered on the rocks of American opposition. Wilson and Lansing had won. There would be no international war crimes courts. There would be no trial to determine the Kaiser's criminal guilt. The charge against him was stated in terms that were opaque and had no roots in international legal doctrine. Furthermore, this boded ill for the prospects of persuading the Dutch to make him available for trial.

## 6

President Wilson left France the day after the Versailles Treaty was signed and embarked on his unsuccessful campaign to obtain Senate ratification. His eventual failure in March 1920 was followed by his severe illness, and Washington's role in treaty matters rapidly dwindled. America's virtual withdrawal weakened both the League of Nations and the treaty, and the European Allies soon learned that it is one thing to get a treaty signed and quite another to enforce it.

Holland was duly asked to make the Kaiser available for trial, but the Allied camp was divided on the wisdom of the project, and the Dutch received hints that the demand was pro forma and there would be no coercion. The Allied request was refused, on the legal ground that the offense charged against the Kaiser was unknown to Dutch law, was not mentioned in any treaties to which Holland was a party, and appeared to be of a political rather than a criminal character. The Kaiser never left Holland, and died in his castle at Doorn in 1941.

No part of the Versailles Treaty aroused more anger in Germany than Article 228, requiring the government to deliver up its own citizens for trial on war crimes charges before tribunals constituted by the victorious army. Credible information reached the Allied leaders that compliance with such demands would threaten the stability of the Weimar Republic and might even lead to a Communist takeover. Lloyd George and Clemenceau were deeply troubled; there was strong demand from their respective publics for strict enforcement of Article 228, but it was obvious that revolution in Germany would jeopardize reparations and have other serious consequences. Nevertheless, on February 3, 1920, the Allies presented to the Germans a list of 854 individuals, including many famous military and political figures, for turnover.

There was an immediate explosion of indignation and defiance in Germany, but within two weeks the immediate crisis was resolved. Accurately sensing Allied misgivings, the Germans had come forward with a proposal that those accused of war crimes be tried before the German Supreme Court in Leipzig. Lloyd George prevailed on the French to accept this solution, and on February 17, 1920, the Germans were so notified.

The Allies then presented the Germans with an initial list of forty-five individuals for prosecution, and a year later the Leipzig trials began. The first accused were four named by the British. Three German enlisted men charged with beating British prisoners with rifle butts were convicted and given sentences of six to ten months. A U-boat commander who had sunk a British hospital ship was acquitted on the ground of superior orders.

The court then heard a Belgian case against a German military policeman charged with torturing small children arrested on suspicion of sabotage. The court acquitted the defendant; the Belgians at once repudiated the trials and refused further participation.

The Leipzig court then took up the case of General Stenger and his subordinate Major Cruscius on the charge of denying quarter and murdering French prisoners. Major Cruscius admitted shooting French wounded, and accused General Stenger of ordering the killings. Stenger denied the charge and was acquitted; Cruscius was sentenced to two years' imprisonment. The trial was turbulent, and the French delegates were taunted and spat upon by the crowd. Four other Germans accused by the French were then acquitted. The French withdrew their delegation and participated no further.

The British had listed for trial Lieutenant Patzig, commander of a U-boat which had sunk a hospital ship and then destroyed two lifeboats with survivors.° Patzig was unavailable for trial, but the German prosecutor on his own initiative brought charges against two subordinates, Lieutenants Dithmar and Boldt. The court ruled that they well knew that Patzig's order to attack the lifeboats was unlawful, convicted them of manslaughter, and sentenced them to four years' imprisonment. Within a few months both escaped, apparently with the connivance of the jailers.

Dismal as the Leipzig record was from a prosecution standpoint, the British did not share the outrage of the French and Belgians, and refused

---

°The incident became known because a third lifeboat crew escaped in the dark.

to join in French proposals for sanctions. By way of compromise, however, in August 1922 the British joined in an Allied note to Germany declaring that the Leipzig court's decisions would not be recognized as valid and reserving all rights under Articles 228–230 of the Versailles Treaty.

There were few other post–World War I war crimes trials worthy of note. A French court convicted two prominent Saarland industrialists, Robert and Hermann Roechling, of wartime spoliation of French-owned property, but the verdict was set aside on appeal. The Allies showed no interest in pursuing war criminals in Austria or Hungary. Among the victorious Balkan states, only Yugoslavia pressed for the punishment of war criminals—in this instance, Bulgarians. Eager for good relations with the Yugoslavs, the Bulgarian government brought to trial and convicted a number of its own soldiers for crimes against Yugoslav civilians.

Allied, and especially British, interest in Turkish crimes was much greater, with regard both to the Armenian massacres and to the mistreatment of British prisoners. The Sultan's government was submissive to Allied demands, and in April 1919 a Turkish military tribunal convicted two officials, one of whom went to the gallows, of murdering Armenians. But the Turkish nationalist movement was growing, and Greek atrocities against Turks in Smyrna put a hypocritical cast on the war crimes issue. The word "genocide" had not yet been coined, but that is what the Armenian massacres were. The Allies failed to establish the criminality of the massacres by judicial process, and in 1923 the Treaty of Lausanne covered the perpetrators with the shield of amnesty.

As for the war crimes provisions of the Versailles Treaty, the best that can be said is that "the mountain labored and brought forth a mouse."

Thus the war crimes prosecutions moved offstage, but the enormous carnage of World War I stimulated public demand for measures to prevent a recurrence of such slaughter and destruction. Military and diplomatic interest was rekindled in the use of multinational treaties not only to limit armaments, but also to govern their use. The airplane, the submarine, and poison gas had profoundly affected the conduct of war, and it was to these relatively new weapons, largely untouched by the Hague Conventions, that attention now turned.

The first efforts, at the five-power Washington Conference of 1922 on the limitation of armaments, failed. The conference also found it impossible to formulate a treaty limiting aerial warfare, but provided for a Commission of Jurists to study and report on the problem. Early in 1923 the commission submitted proposed rules which included a prohibition against "bombardment for the purposes of terrorizing the civilian population" and limiting aerial bombing to specified "military objectives." The rules were never adopted in legally binding form.

Success in these areas was first achieved by the prohibition against the use of poison gas in the 1925 Geneva Protocol, which was soon ratified by most nations and generally recognized as legally binding. The United States, however, did not ratify the protocol until 1975, and both the United States and Great Britain have expressed reservations about its application to tear gas and herbicides.

The 1930 London Treaty for the limitation of naval armaments, signed by eleven nations, provided that "with regard to merchant ships, submarines must conform to the rules of International Law to which surface vessels are subjected" and explicitly required that, unless the merchant ship refused to stop or attacked the submarine, it could not be sunk unless the "passengers, crew and ships papers" had first been put "in a place of safety," with due regard to location and sea and weather conditions. In 1936, pursuant to the London Protocol of that year, these rules were circulated to all other nations, and by the time World War II began it had been accepted by forty-eight countries, including Germany and all other major powers.

For air warfare there were no further treaty developments, and in retrospect it is easy to see why the 1923 draft failed to win adherents. In 1921, the Italian air general Giulio Douhet had published a widely read book, *Command of the Air*, preaching the doctrine that in future years air power would be decisive—a view congenial to the British air staff, which soon was planning a large investment in heavy bombers as the best deterrent to German air attacks against the homeland. The United States was similarly developing the four-engined B-17 and B-24 strategic-range bombers that were to play a major role in World War II. Public opinion, during the years between the two world wars, settled into a fatalistic acceptance that future wars between the great powers would surely involve urban infernos produced by bombers, and that nothing could be done about it. So firm was this belief that, when such attacks failed to materialize during the first months of World War II, people called it the "phony war."

Of more general importance than these discussions and agreements was the 1928 Treaty of Paris, which sought to outlaw war itself. The late 1920s was a period of international amity, which had begun in 1925 with the Locarno security pact among Britain, France, Germany, Belgium, and Italy guaranteeing the German-French and German-Belgian frontiers. The foreign ministers of France and Germany, Aristide Briand and Gustav Stresemann, were seeking to allay old animosities; the French ended their occupation of the Ruhr; Germany resumed reparations payments and in 1926 was admitted to the League of Nations. That year the two men shared the Nobel Peace Prize.

The tenth anniversary of the United States' entry into World War I fell on April 6, 1927, and Briand proposed to celebrate the occasion by a mutual undertaking by the two countries to renounce war. The American Secretary of State, Frank B. Kellogg, proposed making such a treaty multilateral, and on August 27, 1928, the representatives of fifteen nations met at Paris and signed the International Treaty for the Renunciation of War as an Instrument of National Policy, better known today as the Kellogg-Briand Pact and providing as follows:

> Art. I. The High Contracting Parties solemnly declare in the names of their respective peoples that they condemn recourse to war for the solution of international controversies, and renounce it as an instrument of national policy in their relations with one another.
> Art. II. The High Contracting Parties agree that the settlement or solution of all disputes or conflicts of whatever nature or of whatever origin they may be, which may arise among them, shall never be sought except by pacific means.

The treaty was subsequently accepted by forty-four nations, including all the Great Powers except the Soviet Union. It certainly was an impressive antiwar commitment, but did it make engaging in war a crime? Of course it was not intended to condemn resorting to war in self-defense, but what about launching an aggressive war? Opinions differed sharply at the time, and still did when World War II brought the question to a head.

In summary, one could say that when that war ended in 1945, except for the treaty provisions relating to poison gas and submarines, the declared and generally accepted laws of war were not fundamentally different from those embodied in the Hague and Geneva conventions.* But one would have to put that statement in perspective by adding that, in 1945, public and official *attitudes* toward the laws of war had undergone a sea change. The reasons for this will become apparent in the immediate background of the Nuremberg trials.

---

*In July 1929, two conventions, one relating to care of the wounded and the other to the treatment of prisoners of war, were signed at Geneva by representatives of virtually all the nations except the Soviet Union. These conventions dealt in much greater detail with matters already treated by the Hague Convention on Land Warfare and the Red Cross Convention of 1906. The 1929 treaties were technically much superior to their antecedents, but did not break new ground in terms of doctrine or general scope.

# Chapter 2

# THE NUREMBERG IDEAS

I n sharp contrast to the aftermath of World War I, that of World War II witnessed an explosion of war crimes trials in both Europe and the Far East. The differences can be explained in part by the changing outlook of the late 1920s, reflected in international agreements such as the Kellogg-Briand Pact.

A more important reason was that the perceived evil of Nazism in action was far deeper and more pervasive than was that of Imperial Germany. In World War I, U-boats, zeppelins, and poison gas had been brutally and ruthlessly used, but they were weapons of war employed to achieve military victory. The ideology of the Third Reich, however, embraced not only German aggrandizement by force of arms, but also the violent suppression of political opposition and reduction of Jews and Slavs to the status of "subhumans" targeted for enslavement at best. Nazism was a proudly avowed repudiation of the libertarian, humanitarian, and internationalist ideals to which most national governments gave at least lip service.

In Germany, the period between Hitler's ascent to power in 1933 and the attack on Poland in 1939 included the establishment of concentration camps, in which Communists, social democrats, royalists, and other opponents of the Nazi regime were incarcerated; establishment of a totalitarian dictatorship by imposing Nazi Party control over labor unions, professional business associations, and other public organizations; destruction of the rule of law by Nazifying the judiciary and according Hitler as Supreme Judge the power to direct the imprisonment or execution of individuals with no semblance of a trial; and the progressive outlawing of Jews by their expulsion from all positions of private or public authority and, under the 1935 Nuremberg Laws, by depriving them of the rights of German citizenship and making marriage or sexual intimacy between Jews and German citizens a criminal offense.

As for foreign policy, Hitler pulled Germany out of the League of Nations and the 1932 Geneva Disarmament Conference, repudiated the Treaty of Versailles military provisions, launched a vigorous rearmament program, cultivated his fellow dictator Benito Mussolini, and drew Italy, and subsequently Japan, into alliance with Germany. In March 1938, by brutal diplomatic pressure subsequently sharpened by the threat of military force, Austria was annexed to the Reich. Six months later, with the Wehrmacht deployed along the German-Czech border and poised for invasion, at the famous Munich conference Czechoslovakia was rendered defenseless by the forced cession of the Sudetenland to Germany. In March of 1939, just a year after the annexation of Austria, German troops occupied Prague and Hitler proclaimed the incorporation of Bohemia and Moravia into the Reich as a "protectorate," while Slovakia preserved a precarious autonomy as an avowed satellite of Germany.

None of these events prior to September 1, 1939, touched off a war. Yet the systematic, state-mandated mistreatment of the Jews—including such horrifying excesses as Kristallnacht (November 10, 1938), when there was an orgy of looting, arson, harassment of Jews, and destruction of synagogues, homes, and businesses, with many arrests and some killings—had raised the same question as the earlier Turkish massacres of Armenians. Are such actions by a state, against a racial or religious segment of its own citizenry, crimes under international law? The German takeover of Czechoslovakia, though accomplished without any fighting, was plainly the result of a *threat* of war. Was that not, within the spirit if not the letter of the Kellogg-Briand Pact, an aggressive act? These questions had to be addressed as Allied victory in World War II became increasingly probable, and war crimes policies had to be shaped.

However, no such difficulties surrounded the German invasion of Poland in September 1939, and the speedy destruction of the Polish government and occupation of most of its territory by German and Soviet troops.° If launching an aggressive war was to be regarded as an international crime, this was "it."

The provisions of the Hague and Geneva conventions thus became applicable, and violations of the Germans' obligations to the Polish civilian populations were therefore plainly war crimes. And crimes of hideous intent and effect multiplied. Under German administration, the Poles were to

---

°In execution of secret protocols, attached to the German-Soviet nonaggression pact, which was signed shortly before the invasion of Poland, the country was cut up as follows: (1) large areas of western Poland, including the Polish Corridor, Posen, Lodz, and Katowice, were annexed to the Reich, (2) parts of eastern Poland, including Lvov and Bialystok, were annexed to the Soviet Union, (3) the area between, including Warsaw, Cracow, and Lublin, was denominated the "Government-General" and was administered by a German Governor-General (Hans Frank) substantially as a colony of the Reich.

be allowed only "bare living conditions." So that no indigenous Polish leadership could develop, the monied and cultured classes, including intellectuals, landowners, and clergy, were to be stamped out. Jews, wherever located, would be resettled in ghettos established in the larger cities. For Germany, the Government-General was regarded as useful only as a military deployment area and a source of cheap slave labor. "The accomplishment of this task," said Hitler, "will involve a hard racial struggle which will not allow any legal restrictions. The methods used will be incompatible with the principles we otherwise adhere to."

As these murderous policies were put into effect, many of the German soldiers in Poland watched with incredulous horror. In November 1939 a young German staff officer, Major Helmuth Stieff, wrote to his wife: "When one has seen the ruins of Warsaw . . . one feels not like a victor, but as a guilty man. . . . The wildest fantasy of horror propaganda is as nothing to the reality, the organized gangs who murder, rob and plunder with what is said to be the tolerance of the highest authorities. . . . *It shames me to be a German!*" Higher-ranking officers were indignant not only at the savagery but also at what appeared to them the stupidity of these atrocities. In December 1939, General Johannes Blaskowitz, Commander in Chief of all German military forces in the Government-General, sent a stinging criticism of the German civil and police administration to the Army High Command in Berlin. A few months later, Blaskowitz was relieved of his command, his career blighted.

News of these events came to the outside world in January 1940, when the Primate of Poland, August Cardinal Hlond, visited Rome, where he reported that 214 Catholic priests had been executed and some 1,000 imprisoned by the Nazis in Poland. But soon after the broadcast of Hlond's report on the Vatican radio station, the German Ambassador to the Holy See was able to inform Berlin that the broadcasts had been stopped.

Public attention soon shifted in other directions during the spring of 1940, when the Wehrmacht struck north and west and occupied Denmark, Norway, Luxembourg, Holland, and Belgium. France was then forced to accept an armistice under which northern France (including Paris) fell under German occupation. The following year Yugoslavia and Greece were added to the list, shortly before Hitler launched his last and most massive assault, against the Soviet Union. In November 1942, when British and American forces landed in Algeria and Morocco, the Germans occupied the rest of France.

2

And so all of Europe, except Sweden, Switzerland, and the Iberian Peninsula, fell under occupation and administration by Germany or its satellites—Italy, Hungary, Romania, and Bulgaria,° all referred to collectively as the Axis powers. Festung Europa (Fortress Europe) it came to be called, and from the Fortress all normal sources of news were cut off.

But information did come out, through refugees, clandestine agents, neutral travelers, and other sources. And in London, quite apart from British intelligence agencies, there was a most unusual group of persons to whom much of this information was directed and who eagerly collected and recorded it—a group that had no parallel during World War I.

The first members were fugitive Polish military and civil officials who, after the defeat of France, established a Polish government-in-exile in London, with General Vladislav Sikorski as Premier. Simultaneously, there came a procession of monarchs and ministers fleeing the German invasions of their respective countries: King Haakon of Norway, Grand Duchess Charlotte of Luxembourg, Queen Wilhelmina of the Netherlands, the émigré ministers of Belgium, ex-President Eduard Beneš of Czechoslovakia, and General Charles de Gaulle, leader of the Free French forces. In 1941 they were joined by King Peter of Yugoslavia and King George of Greece. By the end of 1941 there were nine governments-in-exile established in London, amassing information on how matters were going in their respective countries under German rule.

In general, the answer was very badly in Western Europe, and far, far worse in Eastern Europe. Early in 1940 the United States Embassy in Berlin transmitted news of the wholesale deportation of German Jews to Poland. In the wake of the Nazi conquests of 1940 and 1941 came reports describing the roundup of millions of men and women from all the occupied countries for forced labor on German farms and in German mines and factories. In the course of invading the Soviet Union, German military orders declared that "the supply of food to local inhabitants and prisoners of war is unnecessary humanitarianism" and ordered all things of value confiscated, including children's boots. Soviet prisoners in German hands froze and starved to death by the millions. And in 1942 came the reports, at first deemed incredible but soon confirmed, of the mass extermination of Jews, from all the occupied countries, at Auschwitz, Treblinka, and other death camps in Poland—the Nazis' "final solution of the Jewish problem," later called the Holocaust.

These outrages were not the work of faceless or anonymous men or agencies. A decade of Nazi rule had made the names of Hitler's principal associates, and the organizations through which they worked, household words in the Western world. Especially familiar to the public at large, inside

°Finland's situation was unique. The country had joined Germany in attacking the Soviet Union, but Finland was not at war with Britain or with the United States. There were German combat troops in Finland, but the Finnish government remained master in its own house.

and beyond German borders, were Hermann Goering, Commander in Chief of the Air Force and Chief of War Economy, and designated by Hitler as his own successor; Rudolf Hess, Deputy to Hitler for Nazi Party matters, and successor-designate in the event of Goering's unavailability; Heinrich Himmler, head of the black-uniformed SS (Schutzstaffel), the Nazi Party's police, intelligence, and security organizations, including the concentration and death camps; the diminutive, clubfooted Dr. Joseph Goebbels, Minister of Public Enlightenment and Propaganda; Hans Frank, the Governor-General in Poland; Hjalmar Horace Greeley Schacht, the banker who had supported Hitler's accession to the chancellorship and directed the financing of rearmament until his replacement by Goering; Joachim von Ribbentrop, Foreign Minister; Julius Streicher, Regional Leader in Franconia and Editor-in-Chief of the lascivious anti-Semitic newspaper *Der Stuermer*; Fritz Sauckel, head of the forced labor program; and Albert Speer, Hitler's favorite architect and, subsequently, director of the armaments program.

What was to be done about these men publicly regarded as murderous villains, and their terrorist organizations? During the first two years of the war, as Britain's allies were bowled over like so many tenpins and Britain herself clung to survival by her fingernails, there was little time to spare for consideration of war crimes. Then, on October 25, 1941, President Roosevelt and Prime Minister Churchill simultaneously issued statements condemning the Germans' execution of "scores of innocent hostages" and other atrocities in the occupied territories. "Retribution" for these crimes was envisaged, but the statements did not address any of the many problems which this prospect presented.

On January 13, 1942, moved by the need for concerted action, representatives of the nine governments-in-exile met at St. James's Palace in London, organized themselves as the Inter-Allied Commission on the Punishment of War Crimes, and issued what became known as the Declaration of St. James's. The salient feature of the declaration was that it explicitly repudiated retribution "by acts of vengeance on the part of the general public" and declared that "the sense of justice of the civilized world" required that the signatory powers

> place among their principal war aims the punishment, through the channel of organized justice, of those guilty of or responsible for these crimes, whether they have ordered them, perpetrated them or participated in them.

Of course, this was only a beginning, but it was the war's first principled utterance about war crimes, and it was accurately predictive. The leaders of these German-occupied lands, on whose peoples the burden of the atrocities directly fell, did not merely want to see the heads of their oppressors roll; they wanted vindication and retribution by *law*, applied through judicial process.

And so it was to be. In July 1942, evidence of new German atrocities in hand, the St. James's signatory powers sought public support from the Big Three—Churchill, Roosevelt, and Stalin. In reply, Churchill and Roosevelt explicitly approved the proposal that those accused of war crimes should stand trial, while Stalin referred to such trials before "a special international tribunal."

Meanwhile the phrase "united nations" had been adopted to signal° the alliance of Britain, the United States, the Soviet Union, China, and twenty-two other nations against the Tripartite Pact powers, Germany, Italy, and Japan. On October 7, 1942, in simultaneous but separate statements, President Roosevelt and the British Lord Chancellor (Sir John Simon) proposed the establishment of a United Nations Commission for the Investigation of War Crimes to identify war crimes suspects and collect and organize evidence of and about war crimes.†

The necessity for some such organization was greatly sharpened on December 17, 1942, when, in a joint declaration by the United States and the European members of the United Nations, the German government was publicly and officially accused of a "bestial policy of extermination of the Jewish people in Europe" in accordance with "Hitler's oft-repeated intention."‡ The Soviet Union did not become party to the commission.

The United Nations War Crimes Commission (UNWCC) was organized in London as a fourteen-member body, comprising the nine governments-in-exile, the United Kingdom, United States, China, Australia, and India. At the first meeting, on January 11, 1944, the British Commissioner, Sir Cecil Hurst, was elected Chairman; he had for many years been Legal Adviser to the Foreign Office, and his selection as the British Commissioner betokened London's belief that the war crimes "problem" was as much a diplomatic as a legal one. The United States Commissioner, Herbert C. Pell, was a New York Democrat and friend of Roosevelt.

The UNWCC was politically weak. A majority of its members repre-

---

°The United Nations alliance was formally established by the Joint Declaration of January 1, 1942. Churchill pointed out to Roosevelt that the words "united nations" had been used by Lord Byron in his poem *Childe Harold's Pilgrimage*, canto 3, stanza XXXV. Byron applied the expression to the allies whose forces defeated Napoleon at Waterloo; the poet appears not to have attached any special significance to the words, as in an earlier stanza (XVIII) of the same canto he called the allies the "banded nations."

†In a phrasing which surely would raise a few eyebrows if used today, President Roosevelt referred to "atrocities which have violated every tenet of the Christian faith."

‡Although this declaration was front-page news, it made astonishingly—indeed shamefully—little impact on the public mind. I myself did not become aware of the Holocaust until my exposure to the relevant documents and witnesses at Nuremberg. See the comparable avowal in George Ball, *The Past Has Another Pattern* (1982), p. 63.

sented shadow governments, who might or might not be restored to power when their countries were liberated. Even as the commission was being organized, there came a pronouncement from a much higher level which significantly limited the prospective scope of its work.

On November 1, 1943, at the Moscow Conference of the Foreign Ministers of Britain, the United States, and the Soviet Union, a declaration on war crimes was promulgated over the names of Churchill, Roosevelt, and Stalin, speaking in behalf of the United Nations. The last paragraph of the Moscow Declaration struck a new note:

> The above declaration is without prejudice to the case of the major criminals whose offenses have no particular location and who will be punished by a joint decision of the Governments of the Allies.

This, in practical effect, removed the principal Nazi leaders from the jurisdiction of the UNWCC. The fate of these "major criminals," and the important issues associated with their punishment, would not be decided by the UNWCC but by consultation among the Allied governments, which as a practical matter meant Britain, the United States, the Soviet Union, and perhaps France.

In fact, the UNWCC was in for a very thin time. It was supposed to investigate and collect evidence of war crimes, but it had no investigatory staff or, for that matter, adequate staff for any substantial undertaking. The governments-in-exile had but meager resources; the commission could do little but record cases referred to it by the member governments. Of these there was a mere trickle; on March 30, 1944, Sir Cecil Hurst reported that the UNWCC had not more than half a dozen cases that could reasonably be regarded as "atrocities." Sir Cecil confessed that "no evidence" of the massacre of Jews in Poland had been received by the commission—and this fifteen months after the Foreign Minister's public disclosure that proof of such massacres was in the British government's hands.

In these frustrating operational circumstances, the members turned their attention to legal issues and considered at length such questions as whether launching an aggressive war should be considered a crime of international law; whether an atrocity committed by a government against its own citizens, frequently described as a "crime against humanity," should be regarded as an international crime; and whether an international tribunal should be created for the trial of war criminals, especially those charged with crimes described in the Moscow Declaration as having no particular geographical location.

These issues had all been raised after World War I, and the discussions in London in 1944 closely tracked those twenty-five years earlier. But neither of the other two questions could be resolved. On the issue of the criminality of aggressive warfare, the members of the commission were sharply split; in December 1944, when the problem came before the full commission, the members were so evenly divided that no consensus could be reached, and no resolution was ever adopted.

The situation with "crimes against humanity" was more complicated. Herbert Pell, no doubt sensitive to ethnic factors in New York politics, took the lead in espousing the view that "crimes committed against . . . any persons because of their race or religion," and especially Nazi atrocities against German Jews and Catholics, should be punishable "as war crimes." A State Department official privately informed the Foreign Office that Pell was "ignorant of law" and "difficult," and had no authority to take this position. Pell's démarche also provoked a personal letter to him from the President (one of Roosevelt's very few interventions on the details of war crimes policies) expressing the opinion that UNWCC jurisdiction comprised "cases arising during the war period," while prewar atrocities, since they "may not fall within the category of war crimes," would "have to be dealt with by the United Nations."

Pell's initiative, however, had won considerable support within the commission, and in May 1944 a draft resolution in line with his opinion was presented for consideration. Apart from the merits of the matter, there was great doubt that the member governments would accept Pell's views, and in consequence Sir Cecil addressed a letter of inquiry to the British government. In November 1944 the Foreign Office replied that the commission should stay within the traditional definitions of "war crimes." And so the matter rested until the end of the war.

The UNWCC had become a pretty discouraging place to work, and at the end of the year Pell resigned and was replaced by the less volatile Colonel J. V. Hodgson. Sir Cecil Hurst resigned on health grounds and was succeeded as Chairman by the Australian Commissioner, Lord Wright of Durley, who remained a respected figure in war crimes activities. However, the UNWCC played no significant role in shaping the Nuremberg enterprise.

The major contribution of the governments-in-exile was their first act—promulgation of the St. James's Declaration, with its decisive emphasis on judicial process as the only acceptable procedure for the trial of persons accused of war crimes.

### 3

On November 12, 1942, Ivan Maisky, the Soviet Ambassador to Britain, sent a note to the Foreign Secretary, Anthony Eden, suggesting that an international tribunal be established for the trial of "major war criminals." There was at that time only one such person actually in custody: Rudolf Hess, who had made a dramatic solo flight from Germany to Britain on May

10, 1941, in the vain hope of persuading the British to negotiate peace with Germany. Eden sharply rejected Maisky's proposal as premature. Nonetheless, the proposal for an "international tribunal" had an importance much more general than that of the Hess case. Several months before Maisky made his proposal, the Foreign Office staff had circulated a memorandum opposing the establishment of any tribunal for the trial of archcriminals such as Himmler on the ground that their "guilt was so black" that it was "beyond the scope of any judicial process." Lord Simon, the Lord Chancellor, was mindful of the views expressed in the St. James's Declaration and doubted that summary execution of the major Nazis would "satisfy public opinion or achieve a measure of substantial justice." But he soon came around to the opinion, strongly held by Eden and Churchill, that while national tribunals for the trial of lesser individuals accused of violating the laws of war would be entirely proper, the creation of an international war crimes tribunal should be strongly opposed and that the principal Nazi leaders should be dealt with by a political decision of the Allied powers.

This was, of course, a complete reversal of the war crimes policies which Britain had pursued after World War I, when Prime Minister Lloyd George had pressed vigorously for the establishment of international tribunals to try the Kaiser and other German leaders. These efforts had been blocked by American opposition, and ultimately the whole war crimes undertaking was trivialized by the fiasco of the Leipzig trials. No doubt this dismal upshot induced in some British officials a feeling of "once bitten twice shy" and helped to establish the atmosphere in which Churchill, Eden, and numerous other British officials concluded that international court trials of the Nazi leaders were all too likely to work more harm than good.

It was plain, however, that this was a matter of deep interest to other countries, and in 1943 Churchill embarked on a program intended to bring the United States and Soviet governments around to the British view. The first move was the Moscow Declaration of November 1, 1943, based on a draft which Churchill had sent to Roosevelt and Stalin a few weeks earlier. The concluding paragraph (a classic example of the tail wagging the dog) did not explicitly state that the major criminals would be given no benefit of trial, but the phrase "punished by a joint decision of the Governments of the Allies" certainly lent itself to that interpretation.

As a practical matter, this and other related issues could, from then on, only be decided by consultation among the Big Three. Opportunity for this came later that same month at their first meeting, which took place at Teheran at the end of November 1943. There was no agenda, but the purposes of the gathering were primarily military, and neither Churchill nor anyone else brought up the subject of war crimes at any of the plenary sessions.

There was, however, a bizarre confrontation between Churchill and

Stalin at a dinner hosted by the latter. The Soviet leader, for some reason, was in a mood to tease Churchill, primarily by accusing him of secret affection for the Germans. Matters came to a head when Stalin, in the course of a long speech, declared that 50,000 German General Staff officers should be liquidated. Churchill took the remark seriously and angrily declared that neither he nor the British public would tolerate mass executions of military officers.

The American diplomat Charles Bohlen, who was serving as Roosevelt's interpreter and was the only Russian-speaking American present, thought that Stalin had made the remark "in semi-jocular fashion, with a sardonic smile and wave of the hand," and meant it "as a jibe at Churchill" rather than as an indication of his actual intentions. It was a very boozy evening, and though several writers have sought to draw important inferences from the episode, the recorded accounts by those present are in sharp conflict,* and I think Bohlen's conclusion is the most reliable.

Meanwhile in London the Foreign Office and the Lord Chancellor were confronting the problem which inevitably arose from their proposed policy of summary disposition: Which German officials were so prominent in the pursuit of evil that they should be given the "honor" of execution without trial? It was the same difficulty that Antony, Lepidus, and Octavius had faced when they "pricked" a list of those to be killed after the murder of Julius Caesar.

In May and June 1944 numerous British officials were preparing such lists, and whoever was "pricked," there were always arguments that other names should be added. Hitler, Goering, Goebbels, Himmler, Ribbentrop, and Field Marshal Wilhelm Keitel (Hitler's military amanuensis) were all obvious choices, but there were several votes to add Admirals Karl Doenitz and Erich Raeder and a few generals, and Clement Attlee (then the Deputy Prime Minister) wanted to add Franz von Papen, Schacht, and several of the bankers and industrialists who had financed Hitler's political rise.

Later that summer Churchill and Roosevelt decided to meet in Quebec in mid-September, and before leaving, Churchill informed the War Cabinet "that he proposed to discuss personally with President Roosevelt the question of war criminals whose crimes had no geographical location." The Prime Minister went to Quebec armed with a memorandum from Lord Simon which began with the pious hope that before the end of the war these criminals would be disposed of by suicide or the action of the German people. Failing this happy outcome, and in accordance with a previously prepared list, the criminals would be executed on proof of identity and on the basis of a political decision. This came to be referred to in government

---

*The confrontation has also been described by Churchill, Admiral William Leahy, Averell Harriman, and Elliott Roosevelt.

circles as the "Napoleonic precedent," since the Little Corporal had been exiled to St. Helena without trial and by political decision.

At Quebec the proposal sailed through smoothly, and on September 15, 1944, the President approved a memorandum stating that "The President and Prime Minister have agreed to put to Marshal Stalin Lord Simon's proposal for dealing with the major war criminals, and to concert with him a list of names." On the same day the two leaders approved a memorandum embodying the so-called Morgenthau Plan to prevent the rearmament of Germany by closing down the Ruhr and Saar industries in order to make Germany "into a country primarily agricultural and pastoral." Both Roosevelt and Churchill soon backed away from the Morgenthau Plan, but the Simon Plan for war criminals had a somewhat longer life.

The following month Churchill flew to Moscow to confer with Stalin. It was a difficult meeting because of disagreement over the future of Poland, and it was here that Churchill first encountered strong opposition to his war crimes proposals. On October 22, 1944, he informed Roosevelt:

> Major War Criminals. U.J.° took an unexpectedly ultrarespectable line. There must be no executions without trial otherwise the world would say we were afraid to try them. I pointed out the difficulties in international law but he replied if there were no trials there must be no death sentences, but only life-long confinements. In face of this view from this quarter I do not wish to press the memo I gave you which you said you would have examined by the State Department. Kindly treat it as withdrawn.

Roosevelt, who by this time regretted his own approval of the Quebec memoranda, replied noncommittally that Churchill's memo about Stalin's attitude was "most interesting" and that these and other matters should be discussed "at the forthcoming three-party meeting."

At Yalta, Churchill brought up the matter near the end of the session on February 9, 1945. Referring to the final paragraph of the Moscow Declaration, he called it "an egg that I myself laid" and made his usual argument for shooting "the leading Nazis" once their identity had been established. Stalin then asked about Rudolf Hess, an inquiry plainly intended to needle Churchill, who replied rather lamely that "events would catch up with Hess," adding that "these men should be given a judicial trial," by which he probably meant that Hess and other war crimes suspects should get a trial, in contrast to the "major criminals," who would face summary execution.†

---

°Initials for "Uncle Joe"—the name by which Roosevelt and Churchill referred to Stalin in their correspondence.

†Stalin probably did not know that in Churchill's private opinion Hess should not be

Churchill first proposed that the conferees should draw up a list of major criminals then and there, but later he withdrew that suggestion, declaring that he merely wanted an exchange of views and that nothing should be given out to the public. Stalin showed no desire for a serious interchange, and the President (who must have been a very tired man) indicated that he was not ready to consider the matter, so the discussion ended inconclusively. The published communiqué at Yalta merely stated that "the question of major war criminals should be the subject of enquiry by the three Foreign Secretaries for report in due course after the close of the conference."

The British summary-execution plan died hard. Early in April 1945, Roosevelt sent his close adviser Judge Samuel Rosenman to discuss war crimes questions in London. En route Rosenman met with Charles de Gaulle, then head of the provisional government of France, who stated that he favored trial rather than summary execution. But Lord Simon met Rosenman with the old arguments for summary execution. On April 12 the War Cabinet, after much discussion, concluded that "for the principal Nazi leaders a full trial under judicial procedure was out of the question."

That same day President Roosevelt died. Rosenman at once returned to Washington, and further negotiations were put over to the United Nations Conference on International Organizations at San Francisco, where the foreign ministers' meeting called for in the Yalta communiqué finally took place. By then the British were being overtaken by events.

Soon after taking office, President Harry Truman made it clear that he opposed summary execution and supported the establishment of a tribunal to try the Nazi leaders. By the end of April, Germany was all but totally overrun by the Allied forces and the Third Reich was disintegrating. On April 28, 1945, Benito Mussolini was shot and his body hung in public in Milan. On April 30 Hitler committed suicide, and the ever faithful Goebbels, with his family, followed his example the next day. Thus the hopes that Lord Simon had voiced at Quebec were in important part fulfilled, for of all the Nazi leaders Hitler and Goebbels had been the two most likely to make an orderly trial difficult.

On May 3 the War Cabinet capitulated and informed Eden, waiting impatiently in San Francisco, of his instructions:

The position as regards the major war criminals has greatly changed since this matter was last considered. Many of these have

---

punished. In *The Grand Alliance* (1950), p. 55, Churchill wrote: "Whatever may be the moral guilt of a German who stood near to Hitler, Hess had, in my view, atoned for this by his completely devoted and frantic deed of lunatic benevolence. He came to us of his own free will, and, though without authority, had something of the quality of an envoy. He was a medical and not a criminal case, and should be so regarded."

already been killed, and the same fate may well overtake others before the fighting is over.

The War Cabinet still see objections to having formal state trials for the most notorious war criminals whose crimes have no geographical location. But if our two major allies remain convinced that this is necessary, we are willing to accept their views on principle.

There were better reasons than the deaths of Hitler and Goebbels, and the imminent prospect of being outvoted, for turning London around. No principled line could be drawn between those who would and those who would not be given opportunity to defend themselves before a court. Summary execution looked like a simple way out of troublesome problems, but it was out of tune with the times. Too many people believed that they had been *wrongfully* hurt by the leaders of the Third Reich and wanted a *judgment* to that effect. Furthermore, and although this may not have been felt as keenly in 1945 as it would have been a few years later, the spectacle of Joseph Stalin, who had sent uncounted thousands of his own countrymen to their deaths by his "political decisions," sitting as one of a triumvirate to "prick" a list of Germans, would have made their decisions a target of mockery as long as memory endured.

## 4

Mankind is supposed to learn from experience, but individuals often "learn" quite different things from much the same experience. In 1944 the United States, like Britain, made a 180-degree turn from its 1919 war crimes policies, but in the opposite direction. In 1945 it was the United States that took the lead in planning and establishing an international tribunal and in expanding international penal law beyond the traditional limits of the laws of war.

In Washington, despite the President's several public denunciations, no significant attention was given to the implementation of war crimes policies until the late summer of 1944, when the Wehrmacht was in desperate easterly retreat through France and Belgium. With an Allied victory apparently imminent, plans for the occupation of Germany became an immediate necessity. Simultaneously, the importance of war crimes as a part of such plans was underlined when Soviet troops advancing into Poland overran the Nazi extermination camp at Maidanek, near Lublin.

At least seven different federal agencies had immediate or potential concern with war crimes questions—the departments of State, War, Navy, Treasury, and Justice, the Office of Strategic Services (OSS), and of course the White House itself. Initially, however, the War and Treasury departments were much the most vigorous participants, and the early discussions led, within a few weeks, to a sharp confrontation between their two chiefs:

Secretary of War Henry L. Stimson and Secretary of the Treasury Henry Morgenthau, Jr.

The Treasury Department was the citadel of the "tough peace" advocates, whose views were embodied in the Morgenthau Plan, known primarily for its proposal to abolish German heavy industry. But it also included a section on war crimes which closely resembled the British proposal,°in that it envisaged the summary execution of those on a list of "archcriminals" by military "firing squads," once their identity had been established. Secretary Stimson, on the other hand, opposed the draconian economic features of the Morgenthau Plan and believed that the United States "should participate in an international tribunal" for trial of "the chief Nazi officials," who would be charged with "offenses against the laws of the Rules of War." These conflicting views were laid before the President in two meetings early in September 1944.

Without reaching any decision, the President went off to the second Quebec meeting with Churchill. On September 13, to the chagrin of both Stimson and Secretary of State Cordell Hull, Roosevelt asked Morgenthau to join him in Quebec, where, on September 15, Roosevelt and Churchill initialed the Morgenthau Plan and agreed that Lord Simon's summary-execution proposal be presented to Stalin.

Morgenthau returned from Quebec the apparent victor. But his triumph was short-lived; news of Stimson's disagreement leaked to the press, and the public reaction to the most punitive features of the Morgenthau Plan was sharply adverse. Stimson sent a critical memorandum to the President, and at a meeting of the two on October 3, 1944, the President expressed great regret that he had initialed the Morgenthau document at Quebec, and declared that Morgenthau had "pulled a boner."

The episode decisively weakened Treasury's influence on planning for the occupation of Germany and, although the subject of war crimes appears not to have been discussed at the Roosevelt-Stimson meeting, the formulation of war crimes policy proceeded thereafter with no significant participation by Morgenthau or his staff. The President, chastened by the Quebec experience, told the State Department that he disliked "making detailed plans for a country which we do not yet occupy" and for several months left Washington officialdom with no presidential guidance on war crimes policy formulation.

In this situation, the War Department emerged as the dominant entity. The Navy Department, with little or no stake in the occupation of Germany, showed no interest in war crimes planning. Neither the Justice Department nor the OSS played a significant role until 1945. The State

---

°Morgenthau had just returned from a trip to Europe, where he had seen both Churchill and Eden, who may very well have told him of their summary-execution preferences.

Department legal adviser, Judge Green Hackworth, participated in the planning process, but Secretary Hull was ill and out of favor at the White House. He resigned early in December 1944, but his successor, Edward R. Stettinius, was so inexperienced and tentative that his department's voice in decision-making was never strong.

Stimson's ascendancy also foreclosed American support for the British summary-execution plan. In his insistence that the Nazi leaders stand trial, the Secretary had the strong support of both the Army Chief of Staff, General George C. Marshall, and the army's principal lawyer, Judge Advocate General Myron C. Cramer. But as the dust of the Stimson-Morgenthau dispute settled, nothing else about the scope or nature of the trial or trials had been determined.

Within the War Department, the unit which, by mission and tradition, would be primarily responsible for war crimes planning was the Office of the Judge Advocate General (JAG). And so it was at the outset; in August JAG submitted a proposed directive to army commanders in the field for the apprehension of enemy individuals suspected of "violations of the laws and customs of war"—a thoroughly conventional approach to the matter. The source of the proposals which eventually blossomed into the "Nuremberg ideas" was found elsewhere in the War Department and first appeared in a memorandum of September 15, 1944, authored by Colonel Murray Bernays, a member of the personnel branch (G-1) of the Army General Staff.

Bernays, in peacetime a successful New York lawyer, had been concerned with the treatment of American prisoners of war in Germany and was aware of the extensive atrocities, against Russian prisoners and others, committed by members of Nazi organizations, such as the SS. He also knew of the demands, then emanating from the American Jewish Conference and the War Refugee Board, for the punishment of Nazi crimes against German Jews during the prewar years, which the State Department regarded as outside the scope of the laws of war. There were "many thousands of war criminals who should be tried for crimes committed all over Europe," Bernays wrote, and pointed out the numerous difficulties which would be confronted in obtaining evidence to convict so many individuals. His memorandum of September 15 proposed methods for resolving these two problems, to wit: finding a legal basis for punishing the prewar German crimes, and developing a procedure for dealing with the hundreds of thousands of members of the SS and other Nazi organizations implicated in German atrocities.

To meet the first difficulty, Bernays resorted to the Anglo-American law of criminal conspiracy, proposing that the Nazi organizations and their leading members be charged, before an international court, not merely with atrocious violations of the laws of war, but with conspiring (presumably from the beginning of the Nazi period in 1933 or earlier) to commit such violations. In Anglo-American law, criminal conspiracy consists of an agreement by two or more persons to engage in unlawful conduct. Bernays reasoned, therefore, that if members of the Nazi organizations had agreed among themselves prior to the war to commit violations of the laws of war when war came, their preparatory conduct before the war would be punishable as a part of the conspiracy to commit the wartime atrocities.°

The second problem—how to cope with defendants numbered in six or seven figures, a ghoulish *embarras de richesses*—Bernays proposed to deal with by indicting the Nazi organizations themselves, and providing that once such an organization was convicted on the conspiracy charge, all its members might thereafter likewise be found guilty on proof of membership alone. The severity of punishment for individual members would be governed by evidence of the extent to which they were involved in or knew of the organization's criminal activities.

There were weighty objections to both of these proposals. The Anglo-American concept of conspiracy was not part of European legal systems and arguably not an element of the internationally recognized laws of war. The proposal that the leading members of Nazi organizations be given a judicial trial, while rank-and-file members of convicted Nazi organizations would be found guilty on mere proof of membership, appeared to turn upside down the British plan to punish the major war criminals by political decision and try the lesser fry before national war crimes tribunals.

However, the problems Bernays had tackled were very real, and no one was coming up with better solutions. His plan picked up support as well as encountering opposition when it was scrutinized in other branches of the War Department. Secretary Stimson had delegated to the Assistant Secretary of War, John J. McCloy, responsibility for developing a war crimes program, and both McCloy and his assistant executive officer, Colonel Ammi Cutter, reacted favorably enough so that, on October 24, Bernays was given opportunity to present his plan at a general conference on war crimes in Stimson's office.

The Secretary was greatly impressed, and especially enthusiastic about the conspiracy concept. No formal approval was given to the Bernays plan, but Stimson promptly passed it on as "worthy of complete investiga-

---

°To illustrate: Assume that a group of Nazis has conspired to lead Germany into war against Poland and France, with the further intention that, after conquering and occupying those nations, all French and Polish Jews would be transported to eastern Poland and slaughtered in death camps. Assume further that the members of the group not only wish to treat German Jews the same way, but believe that it will be impossible to carry out their plan for French and Polish Jews unless the German public has previously been imbued with violent anti-Semitism, and that this can only be accomplished by prewar degradation and harassment of German Jews. Under these circumstances, the domestic German anti-Semitic atrocities would be a necessary preparation for the subsequent violations of the laws of war in France and Poland and would be punishable as part of the conspiracy to violate the laws of war.

tion" to the State and Navy departments, and on November 21, meeting with the President, he outlined the conspiracy approach, with the result, as described in Stimson's diary, that Roosevelt "gave his very frank approval when I said that conspiracy with . . . representatives of all classes of actors brought in from top to bottom, would be the best way to try it and would give us a record and also a trial which would certainly persuade any on-looker of the evil of the Nazi system."

A week after this meeting, a new wellspring of war crimes ideas surfaced in the person of Colonel William C. Chanler, the Deputy Director of Military Government, and in peacetime a law partner, friend, and neigh-bor of Stimson's. Prior to his War Department appointment, Colonel Chanler had been Chief Legal Officer of the Allied Military Government in Italy, and his period of service included the seven weeks during which Mussolini was interned by the Badoglio government of Italy.° This situation had led Chanler, then in Palermo, to ponder a war crimes trial of Mussolini, and he and Colonel Robert O. Gorman drew up an indictment which included a charge of engaging in unlawful warfare against peaceful nations.

Mussolini's escape from Italy to Germany rendered the project aca-demic, but in late November 1944 Chanler, back in the Pentagon and noting that the Bernays plan did not include any charge based on the illegality of Germany's resort to war, revived the ideas he had developed in Italy and embodied them in a memorandum which he submitted directly to Stimson.

Stimson thought Chanler's thesis "a little in advance of the progress of international thought," and in fact the legal theory on which Chanler based his conclusion† was never widely accepted. But the Secretary was highly sympathetic to Chanler's wish to include a charge based on the illegality of aggressive war; and as time went on, Stimson became increas-ingly convinced of the great moral and political importance of securing a judicial decision that launching an aggressive war was criminal under inter-national law.

---

°Mussolini was removed from office on July 26, 1943, and power was entrusted to Marshal Pietro Badoglio, the former Italian Army Chief of Staff. The fallen dictator was interned succes-sively on two small Italian islands and then in a mountain resort in the Abruzzi, from which he was rescued by the German SS officer Otto Skorzeny, and flown to Germany on September 12, 1943.

†Chanler's theory was based on the Kellogg-Briand Pact, and his arguments were in-tended to get around the omission in the pact of any explicit proviso that waging aggressive war was criminal. Since, however, the signatory nations did "condemn recourse to war" and "re-nounce it as an instrument of national policy," Chanler argued that if any of the signatories should violate the pact by aggressively invading another country, the aggressor would lose the rights of a lawful belligerent. Its acts of war in the invaded country would therefore be murders and assaults under the domestic law of the invaded country. Thus Poland, Belgium, and the other countries invaded by Germany could demand the extradition of the German leaders, and the charges against them would not be stated as violations of the pact but as murders and other crimes under those countries' own laws.

Stimson, nonetheless, does not appear to have ever laid such a recommendation before the President, and 1944 came to its end with the lawyers in the several departments still sunk in controversy over all these questions. However, on January 3, 1945, President Roosevelt, for the first and last time, gave direct, though informal and unpublished, instructions to his subordinates on the subject of war crimes. In a memorandum addressed to Secretary of State Stettinius he wrote:

> Please send me a brief report on the state of the proceedings before the War Crimes Commission, and particularly the attitude of the U.S. representative on offenses to be brought against Hitler and the chief Nazi war criminals. The charges should include an indictment for waging aggressive war, in violation of the Kellogg Pact. Perhaps these and other charges might be joined in a conspiracy indictment.

The occasion for the first sentence is plain, for the "U.S. representative" was Roosevelt's friend Herbert Pell, who was continually at loggerheads with the State Department and was even then requesting an audience with the President. In the third sentence, the reference to a "conspiracy indictment" is in line with Roosevelt's approval of Stimson's recommendations at their meeting on November 21, 1944.

But what explains the mandate in the second sentence? There is no sure answer; one writer has plausibly inferred that it was suggested to the President by his special counsel, speech-writer, and valued adviser, Judge Samuel Rosenman, whom the President had recently designated to iron out the departments' conflicting views on war crimes policy.

But there is a more likely explanation. Colonel Chanler had summarized his views in a half-page memorandum which (probably sometime in December 1944) he sent directly to the President via Lieutenant Colonel John Boettiger, Chanler's army colleague and Roosevelt's son-in-law. The President's reference to the "Kellogg Pact," which was the cornerstone of Chanler's thesis, strongly suggests that it was the half-page Chanler memorandum that triggered the President's endorsement of the aggressive war criminality concept.°

The President was soon to depart for the Yalta Conference; Rosenman was under pressure to provide him with a position paper and proved adept

---

°This paragraph and certain other references to Colonel Chanler are based on letters to me from him, dated December 28, 1954, and February 25, 1955. The second letter states that the memorandum to the President was returned with his initialed approval; there is no reason to doubt this, but when he wrote to me, Mr. Chanler was unable to find the document itself.

In private life Mr. Boettiger was at that time publisher of the Seattle *Post-Intelligencer.* He and his wife, Anna (Roosevelt), frequently visited and traveled with the President. Both had a literary bent and from time to time helped with the President's speeches.

at negotiating a compromise. Only the Stimson group had a well-developed position, and the upshot of the negotiations was a document in which the Bernays contributions were included.

It was delivered to the President on January 22 in the form of a memorandum initialed by the Secretaries of State and War and the Attorney General, Francis Biddle. An international tribunal was to be established to try both "the highest ranking German leaders" and the Nazi groups and organizations through which they had acted. These defendants would be charged with both the commission of crimes and conspiracy to commit them, and the crimes would comprise prewar atrocities against their own German nationals, the waging of "an illegal war of aggression," and violations of the laws of war. After the international trial, and assuming that the tribunal had found guilty one or more of the Nazi organizations, individual members of each such organization would be "brought before occupation courts" where "the only necessary proof of guilt of any particular defendant would be his membership," while "the punishment would be made appropriate to the facts of his particular case."

Public pressure for a decision was mounting fast. In December 1944, during the Battle of the Bulge, news of the slaughter of some seventy American prisoners at Malmédy in Belgium by troops of an SS tank regiment sent a wave of indignation throughout the country and convinced the doubters that stories of SS atrocities were no figments of propaganda. Four months later, as British and American troops overran western Germany, the horrors of the concentration camps—Belsen, Dachau, Buchenwald— were exposed. There was growing unrest in Congress at the lack of authoritative information about the government's war crimes plans.

The Yalta communiqué had called for a report from the foreign ministers of the Big Three—Eden, Vyacheslav Molotov, and Stettinius—who were just then gathering at the San Francisco Conference for consideration and adoption of the United Nations Charter. War crimes were not on the agenda, but it was decided to seize the opportunity of San Francisco to bring about a meeting at which the War Department plan would be accepted, at least as a basis for discussion. In preparation for such a meeting, the chief legal craftsmen of the Stimson group spent many hours reviewing and revising the basic memorandum and proposed executive agreement to make them more suitable for foreign scrutiny and approval.

While this was going on President Truman, by an executive order published May 2, 1945, appointed Robert H. Jackson, Associate Justice of the Supreme Court, as Representative of the United States and Chief of Counsel "in preparing and prosecuting charges of atrocities and war crimes against such of the leaders of the European Axis powers . . . as the United States may agree with any of the United Nations to bring to trial before an international military tribunal."

It appears that the major impetus for creating such an office and selecting Jackson to fill it came from the Stimson group. Ordinarily the President would have consulted the Attorney General, but Truman and Biddle were not then on good terms. On April 22 McCloy sent Rosenman a memorandum declaring that there was "imperative need of having counsel designated immediately" to "prepare the United States' side of the main war criminals cases." There followed a list of eight names in alphabetical order, including Supreme Court Justices Owen Roberts (seventy years old and ready to retire) and Robert H. Jackson, Sidney Alderman (lawyer for the Southern Railway), John Harlan, and Theodore Kiendl (the last two litigating partners in large New York firms). Perhaps as a bow to seniority McCloy described Roberts as "probably our first selection," but in fact McCloy, Chanler, Robert Patterson (Under Secretary of War and a former federal judge), and Rosenman were all solidly behind Jackson, whom they had known during the Roosevelt administration as Solicitor General, Attorney General, and Supreme Court Justice.

Shortly before his appointment was announced, Jackson reviewed the documents that had been prepared for San Francisco and suggested some revisions. In particular, he thought the memorandum was "too impassioned and gives the impression that it is setting up a court organized to convict." But he readily accepted the structure and content of the War Department plan, and left it to the Rosenman-McCloy group to "sell it" at San Francisco.

On May 3, 1945, when the Big Three foreign ministers met, Stettinius presided, but Rosenman presented the American plan. Stettinius next called for a decision on the question of French participation; there were no objections, but the French Foreign Minister, Georges Bidault, was not immediately available, so it was agreed that Stettinius would bring him up to date and invite his participation. Eden then announced that his government accepted the decision to bring the "major criminals" before a tribunal and would join in the trial. Molotov declared himself unable to comment on such important matters on short notice.

The American proposals were then remitted to the legal advisers for further consideration, and during the next two weeks Rosenman and his associates met with their British, French, and Soviet opposite members and discussed a wide variety of questions and proposed amendments. But the other governments never authorized their delegations to accept the American proposals, so once again most of the major policy decisions were put off to another day.

5

So ended the first phase of the Nuremberg undertaking, during which the basic concepts of the trials were developed. The ideas of trying defeated leaders before an international tribunal and of extending international criminal law to both domestic atrocities against religious and racial groups and the launching of aggressive war had all been broached, albeit unsuccessfully, at Versailles in 1919. Both the concepts of conspiracy and of organizational guilt were new to international penal law, though not to Anglo-American domestic law.

The initial pressure for postwar trials came from the peoples of the German-occupied nations, but the assemblage of all these concepts in a single trial package was the work of a handful of American lawyers, all but Cutter (who was from Boston) from New York City. Some of them (Stimson, McCloy) were what today we would call "moderate" Republicans; several (Rosenman, Chanler, Herbert Wechsler) were Democrats. Elitist and generally accustomed to personal prosperity, all had strong feelings of noblesse oblige. What moved these men to push out of their way the JAG, the usual repository of war crimes matters, and steer their government into these paths, most of them controversial and some of them novel?

Bernays, originator of two of the most original proposals, appears to have been motivated by the same desires as those of the victims of German occupation. He wanted to visit condign retribution by law on the multitude of Germans who shared complicity in the atrocities. His invocation of organizational responsibility did not broaden the concept of war crimes, but was a juridical device to eliminate the need to prove complicity of the individual members of the organizations, primarily the SS, which were responsible for many if not most of the crimes, by making membership itself sufficient proof of guilt.

There were a few precedents in Anglo-American domestic law for attaching individual guilt to organizational membership, including the then recently enacted Smith Act (1940), in which Congress made it a felony to be a member of any organization which advocated overthrow of the United States government by the use of force and violence. But the Smith Act had been passed over the President's veto and was anathema to civil libertarians. The men of the Stimson group were, in varying degrees, sensitive to the traditional rights of the accused and the dangers of "guilt by association." Why did they accept a procedure which so clearly threatened those safeguards?

No doubt it is difficult for many of today's readers to grasp the utter hatred of the SS which its actions had spread throughout the Western world, especially during the last two years of the war, when there was incontrovertible proof of the wholesale massacre of Jews, the horrors of the concentration camps, and the killings of prisoners of war, as at Malmédy. I remember attending a party in Washington, early in 1945 during a brief home leave, at which the nearly unanimous view of the guests (mostly libertarian New Dealers) was that all members of the SS should be put to death, and I was attacked as "soft on Germany" for expressing a contrary opinion.° With such attitudes afloat, it is hardly surprising that at the Treasury, Morgenthau and his staff were proposing the permanent exile of all SS members and their families. Bernays's organizational guilt plan, insofar as it contemplated a hearing at which the penalty for membership would be based on the individual's degree of complicity, was, obviously, far less arbitrary or draconian.

The other members of the Stimson group no doubt shared the prevailing wish for retribution. However, Colonel Chanler's memorandum on the aggressive war concept inspired a different and greater concern which, for Stimson, became the dominant feature of the Nuremberg process. "With the judgment at Nuremberg," he wrote in 1947, "we at last reach to the very core of international strife, and we set a penalty not merely for war crimes, but for the very act of war itself, except in self defense." In short, it was "war and not its methods" that was "the central moral problem."

It was a matter of chance that the United Nations Charter and the first international consensus on war crimes were contemporaneously achieved at San Francisco. But the coincidence is meaningful. As Justice Jackson's son, William E. Jackson, later wrote: "It is perhaps not commonly apprehended that the principles of Nuremberg . . . go hand in hand with the organization of the United Nations as the twin foundations of an international society ordered by law."

Essentially, in the minds of Stimson and his colleagues, their prime purpose was to bring the weight of law and criminal sanctions to bear in support of the peaceful and humanitarian principles that the United Nations was to promote by consultation and collective action.

---

°My dissent was based on my view that such gargantuan slaughter was unthinkable and that even SS men were not all alike. In the summer of 1944 I had been on duty at Bastia in Corsica, which had just been liberated from German occupation. I was billeted with a Corsican family, and they and the other Corsicans I met all declared that the occupying troops, the SS Brigade Reichsfuehrer SS, had behaved very correctly. The only guest who agreed with me was the late Mark DeWolfe Howe, then a colonel assigned to American Military Government, who also had recently been on duty in Europe.

*Chapter 3*

# JUSTICE JACKSON
# TAKES OVER

After the Rosenman-McCloy delegation returned from San Francisco, full leadership of the Nuremberg venture passed to Jackson. Henceforth, the War (soon to be renamed "Defense") and State departments would only occasionally be involved in war crimes decision-making, though they continued to furnish basic support.

Robert H. Jackson was not one of the legal Brahmins typical of the Stimson group. He had a rural upbringing in western New York State, did not attend college, and his "higher" education consisted of one year at Albany Law School. He was probably the last nationally prominent lawyer to gain admission to the bar by serving an apprenticeship rather than by a law school degree. Despite these academic shortcomings, Jackson developed, in the small city of Jamestown, a successful regional law practice and, more important for present purposes, a superb command of the English language.

Jackson's courtroom success and Democratic Party preference brought him to the attention of New York State's major politicians—Franklin Roosevelt, Herbert Lehman, Henry Morgenthau—and in 1934 he was appointed General Counsel of the Bureau of Internal Revenue. Thereafter promotions came fast: Assistant Attorney General in 1936, Solicitor General in 1938, Attorney General in January 1940, Associate Justice of the United States Supreme Court in July 1941.

Jackson's forensic talents were especially admired during his service as Solicitor General, but it was as Attorney General that he first encountered situations which touched closely on one of the major issues he would later confront in connection with Nuremberg. His tenure as Attorney General comprised most of the uneasy period between the outbreak of war in Europe in September 1939 and the Japanese attack at Pearl Harbor in

December 1941 which threw America into the war. The country as a whole strongly favored the Allies against Nazi Germany, but there was strong sentiment for noninvolvement and neutrality, even at the risk of defeat for the Allies.

In 1940 Roosevelt won reelection to a third term, promising the electorate that "their boys would not be sent to foreign wars." But after the fall of France, with Britain under heavy attack by the Luftwaffe and facing possible invasion, Roosevelt's own views and those of many of his countrymen led to measures in support of Britain which raised grave issues under the international law of neutrality. Early in 1941 Congress passed the Lend-Lease Act, which Jackson as Attorney General interpreted as explicitly adopting "the policy that defense of certain countries now at war, including Great Britain, is vital to our own defense and that the furnishing of aid to such countries is essential to the security of the United States."°

Such measures triggered Jackson's interest in the international law of war, a subject which he publicly addressed in March 1941 in a speech to the Inter-American Bar Association at Havana. Drawing on the old doctrine of just and unjust wars, Jackson flatly rejected the view that all wars are legal and that neutrals invariably owe a duty of impartiality as between one belligerent and another. He declared that "aggressive wars are civil wars against the international community" and, invoking the Kellogg-Briand Pact, accused the Axis powers of shamefully violating their obligations under it. Their guilt, he said, fully justified neutrals in giving aid to the victims of aggression.

Once on the bench, Jackson spoke no further on such matters until April 13, 1945, the day after Roosevelt's death, when he addressed the American Society of International Law on the topic "The Rule of Law Among Nations." For the first time, Jackson gave public evidence of his thinking on war crimes:

> I have no purpose to enter into any controversy as to what shall be done with war criminals, either high or humble. If it is considered good policy for the future peace of the world, if it is believed that the example will outweigh the tendency to create among their own countrymen a myth of martyrdom, then let them be executed. But in that case let the decision to execute them be made as a military or political decision. . . .
>
> Of course, if good faith trials are sought, that is another matter. I am not troubled as some seem to be over problems of jurisdiction of war criminals or of finding existing and recognized law by which

°This statement was made in Jackson's opinion as Attorney General, advising the President that he had statutory authority to provide for the training of British aviators in the United States by members of the United States Army Air Corps.

standards of guilt may be determined. But all experience teaches that there are certain things you cannot do under the guise of judicial trial. Courts try cases, but cases also try courts.

You must put no man on trial before anything that is called a court . . . under the forms of judicial proceedings if you are not willing to see him freed if not proven guilty. . . .

Thus, when Samuel Rosenman entered Justice Jackson's office on April 26, 1945, to convey President Truman's wish to appoint Jackson as his country's Representative and Chief Counsel for war crimes, he was talking to a man who already had a considerable public record on the subject and who would be a strong advocate of a charge based on the illegality of aggressive war. Furthermore, the passage just quoted was a clarion call for just trials. There should be no drumhead court-martial, no Moscow-type show trial, no foregone conclusions; there should be no trials at all unless prosecutors and judges alike were agreed that defendants should be acquitted if the law and facts did not support their conviction.

Jackson was barely two days into his new assignment when that commitment was put to the test. With victory in hand, the question of war reparations from Germany arose, and an Inter-Allied Reparations Commission was established. In Washington an interdepartmental Informal Policy Committee on Germany drafted instructions for the American representative on the Reparations Committee, Edwin W. Pauley, a California corporate executive in the oil business and a member of the Democratic National Committee, whom Roosevelt, and later Truman, often used as a special presidential representative on foreign economic matters. One section of these instructions dealt with compulsory labor service as an element of reparations, and provided that such service could be required from "war criminals and individuals definitely determined by appropriate process to be members of the Gestapo, the S.S., the Sicherheitsdienst, leaders of the S.A., or leading collaborators, supporters of and participants in the Nazi party or administration." This and other parts of the instructions had been drafted by officials in the Treasury Department.

When this document was reviewed at the War Department, Colonel Chanler pointed out to Bernays that it in effect inflicted penal servitude on members of the very organizations which, under the American war crimes plan, were to have their guilt determined by an international tribunal. During the evening of May 3 Bernays telephoned this information to Jackson, who at once concluded that such a provision would prejudge the criminality of these organizations and their members and "make it farcical to conduct trials" on that issue.

Armed with a memorandum urging that liability for penal servitude be limited to "convicted war criminals," on May 12 Jackson met with

Pauley; also present were Averell Harriman (then Ambassador to the Soviet Union), Rosenman, and Isador Lubin (Chief of the Bureau of Labor Statistics), one of the draftsmen of the proposal. When Lubin disclosed that Russia wanted a working force of 5 million to repair her war-devastated areas, Jackson was "shocked at the idea of transporting to Russia masses of people," and Harriman predicted that they would be subjected to atrocious living conditions. After Jackson had stated flatly that "he could not go ahead with pretended trials if this provision were agreed upon," the conferees decided that it would have to be modified.

On the morning of May 15 Jackson took the matter to Truman, who approved the Justice's stance on the matter. Thus Jackson was in a strong position when, on May 18, there was a showdown conference in Morgenthau's office, with over twenty participants representing the interested agencies. There were some hot words, but by this time Morgenthau had little support except from his own staff, and in the end even he felt constrained to vote for an amendment in line with Jackson's viewpoint. Morgenthau resigned shortly thereafter.

Jackson's victory was not without cost. A few days later the widely read Washington columnist Drew Pearson published extracts from Jackson's memorandum to Pauley (which had been classified "top secret"), together with an attack on him for being "soft on Germany." Plainly, Jackson's job was going to have its rough side.

## 2

Jackson's first task was to assemble a staff, and of the Stimson group only Colonel Bernays was available. For fiscal reasons, Jackson wished to rely primarily on personnel loaned to him by other federal agencies, but his first selection was from outside the government and was further surprising in that it was a man with whom he had no personal acquaintance. On May 3 Jackson telephoned Sidney Alderman, whose arguments before the Supreme Court Jackson had greatly admired. He asked Alderman to come aboard as his "first assistant," an invitation which was promptly accepted. At about the same time, Jackson secured from the Justice Department the services of Assistant Attorney General Francis M. Shea, with whom he had had a close personal and professional relation since the early New Deal days. These two men were to be Jackson's principal associates during the next five or six months.

Broader in import, however, was the relation Jackson soon established with Major General William J. Donovan and the organization which he headed, the Office of Strategic Services. As a battalion and regimental National Guard commander in World War I (from which he emerged with the sobriquet "Wild Bill"), Donovan was awarded the Congressional Medal of Honor and many other decorations. Thereafter he held several federal offices and established a highly successful law practice. In 1941 Roosevelt appointed him Coordinator of Information and a year later Director of the OSS, responsible to the Joint Chiefs of Staff.

Donovan had been interested in war crimes at least since 1943, and in 1944 he committed his agency to cooperate with the War Crimes Division of JAG. In March 1945, after discussion with the President's close adviser Harry Hopkins, Donovan sent a memorandum to the President proposing that "the German people themselves" should "undertake to bring to trial and punish certain war criminals under pre-1933 German laws."

Although there was a certain volatility in Donovan's thinking on the subject, it nevertheless is clear that his interest was genuine, for early in April 1945 he directed the OSS General Counsel, Lieutenant James Donovan, "to get us a top-flight staff on war crimes," which were "something on which we must be prepared at once." And as soon as Jackson's appointment was announced, Donovan coupled his letter of congratulations with the information that his agency had "done certain work in the war crimes field" and would "cooperate with you in any manner which you deem desirable."

Sorely pressed for staff and general logistical support, Jackson jumped at the offer and asked for all the assistance that could be given. Soon General Donovan was being referred to as Jackson's "First Deputy" (the hierarchical relation between the General on the one hand and Alderman and Shea on the other was never clarified). James Donovan made an excellent impression on Jackson and joined the inner circle of his advisers.

On June 7, 1945, the relation was formalized by a letter from Jackson to General Donovan. It was a relationship which greatly benefited the Nuremberg project in terms of staff and equipment, but the personal ties between Jackson and Donovan were never strong, and they gave way shortly before the trials began.

Other high-level appointments to Jackson's staff included Colonel John Harlan Amen, a well-known New York lawyer who since 1942 had been in the Inspector General's branch of the army; Gordon Dean, who had been press officer at the Department of Justice, to handle press relations; and Jackson's son William, who had graduated from law school in 1944 and, commissioned a naval ensign, had been serving in the Bureau of Ships. Bernays was appointed as the staff's executive officer.

Jackson had apparently undertaken his task under the impression that the War Department, and perhaps other government agencies, would have evidence connecting the Nazi leaders with the crimes to be charged. But on May 7, and again ten days later, he had rude awakenings to the truth, which was that Washington was little better off than the UNWCC in this respect. James Donovan first disclosed this situation to the Justice, and on May 17 Amen reported that JAG had no cases ready for trial and virtually nothing implicating the major defendants. On May 21 General John Weir of JAG confessed that even with respect to the Malmédy massacre he had no way of identifying the guilty individuals; they had all been in tanks, and in his opinion Malmédy was "washed out as a war crimes case." JAG had but one important piece of evidence: the text of Hitler's Commando Order of October 18, 1942, directing the execution of all enemy commando troops, even if captured in full uniform. This was, of course, a flagrant violation of the Hague Conventions.

On May 22, rightly concluding that neither his evidentiary nor his diplomatic aims could be furthered in Washington, Jackson, with Amen, flew to Paris to see what progress could be made on that side of the Atlantic.

## 3

Accordingly, Justice Jackson was across the ocean on May 24 when, still undecided about my own immediate future, I first visited his staff's offices in the Pentagon Building. I met Sidney Alderman, a gentle-mannered Southerner who was later to be my housemate in Nuremberg, and then had lunch with Frank Shea, a close friend under whom I had worked both at the Agricultural Adjustment Administration in 1934 and at the Department of Justice in 1939.

By the next day I had decided to cast my lot with the Jackson team, and reported for duty to Colonel Bernays, the Executive Officer. Although my relations with him were always cordial, I never came to know him well because he soon went to London, and shortly after I returned to England he resigned, dissatisfied and ailing, and resumed his New York law practice. He was a slender, sallow-complexioned man with white hair and cavernous eyes, and never looked to me like a well man. But his resignation was motivated in large part by disappointment over his decline in the prosecution hierarchy. His initial contributions to the Nuremberg enterprise were unique and substantial, but his talents were conceptual rather than operational, and after the general shape of the project was established, he was edged out of leadership by stronger and more versatile men.

I was assigned a desk and was pleased to find as my office neighbor Lieutenant Colonel Benjamin Kaplan, a contemporary whom I knew by reputation as an exceptionally able New York lawyer; in later years he was a professor at Harvard Law School and then a judge of the Supreme Judicial Court of Massachusetts. During the war he had been working in military procurement under John J. McCloy, Robert Patterson, and General Lucius Clay, my future boss. Kaplan and I soon agreed that the staff was stuck on dead center. Jackson (as well as General Donovan and Colonel Amen) were in Europe; Alderman and Shea were almost as new to the subject matter as we were; Bernays did not seem to know what to do with the new recruits.

But it soon became apparent that there was a deeper cause of this malaise. Our task was to prepare to prosecute the leading Nazis on the criminal charges described in the draft executive agreement presented at the San Francisco Conference. The first question a prosecuting attorney asks in such a situation is "Where's the evidence?" The blunt fact was that, despite what "everybody knew" about the Nazi leaders, virtually no judicially admissible evidence was at hand. Unless it could be found, all the care put into drafting agreements and organization plans would be wasted effort.

The only available veterans of past war crimes activities were Bernays and James Donovan. In mid-May they had drafted a Planning Memorandum and a Memorandum on Trial Preparation, and these documents had been approved by Jackson shortly before he went to Europe. The Planning Memorandum described, in a discursive way, the proposed charges against the defendants (characterizing their "common plan" as aimed at "complete domination of Europe and eventually of the world") and listed some twenty-five ingredients of the proof necessary to prove the charges. The Trial Preparation memo gave the task of providing the necessary evidence to the JAG for aggressive war and violations of the laws of war, and to the OSS for other atrocities and the "common plan."

The responsibilities thus imposed were formidable and fundamental, and I was very doubtful that either agency could fulfill them. Indeed (though I did not know it at the time), Jackson had already been disabused of the notion that the JAG would be an important source of evidence, and my own visits to the JAG offices late in May led me to the same conclusion.

As for the OSS, James Donovan had previously assured Bernays that his agency had "done a great deal of work" and "assembled much material" on its assigned subjects. But his progress report of May 30 did not encourage me to believe that the OSS would be much more productive of real evidence than the JAG. In fact, the OSS staff included a number of able and learned experts on the Third Reich,* but most of what they had to offer, however valuable as background information, was neither documentary nor testimonial evidence suitable for court use.

I soon concluded that Washington was not the right place for Jackson's headquarters and that he should move it to Europe. My wartime duties had not involved captured documents or prisoner interrogation, but I had been working in the world of military intelligence and knew where and by whom those things were handled. I also knew that with the occupation of western Germany, a number of Allied "target" teams, both military and civilian, had gone in behind the front-line troops to collar and sequester all high-

---

*These included Franz Neumann, author of *Behemoth—The Structure and Practice of National Socialism* (1944), Raphael Lemkin, coiner of the word "genocide" and author of *Axis Rule in Occupied Europe* (1944), Carl Schorske, and William L. Langer.

ranking Germans and other informed persons for interrogation, to locate and collect official files and other documentary caches of military or other significance, and to generally sniff out and secure anything and everything of use for governmental purposes. These teams, I was sure, would be the prime source of the evidence we needed.

So thinking, I decided that the best use I could make of my time would be to put my information and thoughts on evidence-gathering into a memorandum, which would also include some general comments on the situation and problems confronting the Jackson staff. I entitled it "An Approach to the Preparation of the Prosecution of Axis Criminality," and submitted it to Alderman on June 2. The memorandum reveals my initial and, to a great extent my continuing, perception of the nature and purpose of the prosecution, and, deservedly or not, it made a considerable impression on Jackson and thus brought me a place among his principal associates.

As I saw it, the two most important things to be accomplished by the trials were:

> To give meaning to the war against Germany. To validate the casualties we have suffered and the destruction and casualties we have caused. To . . . make the war meaningful and valid for the people of the Allied Nations and, it is not beyond hope, for at least some people of the Axis Nations.
>
> To establish and maintain harmonious relations with the other United Nations in the presentation and successful prosecution of the case. Incalculable harm can be done . . . if the trial "bogs down" as the result of disagreement among the United Nations, or if the several nations proceed separately and in a spirit critical of each other.

In view of the criminal charges listed in the draft executive agreement, I had of course been hearing much discussion of the question of whether the launching of aggressive war could legitimately be treated as an international-law crime. I wrote:

> This phase of the case is based on the assumption that it is, or will be declared, a punishable offense to plan and launch (and lose?) an aggressive war, particularly if treaties are thereby violated. Although the phrase "illegal launching" is a "law idea" . . . the thing we want to accomplish is not a legal thing but a political thing. Its accomplishment depends on persuading the several participating nations to take the political step of committing themselves to this doctrine.

The ex post facto problem,° I wrote, was not a bothersome question "if we keep in mind that this is a *political* decision to declare and apply a principle of international law." Furthermore:

> Only the most incorrigible legalists can pretend to be shocked by the conclusion that the perpetrator of an aggressive war acts at peril of being punished for his perpetration, even if no tribunal has ever previously decided that perpetration of an aggressive war is a crime. And, in any event, the ex post facto question is rendered much easier by the fact of treaty violation . . . a man who violates a treaty must act at peril of being punished by the offended party's employing self-help.

What defenses could the Nazi leaders raise against the aggressive-war charge? Much of the British opposition to trying these men had arisen from fear that they would use the courtroom as a forum for accusing the British and French of having grievously injured Germany after World War I by the terms of the Versailles Treaty, the French occupation of the Ruhr in 1923, the failure of the victorious powers to disarm, and other political and economic sins.

I was no historian, but I remembered something of the successful attacks against the Versailles Treaty's imposition of war guilt on Germany and her allies† which had been brought by "revisionist" historians such as Sidney B. Fay and Harry Elmer Barnes.‡ It appeared to me that such issues should be ruled irrelevant, on the familiar legal principle that a destitute man who steals groceries is a thief even though his purpose is to feed his starving children. The paragraph that I wrote on this problem was the one which, as Jackson told me, was most helpful to his own thinking:

> It is important that the trial *not* become an inquiry into the *causes* of the war. It cannot be established that Hitlerism was the sole cause of the war, and there should be no effort to do this. Nor, I believe, should there be any effort or time spent on apportioning out responsibility for causing the war among the many nations and individuals concerned. The question of causation is important and will be discussed for many years, but it has no place in this trial, which must rather stick rigorously to the doctrine that planning and launching an aggressive war is illegal, whatever may be the factors that

----

°I.e., the rule that a criminal law can be applied only prospectively, and not to conduct that has occurred prior to enactment of the law. It is based on the maxim *Nulla poena sine lege*—No punishment without law.

†By Article 231 of the Treaty, Germany accepted "the responsibility of Germany and her allies" for the damages to the Allied governments caused by "the war imposed upon them by the aggression of Germany and her allies."

‡Fay, *The Origins of the World War* (1928); Barnes, *The Genesis of the World War* (1927).

caused the defendants to plan and to launch. Contributing causes may be pleaded by the defendants before the bar of history, but not before the tribunal.

Following these general observations, the balance of the memorandum was devoted to evidence-gathering, including a description of the way in which captured documents were being handled by our occupying forces, and a suggestion of particular ways in which the British could be of great help. In conclusion I wrote:

> If my views as to (a) division of business with the other participating nations, and (b) location of most of the vitally important evidence in Europe, are correct, it would appear that the bulk of the immediate staff should move to Europe . . . as soon as possible, leaving a few members behind for the time being to coordinate the work in progress at OSS, WCO [War Crimes Office], and elsewhere.

### 4

Meanwhile Jackson had spent a busy week in Europe, visiting Paris, the American military headquarters in Frankfurt-am-Main and Wiesbaden, and London. He had luckily encountered the French officials Georges Bidault and Georges Bonnet on the plane to Paris, which enabled him to explain his plans. In Paris he met with General Eisenhower, who agreed that there ought to be a trial, but hoped it would not take too long. The Judge Advocate for the European theater, General Edward C. Betts, gave Jackson the first of several lectures he would be receiving on the bad behavior of the Russians, which the Justice found "somewhat frightening" and made him apprehensive about "the turnover of any prisoners to the Russians."

Leaving Amen in Paris to commence interrogation and document-searching, Jackson stopped next at Eisenhower's headquarters in Frankfurt, where he conferred with the Chief of Staff, General Walter Bedell Smith, who proved "somewhat skeptical" of Jackson's undertaking. Smith, who less than a year later was appointed Ambassador to the Soviet Union, told Jackson that the Russians were speedily resolving the war crimes problem by summary executions. At the JAG forward base in Wiesbaden, Lieutenant Colonel Charles Mickelwaite had a large number of cases against Germans who had killed or injured American aviators shot down in Germany, but nothing involving the Nazi leaders. On returning to Paris, Jackson held a press conference, and obtained valuable evidentiary material (including the diary kept by Galeazzo Ciano, Mussolini's son-in-law and Foreign Minister) from Allen Dulles, who had served the OSS brilliantly in Switzerland.

In London, Jackson joined forces with General Donovan and William D. Whitney, a prominent New York lawyer who had also been admitted to the English bar and had extensive British connections. On May 29, 1945, the three Americans met with the British Attorney General, Sir David Maxwell-Fyfe (whose appointment as Jackson's "opposite number" was announced that day) and other officials representing the Lord Chancellor, the Foreign Office, and the Treasury. This body, subsequently christened the "British War Crimes Executive" (BWCE), became the British government's control group for war crimes policies.

The discussion was disorganized and on all sides reflected confusion about the problems and prospects; all seemed to expect that there would be guilty pleas and recorded their agreement that "the opening trials should be of those, if any, who were weak enough to plead guilty." The conferees also considered whether the convicted Nazis might be subjected to "corporal punishment." Upon Jackson's remonstrance that this "would never be tolerated by the U.S.," the idea was dropped. More important, the British accepted the plan to seek declaratory judgments against the Nazi organizations, and it was agreed that the French and Russians should be invited to a four-power meeting in London for negotiations looking to a protocol along the lines of the San Francisco proposals.

The following day Jackson and General Donovan visited Fedor Gusev, the Soviet Ambassador to Britain. Perhaps as a result of General Betts's indoctrination, Jackson took a rather blunt posture, telling Gusev that the United States would proceed with the trial whether or not the Soviet Union chose to cooperate.

On May 31 Jackson returned to Washington. The following day he saw the President, and it was agreed that there should be a written report for immediate publication. The report, which was released on June 7, 1945, met with wide and generally favorable attention.

After describing his activities during the month since his appointment, Jackson pointed to the "inescapable responsibility" which attached to his country's custody of many of the Nazi leaders:

> ... What shall we do with them? We could, of course, set them at large without a hearing. But it has cost unmeasured thousands of American lives to beat and bind these men. To free them without a trial would mock the dead and make cynics of the living. On the other hand, we could execute or otherwise punish them without a hearing. But undiscriminating executions or punishments without definite findings of guilt, fairly arrived at, would violate pledges repeatedly given, and would not set easily on the American conscience or be remembered by our children with pride. The only other course is to determine the innocence or guilt of the accused after a hearing as dispassionate as

the times and horrors we deal with will permit, and upon a record that will leave our reasons and motives clear.

The prosecution's purpose would be to provide "a well-documented history of what we are convinced was a grand, concerted pattern to incite and coerce the aggressions and barbarities which have shocked the world":

> Unless we write the record of this movement with clarity and precision, we cannot blame the future if in days of peace it finds incredible the accusatory generalities uttered during the war. We must establish incredible events by credible evidence.

The defendants would comprise "a large number of individuals and officials who were in authority in the government, in the military establishment, including the General Staff, and in the financial, industrial, and economic life of Germany who by all civilized standards are provable to be common criminals." The charges against them would be:

> (a) Atrocities and offenses against persons or property constituting violations of International Law, including the laws, rules, and customs of land and naval warfare. . . .
> (b) Atrocities and offenses, including atrocities and persecutions on racial and religious grounds, committed since 1933. This is only to recognize the principles of criminal law as they are generally observed in civilized states. These principles have been assimilated as a part of the International Law at least since 1907. . . .°
> (c) Invasions of other countries and initiation of wars of aggression in violation of International Law or treaties.

For Jackson, the last of these charges was much the most important, as "the crime which comprehends all lesser crimes is the crime of making unjustifiable war." Harking back to his 1941 Havana speech, Jackson not only invoked the Kellogg-Briand Pact but, more compellingly, the history of the English common law, which developed not primarily by acts of Parliament but by "decisions reached from time to time in adapting settled principles to new situations." And now was the critical time for such action:

> Any legal position asserted on behalf of the United States will have considerable significance in the future evolution of International Law. In untroubled times progress toward an effective rule of law in the international community is slow indeed. Inertia rests more heavily

---

°1907 was the year of the second Hague Conference which was, of course, concerned with the laws of war and did not cover the "domestic" atrocities (such as Germans against German Jews) which were the obvious target of this provision.

upon the society of nations than upon any other society. Now we stand at one of those rare moments when the thought and institutions and habits of the world have been shaken by the impact of the world war on the lives of countless millions. Such occasions rarely come and quickly pass. We are put under a heavy responsibility to see that our behavior during this unsettled period will direct the world's thought toward a firmer enforcement of the laws of international conduct, so as to make war less attractive to those who have governments and the destinies of peoples in their power.

As reflected in the press, Jackson's report made a profound public impression. The distinguished publicist Walter Lippmann described it as "an historic state paper." The St. Louis *Post-Dispatch*, under the headline "Justice Jackson's Magnificent Report," called it an "eloquent and many-sided declaration on the job that lies ahead." By no means was criticism lacking, but the dissenting voices were few.

# Chapter 4

## ESTABLISHING THE COURT:
## THE LONDON CHARTER

I took no part in Jackson's report, as early in June I had gone on leave to visit my parents and in-laws. Upon returning, I learned that Jackson had no need of my prompting on moving to London. Back in Washington, he had at once told his senior staff that they should get ready to go in about two weeks. In mid-June, when I first met Jackson in his new capacity, he told me that he and some fifteen others would be leaving within a week and that he wished me to remain in charge of his Washington office until the major local sources of evidence had been combed, after which I should join him in Europe. This fitted my personal desires, as I had been away for two years and wished to stay longer in Washington before again going overseas.

On June 18 Jackson and sixteen of his staff flew to London. Those chosen comprised the Justice and his three personal assistants (his son Ensign William Jackson, Major Lawrence Coleman, and Mrs. Elsie Douglas), Alderman, Shea and his secretary Elizabeth Leonard, Bernays, James Donovan (for whom Jackson had secured a double promotion to Commander), Gordon Dean, Captain Ralph Morgan, and five other secretarial assistants. They were followed a few days later by General Donovan and Robert Storey, a Texas lawyer who, during the war, had been an Air Corps colonel doing both legal and intelligence work. In mid-June Jackson had personally recruited Storey, with whom he was already acquainted.

In London Jackson, General Donovan, Alderman, Shea, and James Donovan were accommodated at the prestigious Claridge's hotel. The others were billeted comfortably but less fashionably. The distinction did not pass unnoticed by Bernays and was a seed of later staff grumbling.

With the departure of the Jackson group, the Washington office became a backwater, and my responsibilities were not onerous. Furthermore,

I had able associates, including Ben Kaplan and several new recruits. Among these were two brilliant lawyers who had been serving in the Coast Guard: Lieutenant Commander Harold Leventhal, in later years a member of the United States Circuit Court for the District of Columbia, and Commander Sidney Kaplan, an old friend with whom I had worked on the staff of the Senate Interstate Commerce Commission and later in the Department of Justice.

Essentially my task was to ensure that the possible sources of evidence in Washington were adequately combed. The evidentiary resources of the JAG had already been discounted, but in support of the aggressive war charges JAG officers were compiling and analyzing the various international treaties and other agreements broken by the Nazi government. Ben Kaplan continued to probe the OSS claims that James Donovan had advanced. They were never borne out, and early in July Kaplan reported that "the OSS studies will be little more than presentations of data generally available, useful chiefly as a basis for further work with richer sources in Europe."

At the State Department, where Sidney Kaplan was conducting our search, we had better luck. Quite a number of German secret records of conferences and interagency communications had been uncovered by target teams in Europe and sent back to the Department, and for the first time we began to realize that the Teutonic penchant for meticulous record keeping would greatly ease our task of proving the criminal charges.

The fruits of our documentary searching in Washington (which Jackson declared were of "great value") arrived in London at about the same time as a much richer haul from the European continent. In Paris, Colonel Amen had been joined by Robert Storey and Colonel Robert Gill, a Baltimore lawyer commissioned in the military police. Storey was given charge of collecting and organizing the documentary evidence, Amen continued in charge of interrogation, and Gill was designated executive officer of Jackson's staff on the Continent.

The evidentiary situation which in June had been so dismal, was very encouraging by the end of July, both as to what was in hand and what might be expected in the near future. In Washington, matters had progressed so rapidly that by July 3 I was able to inform Jackson that the evidentiary search there could "be wound up during the month of July, except for some odds and ends which may tail over into August." And so it worked out; during July all but a few of the Washington staff were transferred to London, and early in August I made ready to follow them.

2

Vital as the evidentiary search was, Jackson rightly gave first priority to concluding an agreement with the other three powers on the establishment of the international tribunal for trial of the Nazi leaders. The Americans took office space at 49 Mount Street (near Park Lane), and their British counterpart (BWCE) was located at Church House on Great Smith Street, where most of the international conferences were held. The French and Russians were not due to arrive until the last week of June.

At this juncture the BWCE was headed by the newly appointed Attorney General, Sir David Maxwell-Fyfe, and its other members including G. D. Roberts, K.C., a prominent member of the criminal bar; Treasury Solicitor Sir Thomas Barnes; and a dozen or so other officials representing the Lord Chancellor, the Foreign Office, and other government agencies. It was decided to appoint working committees, and later that day four were established, of which Committee 2, to draft a protocol, was the most immediately important. Jackson appointed to it Alderman and Shea, and Fyfe designated Sir Thomas Barnes, and Patrick Dean representing the Foreign Office.

Much more important was a Soviet proposal (by N. V. Novikov, Minister in Washington) to delete all the provisions for the trial of the Nazi organizations, on the ground that they had already been dissolved by the occupying governments. However, it was thought that this request was based on a misunderstanding and that the Soviet delegates could be persuaded to drop it.

During most of the period of negotiations on the protocol, the leadership of the British delegation was unstable. The end of the war in Europe triggered pressure in Britain for a general election; in May Churchill resigned as head of the coalition government, and on June 15 the King authorized the dissolution of Parliament. During the period from June 15 to July 26 there was a caretaker government headed by Churchill, and it was in this government that Fyfe was appointed Attorney General. This meant that his tenure as Attorney General would be ended should the Labour Party win the election, as indeed it did.

As the four-nation conference date approached, Jackson had some reason to think that agreement might come easily. In fact, the British and American conceptions of the trial they were planning were not nearly as congruent as the harmony at these meetings might suggest. The British accepted but did not warm to the Americans' wish to establish new principles and procedures in international law and thought convictions of the Nazi leaders could be more easily and rapidly secured by more conventional means. Sir Thomas Barnes was still insisting that the trial should not last more than two weeks. Fyfe, when he began to grasp the scope of the American plan and the size of Jackson's forces, gasped feebly: "You Americans do things on such a vahst scale!" But he and most of his colleagues rapidly adjusted themselves to the American vision, and throughout the preparations and the trial there was good cooperation and harmony between the two delegations.

But Britons and Americans alike had overlooked the virtual certainty that a criminal trial involving them with Russian, French, and German lawyers would raise many basic procedural problems quite apart from war crimes. English and American criminal procedures were not identical, but grew from the same English common law roots, and such differences as had developed posed no serious problems. There were also differences among the French, Russian, and German judicial systems, but they all shared concepts and procedures quite different from those of the Anglo-American legal tradition. But there is no evidence that either group had given any prior attention to the problem of how, if at all, the two systems could be married.

*3*

On June 26, 1945, the four delegations to what is officially known as the International Conference on Military Trials met at Church House in London for the first of what proved to be fifteen sessions. The French were represented by Judge Robert Falco of the Cour de Cassation. The two Soviet representatives were Major General I. T. Nikitchenko, an army judge advocate and Vice President of the Soviet Supreme Court, and Professor A. N. Trainin, a distinguished legal academician and author of a well-known book on war crimes. Their interpreter was Oleg A. Troyanovsky, son of a former Soviet ambassador to the United States, a recent graduate of Dartmouth, and a highly intelligent young man who spoke faultless American English.

There soon were storm signals. Nikitchenko and Trainin, in line with the Soviet conception of law as the servant of the political leadership, had a very limited idea of the trial's purpose. In the Russians' view, the Nazi organizations had already been condemned as criminal by the Big Three at Yalta, and it was "unthinkable" that the international tribunal—an organ of much less authority—could come to any other conclusion. Nikitchenko's attitude was clearly expressed during the second session: "We are dealing here with the chief war criminals who have already been convicted and whose conviction has been already announced by both the Moscow and Crimea declarations by the heads of the governments. . . ." The tribunal's task, he later declared, was "only to determine the measure of guilt of each particular person and mete out the necessary punishment—the sentences."

Such talk was anathema to Jackson, whose position from the beginning had been that "if we are going to have a trial, then it must be an actual trial." He sharply rejected Nikitchenko's statement, and for the first, but by no means the last, time suggested that the differences between the American and Soviet positions might be so basic that perhaps "the idea of separate trials for each nation for the trial of its separate groups of prisoners may be the easiest and most satisfactory way of reconciling it."

Well founded as Jackson's objection to Nikitchenko's declaration was, his proposal of separate national trials drew no support from the other delegations and later was effectively countered by Nikitchenko, who pointed out that such a procedure "would be directly opposed to the Moscow declaration, which laid down that the trial of the war criminals should be a common task of the United Nations." The situation was temporarily eased, however, by the Soviet delegation's decision, after much discussion, to go along with the American plan for trial of the Nazi organizations. There was also some discussion of the place of trial, and Jackson reported that American army authorities had suggested that "Nuremberg would be an appropriate place from the security point of view."

On July 11 the committee distributed a "Draft of Agreement and Charter" which Alderman recommended to Jackson for adoption, subject to further action on a few matters on which no agreement had been reached. The members had approved a Soviet proposal that the court be named "International Military Tribunal," and that its duties and powers be embodied in a "Charter." The most important "reserved" matters were the definitions of the crimes to be charged and the location of the trial or trials.

Beneath the surface, however, there was much more unrest than the subcommittee proceedings reflected. Jackson's emphasis on his disagreement with the Russians, and his references to abandoning the one-court plan in favor of national tribunals, did not pass unremarked by the British. Reporting on July 1 to the Foreign Office, Patrick Dean wrote:

> The Treasury Solicitor [Barnes] and I . . . are both rather worried because the Americans appear to show signs of trying to magnify the differences between their and our views on the one hand, and the Russians' views on the other. Justice Jackson, inspired by General Donovan, appears to be thinking that we should now try and reach agreement to set up four Courts, each under the presidency of one of the four parties concerned, to handle these trials, and that in this way we should avoid being drawn into a trial which is of too Soviet a character. This course may be eventually necessary, but both Sir Thomas Barnes and I are convinced that nothing has yet appeared in the course of the discussions which renders it necessary, and that the Soviet representatives are, in fact, being very reasonable. . . .
>
> In the circumstances, it might be useful if Sir Alexander Cadogan (Permanent Under-Secretary of the Foreign Office) were willing to see Justice Jackson and emphasize to him the importance which we attach to reach agreement with the Russians on the way in which these trials should be conducted, and to one court only, in the first instance, being set up for this purpose. The Americans have no one from the State Department with them, and General Donovan, who clearly does not like the Russians much, is attracted by the idea of running the Courts without Soviet participation.

On July 7, however, Dean informed them that pressure on Jackson was no longer necessary, and Cadogan was not brought into the situation.

Whatever Dean thought, Jackson was not undergoing a change of heart about the Russians. On July 7 he flew to Wiesbaden, where he met Amen, armed with very useful captured documents, and Allen Dulles, bringing prospective German witnesses. The following day, Jackson and General Donovan met in Frankfurt with General Clay and his political adviser, Robert Murphy, neither of whom was likely to tell Jackson that the Russians were easy to deal with. Clay confirmed to them that Nuremberg was the best place in the American Zone of Occupation for a big trial, and the Jackson group promptly went there to have a look.

Symbolically the city was quite appropriate for a trial of the Nazi leaders, as it was here that the Nazi Party had staged its annual mass demonstrations and where the anti-Semitic "Nuremberg Laws" had been decreed in 1935. Physically it was still a shambles, but the outskirts and suburbs were comparatively undamaged, and the courthouse known as the Palace of Justice, though partially in ruins, was reparable and its structural qualities very suitable. There was extensive office space, a courtroom which could be altered and enlarged for a trial of twenty or so accused, a large adjacent jail with a tunnel connecting it to the courthouse, and good external security. All agreed that it would do, though a lot of work would have to be done quickly to get it ready for a trial in the autumn.

After a brief visit to Salzburg in the American zone of Austria, Jackson and General Donovan arrived in Paris on July 10. Here the division of functions among Amen, Storey, and Gill was arranged, and the next day Jackson's group returned to London, accompanied by Storey, who had had his own troubles with the Russians during the last year of the war.

The next day Alderman's report to the committee was scrutinized by Jackson and his aides, and that evening Alderman had to interrupt his dinner to confer with Ensign Jackson and Major Coleman, who were very critical of it, provoking Alderman to tell them that such comments should come from Jackson himself.

The following day, Friday, July 13 (described in Alderman's diary as "bad luck Friday"), the four delegations resumed their sessions. Shea met Jackson on the way to breakfast and was told that the report "had given away a number of our essential plans," primarily in its failure to provide for advance notice to Nazi organization members that their organization would be accused of criminality so that the members would have an opportunity to be heard on the matter. Outside the meeting room at Church House, Jackson, Shea, and Alderman encountered Fyfe and Barnes, both of whom said they were delighted with the report. Jackson replied that "it was a good draft for the Russians." In Shea's words, the Justice "really knocked the wind out of the British."

But when the meeting began, Jackson at first ignored the new draft and instead launched a cross-examination of the other representatives with respect to the scope of their authority. Were they authorized to sign an agreement, or would they have to refer back to their governments? Were they authorized, as he was, to prepare and prosecute the case? The answers disclosed that Fyfe had authority to sign and to prosecute (which, of course, he was soon to lose when the Labour Party won the election), but that Falco and Nikitchenko were authorized only to sign, and the identities of the French and Soviet prosecutors were yet to be determined.

Jackson treated these revelations as a threat to the prospects for rapid progress toward the trial; he described vividly (and with good reason) the need for prompt notice of the place of trial to the military authorities in Germany so that the necessary reconstruction could get underway, claimed that the President had appointed him "on the theory that I would be back the first of October when our court resumes sitting," and warned that the "official policy of the United States" as set forth in his presidentially approved report was "that whether we got an agreement or not we would go ahead and try these people that are in our captivity." Jackson's report to the President of June 7, 1945, had stated: "The American case is being prepared on the assumption that an inescapable responsibility rests upon this country to conduct an inquiry, preferably in association with others, but alone if necessary, into the culpability of those whom there is probable cause to accuse of atrocities and other crimes."

Fyfe soon turned the discussion to the new draft, and some progress was made on minor points. But Jackson remained very prickly, and the atmosphere was tense; Shea, an excellent negotiator, wrote in his diary:

> I doubt that the bare description gives any real feeling of the atmosphere. I was on tenterhooks throughout and so was Bill Whitney. The Justice seemed to be making a show of force, and I had real fear during the morning session that the result might well be to prejudice the chances of an agreement. . . . Bill and I both urged the Justice to take it easy.

In all probability Jackson *was* making "a show of force," and in fact he had a lot of force to show. Of the twenty-two defendants brought to Nuremberg for the first trial, ten (including Goering) were prisoners of the United States, five (including Hess and Ribbentrop) were in British hands, three were in joint Anglo-American custody; the Russians had two (including Hans Fritzsche, a Goebbels aide who was not really a "major" war criminal), and the French one (Constantin von Neurath, formerly Foreign Minister). The Americans had a large staff on the Continent which was bringing in the bulk of the documentary evidence. His recent trip had relieved Jackson's worries about both the evidence and finding a suitable place of trial and had also put him in close company with several highly articulate fellow Americans who had found no pleasure in doing business with the Russians. If the talks were broken off, the United States was in a far better position than any of the other countries to conduct a major war crimes trial on its own.

In private, however, Jackson told Alderman and Shea that he was more worried about Soviet reliability than the language of the report, and distressed them by declaring that he would not much mind a breakup of the conference. But the other delegations were all determined to keep things going. Nikitchenko stuck to his guns without loss of temper, and Fyfe (presiding) was adept in suggesting and promoting compromise solutions of the various problems, of which only a few were really difficult.

Fortunately, the usual weekend break followed bad luck Friday, and when the conferences were resumed the following week real progress was made. Perhaps the most intractable problem was the technical one of stating the respective functions and responsibilities of the Tribunal and the prosecution—a problem caused by the differences between Continental and Anglo-American criminal procedures. Under the Continental system (known to lawyers as the "inquisitorial" system), most of the documentary and testimonial evidence is presented to an examining magistrate, who assembles all of it in a dossier. If this process establishes a sufficient basis for prosecution, copies of the dossier and the indictment based on it are given to the defendant and to the court which is to try the case, and the trial then proceeds with both the court and the concerned parties fully informed in advance of the evidence for and against the defendant. If the court, on its own motion or at the request of one of the parties, decides to take further testimony, the witnesses are usually questioned by the judges, rather than the lawyers, so that cross-examinations by opposing counsel, which play so large a part in Anglo-American trials, do not often occur. The defendant is not allowed to testify under oath, but may make an unsworn statement to the court.

In the "adversarial" Anglo-American system, in which the defendant goes to trial on a comparatively summary indictment to which no evidence need be attached and the trial judge knows in advance only the general nature of the case, the evidence is presented in open court by the lawyers, who examine and cross-examine the witnesses and who may exploit and must confront the element of surprise.° The defendant may testify under oath in his own behalf or decide not to take the witness stand without any adverse inference being drawn.

---

°Contemporary American criminal practice has been somewhat modified so as to give the defendant advance access to some kinds of evidence, but the basic pattern has remained adversarial.

Naturally, the limited role of lawyers in Continental criminal trials had little appeal for British barristers or American advocates. The French and Russians went a long way to meet their allies' psychological needs for the adversarial process, even though they understood it very imperfectly; at the very last meeting Nikitchenko had to ask: "What is meant in the English by 'cross-examine'?" Falco found "a little shocking" the idea that the defense would not, prior to trial, be informed of "the whole case against them" and complained: "It seems there is a possibility under this draft that the defense could be faced during the trial with the opening of a Pandora's box of unhappy surprises, inasmuch as during the trial there is liberty to the prosecution to produce something new." Jackson was driven close to distraction:

> From the very beginning it has been apparent that our greatest problem is how to reconcile two very different systems of procedure. . . . I would not know how to proceed with a trial in which all the evidence had been included in the indictment. I would not see anything left for a trial and, for myself, I would not know what to do in open court.

The differences were resolved by compromises which were crude but proved workable. For example, the Charter would require, contrary to Anglo-American practice, that the indictment "shall include full particulars specifying in detail the charges against the defendants" and that there would be "documents" submitted with the indictment, but, contrary to Continental practice, it did not require that the prosecution present *all* of its evidence with the indictment. Contrary to Continental practice the defendants could testify as witnesses in their own behalf, but contrary to Anglo-American practice, defendants could also make an unsworn statement at the end of the trial. From a practical standpoint, at Nuremberg it was essential that the prosecution be allowed to present evidence additional to what was submitted with the indictment. The gigantic task of finding and sifting Nazi documents and interviewing potential witnesses had barely begun.

While this and other issues of varying importance were being resolved, Jackson invited representatives of the other delegations to join him, on the following Saturday, July 21, in a visit to Nuremberg so that they might see for themselves its suitability as a site for the trial. All three accepted, and Nikitchenko added that his delegation had no objection to conducting "the first trial" in Nuremberg, but that the "permanent headquarters" of the Tribunal should be in Berlin.

Thus all seemed in order for the Saturday trip, but on Friday, during a luncheon given by the Russians at the Savoy Hotel, Nikitchenko, with visible embarrassment, told Jackson that the Soviet delegates would be unable to take part. Jackson offered to change the date to meet the Russians' convenience, but Nikitchenko said that would make no difference. They could not go, and it was apparent that the contretemps must be the result of orders from higher Soviet authority.

Jackson was understandably annoyed, and his first impulse was to call in the press and tell them what had happened. However, Gordon Dean, a very levelheaded man, pointed out that if it was the Justice's purpose to get an agreement, "to break this story would certainly hinder achievement of the objective." Fortunately, his advice was accepted.

The trip to Nuremberg with the British and French representatives was a great success, and Jackson returned to London determined to bring the negotiations to a quick conclusion. With regard to the location of the Tribunal, agreement had been reached by providing that the "permanent seat" should be in Berlin, the first trial in Nuremberg and any subsequent trials at such places as the Tribunal might determine.

But Jackson was more than ever dubious of the Russians' reliability, which probably explains why, when the negotiations were resumed, he grew increasingly impatient even as the areas of disagreement were greatly narrowed. By Wednesday, July 25, the parties were well on their way to agreement on all points except the definition of the crimes to be charged, in Article 6 of the Charter, and here the matter of disagreement was an important question of principle which at first appeared to be intractable.

The issue was whether or not the Charter should follow the American draft in providing, by language binding on the Tribunal, that initiating an aggressive war was a crime under international law. To this the Russians and the French were strongly opposed, and a revision of the American draft was submitted by the Russians that provided:

> The Tribunal shall have power to try any person who has . . . directed or participated in . . . any or all of the following acts . . . namely:
> (a) Aggression against or domination over other nations carried out by the European Axis in violation of the principles of international law and treaties. . . .

The ensuing paragraphs (b) and (c), dealing with atrocities against the civilian population, murder and ill treatment of prisoners, and other violations of the laws of war, did not contain the phrase "carried out by the European Axis." Thus the necessary implication of the phrase was that aggressive war was a crime only when carried out by European Axis defendants, while the laws of war were general laws applicable to all, regardless of nationality. The French submitted a draft of Article 6 in all these respects similar to the Soviet proposal.

The French position was based squarely on legal principle: "We do not consider as a criminal violation the launching of a war of aggression," said Professor André Gros (Falco's alternate), and he referred to the views of Secretary of State Lansing at the Paris Peace Conference in 1919, and the conclusion reached there, as negating any legal basis for imposing criminal responsibility on individuals who launch aggressive wars. To decide otherwise would be "shocking" and constitute "ex post facto legislation." The Nazi leaders were criminals not because they launched an aggressive war, but because, in so doing, they committed atrocities and other violations of the laws of war.

Nikitchenko's exposition was not as lucid. He did not explicitly deny that launching an aggressive war was a crime, but thought that "we should not try to draw up this definition for the future," since there was ample evidence of Nazi guilt of many atrocities. Unspoken but probably contributing to the Soviet position were the circumstances of the Soviet government's participation in the carving up of Poland and the attack against Finland.

Both privately and, in his June 6 report to the President, publicly Jackson had declared it to be the prime purpose of the trial to establish the criminality of aggressive war under general international law. His position was as lucid as that of Gros, and directly contrary:

> I must say that sentiment in the United States and better world opinion have greatly changed since Mr. James Brown Scott [a distinguished academic figure in international law who accompanied Lansing to the Versailles Treaty conference] and Secretary Lansing announced their views as to criminal responsibility for the first World War. . . . If certain acts of violation of treaties are crimes, they are crimes whether the United States does them or whether Germany does them, and we are not prepared to lay down a rule of criminal conduct against others which we would not be willing to have invoked against us. Therefore, we think the clause "carried out by the European Axis" so qualifies the statement that it deprives it of all standing and fairness as a juridical principle.

The argument swayed back and forth through five sessions of the conference, from July 19 to 25, with Jackson expressing discouragement about "conducting an international trial with the conflicting viewpoints" and unacceptable delays. On July 24 he went partway to meet the French and Russian views by proposing to move the phrase "carried out by the European Axis" out of the specification of aggressive war in subparagraph (a) and into the introductory paragraph, thus putting subparagraphs (a), (b), and (c) on the same footing. Although the suggestion was eventually adopted, it did not immediately satisfy the Russians, who on July 25 submitted another draft of Article 6 with the controversial phrase still in subparagraph (a).

The delegations appeared to be at an impasse. Professor Gros lamented that "the Americans want to win the trial on the ground that the Nazi war was illegal, and the French people and other people of the occupied countries just want to show that the Nazis were bandits." Nikitchenko observed "that we have gone one or two steps back during the last few days, that sometime ago we seemed to be nearer agreement than we are now," and suggested a few days adjournment to enable everyone to reconsider the various proposals.

Jackson had had enough: "there are some things worse for me than failing to reach an agreement," he declared, "and one of them is reaching an agreement that would stultify the position which the United States has taken throughout." And he continued:

> I think there are four possible courses here: one is to set up the international Four Power trials we have been considering; another is to refer the war crimes matter back to the Potsdam Conference° for a political decision as to what they will do with these prisoners; another is for the United States, whose interests and views in the matter do not seem to be in accordance with those of the European Allies, to turn over its prisoners to those Allies and permit their trial or disposition by such method as you three agree upon; and the fourth course would be for each of us, by separate trials, to proceed to try those we have as criminals.

Fyfe's efforts to soothe the delegates into a compromise were unsuccessful; it was the day that the results of the British election were to be announced, and he took his departure to "learn my fate at the polls." Sir Thomas Barnes undertook to produce a new draft of Article 6, and the conference was adjourned until July 27. Big changes were in the offing, however, and the next and what proved to be the last meeting did not take place until August 2.

## 4

The Potsdam Conference had been in process since mid-July, but preparations had begun in May. Late that month the British Foreign Office had sent to Washington a proposed agenda which did not mention war crimes. On June 29, however, at about the time Patrick Dean was warning his superiors of Jackson's hostility to the Russians, the British Ambassador in Washington, Lord Halifax, informed the State Department that his government

---

°The Conference of Berlin, better known as the Potsdam Conference, at which Truman, Stalin, and first Churchill and subsequently Clement Attlee comprised the Big Three, was then underway.

wanted to add "war criminals" to the list of subjects for discussion, since it was expected that "there will be matters connected with war crimes still unresolved" at the time of the Potsdam meetings.

When Jackson on July 4 was informed of the British proposal, he sent a message to the Secretary of State, James F. Byrnes:

> Am rather appalled at thought of Big Three trying to discuss subject so technical and involved and one where details so important. Mr. Dean of British Foreign Office explains British suggestion as not intending detailed discussion but rather as intended to allay Russian suspicion that prosecution is being evaded.
>
> If Big Three undertake discussion seems important that I review matter in some detail President and you because important differences lurk in small phrases.

To which Byrnes replied that he agreed with Jackson and that if such discussion became "unavoidable," he would "try to let you know in time for consultation with President and me."

On July 24, as his discontent with the progress of negotiations deepened, Jackson made a bizarre move which he later described as giving the Russians the "absent treatment," by sending all his chief aides to distant parts. His son Bill and Shea flew back to Washington on July 26, and Alderman and Bernays to Paris the next day. General Donovan had left London earlier to deal with OSS responsibilities in the Far East, and Whitney was no longer active on war crimes matters.

Jackson himself had concluded that a visit to Potsdam was now desirable, and after the July 25 session of the London Conference broke up he wired McCloy (who was participating in the Potsdam Conference) that he would arrive with a few assistants in Berlin in time for dinner the following evening, and reported: "Our conference in serious disagreement today over definition war crimes. All European powers would qualify criminality of aggressive war and not go along on view in my report to President. . . . This question basic and will want instructions. Most procedural questions cleared up and agreement apparently depends on this."

In the evening of July 26 Jackson met with Secretary Byrnes, who had with him McCloy, Colonel Cutter, General Betts, and Charles Fahy, the recently appointed Director of the Legal Division under General Clay. After Jackson had reported on the state of negotiations in London, the Secretary decided that, as a matter of American policy, Jackson should not "make any sacrifices of or deviations from principle" or make any agreement "which he felt in any way derogated from fundamental axioms of justice." He should, however, "make reasonable attempts to reach an agreement for complete Russian participation on a sound basis." If "within a fairly short time" Jackson was unable to reach agreement "satisfactory to him," then the Secretary would approve his entering into an agreement, "preferably including the Russians," which would define "in general terms the criminal offenses to be tried" and provide for the trial by each nation, "or any group of one or more of the four nations," of the Nazi leaders held by them in accordance with their own procedures.

But on the merits of the issue between Jackson and the Russians, Byrnes was noncommittal. How international crimes should be defined was "a matter committed by the President to Justice Jackson and to be decided by him."

Thus, when Jackson returned to London the next day, he had been told that, as a matter of national policy, Soviet participation in a four-nation trial should be the goal, and it was his, and not the Secretary's, responsibility to determine whether or not that goal was attainable on acceptable terms. True, Byrnes had agreed that if it was found impossible, Jackson could put forward the substitute procedure. But this alternative, as described by Byrnes, was illusory, as it contemplated agreement on "the criminal offenses to be tried," whereas the definition of the crime of aggression was precisely the point—and by that time the only point—on which the French and Russians had so far refused to accept Jackson's proposals.

In London, the session scheduled for July 27 had been canceled because of both Jackson's absence and the British election results. The Conservative government was thrown out of office, and Fyfe was succeeded as Attorney General by Sir Hartley Shawcross.

On July 28 Jackson, who was working without the assistance of any of his senior staff, met twice with Barnes to discuss two redrafts of Article 6, but apparently he had no contact with the French or Russians. On July 30 Jackson sent Barnes three memoranda: a draft of Article 6 in which the Axis limitation phrase was moved to the introductory paragraph, a memorandum criticizing the Soviet draft, and a memorandum proposing half a dozen less important changes in the protocol and an offer to substitute for the protocol an agreement for separate national trials based on common substantive law provisions.° A meeting of the four delegations was scheduled for August 1.

While Barnes was struggling to bring about a meeting of the minds between Jackson and the Russians, the British Foreign Office was taking other measures to prevent the London talks from collapsing. On July 27, R. D. J. Scott-Fox, of the Foreign Office German Department, asked R. S.

---

°As printed in Jackson's records, this third memorandum purports to be by Sidney Alderman, but he was in Paris at the time; the document speaks in the first person and was obviously composed by Jackson. The published records do not state that it was submitted to the other delegations, but references to it in the meeting of August 2 show that it had been.

Clyde, the Treasury official who had been acting as secretary of the Church House meetings, "for a short description of the points on which the Four Nations Conference has been finding difficulty." Clyde responded the next day with a long memorandum specifying the several areas of disagreement, but indicating that Article 6 was the only serious one remaining. The real trouble, according to Clyde, was not textual but personal. Alderman was "a sound and reasonable lawyer," and Shea had for several years been well and favorably known to the British lawyers:

> But of their leader, Justice Jackson, it would not be fair to the other delegations not to say that the kernel of the trouble has been his explicit distrust of the Soviet. Early in our talks he was explaining (to the English Delegation) that he would be content to see the Russians quit. He would reject their views, not because he disagrees with them, but because he distrusts them. . . . The Russians are not unaware of this; and I think have begun to question . . . whether he is seeking to codify international law for the purpose of Soviet discomfiture. . . . Therefore, let our people in Potsdam know . . . that we are up against an unlucky personal attitude which it is taking great and sustained endeavor to bring into harmony with the idea of partnership.

Such was the information sent to the British delegation at Potsdam, now under the leadership of Clement Attlee and Ernest Bevin, replacing Churchill and Eden. On July 30 the three foreign ministers (Molotov, Byrnes, and Bevin) met and discussed two short drafts of statements on war crimes, one each submitted by Molotov and Bevin, for inclusion in the final conference communiqué. The Russian draft declared the necessity of establishing an international tribunal "in the near future," committed the signatories to taking "all possible means" to lay hands on war criminals who had fled abroad, and named thirteen Nazi leaders for trial "in the first instance." The British draft abundantly reflects the British desire for a firm Big Three commitment to an international trial. Except for the later addition of a final sentence, it was identical with the communiqué eventually published:

> The Three Governments have taken note of the discussions which have been proceeding in recent weeks in London between British, United States, Soviet and French representatives with a view to reaching agreement on the methods of trial of those major war criminals whose crimes under the Moscow Declaration of 1943 have no particular localization. The Three Governments reaffirm their intent to bring those criminals to swift and sure justice. They hope that the negotiations in London will result in a speedy agreement being reached for this purpose, and they regard it as a matter of great

importance that the trial of these major war criminals should begin at the earliest possible date.

At the meeting Byrnes disclosed that he had discussed the situation with Jackson and that there was still disagreement about the definition of war crimes, which he hoped would soon be resolved. As to the communiqué, Byrnes wanted to check the language with Jackson by telephone before reaching a decision. Molotov agreed to the postponement, but added that only two matters remained in dispute in London, one of which was whether the Tribunal should sit in Berlin or Nuremberg; his government would agree to either. Byrnes and Bevin both objected to the Soviet proposal to name defendants.

The next day, July 31, President Truman "raised the matter of war crimes" at the Big Three meeting, which the foreign ministers also attended. Molotov agreed to accept the British draft of the communiqué if a clause were added naming Goering as a defendant. Stalin supported but Attlee and Byrnes opposed the change, and Byrnes stated

> that this morning he had talked to Justice Jackson . . . who represented the United States on the War Crimes Commission° in London. Justice Jackson had expressed hope that the Commission meeting this afternoon or tomorrow would agree on an international tribunal. If the Marshal [Stalin] could instruct his representatives to reach agreement it would be well.

Stalin stated "that this was another question," meaning that he did not wish to be deflected from the controversy about naming the defendants. The President broke in to say that since Byrnes expected to hear from Jackson the next day, the war crimes matters should be postponed until then, and Stalin agreed.

Jackson did call Byrnes the following morning (August 1), but, failing to reach him, spoke to Judge Rosenman, who sent a memorandum of the conversation to Byrnes:†

> Bob Jackson tried to reach you, and when he couldn't, asked for me, and he discussed with me the present situation on war criminals.
> The meeting scheduled for this morning did not take place, because of the opening of Parliament and the necessity of the Lord Chancellor being present at the opening. The meeting has been post-

---

°Secretary Byrnes was apparently unaware of the distinction between the War Crimes Commission and the International Conference on Military Trials.

†Since the memorandum was found among the Truman papers, it is probable that Byrnes passed it to the President.

poned for tomorrow. I told Bob that anything that was to be done had to be done at today's meeting.*

His views are: 1. That we should refuse emphatically to name any of the war criminals.

2. That we should not commit ourselves to an international tribunal for purposes of trial.

As to the second point, Bob has come to feel very strongly that it would be better not to have a joint tribunal because of the difficulty of working with the Russians in a trial. He feels that if the Russians, however, in London accept the various propositions which we have made, that he is committed to favor a joint tribunal, and does not feel that he can back out of it merely on the ground that it would be difficult to get along.

If, however, they do not accede to our suggestions as to definition of a war crime and certain other matters, he will then take the course of having each nation try the criminals in its respective jurisdiction. He was even of the thought that the British, French, and Americans might agree to a joint trial, leaving the Russians out. I expressed to him my personal opinion that that would be quite a slap at the Russians, leading to recriminations, whereas it would not be quite so bad if it was decided that each nation would try its own war criminal prisoners.

At any rate, nothing will be done before tomorrow, and I said I would phone him from some place in England and find out what has happened.

Meanwhile, however, unsure that the communiqué alone would suffice to ensure an agreement in London, the new Lord Chancellor, Sir William Jowitt, sent a message on July 31 to Attlee in Potsdam:

> Have discussed matters today with Maxwell Fyfe. The differences outstanding could easily be solved by good will. Insistence on these difficulties by Americans makes me fear that they will be used as an excuse for breaking away from the idea of a joint trial to trials by individual nations. I have invited the representatives to meet with me in the immediate future. But if you could do anything at your end to promote good will it would greatly assist me.

It was more than a little ironic that the British, who only two months earlier had been opposing the American proposal of an international war crimes tribunal, were now making every effort to protect the project from destruction at the hands of America's chosen representative. It should not

---

*The twelfth and last plenary meeting of the Big Three at Potsdam was to take place that afternoon.

be overlooked, however, that at Potsdam these efforts were made by the new Labour government. Possibly Churchill and Eden would not have responded to the situation with such alacrity. But it was the coalition government, headed by Churchill, that had decided to yield to Stimson's insistence, embrace the international trial concept, and invite the four powers to send representatives to London to organize the Tribunal, and the records yield no indication that the Conservatives wanted the London Conference to fail.

Thus Jackson's desperate effort via Rosenman to prevent the Potsdam conferees from reaffirming the goal of an international tribunal fell on deaf ears. That same day Attlee replied to Jowitt:

> I have spoken to the President today . . . and I am sure that we have his entire good will. He agreed that it was most important that these trials should be conducted on a quadripartite basis and should be started soon. I am sure that he will speak to his people in this sense.° I hope that speedy results will thus follow.

When the Big Three met on August 1 for the last time, nothing more was said about the London negotiations, and the discussion of war crimes was confined to the question of whether the communiqué should name any prospective defendants. Stalin pushed hard, stressing the public interest in the matter, and Hess was still on his mind: the public "wondered why Hess was well fed and cared for." But he got no support from the other conferees. Attlee and Bevin were dead set against naming any defendants at this stage, and Truman remarked that "he did not like any of them and thought that reassuring some might make the others think they might escape." Facing a solid wall of opposition, Stalin settled for adding to the British draft of the communiqué a concluding statement that "the first list of defendants will be published before September 1." So it was agreed, and the communiqué was duly published on August 2, 1945.

While the Potsdam conferees were closing up shop, Jowitt invited Jackson to meet with him in the Lord Chancellor's office in the House of Lords. Jowitt said that he had been given responsibility for further negotiations and was already informed of the points of agreement and disagreement. The new Attorney General, Sir Hartley Shawcross, would be the British Chief Prosecutor, and he had already asked Fyfe to stay on as his deputy. The record of the discussion is very summary; after Jackson had stated "the American point of view as to the unsettled questions," Jowitt

---

°I have found no record of Truman's assurances to Attlee being transmitted to Jackson, but under the circumstances it appears probable that they were so conveyed by Byrnes or Rosenman. If so, no doubt it gave Jackson "more patience," as a Foreign Office official noted.

"expressed general agreement with Mr. Justice Jackson on all except one of the points, namely, the right to terminate the agreement if any of the signatories failed promptly to name prosecutors, which he suggested might be taken to imply a distrust in some signatory." The Lord Chancellor then called a meeting of the delegations for the following day.

And so, when the delegates gathered for their last conference at Church House, the presiding member was the Lord Chancellor, senior member of the Cabinet and a figure of much greater authority than the Attorney General. Furthermore, Jowitt was able to create an atmosphere in which it was assumed that an agreement would promptly be reached.

In short order more than a dozen minor changes, most of them proposed by Jackson and a few by Nikitchenko, were adopted. Only on Article 24, specifying the order of events at the trial (pleas, opening and closing statements, presentation of evidence) did the conferees get into a tangle, owing to the difficulty of finding terms that would be clear to both Continental and Anglo-American lawyers. Although no matter of principle was at stake, Jackson gave way to the impatience reflected in his previous day's call to Rosenman and renewed his proposal for national trials.

But the others would not have it so. Nikitchenko said that he was authorized to sign an agreement for an international tribunal and had "no power to sign an agreement saying we do not need an international tribunal." Falco was almost mocking: "I find Judge Jackson is always optimistic. But I find him more pessimistic toward the end." And the Lord Chancellor ended the matter by stating firmly that "it would be a bad thing before the world, after having declared we should have a joint trial, if we should now declare we are not going to have it."

After all other points had been discussed, Jowitt brought up Article 6. Nikitchenko, on his own responsibility and subject to approval from his government,° accepted Jackson's latest draft, with a few changes which were readily agreed on all round. Nikitchenko promised a final answer within a day or two, and no further obstacles arose.

The text of the Agreement and Charter in English, French, Russian, and German was being proofread and checked for accuracy of translations when the *Enola Gay* dropped the atom bomb at Hiroshima. On August 8 the documents were signed at Church House by Jackson, Falco, Jowitt, Nikitchenko, and Trainin.

---

°This suggests that Nikitchenko had not been previously instructed to accept Jackson's draft of Article 6. Whether or not he had been given a general mandate to reach a prompt agreement, as Byrnes had requested at Potsdam, is not known to me.

5

The London conferees are entitled to great credit for drawing up and reaching agreement on a document which was well organized, coherent, and a generally sensible basis for the anticipated trial or trials.° The Americans (including several who were not in London, in particular Rosenman, McCloy, Cutter, Chanler, and Herbert Wechsler) made a major contribution to the project by developing the basic concepts and furnishing the drafts that were the basis of discussion.

But to what extent did the Charter meet the aims of Stimson and the others who launched the project in the fall of 1944? How successfully did the Charter move beyond the concepts of Francis Lieber and the Hague Conventions to implement Bernays's ideas about organizational guilt and conspiracy, and to establish the criminality of aggressive war?

Bernays had embraced the organizational guilt idea with the purpose of obtaining a judgment of criminality in a single trial, after which convictions of members who had joined voluntarily would follow automatically and punishments could be imposed in summary proceedings against hundreds of thousands of members. Sections 9 and 10 of the Charter provided for such processes, but they failed to specify what, if any, defenses or mitigating circumstances the members could raise or what scale of punishments should be imposed. Even SS men were not all alike in thought or deed. If individual-blame assessments were to be made with any care, the individual trials, even with myriad courts, would last until doomsday. For punishing such a multitude of convicts, neither jails nor exile would serve, and capital sentences would beggar Napoleon's slaughter of a few thousand Mamelukes on the Jaffa beaches. The practical and moral difficulties proved overwhelming, and in the end the organizational guilt plan was of little value.

Bernays's aim in utilizing the charge of conspiracy was to reach prewar Nazi atrocities against Germans (particularly Jews), which could not be independently treated as war crimes but might be punishable as initial steps in a conspiracy to commit war crimes after the war had begun. To this end, all the American drafts defining the crimes to be charged had, until July 28, included a charge of common plan or conspiracy to commit *any* of the crimes described in what had become, and remained, Article 6 of the Charter. On that day, however, Sir Thomas Barnes circulated a redraft of Article 6, intended to accommodate Soviet views, which not only included

°Since the Agreement and Charter furnished the framework for most of the ensuing events described in this book, I have set forth its text in Appendix A.

in the charge of launching aggressive war the "European Axis Powers" limitation, but also made the conspiracy charge applicable *only* to the crime of initiating aggressive war. Jackson's answering redraft of July 30 eliminated the "European Axis" limitation from the aggressive war charge, but embodied Barnes's new placing of the conspiracy charge.

The result was that the text of Article 6 as finally agreed on contained no explicit charge of conspiracy to commit war crimes or other atrocities. This was a disastrous blow to Bernays's original proposal, because while it might plausibly be urged that prewar anti-Jewish actions were a necessary part of a conspiracy to perpetrate greater atrocities after war came, it was difficult to argue that the prewar harassment of Jews was a necessary preparation for aggressive war.

There was no reference to this feature of the new draft at the August 2 meeting. Bernays and Alderman had gone to Paris as part of the "absent treatment,"[*] and Jackson either overlooked the effect of the change or did not care; for him the conspiracy charge had always been important primarily in aid of proving individual guilt for waging aggressive war, and its role as a device for criminalizing prewar atrocities may not have been in the forefront of his mind. Be that as it may, the upshot was that prewar atrocities were not treated as crimes covered by the Charter.

The outcome on the aggressive war charge was, from the American standpoint, much more satisfactory. Inclusion of the "European Axis" limitation in the definition of the crime—particularly since it was not included in the definitions of the other crimes—would have been fatal to the prime purpose of Stimson, Jackson, and the other officials to establish the initiation of aggressive war as a crime under universally applicable international law. Jackson was bound to oppose adamantly the Axis limitation in the definition, and to gain his ends it was a shrewd stroke to propose transferring it to the introductory paragraph of Article 6. This put the aggressive war definition on the same plane of generality with the other defined crimes, and in its new position the "European Axis" limitation was merely repetitive of the provision in Article 1 specifying the Tribunal's jurisdiction as covering "the major war criminals of the European Axis."[†] At the same time, the repetition of that phrase in the introduction to Article 6 made it easier for the Russians and French to yield on a point which, for Jackson, was nonnegotiable.

But it remains a question whether Jackson, at the time of his trip to Potsdam, was trying to bring about a four-way agreement or to get rid of

---

[*]The records of the conference give no indication that the absence of Jackson's chief aides made any particular impression on the Russians. Jackson himself was away on his Potsdam trip for only twenty-four hours, and on his return he was active in the interchange of drafts with the other delegations. It appears probable that Jackson dispersed his counselors because he did not want them present to give him unwelcome advice.

[†]In the long run, however, this jurisdictional limitation, discussed in my concluding chapter, has come to be seen as a major flaw in the juridical structure of the Nuremberg process.

the Russians. His own attitude toward the outcome, partly owing to the ominous warnings about the Russians from Clay, Betts, Storey, and no doubt others, became increasingly ambivalent. On July 12, the day before the tense "bad luck Friday," Jackson dispatched a letter to me in Washington expressing confidence "that on matters of substance we will prevail." Six days later, on July 18, when things appeared to be going more smoothly, he wrote to McCloy that the "Russian situation" was "most discouraging" and "an agreement for a joint trial may be impossible." The next day, July 19, he again wrote to me: "Now looks probable that we will have agreement for international trial which will embody substance of our views. . . ."

Probably his proposal for separate national trials on an agreed substantive law basis was at first intended as a safety net in case the conference broke down, and perhaps Jackson hoped that his repeated references to it might frighten the other delegates into yielding to his demands. But the British account of his handling of the Russians, and his telephone call to Rosenman on August 1, appear to show that by then he really wanted the conference to fail so that he could go to trial without the Russians and perhaps with the British and French.

That is hard to believe, for Jackson's alternative plan was so obviously chimerical. To achieve a four-nation trial the French and Russians might swallow their doubts about the legitimacy of an aggressive war charge, but if each nation were to try its own prisoners, they would have no reason to do other than follow their own inclinations. Jackson's cherished goal of an authoritative pronouncement of the criminality of aggressive war could only be achieved by international action by the major powers. If Jackson were to break up the conference, it was most unlikely that any of those left sitting at the table would thereafter join with him. The British were appalled by the course Jackson seemed to be pursuing, and headed him off at the pass by getting their draft communiqué adopted at Potsdam; it was published the very day of the last meeting in London. The mandate of the Big Three was to reach a "speedy agreement," and by that they certainly did not mean a breakup in London that same day. When Jackson went to the August 2 meeting, he was in no position to say "Take it or leave it."

At least after reflection, Jackson must have realized that the Agreement had given him the only basis on which he could do what he had set out to do. He had a declaration that initiating aggressive war was a crime, he had the agreement to establish an international tribunal, and the trial would take place in Nuremberg, in the American Zone of Occupation, where he would be, comparatively speaking, on home ground.

Accordingly, Jackson's negotiations at London had been generally successful. And now the stress of diplomacy would be diminished, and he could look forward to concentrating on the trial and its legal issues, which were much more congenial to his interests and capacities.

*Chapter 5*

# THE DEFENDANTS AND THE CHARGES: KRUPP AND THE GERMAN GENERAL STAFF

On Wednesday, August 8, 1945, with Shea, Bill Jackson, and most of the staff that had remained in Washington, I set off to London. There were flight delays, and it was not until the evening of August 9 that we landed at Prestwick in Scotland, where we learned that a second atomic bomb had been exploded over Nagasaki. When we reached London, Shea and Bill Jackson were escorted to Claridge's, and the army billeting office assigned me a room at the Mount Royal Hotel near Marble Arch; nothing fancy, but adequate, and conveniently close to Jackson's office on Mount Street. The next evening I attended a dinner at Claridge's given by Jackson in honor of Lord Jowitt and the British delegation. I was seated next to Lord Simon, a forlorn ex–Lord Chancellor who proved *very* difficult to engage in conversation.

That weekend I was cordially welcomed by Jackson at Mount Street, and shortly thereafter he appointed me the American representative on one of the four international committees established to draft the Indictment, the document naming the defendants and specifying the charges against them.

For the first time I found myself in the mainstream of the Nuremberg project, and it soon became apparent that these were very turbulent waters. There had been explosions of dissatisfaction at staff meetings during the very first week in June, at which Jackson's confession that he was "no administrator" was followed by General Donovan's warning that anyone dissatisfied with his assignment could take the next flight home—an attitude ill calculated to soothe the dissidents.

Two weeks later, Bernays wrote a private letter to Ammi Cutter blaming Jackson and Shea for the staff disorganization. Jackson's subsequent actions on "bad luck Friday" stirred renewed dissatisfaction. Then at Claridge's, in the dead of night on July 19—when, owing to the warm summer weather, many windows overlooking a courtyard were open—

Jackson and Shea were awakened by James Donovan's shouting on a long-distance call to General Donovan. The OSS General Counsel was overheard to say that Jackson was too much under the influence of his son, Bill, that the Justice had turned over to Shea "the economic side of the case" and so there was no use trying to push one Dickinson for that job, and that Jackson had promised that "he would not embarrass [General] Donovan and he hoped Donovan would not embarrass him." Jackson and Shea were much disturbed by this gross indiscretion.°

Even on August 5, when the successful negotiation of the London Charter should have spread euphoria in the American camp, there was a staff organizational flare-up so tempestuous that Alderman, who hated confrontations, receded into silent neutrality. When I encountered Bernays at Mount Street his face was like a thundercloud, and in mid-August he resigned and returned to America.

To be sure, some of this sort of dissatisfaction was to be expected from a group of exceptionally able lawyers, suddenly thrown together on a one-time project of uncertain scope in the wake of a war. Jealousies and disappointments were inevitable, and no administrator, no matter how skilled, could have satisfied everyone. But Jackson had neither talent nor inclination to wrestle with these problems, and after the Charter was signed, intrastaff relations continued to worsen.

## 2

The next step for the chief prosecutors (as specified in Article 14) was to decide whom to name as defendants, to prepare the Indictment, and to divide the work among the four delegations. Of the four chiefs, only Jackson and Shawcross had been named and were on hand. Trainin had informed the delegations that Nikitchenko would be so appointed; this prediction proved incorrect, but Nikitchenko acted as such until September 1, when he returned to Moscow. No French Chief Prosecutor was named until September, but Professor Gros was authorized to act in that capacity.

The four chiefs circulated remarkably parallel organizational proposals, and within a few days it was agreed that four working committees should be established. Committee 1 would handle the aggressive war charge, for which the British would take primary responsibility. War crimes and crimes against humanity in Eastern Europe would be handled by Committee 2, led by the Russians, and such crimes in Western Europe by

°Whether or not as a result of this episode, after my arrival in London I only rarely encountered James Donovan at staff conferences, and his responsibility at the trial was limited, as far as I could determine, to the presentation of visual evidence, such as charts and films. In later life as a New York City lawyer, Donovan was Chairman of the Board of Higher Education, unsuccessful Democratic nominee for election to the United States Senate, and executant of spectacular exchanges of captured American and Soviet espionage agents, as recounted in his book *Strangers on a Bridge* (1964).

the French in Committee 3. The American delegation would take care of the common plan and conspiracy, assigned to Committee 4. Within the American delegation, Frank Shea was designated the representative on Committee 1. I was named for Committee 2 and Sidney Alderman for Committee 3. Jackson himself would be the chairman of Committee 4, which had, as he viewed it, the most difficult and important task.

The French and Russians had initially opposed, and only reluctantly agreed to, the aggressive war and conspiracy charges. Furthermore, they were badly understaffed. Trainin had left, and Nikitchenko had only a couple of juniors. For several weeks Gros came to meetings alone. It would have been difficult for either delegation to participate meaningfully in four committees, and anyhow their primary concern was with Committees 2 and 3, on war crimes and crimes against humanity. Since the line between the two was purely geographical and the desirability of a common format for both "Eastern" and "Western" crimes was obvious, my suggestion that the two committees meet together was readily accepted. Joint meetings were held with fair regularity from mid-August until completion of the work on the Indictment early in October.

The conspiracy case, in the form in which it lay close to Jackson's heart, bid fair to swallow the greater part of the entire case. It would cover the pre–World War II story of Nazism, Hitler's seizure and exploitation of power, and his plans for the diplomatic and subsequent military steps to overrun and occupy Austria, Czechoslovakia, Poland, Norway, the Low Countries, France, Yugoslavia, Greece, and the Soviet Union, and (in concert with Japan) to attack the United States. It would be the first count of the Indictment and would comprise the basic narrative of the case as a whole.

Thus it left very little "meat" for Committee 1, which had the task of drafting the second count of the Indictment, charging the actual attacks on and occupations of the victim countries. This involved little more than specifying the dates and basic facts of the attacks on those nations and tabulating the treaties to which Germany was a party and which had been broken by these actions. As it finally emerged in the Indictment, Count Two was barely one page in length, supported by an appendix listing the treaties thus violated. Little consultation was needed for these scribal tasks, and apparently Committee 1 never met. During August, Frank Shea and Sidney Kaplan had several conferences with Fyfe, Barnes, and Clyde, and by early September the job was as good as done.

On July 12, Jackson had asked Shea to handle "the economic aspects of the case," and announced this appointment at a staff meeting.* On July

---

*Shea's designation for this assignment caused friction between Jackson and General Donovan, who had already told one of his staff that he would have "full charge" of the "economic case."

23 Shea produced for Jackson a memorandum outlining his conception of the "economic case" and suggesting as defendants Hjalmar Schacht, Fritz Sauckel, Albert Speer, and Walter Funk (all of whom were subsequently named as defendants before the International Military Tribunal), as well as Alfried Krupp and half a dozen other leading German industrial and financial leaders.

Shortly thereafter Shea went back to Washington, but after his return to London on August 9 the economic case became the main focus of his activities. In Jackson's and Shea's minds it was an important component of the general charge of conspiracy to plan and launch aggressive wars. The guilt of the industrialists and financiers, as Shea saw it, was that they had given Hitler the material means to rearm Germany, *with full knowledge* that Hitler planned to use these armaments to carry out his program of German aggrandizement by military conquest.

This was a coherent theory, but of course proof of criminality depended entirely on finding evidence that the "economic defendants" had sufficient knowledge of Hitler's plans, and shared sufficiently in his criminal purpose, that they might properly be convicted as co-conspirators with the Nazi leaders. Proof that they had provided the sinews of war was easy to establish, but evidence of knowledge and intent might be elusive. The industrialists and financiers did not participate in the diplomatic and military plans for aggression, and while rearmament involved violations of the Treaty of Versailles, it was not otherwise intrinsically unlawful.

Schacht, Sauckel, Speer, and Funk were all government ministers, and official records might tie them into Hitler's plans. But if Krupp and other private business tycoons were to be charged, the evidentiary prospects were at best uncertain. Shea's suggestions on where to look were perceptive. But, as he freely admitted in his memorandum of July 23, "all we have at this point are a few monographs and scattered bits of evidence."

Nobody was better than Shea at recruiting able subordinates, and on August 17, accompanied by four of them, he flew to Paris to start the search for the necessary proof. There Shea confirmed his suspicion that Storey "had gotten nowhere" on the economic case and that he would have to rely on his own staff as evidence-gatherers. Led by Benjamin Deinard, an able and experienced Minneapolis lawyer, Shea's team moved to Frankfurt-am-Main, where there would be easy access to headquarters and records of the Ruhr magnates and the huge I. G. Farben chemicals combine.

This was trenching on the preserve of Storey and Amen, and Shea was not aware of the hostility which he and his economic case had already generated in the Paris group. Alderman had learned of it during his visit to Paris at the end of July. Amen had been very outspoken: the task in hand, he declared, was to convict the major war criminals and then go home, not to "reform European economics." Shea's project would "overload things" and turn a war crimes trial into an "anti-trust case." Storey opined that the economic case was a "balloon that will burst" and "make us all look silly," and stated that Jackson had assured him that he need take no responsibility for it.

Alderman recorded that he was "strongly inclined to agree" with the Storey-Amen view. On his return to London, Alderman apprised Jackson of the Paris attitudes, but neither Jackson nor Alderman adequately warned Shea, and Alderman, though he remained personally friendly to Shea, continued to question the value of the economic case. However, Shea's team of lawyers and document analysts, strengthened by the addition of Lieutenant Colonel Murray Gurfein, an experienced prosecutor and interrogator, eventually accumulated substantial evidence in support of their project.

On August 16 Jackson called a meeting of Committee 4, which was attended by Barnes and Nikitchenko. But, to the bewilderment and chagrin of his staff, Jackson made no further move to commence drafting the conspiracy count of the Indictment. In fact, he never again called a single meeting of Committee 4, of which he was the chairman and which was charged with preparing the part of the Indictment that Jackson himself regarded as all-important.

From mid-August to mid-September, I attended at least a dozen conferences of the leading American prosecution staff members, at half of which Jackson was present. These meetings generally included Alderman, Shea, the Kaplans, and Colonel Leonard Wheeler, an able Boston lawyer whom Jackson had appointed to succeed Bernays as coordinator of evidence-gathering. These meetings were largely devoted to endeavors to organize the staff in an efficient way for drafting the Indictment. But despite Jackson's continuing stress on the importance of the conspiracy charge, he laid down no guidelines, called no committee meetings, and produced no drafts of his own. After the meeting on August 14, Shea noted in his diary that "Everyone is badly discouraged with the disorganization."

In this respect, things did not improve. As late as September 6, in Jackson's absence, his staff was still consulting, both among themselves and with Sir Thomas Barnes, on how to get Committee 4 going on the conspiracy charge. The British, indeed, were both puzzled and angry. In a letter of September 10, 1945, Sir Hartley Shawcross laid his worries before Foreign Secretary Ernest Bevin:

> I think I ought to tell you that I am concerned at the slow progress which is being made in the preparations for the trial of the Major War Criminals. . . .
> Our own preparations are going ahead at a not unsatisfactory rate. . . . Thanks mainly to our own efforts the two committees on atrocities have also made some progress. . . .

But the completion of the case as a whole depends . . . on the extent to which the Americans . . . have gone both in providing us with the material at their disposal in regard to those sectors of the case which are not their especial concern, and also in the preparation of that part of the case which is their responsibility. The Americans are primarily concerned with establishing that the prisoners conspired together to wage a war of aggression—a very vital part of the case. . . . Our difficulties are not diminished by the fact that Mr. Justice Jackson, who alone seems to possess any real authority, has been away in the States for the past 10 days, and is now going to establish himself and his staff at Nuremberg, where we shall have diminished opportunity of influencing the further conduct of the preparatory work. . . .

I write to you now in case you should consider it possible to deal with the matter at a higher level. If the Council of Foreign Ministers could issue a directive to us that the trial must be started by early in November and ought to be as short as possible it would be of great help. . . .

So far as I know, the Foreign Office never acted on Shawcross's suggestion. But his complaint was understandable; Jackson had been unavailable for a large part of the period since the Charter signing. In mid-August he had spent several days in Nuremberg and Paris conferring with his staff and the French Minister of Justice. A week later he flew to Italy, where he visited the Isle of Capri and had an audience with the Pope in Rome. On August 31 he was off again to Washington by way of Paris. He did not return to London until September 12, and the very next day he departed for Nuremberg. There he remained until October 6, when he went to Berlin for the first meeting of the International Military Tribunal.

Jackson's failure to give any guidance or impetus to the work of Committee 4 was disheartening to his staff and incomprehensible to the British. And in the upshot, nothing of moment was done on the conspiracy charge until Jackson settled down in Nuremberg in mid-September.

## 3

While our colleagues assigned to the conspiracy and aggressive war charges were enduring these troubles, Alderman and I were having a comparatively easy time at the joint deliberations of Committees 2 and 3, which were held eight times between mid-August and October 1. There I had a good opportunity to become acquainted with our prosecution colleagues from the other three countries.

Since in form there were two committees dealing with matters of primary concern to the French and Russians, both Nikitchenko and Gros had chairmanship claims. Nikitchenko, however, never asserted his rights, and throughout August, Professor Gros presided. He was a lucid, scholarly, and cooperative man, but not a distinctive personality. As the French representative on the UNWCC he was well informed on war crimes matters, but he was not made part of the French team at Nuremberg, so I never saw much of him.

General Nikitchenko, despite his inability or unwillingness to speak English, was at once impassive and impressive. His dialectical abilities were remarkable and his replies were often pointed, though never discourteous. He never raised his voice or showed irritation, and was the soul of patience. On business matters he was very impersonal, but on the rare social occasions provided or attended by the Russians he was witty and engaging, even through the fog of translation. His young interpreter, Oleg Troyanovsky, was personable and gracious, but, despite his American educational background, he was never alone with foreigners and never went beyond the measured cordiality that the Russians deemed suitable for official entertainment.

For the first several weeks, the dominating figure at these meetings was the British member, Geoffrey Dorling Roberts, known to all as "Khaki" Roberts. He was the oldest (born 1886) and by far the largest of the London group—a huge, beetle-browed man who at Oxford (where he read his law) had won his blue for Rugby football; he played the game for England in 1907–1908. After World War I, in which he served, Khaki became a notable figure at the London criminal bar, and presumably that is why he was appointed to the BWCE as second man to Fyfe. It was not a happy choice: Khaki was energetic, but he oversimplified problems and was not very good on paper. He was gregarious and affable and my relations with him were always friendly, but in his professional personality there was a bullying streak which was to serve him ill before the Tribunal.

Since the charges under Committees 2 and 3 involved specific, discrete German actions which constituted war crimes or crimes against humanity, the committees' tasks were not difficult. Most if not all of these happenings were violations of the Hague and Geneva conventions and fell into one or more of the categories of war crimes (e.g., murder of prisoners of war, killing of hostages) or crimes against humanity (e.g., racial or religious persecutions) specified in Article 6(b) and (c) of the Charter. It was necessary only to identify these actions by place and date, briefly describe each atrocity (e.g., in June 1944 at Oradour-sur-Glane the entire village population was shot or burned alive in the church), and organize the listing of the individual items in accordance with the categories in Article 6, dividing them geographically between Western and Eastern Europe.

Our main difficulty was that we did not have at hand much evidence pertaining to war crimes, for the furnishing of which we had been relying on the German-occupied nations, especially France and the Soviet Union. But Nikitchenko had nothing and said he would be unable to contribute much until he had opportunity to go to Moscow and collect relevant documents. Gros was only a little better off; the French Provisional Government was still getting its act together and made little evidentiary contributions to the Nuremberg process until several months later. In view of Jackson's primary interest in the conspiracy and aggressive war charges, most of what Amen and Storey had sent to London fell into those categories.

The British, however, were soon finding documents highly relevant to the war crimes charges, and beginning with our meeting on August 20, Roberts produced fifty or more eyewitness reports, captured German military orders, and other documents on which grave charges could be based. Since Alderman and I had nothing comparable to offer, our role in these meetings was limited to helping assess the evidentiary value of particular documents and running down leads, suggested by the other delegates, to evidence thought to be in American hands.

## 4

While the Indictment-drafting committees were functioning unimpressively, at a higher level an equally important problem was in process of resolution: Which individuals should be named in the Indictment as defendants? On this matter, the chief prosecutors were under the mandate of the Potsdam Big Four that "the first list of defendants will be published before September 1."

The British already had lists of leading Nazis, made in the spring of 1944, when Churchill and Eden were pushing their plan for summary execution of the Nazi leaders and needed to support their proposal by indicating which individuals might be selected for this fate. When the diplomatic die was finally cast in favor of a trial, the British wanted to limit the number of defendants in order to shorten and simplify the proceedings. At the first meeting of the British and American delegates, on June 21, Fyfe put forward a list of ten defendants.

These comprised Hermann Goering, Rudolf Hess (who, the British warned, might be insane), Joachim von Ribbentrop (Hitler's Foreign Minister), Robert Ley (Leader of the German Labor Front), Field Marshal Wilhelm Keitel (Chief of Hitler's military staff), Julius Streicher (Nazi Party leader in Franconia and editor of the virulently anti-Semitic newspaper *Der Stuermer*), Ernst Kaltenbrunner (after Heinrich Himmler's suicide the senior surviving official of the SS and Gestapo), Alfred Rosenberg (the official Nazi ideologist and Minister of the German-occupied eastern territories), Hans Frank (civilian Governor-General of occupied Poland), and Wilhelm Frick (Minister of the Interior and subsequently Protector of Bohemia and Moravia). Subject to doubt about the inclusion of Hess, Jackson approved the list, but said that he would want to add other names.

Fyfe explained that these ten men had been selected on the basis that their names were well known to the general public. Apparently, little effort had been made to assess the evidence which might be available against them individually, nor had the British selections fully met the need for adequate representation of such organizations as the prosecution might seek to have declared criminal by the Tribunal, as required by Article 9 of the Charter.

The following evening Alderman, Bernays, and James Donovan conferred at length in an effort to amplify the list without making it unwieldy, and to get fuller representation of the several "organizations" or "groups," including the Nazi Party leadership, the SS, the Gestapo, and the "general staff and supreme commanders" of the Wehrmacht.

They tentatively settled on a list of sixteen defendants, which they presented on June 23 at a meeting with a British group headed by Roberts. Hitler (whose death was not yet regarded as firmly established) was added to the list along with five others: Hjalmar H. G. Schacht (who, prior to the war, as head of the Reichsbank and Minister of Economics, had handled the financing necessary to expanded war production), Arthur Seyss-Inquart (an Austrian Nazi, later Commissioner for the occupied Netherlands), Grand Admiral Karl Doenitz (Commander-in-Chief of the German Navy from 1943 to 1945, and named in Hitler's will as President and Supreme Commander in the Reich), Walter Funk (Schacht's successor as head of the Reichsbank and Minister of Economics), and Albert Speer (Hitler's favorite architect, later Minister of Armament and Munitions).

The British delegates were generally pleased with the list, but suggested the addition of Baldur von Schirach, the Nazi Youth leader, on the ground of his "vicious indoctrination" of the young. They were, however, dubious about the inclusion of Doenitz; the Admiralty, after studying his diary, had "found nothing in it that might incriminate him," and their "general view" was that "as compared with land warfare and air warfare, the German Navy came much closer to following the rules of chivalry." All agreed to adding Schirach, but the Doenitz case was left in abeyance.

Shortly thereafter the Soviet and French delegations arrived in London, and attention shifted to the Charter negotiations. No further action was taken on the defendant selections until after the Charter was signed, but informal discussions made it clear to the British that Jackson, and the French and Soviet delegates as well, were planning to expand the list of defendants to include, among others, several "economic" defendants. The Foreign Office took alarm, and urged that Shawcross be admonished to resist this trend on the grounds that the trial would be unnecessarily complicated and that embarrassing acquittals might result.

And so, at a meeting of the four delegations on August 8, immediately after the Charter signing, when Nikitchenko brought up for discussion the selection of defendants, Sir Thomas Barnes announced that his compatriots had "already suggested a list of less than twenty defendants." This, however, at once exposed the issue, for Jackson responded that "Our idea has always been to clean up most of these people in one trial, in that trial to get representatives of the SS, the Gestapo, etc., perhaps less than fifty defendants, perhaps more than twenty, convict them and secure the finding of the criminality of the organizations and groups." Gros chimed in, stating his government's view that "many more than ten ought to be convicted in the first trial."

At the delegates' next meeting, on August 13, Nikitchenko again raised the matter, saying that Schacht, Krupp, and Doenitz were all "part of the common plan or conspiracy" and we "should put all three on the preliminary list." Lord Jowitt (still pinch-hitting for Shawcross) then voiced his understanding "that a man named Bormann was a very bad man" and asked Nikitchenko to find out whether the Russians had him in custody.

Bormann was indeed a "bad man" who had profited greatly from Hess's mad flight to Britain by inheriting his position as Hitler's Deputy for Nazi Party affairs. He later was given the additional office of Secretary to the Fuehrer and soon was rivaling Himmler and Goebbels for authority over the home front. But no one knew whether he was dead or alive; he had been in Hitler's bunker at the time of the Fuehrer's death, but then disappeared in the course of an attempt to escape the Soviet tidal wave.

The Foreign Office did not share the Lord Chancellor's tolerance for expansion of the dock. On August 15, E. J. Passant, Chief Librarian of the Foreign Office, circulated a memorandum cogently criticizing several of the proposed additions. The case against Doenitz, Passant thought, was "very much weaker" than that against Keitel, and in support of his conclusion he wrote:

> (a) On the point of "participation in the criminal plan" of aggressive war Doenitz can plead that, between 1933–9, he was a relatively subordinate officer (1935 Captain in Command of U-boats, 1939 Rear Admiral). . . .
> However completely he may have approved of the Nazi war to dominate Europe by aggressive war it will be impossible to prove that Doenitz knew what those plans were, still less that he contributed to their formulation. . . . So far as is known he played no part at all in politics before the war.
> (b) Specific war crimes: After enquiry at the Admiralty, I gather that the position is as follows:
> > 1. A case of some strength could be made out against Doenitz, from his diary and other documents, for responsibility for increasing ruthlessness in the methods of submarine warfare. . . .
> > 2. It is to be remembered that most of the measures adopted by the Germans were also adopted by ourselves and the Americans, so

that the defence would be in a position to throw a good deal of mud back at the prosecutor.

3. It should perhaps be added that those to whom I have spoken on the Admiralty appear to hold the view that, though tough, the German Navy, with one or two exceptions amongst U-boat commanders, behaved on the whole pretty well.

Equally severe were Passant's strictures on the proposals to prosecute Krupp and Schacht. Concerning Schacht he wrote:

At first sight the case against Schacht under the . . . head of participating in the criminal enterprise appears strong.

(a) It is well known that Schacht's economic policy . . . was of vital assistance to the Nazis in building up their economic system and in bringing the States of south-eastern Europe under German economic influence. But it is obvious that a policy of economic penetration and control does not necessarily imply military conquest, and may, indeed, be ruined by it. Schacht's defence of himself would probably run on the following lines:

1. I set out to create a stable international economic system. . . .

2. This aim did not imply any desire on my part for military adventures. So far from that I protested on many occasions (he can probably produce evidence for this) against the Nazi plans. . . .

3. When my views were overridden I resigned the Ministry of Economics (Nov. 27, 1937), and, when Hitler's aggressive plans became more obvious, I resigned the Presidency of the Reichsbank (January 20, 1939). Note that this second resignation was before Hitler marched into Prague and established the Protectorate. . . .

5. Since 1939 I have had no responsibility at all and, indeed, none for State policy since I ceased to be Minister of Economics in 1937. . . . I have done my best at personal risk to assist Jews (he can almost certainly produce instances). My own attitude and that of my family can be judged from the fact that you found me in a concentration camp. . . .

(b) There can be no charge against Schacht for war crimes in the narrower sense.

Whatever the views of our American and Russian allies I should regard it as most inadvisable to indict Schacht with the others on the list. He is, I believe, in many ways an unpleasant and unreliable character. But, in my considered view, he is not a war criminal in the sense of the prosecution. His defense would be so strong that, if it did not secure an acquittal, the authority of the Tribunal would be seriously reduced.

Such views were uncongenial to the representatives of the other countries. When the four heads of delegations met on August 23 to settle the
final list of defendants, Doenitz, Krupp, and Schacht were included. Five
new names were added: Fritz Sauckel (primary figure in the foreign forced
labor program), Alfred Jodl (Chief of Operations on Hitler's military staff),
Franz von Papen (Reich Chancellor in 1932, Vice Chancellor in the Hitler
Cabinet from 1933 to 1934, and subsequently Ambassador to Austria and
then Turkey), Constantin von Neurath (Ribbentrop's predecessor as Foreign Minister, subsequently Reich Protector of Bohemia and Moravia), and,
at the request of the Russians, Grand Admiral Erich Raeder (Commander
in Chief of the German Navy until his retirement in 1943).

In a memorandum informing his senior staff of these decisions, Jackson explained that Hitler's name had been dropped, but "if found alive
before the date of the trial he would, of course, be included," and that
"Raeder and Bormann were included although it is not known whether they
are alive and in captivity." The list (now including twenty-three names) was
to be made public on August 28.

Jackson shortly took off to Italy, thinking these matters finally resolved, and designated Alderman as his deputy. Problems soon arose. Two
of the delegations thought Raeder's availability too uncertain and left him
off their lists; three of the delegations identified the "Krupp" defendant as
Gustav, while the Jackson list specified his son Alfried. Then, at noon on
August 28, Troyanovsky called Alderman to request an immediate meeting
of the delegations to consider fresh requests from Moscow. Alderman cabled Washington to hold up the press release until August 29.

At the meeting, Nikitchenko resolved the doubts about Raeder; the
Russians had him in captivity, and his inclusion in the list was confirmed.
The Soviet government, however, was distressed at having so few prisoners
of sufficient notoriety to merit a seat in the dock, and Nikitchenko produced
a list of six names which, he hoped, might qualify. Four were too obscure
and unimportant to be taken seriously, but there was considerable discussion of Field Marshal Ferdinand Schoerner (the last German Army commander to achieve that rank), and Hans Fritzsche (a senior but by no means
the highest subordinate of Goebbels at the Propaganda Ministry). Schoerner was finally rejected by the other delegations on the ground that there
was no basis for distinguishing his case from that of numerous other top-
ranking German field commanders, but Fritzsche was accepted, and Shawcross succeeded in soothing Nikitchenko by promising a second look at "the
question of further military men" at a later date.

Accordingly, on August 29, 1945, the chief prosecutors, in compliance
with the Potsdam mandate, announced the "first list of war criminals to be
tried before the International Military Tribunal." The twenty-four named
comprised Goering, Hess, Ribbentrop, Ley, Rosenberg, Frank, Kaltenbrun-

ner, Frick, Streicher, Keitel, Funk, Schacht, Gustav Krupp, Raeder, Doenitz, Schirach, Sauckel, Speer, Bormann, Papen, Jodl, Neurath, Seyss-Inquart, and Fritzsche.

## 5

All in all, the task of selecting the defendants was hastily and negligently
discharged, mainly because no guiding principles of selection had been
agreed on. The only important contribution of the Russians and French was
to support the American proposals to add military and big business defendants, against the British plea for a quick and simple trial of the dozen
"worst." Fritzsche was added only to caress the Soviet ego. Jackson apparently insisted on including Doenitz only because Hitler had appointed him
the successor Chief of State; but under the charges in the Indictment, the
circumstance was wholly irrelevant to guilt. Once Keitel was in the dock
there was little point in adding Jodl; the first was an administrative and the
second a technical aide to Hitler as Commander in Chief of the Wehrmacht.
Kaltenbrunner led only a part of the SS and was insufficient as sole representative of that organization.

Jackson involved his staff deeply in drafting the Indictment, but for
some reason ignored them in the defendant-selecting process. He and Alderman were fine lawyers, but neither was an expert on the structure and
hierarchy of the Third Reich. Neither was I, but my wartime mission had
been in German military and diplomatic intelligence, and I knew where to
look for reliable information. Neither I nor, as far as I know, any of my
friends and contemporaries on Jackson's staff was consulted during these
August meetings. Late in August, hearing rumors of what was afoot, I
enlisted Franz Neumann's aid and circulated a memorandum on defendant
selection in which I suggested some criteria. But the only feedback I ever
got was at a staff meeting on August 31, at which Jackson referred to my
memorandum and then stated that, in his opinion, "this present list is only
window dressing. The people at Potsdam got put on the spot and made this
commitment to publish the list before September 1 without consulting us."
He would "feel no embarrassment about adding other defendants more
adequately to represent the criminal organizations." This prospect never
materialized; the August 29 list of twenty-four remained the full list of
defendants indicted before the International Military Tribunal.

For the most part, the deficiencies in the list worked no lasting harm.
There was, however, one very major exception: the mix-up over Gustav and
Alfried Krupp, which had serious and continuing consequences, and was
entirely due to the sloppiness of the selection process.

To grasp the full significance of this episode, it is well to recall that
while Hitler and Nazism were the primary targets of the Nuremberg pro-

cess, there were also features of the German landscape, pervasively feared and condemned in world public opinion, which dated back to and beyond World War I. In the popular mind, these fears were focused in particular on two groups: German "militarists" and German munitions-makers. And within this second aggregation, the name which led all the rest was that of the huge firm Fried. Krupp of Essen, founded in 1811. Ever since then it had remained a Krupp family enterprise, controlled and directed by the senior family member.

By the time of World War I, the Krupp concern had grown into an industrial empire embracing coal mines, steel mills, munitions factories where guns, and later tanks, were made, and a huge shipyard producing both armored naval surface vessels and submarines. When Hitler came to power, the full might of the Krupp firm was thrown behind the arming of the new Wehrmacht.

In 1902 there had been a break in the Krupp male line, when Friedrich Alfred Krupp died leaving two daughters but no son. Ownership of the Krupp concern passed to the older daughter, Bertha Krupp, after whom were named the long-range "Big Bertha" guns that shelled Paris in 1918.[*] In 1906, probably on the initiative of Kaiser Wilhelm II, Bertha was betrothed to an obscure German diplomat, Gustav von Bohlen und Halbach, and at their wedding the Kaiser rechristened the groom Gustav Krupp von Bohlen und Halbach. Bertha bore him four children, of whom the eldest, Alfried, was born in 1907.

As World War II approached, Alfried turned thirty and Gustav was nearing seventy. He was showing his age, and Alfried was taking a larger share in the Krupp management. In 1941 Gustav suffered a stroke, and from then on it was downhill all the way. In November 1943 Bertha Krupp formally renounced her ownership of the Krupp properties in favor of Alfried, whose leadership of the Krupp concern was certified by Hitler decree, the Lex Krupp.

Against this background, it is no wonder that the surname Krupp was in Jackson's mind when he included in his June report to President Truman a commitment to indict individuals "in the financial, industrial, and economic life of Germany who . . . are provable to be common criminals." But who was to provide the given name: Gustav or Alfried?

The British appear to have assumed from the beginning that a Krupp, if chosen, would be Gustav. Passant's memorandum of August 15, in the section dealing with "Krupp von Bohlen und Halbach," does not even mention Alfried. Passant wrote:

[*]Originally, the name was attached to the heavy siege guns used by the Germans in 1914 against the Belgian forts at Liege and Namur. These were in fact made by Skoda, but the press assumed that they were Krupp products. In 1918 the press revived the name (in German *die dicke Bertha*, literally "fat Bertha") and applied it to the seventy-six-mile-range Paris-shelling guns.

Gustav Krupp is now 75. *So far as I know* there is no evidence that he ever had any part in the political decisions on foreign policy of the Nazi or any other German Government. Nor can he be charged with any direct responsibility for war crimes in the narrower sense. Unless evidence that he played a political role can be produced, the whole case against Krupp must rest on the financial support rendered by him and his fellow manufacturers to the Nazi party. . . .

This, Passant thought, would be quite insufficient; why were contributions to the Nazi Party criminal any more than Vickers's contributions to the Conservative Party or Du Pont's to the Republican or Democratic Party funds?

On the American side, the assumption was otherwise. Frank Shea, in his July 23 memorandum outlining the "economic case," included in his tentative list of defendants "Alfried Krupp, President of the huge munitions company, Friedrich Krupp A.G., and since 1943 its sole owner."

Extraordinary as it appears in retrospect, the British and Americans remained unaware that each was thinking of the other Krupp right up to and including the chief prosecutors' meeting on August 23. The British record of the meeting lists "Gustav Krupp von Bohlen und Halbach" as one of the defendants. Perhaps because Jackson went to the meeting accompanied only by his son there is no American record, but Jackson sent his senior staff members a memorandum summarizing its results, and his list of the defendants specified "Alfried Krupp." Alfried was also named in a cable listing the defendants which Jackson sent to the State Department on August 26.

Jackson then left for Italy, apparently unaware that the British, French, and Russian lists specified Gustav. Shea noticed the discrepancy and on August 25 sent letters to Nikitchenko and Gros informing them that Jackson understood Alfried to have been named. Alderman, however, in a teletype conversation with Gordon Dean in Washington on August 27, directed that the list to be published should include Gustav, not Alfried.

It was a first-rate snafu, and the chief prosecutors, at their meeting on August 28, only made matters worse. Alderman reported that there had been "confusion yesterday on the name of Krupp. We had Alfried, the son, on our list. The other three delegations seemed to have Gustav, the father. We ought to be certain of agreement." To which Sir Hartley Shawcross, whether ignorant of or indifferent to the warning in the Passant memorandum, replied: "We have a much stronger case against Gustav Krupp."

Alderman had no information on which to challenge that opinion; Jackson was in Rome, and Shea was in the air on his way back to London from Frankfurt. And so it was agreed, without further discussion, that Gustav would be named, as indeed he was when the list was published on August 29.

At no time do the prosecutors appear to have compared Gustav and Alfried in terms of the charges. If the main emphasis was to be involvement in the conspiracy to initiate aggressive war, the obvious choice was Gustav, for he had been the active and responsible head of the firm throughout the prewar and early war periods. If the principal charge was to be war crimes, then the defendant should have been Alfried, for the principal acts of plunder, and exploitation of concentration camp and slave labor, had occurred after Alfried had replaced his father as actual head of the family and, in 1943, as sole proprietor of the Krupp enterprise. If the intention was to press both kinds of charges, then both men should have been indicted. There was nothing complicated about these factors, but they were never articulated, much less considered.

But the negligence was much grosser than the failure to observe these comparative factors. Some men of seventy-five are still fit, but many are not. Throughout the many months of planning the Nuremberg trials, Gustav Krupp was bedridden at the Krupps' Austrian villa in Bluhnbach, in an advanced state of senile decay, inarticulate, incontinent, and wholly incapable of standing trial.

It was a very bad show, for which the Americans were by no means blameless. Private individuals, as well as soldiers and government officials, are subject to the applicable laws of war, and Jackson regarded the charges against German industrialists as a vital part of the case. It was he who had suggested "Krupp" in the first place, and he should have left firm instructions on the Alfried-Gustav question before putting himself out of reach in Italy. Alderman should not have so readily assumed that the British were right and should have prepared himself better for the August 28 meeting, or at least requested a postponement in order to consult with Jackson or Shea.

But it was the British, and Shawcross in particular, who were primarily responsible for this disastrous situation. Essen and the Krupp headquarters were in the British-occupied zone of Germany. The British had the Krupp people and properties under their control. Colonel Harry Phillimore and Major Airey Neave, two barristers assigned to the BWCE, were stationed at Essen to examine the files at the Villa Huegel, the Krupp family mansion. It is astonishing, and it was inexcusable, that no one on or connected with the BWCE had taken the trouble to check out Gustav's state of health, which surely could have been accomplished by a simple inquiry to any one of the Krupp family or their retainers.

Soon after the list of defendants had been announced, Phillimore and Neave awoke to the mistake. By September 1 Neave "had found nearly a ton of Krupp documents" but "had little evidence against Gustav Krupp himself" and was puzzled that Gustav "was still our target, although Alfried had been sole owner of the firm since 1943." Later that month Phillimore wrote to the Foreign Office:

> I must confess that I have been somewhat astonished that Gustav Krupp should have been selected, as he is, I understand, virtually dead. So much so that the family has already been to the Villa to collect mourning clothes and I think the Will has already been read. Alfried, who was just as deeply implicated, would, I should have thought, been more likely to get to the Court.

At that time, it would still have been a simple matter to revise the list of defendants by replacing Gustav Krupp (if investigation bore out his incapacity) with Alfried or other implicated industrialists. But there is no indication that Phillimore's warning attracted any attention in London.

The enduring effects of this fiasco will emerge in due course. At this point, it is enough to note that Alfried Krupp was a very lucky man, for, had he been named, he would almost certainly have been convicted and given a very stiff sentence by the International Military Tribunal. In that event, any subsequent clemency would have required the concurrence of all four occupying powers, and it is highly improbable that either the Russians or the French would have been moved in his behalf.

## 6

At the end of August, Jackson returned from Rome well pleased with the interest in war crimes shown by the Pope, and with a memorandum from the Vatican staff on Nazi persecution of Catholic clergy. At a staff meeting on the morning of August 31, Jackson informed us that he would depart London that afternoon and remain in the United States for nearly two weeks, with the principal purpose of expediting the President's appointment of the American members of the Tribunal. He had been hopeful that Justice Owen Roberts, who had just retired from the Supreme Court, would accept such an appointment, but that now appeared unlikely. I made bold to raise questions about the wisdom of prosecutorial participation in picking the judges; Jackson acknowledged the problem but said that he "did not see how he could avoid having a hand in it."

Jackson then went off to a meeting of the chief prosecutors which had been called at his request in order to present a proposal to use a recently developed International Business Machine telephonic system for simultaneous translation of multilingual proceedings. If it could be used for the Tribunal's sessions, it would greatly shorten the trials, so everyone was for it, if it would work. Jackson then took occasion to admonish his fellow prosecutors on the importance of having their governments appoint distinguished jurists to the Tribunal, and disclosed that he planned to discuss the subject with President Truman.

If Jackson had hoped to influence the selection he was disappointed for when he met with Truman on September 5, the President told him that he wished to appoint Francis Biddle, the former Attorney General, who had resigned at Truman's request about six weeks after Roosevelt's death. The President candidly admitted that he wanted to make amends to Biddle for this abrupt dismissal, and Jackson had little choice but to assent. Truman then revealed that Secretary of State Byrnes, a South Carolinian, wanted to appoint a judge from that state as the alternate member of the Tribunal. Jackson countered by suggesting John J. Parker, a North Carolinian, presiding judge of the federal court of appeals for the Fourth Circuit and a jurist of considerable distinction.° Truman approved this proposal.

Despite his friendly personal relations with Biddle, Jackson was disappointed by the selection. Biddle had served for a few months as a federal circuit court judge, but had made no secret of his distaste for the bench, and when Jackson became Attorney General, Biddle had happily left the court to take Jackson's place as Solicitor General. When Jackson was appointed to the Supreme Court, Biddle took his place as Attorney General. Thus, although in age Biddle was six years Jackson's senior, professionally Jackson regarded him as a junior. Biddle was in fact an able lawyer and a charming man, but was not generally regarded as a great jurist. He was not the prestigious judicial figure Jackson had been hoping to attract.

Biddle probably owed his selection to Byrnes, with whom he had established close relations during the war and who telephoned Biddle to offer the appointment. Biddle, who was chafing in inactivity, accepted with alacrity, on condition that his wife be allowed to accompany him. At that time Americans serving in occupied Germany and Austria were not allowed to bring in their families, but Truman gave Biddle a letter of authorization, which did not, however, prove immediately effective and which ultimately led to friction between Biddle and Jackson. Parker, on the other hand, accepted only reluctantly; he was troubled about "leaving home and his comfortable, well-defined life" and felt that "as an alternate he would be a voteless cipher." Biddle assured him that "except for voting, his status would be identical with mine," and on that basis Parker agreed to go.

7

Meanwhile Nuremberg was becoming the focus of the American prosecution's activities. Colonel Gill as Executive Officer and the army personnel supporting the Nuremberg project were busy repairing war damage to the

---

°Parker was a Republican who had been nominated for appointment to the Supreme Court by President Hoover in 1930. The Senate, by a margin of one vote, failed to confirm him, largely because of labor opposition generated by an anti-union decision. In fact, the Fourth Circuit was merely following a rule laid down previously by the Supreme Court.

Palace of Justice and the Grand Hotel, altering and enlarging the courtroom and procuring billets to house the hundreds of lawyers and other staff who would soon be descending on the lovely but sadly battered old city. Jackson had told us that when he returned from Washington he would pay London only a flying visit and then go, with much of the staff, to Nuremberg. On September 1 Bill Jackson started moving his father's files there. Storey, Amen, and most of the Paris group went to Nuremberg early in September.

With Shawcross the only duly appointed Chief Prosecutor in town, and France and the Soviet Union represented only by stand-ins, the work in London became increasingly desultory. Bored and insufficiently occupied by the sessions of the subcommittee on war crimes, and moved by the prevailing malaise among my colleagues, I circulated a memorandum entitled "We are all worried," directed to such matters as dissatisfaction with the published list of defendants, the virtual impossibility of dealing with all major suspects in a single trial, and the difficulty of drawing an indictment with only a small part of the evidence in hand: "It is blinking at the facts to act on any other assumption than that the evidentiary basis of this case is likely to expand (and occasionally contract), right up to the end of the trial or trials themselves."

To resolve these problems I proposed to abandon the goal of a single trial and instead to envisage a series of trials, starting with defendants against whom compelling evidence was already available and moving on later to defendants whose cases required more time to collect evidence and formulate charges. My memorandum raised much discussion and some support within the American staff, and, indeed, as regards the entire Nuremberg process from 1945 to 1950, something very much like my proposals eventually transpired. But in terms of the trial before the Tribunal then in contemplation, these ideas came too late. Furthermore, there is no doubt that a series of smaller trials would have lacked the public impact of a single large trial against the defendants with the biggest names, such as Goering, Hess, and Ribbentrop. As matters had developed by then, Jackson was right in rejecting my proposals.

A more fruitful project grew out of my increasing awareness that the prosecution staffs were poorly equipped to deal with the military and naval defendants, of whom there were five: Goering, Keitel, Jodl, Doenitz, and Raeder. Even the lawyers in uniform had had little or nothing to do with German military organization, order of battle, or kindred subjects. It appeared to me that a small group of experts would greatly strengthen the prosecution team, and that among the British intelligence officers with whom I had worked during the war were some who would fill that role admirably.

To lead such a group I thought of my friend Peter Calvocoressi, who was both a barrister and an exceptionally able air intelligence officer. It is interesting to note that while American intelligence officers included many if not a majority who were lawyers in civilian life, there were very few barristers in British intelligence. Calvocoressi was an exception, but after the war he abandoned the bar and became noteworthy as an editor, historian, and publicist.

Late in August I submitted my proposal to Jackson, and it was approved at the chief prosecutors' meeting on August 31, subject to the concurrence of the British intelligence authorities. On September 11, I appeared before the interservice Joint Intelligence Committee and secured an agreement that "a small intelligence section should be placed at the disposal of the Chief Prosecutors of War Criminals for Britain, America, France, and the U.S.S.R. to give expert advice on the organization and methods of German Armed Forces and Police." Within a few weeks the group was assembled and attached for administration to the American prosecution team. Calvocoressi was to play an important part in the indictment of the "General Staff and High Command of the German Armed Forces" as a criminal organization.

On September 11, Alderman received word that Jackson would come to London the next day, but would go to Nuremberg on the thirteenth, to stay. He wanted Alderman, Shea, and all others working on the Indictment (which included all but a few of the lawyers) to go with him. This raised unexpected problems. Neither the French nor the Soviet Chief Prosecutor was on the scene, and we knew that they would be coming to London. The British wished to finish work on the Indictment in London. I had not yet completed the arrangements for the Calvocoressi group.

On September 12 Alderman called a staff meeting, the upshot of which was that he, Shea, and I jointly signed a rather blunt memorandum to Jackson stressing the necessity of both a staff meeting and a meeting of Chief Prosecutors to settle these matters before his departure to Nuremberg. As it turned out, the British were equally insistent on a prosecutorial meeting, especially since the newly appointed French Chief Prosecutor, François de Menthon, was in London for that purpose.

Jackson arrived in London late on the twelfth, and there was no opportunity for a staff discussion before the chief prosecutors' meeting the following morning. De Menthon made his debut accompanied by Gros and half a dozen other supporters; he was a bit wild-looking, but said nothing out of the way. Mr. Ivanov, Counselor at the Soviet Embassy, was the lone Russian present. Jackson had with him his son and Alderman. Shawcross, Fyfe, and Barnes were all present; Shawcross presided and, after welcoming de Menthon, made a strong statement in favor of keeping the four delegations together in London to complete the Indictment.

Jackson then announced the appointments of Biddle and Parker to the Tribunal, after which Shawcross left, too soon to hear Jackson flatly reject the plea to remain in London: "My view is that our time will not be well spent in London. The case is actually being made in Nuremberg. . . . I shall go to Nuremberg at once." He concluded by declaring that it would be "a great mistake to have a Berlin meeting," despite the fact that Article 22 of the Charter explicitly required that "The first meetings of the members of the Tribunal and of the Chief Prosecutors shall be held at Berlin. . . ."

Jackson failed to sway the other prosecutors, who all agreed that the Charter required the Berlin meeting, and thought that the delegations should remain in London for the time being. Ivanov had no authority to commit his country, but said he was expecting Nikitchenko to return to London "tomorrow or the day after." In view of Jackson's intransigence, however, both Fyfe and de Menthon agreed to visit or send liaison teams to Nuremberg the following week. For his part, Jackson allowed that he would "try to leave such personnel here as can carry on with any work remaining to be done"—a rather slighting way to refer to the announced decision of the other chief prosecutors to continue their work on the Indictment in London. The next meeting was scheduled for the following Monday, September 17.

Jackson then returned to Mount Street and announced that his departure was imminent and that any staff meeting must be held at once. Shea was at lunch and the Kaplans could not be found, so Alderman, James Donovan, and I were the only senior staff available. Jackson told Alderman to stay in London in order to attend the next chief prosecutors' meeting, but directed that the rest of the staff working on the Indictment should go to Nuremberg "as soon as possible." He gave me no specific instructions, but since I had been working only on the war crimes and crimes against humanity counts, and it was plain that Committees 2 and 3 would continue to meet in London, it was understood that I would remain there as long as necessary. Jackson then departed, and three days later Shea° and about fifteen other staff members followed him to Nuremberg.

At the time, Jackson's inattention to the Indictment for five weeks after the Charter was signed and his insistence on moving to Nuremberg in the face of the other chief prosecutors' preference for London baffled and exasperated both the other delegations and his own staff. But in retrospect his purposes are apparent, and in large part sensible. The conspiracy charge required a narrative of the conspiracy's origin and course and a showing of its criminality, for which evidence had to be available. Such evidence began to accumulate in July, and the flow continued throughout the summer and fall. Jackson's sense that the evidentiary basis for final drafting had not been laid until mid-September was sound, and the greater part of the evidence was in Nuremberg.

---

°Shea had barely arrived at Nuremberg when he received word of his father's death. He flew to the United States and did not return to Nuremberg until early October.

But surely he was moved by other factors as well. Jackson did not enjoy his dealings with the Russians and French, and even with the British he was not wholly at ease. Reaching a workable agreement on the Charter had been a great strain, and he must have abhorred the thought of a comparable struggle over the Indictment. Jackson was sure that he and his staff could work more effectively in Nuremberg, where, for the next few weeks, there would at most be visits from the British and perhaps the French. Fyfe saw what was going on and at the September 13 meeting remarked: "It seems to me that the final form of the Indictment will have to be settled at Nuremberg." And for the greater part of the Indictment, that is how it turned out.

Finally, the early move to Nuremberg was part of Jackson's strategy for ensuring American control of the prosecution's case. On September 17, as he was settling in his new domain, Jackson sent a memorandum to Storey, which concluded as follows:

> I do not think that division of the work is advisable in view of the situation concerning our fellow-prosecutors. Candidly, I think we must utilize Committee 4 as the basis for keeping control of the bulk of the case in American hands. To this end, I think . . . that Committee 4 will have to take primary responsibility for the development of the case in all its aspects on the questions of common plan conspiracy and individual and organizational responsibilities.

The reference to "Committee 4" as the locus of power is indeed ironic. Jackson was the Chairman of that committee, but since August 16 he had never once called a meeting. The committee had met once in his absence and was destined never to meet again. For "Committee 4," read "Jackson."

He was feeling feisty that day (September 17), during which he had also cabled to President Truman his indignation that the Soviet government had recalled its prosecutor but had not appointed a replacement, and that so far the Russians had not produced either evidence or a staff. Jackson went so far as to advise the President that, if the delay lasted too long, he should appoint an American military commission to dispose of the charges, replacing the International Military Tribunal. Fortunately for the Nuremberg project, the new Soviet prosecutor appeared in London that same day, so Jackson could turn his attention to other annoyances, but Alderman had to correct the record by calling the State Department.

## 8

As more of the staff left London, the Mount Street offices were quieter and the *ambiance* more leisurely. Sidney Alderman (whom Jackson had left in charge) and I profited by the diminished pressure to improve our acquaintance. I had already concluded that his sensitivity to the ways and moods of others made him an excellent ambassador. He was perhaps not sufficiently inclined to question instructions, and he shunned unpleasantness, but he could be quite pointed in a courteous way if occasion so required. Socially he was most amiable and, like many Southerners, anecdotally humorous. He loved music and could make a pleasant sound on the violin; it was a taste I shared, and our friendship was cemented when I helped him to fulfill a long-held desire to own a baroque violin by a good Italian maker. I have a good ear, which cost Sidney a couple of hundred pounds when I assured him that the more expensive (a Mariani) of the two violins he was considering (at the famous London firm of Hill & Sons) was much the better. At that time I had fair skill at the piano, and we had several good evenings playing Mozart and Beethoven sonatas at the old Sassoon mansion (now gone) opposite the Dorchester Hotel on Park Lane, which then served as the senior American officers' mess in London.

Moved by Jackson's newly kindled interest in the Indictment, Alderman distributed to the other delegations a voluminous compilation of working materials which our staff had produced and which might provide a factual basis for drafting the conspiracy charge. The British promptly used it to produce a rough draft of Counts One (conspiracy) and Two (aggressive war) and combined it with Roberts's draft of Counts Three (war crimes) and Four (crimes against humanity), based on the documents that had been produced for Committees 2 and 3. This was the general structure which the Indictment ultimately assumed, but Fyfe's draft was, by American standards, so skeletonic and dry that we were sure it would require amplification and rearrangement.

Despite Ivanov's assurance as late as September 13 that Nikitchenko would soon return, the very next day Alderman learned from the French that the Soviet Chief Prosecutor would not be Nikitchenko, but Roman A. Rudenko, Chief Prosecutor of Soviet Ukraine. We first met him at the chief prosecutors' meeting on September 17—a short, pallid man wearing the brown Soviet Foreign Office uniform, with shoulder stars showing the rank of lieutenant general, one notch higher than Nikitchenko's army rank of major general. Rudenko was accompanied by his deputy Colonel Yuri Pokrovsky, Ivanov, and a young lady interpreter, who introduced herself as Miss Dmitrieva.

The meeting, which had been called to consider the Anglo-American draft of Counts One and Two, did not go well. Neither de Menthon nor Rudenko was at all familiar with the long negotiations which had led up to the Charter, and de Menthon repeated many of the same arguments against the aggressive war charge that Falco and Gros had voiced earlier. Fyfe had to leave the meeting, and Roberts as chairman was contentious and bullying. Miss Dmitrieva, though personally rather winsome, was wholly unequal to the task of translating legal concepts; discussion with Rudenko was, as Alderman put it, like conversation through a double mattress. All the renditions of Rudenko's comments began: "General Rudenko say, he very glad to be with you in this h[aspirate]onorable work."

Rudenko did, however, produce a large pile of evidentiary material from the Soviet Extraordinary State Commission for War Crimes, together with a few captured German documents. Except for these last, unfortunately, everything was in Russian, and only one copy was provided.

On September 18 Fyfe, Barnes, and Sir Frank Soskice (the Solicitor General) were all on hand, Roberts was subdued, and things went much better. A fresh face at the table was that of Major Elwyn Jones, a young barrister and Labour Party Member of Parliament, newly chosen as a junior member of the British prosecution team. Fyfe had made some changes in the draft of Counts One and Two, which seemed to mollify de Menthon and Rudenko.

Fyfe and de Menthon both disclosed that they planned to visit Nuremberg during the latter part of the week to discuss the Indictment with Jackson. Rudenko said he would remain in London for at least two more weeks. Alderman, after vainly trying to switch the scene for future meetings to Nuremberg, stated that he would move there on the morrow and that I would remain as Jackson's representative in London.

Alderman and seventeen other staff members flew to Nuremberg the next day, and for the second time I found myself in charge of the rear echelon, which by this time had dwindled to some thirty members, including about a dozen lawyers. Working with me on the Indictment were John Hazard, in later years my colleague on the faculty of the Columbia Law School, who spoke fluent Russian, and Major Loftus Becker, a New York lawyer who had been a member of my intelligence group during the war. When Bernays left I had inherited his able and very attractive secretary, Miss Betty Stark. Though not yet formally attached, Peter Calvocoressi was on hand, studying the problems which would arise if it was decided to indict the German General Staff.

When Committees 2 and 3 met on September 22, Soskice presided and all went smoothly. I attended with Hazard, who was translating the Soviet materials that Rudenko had produced, and we circulated a revision of Roberts's draft of the Indictment counts on war crimes and crimes against humanity, based on ideas which Alderman and I had discussed before his departure.

Miss Dmitrieva's interpreting was beginning to improve somewhat, but her lapses were often comical and there was a good deal of mirth, which she took with great good humor. However, she was the soul of propriety, and when someone at the table used the expression "to throw the baby out with the bath water," she blushed to the roots of her hair and declared severely: "I weel not translate that; it eez not *nice.*" Hazard explained the figure of speech in Russian to Colonel Pokrovsky's satisfaction, but the lady still seemed troubled by this vision of a naked baby tumbling out of a tub. All in all, the meeting was both pleasant and useful, as our allotted portion of the Indictment began to take shape.

But collaboration on the draft of the conspiracy count soon ran into difficulties. Both Fyfe and de Menthon went to Nuremberg, Fyfe armed with the Anglo-American draft, and met with Jackson and Alderman on September 21. Fyfe thought that Jackson regarded the "general scheme" of the London draft as "not unacceptable," subject to some shortening.

But late on the twenty-second, just as Fyfe was leaving to return to London, Jackson handed him a redraft of the conspiracy count which Jackson himself had prepared without taking any account of the London draft. The timing could hardly have been more irritating, for Fyfe had just spent two days with Jackson reviewing the London draft under the impression that it had been accepted as a basis for discussion—time largely wasted if Jackson's own draft was to replace it. Furthermore, Jackson had put it forward too late for any effective discussion prior to Fyfe's departure. Fyfe was a very patient negotiator, but this was too much, and when he got back to London the pent-up anger spilled out, some of it on me.

The British were the first to complete their amendatory work on the Indictment and this time decided to entrust the negotiations in Nuremberg to Patrick Dean of the Foreign Office, assisted by Robert Scott-Fox and Colonel Phillimore. They were happy to find that the American draft was "a great improvement on any earlier U.S. text." The negotiations went well, and on September 28 full agreement on the conspiracy and aggressive war counts was reached.

Meanwhile, on September 27 the chief prosecutors met again, and Soskice sought agreement for still another meeting the following week to be attended by Jackson, at which the text of the Indictment would be settled, to be followed on October 5 or 6 by the mandatory meeting in Berlin at which the Indictment would be signed and filed at the opening session of the Tribunal. But Jackson had spoken to me on the telephone earlier that day, and I was obliged to interpose that he had warned that while Anglo-American agreement on the Indictment was probable it was not yet certain and that the American judges might not be able to reach Berlin earlier than October 10. Sir Hartley joined the gathering at this juncture and begged me to "persuade Mr. Justice Jackson to adhere to" the British schedule. I said that I would do my best, but did not add that by this time it was clear to me that Jackson was a man who listened primarily to his own counsels and was not easily moved by alien blandishments or criticisms.

At the last two meetings of Committees 2 and 3, on September 29 and October 1, a new French face appeared in the person of Charles Dubost, de Menthon's deputy. A bald, spectacled man, intense and humorless, he soon became persona non grata to Jackson, who, on what basis I know not, believed him to be a Communist. In these meetings, the war crimes and crimes against humanity charges were brought close to their final form. Over Roberts's objections, we used the word "genocide," newly coined by Raphael Lemkin (at that time a member of the American prosecution staff) to describe "the extermination of racial and national groups . . . particularly Jews and Poles and gypsies and others."

Ever since Jackson had left London, the other delegations, especially the British, had been beseeching him to return there for a meeting at which the Indictment could be finally approved. The Justice had just as consistently declined to commit himself and, after having reached agreement with the British in Nuremberg, on September 29 he announced that he would not make the trip and instead would send Alderman, fully authorized to make a final agreement.

On October 1 Alderman, with Bill Jackson, the Kaplans, and a few others, flew to London. Soon after their arrival I received word from the French that de Menthon had refused to come to London unless Jackson would also be present. Alderman sought out Dubost, explained that he came fully authorized by Jackson to reach an agreement, and then reminded Dubost that Jackson had attended many London meetings at which no authorized French representative appeared. This tumbled Dubost off his high horse, and he promised that de Menthon would arrive the next day.

Alderman had brought to London not only the text of Counts One and Two as agreed to in Nuremberg (and which were to be combined with Counts Three and Four as agreed to in London, thus forming the main body of the Indictment), but also drafts of three appendices.

Appendix A was a "Statement of Individual Responsibility" consisting of a paragraph on each of the twenty-four defendants, describing in each case the principal governmental offices held and the particular areas of personal responsibility and specifying the counts of the Indictment under which each defendant was charged.* Appendix C, initially drafted by Barnes and Shea in London, related exclusively to the aggressive war charges and comprised a descriptive listing of the international treaties and agreements violated by Germany in planning and initiating the aggressive wars.

Appendix B was entitled "Statement of Criminality of Groups and Organizations" and comprised separate sections, each describing one of the groups or organizations against which a declaration of criminality was

---

*In Count One of the Indictment, Adolf Hitler was named as the organizer and leader of the conspiracy, and several of the defendants were mentioned by name in the course of the narrative. In Counts Two, Three, and Four no individual defendants were named.

sought. It had not yet been finally determined which organizations should be so charged, but it had been assumed from the beginning, as appears from Bernays's earliest memorandum, that Himmler's enormous engine of tyranny known as the SS, as well as the closely related Gestapo, would be included.

In the course of meetings and informal discussions during the summer of 1945, a number of proposals for additions had been made. The Nazi Party as a whole was deemed the driving force of the conspiracy, but it was a huge organization with many members who joined for reasons of expediency and played little or no part in its doings. Consequently, it was proposed to draw a line between the leaders and those of no account. It was also proposed to add the branch of the party called the Sturmabteilung (SA), commonly known as "Storm Troopers" or "Brownshirts," a quasi-military force of guards and street fighters that played a leading part in the Nazi seizure of power.

Toward the end of September, as the time for decision neared, there were recommendations to add the Reichsregierung, meaning the official government leadership, comprising the Cabinet of Ministers and other ministerial councils; the Labor Front led by Robert Ley, which had suppressed and replaced the preexisting labor unions; the Einsatzstab Rosenberg, a special staff set up by Alfred Rosenberg for looting valuable works of art; and the General Staff of the German armed forces.

The BWCE consulted Passant on the wisdom of these proposals, and he counseled against indicting any of them. The British took his advice, except in the case of the Reich Cabinet, for the inclusion of which there was apparent logic, inasmuch as a majority of the defendants had been members of it. The draft of Appendix B brought to London by Alderman, however, covered five organizations: the Reich Cabinet, the Leadership Corps of the Nazi Party, the SS, the Gestapo, and the SA.

During the afternoon of October 2, in the absence of de Menthon, the four delegations held a preliminary meeting to consider the draft Indictment as a whole. All went well and, as Alderman later wrote, "We made great strides towards final agreement on the latest redraft of all four counts."

That evening, however, Jackson telephoned his son, conveying further instructions to Alderman. The most important mandate was that Alderman "must not agree to any indictment which did not include the German General Staff or some recognizable category of the High Command as a defendant organization alleged to be criminal." Since this addition was indeed made the following morning, over strong British objections, and since that action was and has remained highly controversial, it deserves to be dealt with in some detail.

## 9

Like the armament makers, of whom Krupp was the symbol, the "militarists" were a category widely regarded as a vicious element of Germanhood, born long before Nazism and all too likely to survive it. And for the idea of "militarism," the symbol, even before World War I, was the German General Staff. In international law, this concept first found recognition in Article 160 of the Treaty of Versailles, wherein (among other restrictions on future German military forces) it was provided that:

> The Great General Staff and all similar organizations shall be dissolved and may not be reconstituted in any form.

This terminology has led to much confusion, and is more readily understood if it is realized that "command" and "staff" designate the two basic elements of military control and discipline. "Commanders" are those who can issue orders on their own authority and over their own names to troops in the units they command, whether large (division, corps) or small (platoon, company). But, except in very small units, a commander cannot function effectively without helpers, who bring him information about the condition of his troops, the whereabouts and intentions of the enemy, and other circumstances which together form the basis for his decisions and orders. These helping officers are a "staff," and if the unit is a large one and the staff correspondingly numerous, it is headed by a "Chief of Staff." This officer may be of high rank and his function very important, but he cannot issue orders (other than to his own staff subordinates) except by the authority and in the name of the unit commander. In the large units, and at the supreme headquarters, the staff is called a "General Staff."

This command-staff relation has presumably existed in some form since very early times, but in the modern era the vocabulary and technical evolution were most evident in Prussia and, later, in Imperial Germany. Frederick the Great was the Commander in Chief of his military forces in fact as well as in name, but the succeeding Prussian and Imperial monarchs rarely essayed the exercise of personal command. As sovereigns, they remained formally commanders in chief, but effective command had to be exercised by someone else. At least since the Franco-Prussian War, that individual was the Chief of the General Staff of the Army. The most important of these were Helmuth von Moltke (1858–1888), Graf Alfred von Schlieffen (1891–1905), and, during the last two years of World War I, Paul von Beneckendorff und von Hindenburg, who relied heavily on his chief assistant, Erich Ludendorff.

It was this group of staff officers at Supreme Headquarters, who actually exercised the Kaiser's powers of command, that became known as the "Great General Staff" and who shared, with their sovereign, condemnation by the victorious Allies. But the effort to "dissolve" and forbid revival of the offending entity failed to distinguish between the staff function and the way it had been exercised by the Germans.

Article 160 of the Versailles Treaty did not abolish the German Army; it drastically limited its future size and armament, but the army was permitted 100,000 men, organized in not more than ten divisions. There was no way in the world that such an army could *be* an army without someone in command, and that someone could not possibly exercise effective command without a staff. To tell the Germans that they could not have any "similar organization" was like telling a boy that he might go swimming but must not get wet.

What happened can easily be guessed; a rose by any other name smelled as sweet. The post-Versailles German Army had a small Great General Staff, but it was called simply the "Truppenamt" (literally "Troops Office"), the Chief of which was, functionally, the Chief of the Army General Staff.

But there was one significant change from Imperial times. The President of the Weimar Republic, like the Emperor, was titular Commander in Chief of the armed forces, but he had no military staff. Effective command of the army was vested in a general (of higher rank than the Chief of the Truppenamt) who bore the title "Chef der Heeresleitung" (literally "Chief of the Army Leadership"), and the Truppenamt was responsible to him, not to the President.

In 1935, when Hitler denounced the Versailles military restrictions, the army's commander was rechristened "Commander in Chief," and the Truppenamt camouflage was shed as its chief became "Chief of the General Staff." But this did not restore the authority of the Moltke-Schlieffen-Hindenburg days, for the Chief remained subordinate, and junior in rank, to the Commander in Chief.°

In 1938 Hitler himself replaced Field Marshal Werner von Blomberg as Commander in Chief of the Armed Forces (Wehrmacht). Hitler's staff, which was not called a General Staff, was headed by Keitel. The Fuehrer rapidly assumed effective as well as titular command, and at the end of 1941, when Field Marshal Walter von Brauchitsch resigned as Commander in Chief of the Army, Hitler appointed himself as successor. Thus Hitler had

---

°The Air Force (Luftwaffe), established as a separate branch of the armed services in 1935 with Goering as Commander in Chief, had a staff structure similar to that of the Army. Raeder was simultaneously titled Commander in Chief of the Navy, but his general staff was called the Seekriegsleitung ("Naval War Leadership").

two staffs, as the Chief of the General Staff of the Army now also became directly responsible to him. Organizationally, Hitler's assumption of full and direct command was a throwback to the days of Frederick the Great.

Accordingly, whatever plausibility might in 1918 have supported the idea that the General Staff was the *fons et origo* of Teutonic frightfulness, by 1945 it was pretty much a paper tiger. While individual staff officers shared the guilt in varying degrees, the main responsibility for the army's war crimes rested within the chain of *command*, from Adolf Hitler right down to the company captains.

This was known to many officers on the Allied side, but symbols acquire a momentum of their own, and throughout the war journalists and politicians continued to excoriate the General Staff. Confusion was compounded because the label itself was imprecise, as was abundantly apparent at the silly wrangle between Stalin and Churchill at the Teheran Conference, when the Soviet leader suggested the liquidation of "50,000 German General Staff Officers." There were General Staffs at the higher field headquarters (Army Group, Army, and Corps) as well as supreme headquarters, and some General Staff officers (meaning those who had general staff training and wore the red trouser-stripes of the "General Staff Corps") were also assigned to divisional and other lower headquarters. Furthermore, the abler German officers, most of whom had general staff training, commonly served sometimes in staff and other times in command appointments. By the end of the war there were several thousand officers qualified for General Staff assignments, but certainly not 50,000, and Stalin was probably thinking (if he was thinking at all) about the entire body of German regular officers rather than those of the General Staff Corps.

Hatred and fear of German "militarism," under whatever symbol, was certainly the dominant public sentiment in 1945, but in military circles there was division of opinion. The affinity among professional military men crosses national and even battle lines, and in both Britain and the United States there were many officers who admired German professionalism and thought their German counterparts were merely "doing their duty" and "obeying orders," and that they deserved respect rather than condemnation. A criminal indictment of the General Staff, or any comparable segment of the German armed forces, was bound to be highly controversial.

However, no doubts about the necessity of harsh punishment for the German General Staff troubled the mind of General Dwight D. Eisenhower, Supreme Commander of the Allied Forces in Europe. In England on July 8, 1944, lunching with Lord Halifax (then the British Ambassador in Washington), Eisenhower held forth (as recorded by his Naval Aide, Captain Harry C. Butcher) as follows:

Ike repeated his views° that the German General Staff regards this war and the preceding one as merely campaigns in their dogged determination first to dominate Europe and eventually the world. He would exterminate all of the General Staff. Or maybe they could be concentrated on some appropriate St. Helena. . . . Halifax asked Ike how many officers are on the German General Staff. Ike guessed about 3,500. He added he would include for liquidation leaders of the Nazi Party from mayors on up and all members of the Gestapo.

There was agreement that extermination could be left to nature if the Russians had a free hand. Ike added that justice would be done if zones of influence in Germany could be temporarily assigned to the small nations overrun by Hitler. He would give Russia the largest position and other areas to the Czechs, Yugoslavs, Poles, Danes, Norwegians, Greeks, and the French.

Extermination or exile for the entire General Staff were, to put it mildly, drastic alternatives. Subsequently, Eisenhower put in writing his personal views, which he "placed before the President and the Secretary of State when they came to Potsdam in July 1945." They included the following recommendations: (1) "Leading Nazis," members of the SS and Gestapo, and soldiers guilty of violations of the laws of land warfare should be "punished by Allied Tribunals," (2) membership in the Gestapo and SS "should be taken as prima facie evidence of guilt," (3) the German General Staff should be "utterly eliminated," all its records destroyed, its members "scattered and rendered powerless to operate as a body," and in "proper cases" they should be "more specifically punished."

There can be little doubt that Eisenhower, given his personality and military eminence, did much to revive the General Staff as the symbol of German militarism and to spread the view that its members should suffer summary and severe punishment. It was not long before these ideas were connected with Bernays's organizational proposal. At the meeting in Morgenthau's office on May 18, 1945, Henry Fowler of the Treasury Department said to Jackson: "As a matter of fact, we discussed other organizations that you might indict." McCloy added: "You might very well indict the General Staff. . . . I think that's a very good thing to indict."

That appears to be the first articulation of the idea, but within ten days it had vaulted the ocean and risen to the highest international level. On May 28, 1945, Harry Hopkins, on his last mission as Presidential Representative (his only one for Truman), was in the Kremlin, flanked by Ambassador Harriman and Chip Bohlen and opposite Stalin and Molotov, for discussions preliminary to the Potsdam Conference. According to the minutes:

°How long Eisenhower had held these views is uncertain. As least since January 27, 1944, he had known that the European Advisory Council had recommended that the surrender terms should include "abolition of the German General Staff."

*Mr. Hopkins* . . . said he had in mind such questions as . . . trial of war criminals and particularly the question of the German General Staff. He said we have already ordered all members of the Gestapo, SS, SD and the General Staff to be placed under arrest. He said in considering the General Staff we must ascertain if we have the same thing in mind when we use the term. For example, do we mean twenty or thirty thousand officers directly connected with the Staff or do we mean a smaller one?

*Marshal Stalin* said that the German General Staff had two aspects, one formal and the other real. He said in its formal aspects it was comprised of the official members of the General Staff which numbered seven thousand. . . . In its real aspect, however, the General Staff should be regarded as composed of the whole agglomeration of staffs since every division and army staff in the German Army was closely linked with the General Staff and operated under its direct orders. Viewed in this light the real General Staff was composed of tens of thousands of officers. . . . He felt we should arrest all these officers and keep them out of the way in order to avoid planning for future war. . . .

*Mr. Hopkins* said they were all prisoners of war and the question was what distinction should be made between the General Staff officers and the ordinary prisoners of war. He said we were considering the possibility of not allowing them to return to Germany.

*Marshal Stalin* said . . . it would be wise to keep these officers under arrest for as long as the period of occupation at least. Possibly for ten or twenty years. He said of course some members of the General Staff would be tried as war criminals.

*Mr. Hopkins* replied that we were considering the possibility of indicting the General Staff as an organization as we proposed to do in the case of the Gestapo and SS.

*Marshal Stalin* replied he thought that was a very good idea if it were legally possible.

Stalin's concern about the legality of indicting the General Staff is reminiscent of his meeting with Churchill in October 1944, when he insisted on a trial rather than summary execution for the Nazi leaders. However, at this stage, neither Hopkins nor Stalin was primarily concerned with judicial process against the General Staff, but rather with the most practical means of permanently suppressing it.

That was the same problem that Eisenhower had been discussing privately with Halifax, Morgenthau, and others, and now the time for action had arrived. On June 5, 1945, Eisenhower cabled the War Department that the policy his headquarters was carrying out was that "members of the German General Staff Corps and equivalent Naval and Air Officers . . . should be arrested and segregated in separate detention camps pending

. . . [Allied] decision as to their disposal." Seeing this message, Colonel Chanler realized that Eisenhower's action was relevant to Jackson's commitment, in his June 7 Report to the President, to bring criminal charges against members of the "military establishment, including the General Staff." Chanler's superior, Major General John R. Hilldring, suggested to McCloy that perhaps "Jackson will dispose of these people without further action on the part of the War Department." But McCloy replied that no final conclusions could be reached until "Jackson's plans are a little better developed."

At this point Eisenhower returned from Europe and in a Pentagon press conference on June 18 made public his views about both the General Staff and the SS:

> The General Staff must be utterly destroyed. These wars of Germany's have been, from the standpoint of the General Staff, merely campaigns—merely incidents. . . . Now, how are you going to destroy that German General Staff is something else again, because many of them have the excuse they did their duty as honorable soldiers. But my own opinion is that it should be made utterly impossible for them even to function again. . . .
>
> To my mind you not only have to get them and eliminate all their archives, but you have to get every man, certainly, that is a trained general staff officer, and I see no way of doing it except segregation in some way, where he simply can't get back to his job. . . .

Then, in answer to a question of whether he considered "the ordinary SS trooper a war criminal":

> That is what I'd say: The SS trooper, up until it began to get desperate, or somewhere in September of 1944, I'd say anyone that was an SS trooper until that time would be a war criminal. At least the full burden of proof would be on him. After that . . . they would put any healthy man in it they could get hold of. He couldn't help himself. . . . Except for the 12th SS. I think that the American Army as a unit will handle the 12th SS, every man they can get a hold of. They are the men that killed our people in cold blood. . . . We hate everybody that ever wore a 12th SS uniform.°

---

° The 12th SS Panzer Division Hitler Jugend was raised in 1943 in Belgium, partly from recruits from the military fitness camps of the Hitler Youth. It took part in the 1944 battles in Normandy and in the Battle of the Bulge (the December 1944 Ardennes offensive). No doubt Eisenhower's hostility to this division was based on reports (confirmed by a Court of Inquiry established at his headquarters) that units of this division, between June 7 and 21, 1944, had shot to death sixty-four Allied prisoners in uniform, some of whom were wounded and none of whom had resisted or attempted escape.

Although it is highly improbable that Eisenhower had ever heard of Bernays, these public statements were certainly in line with the lawyer's ideas of organizational guilt, which Jackson had already embraced. And although Ike does not appear to have contemplated any trial as the basis for "segregating" the General Staff officers, he certainly regarded them as an identifiable "group" to be singled out for special treatment.

Jackson and his party departed for London that same day, and with Eisenhower's words ringing in their ears, it is no wonder that Bernays wished to indict the German General Staff. But nothing further was done by the Jackson group until well into September.

Not so with the American military authorities. At the end of June, Eisenhower's Allied headquarters (SHAEF) was dissolved. Pursuant to the Potsdam Agreement, the administration of occupied Germany came under the Allied Control Council, a quadripartite (Britain, France, Soviet Union, United States) organization of which the American component was the Office of Military Government, U.S. (OMGUS), headed in Berlin by the Deputy Minister Governor, Lieutenant General Lucius D. Clay.

Within OMGUS, the problem of German "demilitarization" was assigned to Major General Ray W. Barker, who had been a Deputy Chief of Staff at SHAEF and had had some experience with war crimes matters during the last weeks of the war. At an OMGUS committee meeting on July 6, 1945, General Barker stated that a staff study was in progress on the "disposition of the officers' corps," and Clay instructed Barker to report at the next meeting on plans for "disposition of the General Staff."

The General Staff officers were already under arrest pursuant to Eisenhower's order of June 5. On August 2 that policy was internationally confirmed by the Potsdam Declaration, which included "the general staff" among the military and Nazi organizations which were to be "completely and finally abolished in such manner as permanently to prevent the revival or reorganization of German militarism and nazism."

But how to achieve so permanent a suppression was, as Ike had succinctly put it, "something else again." On August 9, Barker submitted to Clay a memorandum entitled "Disposition of Potentially Dangerous Officers of the German Armed Forces." Barker divided the officers into two categories: Group I, the "highly dangerous," and Group II, the "less potentially dangerous." Group I comprised (1) officers of "flag rank," i.e., army and air force generals and navy admirals, (2) members of the General Staff Corps and officers of equivalent status in the air force and navy, and (3) individual officers whose personal background or other characteristics stamped them as "potential builders of a resurgent military system."

Three courses of action, Barker wrote, had been proposed for the "disposal" of these officers: (1) Banishment or exile of the "St. Helena nature," (2) "Disposal, individually or in small groups, throughout the world to places under control of the Allied governments," and (3) "Detention in Germany under severe restrictive measures prescribed by the Control Council." The first two of these, Barker very sensibly rejected on the ground that the political difficulties and the scant likelihood that such situations could be maintained on a long-term basis were decisive disadvantages.

Falling back on the third alternative, Barker proposed that the restrictions to be imposed should include (1) prohibition of all foreign travel or emigration, of holding public office, and of access to the public payroll other than as a "laborer"; (2) approval by the occupation authorities for any change of domicile; and (3) close surveillance of all activities and communications and subjection of homes to search at any time.

Barker's proposals came before Clay with the concurrence of the other divisions of OMGUS except for the Director of Intelligence, Brigadier General T. J. Betts, who stated (altogether sensibly) that the proposal called for such extensive surveillance of so many individuals that its execution was wholly impracticable, and proposed (quite absurdly) that the Group I officers should all suffer "banishment of the St. Helena type," with "all members of their immediate families." The Director of the Legal Division, Charles Fahy, pointed out that the General Staff might be indicted as a criminal organization and suggested that Justice Jackson be informed of the Barker proposals.

On September 3 Clay told Barker to follow Fahy's suggestion. Jackson was then in the United States, but the next day Barker met in London with Shea and described his plan to keep the "dangerous" officers in Germany, under strict surveillance. In reply to Barker's question, Shea told him that indictment of the General Staff was not probable, but that no final decision had been reached. After consulting Ben Kaplan and me, Shea assured Barker that we had no objection to presentation of his plan to the Control Council since the German officers would be kept under arrest or close surveillance should we need any of them as witnesses or defendants. Upon his return to Berlin, Barker secured Clay's approval of his general plan.

Barker's visit served as a reminder to us that the chief prosecutors might decide to indict the German military leadership as a criminal organization, and a few days later Calvocoressi and I began discussing how such a group might be defined if matters so fell out. I did not then nor do I now know what Jackson's thinking was in the early stages, and the first record of his views that I have found is in his letter of September 22 to Fyfe, written during the course of their joint work on the Indictment in Nuremberg. In a passage dealing generally with the organizations, Jackson wrote:

> I assume there is no question about the inclusion of the SS, the
> SA and the Gestapo. I do think we should consider whether we should
> not include the Nazi Party leadership down to the level where policy-

making ceased and I think we probably must include the General Staff. Everybody agreed that it is a menace to the peace of Europe, that it is as guilty as any organization of the aggressive warfare and it seems a little peculiar to convict others of aggressive warfare if they [the General Staff] are innocent.

No doubt it was this passage which led the BWCE to consult Passant, who remarked that it would be hard to determine *who* should be the defendants, as the General Staff did what most staffs do (plan), and some of them opposed Hitler. He concluded:

Whilst, therefore, it is clearly necessary to destroy both the General Staff and the Officers' Corps as institutions in the Germany of the future, and to prevent the revival and perpetuation of their traditions, it is felt that to indict either or both as criminal organizations on the same footing as the Gestapo and the SS would be incongruous in itself and would appear unjust to wide circles in many countries. For these reasons their inclusion is not recommended.

These arguments proved persuasive to the BWCE, and the agreement on the Indictment reached on September 28 in Nuremberg did not include the General Staff, which was merely listed in brackets in the draft Alderman brought to London. But after Alderman left Nuremberg, Jackson must have decided to press the issue to a showdown vote, and that accounts for his telephone call on the night of October 2 instructing Alderman not to agree to the Indictment unless the General Staff, or some equivalent category, was accused as a criminal organization.

## 10

When Peter Calvocoressi and I put our heads together on the problem of defining a military "group" for indictment, we had virtually nothing by way of guidance. To the best of my recollection, Jackson never mentioned the General Staff to me during the pretrial months, much less asked for my views on indicting it. So we had no idea what the Justice's underlying purpose was. Did he want a definition which would embrace thousands of officers, with a common denominator of General Staff training or of career professionalism? Did he want every officer above a certain rank? Or a group defined according to its decision-making authority?

There was no telling what Jackson wanted, and we could only use our best judgment. I think we believed that our indictment of thousands on the sole ground that they were German officers would rightly be regarded as both unfair and absurd. Nor did either rank or General Staff membership, without more, seem an adequate criterion. We well knew that "General Staff" was no longer a plausible indicator of high-level responsibility, and that the armed services were run by commanders, not staff officers.

What we were seeking was a credible selection of those officers who had the principal authority, under Hitler, for the plans and actions of the Wehrmacht. Peter hit on the idea of including only those commanders who held the military title of *Oberbefehlshaber*,° which is not a rank but a designation best translated as "Commander in Chief." It was held only by the commanders of one of the three branches of the Wehrmacht (army, navy, air force) or of the largest field and territorial formations. In the army these would be predominantly "army groups" and "armies," in the Luftwaffe "air fleets," and in the navy "sea group commands."

This was at least a plausible line-drawing in the chain of command, but it did not seem sufficient. The Chief of the General Staff of the Army, even though demoted from his World War I supremacy, was still an important participant in decision-making, and, considering all the talk about the General Staff in the highest political and legal circles, to exclude him from the scope of the indicted group would be difficult to explain. Furthermore, Keitel, though neither an *Oberbefehlshaber* nor a Chief of Staff, was Hitler's military "chief" and the highest-ranking army officer, and neither he nor his principal military advisers, such as Jodl, could realistically be excluded. So we sacrificed symmetry for common sense and added to the list the Chiefs of Staff of the army, navy, and air force, plus Keitel and two others from Hitler's Wehrmacht staff.

As finally drawn, Calvocoressi's definition of the "General Staff and High Command of the German Armed Forces" covered all officers who held one or more of the listed positions at any time between February 1938 and May 1945. The beginning date was selected because Hitler's reorganization of the military structure took place in that month as well as his first use of the Wehrmacht for territorial aggrandizement, by the occupation and annexation of Austria. The surviving individuals covered by our formulation numbered about 130 officers.

On the morning of October 3, prior to the chief prosecutors' meeting, Alderman had informed Shawcross of the motion that Jackson had insisted be made, and Shawcross had warned that he would vigorously oppose it. At the meeting, Calvocoressi was seated with our delegation. Alderman proposed adding the General Staff and High Command to the indicted organizations, and Shawcross was as good as his word. Alderman then asked Calvocoressi to explain the language to be used. The situation was a bit

---

°Literally, "chief command holder." Commanders of smaller formations were called "Commanding General" (for corps), "Division Commander" (for division), and "Commander" (for regiments and battalions).

anomalous, for Calvocoressi, wearing his uniform as a Wing Commander in the Royal Air Force, was not a member of our delegation and was providing a technical basis for a proposal that the British were strongly opposing. But Peter made it clear that he was neither supporting nor opposing Alderman's motion but merely providing technical assistance, which he and his group were expected to do for any of the four delegations. His explanation was lucid, and it passed without incident.

When the vote was taken, the French and Russians voted for Alderman's motion, which thus prevailed by three votes to one. The Foreign Office carried the disagreement up to the Cabinet, which wisely concluded that since a majority of the chief prosecutors favored including the General Staff, "there was nothing to be gained by telling the British representatives to oppose it." And so Calvocoressi's embodiment of Jackson's demand became part of Appendix B of the Indictment.

Alderman also made efforts, in which he fared badly, to add to the list of individual defendants. Jackson's same telephone message via his son had instructed Alderman not to sign the Indictment unless several leading industrialists were named. Inasmuch as the Justice proposed no specific names, and there was no one in London working on the economic case, Alderman was in no position to defend such a motion. When he dutifully made it, Shawcross jumped all over it, and the French and Russians, moved by fear that such additions might delay the trial, voted with Shawcross, and the motion lost.

At the afternoon session, Alderman reported that Jackson "was concerned at the small representation among the . . . defendants of two very important groups, namely, the General Staff, and the Police [Gestapo]." Accordingly, Jackson proposed to add three more members of the General Staff and four of the Police. In fact, there were already five members of the defined military group among the twenty-four defendants, which was ample; the case for adding to the Police defendants was stronger, for Kaltenbrunner was the only one already named. But Soskice, who was presiding, said that such last-minute additions "would make the case ridiculous in the eyes of many," and once again the French and Russians sided with the British on the ground that twenty-four defendants were enough and anyhow there would be more than one trial.

The remainder of the October 3 session, and the final London meeting on October 4, were devoted to minor amendments and additions to the text of the Indictment. Final agreement was achieved, the text was duplicated, and the next day Alderman and I with a part of the London staff flew to Berlin, where the Indictment was to be signed and filed with the newly assembled International Military Tribunal.

## Chapter 6

# BERLIN TO NUREMBERG

The Indictment which the chief prosecutors brought to Berlin was, as we have seen, a polygenetic document. The conspiracy and aggressive war counts were the work of a very able group of American and British lawyers; Rudenko had accepted it with only trivial changes, and de Menthon never pressed for the draft he had submitted on September 27. The contents of the war crimes and crimes against humanity counts, apart from early contributions by the British, were provided by the Russians and French, and the extensive listing of individual atrocities reflected the Continental legal approach, though Roberts, Alderman, and I gave these counts an orderly framework. Mercifully, when the Indictment took its final form, the French and Russians tacitly dropped their insistence that it be accompanied by the documents on which the charges were based, apparently because the task of translating them into the other languages would have taken weeks.

Flawless the Indictment was not. The prosecutors had failed to take into account the change in Article 6 of the Charter which Barnes had effected by moving the conspiracy clause from a position where it applied to all three of the substantive charges to one where it related only to crimes against peace. Through the prosecution's oversight, Counts Three and Four of the Indictment accused the defendants of conspiracies, which were beyond the jurisdiction conferred on the Tribunal by the Charter.

However, such errors in draftsmanship were few and unimportant compared to the consequences of flaws in the process of selecting the individuals and organizations named as defendants. Rudolf Hess had been in British custody since 1941, and his keepers well knew and made no secret of the fact that his mental capacity to stand trial was a matter of grave doubt. Yet the chief prosecutors appear to have named him as a matter of course because of his close relation to Hitler and high office in the Nazi Party without carefully assessing the wisdom of their decision.

Jackson's last-minute demand to indict the General Staff and High Command was made without consulting, so far as I know, any members of his staff, except perhaps his son; the definition of the "group" which Calvocoressi and I supplied to bring it within the scope of the Charter was a tour de force performed to carry out Jackson's directive, the purpose of which was not explained to us. The indictment of the Storm Troopers (SA) appears to have been based largely on memories of their importance in the Nazis' attainment of political power during the years prior to 1935, and reflected insufficient awareness of the SA's subsequent decline and replacement by the SS as the core agency of Nazi domestic power.

All of these missteps were regrettable, and in a few cases, such as Krupp's, it is hard, even with the aid of hindsight, to understand how they could have been made. In general, the blunders were the result of too many unfamiliar problems confronting the lawyers in too short a time, and, on the Anglo-American side, of Jackson's and Shawcross's failures to organize their staffs so that the informational resources of men like Passant and Franz Neumann would be adequately considered when the chief prosecutors made the final decisions.

A danger spot of a wholly different nature was the charge in Count Three of the Indictment that "in September, 1941, 925 Polish officers, who were prisoners of war, were killed in the Katyn Forest in Smolensk." There was no doubt that the corpses of many hundreds of Polish soldiers were buried at the place specified, and in the spring of 1943 the German troops then occupying the area claimed that they had exhumed the corpses. The German government publicly accused the Soviet authorities of the murders, and Moscow replied by blaming the Germans. The other prosecutors urged Rudenko to abandon the charge, which, whatever the truth, would give the German defense counsel the right to contest it and thus implicate in a heinous atrocity one of the powers conducting the trial. But the Soviet prosecutor was adamant, and it appeared to me clear that his superiors had concluded that failure to bring the charge would be publicly regarded as an admission of Soviet guilt. The other prosecutors made it clear to Rudenko that he must assume full responsibility for supporting the accusation.

Reaching agreement on the Indictment was easier than it had been on the Charter, for the earlier document had provided the grand outline and basic principles of the enterprise. But there were many issues in connection with the Indictment which might have proved intractable, and in retrospect its most remarkable feature was that four great nations with divergent legal traditions and political attitudes were able to agree on a document which, despite its shortcomings, furnished a viable basis for the joint prosecution.

The formal signing in Berlin was scheduled for the morning of October 6 at the offices of the Allied Control Council, but when Alderman and I arrived there, only the British and French were on hand. When Rudenko came, he declared that the printed copies of the Indictment contained a number of errors, none of which he was then prepared to specify and which would have to be corrected before the Indictment could be filed with the Tribunal.

Jackson and his party came in late that afternoon. The Justice made no mention of Alderman's failure in London to have several German industrialists added to the list of defendants. But he was troubled by the description, in Count Three, of the Soviet Union as including the erstwhile Baltic nations (Estonia, Latvia, and Lithuania), the Soviet incorporation of which in 1939 had never been officially recognized by either the United Kingdom or the United States. Jackson did not insist that the Indictment's language be changed, but presented Rudenko, de Menthon, and Shawcross with identical letters stating that nothing in the Indictment was to be construed as American recognition of the annexations in question.

On this basis, and on the understanding that the final text of the Indictment would be held open for the correction of minor errors, and reconciliation with the still incomplete French and Russian versions, the English text was signed by the four chief prosecutors.

The next intended step was the filing of the Indictment with the Tribunal, which was scheduled to hold its first meeting the following week. But several of the important participants in the Berlin formalities did not stay for that event. Alderman, at Jackson's request, returned the next day to hold the fort at Nuremberg. Lord Chancellor Jowitt wished to take a view of the Nuremberg trial preparations. Furthermore, he had taken a shine to Alderman's secretary, Charlotte Godchaux, so the three took off for Nuremberg in Jowitt's plane with Alderman, whose jokes were sometimes a bit too obvious, addressing his host as the Gilbertian "susceptible Chancellor."

De Menthon and Shawcross departed Berlin, leaving Dubost and Fyfe as their deputies. More noteworthy was Rudenko's unannounced return to London, leaving no one as his deputy, a move which contributed greatly to the delays and confusions of the next ten days.

2

"The first meeting of the Tribunal in Berlin is a chapter that will make you laugh or cry, depending on how you look at it," wrote Justice Jackson in a letter of October 12, 1945, to President Truman. "We had set up the Tribunal's meeting for October 9, and had asked the European Air Transport Service to furnish a plane to bring Biddle, Judge Parker and their party immediately from Southhampton to Berlin on Sunday [the 7th]. . . . Our judges not only did not get there but we could not find out for a long time where they were. . . . Some of our embarrassment was relieved, however, by the fact that the Russians . . . too, were late in arrival. Also, when the Russian judges finally arrived the Russian prosecutor could not be found. . . ." And indeed the fun, if fun it was, lasted for a full week after Jackson penned this acerbic account.

The American judges had sailed from New York on the *Queen Mary* with an exceptionally strong supporting cast. Biddle had engaged the assistance of Professor Quincy Wright of the University of Chicago, a leading specialist in international law; Professor Herbert Wechsler, of the Columbia Law School and during the war an Assistant Attorney General; and James H. Rowe, a Harvard Law School graduate who had been a confidential assistant to President Roosevelt and subsequently second man in the Department of Justice under Biddle, and who had just returned from service in the Pacific theater as a naval intelligence officer. Judge Parker had with him Major Robert Stewart, an able young Carolinian lawyer. Shortly after arriving in Germany the team was further strengthened by the addition of Adrian S. "Butch" Fisher, another Harvard Law graduate who had been law clerk to Justices Brandeis and Frankfurter and held several important government legal posts before his service with the air force as a navigator. Except for Wright, it was a young staff; Wechsler, Rowe, and Fisher were my contemporaries and coworkers during the New Deal days, and the first two were my personal friends of long standing.

At sea, the group was in frequent conference on foreseeable trial problems, especially the Charter provisions on organizational guilt, which greatly troubled Biddle. The *Queen Mary* made port at Southampton at midday on October 7, and an army plane was waiting for them. But it was also waiting to take to Paris Major General Royal B. Lord,° who chose to have lunch on the *Queen Mary* while the Biddle party cooled their heels. The plane reached Paris at about 5:00 p.m., where it was learned that the Tempelhof airport (in the American Zone of Berlin) closed at 6:00 p.m., after which there were no landing facilities. The army lodged the whole party at the Hotel Rafael and the younger members spent the evening on the town, so there was no hardship. But the following morning there was fog, and the group did not reach Berlin until midafternoon. In fact, neither the French nor Russian judges had yet been heard from, so the detour to Paris was not a serious delay. But Jackson made strong complaint, both to the military authorities and in his letter to the President, with what effect upon the fortunes of General Lord I do not know.

°A distinguished engineer officer and inventor of important items of equipment used by the Corps of Engineers. At the time, General Lord had just completed his service as Deputy Chief of Staff to Eisenhower in charge of troop deployment and had been transferred to a headquarters at Versailles.

The British judges—Sir Geoffrey Lawrence and Sir Norman Birkett—
had arrived on the seventh and took occasion to confer privately with
Shawcross and Fyfe that evening. Biddle and Parker first encountered them
at tea soon after arriving from Paris the following day.

Lord Jowitt had not handled the selection of the British judges
smoothly. At the end of August he had invited Birkett, who had an outstanding record as a barrister and since 1941 as Judge of the High Court,
to be "the British judge at the trial of major German war criminals." Birkett
had accepted by telephone, but when he met with Jowitt a few days later
he was told that the Foreign Office wanted someone—preferably a law
lord—who stood higher in the judicial hierarchy. Birkett accepted an appointment as alternate judge, but his diary reveals the "secret anguish" he
felt at his rejection for the principal assignment "because of the absurd
snobbishness of the Foreign Office." His feelings were not soothed by the
eventual selection of Lord Justice Lawrence of the Court of Appeal, who
had a fine military record in World War I and long experience at the bar and
on the bench, but whose legal abilities had won little acclaim. As matters
worked out, however, Lawrence and Birkett were each rightly cast for the
coming trial.

The French appeared the following day: "two funny little men" was
Biddle's description in a letter to his wife. Judge Robert Falco reappeared
on the scene, as Alternate Member to Henri Donnedieu de Vabres, a law
school professor and specialist in international law. Considering that Falco
had long experience on the Cour de Cassation, this seemed a strange
ordering of status.

It was already known that the Soviet judge would be General Nikitchenko. Fog delayed his arrival until late afternoon, when he appeared,
accompanied by his alternate, Lieutenant Colonel A. F. Volchkov, about
whom nothing was known to the others, and Professor Trainin.

At five o'clock the judges and their staffs (the French had none)
gathered, in the general conference room of the Allied Control Council
Building, for their first meeting. Lawrence at once proposed that the Tribunal meet in public the following morning to receive the Indictment, but
Nikitchenko emphatically objected on the ground that the Soviet prosecutor
was "not in Berlin," adding that the prosecutors should not appear in court
until all four were present. This put an end to Lawrence's plan, but to
assuage the curiosity of the press, the Tribunal allowed itself to be photographed and issued a statement that it had met, was ready to receive the
Indictment "when the prosecutors are ready to present it," and would
continue to meet informally to deal with procedural and administrative
matters.

The Tribunal then reconvened, and Biddle at once took umbrage
because Lawrence went on assuming the presiding role and "shoved in

front of our noses a short and wholly inadequate agenda, which did not even include a temporary chairman appointment." Once again, Nikitchenko (whom Birkett found "very troublesome" but to whom Biddle took a liking) objected because he had not seen the agenda prior to the meeting or as yet had it translated. Biddle joined him in securing a general agreement that each member could propose agendas that must be circulated no later than the evening before the next meeting. The British, Biddle wrote to his wife, "are peculiarly inept."

There was some discussion of a few minor issues on Lawrence's agenda—how the judges should dress, how they should be seated at the trial, and whether to use a system of simultaneous translation. No agreements were reached, and the only accomplishment prior to adjournment was the appointment of three staff members as secretaries to the Tribunal.

Jackson's patience was wearing very thin, and early that evening he told Fyfe that if Rudenko or his representative did not arrive that night, he would leave for Nuremberg the next day. Later he invited the American judges and staff and his own staff members still in Berlin to meet with him at the residence of Charles Fahy, where Jackson was staying. The colloquy was largely between Jackson and Biddle and in part involved ways and means of expediting the trial. I privately told Wechsler that this subject did not appear to me appropriate for informal discussion between judges and prosecutors, a view with which he expressed agreement.

To be sure, the British judges and prosecutors had already held two private discussions of the business at hand, though what particular subjects were raised I do not know. Neither do I know of any subsequent judge-prosecutor interchange comparable to this one, which does not now seem to me quite as reprehensible as it did at the time. Nothing of importance resulted from the discussion, and considering the unusual postwar circumstances it is hardly surprising that the bonds of common nationality should have relaxed restraints which would be observed in domestic Anglo-American legal practice. In European countries the line between bench and bar is not so firmly drawn, as was evidenced by both Nikitchenko's and Falco's transmigration to the judicial role.

When the Tribunal met the following morning (October 10), Rudenko was still missing and Nikitchenko was not sure when he would turn up. The other prosecutors (Jackson, Fyfe, and Dubost) had sent word that they wished to have a public meeting with the Tribunal to obtain instructions for lodging the Indictment. Nikitchenko again vetoed any such meeting in Rudenko's absence, but on Biddle's suggestion the prosecutors were summoned for the sole purpose of informing the Tribunal about the extent to which the Indictment had already been signed. When they came in, Jackson correctly stated that it had been signed in English and that it was subject to conforming to French and Russian texts that were not yet complete.

That would have ended the discussion had not Lawrence asked whether the prosecutors wished to add anything. This gave Jackson opportunity to press for an immediate public meeting so that the press could be accurately informed about the situation. With equal candor Nikitchenko pointed out that such an explanation would embarrass him and that he would oppose any public meeting until Rudenko was on hand.

After the luncheon recess, Nikitchenko returned with the news that he had spoken on the telephone to Rudenko in London, who had insisted that he had had no idea that the prosecutors were meeting° and declared that he "had no means to leave London today." The Tribunal continued to meet throughout the afternoon to discuss lesser matters. The members were not yet accustomed to each other's ways of expression; they had no simultaneous translation and made very heavy weather of it. A query from the press about what was going on produced only the reply that the discussion of procedural and administrative matters was continuing.

Lawrence again raised the question of dress, and Biddle impatiently demanded that a decision be reached on this "minor problem"; he would agree to "any arrangement that is made." Nikitchenko remarked wickedly that "the gown reminds me of medieval times," sparking a flash of Gallic fire from de Vabres, who insisted on a "black robe . . . to conform to our intelligence and dignity. . . . I insist on a black gown." Nikitchenko's compromise offer of black business suits found no takers, and the argument ended in a resolution "that each member wear the form of dress he chooses" and a notation of record that the British, French, and American members favored robes and hoped that the Russian members would agree.

But in the upshot, Nikitchenko and Volchkov continued throughout the proceedings to wear their Soviet Army uniforms. The resolution left the other members fancy-free, but an earlier trial run had convinced them that if each judicial team appeared in its native attire, the bench would resemble a costume ball. So the British eschewed their wigs and the French their caps, and all but the Russians wore black gowns, to which the French judges added their white jabots and Falco the ribbons of his decorations.

While these lesser but necessary decisions were being made, Jackson flew off to Nuremberg, leaving Frank Shea as his deputy, armed with a letter authorizing him to "represent the Chief of Counsel for the United States. . . ." Gordon Dean also remained in Berlin, to handle press matters.

Thursday, October 11, was "waiting for Rudenko" day. On information from London that he would arrive at about midday, Fyfe and Shea

---

°This is hard to believe, as the main purpose of the prosecutors' presence in Berlin was to submit the Indictment to the Tribunal, and this could not have been arranged without Rudenko's (or a deputy's) approval. The other chief prosecutors all appointed deputies to carry the task through. Furthermore, the previous evening Scott-Fox of the Foreign Office had been alerted to the urgency of getting Rudenko to Berlin the following morning.

went to meet him at the airport and secure his agreement to an immediate prosecutors' conference. But Rudenko did not appear, and the two greeters returned empty-handed. Then it was reported that the Soviet prosecutor would land at 2:30 p.m., so Shea and Fyfe hastened back to the airport. In fact, their quarry arrived about an hour later than expected, and the four prosecutors (Rudenko was the only titled Chief present) met early in the evening.

Considering the furor that his absence had caused, it was pretty bold of Rudenko to start the meeting with a declaration that "there should be the least possible delay in the presentation of the Indictment to the Tribunal," especially since he then declared that checking the English text and conforming the Russian translation would take two days. Fyfe suggested Saturday, the thirteenth, for submitting and publicizing the Indictment, but Rudenko held out for Monday, the fifteenth, "as final deadline." So it was agreed, and the prosecutors and their staffs spent the next two days on minor amendments and reconciliation of the Russian and English texts. This also gave time for completion of the French text.

While the prosecutors were thus engaged, the Tribunal continued to consider administrative problems and rules of procedure to govern the trial. There were a few important developments. On Thursday, the eleventh, while discussing service of the Indictment on the defendants, Lawrence disclosed that Gustav Krupp was critically ill and that it might not be possible to bring him to Nuremberg. Later that day the Tribunal decided, over Nikitchenko's objection, that there should be no rotation of the presidency of the Tribunal during the trial at Nuremberg. Friday was largely given over to a discussion of the proposed court trial rules, but at the end of the day the prosecutors were called in and it was agreed that the Tribunal would hold a public meeting on the morning of Monday, the fifteenth, at which the Indictment would be submitted to the Tribunal and given to the press for release at 5:00 p.m.

The principal event on Saturday, the thirteenth, was the Tribunal's selection of Lord Justice Lawrence as its president for the Nuremberg trial proceedings. The choice had lain between Lawrence and Biddle; perhaps from awareness that neither was equipped linguistically or logistically to handle the post, neither Nikitchenko nor de Vabres sought it. Biddle wanted it, but Jackson, after consulting Robert Murphy (Clay's diplomatic adviser) and General Donovan, urged him strongly to support Lawrence on the dual ground that the whole enterprise already had too much of an American cast and that if Lawrence were to preside, the British government would be committed to ensuring the success of the undertaking.

Biddle accepted these arguments, but not altogether happily, as his letters to his wife make plain: "My own delegation thinks I should not preside as Jackson has taken such a leading part in the prosecution, and I have reluctantly agreed. . . . There is not the slightest doubt that I could have been made permanent president had I wanted, but Jackson felt very strongly that as the Americans had carried all the burden of the prosecution, and would carry most of the burden of the trial, the British should preside, it being obvious that neither French nor Russians should preside. Of course it would have been fun to preside, but I have no regret as this is the wiser choice. Lawrence depends on me for everything and I'll run the show."

When the matter came up in the Tribunal's meeting, Nikitchenko nominated Biddle and de Vabres proposed Lawrence. Biddle withdrew in favor of Lawrence, who was duly chosen without a formal vote. De Vabres then proposed Nikitchenko to preside at public meetings of the Tribunal in Berlin, and Nikitchenko again proposed Biddle. The Alphonse-Gaston ceremony concluded with Biddle's withdrawing in favor of Nikitchenko for the Berlin presidency. There was good feeling all around, and Biddle was able, despite Nikitchenko's tepid opposition, to secure the selection of Harold B. Willey, a former Deputy Clerk of the United States Supreme Court, as General Secretary of the Tribunal.

But the next day—Sunday, October 14—the orderly course of events was rudely shaken. Late that afternoon, while the Tribunal was discussing details of the morrow's public meeting, Nikitchenko (who was presiding) suddenly reported that he had received disquieting news that the Indictment might not be ready for presentation and that the public meeting might have to be postponed.

Meanwhile, the prosecutors had fallen into sharp disagreement. Rudenko had opened their afternoon meeting by declaring that while checking the Russian text against the English, he had found many errors in the Eastern Europe portions of Counts Three and Four of the English text. The example he cited was the already controversial Katyn Forest massacre charge, which he wished to change by accusing the Germans of killing not 925 but 11,000 Polish officers who were prisoners of war. To correct the several errors would require information from both London and Moscow. Rudenko proposed that the prosecutors ask the Tribunal to postpone the public meeting for "two or three days."

There was an immediate explosion of disagreement. Dubost (whose behavior on at least this occasion did not bear out Jackson's belief that he was "fearful to oppose the Russians") pronounced it "quite impossible" to ask the Tribunal for a postponement. Shea thought it likely to "lower our own prestige with the Court" and "might be ridiculous and so appear in parts of the Press." Fyfe completely agreed with the French and American spokesmen.

A long discussion ensued in which Rudenko's fellow prosecutors proposed various procedures designed to meet Rudenko's needs without requiring a postponement of the public meeting. But Rudenko was adamant;

postponement was absolutely essential, and it would be a "great mistake" if the matter were decided against him by a three-to-one vote. Shea replied that "serious as a 3–1 vote might be, it might not be so serious as an application for an adjournment."

At Dubost's suggestion the prosecutors conferred privately with their respective judges, and Shea took advantage of the break to telephone Jackson in Nuremberg. He reported that the Russians were "thoroughly unreasonable," and that the British and French would probably vote with the Americans to go ahead with the Monday meeting, over Rudenko's objection. Jackson instructed Shea "to force the issue and make the Indictment public if the [two] other powers would join."

All this took so much time that it was well into the evening when the four prosecutors appeared before the Tribunal. Fyfe's explanation of the prosecutors' impasse was courteous, but made clear that its source was Rudenko's dissatisfaction with his Russian text. Biddle, joined at times by Lawrence, Birkett, and Falco, put Rudenko through a long and sharp cross-examination on why the Russian text could not be submitted subject to later corrections.

The Soviet prosecutor did not acquit himself well, but it became plain that he was under orders. In view of the formality of the Tribunal's first public meeting, and the publicity it was likely to generate, it is not hard to understand the Soviet government's reluctance to have it occur without a Russian text to hand in along with the English and French versions.

At long last the prosecutors were excused, but were requested to remain in the building. Lawrence promptly moved that the public meeting be held as scheduled and permission given to the Soviet prosecutor to amend "either the translation or the figures." Biddle seconded the motion and de Vabres expressed agreement. Nikitchenko then made an impassioned plea for postponement; to proceed publicly with no Russian text available "would harm the interests of our country. . . . . if it were known that the Soviet representative had not or would not sign the Indictment, and in spite of that the Tribunal would receive the Indictment, that then would result in more serious harm."

Biddle then suggested a short recess to enable the British, American, and French representatives to confer. Nikitchenko and Volchkov left the room, and Biddle told the others that Nikitchenko "might bolt if we didn't agree" and proposed a three-day postponement, which would be announced in a statement making it "perfectly clear that the other nations were ready and that the request was being made by Russia."

The others agreed, the Russians returned, and Nikitchenko acknowledged his "supreme indebtedness" to his colleagues. The announcement, drafted by Birkett, stated that the British, American, and French prosecutors "were ready to present and lodge the Indictment in their respective languages" but that "some difficulties in the task of translation" of the Russian text had required the Soviet prosecutor to request a delay. The public session of the Tribunal was postponed to Thursday, October 18, at ten-thirty in the morning. By the time the prosecutors had been called back and had the announcement read to them, it was nearing midnight.

Rudenko's last changes were not agreed upon until the evening of October 17. In the course of discussion, Rudenko stepped out of his own area of primary concern to lament that Count Three of the Indictment included no examples of war crimes on the high seas, and to suggest that the British add a charge based on German bombing of England. No such changes were made; with regard to the bombing, Elwyn Jones stated that "consideration had been given to entering a charge for V1 and V2 weapons,° but it had been considered inappropriate," as raising an argument which would be outside the range of the trial. It was only necessary to look out the windows at bomb-ravaged Berlin to divine what the "argument" would have been.

Early in the evening the prosecutors signed the Russian and French texts of the Indictment, and the following morning everything went smoothly at the Tribunal's first public meeting. The judges were sworn, and Nikitchenko, presiding, acknowledged receipt of the Indictment in the several languages and made several announcements bearing on procedures for the coming trial. The meeting took less than an hour, after which the judges planned to fly to Nuremberg for a look (the first for all except Falco) at what was to be the scene of their activities for nearly a year.

## 3

My participation in these Berlin events was limited to the first few days. After the chief prosecutors had signed the English text of the Indictment on October 6, there was little for me to do. Sidney Kaplan was handling the amendment and language reconciliation problems for our delegation and needed no help from me. Rudenko's absence had stalled any significant decision-making. It soon became apparent to me that I would be much better off in Nuremberg, where I could get settled in for the trial work.

It was characteristic of the loose organizational situation that Jackson did not tell me whether to stay or go. So I lingered a few days to sightsee in what was left of Berlin. I had seen plenty of other wrecked German cities during the closing weeks of the war, but Berlin and its buildings were much larger and the impression of desolation correspondingly stronger, especially

---

°The reference is to the unmanned explosive planes (V1s) and rockets (V2s) which were launched against London during the summer of 1944 and subsequently against Brussels, Mastricht, and other targets in the Low Countries.

in the area around the Unter den Linden (the only part I remembered from my earlier visit to Berlin, in 1929), with the shells of the Reichstag and Reichschancellery and the eerie ruins of the Brandenburger Tor.

Sidney Kaplan and I wandered through the rooms and corridors of the Reichschancellery, where the floors were thickly littered with debris of many kinds, including thousands of government documents. Sidney, who was a legal perfectionist but knew little German, went almost crazy trying to decide whether they should all be collected and scanned for war crimes evidence. On a similar tour Justice Jackson, with a party that included Miss Katherine Fite (a State Department lawyer assigned to assist the Justice), had noticed a gleam of metal in the debris. It proved to be a medal attached to a ribbon. With a great show of gallantry, Jackson hung the decoration around Miss Fite's neck. There was a chorus of demand for translation of the German legend on the medal: "Order of Motherhood, Second Class."°

Despite the destruction, Berlin's cultural life revived with astonishing rapidity. One of my intelligence group in England, Major John Bitter, a talented flutist and conductor, had joined Military Government as musical administrator. I attended two fine concerts, one each in the Soviet and American sectors of Berlin.

Several old friends from the New Deal days held important legal positions in Military Government, and there were a couple of reunion evenings, more than slightly bibulous. I might have felt pangs of conscience for this idling had I been in a stable, upbeat frame of mind, but in fact I was feeling a bit irresponsible. My personal involvements in England had come to an abrupt and painful conclusion and, like the lovelorn heroes of Victorian novels who fled to the Continent for wine, women, and song, I welcomed distractions.

When I left Berlin on October 10, I went to Frankfurt, taking advantage of Jackson's circular to the staff announcing that there was still an acute shortage of German-speaking personnel. I had ascertained by telephone that a WAAF (Women's Auxiliary Air Force) intelligence officer whom I had met during the war was in Frankfurt and might welcome an assignment to Nuremberg. I met her (Barbara Pinion) there late that afternoon; she agreed to come to Nuremberg as part of Calvocoressi's group, and I authorized her to make like arrangements for another intelligence WAAF, also fluent in German.

The next morning I ordered a car for the drive to Nuremberg. From Würzburg on, the road was the same one I had taken six months before. Early in the evening of October 11, I reached my destination and was given

---

°*Kinder, Kirche, Küche* was the Nazi idea of women's role in life. During the war, the government publicly encouraged women to have as many babies as possible, in or out of wedlock, with awards for high achievement in fecundity.

a room at the principal hostelry, the Grand Hotel, which had been taken over by the army for senior officers' and VIPs' billeting and messing.

Next to the dining room was a ballroom and a dance band. After dinner I walked in to scan the scene and saw my secretary, Betty Stark (who had preceded me in the move from Berlin to Nuremberg), dancing with a young officer. Ruined Nuremberg had some amenities after all, for those able to enjoy them.

# Chapter 7

## NUREMBERG: PRETRIAL PAINS
## AND PROBLEMS

T he first day in Nuremberg—Friday, October 12—began quietly enough. I went to the Palace of Justice and found myself comfortably officed on the second floor a few doors from Justice Jackson, with Colonel Gill as my neighbor on one side and a well-equipped room for several secretaries, including Betty Stark, on the other. I touched base with the Kaplans and lunched with Alderman, who had spent the morning moving his belongings from the hotel to a house in the western suburbs that had been assigned to him, Shea, and me as our billet.

The Palace of Justice itself was on the Fürtherstrasse, the main thoroughfare running northwest to the closely adjacent city of Fürth-im-Bayern, and on to Würzburg and Frankfurt. It was a large, heavily constructed complex, including a jail, an office building, and a courthouse, which had been the seat of the Court of Appeals for the Nuremberg region. The principal courtroom was still under repair and enlargement to accommodate an audience of several hundred. There was nothing attractive about this edifice, where I was destined to work for the next three years.

The most important event of the previous few days was the arrival at the jail of Rudolf Hess, who appeared to be in a state of both amnesia and apathy. Colonel Amen at once commenced interrogating him, using various devices intended to jog his memory. Alderman had attended one of these sessions, at which Goering, Papen, and other former close associates of Hess were brought into the room to speak with him. Alderman observed no indication that Hess recognized any of the visitors, and described him as looking "like a ghost."

Jackson had asked his son Bill and Alderman to make a short trip to Washington, Bill to deliver the Justice's letter on the doings in Berlin to the President and Alderman to interrogate a few German military prisoners then confined in Virginia. They were scheduled to leave that afternoon, so I accompanied Sidney to the Nuremberg Airport and then returned to the Grand Hotel.

Shea was still in Berlin, but I decided to move out to "our" house, which, if a bit lonely, would be quieter and more restful than the hotel, where the traffic and the dance band set a high-decibel level. So that evening I called for a car, packed my bags, and was driven out there. But the house, when we reached it, was anything but quiet; it was brightly lit, and music and raised voices were audible at some distance. Two army cars were parked by the front door.

I put on my sternest colonel's mien and banged on the door. The noise level sank, and a young woman came to the door, cringed at the sight of me, and explained in a mixture of English and German that the driver for one of the men who lived there (in fact, it was Shea's driver) had invited them in for some evening fun and that he was *sehr beschwipst* (very tipsy). I saw no reason to make a courthouse case of the matter, so I told her that they all had just three minutes to clear out. I retired to my car, and presently about a dozen soldiers and girls poured out, supporting one or two who had trouble navigating, and drove away.

I dismissed my driver, with instructions to pick me up the following morning, and entered the house. It was in reasonably good order and seemed amply spacious, though quite undistinguished. Alderman's luggage was in one of the second-floor bedrooms, and I deposited my own in another. It was a warm night, I was tired, and without bothering to unpack I took off my clothes and went to bed, leaving the ground floor lit.

My head had hardly hit the pillow when I heard a car draw up, running footsteps, and the front door of the house open with a bang. I jumped up, went to my bedroom doorway, and saw a disheveled private mounting the stairs, his hand on the butt of his holstered pistol. I assume my unclothed apparition startled him as much as he did me, for he stopped uncertainly and asked who I was. With such calm as I could muster I replied: "I'm Colonel Taylor, and this is my billet. Who are you?" His face fell as he realized he might be in trouble, and he mumbled that he was "Mr. Shea's driver" and "I didn't know you was going to be here." Then he turned protective: "Sir, have you got a gun?" When I allowed I had none, he came the rest of the way up the stairs, unbuckled his holster, and presented me with holster and pistol, saying: "You can't never tell what might happen around here." I reflected that he had just convinced me of that very proposition, but said only that he could pick up his gun in the morning and that Mr. Shea would probably not be back for several days.

My unexpected guest left quickly. I opened my luggage, armored myself in pajamas, and went back to bed.

The façade of the Palace of Justice on the Fürtherstrasse, where the trial was held. In normal times these buildings housed the German regional appellate court. *Charles W. Alexander*

Henry Stimson, Secretary of War during World War II. Stimson opposed Winston Churchill's plan to shoot the leading Nazis without benefit of trial, and in the summer of 1944 persuaded President Roosevelt that they should be tried under the laws of war before an international court. *Yale University Archives*

Murray Bernays, a New York City lawyer, was a colonel during the war in the personnel branch of the Army General Staff in Washington. In 1944, deeply affected by German atrocities against Jews and Russian prisoners, Bernays proposed novel methods for trying large numbers of putative German war criminals, which were approved by Stimson. *National Archives*

William C. Chanler—shown receiving the Distinguished Service Medal from Maj. Gen. John K. Hilldring—served during World War II as Chief Legal Officer of the American forces in Italy, and in the fall of 1944 was recalled to Washington to assume the War Department post of Deputy Director of Military Government. He conceived the idea that the charges against the Nazis should include the "waging of aggressive war," and, in December 1944, persuaded President Roosevelt to adopt this decision. *Courtesy of Mrs. William Chanler*

Supreme Court Justice Robert H. Jackson (in civilian clothes) was appointed by President Truman, on May 3, 1945, as American Chief Counsel for the prosecution of the surviving Nazi leaders. On his left is Col. John Harlan Amen, his chief of interrogation, and on his right Col. Robert G. Storey, chief of document procurement. On Storey's right is Col. B. C. Andrus, commandant of the Nuremberg prison. *AP/Wide World Photos*

Sidney B. Alderman, General Solicitor of the Southern Railway, had greatly impressed Justice Jackson by his skill in arguing cases before the U.S. Supreme Court. Alderman joined Jackson's staff as his close associate, and presented much of the prosecution's case against the defendants. *AP/Wide World Photos*

LEFT: Francis M. Shea was an Assistant Attorney General in the Justice Department during World War II, under then Attorney General Robert Jackson, who greatly valued his work and abilities. In May 1945, Shea was appointed to a senior position on Jackson's staff at Nuremberg. *Courtesy of Mrs. Francis Shea.* RIGHT: William J. Donovan—a successful lawyer, and a Congressional Medal of Honor winner in World War I—became, in World War II, Director of the Office of Strategic Services (OSS). He collaborated with Chief Counsel Jackson in laying the groundwork for the war crimes trials. The two men did not see eye to eye, however, and in November 1945 Donovan left Nuremberg and returned to the United States to resume his law practice. *AP/Wide World Photos*

The hundreds of journalists covering the trial during the first several months included a number of well-known reporters. Walter Cronkite, along with many of his colleagues, thought the British prosecutors superior to their American counterparts. *National Archives*

LEFT: Sir Hartley Shawcross was Britain's Attorney General, and ipso facto Chief Prosecutor of the British group. Because of his duties in London, Sir Hartley was seldom in Nuremberg, but he came on important occasions, and presented the British prosecutors' opening and closing statements to the Tribunal. RIGHT: Prof. Hermann Jahrreiss, associate counsel for the defendant Jodl, was chosen by the defense to present their argument that waging aggressive war could not be legally considered a war crime. Jahrreiss made an impressive presentation, especially in urging that, even if the London Charter in 1945 had made aggressive war an international crime, this could not be legally applied to the defendants' conduct prior to 1945. *R. D'Addario*

Peter Calvocoressi, shown in uniform as a wing commander in the Royal Air Force, was the chief of a British military intelligence group which assisted the prosecution in the handling of German military documents and in conducting interrogations of German witnesses and suspects.

Dr. Alfred Seidl, defense counsel for Hess and Frank, is at the lectern, quite probably seeking to embarrass both the judges and the prosecutors, especially the Russians, by offering evidence that the Russians were just as guilty as the Germans in the destruction of Poland. At the right, American prosecutor Drexel Sprecher, leaning on his elbow, appears to have heard Seidl's arguments once too often. *National Archives*

Across the Pegnitz River, a panorama of the war-devastated walled city of Nuremberg. The four men are all war photographers; the one in the dark uniform is a Russian, and the other three are members of the U.S. 3264th Photo Service Company. The man at far left is Ray D'Addario, who was the official photographer for the American prosecution. *R. D'Addario*

Seated before the hangings and flags are the eight judges, comprising four voting and four alternate judges. *Left to right:* Lt. Col. A. F. Volchkov, USSR Alternate; Maj. Gen. I. T. Nikitchenko, Member for the USSR; Mr. Justice Norman Birkett, U.K. Alternate; Lord Justice Geoffrey Lawrence, President and Member for the U.K.; Francis Biddle, Member for the USA; Judge John J. Parker, U.S. Alternate; Donnedieux de Vabres, Member for France; and M. Le Couseillet R. Falco, French Alternate. Behind the judges are two interpreters to assist in discussion among the respectively Russian-, French-, and English-speaking judges. *National Archives*

The American judges and their aides. *Left to right:* Capt. Robert Stewart, aide to Judge Parker; Prof. Herbert Wechsler, aide to Judge Biddle; Judge Biddle; Judge Parker; and James Rowe and Capt. Adrian Fisher, aides to Judge Biddle. *Courtesy of Prof. Wechsler*

Seated to the immediate right of the interpreters' box is Col. Leon Dostert, the officer in charge of the simultaneous translation system. To Dostert's right is Tom Brown, an American skilled in German-to-English interpreting. *R. D'Addario*

A typical cell in the prison within the Palace of Justice. The narrow window in the door permitted constant observation of an inmate, except in the toilet—a feature which enabled the defendant Robert Ley (leader of the German Labor Front) to commit suicide there. The defendants were given bedspreads and a straw mattress, blankets, and a small table and chair. *Charles W. Alexander*

## 2

At the Palace of Justice, the prosecution staff was waiting for completion of the Berlin meetings and the Tribunal's arrival in Nuremberg. Meanwhile, Jackson was considering plans for reorganizing his staff. I first learned of them at a staff meeting in his office on October 15. Jackson opened the subject by saying:

> The preparation of the case has entered a new phase with the filing of the Indictment. The proofs must be fitted to the allegations of the Indictment. Any surplus personnel must be let go. . . . The division of the case among the four Powers, under which the United States leads off on Count I and part of Count IV, means practically that we have responsibility for the entire case and set the tone and pace for it.

Jackson declared that "we should set up a reviewing staff . . . to decide on the proportions to be given to each part of the case" and disclosed that he had asked Colonels Storey and Wheeler and Major Frank Wallis (a Boston lawyer recruited by Wheeler) to prepare charts as a basis for reorganizing the staff in accordance with the review board idea. The charts were then distributed to the rest of us for comment.

The entire Tribunal had been expected at Nuremberg on the afternoon of October 18, following the judges' first public meeting in Berlin that morning. But the plane carrying the British judges encountered weather problems, and instead they went to London, where they remained until near the end of October. The French and Russian judges flew to Nuremberg with the Americans in a plane which Eisenhower had made available to Biddle.

The following morning, after an informal meeting and with Lawrence's telephoned approval, the Tribunal announced that the trial would open on Tuesday, November 20, and scheduled their own meeting for October 29. Thereafter the members dispersed, the French to Paris, the Russians to Berlin, and Biddle (on October 23) to Rome.

However, the necessary pretrial measures commenced immediately with service of the Indictment (in German translation) on the defendants, twenty of whom were in the Nuremberg jail. These were served on October 19 by Major Neave, who had been appointed to the Tribunal's secretariat for the special purpose of dealing with the defendants and their lawyers.° While handing them copies of the Indictment, Neave explained that they

---

°Neave's tenure with the BWCE had ended when the British became aware that Gustav Krupp was totally incapacitated for trial. Colonel Phillimore recommended him to Lord Lawrence as an able German-speaking barrister. Neave was a much-decorated officer who had been

were entitled to be defended by counsel and showed them a list of German lawyers who might be available in case they had no choice of their own.

Raeder and Fritzsche, the two defendants in Russian hands, had been served with the Indictment by a Soviet officer the previous day in Berlin. Martin Bormann, whereabouts unknown, was served by publication.

The remaining defendant, Gustav Krupp, was served on October 23 at his hunting lodge in Austria by Jim Rowe, who attached to his certificate of service statements by an Austrian doctor and two American Army medical officers establishing Krupp's incapacity and unfavorable prognosis and warning that moving him would risk "serious detriment to his health." Thus the fact of Krupp's incapacity became a matter of official and public knowledge.

The sight of the Indictment was a severe shock to a number of the defendants, especially those already jittery, such as Ribbentrop, Kaltenbrunner, and Sauckel. But for Robert Ley, former Leader of the German Labor Front, the blow was lethal. Dr. G. M. Gilbert, the official prison psychologist, visited Ley on October 23 and found him posing "crucifix-like" against the cell wall and "gesticulating and stuttering in great agitation." Two days later Ley strangled himself, using a towel tied to the overhead pipe of the toilet in his cell.

Neave found the provision of counsel for the defendants a long and onerous task. Doenitz was the only one who knew at once the man he wanted—Otto Kranzbuehler, a naval judge advocate with the rank (*Flottenrichter*) of captain. Kranzbuehler accepted the assignment and proved to be one of the ablest of the defense lawyers—a success which led to a lucrative postwar career at the bar.

Hans Frank, himself a lawyer and former Reich Commissioner for the Coordination of Justice, must have been well acquainted with the German bar, and several of the defendants consulted him on the matter. But Frank himself was at first uncertain whether or not to ask the Tribunal to appoint his own counsel. He eventually applied (as did Frick, Schirach, and Sauckel) for a Munich lawyer named Scanzoni, who apparently rejected these importunities, as he never appeared at Nuremberg. However, another Munich lawyer mentioned by Frank, Dr. Fritz Sauter, agreed to represent not only Schirach but Ribbentrop and Funk as well. Frank was ultimately represented by a third and much younger Munich attorney, Dr. Alfred Seidl, who

---

captured in 1940 at Dunkirk, escaped from Colditz prison in 1942, and worked with the French Resistance during the remainder of the war. In later years he became a prominent Conservative Member of Parliament and was slated for a Cabinet appointment when he was assassinated, presumably by agents of the Irish Republican Army. Neave described in great detail the reaction of the defendants upon receiving their copies, in his book *On Trial at Nuremberg* (1978), written shortly before his death.

subsequently also took on Hess. Both Sauter and Seidl had been Nazi Party members.

The defendants as a group reacted in a wide variety of ways to the matter of counsel, and some were unable or unwilling to take it seriously. Goering declared that he "had nothing to do with lawyers" and that Neave would "have to find one for me." Lawyers "would be of no use in this trial," and what he really needed was "a good interpreter," apparently to assist him in preparing his own defense. But he ultimately accepted the services of Dr. Otto Stahmer, a judge from Kiel.

Rudolf Hess asked whether he was allowed to be his own counsel and, on being assured that this was permissible, said: "Then I wish to do so," ignoring Neave's advice to the contrary. Julius Streicher declared that the lawyers' names on Neave's list "look like those of Jews" and demanded "a lawyer who is anti-Semitic." He later asked for and got Dr. Hanns Marx, a Nuremberg lawyer and former Nazi Party member.

However, the "upper-class" defendants—the military and naval men, Schacht, Papen, and Neurath—took the matter of counsel very seriously and sought lawyers who had moved in their own circles. Schacht's principal counsel, Dr. Rudolf Dix, was a well-known trial lawyer in his early sixties who made a dignified and reasonable appearance, and emerged as spokesman for the defense counsel as a group.

While Neave was wrestling with these problems, Biddle and Parker had awakened to the imminence of many more. Their arrival in Nuremberg had already started a stream of requests from the defendants regarding lawyers, witnesses, contact with families and friends, and other such questions. Biddle was dissatisfied with the General Secretary, Harold Willey, who was experienced in the ways of Washington but not of occupied and shattered Germany. He had virtually no facilities for communications, transportation, or investigation and, in Biddle's view, had "bogged down hopelessly." In consequence the judges "were considering getting General Clay to appoint a top ranking officer to act in Willey's place."

Fearing that the Tribunal was "in a real jam," Biddle invited Jackson and Charles Fahy (who was in Nuremberg on other business) to come for a luncheon consultation on October 21. Jackson was having his own organizational troubles and was in a querulous mood. Three weeks earlier he had unsuccessfully urged Biddle and Parker to fly from New York to Berlin instead of crossing by ship, and his first reply to Biddle's list of difficulties was to express disappointment "that the members of the court had not arrived earlier so that they could appreciate the situation" in Germany. As for the problems Biddle had described, the prosecution had learned from experience that the only way "to get things and people" was by using the facilities of the American Army. The thrust of his remarks was that the Tribunal should leave the handling of these matters to the prosecution:

He feared the Tribunal was taking on functions which it was not able to carry out. . . . The prosecutors had been prepared to do these things and had written orders ready. They had planned to assign counsel to the defendants if necessary. He felt the problem of interpretation was important and that the General Secretary could not handle it. . . . He would emphasize that the court should avoid to the utmost the taking on of administrative responsibilities.

Biddle interjected that "it had never been his idea that the Tribunal would do much administration," but he thought that the Tribunal, rather than the prosecution, should issue summons for witnesses. Jackson replied: "This is not an ordinary trial. Some of the proprieties went by the way when General Nikitchenko, who had been the Soviet Prosecutor, was made a member of the Tribunal." He went on to predict that the defense witness problem would not be acute:

He did not think the defense would want many witnesses. They did not dispute the fact that crimes had been committed. Their defense would be that a particular individual did not participate. They would attempt to lay everything on Hitler.

This forecast was not borne out during the trial. Beyond that, however, for Jackson to give the judges ex parte his opinion of the defense case was sending the proprieties "by the way" for fair. Considering Jackson's hostility to the Russians, it was extraordinary that he saw fit to take their actions as a standard of permissibility. And if Nikitchenko's appointment violated the "proprieties," could not the same be said of Jackson's efforts to guide Truman's choice of the Nuremberg judicial appointees?

There was, to be sure, a core of fact in Jackson's warnings to the Tribunal. His staff had been in Nuremberg for six weeks and had the manpower and experience to do things which the judges could not possibly undertake without a great increase in staff. Indeed, the prosecution's responsibility for the major share of the administration was a feature destined to last throughout the nearly four years of the Nuremberg trials.

But obviously there had to be limits on these responsibilities. It is astonishing that Jackson seriously contemplated that the prosecution would "assign counsel to the defendants" or issue summons for defense witnesses. Such a situation would destroy the appearance, if not also the actuality, of a fair trial—and the preservation of fairness was vital to fulfillment of the high purposes to which Jackson himself was dedicated.

Fortunately, these things did not happen. Major Neave remained in direct charge of procuring counsel for the defendants. He now was promised assistance from the Control Council, as Charles Fahy undertook to use the resources of his office and his contacts with the army to help with transport and communication facilities and other administrative matters.

A few weeks later, as a result of Biddle's interview with General Eisenhower, Brigadier General William L. Mitchell was made available to serve as General Secretary to the Tribunal, and Willey took charge of the American component of the General Secretariat. The judges' administrative worries were greatly eased, and they were able to focus on the numerous legal questions which the trial soon generated.

3

Thus the Tribunal handled its organizational problems with little friction. The American prosecution staff was not so fortunate. For some six weeks, beginning in mid-October, the staff was riddled with disagreements, tensions, and jealousies that soured the outlook of many of its members and led to the abrupt departure of several.

It was the reorganization project, presented to the senior staff at the meeting on October 15, which triggered this period of rancor. But there was an antecedent source, a situation which was unavoidable and the resolution of which, even under the best circumstances, would have generated disagreements and disappointments.

That situation was the coming together at Nuremberg of the London and Paris components of Jackson's staff at a time when London's Charter- and Indictment-drafting functions were finished, Paris's document-gathering and interrogation functions were withering, and the staff's ultimate functions—preparation for and presentation of the trial itself—were at hand. At the meeting on October 15, Jackson had highlighted these aspects of the "new phase" by directing that "Any general search for new evidence must be stopped, and we must assume we can proceed with what we already have."

It was too much to expect that the distribution of new responsibilities and opportunities for participation in the trial could be accomplished without pleasing some and wounding others. Unfortunately, this was the very kind of leadership problem Jackson hated to confront personally and sought to delegate as much as possible. In this instance, the individual on whom he chiefly relied was Colonel Storey, who had ably headed the Document Division but who had a very strong personal stake in the pending reorganization, particularly since the search for documentary evidence was now to be brought virtually to a halt and his division's task reduced to custodial functions. Indeed, it would have been hard to find any important member of the prosecution staff who did not have a personal stake, which was the very reason Jackson should have kept a firm hand on the tiller.

At the time of the meeting on the fifteenth, I knew Storey only from having dined with him, at the Grand Hotel and at his invitation, a night or two previously. He was pleasant enough, but seemed to be obsessed by his trove of documents ("docamints" in his Texas patois) to a degree that distorted his conception of the trial. He viewed the prosecution's case as comprising little more than presentation to the Tribunal of organized groups of documents in "document books," accompanied by explanatory briefs based on the documents, which he called "self-proving" briefs. I responded, perhaps too bluntly, that the documents could not be effectively handled in so mechanical a way, and that if the prosecution's case was so limited, and devoid of live testimony, the defendants' case might get much more public attention than ours.

Despite these misgivings about Storey, I agreed with the proposal to set up a group of senior lawyers to shape the American presentation and review the evidence, documentary or other, to be laid before the Tribunal. In response to Jackson's request for comments, I submitted a memorandum the next day in which I described the Storey-Wheeler plans as "in general sound," except for two areas of disagreement.

One of these areas harked back to my dinner conversation with Storey, who had included in his memorandum a recommendation that "a uniform method for preparation of trial briefs and presentation of evidence be adopted." To this I replied: "I do not think that any one method will fit all aspects of so varied a case, and under all the circumstances I think that flexibility may be a better common denominator than uniformity." Furthermore, there were unresolved questions which ought to be dealt with promptly. Would oral testimony be used? If so, should we seek out promising witnesses? Should we present information by means of charts, pictures, glossaries, and so forth? Some parts of the case might benefit by these tools, others not, and for such reasons our methods of presentation could not be "uniform."

The other area was one of partial disagreement, and it concerned Colonel Amen's Interrogation Division. It was quite plain that the division should continue to function, both for informational purposes and for the identification of possible witnesses. But its methods left much to be desired. Amen had several able lawyers, but too many were limited by ignorance of the German language, and by insufficient knowledge of German history and government. Usually they came to their interrogations prepared with lists of questions in English which were put to the witness in German by an interpreter, who then translated into English for the benefit of the interrogator. The questions themselves often reflected ignorance, and the interrogators were frequently unable to follow up the answers with further probing.

During the first few days in Nuremberg I attended interrogations of Hess, Kaltenbrunner, Schacht, Goering, and Field Marshal von Blomberg, Commander in Chief of the Wehrmacht from 1935 to 1938, when Hitler sacked him. Of these, only Gurfein's interrogation of Schacht was expert, and his success owed much to Schacht's excellent English and Gurfein's own knowledge of German.

On the other hand, Thomas Dodd, at that time one of Amen's senior staff, did not shine as an interrogator, although he later performed very competently before the Tribunal. Amen assigned to Dodd the interrogation of the defendant Papen, a slippery and knowledgeable customer indeed, and one of the three defendants subsequently acquitted by the Tribunal. In his memoirs, Papen praises Dodd as a person but comments that "he had only a very superficial knowledge of events and the internal development of Germany."

Indeed, some of Dodd's questions were based on mistaken premises, as I observed when Ben Kaplan and I visited Dodd's interrogation room to view his questioning of Field Marshal Walter von Brauchitsch, former Commander in Chief of the German Army. We reached the room before Dodd arrived and found a young man and his guard standing by the wall. Soon Dodd and his interpreter entered the room, and, to my surprise, the young man was told to sit in the witness chair. I was astonished when Dodd looked squarely at his subject and asked: "You are Field Marshal von Brauchitsch, are you not?" The answer was: "Ach! Das ist mein Vater!" The young man was Bernd von Brauchitsch, who had been serving as Goering's military adjutant. It seemed incredible that an interrogator who knew anything about his subject could have taken the son for his sixty-five-year-old father.

I was neither linguist nor interrogator, but from general familiarity with intelligence-gathering I knew that the best results in getting information from enemy captives were obtained by interrogators fluent in the captive's own language and well prepared on the factual context of the questions to be asked. By such means a conversational atmosphere can be induced and a personal relation established between interrogator and subject which is more conducive to disclosures than the slower and more stilted exchanges through an interpreter.

These considerations were especially applicable to interrogation of the military defendants and the General Staff–High Command group. Accordingly, in my memorandum to Jackson I recommended that the prosecution staff be augmented by the addition of several German-speaking intelligence officers who were experienced interrogators of German prisoners.

Shea returned to Nuremberg on October 18, and the next day we went together to a staff meeting called by Jackson. There was a general discussion of the staff reorganization, in the course of which Jackson approved the acquisition of a few experienced military interrogators and indicated that I would be responsible for presenting the case against the General Staff–High Command.

On October 22, without prior consultation with Shea or me (Alderman was then in Washington) or with any of our close associates on the staff, Jackson signed and circulated "General Memorandum No. 5" on "Trial Organization." Storey was appointed Chairman of the Board of Review; the other appointees were Dodd, Ben Kaplan, and Ralph Albrecht, a well-regarded New York lawyer with an international practice who had joined the staff via the OSS. Alderman, Shea, James Donovan, and I were designated "Consultants to the Board of Review."

The Memorandum gave the board very broad powers (subject, of course, to Jackson's supervision) to "plan the coordination of the case as a whole," "proscribe the form of" and "review" all trial briefs, and "direct the activities of Section Heads as to further briefing or other steps to complete the case." There was to be no further search for documents, "field trips," or bringing of witnesses to Nuremberg for interrogation without prior approval by the board.

About fifty lawyers, comprising some two-thirds of the legal staff, were distributed among seven trial-preparation sections, the chiefs of which were directly subordinated to the board. Three sections, headed by Wheeler, Deinard, and Sidney Kaplan, were to prepare the material in support of the conspiracy charge which, by agreement among the chief prosecutors, would be presented by the American team. The other four sections were to organize the evidence concerning war crimes and crimes against humanity, the culpability of the individual defendants, and the criminal organizations, and prepare answers to foreseeable defense arguments.

There were features of this reorganization that Shea and I found puzzling and alarming. Why did the Memorandum make no mention of General Donovan? Shea soon learned that initially the general had been listed among the Consultants to the Board of Review, but that he had struck his name out. That certainly suggested some dissatisfaction on the general's part, and it was easy to see why. The Memorandum assigned no functions to the consultants. It merely provided that Alderman, Shea, and I were to continue as liaison officers with the French, British, and Soviet delegations and that James Donovan would continue to head the section responsible for visual evidence.

But these liaison functions were but a small part of the tasks for which Alderman, Shea, and I had previously been responsible. Likewise, the Memorandum gave us no staff, and all the lawyers (except the Calvocoressi group) who had theretofore reported to us were assigned to the trial-preparation sections, which in turn were responsible to the Board of Review. Furthermore, the broad powers vested in the board appeared to bring the consultants, too, under its authority on a wide range of important matters.

The Memorandum, however, did not touch on the question of which staff members would be chosen to present the case to the Tribunal. Jackson had from the start regarded Alderman and Shea as his principal assistants in the courtroom. From Shea's standpoint, the worst feature of the reorganization was that Sidney Kaplan, Ben Deinard, and others whom Shea had recruited and upon whom he had relied heavily were now to report to the board and not to him.

Shea immediately went to Jackson and pointed out the absurdity of depriving those who would appear in court of direct authority over those who would prepare their briefs and other materials. Jackson replied that he wanted Shea to present the economic case and part of the aggressive war case and that "he saw no difficulty in my directing Kaplan and Deinard in the preparation of those two aspects of the matter . . . and that he would not have to put it down on paper that they . . . report to me." Shea responded that such a situation "was likely to lead to jurisdictional squabbling" and that Kaplan and Deinard "should not be put in the position of coming in the back door." Jackson made no direct reply but said that "a part of the case had to be given to General Donovan to try and Sidney Alderman, and he thought also that Storey, Taylor and John Amen should have a part in the trial."

I fear that my own attitude at the time was a bit cynical, but Shea was very troubled, as his diary reveals:

> 23 October. The boys are deeply upset about the reorganization order. Sid Kaplan wants to leave, so does Ben Deinard and Ben Kaplan has very much that feeling. Telford doesn't give a damn really. He is going to do a good job so far as it is entrusted to him but he has made up his mind to have some fun out of this and he is not going to let it bother him. I spent a great deal of time trying to get the boys back on the track but I don't know how successful I was.
>
> 24 October. It is hard to imagine a more upsetting thing than this order has proved to be. Sidney [Kaplan] came out to dinner and I tried my best to persuade him to stay.

During the course of these woes, Shea and I drafted a proposed "General Memorandum No. 6," which, if Jackson would sign it, might undo some of the mischief of "No. 5." The results were poor, as recorded in Shea's diary entry for October 27:

> During my conversation with Jackson . . . he told me that he had looked over the memorandum which Taylor had prepared and that he did not feel that he could sign it. If he made assignments regarding the trial at this time to some of us it would result in getting orders all upset. He said that apart from that the remainder of the provisions of the [Taylor draft] memorandum were understood. I told him that I

quite understood them but they were certainly not understood generally. That by some at least, General Memorandum No. 5 was interpreted as a vote of no confidence in his associate counsel. He said that no one could so possibly construe it as such and I told him that there was the fact of the matter however he might feel personally about it.

This interchange reflects some tension between Jackson and Shea, and unfortunately other circumstances were arising which increased the strain. They were reminiscent of Jackson's earlier troubles with the Russians, and grew out of a meeting of chief prosecutors—the first held in Nuremberg—on October 26. In the course of the meeting, Jackson called attention to the prosecution's obligation to submit its documentary evidence in the language of the submitting country and in German. He had received a letter from the Soviet delegation stating that it did not have sufficient staff to translate all the Russian documents into German and asking the American delegation "to undertake this work." Jackson reported that his delegation did not include enough German-Russian linguists to do this. "This is a very serious situation," said Jackson, and warned that if the Russian documents were not accompanied with translations into German, "the Soviet case may be inadmissible at the trial."

A discussion ensued, which disclosed that the French were likewise unable to produce German translations of their documents. Jackson repeated his warnings. Shea, Storey, and I were in attendance, and after the meeting ended he asked us to stay, and, in Shea's words, "whipped himself into a rage about the Russians and the French. He said that they were to have no further documents from us until they get their own translations."

Shea had barely reached his office the following morning when he received a telephone call from a very angry Dubost, who reported that members of his delegation had gone to the Document Room that morning and had been referred to Storey for permission to enter. Storey had told them that they would not be allowed to use the room until the French documents had been translated into German and that they were being punished for not fulfilling their translating commitments. Dubost conceded that his people were in difficulties, but declared it "incredible that they should be spanked as if they were little children this way."

The immediate consequence of this episode is described in Shea's diary:

> I went to Jackson and told him of this conversation. I said to him, rather bluntly, that I thought he just could not handle the matter in this way. I said I had not taken him literally the day before and certainly did not think it would have been taken so precisely. He [Jackson] stated he wanted it to be taken literally and to precipitate

a crisis and the only way to deal with the Russians and French was to perpetrate a crisis and made it so Rudenko would cable back to his government that his position was an impossible one and then we could put pressure on through diplomatic channels. I said that I appreciated his exasperation . . . but representatives of great powers could not be treated as bad children. . . . He was finally somewhat moved by the conversations, though obviously from the point of view of our personal relations it is not healthful.

Jackson then authorized Shea to discuss the translation problems with the other delegations:

> I went down to see Fyfe and learned that the British had already translated the Russian documents, with the exception of four into German and into English. They had likewise done the same with the French documents. While we had been spanking the other two governments, the British had been making hay. . . . I took this information back to Bob [Jackson], refraining with some difficulty from pointing out that he had not advanced our diplomatic position very much. This calmed him down a good deal.

And so, at the chief prosecutors' meeting that afternoon (October 27), Rudenko and Dubost announced that, thanks to the British, their German translations would be furnished on time. No one mentioned the morning episode, and it was agreed, without discussion, that "all documents would be available for any Prosecutor's case."

Shea thought that Jackson "was his charming self and handled the thing with great capacity," but I was not sure his inner feelings matched his manner. Two days later Gordon Dean, a shrewd observer with sensitive political antennae, told Shea that he was "not happy about the Justice's strong feeling with regard to the Russians and French."

Shea's sense that his advice to Jackson during the translation tangle was not "healthful" for their relations was accurate, but insufficient to alert him to the insecurity of his own tenure. His diary for October 29 reveals no awareness of impending crisis, but it was the last entry. On October 31 he received a personal letter from Jackson releasing him "from further duty on this staff." The following day Shea sent Jackson a letter submitting his resignation for "personal reasons," which Jackson accepted the same day by a letter expressing "full understanding" and "reluctance." On November 2 Alderman, who had returned from Washington three days earlier, noted in his diary that Shea was leaving the staff and would return to America, adding that Shea "gave me no explanation whatsoever." Neither did he give me any. Two days later Alderman saw Shea and his secretary off to the United States.

Frank Shea was Jackson's oldest friend at Nuremberg, and the second man appointed to his staff. Only two weeks earlier, Jackson had entrusted his representation in Berlin to Shea. Although I was well aware that the two men were having their differences over matters of policy, I was astounded and, since I counted Frank a close friend, saddened that matters had reached a point at which the Justice would insist on a parting of the ways.

In retrospect, the unfortunate upshot is understandable. In July, during the London negotiations on the Charter, Shea had criticized Jackson's handling of the Russians and his apparent willingness to risk their withdrawal from the project. Shea was not the only critic, but he was a vigorous counselor, who perhaps relied too much on his personal relation with Jackson and did not realize the depth of Jackson's distrust of the Russians. At that same time, Shea repeatedly requested authority to give instructions to Storey and Amen, whose antipathy to Shea and the "economic case" was freely voiced to Alderman and, no doubt, to Jackson. Whatever the limitations of the two colonels, they (and Storey in particular) were unearthing the essential fuel for the trial—voluminous documentary evidence of the Nazi leaders' guilt. Whether or not such evidence existed had previously been Jackson's greatest worry.

As soon as Shea returned from Berlin, history began to repeat itself. When Jackson signed the reorganization Memorandum giving Storey general direction of the trial preparations, Shea openly fought back and confronted Jackson with a proposal to restore the primacy of the consultants—a move in which I supported him, although I had no direct confrontation with Jackson, with whom my personal acquaintance was still slight. No doubt Storey learned of this, and his attitude toward Shea can hardly have been improved on October 27 when Shea sent him a note (with a copy to Jackson) admonishing him for asking one of Shea's assistants to appear before the Board of Review and "summarize the Economic Case" without notifying Shea. To be sure, Storey's action was either thoughtless or arrogant, but no one likes to be caught off base by an opponent. There also were personnel disputes between Amen and Shea.

While all this was going on, Jackson's wrath at the Russians and French over their translation problems precipitated the Dubost episode, and it was London in July all over again, with Shea admonishing Jackson in the same old way. The fact that Frank was absolutely right, and that Fyfe came to the rescue and emerged from the fracas smelling like a rose, probably rankled the worse.

Jackson's first letter to Shea made no mention of staff reorganization or problems with the Russians and French and explained his decision to let him go solely on the basis of "difficulties between yourself and other members of this organization." It appears probable that Storey, and perhaps Amen or other members of the Paris group, portrayed their relations with

Shea as obstructing their trial preparations with a force which led Jackson to conclude, as he wrote to Shea, that the necessity of his departure with the trial approaching was "inescapable."

After Frank's departure Jim Rowe, whose friendship with Frank and me dated from the early New Deal days, kidded me about the Paris group's political outmaneuvering of "old Washington hands" like some of those in the London group. There were several reasons for Storey's success, but perhaps the major one was that Storey was "there"—in Nuremberg—at the critical time, while the senior members of the London group were not. When Jackson settled down in Nuremberg in mid-September, Storey and Gill were there for him to lean on. No sooner had Shea arrived in Nuremberg than his father's death drew him back to America, and upon his return to Nuremberg in early October he shortly accompanied Jackson to Berlin and stayed there after Jackson left. When Shea returned on October 18, the Storey plan was already in place. Alderman and Sidney Kaplan were in London or Berlin a good part of the time, Alderman departed Nuremberg for Washington October 12, and I did not reach Nuremberg until October 11.

Apart from proximity, once the Charter and the Indictment had been taken care of, the London group came to Nuremberg equipped only with its legal skills, while Storey and Amen had the evidence and the Paris group had in Colonel Gill the chief administrator of facilities and personnel for the entire enterprise. Thus it is hardly surprising that the Paris group, far more alert to the competitive aspects of the situation than the rest of us, carried the day. But there would later be a price paid for their victory.

## 4

While this crisis in the American staff was running its course, the judges reassembled, and on October 29 the Tribunal held its first full meeting in Nuremberg. The trial was scheduled to begin on November 20. During this period the judges met privately twenty-six times, occasionally with representatives of the prosecution in attendance, and held five public sessions to hear and rule on preliminary trial issues.

The private meetings were recorded as "organizational" or "executive" sessions and were largely devoted to routine administrative matters, such as the appointment and compensation of defense counsel, securing documents and witnesses requested by the defense, reviewing the arrangements for photographing and recording the trial and the accommodations for the press, and testing the IBM system of simultaneous interpretation, which at the time was novel and regarded as experimental.

Only a few of these matters are noteworthy. By November 12 Neave was able to report that all of the individual defendants (including the absent

Gustav Krupp and the missing Martin Bormann) had counsel, although the representation of the two most rickety defendants—Hess and Streicher—remained unstable. Biddle had secured General Eisenhower's approval of compensation for the defense counsel, most of whom were probably attracted more by the prospect of billets and food than by the paper marks in which they would be paid. On November 17 the Tribunal agreed that each of the indicted organizations should have counsel, and Neave was directed to obtain them. The judges remained concerned about the appointment of lawyers who had been Nazi Party members but continued to follow a policy that the defendants could choose Nazi lawyers, though the Tribunal would not recommend them to defendants who asked the Tiubunal to make the selection. Neave reported on the seventeenth that there were eight former Nazis among the defense counsel, including the very able Dr. Theodor Klefisch for Gustav Krupp and Dr. Hans Laternser for the General Staff–High Command.

Jackson, who at the meeting in Biddle's residence on October 21 had admonished the judges not to take on administrative responsibilities and declared the prosecution ready to assign counsel to the defendants, made a volte-face at a meeting with the Tribunal on November 6, when the problem was how best to handle defense requests for documents and witnesses. Unless these were already under the prosecution's control, said Jackson, "it should be a matter for the Tribunal and not for the prosecution." That was plainly right, and so it was agreed the more readily as the proximate arrival of General Mitchell as General Secretary gave the judges reassurance that their staff could handle the necessary dealings with the American Army.

Other generals, however, were giving Jackson fits. Late in October, when Eisenhower was about to return to Washington and his successor, General Joseph T. McNarney, had not yet taken over, George Patton was temporarily in command of the American forces in Europe. Apparently on Patton's orders, Nuremberg and the surrounding area were constituted a discrete military area called the Nuremberg-Fürth Enclave, in order to cope with the security and logistical problems which the trial was presenting. Brigadier General Leroy H. Watson was appointed commander of the Enclave, under orders which gave him administrative authority over everyone connected with the trial, military and civilian alike.

General Watson, unaware that Jackson was responsible only to the President and that Nuremberg participants were not subject to military administration, at once asserted the authority with which his superiors had vested him. Finding motor transport in short supply, he deprived all but generals, judges, and chief prosecutors of their cars. Overzealous officers on Watson's staff entered Colonel Gill's office and removed the window draperies in order to furnish Watson's office with proper dignity.

Astonished and outraged, on November 2 Jackson drafted a five-page message of complaint to the President. Fortunately for all concerned, General Bedell Smith, still acting as Chief of Staff, happened to telephone Jackson on another matter, and when the Justice described his predicament, Smith persuaded him not to appeal to the President, promising to send General Lucian K. Truscott, Commander of the Third Army (the occupying force in Bavaria), to straighten things out. The next day Truscott and Watson appeared at Jackson's office, where they received what the Justice later described as a "bawling out."

The order giving Watson authority over the trial personnel was rescinded, and Watson proved to be a generous and sensible officer. General Mitchell, however, continued to get on Jackson's nerves. The man who came most happily out of this imbroglio was Gill, who not only recovered his draperies but also won a promotion to brigadier general, arranged by Jackson in order to strengthen Gill's hand in dealing with Mitchell and other rank-conscious army types.

For the time being, Jackson's relations with the Russians and French were untroubled. Disagreement arose with the British over the division of responsibility in the presentation of Counts One (conspiracy, assigned to the Americans) and Two (crimes against peace, assigned to the British). As the Indictment was drawn, all the factual allegations concerning Germany's multiple aggressions were in Count One, and Count Two contained only the particulars of treaty violations—a dull matter indeed, involving none of the sensational documentary evidence of Hitler's deliberate aggressions.

Naturally, the British did not want their role in presenting the prosecution's cases to be so trivial. But the conflict was resolved in gentlemanly fashion on the basis of a compromise proposed by Sidney Kaplan, under which (1) the Americans would deal with conspiracy through the German takeover in Czechoslovakia in 1938 and the launching of the attack on Poland in early September 1939, (2) the British would complete the presentation on Poland and cover the ensuing conquests of Denmark, Norway, Belgium, the Netherlands, Luxembourg, Yugoslavia, and Greece, and (3) the Americans would then establish the aggressive character of the attack against the Soviet Union and the German declaration of war against the United States. All of this was agreed at the chief prosecutors' meeting on November 7.

## 5

Meanwhile, among the American prosecutors, Storey was riding the crest of his wave of authority. On October 26, as Chairman of the Board of Review, he issued a directive assigning particular portions of the Indictment to specified sections of the staff for preparation of "self-proving trial briefs."

In a second directive three days later, Storey reported Jackson's opinion that in view of the language difficulties, the trial briefs should be "self-proving" and include "just as little talk and as many documents as possible." On November 1 a further directive provided for the "Uniform Method of Preparation of Trial Briefs"; my strictures of October 15 on this approach had fallen on deaf ears. On November 5 an order from Jackson designated Storey as Executive Trial Counsel and established a Panel of Trial Counsel comprising General Donovan, Storey, Alderman, Amen, Albrecht, Dodd, Gurfein, Wallis, Ben Kaplan, and me. Ten days later, by which time most of the trial briefs had been submitted, the Board of Review was dissolved and its directive functions taken over by a Planning Committee of the Trial Panel, comprising General Donovan, Alderman, Dodd, Jackson ex officio, and Storey as Chairman.

Storey's ascendancy did not, fortunately, signify any loss of Jackson's confidence in Alderman. On November 2 the two men had what Alderman described as a "satisfactory conference." Alderman continued to represent Jackson at such chief prosecutors' meetings as the Justice did not attend and to handle liaison with the French and (now that Shea was gone) the British delegations. At trial, Alderman would handle the four most promising witnesses he had interrogated in Virginia and reply to legal arguments the defense might raise, such as ex post facto and superior orders. On November 17 Storey informed Alderman that Jackson wished him to present the American prosecution's evidence of the defendants' conspiracy to launch and wage aggressive wars—the single most important part of the American prosecution's case.

Although I had joined Shea in the abortive effort to reduce Storey's authority, my own status was not much altered after Shea's departure. I continued to handle liaison with the Soviet delegation, I was appointed to the Trial Panel and Jackson generally asked me to attend chief prosecutors' and senior staff meetings. It had already been settled that at the trial I would handle the case against the General Staff–High Command. This was a limited but important role, and in its performance I was responsible directly to Jackson; Storey had no supervisory authority, and Jackson allowed me to go my own way. For staff I was well served by Calvocoressi and his group, together with Major Loftus Becker (who had taken charge at the London office after my departure and had just arrived in Nuremberg) and two American Army interrogators who were assigned to us.

During the first half of November there were several joint meetings of the Trial Panel, and later of the Planning Committee, during which there was acrimonious discussion of such trial questions as the use of witnesses, the value of "self-proving briefs," and the scheduling of the various portions of the American prosecution's case. General Donovan, Alderman, and I all thought that the idea of briefs in which the documents would "prove" the case without supporting argument was absurd, and that we should not back away from the use of witnesses. On November 5 there was a particularly sharp set-to, during which Donovan denounced the whole basis of Storey's planning as "foolish." Alderman wrote in his diary: "It was a most extraordinary meeting, a most extraordinary discussion, and it left me with a very painful impression of the whole situation." A week later there was another unpleasant flare-up, and it was during these weeks that the relations between Jackson and Donovan became so badly strained that soon thereafter they reached the breaking point.

The two men, old acquaintances but not close friends, had collaborated with little friction during the early months of their war crimes association. Jackson had benefited greatly from the personnel, facilities, and contacts provided by OSS, and there is no apparent reason to question the good faith of Donovan's support or to believe he was any more self-seeking than the rest of us, as we all naturally hoped that outstanding performance in a unique and noteworthy cause would bring both private satisfaction and public credit. But Donovan had left the scene during the London Charter negotiations to handle OSS business in the Far East and did not return until the meeting in Berlin for filing the Indictment, in the framing of which he had had no hand.

The first note of serious disagreement was struck when Donovan found in the Indictment the charges against the General Staff–High Command. According to Donovan:

> When in Berlin you [Jackson] first showed me the Indictment I said it was unbecoming to our country to use such a device as there employed against the General Staff. I still think so. The young British officer [Calvocoressi] who prepared it told me he was not very proud of the job. I urged a revision so that such members as were participants be charged individually and not by position and by function. . . .
> I have never agreed with those of our Regular Army who think that there should be no criminal charge against the General Staff.°
> That I made clear to General Bedell Smith, Chief of Staff, when you and I were in Frankfurt. Perhaps it would have been better to have shot the guilty ones. Since we elected to proceed by indictment I think we should do it properly. It is repugnant to me that there should be any pretext as we find in the trial today for the defendants to assert that the prosecution is unfair.

At the time I knew nothing of this rift over the organizational charge against the General Staff. The subject had not arisen at any of the few staff

°This is ambiguously expressed, but in the context must mean "criminal charges against individual members of the General Staff."

meetings which both Donovan and I attended. At my one private conference with General Donovan (in his office and at his request), he made no
mention of the Indictment. He did, however, suggest to me that a distinction might be drawn between the German Army field commanders (who
were "just doing their duty") and the staff officers at Hitler's military
headquarters (OKW, Supreme Command of the Armed Forces). I left
Donovan with a suspicion that he had been in touch with some of the field
commanders in the hope of getting them to testify against the two army
defendants, Field Marshal Keitel and General Jodl, who were both in the
second of Donovan's categories.

Much more important than the General Staff issue was the matter of
our use of witnesses, which involved not only how many (if any) we might
call but also what methods might properly be used in "developing" witnesses who could be relied upon to give testimony helpful to the prosecution. Jackson was, if anything, even more opposed than Storey to any
departures from the documentary approach; as he later declared, he had
decided "to put on no witnesses we could reasonably avoid."°

In view of Donovan's contempt for the purely documentary approach,
it was apparent that he would have no interest in participating in its presentation. What, then, would he do at the trial? On November 7 Jackson sent
Storey to ask him that question. Considering that Storey had become the
main source of Donovan's discontent, that Donovan outranked Storey and
was nearly a decade older than Jackson, and that Jackson was much indebted to Donovan for material support, Jackson's manner of raising the
question was either a deliberate provocation or extraordinarily tactless.
Understandably angry,†Donovan at once sent Jackson a note:

> To prevent misunderstanding, let me tell you of my talk with
> Bob Storey—today.
> He said that he came to ask me what part I wanted to take in
> the trial.
> I replied that you not he should ask that question. However
> today I could only conclude that you took this means of cancelling our
> original arrangement and of indicating that you considered that you

---

°In the light of this attitude, it is puzzling that Jackson had sent Alderman to Washington
in October to interrogate possible witnesses, at the very time trial preparations were getting
underway. Furthermore, such a task would normally have been assigned to Amen. I cannot
escape the suspicion that Jackson wanted Alderman out of the way at the time Storey was to be
given virtual control of the trial planning. Although Jackson expressed himself as pleased with the
results of Alderman's trip, none of the men Alderman interrogated was ever called as a witness.

†When Donovan rejoined Jackson early in October, he was undoubtedly in a sensitive and
unhappy mood. On September 20, President Truman had issued an executive order abolishing
OSS and dividing its staff and functions between the State and War departments. Donovan
remained on active duty as a major general until January 1946, but he no longer had the logistic
or organizational clout which had theretofore made him so useful to Jackson.

saw no place for me. . . . I am sorry you did not take a different means of telling me. . . .

   Accordingly—I will finish up the various matters I am doing which I should complete early in December. . . . I shall be here until this time is completed.

Jackson replied the next day in a letter which was conciliatory in wording but not in substance. Storey's visit, Jackson declared, "was by no means intended to convey to you that you should take no part but was to learn your judgment and preferences before I made any assignments." But the letter then laid out various factors which presented difficulty. Donovan "did not think highly of reliance on captured documents" and probably "would not be interested in the documentary aspects of the case"; Jackson "anticipated you would prefer to work with live witnesses or cross-examination of defendants and defense witnesses," but what witnesses the prosecution might use was still unsettled, and the defense part of the case would probably not be reached "until after the first of the year"; it was Jackson's understanding that Donovan must be back to his own law practice "by the first of the year." Therefore:

> If you are of the opinion that the trial as it is now shaping up does not present a place of interest to you, I shall understand and accept your decision. But I do not want you to reach that conclusion on any misunderstanding of the motives either of myself or of Colonel Storey.

Donovan's note depicted himself as having been fired, but stated that he would remain on the job for another month to "finish up" unspecified matters, thus leaving time for adjustments. Jackson's reply was unyielding on the policy issues between them, but denied any intention to discharge Donovan, and rather deftly left it up to him to say what would happen next. And so matters rested for the next three weeks, but it became common knowledge that all was not well between the American prosecution's two foremost figures. In his diary note of November 12 Biddle mordantly recorded: "Donovan restless because nothing to do, and Jackson says, is doing nothing."

## 6

The suicide of Robert Ley had forcefully reminded all parties to the Nuremberg proceedings that physical or mental frailties among the defendants might prevent one or more of them from staying the course to final judgment. For the trial itself, the chief events of these last pretrial weeks involved, in ascending order of importance, the weaknesses of Julius Streicher, Rudolf Hess, and Gustav Krupp.

Streicher's case was settled first. On November 15, at the Tribunal's second pretrial public session in Nuremberg, Streicher's attorney (Dr. Hanns Marx) requested a psychiatric examination of his client "in view of the exceptional nature of the case and of the difficulties of the defense in handling it." The lawyer explained that he was not making a formal motion because Streicher himself "does not desire an examination of this sort." Lawrence, presiding, ruled that a written motion must be made.

Colonel Pokrovsky (Rudenko was away at the time) then rose and informed the Tribunal that at the last interrogation of Streicher conducted by the Soviet delegation, Streicher had stated that, in his remarks about Jews, "he had been speaking from a Zionist point of view." This declaration, said Pokrovsky, "immediately produced certain doubts as to the mental stability of the defendant." Accordingly, he supported Dr. Marx's request. Written motions were duly made, and the Tribunal appointed three physicians from the medical commission assembled to examine Hess to conduct the inquiry into Streicher's sanity.

Streicher had in fact been giving Marx a very hard time. He had greeted the Indictment by announcing: "This trial is the triumph of world Jewry." When the psychiatric examining commission arrived, he lectured the doctors, telling them that he had studied the "Jewish problem" for twenty-five years, and "knew more about it than anyone else." His anti-Semitic obsession was so dominant in his behavior that Marx could get nowhere with him in preparing a defense, and concluded that his client had a "diseased mind." Furthermore, Streicher was neither attractive nor bright; he scored lower than any other defendant on the intelligence tests administered by the prison psychologist, Dr. Gilbert.

But in the opinion of the examining physicians these shortcomings did not amount to insanity. On November 18 the commission submitted a unanimous report finding that Streicher was "sane" and "fit to appear before the Tribunal and to present his defense." The following day the Tribunal recorded its approval of the report.

Rudolf Hess, of course, had been a problem since his arrival in Nuremberg early in October, but for the next few weeks the problem was his amnesia, genuine or feigned, rather than his sanity. Amen made numerous unsuccessful efforts to lift the seeming curtain on his memory and eventually came upon the idea of showing Hess *Triumph of the Will*, a Nazi documentary film about the creation of the Third Reich, in which Hess figured prominently.

The event was staged on November 8 in a large room with some twenty-five onlookers, of whom I was one. When the film had finished, Amen (through an interpreter) asked, "Do you remember?" to which Hess replied that he recognized Hitler and Goering, but added, "I must have been there because obviously I was there. But I don't remember."

The experiment was not a bad idea, but had been amateurishly executed. The presence of so many kibitzers was ill calculated to put Hess at ease. The film should have been shown to him under more casual and private circumstances, with one or two knowledgeable German-speaking questioners, preferably known to Hess in a nonadversarial way, who could converse with him during the showing. Of course, this method might well have worked no better, but the chances of tripping up Hess, if he was indeed feigning, would have been much greater, and if not, his replies to factual questions and comments might have led to better understanding of his ailment.

By this time, doubts had also arisen about Hess's mental fitness to stand trial. On November 6, at a joint meeting of the Tribunal and chief prosecutors, in the course of discussing the Gustav Krupp situation, Biddle remarked that "the same problem would arise in connection with Hess." Jackson replied that "it was a different problem" because "The question was whether Hess was pretending to have lost his memory or not. . . . It would be a very serious matter to omit Hess from the trial and, as he was perfectly in command of his mind, there was no reason why . . . we should anticipate an application for examination, by Counsel on his behalf."

But Biddle said that such an application would soon be filed. He was well informed, for the next day Hess's counsel (Dr. Gunther von Rohrscheidt) submitted an application that the Tribunal appoint a medical expert to determine whether Hess was "mentally competent" and "capable of being tried," on the ground that Hess "was unable to give his Counsel any information whatsoever regarding the crimes imputed to him in the Indictment." Hess had declared that "he has completely lost his memory since a long period of time, the period of which he can no longer determine."

On November 8 the Tribunal members agreed to appoint a commission consisting of physicians from each of the four countries (the leading British doctor was Churchill's personal physician, the famous Lord Moran) to examine Hess "with reference to his mental competence and capacity to stand trial." On November 19 (the day before the trial was to begin) the commission's final report had not yet been received, and the Tribunal decided to take no action on the Hess situation until the report was available. Consequently, Hess was in the dock with his fellow defendants when the trial opened, and another ten days were to elapse before the problem was resolved.

The extraordinary controversy involving Gustav and Alfried Krupp began as soon as Jim Rowe returned from serving the Indictment on the uncomprehending Gustav in Austria on October 23. Jackson at once asked

Shea for a memorandum on "the possibility for addition to the Economic Defendants," and on October 25 Shea submitted the names of Alfried Krupp and Herman Schmitz, Chairman of the Vorstand (managing directorate) of the huge I. G. Farben industrial combine. Aware of the undesirability of delaying the trial, Shea gave the nod to Alfried on the ground that the case against him could be prepared more rapidly. He also raised "the question as to whether public reaction may be that we are going after the son because the father cannot be tried." Jackson promptly addressed a memorandum to the other chief prosecutors proposing a meeting to add to the Indictment either Alfried Krupp or Schmitz, as well as two more high-ranking SS officials. Such additions, he optimistically predicted, would not be likely to "delay substantially the opening of the trial."

Dubost, in de Menthon's absence, visited the British delegation to discuss the matter with Colonel Phillimore. Dubost had already heard that Jackson was considering the substitution of Alfried for Gustav, but he had other ideas. "French public opinion would not be content unless Bertha Krupp was indicted," Dubost declared, "as she had held 99% of the shares from 1913 onwards, had been the power behind the throne . . . and it was her name that was associated with the gun that had shelled Paris in the last war."

However, Dubost's prior consultations with de Menthon and the Russians had produced a consensus that "it would be fatal to risk any delay in the commencement of the trial," and therefore: "He had in mind a compromise involving a second trial covering the names put forward by Mr. Alderman (in London on October 3), and also Bertha Krupp."

Phillimore, who had spent several weeks among the Krupp documents in Essen, doubted that there was much evidence against Bertha, and certainly it would be incongruous to charge the lady with war crimes because of Big Bertha's ineffectual shelling of Paris in World War I, when in World War II the Royal Air Force had sown death and destruction in Berlin, Dresden, Hamburg, and numerous other German cities. Phillimore was certain only that the British would oppose "any proposal which might either delay the start of the trial or prolong its duration."

The chief prosecutors met on October 26 and again the next day to consider the Jackson and Dubost proposals. Dubost's wish to indict Bertha Krupp drew no support, but Rudenko agreed with his plan for a second trial. Fyfe and Jackson were both cool to the idea of a second trial. Jackson's motion to add Alfried Krupp to the pending Indictment was defeated by a vote of three to one because of the certainty that it would delay the trial.

So matters stood when the Tribunal, on October 30, approved the appointment of a medical commission to examine the condition of Gustav Krupp. On November 4, Dr. Theodor Klefisch, representing Krupp, submitted to the Tribunal a petition that the case against his client be deferred, on the ground that he was incapable of defending himself. The petition was supported by medical certificates from two German doctors describing his illness.

The Tribunal's medical commission reported on November 7 that Gustav Krupp was incapable of standing trial, that he could not be moved without endangering his life, and that "his condition was unlikely to improve." At a chief prosecutors' meeting later that day Fyfe produced a copy of the commission's report and commented that in view of its contents, "He did not see how we could resist his Counsel's [Klefisch's] motion to sever." Alderman reported to Jackson that "The meeting was unanimous in the view that . . . the Prosecutors should not offer any resistance to his Counsel's motion to sever him from the case." But Jackson appeared at Alderman's office early on November 8 much upset by the disappearance of any Krupp from the case. He wanted either to persuade the other prosecutors to substitute Alfried for Gustav or to urge the Tribunal to try Gustav in absentia under Article 12 of the Charter. Alderman responded that Gustav was not in absentia within the meaning of Article 12 and that Alfried could not be put into Gustav's shoes because it would appear unfair and delay the trial. That evening Alderman and I discussed the situation and agreed that Jackson's course of action was unsound and unlikely to be successful.

On November 8 the Tribunal announced that on November 14 it would hold a public hearing on Klefisch's application to postpone the proceedings against his client. Accordingly, when the chief prosecutors met on November 9, they knew they were facing a showdown on the controversy. The Russians did not attend, and the other three found themselves still at odds. Jackson justified reopening the question by invoking American public opinion in a threatening way:

> He [Jackson] said public opinion in the United States would not allow his assuming the responsibility for the situation which resulted from the sickness of Gustav Krupp. He would have to tell the United States public that the American Delegation were outvoted by a three to one vote on the question of joining [i.e., indicting] industrialists. The firm of Krupp had made weapons for four generations and it was their weapons that had made Europe a battleground. . . . Krupp typified the sinister forces which he, Mr. Justice Jackson, was sent to Europe to punish. He realized that this would put the other delegations on the spot and such a line would be keenly felt by public opinion in Moscow and he did not wish to put his colleagues in that position. He could see only two ways out: (1) To try Gustav *in absentia*; (2) To insist on the substitution of Alfried. He realized that this would take time and cause delay but twenty days . . . was not such a very long time anyway.

Alderman, suppressing his personal opinions, supported Jackson loyally, but to no purpose. Dubost merely repeated his solution, that of a second trial, to which both Fyfe and Jackson were unreceptive. Fyfe remained adamant against Alfried's substitution because of the consequent postponement, and declared that British opinion was already incensed by the trial's delays. But he wanted the prosecutors to present a united front and to that end was prepared to support trying Gustav in absentia. No decision was reached.

On November 12 the prosecutors met for further discussion. After Jackson had repeated his argument for indicting Alfried, Fyfe announced that "the highest quarters of the [British] Government" had been consulted and that they "attached the greatest importance" to starting the trial on schedule. His superiors had authorized him to support a motion for Gustav's trial in absentia, but only if this "would mean a united stand by the prosecution." Fyfe "tried for about an hour to get Mr. Justice Jackson to agree to a common front" on that basis, but without success, and he got no help from the Russians or French.

Jackson waited no longer for support from the other delegations. Later that day he filed with the Tribunal an Answer for the United States to Klefisch's petition. It was a long document, tuned for public consumption as much as for judicial consideration. Indeed, the greater part of the text was a portrayal of the Krupps as a family which for "over 130 years" had been "the focus, the symbol, and the beneficiary of the most sinister forces engaged in menacing the peace of Europe," and as the industrial linchpin of Hitler's rise to power and Germany's rearmament. All this was supported by extracts from Krupp documents included among the trial briefs which the American prosecution had prepared. The bottom line of Jackson's answer was that Klefisch's motion should be denied and that Gustav should be tried in absentia, "unless some other representative of the Krupp armament and munitions interests should be substituted." The ensuing text made it clear that the "substitute" should be Alfried Krupp.

The British answer, filed the same day and signed by Shawcross, "strongly opposed any postponement" of the trial and recommended that Gustav be tried in absentia. Acknowledging that "in an ordinary case it is undesirable that a defendant should be tried when he is unable to comprehend the charges made against him," Shawcross contended that the Indictment's broad conspiracy charge raised "special considerations" which made the in absentia procedure "essential." Whether or not he was to be tried as a defendant, Krupp was charged as a coconspirator, and under conspiracy law the evidence of Krupp's participation would be admissible against the other defendants. In these circumstances, Shawcross argued, "It is preferable for . . . [Krupp] to be represented so that his lawyer can deal with such evidence to the best of his ability." Shawcross made no reference to Jackson's plea to substitute Alfried, other than firm objection to any delay.

The Soviet delegation submitted no answer. Dubost's reply was, depending on the point of view, charmingly or ridiculously artless:

> France is formally opposed to dropping the firm of Krupp from the Trial since the other prosecutors do not contemplate the possibility of preparing at this time a second trial directed against the big German industrialists.
>
> France objects therefore to a simple severance.
>
> The remaining possibilities are either the trial of Krupp Sr. *in absentia* or the substitution of Krupp Jr. in his father's place and stead.
>
> The trial of an old man who is about to die and who is not before the Court is difficult in itself.
>
> France would prefer to substitute his son against whom there are serious charges.
>
> For simple reasons of expediency, France requests that there be no delay in excess of the delay that will result in all probability from the motions of the Defense.
>
> If the Tribunal denies these motions of the Defense, the trial of Krupp Sr. should take place in his absence.
>
> However, this is in our opinion the lesser of two evils.

Early in the morning of November 14, Jackson and Dubost received notice by telephone from General Rudenko, then in Moscow, that the Soviet Union was joining in Jackson's application for the addition of Alfried Krupp to the Indictment. Dubost then submitted to the Tribunal a second and equally candid memorandum categorically opposing Gustav's trial in absentia, and requesting the substitution of Alfried even though the trial might thereby be delayed. The Frenchman attributed his change of position to the circumstance that "the Soviet Delegation has concurred in Mr. Jackson's thesis."

Later that morning the Tribunal held its first public session at Nuremberg, in the enlarged and rearranged courtroom, which was soon to provide the setting for the trial itself. The judges filed in behind the bench in the prearranged order of seating: facing the bench, from right to left, Falco, de Vabres, Parker, Biddle, Lawrence (presiding), Birkett, Nikitchenko (who was absent), and Volchkov. Thus each member sat beside his alternate, but Biddle and Lawrence in the center were the only two voting members next to each other—an arrangement carefully contrived by Biddle so that he could pour advice into Lawrence's ears.

Without prelude, Lawrence called on Klefisch to present his motion for severance. The German lawyer was commendably lucid and brief. The medical report plainly showed that Gustav Krupp was wholly incapable of standing trial; Article 12 of the Charter was primarily intended to cover fugitive defendants whose absence from the trial was voluntary rather than defendants physically incapable of defending themselves or exercising any of the procedural rights conferred on defendants by the Charter; Gustav Krupp could not, in his condition, be tried in absentia under German law, nor under any Continental legal system; the gross unfairness of trying Gustav in absentia should especially be avoided by "a court of such unequalled world historical importance" as the Nuremberg Tribunal.

Jackson made no effort to controvert these solid points. He conceded that Gustav's trial in absentia "would not comply with the constitutional standard for citizens of the United States in prosecutions conducted in our country." He sought to justify his position on the ground that the "great Krupp organization" had ample resources to defend Gustav—a point which, however true, quite overlooked the fact that if Gustav remained a defendant it would be *his* life, liberty, and *name* that would be tried and that from the standpoint of the Krupp enterprise, they would be defended through a principal who was, functionally, incompetent.

Jackson was leading from weakness, and he made matters worse by arguments unworthy of him. He sought to mitigate the fact that Gustav Krupp would be unable to come to court and testify in his own defense by suggesting that Krupp would not dare to take the stand even if he were able to. When Lawrence asked Jackson whether Alfried, if indicted, would not be entitled to thirty days' time to prepare a defense before being brought to trial (as the Tribunal's rules provided, and which would delay the trial until mid-December), the Justice replied that Alfried's preparation time could be shortened because "the work that has already been done [in defense of Gustav] presumably would be available to him [Alfried]." This argument assumed that the evidentiary cases against father and son were substantially similar—an assumption which the Tribunal had no right to make, and which Jackson himself knew, from what Shea had told him weeks earlier, was incorrect. Worse, Jackson suggested that Alfried "might be willing to step into his father's place without delay," a preposterous and unseemly speculation which served only to strengthen the inference that the sins of the father were to be visited upon the son.

Shawcross, who spoke next, professed that there was "no kind of difference of principle between myself and my colleagues representing the other three prosecution Powers," and then promptly revealed that there were in fact such differences by sharply criticizing Jackson's efforts to bring in Alfried. "This is a court of justice," Shawcross declaimed, "and not a game in which you can play a substitute, if one member of a team falls sick." He repeated his written argument in favor of trying Gustav in absentia, but responded only halfheartedly to Lawrence's pointed questions.

Pokrovsky, representing Rudenko, declined the opportunity to speak. Dubost was as frank *viva voce* as he had been on paper. In reply to a question from Volchkov, he echoed Klefisch's contention that Gustav Krupp could not be tried. As for Alfried, France had wanted to try him and other industrialists in a second trial, but, since the other powers did not agree, Dubost said he should be tried now, regardless of delay. De Vabres criticized Dubost for using the word "substituted" (which Jackson had also used in his written submission), but Dubost was not one to wriggle away from words that disclosed reality, even if impolitic. Klefisch, in rebuttal, told the Tribunal that if Alfried was to be tried he would request the full thirty-day period specified in the rules and drew on Shawcross's imagery by describing "a certain game being played by representatives of the United States which cannot be sanctioned by the Court in my opinion."

At this first public session in Nuremberg, the prosecution had certainly not distinguished itself. Alderman recorded ruefully his "uncomfortable feeling" that only Klefisch and Dubost had taken "defensible positions." Biddle thought that Jackson's argument was a "cheap speech." Lawrence and Birkett described the proposal to substitute Alfried for Gustav as "shocking."

When the Tribunal met privately that afternoon, all wished to grant Klefisch's motion for severance and only Volchkov (Nikitchenko was still absent) looked on the substitution of Alfried with any favor. Since there was unanimity on the severance of Gustav, Lawrence prepared a short decision declaring that his trial would not be "in accordance with justice" and granting Klefisch's application, which the Tribunal adopted and announced on November 15.°

The Tribunal had been putting off a final decision on Alfried in the hope that Nikitchenko would arrive, but on the morning of November 16, the members formally agreed to come to a conclusion that afternoon. News of this plan reached Jackson, who was worried that the Tribunal might rest on the technical point that no formal resolution of the chief prosecutors for the designation of Alfried Krupp as a defendant (as required by Article 14 of the Charter) had been made. The defect was remedied at a midday meeting of the chiefs, who adopted and immediately submitted to the Tribunal a formal motion for amendment of the Indictment by adding Alfried's name, together with "appropriate allegations in reference to him." The prosecutors also moved that "the time of Alfried Krupp be shortened from thirty days to 2 December 1945." This ungrammatical and sketchy document was signed by Jackson, Pokrovsky, and de Menthon.

When the Tribunal met that afternoon, Nikitchenko was still absent. Volchkov made several unsuccessful efforts to postpone a decision, but the

°Technically, the Tribunal "postponed" the proceedings against Gustav Krupp so as to make possible his subsequent trial if his condition should improve. But no one expected any such development. Gustav, his condition unchanged, remained in Austria, where he died on June 16, 1950.

members ultimately voted by three to one, Volchkov dissenting, to deny the chief prosecutors' motion to amend the Indictment. The following morning Biddle and de Vabres produced draft opinions in support of the decision. Nikitchenko was now on hand, and he made a long but unsuccessful argument to reopen the issue. It then proved impossible for the American and French judges to agree on an opinion, so the Tribunal members finally decided to reject the prosecution's motion without opinion.

Accordingly, that afternoon the Tribunal again met in public session and announced that

> ON CONSIDERATION of the motion to amend the Indictment by adding the name of Alfried Krupp.
> IT IS ORDERED that the motion be, and the same hereby is, rejected.

This order put an end to the Krupp issue as far as the Tribunal was concerned, but the prosecutors had various continuing problems. Jackson, for example, was disturbed by the reference, in the Tribunal's order on Gustav Krupp, to the possibility of a "trial hereafter" and filed with the Tribunal a memorandum making it a matter of record that "the United States has not been, and is not by this order, committed to participate in any subsequent Four Party trial."

On the morning of November 19, the day before the trial was scheduled to begin, the Alfried Krupp issue broke open again, this time in close connection with a new crisis, which had been foreshadowed two days earlier when Nikitchenko returned to Nuremberg. While arguing for the indictment of Alfried, Nikitchenko had stated that Rudenko was in Moscow, ill with malaria, and would be unable to return to Nuremberg "for a few days," implying that the delay necessary to be accorded Alfried's lawyers would not matter since Rudenko's illness would require postponement of the trial.

In line with this warning, on the morning of November 19 Pokrovsky visited each of the chief prosecutors and informed them that Rudenko's continued illness required postponement of the trial "for some time." Simultaneously, Nikitchenko offered the same information, specifying a postponement of "about twelve days" at the Tribunal's morning meeting. After some discussion in strict privacy, the Tribunal directed the chief prosecutors to meet with them early that afternoon.

Meanwhile Pokrovsky and Dubost separately requested an immediate chief prosecutors' meeting, the former for discussion of the Rudenko problem, the latter for a reopening of the Alfried Krupp matter. There ensued one of the most tense and rancorous of these gatherings.

Dubost opened the meeting with a bitter complaint that the French delegation had not been notified of the Tribunal's meeting at which the adverse ruling on Alfried Krupp had been announced, and that the Tribunal had ignored a French request to argue in support of the three prosecutors' motion. He made the point that under the Charter the chief prosecutors were empowered to designate the defendants and that the Tribunal had no authority to reject their decisions.

There followed a rapid interchange among Dubost, Shawcross, and Jackson in which the other two pointed out to Dubost that it was for the Tribunal to decide how and when a named defendant would be tried and that no indictment of Alfried had been signed or submitted.

Dubost then produced a document which he described as "a draft of an indictment against Alfried." He requested Jackson and Pokrovsky to join in signing and submitting the document to the Tribunal and thereafter in a motion "to consolidate the proceedings under this indictment with the proceedings against the other defendants." Dubost grew more and more heated and insistent and orated at length on the miseries of France under German occupation and the sins of the Krupps.

This diatribe was not without effect on Shawcross, who now declared: "I will publicly announce my attention of indicting others for a second trial if it will be of any assistance here in order to make it known that Alfried and other industrialists will not escape trial." Dubost was not mollified; it might not be feasible to have a second trial, and that was "the reason why the French want to catch at least one industrialist in this trial."

Pokrovsky now spoke in support of Dubost, but soon introduced the Rudenko situation, making the point that the addition of Alfried would cause no delay beyond what Rudenko's illness would require. He then declared that

> . . . no one except Rudenko had been authorized to represent the Soviet, that there could be no substitute at this point, and that the Soviets would not attend the session tomorrow if the trial should open in the absence of General Rudenko. He suggested a 10-day delay on account of Rudenko which would make it possible to indict Alfried and join the second indictment to the first. Since he must report the chief prosecutors' and the Tribunal's decision to Moscow he would like to know what he should report.

Thus Pokrovsky explicitly linked the two matters, perhaps hoping to induce Jackson, the principal engineer of the move to indict Alfried, to join in Dubost's plan. But Jackson did not rise to the bait. For him, the Krupp "chapter seems closed." Any delay in opening the trial "will impair our good faith with the world." Furthermore: "The Soviets should be represented all through the trial and from its very beginning." Dubost interrupted Jackson to declare that "The French delegation will not attend the session tomorrow if the trial goes ahead without General Rudenko." Jackson continued:

> There are Frenchmen and Russians on the court. If they order us to proceed [with the trial] we will do so. We will not interfere with your presenting your position to the court, but I must urge that delay will impugn our good faith and demoralize our staff. . . . A failure of the Russians and French to attend tomorrow's opening session will cause an unfortunate reaction in the United States, with implications far more important than the progress of this trial. I beg you to consider these things before you act.

It is an impressive statement, but Dubost responded with a peremptory demand to know whether Jackson would "sign an indictment of Alfried now." Jackson answered that he could not be "diverted to this problem if we are going to start this trial tomorrow. I have an opening speech to prepare." Shawcross, still working for a compromise, responded that he would "sign a proper indictment against Alfried for a second trial," but rejected Dubost's document as "totally inadequate as an indictment."

The four men were at an impasse when Jackson announced that he had received word that the Tribunal had requested a private meeting at two o'clock. Pokrovsky, a sensitive man, was most unhappy about the position he was obliged to take, and even unhappier because he had nothing to "report to Moscow," for the prosecutors had reached no decision on either Dubost's proposal to pursue Alfried further or Pokrovsky's to postpone the trial. Since Pokrovsky was not authorized to act for Rudenko, he could not even submit a motion to postpone to the Tribunal. The only whiff of compromise in the air was Dubost's remark that "We cannot start the first trial without an assurance that a second trial against the industrialists will follow." Maybe Shawcross's offer of such a commitment might help.

The Tribunal had decided that the meeting should comprise only members and alternates, the interpreters, and the four chief prosecutors. Jackson came accompanied by his son, Gordon Dean, and his aide Mrs. Douglas. All were excluded, over Jackson's strong objection in the case of Mrs. Douglas, who he said was entitled to record the proceedings.°

After Nikitchenko had spoken briefly in support of Rudenko's request for delay, Dubost made it clear that he had no independent objection to proceeding with the trial on schedule; his orders were simply to absent himself if the Russians were unwilling to attend.

---

° As far as I know, the only surviving records of this meeting consist of a few pages of rough notes by Biddle, Jackson's recollection in his Columbia oral history deposit, and a brief reference in the British delegation's report to the Foreign Office.

When Pokrovsky (who had been telephoning Moscow) arrived, he reported that he was now authorized to file a formal motion for postponement of the trial. Rudenko had refused to designate anyone to represent him at the opening of the trial, which would be "a high solemn moment, of supreme importance." Pokrovsky did not "know what his Government would decide if postponement was refused." After hearing all this, Jackson "hardly knew what to say." He regarded delay as disastrous, but also thought that "some Russian should be present throughout the trial." The Tribunal took no action while the prosecutors were present, but de Vabres, Falco, and Lawrence made comments indicating opposition to postponement.

About midafternoon the private session was suspended. Pokrovsky called Moscow for further instructions, and no doubt there were informal discussions among the chief prosecutors. At about six o'clock they informed the Tribunal that they had "a statement to make," and the private meeting was resumed. Pokrovsky reported that under his new instructions from Moscow, the trial should start the next day; the Indictment should be read in open court (as had been planned), the defendants should be called upon to plead guilty or not guilty, and Jackson could make his opening statement. The only condition they insisted on was that no other statements by counsel should be made pending Rudenko's return, which was expected within five days. The meeting ended with this burst of sunshine and profuse compliments to Pokrovsky; Nikitchenko and Biddle saluted him as "a distinguished soldier, lawyer, and diplomat."

The next day, however, Dubost had the last word. He submitted to the Tribunal a sort of manifesto, which began by admonishing the Tribunal that their decision rejecting the motion to add Alfried Krupp to the Indictment "cannot reject the declaration" in that motion, based on Article 14(b) of the Charter, designating Alfried as a defendant. More important, the document then set forth the text of a "declaration published by the Chief Prosecutors representing Great Britain and the Government of the French Republic," the operative part of which announced that

> . . . the French and British Delegations are now engaged in the examination of the cases of other leading German industrialists, as well as certain other major war criminals, with a view to their attachment with Alfried Krupp, in an indictment to be presented at a subsequent trial.

This was the first official indication of further war crimes projects, which were destined to prolong and amplify the scope of the Nuremberg trials.

## 7

In his oral history recollections, Jackson said he had "never understood" what brought about the Rudenko malaria crisis. Birkett (and no doubt others) thought he was not ill at all, and of course that is quite possible. But it has always seemed to me that if the disability was strictly diplomatic, the Kremlin would have attributed it to a more superficially plausible malady than malaria, which is not commonly associated with Moscow in November.° The more important question, it appears to me, is why, even assuming that Rudenko was truly disabled, were the Soviet authorities so insistent that the trial be postponed until he could be present? And why did they change their minds at the last moment and consent to its commencement on schedule?

A contemporaneous report to the Foreign Office from the British delegation (probably from Patrick Dean, who represented the Foreign Office at Nuremberg) states that on November 19 it became "apparent at an early stage that the true reason for their [referring to the Soviet and French delegations] wish to secure a postponement and possibly for their previous attitude in the matter of joining Alfried Krupp was that neither Delegation was ready to begin, although both stated publicly to the Press the contrary." I believe that this is almost certainly incorrect. It was well known to all the delegations that the United States would present their part of the case first, the British second, and that therefore a number of weeks if not months would elapse before French or Russians would be called upon. In fact, de Menthon did not open the French case until January 17, and Rudenko began the Soviet case on February 8, 1946. Under these circumstances, it is most unlikely that the need of time for preparation played any part in either Rudenko's or Dubost's conduct on November 19.

In my opinion, either Rudenko was indeed ill and deeply desired, for personal or policy reasons, to be present at the trial's opening, or he was collaborating with Dubost to cause delay as a device to reopen the Alfried Krupp matter on the basis that his inclusion in the trial would no longer cause additional delay. As for Dubost, Jackson thought him "probably" a Communist lining up with the Soviets. But whether he was or was not a Communist, there is no reason to question the sincerity of his desire, prompted by Jackson himself, to get Alfried Krupp into the dock. Certainly he was happy to collaborate with Rudenko to that end, just as Jackson had been. And if there was no such collaboration on November 19, still

---

°Although malaria is initially contracted from the Anopheles mosquito, which flourishes in southern climes, it is a lingering disease which may occur and recur for years after the initial infection. There was nothing intrinsically incredible about suffering from malaria in Moscow.

Rudenko's illness would appear to Dubost as a golden opportunity to renew the effort.

As for Rudenko's last-minute change of heart, it is clear that Moscow had no stomach for public disclosure that the Soviets were responsible for delaying the trial. That is why Pokrovsky worked so hard for postponement by action of the Tribunal or by the chief prosecutors as a group. But Shawcross and Jackson refused to let the Russians off the hook and, as the British delegation reported to London, "forced them into the position that they must make a public application in Court and state the true grounds for it if they wished to secure a postponement." It is virtually certain that the British, American, and French judges took the same attitude. Furthermore, Shawcross had sweetened the deal for both French and Russians by agreeing to sponsor publicly a second trial at which Alfried and others would be defendants.

Finally, it is very unlikely that either the Russians or French, any more than the British and Americans, were prepared to confront a commencement of the trial with their prosecutors absent. It is possible that Nikitchenko and Volchkov would have stayed away, but very unlikely that de Vabres or Falco would have followed suit. How would the French have looked with their judges on the bench while their prosecutors were sulking in their tents? The strands holding the four nations together in this unique judicial venture were strained almost to the breaking point, but at Nuremberg in November, just as at London in August, the centrifugal finally overcame the centripetal forces.

Jackson's desperate efforts to bring the Russians and French back to their senses in Nuremberg displayed an awareness of the values at stake which contrasts sharply with the petulant hostility he had displayed in London. In his oral history, he speculated that if the Russian and French prosecutors had withdrawn, the British and Americans would probably have carried on the trial without them. He added, with the benefit of hindsight, that such an outcome "would have destroyed much of the good that could come from a four-power trial."

So the postponement crisis was resolved, and the Tribunal's handling of the Krupp motions showed that it was determined to observe standards of fairness and reject prosecution attempts to cut corners. But this second chapter of the Krupp fiasco was not merely a blunder but a disaster, and this time it was Jackson instead of Shawcross who was primarily to blame. The damage lay not in the fact that his efforts to indict Alfried failed, but in the fact that they were made at all. It is hard to believe that a lawyer of Jackson's stature could have seriously expected the Tribunal to go along with what he was proposing, and equally hard to escape the conclusion that he was primarily concerned with making a record to protect himself from political criticism.

The circumstances of Gustav's incapacity and Alfried's comparative youth, as Shea had foreseen at the very beginning of the affair, would inevitably have aroused suspicion that it was not primarily Alfried's individual guilt but his name and filial relation which were putting him in jeopardy. Jackson's distressing answers to the Tribunal's questions went far to turn suspicion into belief and fostered the wholly erroneous public impression that Alfried was *only* a stand-in. Thus he came to be seen by many as a fabulously wealthy young playboy, not to be taken seriously as an industrial magnate.

Once again Alfried was lucky, for this image, with which Jackson unthinkingly endowed him, was to stand him in good stead five years later, when Alfried's conviction was commuted by John J. McCloy.

# Chapter 8

# ON TRIAL

When the trial opened on the morning of November 20, 1945, we had our first look at the defendants in a group. The circumstance that they had all been officials of the Nazi regime, and in consequence were now sitting in the same dock, did not produce any other visible common denominator. As a group, they could only be described as nondescript, and until they began to react individually to the trial itself, it would have been difficult to deduce, from visual scrutiny alone, what manner of men they were. One was missing; three days earlier Ernst Kaltenbrunner had suffered a minor cerebral hemorrhage, and he did not appear in the dock until December 10.

Lord Lawrence began the proceedings by noting "with great satisfaction . . . the steps which have been taken by the Chief Prosecutors to make available to defending counsel the numerous documents upon which the Prosecution rely, with the aim of giving to the defendants every possibility for a just defense." It soon emerged that this matter had not yet been satisfactorily resolved.

In accordance with Article 24(a) of the Charter, Lawrence next directed that the Indictment be read. In view of its length, the prosecutors and defense counsel had joined in a stipulation that it be summarized. The Tribunal, however, insisted on a full reading, partly to take up time pending Rudenko's return. Consequently, the rest of the first day was consumed by the reading, accomplished by Alderman, Fyfe, and two French and two Russian junior prosecutors. It was a very dull beginning, but the novelty of the scene and the number and variety of personalities gave the press plenty to write about, while the leisurely pace enabled participants and audience to get acquainted with the simultaneous translation system, which still failed from time to time.

The previous day, all defense counsel had joined in a petition to the Tribunal, signed by Goering's counsel, Dr. Otto Stahmer, which challenged the juristic foundations of the trial. It contained nothing original or surprising; the bulk of it was an exposition of the view of many international lawyers that neither the Kellogg-Briand Pact nor any international action had established the criminality of "starting an unjust war." It also complained that the Tribunal was composed exclusively of judges from the victorious powers. The document requested that the Tribunal procure "an opinion . . . by internationally recognized authorities on international law on the legal elements of this Trial under the Charter of the Tribunal."

The petition was summarily denied at the beginning of the Tribunal's second session on the ground that it conflicted with Article 3 of the Charter, which provided that neither the Tribunal nor its membership could be challenged by either the prosecution or the defense. The ruling did, however, allow for further consideration of these issues at a later time.

Lawrence then called upon the defendants to plead "guilty or not guilty," but Dr. Rudolf Dix, interrupted the order of business by protesting that he and his colleagues had not been allowed to consult with their clients that morning in the courtroom before the session began. Lawrence at first upheld the prohibition, but Dr. Alfred Thoma, Rosenberg's counsel, then rose and said that the previous day his client had given him "a statement as regards the question of guilt or innocence" which they had agreed to discuss the following morning. Since he had not been allowed to speak to Rosenberg, Thoma said, "neither I nor my client are in a position to make a statement today as to whether he is guilty or not guilty." The request could not be refused, and Lawrence called a short recess so that all defense counsel could consult with their clients before their pleas were taken.

When the session resumed, a guard approached the dock with a portable microphone and Lawrence called on Goering to plead. During the reading of the Indictment Goering had been endeavoring to draw attention to himself, and establish his primacy among the defendants, by gesturing, mugging, and muttering comments on the proceedings. Prison diet and enforced withdrawal from drugs had thinned him and restored much of his former energy and ability. He now rose, holding a sheet of paper, and began: "Before I answer the question of the Tribunal whether or not I am guilty . . ." He got no further; Lawrence interrupted with the admonition that "defendants are not entitled to make a statement" and told Goering that he "must plead guilty or not guilty." Goering stared at Lawrence for a moment, apparently reflecting on the wisdom of defiance, and then snarled: "In the sense of the Indictment, not guilty."* He sat down.

---

*Im sinne der Anklage nicht schuldig. This wording of a not guilty plea came to be used by many German defendants in subsequent war crimes trials and was adopted by Adolf Eichmann at his Jerusalem trial in 1961.

Hess, the next called on, shouted hoarsely into the microphone: "Nein!" Lawrence calmly stated: "That will be entered as a plea of not guilty." There was a ripple of laughter in the room, which elicited his prompt warning: "If there is any disturbance in court, those who make it will have to leave the court." Whatever his shortcomings as a legal scholar, Lawrence was handling sudden developments with firmness and aplomb.

Ribbentrop echoed Goering's response, as did Rosenberg and Schirach. Schacht declared himself "not guilty in any respect." The others simply pleaded "not guilty," with minor variations, except Sauckel and Jodl, who embellished their denials by avowing their innocence before God, history, and the German people.

After all the defendants had pleaded, Goering made another effort to speak° and once again was put to silence by Lawrence, who then called upon "the Chief Prosecutor for the United States of America."

2

The Nuremberg trials began with Jackson's opening statement, and in my opinion, nothing said at Nuremberg thereafter matched its force, perception, and eloquence. Indeed, I know of nothing else in modern juristic literature that equally projects the controlled passion and moral intensity of many passages. It won wide acclaim, has frequently been reproduced, and is often quoted. I will, therefore, forgo a lengthy recapitulation and discuss only what appear to me as its most important and impressive portions. Jackson began:

> The privilege of opening the first trial in history for crimes against the peace of the world imposes a grave responsibility. The wrongs which we seek to condemn and punish have been so calculated, so malignant, and so devastating, that civilization cannot tolerate their being ignored, because it cannot survive their being repeated. That four great nations, flushed with victory and stung with injury, stay the hand of vengeance and voluntarily submit their captive enemies to the judgment of the law is one of the most significant tributes that Power has ever paid to reason.

Soon thereafter, Jackson squarely confronted the question of "victor's justice":

---

°The statement which Goering had planned to read was given to the press. In it Goering acknowledged "political responsibility" for his acts, denied that they were criminal, and challenged the jurisdiction of the Tribunal. Additionally, he rejected responsibility for "acts of other persons which were not known to me" and which he did not approve but could not have prevented.

Before I discuss particulars of evidence, some general considerations which may affect the credit of this trial in the eyes of the world should be candidly faced. There is a dramatic disparity between the circumstances of the accusers and the accused that might discredit our work if we should falter, in even minor matters, in being fair and temperate.

Unfortunately, the nature of these crimes is such that both prosecution and judgment must be by victor nations over vanquished foes. The worldwide scope of the aggressions carried out by these men has left but few real neutrals. . . . We must never forget that the record on which we judge these defendants is the record on which history will judge us tomorrow. To pass these defendants a poisoned chalice is to put it to our lips as well. We must summon such detachment and intellectual integrity to our task that this Trial will commend itself to posterity as fulfilling humanity's aspirations to do justice.

There was no basis, Jackson pointed out, for regarding the trial as an "injustice" to the defendants, "who may be hard pressed, but they are not ill used":

If these men are the first war leaders of a defeated nation to be prosecuted in the name of the law, they are also the first to be given a chance to plead for their lives in the name of the law. Realistically, the Charter of this Tribunal, which gives them a hearing, is also the source of their only hope.

He continued:

We would also make clear that we have no purpose to incriminate the whole German people. . . . If the German populace had willingly accepted the Nazi program, no storm troopers would have been needed in the early days of the Party and there would have been no need for concentration camps or the Gestapo. . . . The German, no less than the non-German world, has accounts to settle with these defendants.

Jackson promised the Tribunal members that the prosecution would give them "undeniable proofs of the incredible events" and that

The catalog of crimes will omit nothing that could be conceived by a pathological prince, cruelty, and lust for power. . . . Against their opponents, including Jews, Catholics, and free labor, the Nazis directed such a campaign of arrogance, brutality, and annihilation as the world has not witnessed since the pre-Christian era. . . . At length bestiality and bad faith reached such excess that they aroused the sleeping strength of imperiled civilization. Its united efforts have ground the Nazi war machine to fragments. But the struggle has left Europe a liberated yet prostrate land where a demoralized society struggles to survive. These are the fruits of the sinister forces that sit with these defendants in the prisoners' dock.

Jackson then devoted the bulk of his statement to a summary of the evidence in support of the conspiracy charge, some his own narrative, some selections from particularly striking documents. He dealt succinctly with the Nazi rise to power and Hitler's appointment as Chancellor, and his clever use of the Reichstag fire as a means of obtaining from the aged and failing President von Hindenburg a decree suspending the libertarian guarantees of the Weimar Constitution. He described more fully the Nazis' exploitation of that decree, and the excesses and atrocities accompanying Hitler's consolidation of power: the wholesale arrests of opponents of the Nazi regime, beatings and killings, and the advent of concentration camps, whose names—Belsen, Buchenwald, Dachau*—had since acquired worldwide and sinister familiarity. He described at length the conversion of mere anti-Semitism into the virtual outlawry of Judaism, which led eventually to the ghettos and the deliberate extermination of European Jewry.

Jackson more than made good on his promise to produce proof of "incredible events," so incredible, indeed, that despite compelling evidence during the war of the death camps in Poland, few people had believed such reports. One such person was Jackson, who now described himself as "one who received during this war most atrocity tales with suspicion and skepticism." I was another who had shared this attitude, and, judging by the shocked reaction of Jackson's listeners, most of them were also erstwhile skeptics.

Jackson read from the reports of the SS Einsatzgruppen, the paramilitary SS units that followed the German front-line troops into the Soviet Union with the mission of collecting and killing all Jews, Gypsies, and other categories thought hostile to the German invaders. For example:

In Vitebsk, 3,000 Jews were liquidated because of the danger of epidemics. In Kiev 33,771 Jews were executed on September 29 and 30 [this was the massacre at Babi Yar] in retaliation for some fires

---

*Today's readers of Jackson's address may wonder why Jackson made no reference to Auschwitz and the other death camps in Poland, where the major part of the Holocaust occurred. Auschwitz remained in German hands until January 1945, and when then overrun by Soviet forces the camp was virtually deserted, as the staff had fled westward, driving most of the surviving inmates with them. In contrast, camps such as Dachau, Belsen, and Buchenwald were captured by American or British troops while still in operation, and their horrors were witnessed by hundreds of Allied soldiers and widely pictured in the press, as Eisenhower and other notables visited them. Nothing comparable occurred at the camps in Poland.

which were set off there. In Zhitomir 3,145 Jews had to be shot because, judging from experience, they had to be considered as the carriers of Bolshevik propaganda.

Jackson read from SS General Juergen Stroop's report on the destruction of the Warsaw Ghetto:

> The resistance put up by the Jews and bandits could only be suppressed by energetic actions of our troops day and night. The Reichsfuehrer SS [Himmler] ordered, therefore, on 23 April 1943, the clearing out of the Ghetto with ruthlessness and murderous tenacity. I, therefore, decided to destroy and burn down the entire ghetto. . . . Jews usually left their hideouts, but frequently remained in the burning buildings and jumped out of the windows only when the heat became unbearable. They then tried to crawl with broken bones across the street into buildings which were not afire. . . . Countless Jews were liquidated in sewers and bunkers through blasting. . . . This action eliminated . . . a proved total of 56,065. To that we have to add the number killed through blasting, fire, etc., which cannot be counted.

In keeping with his belief that the charge of launching aggressive wars was the core of the entire case, Jackson read from the military records of the German attack against Poland which began World War II. In May 1939, Hitler had told the principal military leaders:

> It is a question of expanding our living space in the East and of securing our food supplies. . . . There is therefore no question of sparing Poland, and we are left with the decision: *To attack Poland at the first suitable opportunity.*

Ten days before the initial assault, addressing a much larger meeting of military commanders and chiefs of staff, Hitler declared that he would give a reason for the attack only for propaganda purposes, but added: "It will make no difference whether the reasons will sound convincing or not. After all, the victor will not be asked whether he spoke the truth or not. We have to proceed brutally. The stronger is always right."

Jackson continued by reading comparable documents relating to Germany's subsequent aggressions. He then turned to the subject of war crimes, committed in furtherance of the overall conspiracy. He quoted from a letter sent in February 1942 from Rosenberg to Keitel stating that of 3,600,000 Soviet prisoners of war, "only several hundred thousand are still able to work fully." The others had "starved or died because of the hazards of the weather." The commanders of the prisoner-of-war camps "have forbidden the civilian population to put food at the disposal of the prisoners, and they have rather let them starve."[*]

If freezing and starving to death literally millions of Soviet prisoners beggared the imagination, Jackson's description of "medical" experiments performed on concentration camp inmates turned the stomach:

> At Dachau the reports of the "doctor" in charge show that the victims were immersed in cold water until their body temperature was reduced to 28 degrees centigrade (82.4 degrees Fahrenheit) when they all died immediately. This was in August 1942. But the "doctor's" technique improved. By February 1943 he was able to report that 30 persons were chilled to 27 to 29 degrees, their hands and feet frozen white, and their bodies "rewarmed" by a hot bath. But the Nazi scientific triumph was "rewarming with animal heat." The victim, all but frozen to death, was surrounded by bodies of living women until he revived and responded to his environment by having sexual intercourse. Here Nazi degeneracy reached its nadir.

The last part of Jackson's address was devoted to legal issues: the justification for treating aggressive war as a crime, the personal liability of government officials, the defense of superior orders, and the purpose of indicting the principal Nazi agencies and the General Staff–High Command as criminal organizations. Finally, Jackson delivered a moving peroration:

> The real complaining party at your bar is Civilization. In all our countries it is still a struggling and imperfect thing. It does not plead that the United States or any other country has been blameless of the conditions which made the German people easy victims to the blandishments and intimidations of the Nazi conspirators.
>
> But it points to the dreadful sequence of aggressions and crimes I have recited, it points to the weariness of flesh, the exhaustion of resources, and the destruction of all that was beautiful or useful in this world, and to greater potentialities in the days to come. It is not necessary among the ruins of this ancient and beautiful city with untold numbers of its civilian inhabitants buried in its rubble, to argue the proposition that to start or wage an aggressive war has the moral qualities of the worst of crimes. . . .
>
> Civilization asks whether law is so laggard as to be utterly helpless to deal with crimes of this magnitude by criminals of this order of importance. It does not expect that you [the Tribunal] can make war impossible. It does expect that your juridical action will put the forms of international law, its precepts, its prohibitions and, most of all, its sanctions, on the side of peace, so that men and women of

---

[*]Some of the translations from German are not in idiomatic English.

good will, in all countries, may have "leave to live by no man's leave, underneath the law."

The Tribunal adjourned, and Jackson became the focus of unanimous acclaim. Biddle described his address as "eloquent and moving," and the Philadelphia *Inquirer* called it "one of the greatest opening statements ever delivered before any court." The British, whose praise for American efforts was rarely unqualified, joined the chorus; Birkett called the statement "very fine," and the BWCE's report to London judged it "exceedingly good and generally acclaimed."

All this and more was abundantly justified; the quality of the speech was the product of hard work as well as Jackson's rhetorical gifts. Most of the work was done in the quiet of his Lindenstrasse house and for the most part was written in longhand, though some was dictated directly to Mrs. Douglas. The evidentiary material was supplied by a team comprising Storey, Bill Jackson, Gordon Dean, and Lieutenant Whitney Harris.

Jackson regarded the address as "the most important task of my life," and its preparation must have been a taxing period of intense concentration. I am inclined to believe that Jackson's actions and attitudes during the six weeks preceding the trial, some of which appear ill-considered and difficult to reconcile with the high standards of fairness which he articulated in his own opening statement, must have been the consequence of absorption in its creation and irritation at the intrusion of other problems.

But if amends from Jackson were due, they were more than made. Jackson had started this great trial at a level of force, feeling, and dignity which, I believe, no other man could have attained.

### 3

In Jackson's oral history memoir, the section dealing with his opening statement is immediately followed by one entitled "Flood Tide to a Walk." The import of these metaphors is that after the great success of his statement, the ensuing presentations by members of his staff were not so well received. Indeed, the compliments which he and Storey had been anticipating were not forthcoming. As Jackson described the scene during the next few days, his lawyers "glutted" the court with a mass of documents. The press raised a "tremendous fuss," and the Tribunal was "in a tizzy." In retrospect, Jackson wrote: "I suppose there was a good deal of justification for it [i.e., the complaints], although I didn't see much at the time." But plenty of other people did.

To be sure, Jackson was a hard act to follow, and no one expected that such a level of eloquence could be maintained. In fact, it is hard to see how the next few sessions, consisting as they did of expositions of the evidentiary background of the case and descriptions of the early days of the Nazi conspiracy, could have been turned into high drama. But things were a lot worse than they should have been, and the price of leaving management of the American presentation to Storey was now to be paid.

Storey started the second day of the trial well enough by describing to the Tribunal the process by which the prosecution's documents had been collected, sorted, and authenticated, and the nature of the briefs and document books which would be submitted to the Tribunal. He then announced that the first evidentiary presentation would cover "the Common Plan and Conspiracy up to 1939" and called on Ralph Albrecht to describe the structure of the German government and the Nazi Party. This took the rest of the morning session and, since no documents other than two certified charts were offered in evidence, aroused no objections.

The troubles began in the afternoon, while Major Frank Wallis was presenting evidence showing "the aims of the Nazi Party, their doctrinal techniques, their rise to power, and the consolidation of control over Germany between 1933 and 1939 in preparation for aggressive war." After discussing the first of these subjects without referring to either document books or briefs, Wallis said:

> I now offer the documents which establish the aims of the Nazi Party and their doctrinal techniques. I also have for the assistance of the Court and Defense Counsel, briefs which make the arguments from these documents.

Document books and briefs were then given to the Tribunal clerk. Wallis turned to his next subject, but was interrupted by a question from Lawrence as to whether he had copies for defense counsel. Wallis replied that six copies of each document book and brief had been deposited in the Defendant's Document Room. Lawrence at once announced: "The Tribunal thinks that the Defense Counsel should each have a copy of these briefs." Wallis promised that this would be done. Dr. Dix (Schacht's lawyer) rose and thanked the Tribunal for the directive, but complained that "none of us has seen any of these documents so far."

Wallis finally got going again, but the next time he offered documents and briefs Lawrence pressed him to get some copies for defense counsel as soon as possible. Storey intervened, but had to admit that the briefs furnished to the Defendant's Documents Room were in English, not German. Dix, though conciliatory in tone, again stressed the "great difficulties" under which he and his colleagues were laboring.

There was more interchange of this sort when Wallis finished his assignment. Tom Dodd followed him with a short presentation on "economic preparation for aggressive war," but when he finished Lawrence would not accept his documents until the defense counsel had opportunity to examine them.

It had taken less than two days of the trial to expose two serious prosecution errors, for both of which Storey was primarily responsible. The first arose from his obsession with the notion of "self-proving briefs," which apparently led him to believe that all his lawyers had to do was get the briefs and documents into the record. Originally, it had been planned that the lawyers would read the briefs to the Tribunal, but to save time Wallis and Dodd read summaries of the briefs, with the result that the documents lost all individuality and became merely a library to support the contentions in the briefs. This deprived the oral presentations of emphasis and color, for essentially Wallis and Dodd were doing no more than telling their listeners: "This is what the Nazis did, and take it from me, the documents in these books will prove that I'm giving it to you straight."

This technique also enabled Storey to get an enormous mass of documents into the record in a very short time. At a subsequent chief prosecutors' meeting Jackson boasted that his team had put in 331 documents during "the first four hours of this trial." No wonder the press raised a "fuss" and the Tribunal "was in a tizzy." The BWCE reported to London:

> Mr. Justice Jackson's speech . . . left the prosecution well on top but its effect was unfortunately somewhat dissipated in the following two days during which the American Prosecution proceeded to put in the evidence. A self-proving brief had been prepared on each aspect of the case, comprising a summary based on the principal documents and when necessary quoting or giving the reference for any statement in the brief. Each of these briefs was accompanied by a bundle of documents containing all those referred to or quoted from in the brief. Each member of the American team who presented a part of the evidence merely confined himself, however, to reading a summary of the brief (i.e., a summary of a summary) and then handing in the latter with the bundle of documents. In this way a number of lengthy briefs and very large bundles of documents were handed up to the Court at a pace which nobody could digest, and it became virtually impossible for the Judges, let alone the Defence, the other Prosecution Teams, or the Press, to understand, much less follow what was being proved. The Judges gave very clear indications . . . that they would not allow the case to go on in this way.

Storey's other major mistake was that he approached the presentations as if they concerned only the American prosecutors and the English-speaking members of the Tribunal, with little consideration for the legitimate needs of the other prosecuting delegations, the defense lawyers, or the Russian and French judges. The six copies of the document books and briefs which were sent to the defense lawyers were obviously and utterly inadequate, particularly since all of the defendants and the five organizations were indicted for conspiracy, which was the crime the American lawyers undertook to prove. While it was true that some of the defense lawyers had a good command of English, others did not, and in any event all the lawyers were entitled to documents in both their original language and as translated, so that errors or ambiguities in the translations could be checked.

To hand to the Tribunal briefs and documents in English, which only half the bench could read, was the sheerest folly, as was the failure to have copies for the other delegations. Even the British, for whom no translation was needed, reported to London that "the British Prosecutors were unable to secure a single copy [of the document books] and were only able to get two copies of the briefs."

To be sure, making adequate documentary provision for everyone who had a claim was a mountainous task, and no one could accuse Storey and his staff of not trying, to the extent of laboring into the wee hours. But these problems, which were in part due to the frantic pace at which the documents were poured in, should have been foreseen.

Furthermore, the excuse that a shortage of duplication facilities was to blame wore thin at the next trial session when Dr. Stahmer (Goering's lawyer) complained that a document which had not been offered in evidence was given to the press. This caused Lawrence to ask Storey how many copies of the prosecution's documents were given to the press, and when that harassed gentleman replied that "about 200 or 250 mimeographed copies" went to the press, there were audible snickers. Storey's failure to recognize the ridiculous aspect of this distribution vastly irritated Lawrence, who admonished him:

> You don't seem to understand what I am putting to you, which is this: That if you can afford to give 250 copies of the documents in English to the press, you can afford to give more than five copies to the defendants' counsel—one each. Well, we don't need to discuss it further. In the future that will be done.

When Dodd finished his presentation during the afternoon session on Friday, November 23, Sidney Alderman took over the lectern to present the evidence of conspiracy to initiate and wage aggressive wars. He wore the morning coat and striped trousers that, in those days, were de rigueur for arguments before the United States Supreme Court, and spoke with the ease and polish of the experienced appellate advocate. He quoted Justice Oliver Wendell Holmes, for whom both Biddle and Jim Rowe had clerked, and there were approving smiles at the bench. The American and British judges had previously spoken to Alderman privately and exhorted him to keep the case going and avoid any necessity for a recess.

Alderman had assembled a remarkable array of German military and diplomatic documents, of great historical interest and utmost value for the proof of Hitler's aggressive intentions and the involvement of others in his war plans, including the substance of Hitler's meetings with the principal military commanders and other high officials. He had the benefit of excellent trial briefs prepared by bright young lawyers working under the supervision of Sidney Kaplan. However, he did not plan to submit these briefs to the Tribunal, but rather to use them as the basis for his own running commentary on the documents which he would read to the Tribunal. That would constitute his presentation and make a written brief unnecessary. It would also eliminate any problem of making copies of the briefs for the Tribunal, defense counsel, or others, since no briefs would be submitted to the Tribunal.

But Alderman had been able to extract from the overworked clerical force only two sets of the English translations of these documents, and he knew, from what had happened with his predecessors, that this would cause trouble. He was ready for it, and when Dr. Dix declined to accept the single set of copies offered for the defense counsel, Alderman said:

> If Your Honor please, may I make this suggestion . . . I expect to read the pertinent parts of the documents into the [interpreting] system so that they will go into the transcript of record. Counsel for the German defendants will get their transcripts in German; our French and Russian Allies will get their transcripts in their language, and it seems to me that that is the most helpful way to overcome this language barrier.

That was essentially the way the Tribunal resolved the document problem at a closed meeting the next day. Storey's physical facilities simply could not produce enough copies to meet the needs of the trial participants, and nobody could cope with the flood of documents that Storey's lawyers had let loose. Reading the documents into the record would ensure that after each session, when the record was typed and duplicated in the four languages of the trial, all concerned would have both the text of the documents, and what Alderman had said in connection with them, in their own languages. It would also slow the previously mad documentary pace of the trial so that the import of the documents could be grasped as they were read. But would it slow the trial process too much?

Pending the expansion of the prosecution's translating and duplicating facilities, no better solution was suggested. When the trial sessions resumed on November 26, the Tribunal announced new rules for the prosecution's use of documents. The first and most important of these was "That in the future only such parts of documents as are read in court by the Prosecution shall in the first instance be part of the record." Inclusion of the phrase "in the first instance" was to make clear that the parts of a document not so read could later become part of the record if read by the same or another lawyer.

The only reason for such a rule was, of course, the continuing lack of a sufficient supply of documents and briefs in the four languages. Initially, the new rule did not much hamper Alderman, who had planned in any event to read his better documents in full. But the rule did greatly slow the proceedings, and Jackson soon sought ways and means to alter it. Nonetheless, the rule remained in effect until mid-December.

Alderman's presentation continued until the afternoon of November 29, by which time he had completed the detailed evidence through the German annexation of Austria in March 1938. Other matters were taken up during the next two days, after which Alderman returned to the lectern.

## 4

Rudolf Hess's bizarre denial of guilt had been followed by equally bizarre behavior in the dock as well as in his cell. He was apathetic most of the time, and inattentive in the dock, where he sometimes read pocket novels and occasionally suffered what appeared to be stomach cramps which required a temporary departure from the courtroom. Hess continued to maintain that he could remember virtually nothing of his Nazi past, and Dr. Gilbert, who often talked with Hess, was convinced that the amnesia was genuine.

The members of the examining medical commission which the Tribunal had appointed filed their reports shortly before the trial began. None of them suggested that Hess was feigning amnesia, but the American members found "a conscious exaggeration" of his loss of memory and a tendency to exploit it to protect himself against examination. Neither did any members find that he should not be tried. On November 24 the Tribunal scheduled a hearing "on the issues presented by the reports" during the afternoon of November 30.

On the third day of the trial I witnessed, by chance, an episode which, apparently, no one else noticed and which gave me an impression of Hess's condition. I was sitting in the courtroom at the American prosecution table while Ralph Albrecht was delivering his lecture on German governmental structure. It was my first opportunity to scrutinize the defendants and their counsel at leisure and close range. I was not paying close attention to Albrecht's presentation, but I heard him say that Hitler's "successor-designate was first the defendant Hess and subsequently defendant Goering."

This I well knew to be an error. The names were right but the order was wrong; Goering was number two and Hess number three. Since I was sitting barely twenty feet from those two gentlemen, I looked to see whether either of them had noticed the slip and, if so, how he reacted. Goering was already waving his arms to attract attention, pointing to himself, and saying repeatedly: *"Ich war der Zweite!"* ("I was the second!"). As these protests were pouring out of Goering, Hess turned and looked at him and burst into laughter. It appeared to me that Hess also knew that Albrecht had misspoken (Albrecht corrected the order of succession at the end of his presentation), and was vastly amused by Goering's characteristically vain reaction. I inferred from this occurrence that Hess's amnesia was not as complete as he had given out.

On November 29 the chief prosecutors met to consider, inter alia, the Hess case. It was unanimously agreed that they would take the position that Hess should be tried.

At the Tribunal's hearing the following afternoon, Hess was the only defendant present. His counsel, Dr. von Rohrscheidt, revealed at the outset that Hess considered himself fit to plead. Rohrscheidt stressed, however, those portions of the medical commission's reports which recognized the existence of amnesia, and acknowledged that Hess's ability to defend himself would thereby be impaired.

In keeping with the past history of the Hess affair, Rudenko merely stated that the medical commission and the prosecution had concluded that Hess was sane and able to stand trial. Fyfe spoke at greater length, but contributed little to the problem.

Jackson's argument was more belligerent and made much of the fact that Hess had refused to submit to medical tests or take medications which might "bring him out of his hysterical situation." The drugs could not safely be forced on him, even if they were quite safe in themselves, because if Hess were subsequently to die, from no matter what cause, his death would inevitably be charged to the prosecutors' ministrations. On this basis, Jackson argued that

> a man cannot stand at the bar of the Court and assert that his amnesia is a defense to his being tried and at the same time refuse the simple medical expedients which all agree might be useful. He is in the volunteer class with his amnesia.

After a brief interchange between Jackson and Rohrscheidt, Lawrence, at Biddle's urging, gave Hess an opportunity to speak for himself:

> Mr. President, I would like to say this: At the beginning of the proceedings this afternoon I gave my defense counsel a note saying that I thought the proceedings could be shortened if I would be allowed to speak. I wish to say the following:

In order to forestall the possibility of my being pronounced incapable of pleading, in spite of my willingness to take part in the proceedings and to hear the verdict alongside my comrades, I would like to make the following declaration before the Tribunal, although originally, I intended to make it during a later stage of the trial:

Henceforth my memory will again respond to the outside world. The reasons for simulating loss of memory were of a tactical nature. Only my ability to concentrate is, in fact, somewhat reduced. But my capacity to follow the trial, to defend myself, to put questions to witnesses, or to answer questions myself is not affected thereby.

I emphasize that I bear full responsibility for everything that I did, signed, or co-signed. My fundamental attitude that the Tribunal is not competent, is not affected by the statement that I have just made. I also simulated loss of memory in consultations with my officially appointed defense counsel. He has, therefore, represented me in good faith.

There was dead silence, then a ripple of laughter and an outward rush of the press. Lawrence announced that the session was adjourned, and the Tribunal retired. The following morning, with no further analysis of the matter, the Tribunal announced that "the defendant Hess is capable of standing his trial at the present time," the motion of his counsel was denied, and the trial would proceed.

The Tribunal's decision resolved the issue of whether or not Hess would be tried. But it did not put an end to the questions of whether or not he was sane, or had amnesia, or should not have been tried. Dr. Douglas Kelley, the prison psychiatrist, thought that Hess's performance was "a typical dramatic, hysterical gesture, which confirmed my opinions and those of the consulting psychiatrists"—to wit, that despite denials Hess had in fact been suffering from amnesia rooted in hysteria. Dr. Gilbert attributed Hess's insistence on being tried to a hysterical fear of being separated from his fellow defendants. Hess himself sought praise for his action, and his memory and general mental condition temporarily improved.

Questions such as whether Hess was insane under British law and whether his amnesia was feigned or genuine, were beyond my ken. The Albrecht episode appeared to have caught him off his guard, but as a lawyer I felt that the relevant questions were whether it would appear fair to put him on trial and whether his behavior in the dock would comport with the dignity of the proceeding. I certainly did not regard Hess's own statement as providing an answer to these questions. Indeed, if the book had already been written, I would have thought of Joseph Heller's *Catch-22*, one theme of which was that "if he says he's sane, he must be crazy." As the trial went on, his behavior gradually convinced me that the answer to both questions should have been negative.

For political reasons, these considerations were academic. The judges and senior prosecutors all knew that the Russians were out to "get" Hess. Once the doctors had found him sane, it was clear that dismissing him from the trial would have prompted Stalin to revive his accusations that Britain (and now her allies) were coddling and shielding Hess, who had flown to England to forge an alliance against the Soviet Union. As a result of Soviet enmity, for more than forty years until his death, Hess was a prisoner for life under the Tribunal's judgment. Alfried Krupp had all the luck, Rudolf Hess had none.

5

The first two weeks of the trial also witnessed the final rupture between Jackson and General Donovan and the general's departure from the Nuremberg scene.

The general had certainly not been acting like a team member. I never saw him in the courtroom, and I doubt that he ever attended a public session of the Tribunal. He asked Calvocoressi to his office, but treated him with manifest hostility, probably because of Peter's connection with the General Staff indictment. He summoned Bernard Meltzer, of Shea's staff, asked him what the economic group's "best" pieces of evidence were, and then called for Meltzer's opinion on how the presentation of the American case should be divided among the senior lawyers—a question which Meltzer (then a naval lieutenant, junior grade) could not have answered with either propriety or adequate knowledge.

The friction between Donovan and Jackson early in November had not diminished Donovan's belief that the prosecution should call witnesses, and most of his activities continued to be directed to that end. He was privately seeking prominent German witnesses who would testify against one or more of the defendants. These included defendants who would testify against other defendants, and it was this feature of his actions which led Jackson to lower the boom.

My suspicion that Donovan was trying to turn some of the German generals into witnesses against Keitel and Jodl was sound. He had been in touch with what he called the "Brauchitsch Group" and had secured Jackson's permission to allow it to submit a statement in behalf of the German Army. Dated November 19, 1945, it was signed by Field Marshal Walter von Brauchitsch (Commander in Chief of the German Army, 1938–41), Field Marshal Erich von Manstein (perhaps the ablest German field commander of World War II), General Franz Halder (Chief of the Army General Staff, 1938–42), and two generals of lesser rank. Their document proved worthless for Donovan's purpose, as he himself saw, since it pointed the finger of blame for Germany's sorry state at Hitler and away from the army, and attributed no individual responsibility to Keitel or Jodl.

Early in November, Donovan attended interrogations of Schacht and of Goering. Apparently as a result, Donovan received from Schacht a letter dated November 14, 1945, reading in part as follows:

> I am among the few people who have watched and gone through the frightful events of the last twelve years in Germany and with open eyes. Thanks to my official position I think I know more of the background of Hitler's policy than many others.
>
> I welcome the installation of the International Military Tribunal, the competence of which nobody can doubt. . . .
>
> I would therefore be very grateful, if an officer of your high standing . . . would be willing to look into a brief summary of the underlying reasons and conditions of the dreadful Nazi regime, as I have perceived them.

The same day, Donovan sent a memorandum to Jackson, which began:

> I have carefully gone over the briefs and proofs on the Schacht matter. . . . Schacht made possible the rearmament project. It was his support in financial matters that strengthened Hitler's position. Aided by influences and what he should have known about Hitler's character, we may have enough to hold him for aggressive war. There is strong argument in this.

Donovan then referred to several mitigating factors: Schacht's breach with Hitler, his relations with the resistance movement and eventual commitment to a concentration camp, his close relations with the American Embassy staff in Berlin, and his giving the embassy "advance notice of the attack on Russia." Then he added:

> In view of all this I return to the suggestion that consideration be given to the possibility of giving him the opportunity to fight his way out by actual testimony dealing with the facts. He could strengthen the case considerably and without promises he could be given the chance in the direct case to state his position. As I have already told you there have come certain suggestions that he would like to talk with me. If anything develops I will let you know.

Goering, too, had sensed that Donovan was approachable, and the general had discussed with Dr. Stahmer his client's "attitude" about testifying. Their dealings became known among the defense lawyers. Dr. Victor von der Lippe, assisting Dr. Walter Siemers in the defense of Raeder, kept a diary, in which he recorded on November 23:

> Among the American prosecutors General Donovan . . . played a special role. A lawyer by profession, during the War he was head of

the American military intelligence system. The relations between Donovan and the Chief Prosecutor Jackson were very tense. From an apparently well informed source it was heard that Donovan had a very different plan for the trial than Jackson and his men. He had the intention of making Goering, second man in the Third Reich, a privileged witness for the prosecution, and giving him opportunity . . . to save his head. Goering, in discussion with Donovan, accepted this plan. The plan collapsed because of Jackson's opposition. . . . Also as regards the handling of . . . the greater part of the military, Donovan had his own opinions.

While Donovan was putting out these feelers toward Schacht and Goering, he fell into controversy with Amen, who was preparing to call as a prosecution witness General Erwin Lahousen, an Austrian Army intelligence officer who, after Austria was annexed in 1938, was commissioned in the German Army and assigned to the Abwehr, the German military intelligence service headed by Admiral Wilhelm Canaris. Many of the officers in this agency were hostile to the Hitler regime and involved to some degree in the German resistance.

Several years prior to the war, Donovan had become acquainted with a German lawyer, Paul Leverkuehn, who like Donovan had connections with the intelligence world. During the war, Canaris put Leverkuehn in charge of Abwehr activities in Turkey, where Canaris appears to have had some contacts with an American assistant naval attaché in Istanbul, George Earle.* As head of the OSS, Donovan must have known of Leverkuehn's Abwehr activities, and after the war brought him to Nuremberg as a consultant. The general may also have had prior information about Lahousen, but in any event became interested in him at Nuremberg, where Lahousen was staying in the prosecution's "guest house," despite the fact that he was a prisoner of war.

Leverkuehn was also billeted there, and on November 22, on Donovan's instructions, he invited Lahousen to dine that evening at the general's house. Lahousen had been requested to remain available for "work" that evening with Richard Sonnenfeldt, an able interpreter whom Amen used for the most important interrogations. However, Donovan's rank and Leverkuehn's assurance that "he would straighten out" the problem with Sonnenfeldt persuaded Lahousen to accept the invitation.

The affair appears to have been casual rather than conspiratorial, for Donovan was not at dinner, and when he later arrived he said nothing to Lahousen except hello and good-bye. The others present were four ladies (of whom one was Donovan's daughter), an American naval lieutenant, and Ralph Albrecht, who asked Lahousen a few questions about Canaris.

*Former Governor of Pennsylvania and Ambassador to Bulgaria (January 1940–December 1941).

Innocuous the occasion may have been, but Amen was enraged that Sonnenfeldt's appointment with Lahousen had been trumped and suspected that Donovan was trying to steal his star witness. He sharply cross-examined the unhappy Lahousen, who was far from well, and then complained to Jackson.

The result was a Jackson memorandum, addressed to Donovan and the other senior staff lawyers, which, after referring to "Matters which I think may cause criticism, and confusion in reference to high-ranking prisoners of war," laid down new regulations obviously aimed at Donovan's activities. No persons, other than guards and staff, were to be billeted with prisoners of war; no member of Jackson's staff should entertain a prisoner of war socially; witnesses could be interrogated "only by persons authorized in writing to do so"; no promise or intimation of leniency should be made to any defendant or his counsel "under any circumstances whatever"; and

> No agreement shall be made with any defense council on behalf of this office for the use by the United States of any defendant as a witness except upon written authorization. It will be the general policy that no defendant will be used as a witness for the prosecution who does not in advance make a written and signed statement incriminating other defendants against whom other evidence in our possession is deemed weak or insufficient to establish guilt.

If Donovan was upset by this sharp rebuff, he did not show it, and he continued to press the proposal of Goering as a witness. He immediately dispatched a reply memorandum pointing out that copies of letters to him from Schacht and Goering had already been sent to Jackson.* Donovan wrote that he had refused to see Schacht "until he made clear what he was prepared to do." Goering, in contrast, "has offered to testify before the Tribunal" and "in interviews with him he has already incriminated certain of the defendants." The general declared that he did not want to press Jackson for a decision on the Goering project until he had in hand "a full written question and answer statement containing the necessary safeguards usually surrounding a confession." In order to obtain such a document:

> I suggest that you [Jackson] request Security Control that the defendant Goering be made available beginning on Sunday afternoon, 25 November and thereafter as required. It is not my wish to see him except with his own counsel, who is anxious that I should continue to see him.
> This is damn hard work and if he is to be ready the present momentum must not be lost.

---

*The collection of Jackson-Donovan documents which Jackson later sent to Truman did not contain the letter from Goering, and I have not found it elsewhere.

Up to this time, Jackson had not replied directly to Donovan's proposals for testimony by Schacht or Goering. But the Lahousen-Leverkuehn episode, simultaneous with Donovan's memorandum on Goering, triggered Jackson's decision to bring matters to a head by excluding Donovan from participation in the trial. The virtual dismissal was accomplished by a letter dated November 26, 1945. After mentioning long-standing differences of opinion about the General Staff indictment and reliance on documentary rather than testimonial evidence, Jackson turned to recent matters and the conclusion he had drawn from them:

> In short, I do not think we can afford to negotiate with any of these defendants or their counsel for testimony. . . . To use one of them ourselves will create the impression that there was some kind of a bargain about his testimony, opening the door for that defendant to plead for leniency on the ground he was "helpful" and may give a background for claims that promises were made to that effect. My view is, therefore, that we should prove our case against these defendants with no use of them as witnesses. . . .
>
> Partly because of this feeling, perhaps, but also for other reasons, I disapprove the use being made of the German lawyer Leverkuehn. You told me you were consulting with him and to that I saw no objection. But Saturday [the 24th] I learned he is living in the house with some of our prisoner of war witnesses with whom Amen has been working under my instructions. Apparently on your behalf, Leverkuehn was extending one of them social entertainment at a time when Amen had an appointment to complete his written statement and Leverkuehn assumed to set aside Amen's instructions to Lahousen. . . . Leverkuehn must get out of these billets and out of Nuremberg. His presence here will cause trouble as sure as night follows day. . . .
>
> Frankly, Bill, your views and mine appear to be so far apart that I do not consider it possible to assign to you examination or cross-examination of witnesses.
>
> Therefore, I did not respond to your request for access to Goering. I repeat that time may prove you right and me wrong. I do not claim any great wisdom in so novel and complex a matter. I only have responsibility.

On the twenty-seventh Donovan wrote his final letter to Jackson, comprising a point-by-point reply to Jackson's complaints. With regard to Leverkuehn, he remarked that Jackson and Amen had been told "all I know about him," that both of them thought Leverkuehn "would be useful and he has been," and that Jackson's criticism "might in fairness be deferred until you know the facts." In conclusion he wrote:

It is true that I have frequently told you squarely and honestly that (1) the case needed centralized administrative control. (2) that there was a lack of intellectual direction. (3) that it was not handled as an entity. (4) that because it was a lawsuit plus something else it needed an affirmative human aspect with German as well as foreign witnesses.

I never knew there was ever disagreement on these points.

As I told you several weeks ago I am leaving within a few days. Time will not be concerned with our opinions—right or wrong.

The general was as good as his word. The following day he paid farewell visits, including one to Biddle, to whom he described the prosecution's case as "confused and flat from so much paper evidence" and related his efforts to persuade Jackson to call Goering, who "would come through." By the end of the month Donovan was gone.°

The press reported Donovan's departure, and some of the British newspapers, which had become increasingly critical of the American prosecution's performance, put the blame on Jackson. But neither of the men had much to say publicly about the affair. Jackson could reap no benefit from evidence of dissension in his staff, nor could Donovan by revealing that he had been fired.

Because of Donovan's political and military eminence and the help he had given the prosecution in its early stages, it is probable that Jackson approached the showdown point with caution. No doubt the acclaim that followed his opening statement gave him added courage, but after he had shown the general the door he feared repercussions and found it wise to write a letter to President Truman, attaching copies of the relevant documents. After describing the trial as "going very well," which at that point many would have disputed, Jackson wrote:

> One matter that I think you should be informed about is the departure of General Donovan. . . . In the early stages of the case, General Donovan personally was very helpful. He then took a long trip to China during which he was entirely out of touch with the case. Since he came back, his ideas and mine of handling the case were far apart. They were so far apart that I had to tell him I would not put him on the floor to conduct any part of the case. . . .
>
> I am sure I have made a good many mistakes here, but this is not one of them.

The President sent Jackson's letter to the State Department with no written comment other than that it was "self-explanatory."

---

°Murray Gurfein left at the same time, but whether it was in concert with Donovan, or because Jackson had assigned him no courtroom role, I do not know.

In my opinion Jackson was quite right in his last statement. Although I was in general agreement with Donovan's view that the American case should include witnesses, his proposals with regard to Goering and Schacht were ill conceived and dangerous. Each of the two would gladly have seen the other boiled in oil, and if called by the prosecution each would have tried to strip the other of whatever shreds of credibility he still retained. Efforts to tie them down to prepared question-and-answer statements would have collapsed under the pressure of cross-examination, and reliance on prior undertakings by Goering would have been about as sensible as entering into a no-first-strike treaty with a cobra.

But the issue lay deeper than the hatred between Goering and Schacht. With Hitler, Himmler, and Goebbels dead, Goering was the surviving leader and symbol of Nazism. To put him forward as the man who could tell the truth about the Third Reich and lay bare the guilt of its leaders, as Donovan appeared to expect, was nothing short of ludicrous. To his fellow defendants and everyone else Goering had made it clear that his aim was to defend the record of the Nazi years and discredit the trial, to the best of his ability.

"Set a thief to catch a thief" may be a useful tactic for a district attorney fighting gangland. But summoning Goering to speak, in any other role than that of an accused murderer being given the opportunity to defend himself, could have no place in an avowedly idealistic proceeding dedicated to the future peace of the world and the advancement of international human rights.

## 6

On the afternoon of November 29, when Alderman had finished his presentation of documents on the annexation of Austria, there was an abrupt change in the nature and subject matter of the proceeding. Despite the evidentiary importance and intrinsic interest of Alderman's documents and commentary, even Storey saw that there could be too much of a good thing.

What came next was dictated not by logic but by felt necessity. James Donovan had a chillingly graphic film of German concentration camps ready for showing, and Amen had Lahousen ready to take the stand. Neither film nor witness had much to do with initiating aggressive war, but the umbrella of conspiracy was large enough to cover both.

Donovan explained that the film "has been compiled from motion pictures taken by Allied military photographers as the Allied armies in the West liberated the areas in which these camps were located." The narration, he stated, was "taken directly from the reports of the military photographers who filmed the camps."

Dachau, Buchenwald, and Bergen-Belsen were shown in the condition that American and British troops found them. Even for those who, like me, had had an earlier viewing, these pictures were hard to bear. The defendants were among the many who had not seen them, and the effect was stunning. The frightful condition of the living and the cascade of naked corpses pushed by bulldozers into an immense burial ditch, were wrenching sights. Dr. von der Lippe recorded that the film would rob its viewers of sleep and that he had heard one of the defense counsel say it had become intolerable to sit in the same room with men like Kaltenbrunner and Frank. Schacht turned his back on the screen to show that he had had no connection with such bestiality; Goering tried to brazen it out; the weaker ones like Ribbentrop, Frank, and Funk appeared shattered.

Dr. Gilbert, who from time to time passed information about the defendants to Jackson, made a round of the cells that evening. Schacht and Doenitz were highly indignant that they had been obliged to sit through a public showing of despicable actions with which, in their view, they had nothing to do. Raeder declared that he "had hardly heard of concentration camps before." Frank, Funk, and Fritzsche were weeping tears of shame and fear; Sauckel and Ribbentrop were also deeply stricken. The others were in better self-command, but visibly depressed. Goering, who had succeeded in raising a laugh earlier in the session when Alderman read transcripts of Goering's telephone conversations during the Austrian take-over, lamented that "then they showed that awful film, and it just spoiled everything."

The public showing of the film certainly hardened sentiment against the defendants generally, but it contributed little to the determination of their individual guilt. Lahousen's testimony the next day was more particularly targeted.

Tall, painfully thin, bald, and bony-faced, Lahousen appeared a walking skeleton as he entered the witness box. But physical frailty was not reflected in the tone or content of his testimony. Amen conducted the direct examination competently, and Lahousen made a strong impression on his audience. His evidence was disquieting to many of the defendants, especially Keitel and Ribbentrop, his principal targets.

As head of the Abwehr, Admiral Canaris was, next to Keitel, the senior staff officer of OKW, Hitler's personal headquarters, as Commander in Chief of the Wehrmacht. Canaris had taken a strong liking to Lahousen, whom he appointed one of his four section chiefs—surprising preferment to an officer only recently transferred from the Austrian Army. But Canaris apparently trusted him completely and took him to a number of high-level conferences in which Keitel and other generals and Cabinet ministers, and occasionally Hitler, participated.

Canaris kept a diary which included descriptions of these conferences. It has disappeared, perhaps destroyed by his jailers near the end of the war.

But when Lahousen was present at these meetings, he made notes for inclusion in the diary, and he had retained copies of them. They had suffered damage, but a number of them remained legible and furnished the basis of his Nuremberg testimony. Because of their sporadic nature, the notes do not establish a narrative. They are episodic, and Lahousen's testimony based on them was unorganized, consisting as it does of Amen's selections from the diary notes and Lahousen's recollections.

The witness's most damaging evidence related to a series of meetings in or near Keitel's railroad car in Poland on September 12, 1939, during the German invasion of Poland, and at a time when her total defeat appeared certain. Lahousen testified that, in the presence of Keitel and Ribbentrop,

> Canaris very urgently warned against the measures which had come to his knowledge, namely the proposed shootings and extermination measures directed particularly against the Polish intelligentsia, the nobility, the clergy, and in fact all elements which could be regarded as leaders of a national resistance. Canaris said at the time—I [Lahousen] am quoting his approximate words: "One day the world will also hold the Wehrmacht, under whose eyes these events occurred, responsible for such methods."
>
> The Chief of the OKW [Keitel] replied—and this is also based on my notes, which I re-read a few days ago—that these things had been decided by the Fuehrer, . . . [who] had let it be known that, should the Armed Forces be unwilling to carry through these measures . . . they would have to accept the presence at their side of the SS, the SIPO [Security Police] and similar units who would carry them through. . . . [Keitel] used an expression which was certainly derived from Hitler and which characterized these measures as "political housecleaning." . . . According to the Chief of the OKW, the bombardment of Warsaw and the shooting of the categories of people which I mentioned before had been agreed upon already.

In reply to a question from Amen, Lahousen specified these "categories" as "Mainly the Polish intelligentsia, the nobility, the clergy, and, of course, the Jews."

Keitel next ordered Canaris to put into execution a directive from Ribbentrop "to instigate in the Galician Ukraine an uprising aimed at the extermination of Jews and Poles." Canaris, Lahousen, and Ribbentrop then left the railway car and had a short talk during which Ribbentrop repeated the instruction that "The uprising should be so staged that all farms and dwellings of the Poles would go up in flames, and all Jews be killed."

Subsequently, Lahousen testified about an order from Keitel to Canaris, which the admiral never carried out, to arrange the assassination of Marshal Maxime Weygand, Commander in Chief of the Allied forces during the last days of the Battle of France and subsequently Governor-General in Algeria. Some months later, Keitel gave Canaris a comparable order for the assassination of General Henri Giraud, who had been captured during the German attack in northern France and, after a dramatic escape from Koenigstein prison, reached southern France, which was not yet under German occupation. In both cases the purpose of the assassination was to eliminate a potential leader of the French Resistance.

More important for the prosecution was Lahousen's description of a meeting in the summer of 1941, during the early stages of the German invasion of the Soviet Union, when the German forces were capturing hundreds of thousands (and eventually millions) of prisoners. As Canaris's representative, Lahousen attended a conference called by General Reinecke, chief of the division of OKW responsible for, among other duties, the supervision of prisoner-of-war matters. The other participants were Heinrich Mueller, Chief of the Gestapo, and Colonel Breyer, of Reinecke's prisoner-of-war section.

The purpose of the meeting was to present the orders which had been issued for the treatment of Soviet prisoners. Reinecke first explained:

> The war between Germany and Russia is not a war between the two states or two armies, but between two ideologies—namely, the National Socialist and the Bolshevist ideology. The Red Army must be looked upon not as a soldier in the sense of the word applying to our western opponents, but as an ideological enemy. He must be regarded as the archenemy of National Socialism, and must be treated accordingly.

Reinecke added that these ideas must be made plain to the German officer corps, "since they were apparently still entertaining ideas which belonged to the Ice Age and not to the present age of National Socialism." On the basis of this philosophy, the new orders provided that immediately after capture all Soviet "commissars" should be killed and that thereafter, under a "special selection program of the SD," all those prisoners should be killed who "could be identified as thoroughly bolshevized or as active representatives of the Bolshevist ideology." The distinction between the two categories was made because the "commissars," who were at once fighting soldiers in Soviet military uniform and Communist Party members responsible for ensuring the loyalty and stimulating the determination of the troops, wore red armbands identifying them as "commissars."

Lahousen also testified to the terrible conditions, deliberately fostered by the OKW, under which Soviet prisoners were held—without shelter, food, or medical care—with the result that they died literally by the millions. All these orders and practices were, of course, flagrant and gross violations of the Hague and Geneva conventions, to which Germany, like virtually all other sovereign nations, had subscribed. They might have been understandable in the days of the Crusades against the Infidel, but in the Civil War days would have scandalized Francis Lieber and the soldiers of that time. Even Napoleon had sought to make a case for the legality of his 1799 massacre of the Mamelukes.

Soon we had our first opportunity to see how our German opponents would fare as cross-examiners, a role to which they were little accustomed. Not surprisingly, the most protracted cross-examinations were by the lawyers for Keitel and Ribbentrop. Dr. Otto Nelte, for Keitel, made the usual beginner's mistake of asking long, complex questions which did not pin the witness down to a single point, or which raised new issues to which the witness's answers might be unfavorable. For example, Nelte did his client little good by trying to get Lahousen to say that Keitel had never given his staff instructions about political rather than military matters. The answer he drew was that Keitel had made it clear at OKW staff meetings that only dedicated Nazi officers were welcome there.

Dr. Sauter, for Ribbentrop, asked even longer questions and made absolutely no headway with the witness. Furthermore, he made himself ridiculous by asking Lahousen whether he had reported to the police the "murderous" orders Canaris had been given by Keitel. Dr. von der Lippe recorded that "Ribbentrop and especially Goering were visibly angered by this type of questioning and wanted to put questions to the witness themselves." And indeed, after the cross-examinations were concluded, Dr. Stahmer requested the Tribunal to rule that the defendants could personally question witnesses. Although the Charter, in particular Section 16(e), was susceptible to this interpretation, after a short recess the judges—no doubt moved both by the fact that none of their own legal systems recognized any such procedure and by concern that Goering might exploit such an opportunity to seize the spotlight—rejected Stahmer's request.

Of the other defense counsel, only Dr. Kubuschok, for Papen, accomplished anything for his client. In response to Kubuschok's commendably brief questions, Lahousen gave his opinion that Papen had shared Canaris's negative attitude toward Hitler's war policies and violent methods and had sought to "exercise a mitigating influence."

Coming on the heels of the concentration camp film, Lahousen's testimony about the Nazis' murderous policies in Poland and with regard to Soviet prisoners of war was another heavy shock to the defense. Dr. Gilbert found Goering "fuming" and denouncing the witness: "That traitor! That's one we forgot on the 20th of July!° Hitler was right—the Abwehr was a

---

°Goering was referring to the unsuccessful military attempt to assassinate Hitler on July 20, 1944, and the subsequent executions of many of the participants and suspects, including Canaris and several other Abwehr officers.

traitor's organization!" Jodl was also critical, but equally unable to challenge the truth of Lahousen's accusations. Keitel was beginning to feel contrite: "I don't know what to say—that Giraud affair—well, I knew that was coming up, but what can I say? . . . I don't care if they accuse me of starting the war—I was only doing my duty and following orders—But these assassination stories—I don't know how I ever got mixed up in this thing." From the prosecution's standpoint, Lahousen the witness was a success.

Two days later, Alderman's presentation of the aggressive war documentation was again interrupted so that Sir Hartley Shawcross might open the case for the British prosecution. Sir Hartley was a strikingly handsome man in his early forties. He cut a fine figure at the lectern, displayed a well-controlled vocal delivery, and his text was well organized and crisply written.

The Attorney General started by stressing the value of the trial itself:

> There are those who would perhaps say that these wretched men should have been dealt with summarily without trial by "executive action." . . . But that was not the view of the British Government. Not so would the rule of law be raised and strengthened on the international as well as upon the municipal plane; . . . not so would the world be made aware that the waging of aggressive war is not only a dangerous venture but a criminal one.

That was very true, but coming from Shawcross it sounded hollow to those who knew the background of that issue—that the British government, including Clement Attlee (Shawcross's Labour Party chief) as well as Churchill and Eden, had held out for "executive action" right up to the San Francisco Conference, when it finally gave way when confronted with the combined opposition of the American, Soviet, and French governments.

Shawcross then defined his task as presentation of "the case on Count Two of the Indictment" and stated that his address would comprise two parts: demonstration of "the nature and basis of the Crime against Peace," which consists of "waging wars of aggression and in violation of treaties," and proof "that such wars were waged by these defendants."

In accordance with this prospectus, the first third of Shawcross's address comprised a carefully prepared argument that beginning with the establishment of the League of Nations in 1920, the "statesmen of the world deliberately set out to make wars of aggression an international crime" and carried out that intention "in numerous treaties, in governmental pronouncements, and in the declarations of statesmen in the period preceding the Second World War." He mentioned the numerous intergovernmental treaties of nonaggression, the Geneva Protocol of 1925, the Locarno Treaty of 1925, and, of course, the Kellogg-Briand Pact of 1928, stressing the frequency of German participation in such agreements and declarations. Shawcross thus laid the basis for his conclusion that: "International law had already, before the [London] Charter was adopted, constituted aggressive war a criminal act." Accordingly, there was "no substantial retroactivity"—i.e., no element of ex post facto—in enforcing the Charter's condemnation of crimes against peace.

The balance of Sir Hartley's presentation was not intrinsically different from what Sidney Alderman had been doing—that is, reading and commenting on captured documents which portrayed the intentions, plans, and actions constituting Hitler's aggressive wars. The pace was much quicker because Shawcross did not offer any documents in evidence and read only those parts that were most striking.

Thus, hitting the highlights, Shawcross covered the invasions of Poland, Denmark and Norway, the Low Countries, Greece, Yugoslavia, and the Soviet Union. He closed with a fine peroration:

> The governments of the United Kingdom and the British Commonwealth, of the United States of America, of the Union of Soviet Socialist Republics, and of France, backed by and on behalf of every other peaceloving nation of the world, have therefore joined to bring the inventors and perpetrators of this Nazi conception of international relationship before the bar of this Tribunal. They do so, that these defendants may be punished for their crimes. They do so, also, that their conduct may be exposed in all its naked wickedness and they do so in the hope that the conscience and good sense of all the world will see the consequences of such conduct and the end to which inevitably it must lead. Let us once again restore sanity and with it also the sanctity of our obligations toward each other.

There were a few tender spots in Sir Hartley's reckoning of responsibility. One was the Anglo-German Naval Treaty of 1935 (which he did not mention), wherein Britain acquiesced in Germany's violation of the Versailles Treaty. Another was the Munich Agreement of September 29, 1938, under which Britain and France sacrificed Czechoslovakia in the vain hope of propitiating the Nazi dictator. Shawcross rather ambivalently attributed Munich to "the love of peace, the lack of preparedness, the patience, the cowardice—call it what you will—of the democratic powers."

With Russians both on the bench and at the bar, a very ticklish matter was the Hitler-Stalin Pact, which had immediately preceded the attack on Poland and insured Hitler, for the time being, against a two-front war with major powers. Jackson, in his opening statement, had made a passing reference to the Hitler-Stalin Pact as "a deceitful, delaying peace with Russia." In the draft of his speech previously circulated to the other chief prosecutors, Shawcross, thinking to give the Russians an out, had attributed Stalin's action to Hitler's false assurances of future peace and friendship. Instead, Rudenko, highly indignant, had rushed to Jackson's office and urged that Shawcross be requested to delete what Rudenko regarded as insulting to his government which, he insisted, was all along that Hitler intended the Soviet Union no good. Jackson, amused but anxious to preserve the peace, called Shawcross and told him that the Russians "didn't mind being called knaves as long as they weren't called fools." Shawcross thereupon deleted the offending passage and made no mention of the pact.

Sir Hartley's toughest problem, however, involved the charge that Germany had initiated aggressive war against Norway. As he acknowledged, there were widespread contentions that Germany had invaded that country only because "Britain and France were themselves making plans to invade and occupy Norway and . . . the Government of Norway was prepared to acquiesce in such an event." Shawcross stated:

> I do not propose to argue the question whether or not these allegations were true or false. That question is irrelevant to the issues before this Court. Even if the allegations were true—and they were patently false—they would afford no conceivable justification for the [German] action of invading without warning, without declaration of war, without any attempt at mediation or conciliation.

Shawcross sought to buttress this position by referring to German documents establishing the dates and other circumstances surrounding Hitler's decision to invade and occupy Norway. These documents, he declared, proved that the German invasion was not undertaken for the purpose of forestalling a British action in Norway. But he said nothing about what Britain's aims and acts vis-à-vis Norway were at that time. This failure left a gap in Shawcross's analysis, for if Britain was indeed on the point of landing troops in Norway as a means of waging war against Germany, it could hardly be argued that Germany had no right to take countervailing measures. And later disclosures of British plans and actions raised questions that are far from simple.

But these matters detracted little from an otherwise excellent performance. Sir Hartley's address was of high professional quality and reflected great credit on him and his colleagues.

## 7

Sidney Alderman had resumed his presentation of the aggressive war conspiracy documents on the day (December 3) between Lahousen's testimony and Sir Hartley's opening, and he continued in the afternoon of December

4 after Sir Hartley had finished and into the following morning, completing the documents relating to the dismemberment and subsequent annexation of Czechoslovakia. The documentation of this subject was exceptionally full and vivid because Hitler's military adjutant, Lieutenant Colonel Rudolf Schmundt, had kept an extensive file of memoranda, orders, and conference minutes leading to the mobilization of the Wehrmacht and its deployment on Czechoslovakia's borders. These preparations culminated in Hitler's order to invade that country at the end of September 1938—an attack which was forestalled by the Munich Agreement and followed six months later by the annexation of Bohemia and Moravia and domination of a nominally independent Slovakia.

At this point, pursuant to the agreement reached between the British and American delegations on November 7, Alderman relinquished the lectern to Fyfe. Sir David informed the Tribunal that his delegation would call no witnesses. He himself would describe the treaty obligations into which Germany had entered and which had been breached by the Wehrmacht's attacks and invasions. The plans which led to the aggressive wars launched by the Third Reich would then be described, with supporting documentation, by other members of the British delegation.

Except that British replaced American English, the trial process continued virtually unchanged. Fyfe's description and analysis of the violated treaties, which took only half of the day (December 5), was competent and there was no way it could have been made dramatic.

Sir David was followed at the lectern by one of the British junior barristers, Mervyn Griffith-Jones, a decorated officer of the Coldstream Guards and a handsome young upper-class Englishman who spoke and moved as if he had been born in a dress shirt and high stiff collar. His task was to present the documentation on the attack against Poland. The most striking documents had already been read by Sir Hartley Shawcross, but there was additional material of considerable interest which was well presented. The Guards officer was generally dispassionate, but permitted himself one touch of color by describing Hitler's letter to Neville Chamberlain on the evening before the attack, which declared that "the German government have never had any intention of touching Poland's vital interests," as sounding "like the letters of some common swindler rather than of the government of a great nation."

My friend Major Elwyn Jones then made his debut at the lectern to document the invasion and occupation of Norway and Denmark, a subject which particularly implicated Raeder and Rosenberg in the early stages and subsequently Keitel and Jodl. Jones pointed out that

> The Norwegian invasion is, in one respect, not a typical Nazi aggression in that Hitler had to be persuaded to embark upon it. The

chief instruments of persuasion were Raeder and Rosenberg; Raeder because he thought Norway strategically important and because he coveted glory for the Navy; Rosenberg because of his political connections in Norway which he sought to develop.

As the Tribunal will shortly see, in the Norwegian Vidkun Quisling, the defendant Rosenberg found a very model of the Fifth Column agent, the very personification of perfidy.

And, indeed, Quisling's name soon became the international byword for a traitor. Jones's documentation traced the process by which Raeder and Rosenberg, turning Quisling's treason to their purposes, persuaded Hitler to embrace their view that a German occupation of Norway was necessary to secure northern bases for air and naval operations; to protect the flow of Swedish iron ore, which in winter came to Germany by way of Narvik and Norwegian coastal waters; and to protect against the possibility of an Allied occupation of Norway's Atlantic coast. Denmark was included in the operation in order to protect Germany's line of communications with Norway.

In personal style, Elwyn Jones was as relaxed and easygoing as Griffith-Jones was stiff and formal. Elwyn's presentation was well organized and his documentation unassailable, but, following Shawcross's line, he made no mention of Britain's contemporaneous role vis-à-vis Norway.

The mountainous Khaki Roberts, despite his years of court experience and rank (he was the only King's Counsel other than Shawcross and Fyfe and was listed in the British delegation as "Leading Counsel"), did not fare so well as his juniors. Actually, his task was too simple to be interesting, for plainly the Low Countries—Belgium, the Netherlands, and Luxembourg— were not Hitler's real targets and were overrun only to field the German deployment against France and to procure air and naval bases along the North Sea coast in order to threaten Britain and defend the Reich against British air attack.

There was ample documentation to establish these military purposes, which Roberts had only to read. But Khaki could not shake off his overbearing Old Bailey manner. Furthermore, he addressed every paragraph and sometimes every sentence to "My Lord" or "My Lords," which irritated the bench, and when he characterized the Germans' actions as those of "the common criminal"—which Griffith-Jones had done with impunity—Lawrence admonished him: "Mr. Roberts, I think we would like you so far as possible to confine yourself to the documents."

Last came Colonel Harry Phillimore, to deal with the invasion and occupation of Yugoslavia and Greece in the spring of 1941. This, too, was an easy assignment, for the documentation clearly disclosed the reasons for these actions and the preparations which were made. Mussolini, jealous of his fellow dictator's military triumphs, had attacked Greece in October

1940, but soon was getting the worst of the encounter. This development increased the possibility that Britain might send forces into Greece and thus establish a base for operations in southeastern Europe. Hitler therefore planned to come to Mussolini's aid by mobilizing a large German force in Romania which could cross Bulgaria and invade Greece from the north in the spring of 1941. The situation became more complex late in March, when a political coup in Yugoslavia produced a government less favorably inclined toward Nazi Germany, and Hitler at once decided to occupy that country as well as Greece. The invasions of both countries were launched, without warning, on April 6, 1941.

Thus the British completed their portion of the case for the prosecution in less than four days of court time. It was a neat piece of work, and the judges were favorably impressed. Judge Birkett entered in his trial notebook an assessment of his compatriots:

> Shawcross made good opening speech. . . . I think Shawcross is marked for high distinction. David Maxwell Fyfe . . . presented a dull section with lucidity. . . . G. D. Roberts did not shine. Griffith-Jones and Elwyn Jones were good: Phillimore I thought good. . . . Biddle said that Elwyn Jones was always relevant and lucid and was of great assistance to the Tribunal. He said to me it was the best presentation we have yet heard.

Alderman then resumed the lectern to present the documents concerning Hitler's decision to invade the Soviet Union and the preparations for the attack, launched in July 1941. This was a much larger and more complex undertaking than any of the other Nazi aggrandizements, for it envisaged not only military defeat of the Soviet forces, but also (as in the much smaller case of Poland) destruction of the government itself and permanent occupation and exploitation of huge areas, embracing all Soviet territory west of the Urals and perhaps beyond. Not only the military defendants but also most of the others were involved to a greater or lesser extent. The documentation was extensive, and many of the individual items were lengthy. The Tribunal's ruling that only those portions read in court would be received in evidence was still in effect, so Alderman had a heavy load to carry.

After coping with this weighty subject, Alderman turned to "the final phase of the detailed presentation of the aggressive war part of the case": to wit, German collaboration with Japan in bringing about that country's attack against the United States, which led, four days after Pearl Harbor, to Germany's declaration of war against the United States.

Alderman traced the German-Japanese connection from the Anti-Comintern Pact of 1936 through the formal alliance cemented by the Tripartite (Germany, Japan, and Italy) Pact of 1940. He read documents which conclusively established that Hitler urged the Japanese to join in the war against Britain and later to attack the Soviet Union. The documents also made it clear that both German and Japanese officials were aware that Japanese attacks against British bases in the Far East might well lead to war between Japan and the United States. But it was also plain that Hitler would have preferred to see Japan attack the Russians rather than draw the United States into the conflict.

Thus Hitler's declaration of war on December 11 was in compliance with commitments he had made to Japan rather than a matter of original preference. But it was a resort to hostilities in support of Japan's aggressive attack against both Britain and the United States, and in that sense Germany's action could be characterized as initiating an aggressive war, as the Tribunal ultimately found.

And so, at the end of the session on December 10, Alderman completed much the longest of the individual presentations to the Tribunal. It took over fifty hours of court time and covered the greater part of Count One of the Indictment, including what Jackson regarded as its most important charges.

Before Alderman began, Storey had told him to take no more than four hours. Alderman, who was taking his orders from Jackson, told Storey that such a limit was impossible and absurd. Storey, dismayed as Alderman went on from day to day, accosted him in a hallway: "Sidney, I had a plan—I had a plan—but the case has gone to Hell!" Alderman replied: "Your plan has gone just where it ought to have gone. But the case is in good shape, and is just now being set on ice."

Storey was furious, but Alderman was doing what Jackson wanted done. He was establishing documentary proof of a conspiracy embracing most of the defendants to plan and launch aggressive wars.

Necessarily, it took time—lots of time—to read and explain the documents so that the Tribunal might see and understand the force and continuity of the evidence. The presentation took much more time than it would have if there had been plenty of copies in their own language for German-speaking defendants and their lawyers, and for Russian- and French-speaking judges and prosecutors. But that was not Alderman's responsibility.

The press might and did complain of the lack of drama, but the case was being tried to the judges, not the press. Whatever others may have thought, the Tribunal was well pleased with Alderman's style and process. Biddle wrote to his wife:

> Last week following Jackson and Albrecht, Dodd put in a lot of
> trivial nonsense. Alderman has now begun presenting his case in a

first-rate lawyer-like brief. It is packed with interesting material from captured secret documents.

A recent book on the trial levels a vigorous attack on the American presentation of the aggressive war charges, contrasting it unfavorably with the British handling of the subject:

> The British case could be presented so quickly and clearly largely because the thinking behind it had been deliberately simple. . . . The British prosecutors had hardly discussed intentions; they had concentrated on plans which had actually been put into operation and the events which had resulted.
> In this the British approach was in stark contrast to that of the Americans. . . . The British stuck to documents and events that could not be contested; the Americans put heavy emphasis on documents open to challenge . . . the Hossbach memorandum in particular . . . [and] the Schmundt minutes of Hitler's conferences of 23 May 1939. . . .°

The book has many merits, but in this instance it is inaccurate and based on misunderstanding. The authors completely overlook the fact that the Americans were presenting evidence in support of Count One—conspiracy—and that specific *intention* or *purpose* to commit crime is an essential element of a criminal conspiracy. The British presented evidence in support of Count Two—initiating and waging wars of aggression and in violation of treaties—which requires no special proof of purpose and in any event can be inferred from the acts themselves. The difference can readily be seen in a case such as that of Schacht who, during the early years of the Nazi regime, provided Hitler with the financial basis for rearmament. But these acts would not support a charge of conspiracy unless Schacht acted with the *purpose* of enabling Hitler to launch aggressive wars.

Far from avoiding use of the documents cited by these authors, Shawcross relied upon and quoted from both of them in his opening statement, and Griffith-Jones likewise utilized the Schmundt minutes. In challenging the value of the Hossbach document, the authors declare that therein Hitler "had suggested 1943 as the earliest opportunity for aggression," when in fact Hitler said that Germany should strike "not later than 1943" and

---

°Ann and John Tusa, *The Nuremberg Trial* (1984), pp. 181–82. The Hossbach memorandum was a record by Hitler's military aide, Colonel Friedrich Hossbach, describing a November 1937 meeting of Hitler and the highest military and diplomatic officials, at which Hitler discussed plans and prospects for German territorial aggrandizement. The Schmundt minutes were those of Hossbach's successor, Colonel Rudolf Schmundt, describing a meeting of Hitler and his highest military commanders at which they discussed the projected attack on Poland. There was no question of the authenticity of these documents, though question was raised by the defendants regarding the accuracy and significance of the Hossbach document.

speculated at length on the opportunities for war much sooner. As for the Schmundt minutes, the authors say that this document "existed in more than one version, with substantial discrepancies between them." That is not so; the authors confused it with several versions of a Hitler speech on a comparable occasion three months later.

As for "stark contrast" between the British and American presentations, there certainly was one insofar as the British took fewer than four court days, while Alderman took about twice that time. But the reason for this had nothing to do with a difference in "approach"; indeed, several American lawyers had assisted the British in preparing their presentations. The differences lay in the nature of their respective tasks.

Fyfe presented a compilation and exegesis of the violated treaties. Griffith-Jones, Elwyn Jones, Roberts, and Phillimore all dealt with the planning and execution of the actual attacks against particular countries. Apart from recapitulating the treaties involved, none of these presentations covered more than a few months, from inception of the intention to attack at a certain time to the attack itself. As far as "intention" was involved, the relevant documents spoke for themselves. The "simplicity" of the presentation was due not to a difference in method but to the simplicity of the British task itself.

That observation in no way involves criticism of the British lawyers' performance, for they did what they undertook with efficiency and dispatch. But it went only part of the way to proving the guilt of all or most of the men in the dock. The British presentations heavily implicated Ribbentrop, Keitel, Rosenberg, Raeder, and Jodl and touched, though rather lightly, Goering and Doenitz. But there the task stopped.

The ambit of Alderman's evidence was much broader, bringing in Goering, Papen, Neurath, and Seyss-Inquart during the prewar Nazi years and Goering, Keitel, Jodl, Rosenberg, Frick, Funk, Schirach, Fritzsche, and the accused organizations in connection with the invasion of the Soviet Union. The pre-1939 documentation was, of course, more remote in time from the war itself, and questions of individual intent to initiate aggressive wars inevitably arose—questions which were decisive in the cases of Schacht, Papen, and Fritzsche, all of whom were ultimately acquitted. These were the factors which explain the comparative length of Alderman's presentation.

Alderman was not a strong person physically or emotionally. He was very tired, and Jackson sent him home for a long rest. At Orly airport he ran into General Donovan, who sublimated his Nuremberg frustrations by a sneering reference to Alderman's total reliance on documents. Sidney did not return to Nuremberg until mid-January of 1946.

8

Alderman's presentation was followed on December 11 by the showing of a long documentary film which James Donovan offered in evidence under the title *The Nazi Plan*. He explained that it was a compilation of "films made by the Nazis themselves" which had been given continuity by their assemblage chronologically in four parts: the rise of the Nazi Party (1921–1933), the seizure of totalitarian power (1933–1935), preparing for wars of aggression (1935–1939), and wars of aggression (1939–1944). The film had been prepared by professional motion picture artists, including the screenwriter Budd Schulberg, and it incorporated excerpts from Leni Riefenstahl's *Triumph of the Will*.

Donovan presented the film on the basis that "it sums up the case thus far presented under Counts One and Two of the Indictment." That was true chronologically, but it would be hard to say that it added any new evidence of criminal guilt. However, the film portrayed the defendants, often in groups, in their public guise during the period of the conspiracy and perhaps added another dimension to the judges' mental pictures of the alleged conspirators.

The reaction of those conspirators surprised many of us. Far from viewing the film as another nail in their coffins, they enjoyed it hugely. Dr. von der Lippe wrote: "Goering was visibly delighted to see himself once more 'in the good old times,' Ribbentrop spoke of the gripping force of Hitler's personality, another defendant declared himself happy that the Tribunal would see him at least once in full uniform, and with the dignity of his office." That evening in the jail, Dr. Gilbert found Goering cocky and gloating over his own past accomplishments, Hess predicting that Germany would rise again, and Ribbentrop, "half moved to tears," confessing that "if Hitler should come to me in this cell now, and say 'Do this!'—I would still do it—isn't it amazing?" After the film was ended, Storey and Tom Dodd told the Tribunal that the remainder of the American case would comprise two parts: the conspiracy to commit war crimes and crimes against humanity, and the guilt of the organizations. The first part was based on the assumption that Article 6 of the London Charter declared such a conspiracy to be a crime—an assumption undermined by the amendment to the proposed language of Article 6 effected by Sir Thomas Barnes on July 28.° At this point, however, neither the defense nor the Tribunal raised any objection to the introduction of evidence in support of this charge.

---

°Supra, pp. 75–76. The Tribunal ultimately ruled that the conspiracies covered by the Charter were only those to commit crimes against peace.

Dodd led off with a two-day documentary exposé of the Nazis' use of slave labor and of the concentration camps. The lift that some of the defendants had felt from *The Nazi Plan* soon turned to deep depression, as the scope and horror of their activities emerged from the avalanche of documents. One after another of the defendants—Rosenberg, Frank, Keitel, Seyss-Inquart, and especially Sauckel and Speer—were self-condemned by what they had said or written.

The documents contained no suggestion that the shanghaied hordes from Russia, Poland, France, and the Low Countries had joined the German labor force voluntarily. How could they, when Sauckel had declared in March 1944: "Out of 5 million foreign workers who arrived in Germany, not even 200,000 came voluntarily." Enslaved laborers and Russian prisoners of war alike, in flagrant violation of the laws of war, were set to work on military armament, or even used in combat. At a meeting in February 1943 attended by Speer and Sauckel, Goering's second-in-command, Field Marshal Erhard Milch, announced:

> We have made a request for an order that a certain percentage of men in the antiaircraft artillery must be Russians. Fifty thousand will be taken altogether, thirty thousand are already employed as gunners. It is amusing that Russians must work the guns.

When Major William F. Walsh took over the presentation on the persecution of Jews, he unloaded on the defendants accusations even more lacerating than Dodd's had been.° Somehow, the blandness, and often boastfulness, with which the Nazis recorded their criminal exploits were even more shocking than the deeds themselves. Thus Hans Frank, addressing a meeting of German officials at Cracow in December 1941, declared:

> As far as the Jews are concerned, I want to tell you quite frankly that they must be done away with one way or another. . . . We will principally have pity on the German people only and nobody else in the whole world. As an old National Socialist I must also say: This war would be only a partial success if the whole lot of Jewry would survive it, while we would have shed our last blood to save Europe. . . . Gentlemen, I must ask you to arm yourselves against all feeling of pity. We must annihilate the Jews, wherever it is possible, in order to maintain the structure of the Reich as a whole.

---

°Walsh began his presentation with documents dealing with Nazi persecution of Jews during the prewar years on the stated basis that prewar crimes against German Jews were part of the preparation for waging aggressive wars. No objection was raised at the time, but ultimately the Tribunal held that the evidence did not support such a conclusion and declined to treat prewar persecutions as crimes under the Charter.

Walsh then quoted extensively from the Stroop report on the final destruction of the Warsaw Ghetto in April 1943 and from reports of the SS Einsatzgruppen, both of which had been used by Jackson in his opening statement. Other documents described in detail the construction of the SS gas extermination vans and the extraction of gold from the teeth of the Jewish victims. An affidavit by Dr. Wilhelm Hoettl, an assistant to Adolf Eichmann, established that approximately 4 million Jews had been killed in the concentration and death camps and 2 million by the Einsatzgruppen and other SS agencies.

Dr. Von der Lippe was horrified:

> No words can express the brutality, cynicism, and villainy of these ideas of Hitler, Himmler, and their agents and helpers! "Outrageous" is too weak, "devilish" and "satanic" are more like it. It is contemptible that Stroop should call his operation a "battle" although the SS suffered 16 "casualties," while 65,000 Jews were "destroyed." . . . Now we must acknowledge that even such bestialities actually occurred. It drives me to despair! How the German name has been sullied!

Major Walsh was followed at the lectern by Captain Samuel Harris, an able young lawyer and in later years a successful New York practitioner. His nerves got the better of him, and he saluted the Tribunal with the information that "My knees haven't knocked so much since I asked my wonderful wife to marry me." Birkett recorded that "the shocking taste is really almost unbelievable," and Biddle simply said, "Jesus!"

More understanding hands excised the lapse from the official transcript, and Harris acquitted himself competently while documenting the Nazi policies of Germanization and looting in the German-occupied countries. In Eastern Europe, Germanization meant the extermination or expulsion of unwanted Poles and others from the areas annexed to the Reich and the selection or, if necessary, seizure of ethnic Germans and Germanic types for transfer to Reich territory. The parade of horrors continued; Harris read from captured copies of two Himmler speeches, one in October 1943 and the other (undated) somewhat earlier:

> Often the member of the Waffen-SS thinks about the deportation of the people here. . . . Exactly the same thing happened in Poland in weather 40 degrees below zero, when we had to haul away thousands, ten thousands, a hundred thousand; where we have to have the toughness—you should hear this but also forget it—to shoot thousands of leading Poles.

o o o

I consider that in dealing with members of a foreign country, especially some Slav nationality . . . in such a mixture of peoples there will always be some racially good types. Therefore I think that it is our duty to take their children with us, to remove them from their environment, if necessary, by robbing, or stealing them. . . .

For us the end of this will mean an open road to the East . . . the fetching home of 30 million human beings of our blood, so that still in our lifetime we shall be a people of 120 million Germanic souls. That means we shall be pushing the borders of our German race 500 kilometers farther to the East.

When the Tribunal opened its morning session on Monday, December 17, Lord Justice Lawrence made several procedural announcements, one of which was especially welcome to the prosecution. Jackson, some days earlier, had requested the Tribunal to modify the ruling that only those parts of documents read in open court would be received as evidence. The Tribunal now ruled that documents, in whole or in part, would be received in evidence "on the condition that they have been translated into the respective languages of the members of the Tribunal for their use and that sufficient numbers in German are filed in the Information Center for the use of defense counsel." Translating and duplicating resources had improved to the extent that these requirements could often be fulfilled, and the result was a considerable quickening of the trial's pace.

After Harris had finished, the focus of the prosecution's presentation shifted to the indicted organizations. The General Staff–High Command was one of these, and I had expected to appear before the Tribunal in that connection during this last week before the Christmas recess. But the General Staff was the organization listed last in the Indictment, and by this time it was plain that my presentation would not be due until after the recess.

Storey himself now took over the lectern to present the case against (as designated in the Indictment) "The Corps of Political Leaders of the Nazi Party." Hitler had been the Leader (Fuehrer) of the Party, with day-to-day administration exercised by Hess until his flight to Britain and then by Martin Bormann. Under them were the chiefs of functional Party departments (e.g., Youth, Labor) with the title of *Reichsleiter* and the geographical chiefs, the highest in command of a large district (*Gau*) and the lowest in charge of a block (*Blockleiter*). In response to questions, Storey told the Tribunal that there were some 600,000 members of the Leadership Corps as thus defined.

Storey had considerable documentary proof that members of this aggregation participated extensively in the prewar persecution of Jews and political dissidents, and in a number of the war crimes committed in areas annexed to the Reich, such as Alsace and western Poland. A number of the defendants had held the title of *Reichsleiter*, and Streicher, Sauckel, and Schirach that of *Gauleiter*. But the proof consisted largely of interoffice memoranda and letters establishing responsibility, rather than descriptions of actual events. Furthermore, since much of the wickedness disclosed lay at the door of Ley, recently a suicide, or of Bormann, dead or missing, there was often no live body in the dock to shoulder the guilt. After the horrors described in the documents read by Dodd, Walsh, and Sam Harris, Storey's material was pallid by comparison.

More than a full day of the trial proceedings had passed when Storey finished with the Leadership Corps, and time was hanging heavy. Over the course of his presentation, several exchanges between him and Lawrence had revealed that Storey was not in full command of his material, and Lawrence was running short of patience.

Next Storey went to work on the Reich Cabinet (Reichsregierung), defined in the Indictment as comprising members of the "ordinary cabinet" of ministers, of the Council of Ministers for Defense of the Reich, and of the Secret Cabinet Council. Storey's task was a thankless and unnecessary one. Bernays's purpose in proposing the "organizational guilt" idea was to make possible the prosecution of multitudinous members, but there were only some forty surviving members of this defined group, and these included (by Storey's reckoning) seventeen of the defendants—all but Streicher, Schirach, Sauckel, and Fritzsche. Furthermore, the sins of the ministerial defendants, heinous though they were, had not been committed by means of the indicted group. As was later disclosed, the Reich Cabinet never met after 1937, and the Secret Cabinet Council never even once.

The best advocate imaginable could not have made much out of so feeble a case, and Storey was far from that. Lawrence and Biddle were exasperated beyond the reach of compassion for the unhappy Texan: "Colonel Storey," said Lawrence, "it would help me if you explained to me what conclusions you are asking us to draw from these documents." "If your Honor pleases, we were trying to show the progressive domination of the Reich Cabinet by the defendants and members of this group" was the hopelessly redundant reply. The exchanges became excruciating:

BIDDLE: Colonel Storey, the last document showed only that certain members of the Cabinet came to a Cabinet meeting. Did it show more than that?

STOREY: It shows no more than that. I was just going on a little farther to show that an SS Gruppenfuehrer [equivalent to an army major-general] was present also, and other people were present.

BIDDLE: What would that show?

STOREY: In other words, that they called in these subordinate people, as in the meeting of the ministers.

BIDDLE: What would that show?

STOREY: Well, it just shows the permeation of the Party and its subordinate agencies. . . .

LAWRENCE: There can be no doubt, can there, that there was a Reich Cabinet?

STOREY: No, sir.

LAWRENCE: And that the Reich Cabinet made decrees by the circulatory method? There is no doubt about that?

STOREY: That is right, sir.

LAWRENCE: What does the document add to that?

STOREY: It shows who participated, and how they went out into Party ranks to bring others. . . .

LAWRENCE: But we have had ample evidence before, haven't we, as to who formed the Reich Cabinet?

STOREY: Yes, sir. Well, I will skip the rest of the references. . . .

The best you could say for Storey was that he took this and much more on the chin without quailing. When he had finished with the Reich Cabinet, he bravely embarked on the case against a third of the indicted organizations, the Sturmabteilung (SA) of the Nazi Party, commonly referred to as "Storm Troopers" or "Brownshirts."

There was, of course, abundant proof of the vital role that the SA played as the Nazi Party's paramilitary arm in its rise to power. It was the brutalities and other excesses of the SA that had first given Nazism a bad name in the Western democracies. But after the killing of the SA chief, Ernst Roehm, and many other SA leaders during the so-called Roehm purge in the summer of 1934, the SA dwindled rapidly in both numbers and influence and played no significant part in the further development of the Third Reich or in the war.

Storey's material was correspondingly dated and dull. The Tribunal, apparently tired of baiting him, endured his presentation in comparative silence. There was general relief when, at the close of the morning session on December 19, Storey left the lectern.

The Tribunal's dissatisfaction with Storey did not pass unnoticed in the dock. Statements that the defendants "were in transports of delight" and "roared with laughter every time Storey was reprimanded" are gross exaggerations (Lawrence would not have tolerated such a demonstration), but Goering, as usual, exhibited amusement by mugging. Dr. von der Lippe thought this "tactically unwise," and another defense counsel compared Goering to "a schoolchild who delights when the teacher is censured by the principal."

Major Warren Farr of Boston next presented the case against the SS.

During the afternoon he gave a lucid account of the history and organization of the SS, which was indeed a complex and multifarious entity. Farr had his troubles with the Tribunal; its members were still nursing the irritation Storey had aroused and perhaps wanted to avoid giving the impression that he had been singled out for criticism. Furthermore, it was the next-to-last day before the Christmas break, and everybody was tired and eager to get away.

But, in contrast to the colloquies between the bench and Storey, when Farr was taxed with questions about the necessity of reading particular documents, he responded firmly and with good reasons. There were arguments being aired that the Waffen-SS members were really part of the army and only nominally associated with the other SS branches; that some parts of the SS had nothing to do with the atrocities and could not be regarded as criminal; that many of the members were conscripts rather than volunteers. The validity of these arguments could not be appraised, Farr explained, unless the organization of the SS as a whole was understood and made plain on the record.

The following morning the judges were in a better mood and Farr's documents were less technical and more shocking. He developed the leadership role of the SS in the concentration camps, the atrocious medical experiments perpetrated on the inmates, and the activities of the SS Einsatzgruppen in the death camps, and he concluded with the killing of Allied prisoners by the 12th SS Hitler Jugend Division.

During the afternoon session Storey returned to the lectern and began the presentation of evidence dealing with the Gestapo and SD. Lawrence was not overjoyed to see Storey again, and acidly remarked on his reading of documents previously read to the Tribunal. Storey had time only to describe the organization of the German police and security agencies before four o'clock, when the Tribunal adjourned. Despite Farr's commendable efforts, the American prosecution did not end its 1945 presentations with a bang.

On the morning of December 6, over Jackson's opposition, Lawrence had announced that after the session on Thursday, December 20, the Tribunal would not sit again until Wednesday, January 2. Jackson, "in justice to my staff," noted "the American objection to the adjournment for the benefit of the defendants."

The defendants, however, were not the only ones who benefited. Jackson himself promptly took off in an army airplane, accompanied by his son, his secretary, Gordon Dean and his secretary, and two administrative assistants, on what he described in his oral history as a "holiday jaunt." The itinerary was Rome, Athens, Cairo, Jerusalem, Bethlehem, Luxor, Tunis, and Cannes. Parker paid his home a flying visit, and Biddle was Birkett's guest in England. The other judges and most members of the British,

French, and Soviet delegations disappeared, at least some of them to their homes.

I flew to England to enjoy Christmas with friends and returned to Nuremberg at the end of December to make final preparations for my General Staff presentation.

## Chapter 9

# THE NUREMBERG WAR CRIMES
# COMMUNITY

My wife, Mary, was born of missionary parents in Shanghai and
lived her first seventeen years on the campus of St. John's University in the International Settlement—the part of Shanghai
comprising the British and American extraterritorial concessions. Shortly
after she joined me in Nuremberg in the spring of 1946, she remarked that
living in Nuremberg reminded her of the colonial life-style of the foreign
inhabitants of the Settlement.

I had no such basis of comparison, but what she said expressed what
I had for some time felt but been unable to articulate. The feeling of
remoteness from one's homeland, of separation from (and too often ostenta-
tious superiority to) the indigenous population, and of living in a closed
society—all these indicia of colonialism were part and parcel of life in the
Nuremberg war crimes community.

Such feelings were particularly strong among the Americans and, I am
sure, the Russians. Even in the slow aircraft of those times, London and
Paris were but a few hours distant, and the British and French were
accustomed to European travel and living abroad. Moscow, however,
though not as far away as America, was much farther than London and
Paris, and the Russians, even more than the Americans, were not used to
life in foreign lands.

The Nuremberg war crimes community was exceedingly heterogen-
eous. The four national delegations constituted its main body, comprising
small judicial and larger prosecutorial and administrative components. Op-
erationally, these delegations were directed by the judges and chief
prosecutors. They all lived and worked, however, in the Nuremberg-Fürth
Enclave, commanded by Brigadier General Leroy Watson. His troops provided the prison and courtroom guards, the motor pool and drivers, and

numerous other facilities and services such as billets and the post exchange, as well as general security. Much in evidence at the trial sessions but rarely seen elsewhere was the press, furnishing the window through which our doings were observed in the world outside. Socially, the defendants and defense counsel were no part of the war crimes community, but they were its raison d'être, and provided much of the content and color of our workaday lives.

All of these components formed an island which suddenly emerged from a sea of Germanism and Germans. Nuremberg and its people created the atmosphere in which, outside the Palace of Justice and a few social enclaves such as the Grand Hotel, we all lived.

## 2

As a group the Russians were part of the war crimes community, but as individuals they were in but not of it. The delegation members were expected to be and were courteous as well as professionally cooperative with the other delegations to the extent specified by higher authority. In controlled groups they were, from time to time, permitted to be sociable. But to establish a relation with a Russian in any capacity other than as a member of his delegation was impossible; all such efforts, as far as I know, failed immediately.

This did not mean that an individual Russian could not be likable; many if not most of them were. From the time of my arrival in London to my temporary departure from Nuremberg in February 1946, I was the designated American liaison with the Russian delegation and had abundant opportunity to deal professionally with Troyanovsky, Rudenko, Pokrovsky, Miss Dmitrieva, and several other Russians, all of whom were agreeable. But in Nuremberg, as time went on, I felt increasingly sorry for them. The tight reins from Moscow which restricted them professionally caused them embarrassment, often visible though rarely acknowledged. The total prohibition of personal relations with any non-Soviet person meant that the delegation members could have such relations only with each other. This must have been boring and nerve-racking through the long months of the trial, and I thought that finally they must have come to hate each other.

The only requests the Russians ever put to me were for minor omissions or alterations in our documents or briefs, when a phrase or fact touched a tender nerve. Most of my visits to Rudenko were in the hope that he might be able to produce witnesses or documents helpful to our case. Invariably, Rudenko would affably promise "to call Moscow."* Often the

---

*I never heard Rudenko say that he would call Berlin, which indicates (assuming no misrepresentation) that the Soviet delegation was not responsible to the Soviet member of the

answer was negative or there was no answer that he revealed to me; occasionally, it was positive.

Oleg Troyanovsky was seldom in Nuremberg, and Miss Dmitrieva took over as the Russian prosecution's principal secretary and interpreter. Her English improved, and she remained her winsome and very proper self. On one rare occasion when Rudenko had evidence to show me, it included some photographs. As Rudenko picked up a batch of them, Miss Dmitrieva solemnly announced: "Now I leave the room, Colonel Taylor." Rudenko then showed me several photographs of naked women prisoners running across a courtyard as German guards watched. She then returned, saying: "Those not very nice, Colonel Taylor." It was easy to agree but, despite the revolting photographs, less easy to keep a straight face.

At the Palace of Justice we had virtually no occasion to converse with Soviet prosecutors other than Rudenko and Pokrovsky or with the two or three dozen interpreters and clerks under Major Arkady Poltorak, the Soviet Chief Secretary to the Tribunal. An important exception, however, was I. V. Rasumov, listed in the Soviet directory as "Chief of the Translation Division" of the Tribunal's staff. He was much more than that; it soon became apparent that he was the disciplinary chief of the entire Soviet delegation. Much in evidence at all social functions, he played light music on the piano, cracked bad jokes in English, and kept an eagle eye on the behavior of the delegation members, especially when they were guests. If his flock became overstimulated, a gesture from Rasumov would effect their abrupt departure.

A large part of the war crimes community was housed in the Erlenstegen sector on the eastern edge of the city. The Soviet prosecutors, and virtually all the other Soviet delegation members except the judges and staff, lived in a compound on the Eichendorffstrasse, and it was there that the Russian prosecutors entertained their foreign guests.

The first such occasion that I attended was an early November celebration of the October Revolution, hosted by Pokrovsky and one of the other Soviet prosecutors, General G. A. Alexandrov. After the introductions we stood around for what seemed hours with nothing to do or drink. At length we learned that we were waiting for Justice Jackson and then that his invitation had never reached him. Alexandrov drove to Jackson's house, but the Justice would not be moved, so finally we sat down without him.

The liquor situation at Nuremberg was not yet well organized, and standard spirits such as whiskey and vodka were still scarce, although there was an oversupply of French brandies and liqueurs. Our table was set with

---

Control Commission in Berlin. Whom the delegation called in Moscow was never revealed to me; possibly it was the Procurator General.

alternate bottles of whiskey, brandy, and Cointreau—one for every three diners. My part of the table drew Cointreau.

I was seated next to a Russian general whose name escapes me. To my horror he filled his and my large tumblers with Cointreau and raised his in obvious expectation of "bottoms up." Cointreau is colorless, and I assume he mistook it for vodka. My Russian was equal only to a panicky "Nyet!" He looked at me disgustedly, tilted back his head, and down went the Cointreau—but only part of it, because the sweet, heavy liquid in such quantity was too much for him and he choked and left the table in a hurry. Live and learn.

In the absence of the four chief prosecutors, the toasts were by Pokrovsky, Fyfe ("To the Red Army"), General Donovan ("To the Russian people"), and Dubost. The Frenchman ended his speech with a very neat pun: *"La France est connue comme le pays de la revolution. Nous pouvons l'avouer sans rougir."* (France is known as the country of revolution. We can admit it without blushing [turning red politically]).

Three weeks later there was a higher-level affair when Andrei I. Vishinsky, Soviet Deputy Foreign Minister and Delegate to the United Nations, and General K. P. Gorshenin, Chief Prosecutor of the U.S.S.R., visited Nuremberg. They arrived on November 26, 1945, and that night I attended a dinner in their honor, hosted by Jackson at the Grand Hotel, that included all the senior people except the British, who had prior commitments.

Vishinsky was, to most of us, an ominous figure because of his performance in his former capacity as Soviet Chief Prosecutor at the infamous Soviet "purge trials" of 1936–1938, which resulted in the execution of thousands of military and political officials. In person he did not seem so very terrible, but he certainly struck a decisive note when he rose to give a toast: "I propose a toast to the defendants. May their paths lead straight from the courthouse to the grave!" Vishinsky drained his glass before the translation was completed, as did almost everyone, and some of the Americans were troubled when they learned what they had drunk to. Poor Judge Parker was particularly upset, bedeviled by imagined prospects of newspaper columnists scoring judges who "drink to the death sentences of the men whom they are trying." Biddle, a more casual sort, did his unsuccessful best to allay his colleague's fears.

The next day Jackson introduced Vishinsky and Gorshenin at a session of the Tribunal, and that evening the British gave them another dinner, at which Fyfe, who was part Scottish, introduced the Russians to the blandishments of the bagpipe, played by a piper of the Scots Guards. On November 30 it was Rudenko's turn as host at a dinner featuring no fewer than twenty-five vodka toasts. Fyfe found Vishinsky "amiable, cheerful, downright, and somewhat rumbustious," but I found him no more attractive than

Rasumov. Vishinsky told Patrick Dean that the trial was going too slowly (in which he was quite right), but as far as I could see the Vishinsky-Gorshenin visit in no way modified the conduct of the Soviet prosecution.

The Soviet judges also lived in the Erlenstegen area, but I was only once asked there and as far as I know they did not otherwise invite any of the non-Russian prosecutors. Consequently, I met Nikitchenko and Volchkov only at a few special occasions when judges and prosecutors mingled. Biddle's memoirs, however, describe frequent dining and visiting among the judges, and he continued to find the Russians companionable. So did Parker's aide Bob Stewart, who found one Tania, a Russian interpreter, quite irresistible. The attraction was noticed, probably by Rasumov, and Tania soon returned to Moscow.

Among these courteous Russians there was, in my opinion, only one who had real charm. That was Colonel Rudenko's aide, Yuri Pokrovsky, an older man who had fought in the Tsar's army before joining the Bolshevik forces. He had an Old World elegance and warmth of manner that were most attractive. I occasionally indulged the hope that courtesy might one day ripen into friendship, but the day never came.

### 3

The French and the British found their principal billeting area in Zirndorf, a small town a few miles west of the Nuremberg city limits.

The French presence in the war crimes community was subdued, especially during the opening two months of the trial, before the presentation of their own case. In June, General de Gaulle had resigned his war-born leadership and Georges Bidault was elected President of the provisional government. Reconstruction of the French state, following years of German occupation, was a halting and contentious process, and government financial resources were slender.

The French Chief Prosecutor, François de Menthon, was active in French politics and spent little time in Nuremberg. Early in 1946, immediately after opening the French case, he resigned his Nuremberg post and soon became a member of the French Cabinet. Edgar Faure, who shared with Dubost the title of Deputy Chief Prosecutor, was also an aspiring politician and later was twice Premier. Faure, like de Menthon, was generally in France except when appearing before the Tribunal.

The French judges—de Vabres the professor and Falco of the Cour de Cassation—were not, so far as I know, politically active. They were, of course, in Nuremberg for all trial days; whether or not they returned to Paris on weekends I do not know. However that may have been, they certainly kept a low profile in Nuremberg. Neither Biddle, Fyfe, nor Birkett mentions in his memoirs any social evenings with the French judges, and I never heard of their offering hospitality to prosecutors.

The only senior members of the French delegation with whom we became well acquainted were Dubost, who was an interesting man but not given to small talk, and Mme. Aline Chalufour, an administrator who spoke excellent English and served as interpreter on important occasions. But some of the junior members added greatly to the social scene.

Zirndorf was a pleasant suburb, and the French, with commendable initiative, had established there a *club*, with music, dancing, and suitable potables. It was not so large and garish as the Grand Hotel but pleasantly *intime*, and I spent a number of delightful evenings there as the guest of a young prosecutor, Henri Monneray, who became well known to several American lawyers, leading to subsequent mutual profit in international legal matters. The company was always gay, especially since among the French interpreters and secretaries were several very attractive young women.

### 4

Although relations between the American and British prosecution staffs began and remained amicable and cooperative, the British group could hardly have been more different than it was from the huge, sprawling, poorly led and sharply divided American contingent. Including Shawcross, the British numbered only seven barristers who would appear in court; they were supported by a staff which included Patrick Dean and E. J. Passant from the Foreign Office and approximately ten army "investigating officers" to assist in the procurement, translation, and organization of the documentary evidence. The British aim was to keep things as simple and lucid as possible—an aim greatly furthered by their decision to call no witnesses and leave proof of conspiracy to the Americans.

In addition to these some twenty persons to handle the trial presentations, the delegation included secretaries, interpreters, a detachment of Scots Guards and, of course, the judges and their aides. The entire British contingent comprised about 170 persons—larger than the French and Soviet delegations, but about one-tenth the strength of the Americans, including the military and all employees.

Fyfe consulted Shawcross on important problems, and Dean's reports to the Foreign Office enabled that august ministry to assert its influence, most often exercised to prevent the publication of documents which might be embarrassing to His Majesty's Government. In Nuremberg, Fyfe was very much in charge, and he ran a tight ship; every working day the British prosecution staff met in the morning to hear reports, allocate the work, and iron out problems. Fyfe's task required administration as well as lawyering, as is manifest from a letter to his wife on November 1, 1945:

> My part is partly conducting a seemingly unending international con
> ference, partly running a small department, and lastly getting up a

case for trial. Everyone has something wrong. Lord Justice Lawrence has no top sheet and one straw pillow. Mr. Justice Birkett has no separate house; if the military counsel of the delegation are billeted separately from civilian counsel, the delegation will fall into camps, if they remain mixed, Colonel Turrell will get on Mr. Elwyn Jones' sensitive socialist nerves. Miss Kentish's bathroom has no curtains and none of the female staff can have a bath for fear of being overlooked; there are no driers for the photostat machine; Khaki Roberts has failed to remember to bring a towel and has pinched mine just as I was going to have a bath; the Russians wish to add 28 new documents at the last moment; Jackson thinks that there will be trouble about Katyn; Scott-Fox thinks that he had better telephone the Foreign Office about some 5-year-old secrets possibly being mentioned some six weeks from now; the female staff have got to pay for their meals 1/6 each, and have no marks because they understood that they would not have to pay; Khaki and Robey say that nothing can be done in time. °

The slighting reference to Elwyn Jones (a Labour Member of Parliament) disclosed political friction beneath the outwardly smooth appearance of relations among the British barristers. Fyfe and most of the others were Conservatives, and Fyfe's coolness toward Elwyn was further revealed, obliquely, by a passage in his memoirs praising the other three junior counsel (Griffith-Jones, Phillimore, and Barrington) as among "the most unselfish and industrious people that I have ever known." Relations between Fyfe and Elwyn grew tense to the extent that Shawcross felt obliged to intervene in order to ensure that Jones would be assigned a fair share of the court work.

Fyfe was an able leader and a fine lawyer, but his success was the product of competence and drive, not of brilliance or charm. What humor he had was heavy, and as a speaker he could be very dull. I greatly respected him, but he was a bit too stiff for my taste. The same was true of Griffith-Jones, who was all that and more than a Guards officer should be. In later years he represented the Crown in an obscenity case against D. H. Lawrence's novel *Lady Chatterley's Lover* and won renown (of a sort) by asking the jury rhetorically: "Is this the sort of book you would want to see in the hands of your *servants?*"

The two most sociable British prosecutors were Roberts and Jones; association with the former was usually, and with the latter always, pleasurable. Khaki's leisure tastes were bacchic and terpsichorean, and sometimes he did not know when enough was enough. Elwyn never made such mis-

---

°Birkett soon was assigned a house in Erlenstegen; Lieutenant Colonel Turrell commanded the British Army "investigating officers"; Miss Kentish was Fyfe's secretary; E. G. Robey, son of a famous British comedian, was a barrister on loan to the BWCE from the Director of Public Prosecutions.

takes; his style was light and lively, and he was a consistent source of good humor and good sense.

As President of the Tribunal, Lord Justice Lawrence undertook to host the numerous British celebrities who descended on Nuremberg to see the goings-on at this unique and memorable trial: Jowitt and Maugham (brother of Somerset Maugham), Lord Chancellors present and past; one-time Secretary of State for War Leslie Hore-Belisha and other former ministers; Lord Wright of the UNWCC and his lady, a champion horse jumper; Harold Nicolson of literary fame, and the historian John Wheeler-Bennett. Senior prosecutors were often invited to dinners and receptions for these distinguished guests, so we became well acquainted with the plump, Pickwickian Lawrence and the tall, intensely intellectual Birkett. Soon their wives appeared on the scene, to the annoyance of Jackson, who thought the "foreigners" should preserve the same wifeless condition that Eisenhower had imposed on the American occupation forces.

Perhaps the centuries had worked an affinity for colonial life into British upper-class genes. For whatever reason, they appeared to handle the long exile in war-shattered Nuremberg more easily than the rest of us.

## 5

The main deficiency of the American delegation was that it had no focal point of morale. Jackson was a solo performer rather than a conductor, and the lieutenants to whom he delegated his administrative authority—Storey, Gill, and later Dodd—lacked the stature to achieve leadership. Furthermore, the delegation's size required that their billets be geographically scattered, and they were present in large numbers in all the Nuremberg billeting areas except Zirndorf. There were many individuals who worked with dedication, but the delegation was an aggregation of interlocking, semiautonomous groups rather than an entity with a core.

Among the chief prosecutors, however, Jackson was much the most powerful in that he was his own boss. No one stood between him and the President, and Truman, favorably disposed toward Nuremberg in general, was not one to peer over Jackson's shoulder. Truman was new in the office, not a lawyer, and buried in a multitude of other major matters. From time to time Jackson sent Truman informative letters, but as far as I could see, the idea of consulting him about problems never crossed Jackson's mind.

As for the diplomatic side of his task, while in London Jackson brought over Miss Fite as a State Department adviser, but she stayed with him only a few months. When Jackson went to Potsdam he was not so much consulting Secretary Byrnes as seeking his help in bringing the Russians into line, and the Secretary emphasized that final decisions on the Nuremberg project were not up to him but to Jackson.

Furthermore, the senior officials who had provided the ideas and impetus for that project left the government soon after the end of the war. Stimson and McCloy resigned in the fall of 1945; Biddle and Morgenthau were asked to resign shortly after Truman took office. Rosenman resigned early in 1946 and except at Potsdam seems to have taken no part in war crimes matters once Jackson was fairly launched. Robert Patterson, who succeeded Stimson as Secretary of War, had had no connection with war crimes planning during his previous service as Under-Secretary. Howard C. Petersen, who succeeded McCloy as Assistant Secretary, was an able young lawyer and subsequently endeavored to influence Jackson's handling of the charges against the Nazi organizations. But he lacked McCloy's political clout, and Jackson saw no reason to consult him on Nuremberg problems.

Accordingly, Jackson, generally if not invariably, made his own decisions without clearing them with anyone, in Washington or elsewhere. The results were not always happy, but the other chief prosecutors soon came to realize that he spoke with authority and never had to "call Moscow." Nor was there any flow of volunteered advice coming from Washington. Neither during the Krupp fracas nor any other contentious matter did I ever hear mention of any official pressure from Washington, formal or informal, relating to the matter at hand. My own experience when I succeeded Jackson was much the same.

Jackson and the staff who worked most closely with him were housed in seven villas on the Lindenstrasse in Dambach, a tiny village on the western edge of Nuremberg, just south of Fürth. Jackson himself, with his son and Mrs. Douglas, were at number 33, a large and well-equipped residence, dark and heavy in the worst Germanic style, but blessed with an attractive garden and a good tennis court. Storey, Gill, Amen, Gordon Dean, Dodd, Whitney Harris, and others of Jackson's group were in the other Lindenstrasse dwellings. Alderman, Calvocoressi, and I were a few blocks away on the Schwedenstrasse.

Jackson often played host to his senior staff; Sidney Alderman was frequently there for dinner and music, and to my great pleasure the tennis court was generally available on weekends. But there were few large parties, although I recall one when Senator Claude Pepper of Florida, visiting Nuremberg, toasted Jackson as "America's international district attorney." For Jackson, however, the house was a place of quiet and repose, where he could work on his court presentations.

Life was much livelier at number 2 Hebelstrasse in Erlenstegen, where Biddle and Parker lived with their aides Rowe, Wechsler, Fisher, and Stewart. It would have been hard to find a brighter bunch of young men, and past acquaintance ensured me frequent invitations for an evening of drink and talk. They were careful not to mention the Tribunal's inner workings, but other events and personalities were freely discussed.

For most members of the American delegation, living in rooms wherein group entertainment was not practicable, the focus of social life was the Grand Hotel. Situated in the center of the city near the main railroad station, this hostelry was open to all civilian employees of the occupying powers and to all military personnel of officer rank. One wing of the large edifice had suffered war damage and was under repair during the trial's early months, but the lobbies, dining rooms, and main ballroom were intact and elaborately furnished in the German style.

The food was cheap and reasonably good, the liquor situation soon improved, and the Marble Room featured a dance band and often a floor show. The German staff was obsequiously efficient, and well satisfied with a couple of cigarettes as a tip. The Russians never appeared at the Grand and the French and British only rarely. It was essentially an American gathering place, as was also the nearby enlisted men's club.

In order not to drain the slender food supplies available in the German economy, the American occupiers were not allowed to patronize the few German restaurants but were expected to rely on the army messes and, as soon as it was established, the PX. For similar reasons, none of the American occupiers, military or civilian, were allowed to bring in their wives, children, or other dependents. Consequently, the war crimes community included very few married couples.° Most of the senior personnel, including the lawyers, were married men, while most of the women were single and young and not a few very attractive. This gave the society a relaxed, tolerant, and philanderous ambience which many of us found agreeable.

All in all, the members of the war crimes community lived fairly well and the Americans, who were paid more than the others, very well. We generally worked long hours, but there were breaks in the schedule, and, when it appeared that my own courtroom responsibilities were not imminent, weekend trips to see the cities and sights of Bavaria were frequent. As a colonel I was assigned a car and an excellent driver named Drazba, but those of less seniority could usually get a jeep or the unwieldy vehicle called a "command car" from the motor pool.

Franconian Bavaria is a splendid place for rubbernecking, at which I am very good, and I made the most of my opportunities. The presence of friends, male and female, from both prewar Washington and wartime England ensured pleasant company on drives southward to Augsburg of the famous Fuggers banking family, and, on the Danube, to Donauwörth, Ingolstadt, and Regensburg (Ratisbon to Latins and to Robert Browning in his "Incident of the French Camp") with its lovely cathedral; on the west to

---

°No wives or other dependents joined the Russians, but the British and French judges disregarded the restrictions to the extent that their wives and grown children sometimes visited Nuremberg. In the American delegation, Daniel Margolies and Harriet Zetterberg, both lawyers, created a piquant situation by sharing a room at the Grand Hotel, a situation to which the authorities raised no objection, unaware that the two were in fact married.

Würzburg, sadly battered but still impressive; and northward to Erlangen and its university, Bamberg, Coburg, Bayreuth, and the area called the Frankische Schweiz (Franconian Switzerland) for wonderful scenery, quaint villages, and castles such as Pottenstein.

Two-day or longer holidays could be spent in the Bavarian and Austrian Alps. The army requisitioned hotels and villages for R and R in such resorts as Garmisch-Partenkirchen, Berchtesgaden, and Salzburg, each of which I was able to enjoy during the 1945–1946 winter. Barbara Pinion, the WAAF officer I had recruited in Frankfurt for Calvocoressi's group, was well acquainted with Colonel Paul Sapieha of a noble Polish family (Cardinal Sapieha of Cracow was his uncle), and through him we got accommodations just east of Salzburg on the Fuschlsee in Fuschl Castle, an old monastery which Ribbentrop had confiscated for his personal use as a country retreat. There, and next day at an inn on the nearby Mondsee, we met many Polish officers recently demobilized from the Polish Corps commanded by General Wladyslaw Anders, which, as part of the British Eighth Army, had fought its way north on the Italian peninsula and into Austria.

Most of the officers, including General Anders, had been prisoners of the Russians until released to form the Corps, and some had lost relatives or friends at Katyn. These factors did nothing to diminish the Poles' traditional hostility to Russia, and now their homeland was under Moscow's thumb and the Warsaw government increasingly Communist-dominated. These officers, mostly of upper- or middle-class lineage, could not return home safely, let alone happily. They were educated, attractive men and very good company, but bewildered and lost in the postwar turmoil. I fear that few of them were capable of adjusting to a world from which their cultural heritage had been swept away.

While the other three Nuremberg delegations were homogeneous, the American work force comprised many who were not American by birth or nationality. There had been initial hesitancy about employing local Germans, but the insatiable need for translators, clerks, and deckhands of all sorts resulted in a growing number of Germans in such positions. Other Germans who had fled the Nazi regime, some naturalized in Britain or the United States, some not, were used in linguistic and research capacities, and one, Dr. Robert Kempner, appeared as counsel before the Tribunal.

The international character of the war crimes community was further enhanced by small delegations from the countries occupied by the Nazi forces —Poland, Yugoslavia, Czechoslovakia, Denmark, Norway, the Low Countries, and Greece. Of these the first three worked closely with the Soviet delegation and the others with the British. These representatives, the Poles and Czechs particularly, pressed the four major delegations for permission to appear before the Tribunal to present evidence dealing with their own countries. But these requests were refused, in part because of reluctance to introduce additional languages into the courtroom, since the simultaneous interpreting system could not cope with more than four languages. Accordingly, the minor delegations functioned only as observers or, sometimes, as sources of additional evidence.

## 6

In 1760 Kaspar Faber established a small lead pencil factory in Stein, a suburb of Nuremberg a few miles southwest of the city. His descendants prospered mightily, and a century or more later a huge "castle" and satellite buildings were built on the Faber estate by the proprietor, Baron Faber-Castell. Interior murals displayed mounted knights with pencils as lances; artistically, the whole complex was a fright.

It was here that the members of the Fourth Estate who covered the Nuremberg trials were billeted, under the auspices of the United States Army. The buildings' interiors were so heavy and garish, as well as marred by stains, smells, and dents remaining from military use during the war, that Jackson had rejected them for billeting the Nuremberg staffs. But several hundred members of the press were converging on the old city, and there was no other place large enough to accommodate them.

The reporters and commentators came from more than twenty nations; some eighty from the United States, fifty from Britain, forty from France, thirty-five from the Soviet Union, twenty from Poland, and a dozen from Czechoslovakia. Among the American and British journalists many were, or were soon to become, famous in their field: H. R. Baukhage, Walter Cronkite, Ray Daniell, Wes Gallagher, Marguerite Higgins, Louis Lochner, Roy Porter, William L. Shirer, Richard Stokes, from England Robert Cooper (*The Times* of London), Ossian Goulding (*Daily Telegraph*), David Low (*Evening Standard*), and Peter Mendelsohn (*New Statesman*); from the Soviet Union Ilya Ehrenburg.

Some of the Faber flock, such as Cronkite, put up with the crowded and chaotic conditions without much complaint. Not so Bill Shirer, whose dispatch to the New York *Herald-Tribune* on December 8, 1945, began:

> Give a cheer for your foreign correspondents who, despite the beating of their lives they are receiving from the United States Army, are still trying to report the truth from Germany under the most appalling conditions I have seen in twenty years of reporting from abroad.
>
> As I write half of them trying to cover the trial of Nazi war criminals are ill from vile food which the Army never would dream of serving to the German war prisoners. Packed eight or ten in a room in a ramshackle building which serves as a press camp, they are forced

to live under sanitary conditions—or rather the lack of them—which the State of New York never would permit in Sing Sing.

At the Palace of Justice, the press was better served. In the courtroom 240 seats were reserved for them, and, in a large press room, the trial proceedings could also be followed from loudspeakers. Gordon Dean, whom Shirer described as the "silver lining in the darkest clouds," needled Storey for more copies of documents for the press and did wonders in convincing the tough newsmen that they were being fairly treated, despite the shortages and misunderstandings. Transmission agencies at the Palace included RCA, Mackey, Press Wireless, and Tass, and teletype machines were installed for traffic to London and Paris.

Despite the horrendous décor and the shortcomings of bed and board, visits to Faber Castle were enjoyable. The army commandant, Major Ernest Dean, had formed a small female chorus of German waitresses with lovely voices who sang German folk songs and, as comic relief, heavily German-accented versions of American pop songs; a general favorite was "Mairzy Doats." Walter Cronkite ended my string of victories at table tennis. The conversation was good, and visitors, starved for news other than the contents of the army's *Stars and Stripes*, picked up welcome information and commentary from the world outside.

I rarely saw what the denizens of Faber Castle were writing about the trials. I assume that Jackson was better served by Gordon Dean, but except during the press "revolt" against Storey's methods with the documents at the beginning of the trial, I never heard Jackson mention any press reactions, and I do not believe that the newspapers had much effect on the conduct of the trial.

The British and American components of the press soon formed the opinion that the British prosecution team was plainly superior to our own. I became aware, from press clippings I saw in 1946, that the British reporters were overly chauvinistic in the comparisons they were drawing. But I had no idea that the American journalists shared this negative view of Jackson's team (though not so openly) until years later when I asked Cronkite and Shirer.

Like other spectators of the trial, the American journalists were scornful of Storey's management of the American case and thought Alderman had gone on too long—a natural complaint from reporters who wanted something new every day and did not understand that Alderman was doing exactly what was needed to prove the prosecution's case. Furthermore, despite the eloquence of Jackson's opening, they were put off by his inaccessibility and apparent indifference, while Fyfe was always available for explanation or other assistance.

The British press, to be sure, had every reason to be proud of its

Nuremberg team. Roberts was the only misfit, and all of the British court-room participants were barristers of recognized ability, accustomed to steady and varied court appearances. Their experience and talents at trial work produced excellent results, for they fully accomplished what they set out to do, with economy of time and manpower. Likewise, as time went on, Fyfe emerged as the day-to-day courtroom leader of the prosecution as a whole.

But it is easier to assemble a staff of a dozen lawyers of high quality than one ten times that size and easier to prove that *Nazi Germany* attacked Poland, Denmark, Yugoslavia, and other countries than that *the defendants* conspired to wage aggressive war. While much of the published criticism of the American team was justified, the invidious comparisons drawn by the British reporters took insufficient account of Jackson's brilliant success in setting an epic and elevated tone to the proceeding; of the wealth and compelling organization of the proof offered by Alderman and other Americans; of the sensational revelations of witnesses like Lahousen and Ohlendorf; and of the crushing effect of photographs showing the concentration camps, the destruction of the Warsaw Ghetto, and Nazi justice at work on the insurgents of July 20, 1944. It appeared to me that after the size and resources of the United States had given it first place during the war among the Western Allies, the British journalists were moved to overstate the superiority of their Nuremberg barristers.

The press corps did not, of course, remain throughout the trial at its initial strength. As it became increasingly clear that the proceedings would continue for at least several months, many reporters left, some to new assignments (Cronkite, for example, was transferred to Moscow), others to cover different areas or events from which they could return to Nuremberg for particularly newsworthy episodes.

7

Except for the people themselves, the United States Army *made* the Nuremberg war crimes community. It was the army that proposed Nuremberg as the site of the trial; repaired and adapted the Palace of Justice to make it usable for the trial; brought the defendants and witnesses to Nuremberg and guarded and safeguarded them; procured the necessary duplicating, recording, and communications facilities for the trial staff and the press, and a large part of the administrative and clerical personnel; selected, assigned, and repaired the billets and furnished automotive transportation and the drivers; secured and distributed the food, drink, heat, and help for the community; provided overall security throughout the Nuremberg-Fürth Enclave; and took care of other necessities and amenities too numerous to list here.

In short, the army enabled a large and diverse alien group to settle, within a few weeks, in the battered and largely shattered city of Nuremberg and hold a unique and momentous trial of worldwide import. It was a magnificent feat of construction and management under pressure.

But the army is not faultless, and while the trial was being prepared and gotten underway, the army in Germany was having its troubles. Their name was "redeployment," which had begun even before the end of the war. By midspring of 1945 it was clear that a total collapse of the Third Reich was imminent, and in May the transfer of troops from Germany to the Pacific theater began, in preparation for the assault on the Japanese mainland which, it was feared, might be necessary for final victory in the Far East. By the end of 1945 over two and a half million American troops had left Europe, and by June 30, 1946, 99 percent of the troops there on V-E Day had left, some for further service elsewhere but over 2 million for demobilization and return to civilian life.

The results were disastrous to the morale and competence of the occupation army, as was very noticeable in Nuremberg. The troops there were drawn from the First Infantry Division—the Big Red One (after the shoulder flash), a famous division with a fine combat record. When I reached Nuremberg in October, the soldiers were mostly combat troops who had fought their way into Germany. Except for a lamentable tendency to race their vehicles through the streets with little concern for the safety of German pedestrians, for whom they had little use, they were mature, confident, and capable. But they were soon redeployed, and many of their replacements were callow, poorly trained kids with little professional pride or interest in the tasks they were expected to perform.

After the Japanese surrendered, the flow of redeployment became a torrent. By July 1947 the size of the American forces in Europe had dwindled to 135,000. The rapidity of the shrinkage undermined the effectiveness of the forces, especially of the small units. An engineer battalion found itself with six officers and fifty-six men; an ordnance company, after redeployment, had only eighteen men. Vehicle maintenance became a bad joke. More often than not, my weekend sightseeing trips were interrupted by vehicle breakdowns and long waits for repairs.

Redeployment was accompanied by the departure or dissolution of most of the wartime top headquarters and a simplification of the occupation army's structure. The Supreme Headquarters of the Western Allies (SHAEF) was dissolved and in July 1945, its American components became the United States Forces European Theatre (USFET), in Frankfurt-am-Main. The First Army had already gone to the Pacific and the Ninth Army to the United States, and the two American Army Groups (Devers's Sixth and Bradley's Twelfth) were dissolved late in July.

General Eisenhower remained in command at USFET until November 11, when he returned to Washington to succeed General Marshall as Army Chief of Staff. In what must have been a fit of absent-mindedness he turned over the USFET command to General Patton. That justly celebrated war hero could do nothing right as an occupation commander. General Leroy Watson was sent to command the Nuremberg-Fürth Enclave without adequate briefing on the nature and hierarchical status of Jackson's office, with the results already described. When Patton publicly compared Nazis and anti-Nazis to Republicans and Democrats, he was unceremoniously relieved after two weeks in command and sent to head the Fifteenth Army, a headquarters of little military importance. Shortly thereafter he was killed in an automobile accident.

On November 26, General Joseph T. McNarney took command at USFET. Under him were the Third Army in the eastern part of the American Zone (Bavaria) and the Seventh Army in the west (Württemberg-Baden and Hesse). Toward the end of 1945, however, the military authorities concluded that there was need for a separate force for the maintenance of security, described as "an active patrol system designed to take quick and effective action to forestall and suppress riots, rebellion, and other acts prejudicial to the security of the occupation forces as a whole." It was to be a well-trained, snappily turned out, elite force called the Zone Constabulary, responsible for law and order throughout the American Zone of Occupation, except in a few special areas, including Nuremberg-Fürth.

Selected as Commander of the constabulary was Major General Ernest N. Harmon, wartime commander of the Second Armored Division and known as the "Pocket Patton." He has been described as "short, barrel-chested, gravelly voiced" and as a "tough disciplinarian, profane, bombastic, vain of his cavalry boots-and-breeches turnout."

Harmon proved as good at training the constabulary as he had been as an armored forces commander. But Harmon off duty was certainly a "caution," as we saw when he came to Nuremberg to consult with General Watson. His visit happened to coincide with a reception given by Lord Justice and Lady Lawrence. She was comely and a bit statuesque. As the two generals entered the premises, Lady Lawrence was standing sideways to the entrance, receiving the guests. Finding her posterior prepossessing, Harmon saluted it with a huge pinch. Lady Lawrence turned and confronted Watson, speechless with embarrassment, and Harmon, grinning and extending a hand in friendly greeting. With admirable aplomb she ignored the *coup d'amour* and chatted courteously before turning her attention elsewhere. Later that evening General Harmon was seen in the Marble Room dancing with great vigor and occasionally raising his partners over his head. After his retirement in 1947, Harmon finished his career as President of Norwich University.

Leroy Watson could hardly have been more dissimilar—quiet, unostentatious, and flexible. Some of his guards at the Palace of Justice, checking identification cards, were brusque with the British press men and remarked loudly that the "limeys" were living off Uncle Sam's bounty. But no crises erupted, and gradually Watson raised the caliber of his troops, improved the motor pool, and pulled his command out of the mess that redeployment had made of the American occupation army.

But although the army furnished virtually all the logistic and most of the societal resources of the war crimes community, the army was not part of the Nuremberg project. The President as Commander in Chief had ordered the army to give Jackson, and those associated with him, all possible support, and that was done. But the GIs in general knew little and cared less about what was going on at the Palace of Justice. At the higher levels of command, especially among the regular officers, there were few who applauded and some who openly questioned the wisdom of the Nuremberg undertaking. As time went on, and especially after Winston Churchill in his famous speech at Fulton, Missouri, accused the Soviet Union of hanging an "iron curtain" between Eastern and Western Europe, the voices of doubt grew louder.

*8*

By the time the Tribunal adjourned for the Christmas recess, it had conducted five weeks of sessions. During that period the principal mechanical and procedural problems had been tolerably handled; documents, films, and other physical evidence and briefs were being prepared in time and in sufficient quantity. Glitches in the simultaneous interpretation system had been corrected, and both prosecution and defense lawyers were getting the hang of things procedurally. At the Palace of Justice, the work of the war crimes community was more relaxed and had developed a routine.

The judges sat in public session morning and afternoon (10:00 a.m.) to 1:00 p.m. and 2:00 to 5:00 p.m.) Monday to Friday and occasionally on Saturday morning. Most of the staff lunched in the Palace cafeteria. So, at first, did the judges, but soon they were provided with a private dining room. Those of us blessed with personal transportation often went to the Grand Hotel, where lunching was quieter and better than at the Palace.

Throughout the trial the judges retained their initial seating, with (facing the bench) the Russians, British, Americans, and French in that order from left to right. Since they entered from the left, the French led the incoming procession, with the diminutive Falco in the van and setting a brisk pace.

There had been an embarrassment during the very first public session because the army, rank-conscious as always, had carefully provided smaller chairs for the alternate judges than for the voting members. Parker was very angry, and after the public session lost no time in complaining to his colleagues that this was a "deliberate belittling" of the alternates' status. He then raised a larger question: "What part does an alternate have as a matter of right?" The unpleasantness blew over when Lawrence declared that the chairs should be the same for both members and alternates. After discussion it was agreed that alternates could participate fully in the Tribunal's deliberations and express their opinions on issues before votes were taken.

Behind the judges on the bench sat two or three interpreters to enable communication between the Russian and French judges and between them and the English-speaking judges. The Tribunal did not, however, decide questions of any difficulty in bench conferences, preferring to recess and reach decisions in chamber. Everything said openly in any of the four languages was translated on the simultaneous interpretation system, so the interpreters behind the judges were used only for private communication among them and to clarify obscure passages in the simultaneous interpretation.

As the trial went on, individuals constantly or frequently in the limelight developed "courtroom personalities." On the bench, Lawrence made all the announcements and rulings. In appearance and manner he was dignified and without pomposity, firm but not severe, and homely in a way that suggested personal warmth, utter fairness, and an English Christmas dinner. Nobody could better have dispelled fears of vengeance exacted by "victors trying vanquished."

Lawrence's contribution to the success of the trial was immense, and he was the dominant figure on the bench. But he was not an intellectual or subtle man, and he had his share of amiable weaknesses, one of which was attractive women. On weekends he was often observed in his sedan being driven in and around Nuremberg in company with a sprightly Frenchwoman. He soon spotted Betty Stark when she appeared in the courtroom audience, and Biddle was amused to catch sight of a note Lawrence was sending her via one of the British clerks: "How are you doing Pops—bored as we are?"

The Russian and French judges, as well as Parker and Birkett, said so little in public session that their impact was visual, not aural. Volchkov was wooden, Nikitchenko impassive and rather steely; Parker's heavy frame and moon face revealed little of his friendliness and common sense. Falco appeared insignificant, and de Vabres noteworthy chiefly for his enormous walrus mustache.

In their grasp of the legal and evidentiary issues of the trial, the leaders of the bench were Biddle and Birkett, and Lawrence's success as President owed much to their reminders and suggestions. As a voting member, and one who might have been chosen as President, Biddle was more self-assured and spoke much more from the bench than Birkett as alternate. But the two had much in common. Both were discontented; Biddle because he was not President and Birkett because he was not a voting member. Psychologists believing in such categories would have called them ectomorphs. They were tall and lean, restless and critical, intellectually gifted, prideful, and resentful if their merits were not recognized to the extent they thought they deserved.

Birkett was much the better advocate and the more scholarly jurist of the two. He was less jaunty and charming than Biddle and took the trial even more seriously. On January 20, 1946, he wrote to a friend:

> The thing that sustains me is the knowledge that this trial can be a very great landmark in the history of International Law. There will be a precedent of the highest standing for all successive generations, and aggressor nations great and small will embark on war with the certain knowledge that *if they fail* they will be held to grim account.

And the following day he recorded in his diary:

> This is supposed to be, and no doubt is, the greatest trial in history. The historian of the future will look back to it with fascinated eyes. It will have a glamour, an intensity, an ever-present sense of tragedy that will enthrall the mind engaged upon its consideration. But to have been present every moment of it is to occupy a position of advantage given to but few. . . .

Biddle, too, saw the trial as a great event, but he was cast in a lighter mold. As scion of an old and prestigious Philadelphia family, he was a bit of a "swell," loved the lighter amenities, and could on occasion be patronizing or arrogant. At least for the public sessions, he would have been unsuitable as President, for he was impatient, often caustic, did not suffer fools gladly, and could never have projected the aura of fairness that Lawrence radiated. Furthermore, privately he was scornful of most of his colleagues. He was forever nursing his own ego, at the expense of others, in letters to his wife:

> [Feb. 13, 1946] This is not an able crowd on the "bench"— Lawrence never has a thought of his own except that, largely guided by Birkett and me, he does make an admirable presiding officer. The French add almost nothing, Falco goes along.
> [Mar. 13, 1946] I do really run this show, have won every point, single-handed, except for Parker, who is often a nuisance, and Herb [Wechsler], who is grand. The Tribunal lack intelligence almost as much as they lack guts. . . .

[May 22, 1946, referring to Lawrence] But the old goat is so dumb, so inept, that it becomes a long series of petty annoyances.

Much as the judges admired Jackson's opening statement, his relations with them did not develop well. When they first encountered him in Berlin and Nuremberg, Jackson addressed them like an old hand instructing a bunch of greenhorns. Nikitchenko and Falco had already been at odds with him in London. Biddle respected and liked Jackson, but was dismayed by his arguments for substituting Alfried for Gustav Krupp, and later developments did little to restore his confidence in Jackson's judgment. He could not stand Mrs. Elsie Douglas and regarded her as a bad influence on the Justice.

Immediately in front of the bench, with their backs to the judges, sat a row of members of the Tribunal's Secretariat, who kept records of the various events and the documents offered in evidence and ran errands for the judges. In front of the Secretariat members, opposite the French end of the bench, was the lectern from which the lawyers addressed the Tribunal and examined witnesses. There was a side table where the lawyers' assistants sat with whatever documents were being used or offered in evidence.

In front of the Secretariat along the rest of the bench were the court reporters, usually eight in number at one time. This part of the courtroom was in nearly constant motion. As a court reporter finished his or (usually) her stint, a replacement would come in via the aisle between the reporters and the defense counsel, who sat, facing the court, on the opposite side of the aisle. Secretariat clerks and officers would come in and out by the same route.

The court reporters were the publicly visible component of the large behind-the-scenes staff who handled the typing and duplication of the documents and briefs and, most important, of the trial's daily record. As each reporter returned from the courtroom with the stenographic notes of the proceedings, he or she would dictate them into a recording device, to which a stenographer would then listen through earphones and type a fair copy for duplication by the mimeograph operators. Thus it was possible to produce, before the next day of trial, sufficient copies of the record, in the four languages, to meet the needs of lawyers, judges, and the press.

The defense counsel sat behind five narrow, straight tables which could accommodate twenty-two persons so that each of the twenty-one defendants in the dock would have but one of his counsel in the courtroom. Most of them wore simple black robes, but a few were silk-lined and more colorful. Doenitz's counsel, Otto Kranzbuehler, was still in his naval uniform during the early weeks of the trial, with the four gold stripes of a naval captain (he held that rank, *Flottenrichter*, as a naval judge advocate) on his sleeves. Each lawyer sat as near as he could to his client or clients (some had two), but conversation with the defendants was not allowed during the course of trial. Tall, dignified, and well-spoken, Dr. Rudolf Dix, representing Schacht, often served as spokesman for the defense. He, Kranzbuehler, and perhaps half a dozen others were lawyers of superior ability. The others appeared to me as men of average quality, but a few were painfully incompetent.

In the dock behind their lawyers, the defendants remained the magnet for the eyes of all those visiting the trial for the first few times. For those frequently there, the drama and curiosity soon wore thin. As the trial went on and on, the defendants, like others condemned to attendance most of the time, showed signs of boredom.

Even Goering, who continued to essay the role of defense ringmaster, sometimes lapsed into lassitude, but usually he was the most attentive and expressive of the group. The trimmest were Keitel and Jodl, sitting straight-shouldered in their army uniforms stripped of insignia; Keitel stiff and impassive, Jodl more mobile and often scowling angrily. Kaltenbrunner and Streicher were the most repellent and, according to Dr. Gilbert's tests, the dumbest, the first a brutish, scar-faced hulk, the second ogling the lady court reporters' legs, utterly vulgar. Rebecca West described him as "a dirty old man of the sort that gives trouble in parks." Funk was almost equally unappetizing, rolling his eyes desperately and slumping like a melting lump of rancid butter. Schacht, like Jodl, was a visibly angry man, with his chin high and body turned to set himself above and apart from the others. Doenitz and Hans Frank wore dark glasses most of the time. Hess was inattentive, apparently suffering from recurrent cramps, and appeared to me wholly incapable of defending himself.

Behind the defendants was the door through which they entered and left the dock. Rigid against the back wall of the courtroom was a row of seven American soldiers, with white helmet liners and belts setting off the khaki uniforms. During the early months they wore the insignia and ribbons of combat-experienced troops, but after redeployment they lost much of their snap. Three or four more soldiers were stationed at each end of the dock and at the courtroom's main door to the left of the dock. Each of the courtroom's doors was surmounted by a large medallion of the German regional appellate court—the Oberlandesgericht—which normally sat in the building.

At the back of the courtroom, where the floor was three steps elevated, and next to the junior end of the dock was the box for the linguistic experts who handled the simultaneous interpretation. Generally intelligent, well educated, and displaying much individuality, they were heard and seen more than anyone else in the courtroom. Twelve in number at any one time, they were headed by a chief in the front left corner who flashed yellow lights at the bench and lecterns if the speech was too fast and red ones if the system broke down, as it sometimes did if the connecting wires under the carpet were severed or an interpreter unexpectedly had to be relieved.

A standout among the interpreters was Wolfe Frank, a handsome young Bavarian who had fled to England before the war and mastered English so perfectly that, unlike the others, he was used to render English into German and vice versa. A Russian-language interpreter, Georgi Vassilitchikoff, stammered in conversation, but never when at work. Productive of both admiration and amusement was a young American lady from the Midwest who acted out the content of her renditions with sweeping gestures and dramatic vocal inflections. She wore her corn-silk hair in a towering bun and was known to all but herself as the "Passionate Haystack."

Alongside the interpreters and immediately beyond the defense counsel was the desk for the Marshal, Colonel Charles W. Mayes. On the side of the aisle was the witness box. The wall beyond had a door at the left for the interpreters, and another at the right for the Tribunal. Between was a large blank wall space for display of charts and films.

At the front of the courtroom, separated by an aisle from its center, were four long tables, each accommodating nine persons. In order from the main entrance were those for the members of the French, Soviet, American, and British prosecutions. Beyond the British was a fifth table and an area for the judges' personal assistants.

Behind these tables was a row of chairs backed against the barrier separating the court area from the audience. When attendance was heavy, these seats would be occupied by overflow from the prosecution tables and VIP officials. When demand for seating was slack, the patronage of these chairs would usually be lawyers' secretaries and other junior staff taking advantage of an idle spell to rubberneck in the courtroom.

Behind the barrier, the audience area was two-tiered. The nether and larger area, seating over two hundred, was primarily but not exclusively the domain of the press. The upper tier was considerably smaller but offered a fine view of the whole courtroom and was used mainly by distinguished official or otherwise worthy visitors.

High along the walls behind the defendants and the interpreters, just below the ceiling, were apertures through which cameras protruded, making a visual record of the trial. For closer shots on the floor, cameras could be placed on tripods in the corner by the judges' entrance door.

The prison was in a separate building, reached from the Palace by a covered walkway. There were several hundred cells in the prison, deployed in three tiers. Upon their arrival at the Palace, the twenty-two defendants (soon reduced to twenty-one by Robert Ley's suicide) were put into single cells on the ground-floor tier; other cells were occupied by potential future defendants and individuals wanted for interrogation and as possible witnesses.

The defendants' cells were spartan, containing little more than a bed, table and chair, and water closet. These inmates were kept under close surveillance by American Army guards, who watched them constantly through holes in the cell doors. Partial privacy was available only at the water closet, which was so situated that the guard could see only the user's feet.

The commandant of the prison and guardian of its security was Colonel Burton C. Andrus, a meticulous, go-by-the-book regular officer, stocky and pompous, usually seen under a bright green helmet liner and carrying a riding crop. Most of the defendants, as former holders of high positions, detested the colonel, who addressed them like a martinet drill sergeant. Goering, Papen, and Schacht railed at him, but Andrus, regardless of past rank, treated all the inmates alike. He could be vastly irritating, but he did his best to be fair.

Most trying for the defendants were the limits imposed on them for security. They could write and receive only one letter per week and could not receive packages at all. Once a day they could walk in the prison yard, but they were required to keep a distance from their fellows and not converse. Their only opportunities to talk to each other came in the courtroom when the court rose and at lunch, when they were seated by fours in different rooms. The defendants could not be required to respond to questions from the prosecutors, but such sessions were both sources of information and a relief from solitude, so virtually all the defendants accepted. Conferences with their lawyers required screens so that papers could pass between them only through the guard's hands.

Many of the defendants had come to Nuremberg with trunks or bags full of various commodities which they could not keep in their cells, but there was an area near the cells where they were kept, and officer guards authorized to hold the keys could bring the defendants whatever things they reasonably needed. They were expected to be decently dressed in court, and clothes would be provided for any defendant who lacked suitable apparel.

Coal and food were in short supply, and during the winter of 1945-1946 the defendants were often cold. Their food was provided in the same amounts made available to the German population. The defendants were thinned, especially Goering, whose health and appearance were greatly improved. Certainly the defendants were much better off than the millions of Germans huddling in the cellars of bombed-out buildings and scratching for food or fuels in unpleasant and degrading ways.

The Palace of Justice itself was a complex of four linked structures, stretching for some three blocks along the Fürtherstrasse. The river Pegnitz ran through Nuremberg just behind the Palace. The courtroom was on the second floor of the easternmost wing, and the Palace's main entrance was a few yards to the west, plentifully guarded by well-armed American soldiers who checked everyone's credentials, often rather brusquely. The prosecution's offices were in the next building to the west; it was the longest one and was furnished with a frontal parking lot, with placards naming the individuals entitled to the spaces. Justice Jackson's name quite rightly led all the rest, followed by Alderman, Shea (while he was there), Gill, Gordon Dean, and the several eagle colonels, as well as Ensign Jackson, the Justice's son, whose inclusion provoked a few snide remarks from those of considerably senior rank but not so favored.

The American prosecution controlled an annex to the Palace jail which consisted of a large residence in Erlenstegen known as "The Guest House"—the place where Leverkuehn seduced Lahousen to accept General Donovan's invitation to dinner and break his date with Richard Sonnenfeldt. The purpose of the house was to furnish a safe haven with a measure of surveillance for individuals who were not war crimes suspects but who, because of relationships or other connections with important Nazis or Nazi events, might be useful sources of information or possible witnesses.

In charge of the Guest House was a handsome Hungarian countess of German birth, Ingeborg Kalnoky, who functioned as house manager and, to some extent, as confidante and supervisor of the guests. Hitler's personal photographer, Heinrich Hoffmann—whose daughter Henriette was married to the defendant Baldur von Schirach and who was employed by the Americans to organize and index his thousands of Nazi-period photographs—was a permanent resident. Others, besides Lahousen and Leverkuehn (until Jackson ordered the latter's exile from Nuremberg), included Dr. Karl Haushofer (patron saint of geopolitics, mentor of Rudolf Hess, and counselor to Hitler), Rudolf Diels (briefly Chief of the Gestapo, who soon fell out of favor but survived), and the three generals whom Alderman had interrogated in Virginia, one of whom was General Ernst Koestring, military attaché in Moscow until Hitler turned the Wehrmacht against the Soviet Union. With such varied and knowledgeable guests, dinner conversation in Countess Kalnoky's boardinghouse was lively and often contentious.

# 9

The war crimes community landed in Nuremberg like stones dropping from the sky. Whether they were diamonds or dross, the inhabitants knew and cared naught. As far as they were concerned, the newcomers might well have been Martians, for they were doing strange and bewildering things, and figuring it out was not a priority problem for the natives.

In Nuremberg everything lay in shambles. There was no money and not much to buy with it anyhow. Winter was coming. How to find a roof over the head, a stick of wood or lump of coal to burn, a bit of food, a cigarette? How to keep body and soul together? For the moment, that was all that really mattered.

The Fuehrer was apparently dead, Goebbels and Himmler too. *Der*

*Dicke* and a bunch of other Nazi *Bonzen* ("Bigwigs") were on trial in the old courthouse, but it was all mixed up, and anyhow nobody in authority told the truth. Let the "Amis" take care of the mess.

Strange as it may seem today, we (other than those who had lived in Germany) were about as indifferent to the Germans as they to us. By this I do not mean that Germans and occupiers were unaware of each other's existence or of their mutual dependence. The occupiers, particularly the Americans, were vital to the occupied for aid in distributing the necessities of life, whether coal and food, or jobs which brought the lucky owner into the occupiers' oases of comfort. And for their part the occupiers well knew that only Germans could get Germany going again or provide the workers necessary for many of the projects they wished to carry out.

But still there was a great gulf fixed, despite the easing of social relations following abandonment of the nonfraternization policy in the fall of 1945. In Nuremberg the gulf was probably wider than elsewhere. Compared to Berlin, Frankfurt, and Munich it was a small city, and virtually all occupiers were engaged in a single project, which drew them together in the same places every day. The male members were bachelors or wifeless husbands; few of the females were married, and many were attractive. Under these circumstances the occupiers had less need to rely on Fräuleins for mixed companionship than did the average occupying soldier. In age and sex, the Nuremberg war crimes community was fairly well balanced.

Then, too, there was the nature of the mission in which we were engaged—to prove, expose, and justify severe punishment for atrocities committed by *Germans*. Even if one rejected the idea of criminal guilt for the German people as a whole, there was no denying that those guilty of the charged offenses were Germans. Furthermore, too many Germans, when such unpleasant subjects arose, were prone to deny all knowledge of atrocities or blame them entirely on Hitler. All these factors fostered a standoffish attitude toward the Germans, compounded by self-consciousness and suspicion, even among those who, like myself, had not felt it before exposure to the Nuremberg evidence.

For much the same reasons, relations between the prosecution and defense counsel were strictly business. Of course the German lawyers were essential to the proceeding; if they had not served the defendants, there could have been no meaningful trial. Civility and a fair opportunity to defend their clients were not only their due, but as necessary to us as to them. However, the relation between the German lawyers and ourselves could not be like that of British barristers on circuit, where those who had been at each other's throats in court that day could settle down together that evening for a friendly drink and chat. The appalling organized atrocities of the Nazi leaders lay between us, and we seldom encountered the German counsel outside the Palace of Justice.

But if there were explanations and, perhaps, justifications for drawing these lines, there was a different facet of the German presence, having nothing to do with personal interrelations, with which we did not deal effectively. That was the problem of bringing the Germans into the audience of the trial itself. Given the shock, destitution, and destruction under which Germany lay, that was at best a very difficult undertaking, but much more could have been accomplished than the very little that was attempted.

Jackson made no mention of this matter either in his June 1945 report to Truman or in his opening statement. His stage was the world, his targets a successful trial of the defendants, exposure of their horrendous crimes, and establishment of the London Charter principles as law. The German people had appeared to him only as a dim background to these lofty goals, but after he had seen a bit of the shattered country he realized the importance of showing the Germans what the Nazism they had supported had really been. He wrote to Gordon Dean: "This story must be got to the German people by their own journalists, who must not suffer discrimination, but be helped with the fullest courtroom facilities."

German journalism, however, was in the process of rebirth and barely out of the womb. Initially, the Nazi-controlled press had been suppressed as the Allied forces swept across Germany, and soon after V-E Day it had been totally eliminated. In the American Zone it was temporarily replaced by army publications such as *The Stars and Stripes*. After rejection of the initial plans for prepublication censorship, licensing of German newspapers in the American Zone began on July 31, 1945, and by the time the trial began there were twenty American-licensed newspapers,° only five of them dailies.

The United States, Britain, France, and the Soviet Union maintained staffs which covered the Palace of Justice for the licensed German newspapers in their respective zones. Shortly after the trial began, however, German journalists appeared in Nuremberg, and by November 29 there were twelve from United States–licensed newspapers on hand, who rotated in using the seven seats assigned them in the courtroom. The Russians gave up five of their courtroom seats to German correspondents from their zone. Records of the USFET information service indicated that, on the average, the German papers in the American Zone were devoting 19 percent of their news columns to the Nuremberg trial.

Since the new German journals appeared as the quickest way to get information about the trials to the German public through their own report-

---

°The *Frankfurter Rundschau* was licensed on July 31 and thereafter nine in Bavaria, five more in Hesse, four in Württemberg-Baden, and one each in Bremen (an American port enclave) and Berlin. Only the Hesse papers were dailies; the Berlin *Tagespiel* was published every day except Monday and the others three or four days a week.

ers, it is hardly surprising that Jackson turned in that direction to get his "story" to the people. Yet it soon became apparent that this course of action had its drawbacks. The credibility of the Nazi press had worn thin as the war became a series of Nazi retreats and enemy bombers tore up the cities. While the Third Reich disintegrated, the pronouncements of officialdom and the "news" in the press found few believers. Since the disclosures at Nuremberg were so horrifying that even those of us who encountered them daily in the documents we handled could hardly believe what we read, why should it be expected that the Germans would readily believe these ghoulish tales in newspapers licensed by their recent enemies?

Answers to such questions were soon forthcoming. Early in January 1946, Dr. Robert Kempner passed on to Jackson a letter he had just received from Dr. Friedrich Bergold, who had the unenviable task of defending the absent Martin Bormann. Dr. Bergold, just returned from a Christmas visit to his family, reported:

> Numerous conversations with the population have proved to me that the present Trial is considered in the eyes of wide circles as something taking place on the moon. No one believes that the terrible facts which horrify all feeling people are actually true. My attempts to inform them of the true circumstances are hindered because no one among the German people believes newspaper stories any longer. . . .The people declare that the entire Trial is exaggerated propaganda, they all refuse to believe in the atrocities revealed. . . . To use an oft repeated word in Germany the entire Trial is considered a swindle.

> My exact descriptions awakened everywhere the greatest interest and I was able to enlighten most of my listeners about the truth of this Trial. Horror over the facts was thereby all the greater.

> These experiences led me to the thought that it would be better in the interests of the German people and at the same time that of the other nations, if so many rows of the gallery were not filled unnecessarily with men in uniform (who, in most cases are only satisfying their private curiosity), but instead several rows were allocated to German spectators from all parts of Germany. Thus the Trial would have an entirely different moral effect.

> The best propaganda against the deep mistrust of the German population towards newspaper stories is the so-called "oral" propaganda. The German spectators at the Trial would be far more effectively able to convince wide circles of the population of the truth and importance of the Trial.

> I therefore beg to suggest that permission be granted for German spectators to attend [the Trial]. I would also suggest that not only anti-Fascist circles but also the so-called Fascist circles be included so that these deceived people can be healed by a sight of the truth.

Courtroom space was made available and some Germans came, but more had neither time nor taste for the experience. Of course, even if half the courtroom were filled by Germans every day, the total would still have been a drop in the bucket.

Yet Bergold was right that immediate contact with the proofs was far more effective than newspaper articles. General Eisenhower had perceived this when he ordered that the local burgomasters and other town leaders be forced to view the shame of Buchenwald. But to make effective use of the Nuremberg proofs on a broad basis would have been a major undertaking, requiring pamphlets, lecturers, photographs, motion pictures, and much more.

In later years Jackson lamented the "neglected opportunity": "I think the Americans have done a very bad job in making the proceedings available to the Germans." For some reason the American military authorities opposed public showing of the Nuremberg films and gave little support to the efforts of motion picture directors such as Pare Lorentz, who hoped to organize the loose collection into an effective, comprehensive presentation.

Interest in these projects within the war crimes community was not extensive. I do not recall that the fostering of German attendance at the Palace of Justice crossed my own mind until after I became responsible for conducting the later Nuremberg trials.

# Chapter 10

# THE SS AND THE GENERAL STAFF—
# HIGH COMMAND

I n accordance with Jackson's instructions, soon after arriving in Nuremberg I embarked on preparations for presenting the charges in the
Indictment against the organization or group described as the "General
Staff and High Command of the German Armed Forces." From then until
early January 1946, when the case was heard by the Tribunal, this project,
except for general consultation with Jackson and liaison with the Soviet
delegation, was my sole employment.

From the beginning I was aware that this was going to be a difficult
and, in some quarters, an unpopular undertaking. Within ten days an
extraneous problem arose. After General Barker's go-ahead in early September from Shea, he soon got approval from General Clay for the plan to
allow German generals and General Staff officers to be discharged and live
at home, but under severe restrictions and strict surveillance. But when the
proposal was brought before the Control Council, the British, French, and
Soviet representatives all objected, declaring that the German officers in
question should be held "in detention outside of Germany"—a proposal
tantamount to exile.

On October 17, 1945, Jackson's office was informed of this situation.
It was then suggested to Jackson (by whom I do not know) that the General
Staff–High Command should "be dropped from the Indictment" in view of
the apparent prospect that this or a very similar group would be dealt with
by "political decision" of the Control Council. Jackson then requested Ben
Kaplan and me to prepare a memorandum commenting on the proposal.
Submitted to him on October 22, 1945, it read, in part:

> If the entire question of punishing the Germans who were re-
> sponsible for waging the war and committing atrocities had been dealt

with by political or military decision, it would, of course, have been possible to deal with the German High Command in the same fashion and as part of the same process. . . . But we are now faced with the situation where 24 Germans, including 4 members of the German High Command, and 7 principal German organizations or groups,° have been solemnly indicted for criminality and the public is expecting their trial before the International Military Tribunal. The proposal to drop the High Command from the Indictment must be examined in the light of this existing situation.

Viewed in this light, we do not think that any of the three alternatives for "political treatment" . . . are feasible and satisfactory. As for the first alternative, it would be hard to justify long prison terms for the principal German officers, merely on the basis of their status as officers. . . . The same is almost equally true of the proposal to exile the officers. . . .The third alternative, i.e., a quiet home life under surveillance, is clearly inadequate, standing by itself. . . .

Trial of the German High Command before the International Military Tribunal is another method of approach to the problem. In view of the difficulty of defining the German High Command as a group within the meaning of the Protocol, it may or may not have been wise to cover them into the Indictment, but that is water over the dam. If we lose, we are likely to lose on a technical point arising out of the language of the Protocol rather than on the merits. . . .

Under all the circumstances, the proposal to drop the "General Staff and High Command" from the Indictment seems to us of very dubious merit. The following additional arguments seem in point:

(a) If such action is taken the public would be led to think that there never was a convincing case against the High Command. . . .

(b) The public may not understand why political action is taken against the military group but not against the other defendants and groups, notably the SS and the Gestapo. . . .

(c) To drop a group out of the Indictment solemnly filed before the International Military Tribunal and dispose of that group politically might well put the rest of the case in a curious if not sinister light. It might lend force to the view that the entire proceeding has always been a sham; that it is merely a means to a political end determined upon in advance. . . .

We must also mention the fact that the "General Staff and High Command" group was added to the Indictment at the urgent insistence of the American chief prosecutor and in spite of strong opposition by the British. The Russian chief prosecutor supported the American view with great vigor. If a suggestion to drop the High

°When this was written, Ley had not yet committed suicide and Gustav Krupp's unavailability had not yet been established—hence the "24" defendants. Counting Goering there were in fact five members of the High Command. Appendix B of the Indictment listed six, not seven, groups or organizations.

Command from the Indictment now originates with the Americans, the reaction of the other chief prosecutors may be decidedly unfavorable.

The same day, Peter Calvocoressi submitted to Jackson a short memorandum explaining the difficulty of portraying the "General Staff and High Command," as defined in the Indictment, to be a "group or organization" within the meaning of the London Charter. The officers described in the Indictment, he observed, "are in fact the top men in the chain of command. Clearly a line had to be drawn somewhere. The difficulty is to show that by drawing the line as in fact drawn [i.e., between the *Oberbefehlshaber* and those of lesser command status] something coherent has emerged." Apart from command of troops, authority over the enemy civilians in a theater of war (an authority denominated *Vollziehende Gewalt*, executive power) had generally been given only to *Oberbefehlshaber*, but this might be difficult to prove, and success would "depend on the at present unpredictable prospects of getting information by . . . interrogation and then converting the information into evidence by getting suitable witnesses at the trial."

Despite the uncertain prospects of success, Jackson decided not to drop the General Staff project. But a few weeks later it was sharply attacked in the press by unnamed American Army officers. How much General Donovan had to do with this is not clear, but on November 26, at the time of his departure from Nuremberg, the *New York Times* carried an article, by Frank E. Mason of the North American Newspaper Alliance, which began: "For weeks regular Army officers in Germany have viewed the development of Justice Robert H. Jackson's new theories of international law with distrust." The "new principle" espoused by Jackson, the article declared, was "that all General Staff and High Command officers be condemned as a criminal group . . . on no more evidence than their membership in the General Staff. Our regular officers in Europe are becoming increasingly vocal in expressing opposition to any such international law." Comparable attacks in other periodicals, some referring by name to General Donovan, subsequently appeared.

The unnamed American officers were probably unaware that their complaint would be equally applicable to the other five indicted organizations if individual criminal guilt were to rest on membership and nothing more. That view was held by some members of the prosecution staff, but had not been and never was established as the legal consequence of a finding of organizational criminality.

However, at the time in question there could be no objection to attacking a "guilt by membership" legal doctrine. What was ironic was the source from which the attack was launched. For "guilt by membership" in the German General Staff was precisely the doctrine that General Eisenhower had been preaching ever since 1944 and precisely the method which General Clay, General Barker, and various members of the other delegations to the Control Council in Berlin were planning to utilize against the German General Staff—some recommending exile, others virtual house arrest. These plans carried the "guilt by membership" principle far beyond anything that had been or ever was accepted at Nuremberg, but as far as I know they triggered no public animadversions.

Plainly, high-level American Regular Army attitudes toward their defeated German compeers were remarkably inconsistent. Clarity was by no means served by the fact that at this very time, in the Philippines, five Regular Army U.S. generals, at the behest of General Douglas MacArthur, were trying General Tomoyuki Yamashita for failing to prevent his troops from massacring numerous Filipino civilians. There was no specific allegation that Yamashita had ordered these atrocities, or even that he knew at the time that they were in process, or that he could have stopped them had he known. On such a record, the indictment of a German general, much less the conviction and execution imposed on Yamashita, would have been highly unlikely. Apparently, in old-line military circles yellow generals did not rank as high in the scale of virtue as Nordic white ones.

A very different diagnosis of the General Staff–High Command situation has been published by General Donovan's biographer, Anthony Cave Brown. After describing Donovan's hostility to the charge against the General Staff–High Command, Brown writes:

> The issue caused Donovan's resignation from Jackson's staff, for when Truman agreed that the General Staff and the officers' corps should be regarded as war criminals, Donovan objected, first gently, then forcefully. When Jackson refused to advise the President not to support the Russian demand for the indictment of the General Staff, Donovan decided he should return to the full-time directorship of the OSS.

Much of this passage is plainly incorrect. The Russians never made any "demand" for indictment of the General Staff. The entire initiative came from the United States, from Harry Hopkins's interview with Stalin in May 1945 to Jackson's last-minute insistence, on October 2, that the General Staff be added to the Indictment as a criminal organization. The Soviet Union, together with France, supported Jackson's proposal, but at no time took any initiative on the matter.

Furthermore, Brown's chronology is inaccurate in picturing Donovan as returning to "full-time directorship of the OSS." That agency, as Brown himself accurately states elsewhere, was abolished by Truman's executive order on September 20, 1945. The rift between Donovan and Jackson over the General Staff Indictment did not arise until the second week in October, when Donovan and Jackson met in Berlin after the General's long absence from the war crimes scene. As mentioned earlier, Donovan did not leave Nuremberg until the end of November.

Finally, it is altogether unlikely that Donovan approached Truman on the issue or regarded him as a factor in the situation. As Brown rightly points out, there was no rapport between Truman and Donovan, and Truman had, with alacrity, abolished the OSS. Jackson's letter to Truman, informing the President of Donovan's departure, is quite inconsistent with any idea that Truman had any prior knowledge of the General Staff matter, much less that he had been "supporting the Russian demand."

No source is cited by Brown for the passage in question, and my repeated inquiries to him went unanswered, as did my questions to Jackson's son, Bill.

2

Despite these several obstacles to the continued life of the General Staff charge, Jackson never displayed to me any uncertainty of its status as an important part of the prosecution case. We moved ahead with the preparations, and by early December the greater part of the evidence was in hand.

Calvocoressi's prediction to Jackson that support for the Indictment's definition of the General Staff–High Command group would depend on information to be obtained from German officers and presented in evidentiary form proved correct. In retrospect it is clear to me that my own principal contribution to the General Staff case was my success in proposing and obtaining in London the attachment of Calvocoressi and his associates to the prosecution staff and subsequently in Nuremberg the addition to my own staff of two experienced American Army interrogators, Major Paul Neuland and Captain Walter H. Rapp.

For the purposes at hand, I could not have been better served. I had sound legal assistance from Loftus Becker and excellent secretarial service from Betty Stark. Calvocoressi and his associates were all fluent in German and well trained in military intelligence methods and German military organization. Neuland and Rapp had a good general knowledge of the German Army, and proved to be excellent interrogators.

During November the work of this group bore evidentiary fruit of a quantity and quality far beyond my expectations. I remember my astonishment when Peter appeared in my office with a huge chart of the top organizations of the Wehrmacht, drawn in complete conformity with the General Staff–High Command as defined in the Indictment and certified on oath by General Franz Halder, Chief of Staff of the German Army from 1938 to 1942, as "in effect the General Staff and High Command of the

German Armed Forces." There followed like affidavits signed by Field Marshal Walter von Brauchitsch, Commander in Chief of the German Army during the early years of the war, and General Johannes Blaskowitz who, as an *Oberbefehlshaber*, had held the highest field commands (of army groups) throughout the war. Other affidavits from Blaskowitz and Field Marshal Werner von Blomberg, Commander in Chief of the Wehrmacht until his discharge by Hitler in 1938, stated that the General Staff officers virtually all supported Hitler's prewar policies and favored military aggression against Poland, if necessary, to annex the Polish Corridor established by the Versailles Treaty between East and West Prussia. Still another affidavit, signed by Walter Schellenberg, an SS foreign intelligence section chief, established the involvement of the German Army leaders in the mass murders committed by the SS Einsatzgruppen in the German-occupied areas of the Soviet Union.

But would the Tribunal receive these affidavits in evidence? Since affidavits cannot be cross-examined, they are not generally accepted as evidence in criminal trials. On the morning of November 28, however, the Tribunal had received, over defense objections, an affidavit offered by Alderman and signed by George S. Messersmith, who had been the American Minister to Austria during the time of the Anschluss. The Tribunal appears to have been moved by the circumstance that Messersmith was the Ambassador in Mexico City, and both his obligations there and his age (he was in his seventies) made him reluctant to make the trip to Nuremberg.

That afternoon the Tribunal refused to receive an affidavit offered by Alderman and signed by Kurt von Schuschnigg, Prime Minister of Austria and a leading participant in the Anschluss crisis. Schuschnigg, in contrast to Messersmith, was nearby and readily available for court testimony.

So were the German officers and officials who had signed the affidavits that my staff had procured. If the Schuschnigg decision meant that I must call all those affidavit signers to give their testimony in court, that would greatly prolong my presentation. Furthermore, it was likely that the defense lawyers might seek to draw statements from the witnesses which would greatly weaken their direct testimony. Since we as prosecutors would be offering the affidavits and have called the witnesses, the Tribunal might well not allow us to cross-examine them.

Early in December I described this problem to Jackson, and on December 5 he raised the matter at a meeting of the chief prosecutors. He described the Halder affidavit and reported that Halder would surely confirm its contents. Halder would, however, insist on exonerating the General Staff of all criminal responsibility, and in all probability the prosecution would not be permitted to cross-examine him, as he would be their own witness. Jackson proposed, and the other prosecutors agreed, that the Tribunal should be requested to permit the evidentiary use of affidavits which were not directed against any individual defendant, subject to the right of the defense to call the affidavit signers for questioning in court.

Two days later I sent Jackson a comprehensive memorandum on the presentation of evidence in the General Staff–High Command case. I told him that my staff had twenty affidavits from about a dozen witnesses, available in all the court languages, and urged him to proceed with efforts to persuade the Tribunal to modify its position, as taken in the Schuschnigg case, so as to permit the reception of affidavits, subject to the right of the defense "to call any of them for cross-examination within the scope of the written statement."

There were further developments the following week. On December 13, while presenting evidence with respect to concentration camps, Dodd produced a report which included an affidavit by one Andreas Pfaffenberger, a prisoner at the Buchenwald concentration camp who reported that he had seen tattooed prisoners killed so that their tattooed skin could be used for the manufacture of lamp shades for the use of Ilse Koch, wife of the camp commandant.

The following morning Dr. Kurt Kauffmann, counsel for Kaltenbrunner, requested that the Tribunal strike from the record the Pfaffenberger affidavit and declare a general rule that the testimony of witnesses living in Germany and available to testify in court could not be given by affidavit. In support of these points he referred to the Tribunal's exclusion of the Schuschnigg affidavit previously offered by Alderman.

Jackson and Rudenko (as well as Roberts and Faure) were both in court, which suggests that they were forewarned of Kauffmann's demarche. Replying to Kauffmann, Jackson laid primary stress on Article 19 of the Charter, which freed the Tribunal from "technical rules of evidence" and adjured it to adopt "expeditious and nontechnical" procedures. Acceptance of affidavits was essential "if we are to make progress with this case." In reply to a question from Lawrence, Jackson acknowledged that he did not know where Pfaffenberger was; he would try to find out. There was further colloquy, in the course of which Rudenko, Roberts, and Faure supported Jackson's position and several defense counsel sided with Kauffmann.

After the luncheon recess, Lawrence announced that Kauffmann's motion to strike the Pfaffenberger affidavit was denied, subject to the defendants' right to call him for cross-examination. Kauffmann at once rose and moved that an affidavit offered by Major Walsh at the close of the morning session be stricken from the record. This affidavit had been signed on November 28 in Nuremberg by Dr. Wilhelm Hoettl, an SS functionary and former assistant to Adolf Eichmann, and it recorded a statement to Hoettl by Eichmann in 1944 that 4 million Jews had been killed in concentration camps and 2 million others by the Einsatzgruppen in other ways. Kauffmann pointed out that Hoettl, unlike Pfaffenberger, was in Nuremberg, in the prosecution's custody, and could promptly be made available to testify in court.

Walsh raised no objection to Hoettl's being called. Lawrence, without more ado, denied the motion to strike his affidavit, subject to the same condition as in the Pfaffenberger case. In neither decision did Lawrence give reasons or make any statement other than the bare result. The Hoettl decision appeared to be directly contrary to the earlier rejection of the Schuschnigg affidavit, but the Tribunal's failure to lay down any general rule left us uncertain of its action on future affidavit presentations. As for the affidavits that I was planning to offer, I was left in a state of nervous hope.

Of course, preparation of the General Staff case involved much more than the affidavits. As in the prosecution's case in general, documents would play the major role. We had not initially planned to call any witnesses unless obliged to if the Tribunal rejected our affidavits. Late in November, however, Peter came into my office with the news that our interrogators had come upon a German prisoner of high military rank who might make a very useful witness.

Erich von dem Bach-Zelewski was a German Army soldier during World War I and a junior officer in the postwar army until 1924, when he resigned. He joined the SS in 1930 and subsequently the military SS (Waffen-SS); by November 1941 he had risen to the rank of *Obergruppenfuehrer* (the equivalent of a lieutenant general in the American Army), commanding the SS troops in the central section of the German front in the Soviet Union. At the end of 1942 he was appointed Chief of Anti-Partisan Combat Units on the Eastern Front.

Bach-Zelewski was in command of military operations waged with utter ruthlessness, including suppression of the Warsaw uprising in 1944. He was certainly no angel and did not claim to be, but he was thoroughly familiar with the army's conduct of the war on the Eastern Front and its involvement in war crimes, and he was willing to testify on those matters. Peter and our interrogators believed that he would be as good as his word, and after participating in several interviews, I concluded that he should testify. Under staff rules I was required to clear this decision with Amen and Dodd, with neither of whom I had much rapport. But I think they knew that Jackson would back me up, and they rather sourly accepted my decision.

By the time of the Christmas recess, despite a lingering unease about the affidavits, I felt that we were well prepared. Indeed, success with the Brauchitsch and Halder affidavits had turned my head to the point that I assured Jackson that the Indictment's definition of the General Staff–High Command was "thoroughly sound"—a spasm of overconfidence that wore off long before the end of the trial. But the evidence of widespread involvement of the army leaders in atrocious war crimes was so compelling that I felt sure we would in any event make a forceful and effective presentation.

*3*

When I returned from a brief Christmas vacation in England, Nuremberg was a dreary place. Everyone wished he was somewhere else, some were already, and many others were soon to be; the American staff was rapidly dwindling. Among those who had departed before Christmas were Harold Leventhal, Ben Kaplan, and Sidney Kaplan—all brilliant lawyers whose exceptional services were behind the scenes and who might well have remained longer if Jackson had given them the shares which they richly deserved in the presentation of the case.

Peter and his group returned from England, and we made final preparations to present our case. But we were not quite yet on deck, and when the Tribunal reassembled on Wednesday, January 2, 1946, Storey was again at the lectern, presenting documents concerning the Gestapo.

Storey opened his presentation by reading a document as horrifying as any in the annals of Nazism. It was one of two affidavits by Hermann Friedrich Graebe, a German building construction manager who, in a civilian capacity, was employed by the German Army in occupied Ukraine from 1941 to 1944. On several occasions he observed mass murders of local Jews committed by the SS with the assistance of Ukrainian militiamen, including one which occurred on October 5, 1942, near the city of Dubno. That morning he was told that, near his building site, all of the some 5,000 Jews in Dubno were being shot and buried in large pits. Graebe's affidavit continues:

> Thereupon I drove to the site . . . and saw near it great mounds of earth, about 30 meters long and 2 meters high. Several trucks stood in front of the mounds. Armed Ukrainian militia drove the people off the trucks under the supervision of an SS-man. The militia men acted as guards on the trucks and drove them to and from the pit. All these people had the regulation yellow patches on the front and back of their clothes, and thus could be recognized as Jews. . . .
> . . . Now I heard rifle shots in quick succession, from behind one of the earth mounds. The people who had got off the trucks—men, women, and children of all ages—had to undress upon the order of an SS-man, who carried a riding or dog whip. They had to put down their clothes in fixed places, sorted according to shoes, top clothing and underclothing. I saw a heap of shoes of about 800 to 1000 pairs, great piles of under-linen and clothing. Without screaming or weeping these people undressed, stood around in family groups, kissed each other, said farewells and waited for a sign from another SS-man, who stood near the pit, also with a whip in his hand. During the 15 minutes that I stood near the pit I heard no complaint or plea for mercy. I watched

a family of about 8 persons, a man and a woman, both about 50 with their children of about 1, 8 and 10, and two grownup daughters of about 20 to 24. An old woman with snow-white hair was holding the one-year old child in her arms and singing to it, and tickling it. The child was cooing with delight. The couple were looking on with tears in their eyes. The father was holding the hand of a boy about 10 years old and speaking to him softly; the boy was fighting his tears. The father pointed toward the sky, stroked his head, and seemed to explain something to him. At that moment the SS-man at the pit shouted something to his comrade. The latter counted off about 20 persons and instructed them to go behind the earth mound. Among them was the family, which I have mentioned. I well remember a girl, slim and with black hair, who, as she passed close to me, pointed to herself and said, "23". I walked around the mound, and found myself confronted by a tremendous grave. People were closely wedged together and lying on top of each other so that only their heads were visible. Nearly all had blood running over their shoulders from their heads. Some of the people shot were still moving. Some were lifting their arms and turning their heads to show that they were still alive. The pit was already $2/3$ full. I estimated that it already contained about 1000 people. I looked for the man who did the shooting. He was an SS-man, who sat at the edge of the narrow end of the pit, his feet dangling into the pit. He had a tommy gun on his knees and was smoking a cigarette. The people, completely naked, went down some steps which were cut in the clay wall of the pit and clambered over the heads of the people lying there, to the place to which the SS-man directed them. They lay down in front of the dead or injured people; some caressed those who were still alive and spoke to them in a low voice. Then I heard a series of shots. I looked into the pit and saw that the bodies were twitching or the heads lying already motionless on top of the bodies that lay before them. Blood was running from their necks. I was surprised that I was not ordered away, but I saw that there were two or three postmen in uniform nearby. The next batch was approaching already. They went down into the pit, lined themselves up against the previous victims and were shot. When I walked back, round the mound I noticed another truckload of people which had just arrived. This time it included sick and infirm people. An old, very thin woman with terribly thin legs was undressed by the others who were already naked, while two people held her up. The woman appeared to be paralyzed. The naked people carried the woman around the mound. . . .*

---

*Defense counsel did not object to acceptance of Graebe's two affidavits. The portions read by Storey, though sufficiently shocking, do not comprise the most vivid passages, which were later read by Sir Hartley Shawcross in his closing statement, included in the Tribunal's judgment, and set forth here. Graebe, for his pains, found postwar life in Germany unpleasant and emigrated to the United States. He settled in San Francisco, where he died at the age of eighty-five in 1986.

Comparable episodes, for which the Einsatzgruppen were chiefly responsible, had been occurring behind the German battle lines ever since the start of the Nazi-Soviet war, but few eyewitness accounts of the mass killings have come to light. Storey did not undertake to develop the dimensions of the Graebe affidavits. He continued his production of Gestapo and other documents, establishing what Dr. von der Lippe described as "a chain of atrocities," until the noon recess. He then turned the lectern over to Lieutenant Commander Whitney Harris, who presented a series of documents that focused on the criminal activities of Kaltenbrunner, the only SS official among the defendants.

Harris finished early the following morning, after which Amen called a witness who proved to be, in an evidentiary sense, a real blockbuster. Otto Ohlendorf was an SS official who had commanded one of the four Einsatzgruppen during the first year of the German-Soviet war. He had joined the Nazi Party in 1925 at the age of eighteen, had risen rapidly in the SS hierarchy, and by 1939 had become a section chief in the SS intelligence and security service and was regarded as one of Himmler's bright young men.

Under Amen's questioning, the witness vouched for the accuracy of a chart which showed that Einsatzgruppen A, B, and C were attached respectively to the northern, central, and southern German army groups on the front in Russia and that Einsatzgruppe D, commanded by Ohlendorf, was attached to the 11th Army, which, operating independently of the army groups, entered the Ukraine from Romania and drove easterly along the Black Sea coast to Odessa and the Crimea. The Einsatzgruppen were the headquarters, subordinate to which were several Einsatzcommandos comprising the troops which would conduct the field operations. Further interchanges between Amen and Ohlendorf included the following:

A: State, if you know, whether prior to the campaign against Soviet Russia, any agreement was entered into between the OKW, OKH, and RSHA?°

o: Yes, the Einsatzgruppen and Einsatzcommandos . . . were used on the basis of a written agreement between the OKW, OKH, and RSHA. . . .

A: To the best of your knowledge and recollection, please explain to the Tribunal the entire substance of this written agreement.

o: First of all, the agreement specified that the Einsatzgruppen and Einsatzcommandos would be set up and used in the operational areas. . . . The agreement specified that the army groups or armies would be responsible for the movements and supply of Einsatzgruppen, but that instructions for their activities would come from the Chief of the Sipo and SD [i.e., Reinhard Heydrich]. . . . Even though the Chiefs of the Sipo and SD had the right to issue instructions to them on their work, there existed a general agreement

°OKW was Hitler's military headquarters, OKH was the German Army headquarters, and RSHA was one of Himmler's headquarters.

that the army was also entitled to issue instructions to the Einsatzgruppen, if the operational situation made it necessary. . . .

A: In what respects, if any, were the official duties of the Einsatz groups concerned with Jews and Communist Commissars [Communists who provided political leadership in the field]?

O: On the question of Jews and Communists, the Einsatzgruppen and the commanders of the Einsatzcommandos were orally instructed before their mission.

A: What were their instructions with respect to the Jews and Communists?

O: The instructions were that in the Russian operational areas of the Einsatzgruppen the Jews, as well as the Soviet political commissars, were to be liquidated.

A: And when you say "liquidated" do you mean "killed"?

O: Yes, I mean "killed." . . .

A: Do you know whether this mission of the Einsatz group was known to the army group commanders?

O: This order and the execution of these orders were known to the commanding general of the army.

A: How do you know that?

O: Through conference with the army and through instructions which were given by the army on the execution of the order. . . .

A: Who was the commanding officer of the 11th Army?

O: At first, Ritter von Schober [*sic*, Schobert], later, von Manstein.

A: Will you tell the Tribunal in what way or ways the commanding officer of the 11th Army directed or supervised Einsatz Group D in carrying out the liquidation activities?

O: An order from the 11th Army was sent to Nikolaiev stating that liquidations were to take place only at a distance of not less than 200 kilometers° from the headquarters of the commanding general.

A: Do you recall any other occasion?

O: In Simferopol the army commander requested the Einsatzcommandos in the area to hasten the liquidations, because famine was threatening and there was a great housing shortage.

A: Do you know how many persons were liquidated by Einsatz Group D under your direction?

O: In the year between June 1941 and June 1942 the Einsatzcommandos reported 90,000 people liquidated.

A: Did that include men, women, and children?

O: Yes.

---

°200 kilometers (126 miles) is what the transcript states, but so long a distance seems improbable.

During Ohlendorf's testimony, the judges' attention had visibly intensified. There were also gestures of bewilderment, readily explicable. No one could have looked less like a brutish SS thug such as Kaltenbrunner. Ohlendorf was small of stature, young-looking, and rather comely. He spoke quietly, with great precision, dispassion, and apparent intelligence. How could he have done what he now so calmly described? Biddle spoke of Jekyll and Hyde; Dr. von der Lippe called him "ice cold."

Ohlendorf's testimony was in his mind not a confession but an avowal. His cross-examination by Ludwig Babel, counsel for the SS, is revealing:

B: But did you have no scruples in regard to the execution of these orders?

O: Yes, of course.

B: And how is it that they were carried out regardless of these scruples?

O: Because to me it is inconceivable that a subordinate leader should not carry out orders given by the leaders of the state. . . .

B: Was the legality of these orders explained to these people under false pretenses?

O: I do not understand your question; since the order was issued by the superior authorities, the question of illegality could not arise in the minds of these individuals, for they had sworn obedience to the people who had issued the orders.

That was carrying the defense of "superior orders" to the absolute: *Befehl ist Befehl* (orders are orders). Ohlendorf was nothing if not logical, as the ten defense counsel who cross-examined him soon discovered. But at the defendants' lunch hour only Goering was critical, calling Ohlendorf a "swine" who was "selling his soul to the enemy." Frank spoke up for him as "a man who signed his own death warrant to serve the truth," Funk talked in the same vein, and several other defendants agreed that "there was absolutely no question about the reliability of his testimony."

When Ohlendorf finished, Lieutenant Colonel Smith W. Brookhart (son of a well-known senator from Iowa) called as a witness Dieter Wisliceny, an SS official and assistant to Adolf Eichmann, whose whereabouts was unknown. For the most part, Wisliceny's testimony consisted of stating the time, manner, and quantity of the transports of Jews to Auschwitz from Slovakia, Hungary, Greece, Croatia, and Bulgaria. Wisliceny also reported various acts, decisions, and statements by Eichmann, including his often quoted statement near the end of the war that "he would leap laughing into the grave because the feeling that he had 5 million people on his conscience would be for him a source of extraordinary satisfaction."

The following morning, January 4, Amen resumed the lectern and called to the stand SS intelligence chief Walter Schellenberg. His direct testimony was very brief; he corroborated and enlarged on Ohlendorf's testimony about the agreement between the army and the SS with respect to formation of the Einsatzgruppen and their operations behind the battle lines in the Soviet Union. The most important new detail was that the agreement had been negotiated and signed for the army by General Eduard Wagner, the General Quartermaster.°

The last of Amen's witnesses was Alois Hoellriegel, an Austrian non-commissioned officer in the SS who had been a guard at the Mauthausen concentration camp. He was called to establish that both Kaltenbrunner and Schirach had visited the camp in 1942 and that two SS guards had killed prisoners by pushing them off a cliff. Hoellriegel's otherwise somber account produced laughter when Schirach's counsel, Dr. Sauter, asked how many other visitors had accompanied Schirach. The witness replied that he "did not know at the time that I might have to use these figures, so I did not count them."

## 4

Two of Amen's witnesses, Ohlendorf and Schellenberg, by establishing cooperation between the German Army and the Einsatzgruppen, had certainly helped the General Staff–High Command case. Furthermore, during the first two days of the January hearings, several affidavits had been received in evidence without objection. Thus encouraged, we began our presentation on Friday after the midmorning recess.

Because of the public criticism of the Indictment's charges against the German military leaders and awareness of the Tribunal's growing concern over the handling of the "criminal organization" cases, including particularly the General Staff accusations, I took steps to dispel what I believed to be serious misconceptions about the nature of the case:

> Now, needless to say, it is not the Prosecution's position that it is a crime to be a soldier or a sailor or to serve one's country as a soldier or sailor in time of war. The profession of arms is an honorable one and can be honorably practiced. But it is too clear for argument that a man who commits crimes cannot plead as a defense that he committed them in uniform.
>
> It is not in the nature of things and it is not the Prosecution's contention that every member of this group was a wicked man or that they were all equally culpable. But we will show that this group . . . , like Hitler, wanted to aggrandize Germany at the expense of neighboring countries and were prepared to do so by force or threat of force.

°General Wagner occupied that position from 1940 to 1944, when he became involved in the military conspiracy against Hitler of July 20, 1944. When it failed, he committed suicide.

I then took up the most debatable issue: whether the General Staff–High Command was a "group" within the meaning of Article 9 of the Charter. Since this was the most technical part of the case, I had circulated to the Tribunal and the defense counsel a six-page mimeographed pamphlet entitled "Basic Information on the Organization of the German Armed Forces," comprising a brief history of the Wehrmacht's structure under Hitler and its reorganization in 1938; a glossary of German military terms; and a table of German military ranks and their equivalents in American and British military nomenclature.

I had the chart of the group as defined in the Indictment displayed, explained it, and pointed out the boxes in the chart occupied by each of the five member defendants. Then the Brauchitsch and Halder affidavits, certifying the chart as accurate and authentic, were offered and received in evidence. There was no objection, and the most ticklish part of our presentation was behind us.

We concluded the argument on the definition of the group with a few factually explanatory affidavits by Halder, Brauchitsch, and his air force son, Colonel Bernd von Brauchitsch, and a document listing officers in attendance at a conference Hitler called in June 1941, shortly before the attack against the Soviet Union. This showed that those present made up virtually all of the army *Oberbefehlshaber*.

After the luncheon recess, during which Goering and Jodl fulminated against Brauchitsch and Halder for "double-crossing" and "squealing on us as witnesses to save their damn necks," I took up the aggressive war charges. Proof of the military leadership's complicity in these crimes required us to show that the members of the group *knew* that Hitler's military plans were aggressive, and that they *willingly joined* in the execution of those plans.

Their knowledge was readily established by their attendance at Hitler's meetings, the records of which had already been put in evidence by Alderman and the British prosecutors. To show the group's willing participation, we first submitted an affidavit by Blomberg:

From 1919, and particularly from 1924, three essential territorial questions occupied attention in Germany. These were the questions of the Polish Corridor, the Ruhr, and Memel [a Baltic seaport in Lithuania, claimed by Germany].

I, myself, as well as the whole group of German staff officers, believed that these three questions, outstanding among which was the question of the Polish Corridor, would have to be settled some day, if necessary by force of arms. About 90 percent of the German people were of the same mind as the officers on the Polish question. A war to wipe out the outrage perpetrated by the creation of the Polish Corridor and to lessen the threat to separated East Prussia, surrounded by Poland and Lithuania, was regarded as a sacred duty, though a sad necessity. This was one of the chief reasons behind the secret rearmament which began about 10 years before Hitler came to power and was accentuated under Nazi rule.

Comparable views were expressed in an affidavit by Blaskowitz. Blomberg's affidavit continued with his opinions on the German officers' attitude toward Hitler:

> Before 1938-39 the German generals were not opposed to Hitler. There was no reason to oppose Hitler, since he produced the results which they desired. . . .
>
> Shortly before my removal from the post of Commander-in-Chief of the Armed Forces, in January 1938, Hitler asked me to recommend a successor. I suggested Goering, who was the ranking officer, but Hitler objected because of his lack of patience and diligence. . . . Hitler personally took over my function as Commander. Keitel was recommended by me as a *chef de bureau*. . . .
>
> As far as I heard, Keitel did not oppose any of Hitler's measures. He became a willing tool in Hitler's hands for every one of his decisions.

Goering was far from pleased by this publicity, and Keitel was surprised and wounded by Blomberg's appraisal, especially since his eldest son had married Blomberg's youngest daughter.

I continued by reading extracts from a personal diary that Jodl kept while serving under Blomberg and later as Chief of Operations under Keitel. These entries established beyond question Jodl's own fervid support of Hitler's aggressive plans and acts. Other documents, some of which had previously been introduced, and some found by Calvocoressi's team, completed the evidentiary presentation of the aggressive war charges against the group.

At this point I thought it necessary to discuss again, and in greater depth, the criticisms of our case that had been circulated in American military circles. With respect to war crimes, charged as violations of the Hague Conventions and other officially recognized laws of war, it appeared to me that the Yamashita trial and other court-martial proceedings then under way showed conclusively that the American Army, as an institution, recognized that those laws should be enforced and convicted offenders punished. But the "crimes against peace" charged in Counts One and Two of the Indictment as applied to military officers raised more complicated issues.

In the first place, the legal basis for treating aggressive war as a punishable crime was sharply disputed. To be sure, that problem was not confined to the military charges. But even if the concept of crimes against peace is generally accepted, its application to the military profession troubles many who believe that military leaders are duty-bound to follow the orders of the Chief of State and that within the military chain of command superior orders must always be obeyed. With such conceptions, it is easy to conclude that, so far as concerned the charge of crimes against peace, Keitel, Jodl, Raeder, and Doenitz were "only following orders"—"only doing their duty." I omit Goering from those names only because few if any thought that he was "only obeying orders," and it was obvious that he himself did not think so.

I spoke at some length in an effort to clarify these matters, saying in part:

> I want to make clear again the nature of the accusations against this group under Counts One and Two. They are not accused on the ground that they are soldiers. They are not accused merely for doing the usual things that a soldier is expected to do, such as making military plans and commanding troops. . . .
>
> It is an innocent and respectable business to be a locksmith; but it is nonetheless a crime if the locksmith turns his talents to picking the locks of neighbors and looting their homes. And that is the nature of the charge under Counts One and Two against the defendants and the General Staff and High Command group. The charge is that in performing the functions of diplomats, politicians, soldiers, sailors, or whatever they happened to be, they conspired, and did plan, prepare, initiate, and wage illegal wars and thereby committed crimes under Article 6(a) of the Charter. . . .
>
> The military defendants will perhaps argue that they are pure technicians. This amounts to saying that military men are a race apart from and different from the ordinary run of human beings—men above and beyond the moral and legal requirements that apply to others, incapable of exercising moral judgment on their own behalf. . . .
>
> The prevalence of such a view would be particularly unfortunate today, when military leaders control forces infinitely more powerful and destructive than ever before. Should the military leaders be declared exempt from the declaration in the Charter that planning and waging aggressive war is a crime, it would be a crippling, if not a fatal blow to the efficacy of that declaration.
>
> Such is not the view of the United States. The prosecution here representing the United States believe that the profession of arms is a distinguished profession. We believe that the practice of that profession by its leaders calls for the highest degree of integrity and moral wisdom no less than for technical skill. We believe that, in consulting and planning with the leaders in other fields of national activity, the military leaders must act in accordance with international law and the

dictates of the public conscience. Otherwise the military resources of
the nation will be used, not in accordance with the laws of modern
society, but in accordance with the law of the jungle.

If such words sound overly optimistic today, at the time they mirrored the
sentiments and hopes of a nation in the first few months of postwar peace,
engaged in creating the United Nations as a shield against future wars.

The Tribunal adjourned for the weekend; it returned on Monday,
January 7. We then presented our case against the group under Counts
Three and Four of the Indictment, embracing primarily war crimes as
defined in the laws of war. Our task was now much less controversial
because the charges were based on over a century of tradition, practice, and
both national and international law, and because our documentary and
other proofs were numerous and incontrovertible.

During the first half of the morning I presented documents dealing
with what became known as the "Commando Order," which referred to
small enemy troop units deposited by sea or air in German-occupied areas
for purposes of sabotage and intelligence-gathering. In part the order read:

> From now on all enemies on so-called commando missions in
> Europe or Africa . . . even if they are to all appearances soldiers in
> uniform or demolition troops, whether armed or unarmed, in battle or
> in flight, are to be slaughtered to the last man. . . . Even if these
> individuals, when found, should apparently be prepared to give them-
> selves up, no pardon is to be granted them. . . .
>
> I will hold responsible under military law, for failing to carry out
> this order, all commanders and officers who either have neglected
> their duty of instructing the troops about this order, or acted against
> the order when it was to be executed.

An explanatory preface to Hitler's order declared that enemy commandos who took German prisoners were killing them, implying that the
order was in the nature of a reprisal. Commando operations are a particular
kind of raid, an operation long recognized as a legitimate military tactic. Not
uncommonly commandos encounter situations in which an enemy sentry is
killed instantly to prevent his disclosing the proximity of the raiding party,
or a captured enemy soldier is killed because the raiding party has no means
of safeguarding him.

The laws of war make no exception for such circumstances; some
soldiers believe an exception should be implied on the basis of military
necessity, but military lawyers generally reject any such departure from the
explicit language of Article 23(c) of the Hague Convention: "To kill or
wound an enemy who, having laid down his arms, or no longer having
means of defense, has surrendered . . . is particularly forbidden."

But there was no need to resolve this controversial question in order to establish the lawlessness of Hitler's Commando Order. Whatever one might say about the action of a commander of a raid who orders a captured enemy killed on grounds of military necessity, that has little to do with an order for the execution of *all* commandos engaged in a perfectly legitimate raid, in uniform, innocent of any criminal conduct, who are captured, unarmed, helpless, and surrendering. Such a blanket order of "extermination" was beyond question a flagrant violation of the laws of war and a capital war crime.

In fact, the motivation of the Commando Order had little to do with reprisals. Supplemental orders, simultaneously distributed, showed that the real purpose was to counteract the raids (not all by commando troops) the British had launched along Europe's Atlantic coast during 1942, many of which had been highly successful in destroying important German war installations and carrying off newly developed equipment and technical devices, to the dismay of the German High Command. "If the German conduct of the war is not to suffer grievous damage through these incidents," Hitler wrote, "it must be made clear to the adversary that all sabotage troops will be exterminated, without exception, to the last man." That is why Hitler ordered that information of the killing of captured commandos should be publicized by printing the reports in Wehrmacht communiqués, while directing that the orders themselves "must not, under any circumstances, fall into enemy hands."

These orders, signed by Hitler, with the covering memorandum signed by Jodl, were distributed to the army,° navy, and air force high ommands. We next submitted documents showing receipt of the Commando Orders by the Naval War Staff and their distribution ten days later to subordinate naval commands. In February 1943, a few days after Doenitz replaced Raeder as Commander in Chief, a memorandum was distributed to lower naval commands reaffirming and emphasizing the duty of enforcing the Commando Order.

Most of the victims of the order were British and Canadian soldiers, sometimes accompanied by Norwegians, and most of the killings of which we then had records occurred in Norway. We first submitted the German documents reporting that a British glider had crashed near Egersund on the night of November 19–20, 1942, carrying a British commando unit of seventeen men in British uniform, three of whom were killed in the crash. Six of the fourteen survivors were seriously injured. Pursuant to the Commando Order, all fourteen were shot, on the evening of November 20, by troops of

---

°By this time Brauchitsch had retired and Hitler himself was Commander in Chief of the army as well as of the Wehrmacht as a whole. Halder had retired a few weeks before the Commando Order was issued and had been replaced as Chief of the Army General Staff by General Kurt Zeitzler. Raeder and Goering were still in command of the navy and air force.

the 280th Infantry Division. They had not been interrogated during the few hours that they were held, which resulted in a reproof from the headquarters of General Nikolaus von Falkenhorst, commander of all German armed forces in Norway, emphasizing that captured commandos should be interrogated by German intelligence officers before being executed.

We next submitted records of three other shootings of smaller commando units in Norway in 1942 and 1943. Although I did not know it at the time, Falkenhorst had been tried by a British court-martial and, on August 2, 1945, condemned to death on the basis of his distribution and enforcement of the Commando Order. The sentence was later reduced to life imprisonment.

We also had records of Commando Order enforcement in Italy, including the execution of three British soldiers at Pescara in November 1943. On March 24, 1944, a group of fifteen United States Army soldiers in uniform was captured near La Spezia, in the course of efforts to demolish the railway tunnel between La Spezia and Genoa. They were taken to the headquarters of the 135th Fortress Brigade, whose commander, Colonel Almers, reported the capture to the headquarters of the 75th Infantry Corps, commanded by General Anton Dostler. On the morning of March 25 Dostler ordered the captives shot immediately. Almers endeavored to secure a postponement, but later in the day Dostler repeated his order, and all fifteen Americans were shot the following morning. There was no evidence that Dostler had received any such orders from his superiors. After the war he was apprehended and tried by an American military court-martial in Rome, found guilty, and shot in October 1945. As far as I know, Dostler was the only German general executed on the sole authority of the United States.

The Commando Order took effect almost exclusively in Western Europe. After the midmorning recess, we turned our attention to the East, but to protect Soviet sensibilities I disavowed any intention "to make a full or even partial showing of war crimes on the Eastern Front."

Our first document, in terms of human lives, was thousands of times more nefarious than the Commando Order. It was issued on Hitler's authority and over Keitel's signature on May 13, 1941, in preparation for the coming invasion of the Soviet Union. It was entitled "Order Concerning the Exercise of Martial Jurisdiction and Procedure in the Area 'Barbarossa' and Special Military Measures." Known as the Barbarossa order, the code word for the German invasion of the Soviet Union, its numerous provisions included the following:

I. Treatment of offenses committed by enemy civilians.

   1. Until further notice the military courts and the courts-martial will not be competent for crimes committed by enemy civilians.

2. Guerrillas should be disposed of ruthlessly by the military, whether they are fighting or in flight.

3. Likewise all other attacks by enemy civilians on the Armed Forces . . . are to be suppressed at once by the military, using the most extreme methods, until the assailants are destroyed.

4. Where such measures . . . were not at first possible, persons suspected of criminal action will be brought at once before an officer. The officer will decide whether they are to be shot.

On the orders of an officer with the powers at least of a battalion commander, collective drastic measures will be taken against localities from which cunning or malicious attacks are made on the Armed Forces, if circumstances do not permit of a quick identification of individual offenders . . .

II. Treatment of offenses committed against inhabitants by members of the Armed Forces and its employees.

1. With regard to offenses committed against enemy civilians by members of the Wehrmacht and its employees, prosecution is not obligatory even where the deed is at the same time a military crime or offense.

2. When judging such offenses, it must be borne in mind, whatever the circumstances, that the collapse of Germany in 1918, the subsequent sufferings of the German people, and the fight against National Socialism which cost the blood of innumerable supporters of the movement, were caused primarily by Bolshevistic influences and that no German has forgotten this fact.

The plain purpose and effect of this directive, which was distributed to the commanders in the field, was to deprive all Soviet civilians, in the areas overrun by the German forces, of the protection of military law and justice and to exempt the German invading forces from the requirements of the laws of war, and thus to declare "open season" on the Soviet people. This criminal and murderous military policy was adopted and given as binding orders to the troops two months before the attack, unprovoked by any Soviet action, was launched.

Hitler and the OKW were not the only generators of criminal and atrocious orders to the troops. I submitted to the Tribunal an order circulated in the Sixth Army by its Commander in Chief, Field Marshal Walter von Reichenau, entitled "Conduct of the Troops in the Field":

Regarding the conduct of troops toward the Bolshevistic system, vague ideas are still prevalent in many cases. The most essential aim of war against the Jewish-Bolshevistic system is a complete destruction of their means of power and the elimination of Asiatic influence from the European culture. In this connection the troops are facing tasks which exceed the one-sided routine of soldiering. The soldier in the Eastern Territories is not merely a fighter according to the rules of the art of war, but also a bearer of ruthless national ideology and the avenger of bestialities which have been inflicted upon Germany and racially related nations.

Therefore, the soldiers must have full understanding for the necessity of a severe but just revenge on subhuman Jewry. The Army has to aim at another purpose that is the annihilation of revolts in the hinterland,° which as experience proves, have always been caused by Jews. . . .

That is our only way to fulfill our historic task to liberate the German people once and forever from the Asiatic-Jewish danger. Signed: von Reichenau, Oberbefehlshaber.†

Subsequent documents showed that Hitler saw and approved the Reichenau directive and that Brauchitsch ordered its distribution to other field commands in Russia, down to the divisional level.

After reading some extracts from Einsatzgruppen reports and from documents on army participation in antipartisan warfare and in the destruction of the Warsaw Ghetto, I turned to some affidavits by army and SS officers dealing with warfare on the Eastern Front. Three extracts follow.

### BY GENERAL HANS RÖTTIGER:

As Chief of Staff of the 4th Army from May 1942 to June 1943 . . . I often had occasion to concern myself with antipartisan warfare. For the execution of these operations the troops received orders from the highest authority, as for example even the OKH, to use the harshest methods. These operations were carried out by troops of the army group and the army, for example by security battalions.

At the beginning, in accordance with orders which were issued through official channels, only a few prisoners were taken. In accordance with orders Jews, political commissars, and agents were delivered to the SD [for liquidation].

### BY SS GENERAL ERNST RODE:

I, Ernst Rode, was formerly Chief of the Command Staff of the Reichsfuehrer SS [Himmler]. . . . My last rank was Major General of Police and of the Waffen SS. . . .

As far as I know, the SD Einsatz groups with the individual army groups were completely subordinate to them, that is to say tactically as well as in every other way. The commanders were therefore thoroughly cognizant of the missions and operational methods of these units. . . . The fact that prisoners, such as Jews, agents, and commissars, who were handed over to the SD, underwent the same cruel

---

°The translation in the Tribunal's record is awkward; "crush the seeds of revolt in the rear of the army" is better.

†Reichenau died of a stroke three months later.

death . . . is a proof that the executors had their approval. . . . Frequent mention of these methods was naturally made in my presence at the OKW and OKH. . . .

BY GENERAL ADOLF HEUSINGER, CHIEF OF THE
OPERATIONS SECTION OF OKH, 1940 TO 1944:

The detailed working out of all matters involving the treatment of the local populace, as well as antipartisan warfare in operational areas in pursuance of orders from OKW, was the responsibility of the Quartermaster General of the OKH [Wagner].

It had always been my personal impression that the treatment of the civilian population and the methods of antipartisan warfare in operational areas presented the highest political and military leaders with a welcomed opportunity of carrying out their plans, namely, the systematic extermination of Slavism and Jewry. Entirely independent of this, I always regarded these cruel methods as military insanity, because they only helped to make combat against the enemy unnecessarily more difficult.

After the midday recess I called Bach-Zelewski to the stand; Lawrence had trouble with the complicated name and had it repeated several times. Neatly dressed, Bach-Zelewski looked little more threatening than Ohlendorf. Biddle saw him as "a mild and rather serious accountant." But the defendants took a less neutral view. Funk called him a swine, and when Gilbert remarked that Bach-Zelewski's cross-examination "ought to be interesting," Goering snapped: "You won't see me bothering to ask such a swine any questions."

My sole purpose in calling Bach-Zelewski was to bring eyewitness testimony of the army's involvement in the atrocities planned and rendered inevitable by the Barbarossa order and later directives to ensure its execution. Accordingly, my examination was brief—barely fifteen minutes.

Since Bach-Zelewski was basically an "expert witness," I took pains to establish his credentials: officer in the Reichswehr, wounded and an Iron Cross recipient; SS official in East Prussia and Silesia in the Nazi prewar years; *Obergruppenfuehrer* and general of the Waffen SS and leader of all SS and police forces in the central sector of the Eastern Front, answerable to the commander of the Rear Area, General Max von Schenckendorff; within the SS, directly responsible to Himmler; late in 1942 appointed by Himmler Chief of Anti-Partisan Combat Units on the Eastern Front; recipient of the Knight's Cross, 1944. In his last two capacities Bach-Zelewski's functions covered the entire Soviet front and Yugoslavia, but it was an intelligence and advisory rather than a command position, in which he kept track of virtually all partisan operations and advised the army group and SS leaders where antipartisan troops would be most needed. Occasionally, he took personal command of very large antipartisan operations. The most important parts of the dialogue follow:

T: Are you generally familiar with the operations of the so-called Einsatz-gruppen of the SD?

BZ: Yes.

T: Did these units play any important part in large-scale anti-Russian operations?

BZ: No.

T: What was the principal task of the Einsatzgruppen?

BZ: The principal task . . . was the annihilation of the Jews, gypsies, and political commissars.

T: Then what forces were used for large-scale antipartisan operations?

BZ: For antipartisan activities formations of the Waffen SS, of the Ordnungs-polizei [the regular "order keeping" police], and above all, of the Wehrmacht were used. . . .

T: What proportion of Wehrmacht troops was used in antipartisan operations as compared to police and SD troops?

BZ: Since the number of police and SD troops was very small, antipartisan operations were undertaken mainly by Wehrmacht formations. . . .

T: Was an order ever issued by the highest authorities that German soldiers who committed offenses against the civilian population were not to be punished by the military courts?

BZ: Yes, this order was issued.

T: Was this order an obstacle to correcting the excesses of the troops?

BZ: Yes, in my opinion this order prevented the orderly conduct of operations, since one can train troops only if one has adequate disciplinary powers and jurisdiction over them and is able to check excesses.

The defense counsel then launched their cross-examination with an obvious desire to tear Bach-Zelewski's credibility, if not the man himself, to shreds. His testimony had reduced Goering, Funk, and Jodl especially to apoplectic rage—Goering denouncing Bach-Zelewski as a "swine," a "skunk," and "the bloodiest murderer in the whole damn setup . . . selling his soul to save his stinking neck," while Jodl exhorted his attorney to ask the witness "if he knows that Hitler held him up to us [i.e., the army officers] as a model partisan-fighter. . . . Ask the dirty pig that!"

Dr. Exner, still representing both Jodl and the General Staff–High Command, knew better than to follow such fatuous advice, but his efforts to put the witness in a hole achieved nothing. Dr. Stahmer did put Jodl's question, but drew only a denial.

Since witness and lawyers were speaking the same language and had no need to listen to the interpreters, the tension caused the interchanges to accelerate in speed beyond the capacity of the interpreters to keep up, and Lord Lawrence had to intervene repeatedly in an effort to slow down the antagonists. None of the cross-examiners made any headway, and Dr. Alfred Thoma (representing Rosenberg) courted and met disaster by implying that Bach-Zelewski was a Nazi whose apparent change of heart was contrived:

> TH: Do you believe that Himmler's speech, in which he demanded the extermination of 30 million Slavs, expressed only his personal opinion; or do you consider that it corresponded to the National Socialist ideology?
>
> BZ: Today I believe that it was the logical consequence of our ideology. . . .
>
> TH: What was your opinion at that time?
>
> BZ: It is difficult for a German to fight through to this conviction. It took me a long time.
>
> TH: Then how is it that a few days ago a witness, namely, the witness Ohlendorf, appeared here and admitted that through the Einsatzgruppen he had killed 90,000 people, but told the Tribunal that this did not harmonize with the National Socialist ideology?
>
> BZ: I am of a different opinion. If for years, for decades, a doctrine is preached to the effect that the Slav race is an inferior race, that the Jews are not even human beings, then an explosion of this sort is inevitable.

Sincere or not, Bach-Zelewski's last response epitomized the course and consequence of Nazism. It was quoted in the Tribunal's opinion, with direct relation to the charges against Rosenberg, the reputed philosophical sage of Nazism.

Thoma sat down, and the questioning of Bach-Zelewski soon ended. The cross-examination had been so futile that it would have been folly for me to ask another question, especially since Lawrence was plainly telling rather than asking when he said: "You don't want to re-examine?" Bach-Zelewski left the witness box and walked out by the specified route, which took him close to the corner of the dock occupied by Goering, who glared at him and snarled, "Schweinehund und Verrater" (Pig-dog and traitor). Back in his cell, Bach-Zelewski remarked to our interrogator, Captain Rapp: "At least I got my Iron Cross at the front!" Goering, much decorated as a fighter pilot in World War I, had gotten his World War II Knight's Cross for high rank rather than combat exploits.

I then spoke for a few more minutes, concluding:

> . . . the General Staff and High Command group planned and carried through manifold acts of aggression which turned Europe into a charnel house, and caused the Armed Forces to be used for foul

practices, foully executed, of terror, pillage, and wholesale slaughter. Let no one be heard to say that the military uniform shall be a cloak, or that they may find sanctuary by pleading membership in the profession to which their actions were a disgrace.

Our presentation was treated well in the press, and generously complimented by our associates. Jackson was especially pleased by Bach-Zelewski's testimony. Press coverage of the affidavits was extensive; the *New York Times* printed my summation in its entirety, and the Washington *Post* editorialized that "Any lingering doubts" about the wisdom of indicting the German General Staff "should be relieved by the evidence now available."

# Chapter 11

## INDIVIDUAL DEFENDANTS, FUTURE TRIALS, AND CRIMINAL ORGANIZATIONS

After the General Staff presentation, Colonel Leonard Wheeler described the prosecution's evidence on the Nazis' suppression of the German churches and of the citizens in German-occupied countries. The next day, January 8, 1946, Fyfe told the Tribunal that the prosecution was coming to a new phase of the hearings and explained that "The object of this part of the case is to collect . . . the evidence against each defendant under Counts One and Two [conspiracy to wage and waging aggressive war] . . . presented by the American and British Delegations." That purpose was in the nature of a summing-up, which under traditional procedures comes at the end of a trial, when all the evidence has been presented. Indeed, when the idea of these hearings arose at a chief prosecutors' meeting in early December 1945, Rudenko, supported by the French, had objected: "To treat individual responsibility before proof of the other two counts [i.e., Counts Three and Four] is premature. In Soviet procedure this matter comes only after the whole case is in."

That was equally true of Anglo-American procedure. Jackson and Fyfe had reasons, not revealed to their French and Soviet colleagues, for insisting on individual defendant summaries confined to Counts One and Two. For Jackson, the establishment of crimes against peace as an acknowledged part of international law was the crux of the entire case. The British supported that goal.

But the French and Soviet governments had accepted these parts of the Charter so reluctantly that neither of their delegations were in any position to give even plausible, let alone forceful, support to Counts One and Two. Accordingly, Jackson and Fyfe decided it would be best for them to handle these counts separately and complete their presentations before the French and Russians took over the lectern. The Anglo-American prosecution had the upper hand because neither the French nor the Russians were as yet ready to present their own cases.

Ralph Albrecht began the series with a general introduction during which he declared that there was no need of presentations against Sauckel, Speer, and Kaltenbrunner, whose guilt under Counts One and Two had already been adequately compiled. This reduced from twenty-one to eighteen the number of defendants to be dealt with and must have pleased the judges, who had already been warned by Fyfe that the process would involve "overlapping and repetition."

Albrecht launched into the guilt of Goering—"in some respects even more dangerous than the Fuehrer and other leading party leaders." He was soon in difficulties because of a silly effort to poke fun at Goering's courtroom behavior: "His ready affirmation, by a pleasant nod for all to see, of the correctness of statements made on the contents of documents offered by counsel, his chiding shake of the head when he disagreed with such facts, were commonplace. . . ." The judges had already had abundant opportunity to see all this for themselves; Biddle scowled, and Lawrence cut in sharply: "I don't think the Tribunal is interested in this, Mr. Albrecht."

Nor was the Tribunal much better pleased with what followed, for Goering's career and crimes were already well known, and Albrecht's recital did not, and indeed could not, bring anything fresh to the lectern. Following the afternoon break, Lawrence admonished Albrecht that the Tribunal "already had under consideration" what he was presenting, and that he should turn to "summarizing more" than he was, which would "be more useful to the Tribunal and will save time." Lawrence added that "the same observation will apply to the ones who follow."

Indeed, the fault lay with the system of these presentations rather than Albrecht individually. Fyfe, who followed him with a summation on Ribbentrop, took even more time, without accomplishing anything more than an assemblage of generally familiar material.

Furthermore, by the time Fyfe finished it was clear that the American and British lawyers were not going to adhere to their earlier promise to the French and Russians to deal only with Counts One and Two. Both Albrecht and Fyfe devoted substantial parts of their statements to evidence pertaining to Counts Three and Four. Albrecht also offered several documents which had recently come to the prosecution's attention and, as we shall soon see, new witnesses were also called.

Khaki Roberts had either anticipated the need for brevity or learned from Albrecht's experience. Dealing simultaneously with Keitel and Jodl, in half the time taken by each of his predecessors, Khaki presented a compendious and well-organized summary of the evidence against the two army defendants.

After Roberts, two junior members of the American staff took the lectern to present the evidence against Alfred Rosenberg and Hans Frank. Walter Brudno, a lawyer who had been plucked by the American staff from his duties as an army private, handled the Rosenberg case, and Lieutenant Colonel William Baldwin that of Hans Frank. Both presentations were well organized, but they were long, and the evidence against each of the defendants was so damning and voluminous that little needed to be explained. The Tribunal was bored and testy; Lawrence rebuked Brudno half a dozen times for excessive detail. Baldwin tried to shorten his discourse by reading only short excerpts from the documents he introduced, but Seidl, representing Frank, told the Tribunal that Baldwin was not reading passages helpful to his client. The upshot was that Baldwin was roasted by both Lawrence and Biddle for failing to disclose "the real purport of the document."

The immaculate ex–Coldstream Guards officer, Lieutenant Colonel Griffith-Jones, next rose to present the case against the least appetizing of the defendants, Julius Streicher. The preceding defendants had all been buried under documents undeniably establishing their monstrous guilt. But Streicher had had nothing to do with military decisions and had been a political nonentity since 1940. Virtually all of his Nazism had gone into anti-Semitism, most of it embodied in his journal, Der Stuermer. Beyond question he had been an important force in sowing the seeds of the anti-Jewish atrocities, but was that a crime under international law?

Nearly all of Griffith-Jones's presentation was a compilation of the defendant's speeches and publications, as proof of the intensity and quantity of Streicher's portrayal of Jews as the major source of evil, and insistence on the necessity of their extermination. Only in conclusion, and very summarily, did he address the legal issues:

> In the early days he preached persecution. As persecutions took place he preached extermination and annihilation; and . . . as millions of Jews were being exterminated and annihilated, he cried out for more and more.
>
> That is the crime he has committed. It is the submission of the Prosecution that he made these things possible . . . which could never have happened but for him and others like him.

This was well spoken, but was the publication of a German newspaper in Germany, no matter how scurrilous, an international crime? And what did it have to do with Counts One and Two, supposedly the business at hand?

Next, the two banker defendants—Hjalmar Schacht and Walter Funk—were dealt with by two American junior counsel, respectively Brady Bryson and Bernard Meltzer, both naval lieutenants. Schacht's case was complicated, because after 1937 he had increasingly distanced himself from Hitler and the Nazi government. Jackson had set his heart on the conviction of Schacht, and I was surprised that he did not handle the presentation, especially since Shea, Gurfein, and several other members of the "economic" staff had left Nuremberg.

Nothing was lost, however, as Bryson made a poised and well-organized presentation. The crucial question was whether Schacht, during the early years of the Nazi government, had assisted Hitler's rise to power and the financing of rearmament with the knowledge that the Fuehrer intended to resort to war if necessary to aggrandize the Reich. Bryson produced a number of statements that Schacht made between 1934 and 1938 indicating that he "knew Hitler's aggressive intentions" and "personally favored aggression." But the case against Schacht was based mostly on words and inferences, not on action. Dr. von der Lippe found it "unconvincing"; so did I.

Funk was a somewhat less difficult and much less interesting case. He was an important part of the Nazi government throughout its life and succeeded Schacht as Minister of Economics and later as President of the Reichsbank. But he was under Goering's thumb, the available evidence of his involvement in violent crime was not extensive, and the judges grew restive. Wisely, Meltzer was brief.

On January 14, however, the proceedings were enlivened when Colonel Harry Phillimore of the British delegation presented the case against Grand Admiral Karl Doenitz, commander of the U-boat arm during the first three years of the war and in 1943 successor to Grand Admiral Erich Raeder as Commander in Chief of the German Navy. The weakness of the Schacht case was that he appeared to have relinquished his authority before the major Nazi atrocities; Doenitz, in contrast, had not even reached the rank of rear admiral when the war began and did not attain high authority until 1943.

As commander of U-boats Doenitz held a very important combat command, but it seemed most unlikely that the Tribunal would hold field and sea officers, who were in no way responsible for the decisions to attack other countries, guilty under Counts One and Two. As for war crimes committed in the course of naval warfare, the British Admiralty generally regarded the German Navy as having behaved correctly during the war. In London there had been opposition to indicting Doenitz, but the chief prosecutors had decided to include him, in part because Hitler in his will had named him as his successor and because he had acted as Chief of State for some two weeks after Hitler's death, until his arrest on May 22, 1945. That, in my view, was not a reason for indicting him for international crimes.

Phillimore was thus on a sticky wicket. Although the defendant was indicted under Counts One, Two, and Three, the colonel put the major emphasis on the accusation of war crimes committed by U-boat crews pursuant to Doenitz's orders. There was abundant evidence that the U-boats had regularly sunk ships without warning, in apparent violation of the London Submarine Agreement of 1936, but it was common knowledge that other maritime belligerents had done likewise.

Accordingly, Phillimore undertook to establish that under Doenitz's orders, the U-boats had not only abandoned all efforts to assist the crews of torpedoed ships in life-boats or clinging to flotsam, but also had machine-gunned ships' crewmen who had taken to the boats. To establish these charges, Phillimore read the texts of several Doenitz orders and then called two former submarine officers, Peter Heisig and Karl Heinz Moehle, as witnesses. Both testified that Doenitz, in speeches to U-boat officers in training, and by implication in an order issued in September 1942, had encouraged the killing of enemy crews to prevent their manning ships again in the future.

Otto Kranzbuehler, representing Doenitz, cross-examined the two officers in a manner much superior to any prior cross-examinations by defense counsel. Although both witnesses were intelligent and articulate and stood firm on their testimony, Kranzbuehler drew from Moehle (a decorated lieutenant commander whose boats had sunk twenty ships) admissions that the standing orders of the U-boat's High Command contained no directive for the killing of shipwrecked crews and that he knew of no instance of its happening as a result of instructions from the German submarine command.° Dr. von der Lippe declared the cross-examination "short, effective, and shrewd," and Kranzbuehler's performance made him a standout among the defense counsel for the rest of his time at Nuremberg.

Elwyn Jones then took up the much easier Raeder case. Captured German documents established beyond controversy that Raeder had persuaded Hitler to give orders for the attack against and occupation of Norway for the purpose of expanding the Atlantic coastal areas from which the German Navy could mount operations on the high seas. Raeder's culpability under Counts One and Two was thus readily established. But once again Jones ignored the possibility of a so-called *tu quoque* ("You did it, too") defense based on British preparations for occupying the northern Atlantic coast of Norway. Apart from Norway, the British case chiefly involved Raeder's responsibility for enforcement of the Commando Order, which was an important feature of my own case against the General Staff.

---

°Kranzbuehler's question was carefully phrased. There had, in fact, been a case in which a German submarine crew, in March 1944, had machine-gunned and thrown hand grenades at some thirty crew members of a ship the U-boat had sunk who were struggling for survival on rafts and flotsam. At a trial before a British military court in October 1945, five members of the U-boat crew were found guilty of war crimes. The U-boat captain, Lieutenant Heinz Eck, and two others were shot. But these defendants did not claim that the killings had occurred as a result of any orders from the U-boat's High Command.

Captain Drexel Sprecher took the lectern for the case against Baldur von Schirach, best known to the outside world as chief of the Hitler Jugend. It was not an easy assignment, for Schirach had held no major political office and had nothing significant to do with military matters. Sprecher offered evidence of the military ethos of the Hitler Youth and showed that its members were a source of recruits for the SS, but the judges badgered him constantly. Sprecher made better headway when he turned to Schirach's responsibilities during the war as Gauleiter of Vienna. There he participated in administering the use of slave labor and the deportation of Jews from the Vienna area.

The three defendants dealt with on January 16—Martin Bormann, Arthur Seyss-Inquart, and Wilhelm Frick—presented no such problems to the prosecution. Lieutenant Thomas Lambert told the Tribunal that "because of the absence of the Defendant Bormann from the dock we believe we should make an extra effort to make a solid record in the case against Bormann. . . ." A Nazi Party member since 1925, Bormann had been deputy to Hess and upon the latter's flight to Britain succeeded to his office as Chief of the Party Chancellery. In 1943 he was named Secretary to the Fuehrer, and became, next to Hitler, the most powerful man in the Reich. He was importantly involved in many of the worst atrocities, including the crimes against prisoners of war, the forced labor program, and the systematic slaughter of Jews.

Lieutenant Henry Atherton followed with a brief presentation on Seyss-Inquart, an Austrian who had helped Hitler to annex his country. After the war began he was deputy to Hans Frank in Poland until the spring of 1940 and thereafter, with the title Reich Commissioner, was chief of the German occupation of the Netherlands until the end of the war. While in these capacities, suppressive and atrocious Nazi occupation policies were practiced, including the forced labor program and the deportation of Dutch Jews to Eastern Europe.

The case against Frick was entrusted to Dr. Robert Kempner, a German lawyer who, before he emigrated to the United States, had served as Chief Legal Adviser to the Prussian Police Administration. He was thus well qualified to deal with Frick, a stiff, systematic man who was appointed Minister of the Interior when Hitler came to power. He was well described by Kempner as "the administrative brain who [sic] devised the machinery of state for Nazism, who geared that machinery for aggressive war." His administrative authority in the Reich, and later in the German-occupied countries, was very broad, and like Bormann, Frick was involved in virtually all of the Nazi government's criminal policies.

On January 17 the French began the presentation of their case, but six days later they gave way to allow the Americans to deal with three of the remaining four defendants. Captain Sprecher was again at the lectern with an even more thankless task than before, for his subject, Hans Fritzsche, was a very minor figure in comparison to the other defendants.

Fritzsche was a section chief in the Propaganda Ministry who reported to the Reich Press Chief, Otto Dietrich, who in turn reported to Goebbels. Within the ministry Fritzsche was not unimportant, and his own radio news program, "Hans Fritzsche Speaks," was widely heard. But as a third-level official he had little to say about policy questions. Of course his programs hailed the Wehrmacht's aggressions and denounced the Jews. Thus Fritzsche's case was somewhat analogous to Streicher's, but compared to *Der Stuermer*, Fritzsche's output was pallid indeed.

Next came the two aristocrats of the dock, Franz von Papen and Constantin von Neurath. The former was dealt with by Major J. Harcourt Barrington, and thus the British, like the Americans, appeared to be giving the most difficult cases to their most junior lawyers. Papen was selfish and unprincipled and no doubt connived with Hitler to bring about the German annexation of Austria. But that was not in itself criminal, and Lawrence's questions and comments gave the prosecution little hope of ultimate success.

Since Fyfe had handled Ribbentrop, it was in order for him also to deal with Ribbentrop's predecessor as Minister of Foreign Affairs. Neurath had held that position from 1932 to 1938. He had been present at the now famous Hossbach conference of November 1937, when Hitler revealed his intent to use force for the aggrandizement of Germany. Neurath had continued in office with full knowledge of these plans, and during the German annexation of Austria he knowingly gave false assurances to the Czechoslovak government that Germany would respect its independence. But the stronger part of the case against Neurath was his activity as Reich Protector of Bohemia and Moravia from March 1939 (when the Wehrmacht occupied those lands) until September 1941. By accepting the post Neurath took responsibility for what was certainly a forceful occupation and annexation, as well as for the ensuing acts of the repressive, anti-Semitic regime which the Germans imposed on the Czechs.

Because Hess's counsel, Dr. von Rohrscheidt, had broken his foot, this case was postponed and Griffith-Jones did not present it until the French case was concluded, on February 7. By then Hess was represented by Dr. Alfred Seidl, who also represented Hans Frank. Apart from Hess's dubious mental health, the main prosecution problem was, of course, his removal from the Nazi scene by his flight to Scotland in May 1941. Perhaps because of this circumstance, Griffith-Jones asserted a very broad principle of criminal liability, declaring "that it is sufficient to justify and bring home the conviction of this man and his colleagues to produce simply evidence of their positions in the Nazi State . . . and also the general evidence of the crimes which were committed by the German people."

But there was no need in this case for any such loose view of criminal liability. Like Bormann after him, Hess had a central position in the Nazi government, and the documents he signed and the meetings he attended adequately proved his knowledge of and participation in Hitler's plans and decisions to conquer Czechoslovakia and crush Poland, the Low Countries, and France.

So ended the Anglo-American submissions on the individual defendants. In all, they had taken some eight days of trial time, and it is hard to see that so much time was well spent. The lawyers' presentations were based upon documents which judges and defense counsel could read, and on the whole what was said orally added little. But neither the French nor the Russians had been ready to proceed, and for the Tribunal to shut down temporarily would have been very awkward.

In defense of the proceedings, it may be said that the evidentiary situation, at that stage of the trial, with respect to each defendant was competently assessed. For those who did not already know these things, it became apparent that the cases against Schacht, Doenitz, Papen, and Fritzsche were in trouble and that the evidence with respect to Streicher, Schirach, and Neurath, though apparently sufficient to convict, might not warrant capital sentences. All this was useful information, but the exercise would have been much more meaningful if performed after the French and Russians, and above all the defendants, had been heard from.

2

The Moscow Declaration of November 1943 had distinguished between "major war criminals" who would be "punished by the joint decision" of the Allied governments and those miscreants of lesser stature who would be dealt with by national courts. The International Military Tribunal was established to deal with the major war criminals. From the summer of 1945 until it rendered judgment on October 1, 1946, the Tribunal at Nuremberg was the cynosure of world attention to the great issues of war guilt. But quantitatively, Nuremberg was a small part of the whole. The Nuremberg Tribunal's functions were to pronounce on only the most notorious of those accused under the law as declared in the London Charter and thereby to set a precedent and guidelines for trials and treaties in the years to come.

In the United States, however, the very preeminence of the Nuremberg founders had checked the growth of other agencies badly needed for war crimes tasks. The army JAG's proposed directive for war crimes trials in Europe (officially designated J.C.S. 1023/3) had been approved by the American Joint Chiefs of Staff on October 1, 1944, and presented for approval by the Combined Chiefs of Staff. But there it remained without action for over six months because the much more far-reaching proposals of

Stimson, Bernays, and Chanler were under consideration at the highest levels of the White House and the State, War, and Justice departments. In April 1945 J.C.S. 1023/3 was therefore withdrawn from consideration. Thus, as the war neared its victorious conclusion, the American forces in Europe remained with no war crimes directive from Washington other than the order to support Jackson's international project, which was limited to at most a few score defendants.

Furthermore, both fearing German reprisals and uncertain of future policy, in December 1944 the War Department ordered the European theater commanders not to conduct any war crimes trials except those that appeared necessary for immediate military purposes. However, recognizing the necessity of preparing for trials in the near future, the theater headquarters in Paris (ETOUSA), in February 1945, established a War Crimes Group under the Theater Judge Advocate, General E. C. Betts. The group was commanded by Lieutenant Colonel Clio E. Straight, a reserve officer who, though able and willing, had no prior experience with war crimes and no clout with the JAG regulars.° During June and early·July, the group moved to Wiesbaden, and Straight's staff and facilities began to improve.

At the same time, the Combined Chiefs of Staff authorized the occupation forces to "apprehend and detain" war crimes suspects. Of the American field commands, the Third and Seventh Armies were the only ones that remained in Germany long enough to carry out this mission. The Third collected its suspects at the Dachau concentration camp near Munich, the Seventh in a "civilian internment enclosure" near Ludwigsburg.

It was not until June 19, 1945, that the Combined Chiefs of Staff, at General Eisenhower's request, lifted the previous restrictions on war crimes trials in the American Occupation Zone. The previous day, the British War Office published the Royal Warrant, signed by command of the King, which prescribed regulations for the trial of war crimes before Military Courts in the British Zone. The zealous French had authorized the prosecution of war crimes in the Ordinance of August 24, 1944, when the French government was still in Algiers.

American and British military trials—including the Dostler and Falkenhorst cases already mentioned—commenced soon after the promulgation of these directives. By far the largest and most publicized of those that preceded Nuremberg was the trial at Lüneburg of Josef Kramer and forty-four other staff members of the Bergen-Belsen concentration camp. It lasted from September 17 to November 17, the court heard thirty-one witnesses for the prosecution and seventy-five for the defense, and an audience of some four hundred attended the opening session.

---

°Straight held this difficult and important command assignment for over three years without promotion. Years later he was promoted to brigadier general.

But the trial got a very bad press because the defense lawyers, nearly all British army officers, made arguments supporting the legality of concentration camps under German law, leading to the conclusion that murder in concentration camps was not a crime, and referring to the Belsen victims as "the dregs of the ghettos of Eastern Europe." Of course, the Soviet press excoriated the court for permitting such remarks, and when fifteen of the defendants were acquitted there was a flood of criticism, despite the fact that the fifteen were *Kapos* (inmate trustees) rather than SS guards.

Since the Belsen inmates included many Polish nationals, as well as British, French, Dutch, Belgians, Greeks, and Russians, all nationals of countries at war with Germany, there was no question that Germans responsible for their treatment had committed war crimes. From a factual standpoint, the Belsen and other concentration camp cases were a throwback to the Andersonville case of the Civil War period.* But the evidence was unusual insofar as many of the defendants were civilians, whereas in earlier war crimes trials the defendants had usually, if not always, been in military service.

All seven defendants were civilians in an American trial held at Wiesbaden in October 1945. They were the chief administrator, the doctor, three nurses, and two clerical employees in a small state sanitarium at Hadamar, a town some twenty miles north of Wiesbaden. They were charged with killing, by lethal injection, over four hundred Polish and Russian men, women, and children who were brought to the sanitarium in 1944 and 1945 to be killed in accordance with Nazi policy on the ground that they were incurably ill. The three senior employees were hanged, and the others given long prison terms.† As in the Belsen case, since the victims were Allied nationals, these acts were undeniably war crimes.

The Royal Warrant regulations explicitly limited the jurisdiction of the British Military Courts to war crimes, defined as "violations of the laws and usages of war." The authorized scope of the American JAG trials was at first less clearly prescribed, and the Hadamar trial was not typical of what followed. The trials soon fell into two principal categories: first, offenses under the laws of war against American troops, including battlefield killing or mistreatment of surrendered troops, as in the Malmédy massacre, or of American airmen shot down behind the German lines and attacked by German soldiers or (more often) civilians; second, the killing or mistreating of Allied nationals in German concentration camps, later liberated by

---

*After the Civil War, Captain Henry Wirz, commandant of the notorious Confederate prisoner-of-war camp at Andersonville, Georgia, was tried, convicted, and hanged for cruelties that resulted in many deaths among the Union prisoners. The trial was conducted by a Union Army military commission, pursuant to the Lieber Code, General Orders 100.

†The Trial Judge Advocate in the Hadamar case was Colonel Leon Jaworski, in later years a prominent Texas lawyer and politician.

American troops, in particular Dachau, Buchenwald, Flossenburg, and Mauthausen.

## 3

But the scope of the occupying armies' war crimes obligations in all four of the zones was about to be greatly expanded. Back in Washington, J.C.S. 1023 had gone through numerous revised editions since the Stimson group's broader designs had put it out of circulation in April 1945. Eventually, J.C.S. 1023/10, which closely tracked portions of Jackson's Report to the President of June 6, was approved by the Joint Chiefs of Staff on July 15, 1945, and was received at Eisenhower's headquarters in September. Its effect was electrifying.

Under J.C.S. 1023/10, the conduct defined as "criminal" corresponded very closely to the definitions in the London Charter, to wit:

(a) Atrocities and offenses against persons or property constituting violations of international law, including the rules and customs of land and naval warfare.

(b) Initiation of invasions of other countries and of wars of aggression in violation of international laws and treaties.

(c) Other atrocities and offenses, including atrocities and persecutions on racial, religious or political grounds, committed since 30 January 1933.

A subsequent paragraph provided that "criminality" under clause (b) would include "members of organizations or groups connected with the commission of" such crimes. Furthermore, Eisenhower was instructed not only to follow this directive in the American Zone but also, in his capacity as a member of the Control Council, to "urge the adoption by the other occupying powers of the principles and policies set forth in this directive" by securing its approval in the Control Council.

The last of those tasks required action by the Theater Commander himself, with the aid of General Clay and the OMGUS staff in Berlin. The problem of arranging for compliance with the directive in the American Zone was assigned to General Betts as Theater Judge Advocate. Betts, in turn, referred the directive to Colonel Charles Fairman, Chief of the International Law Section of his staff.

Betts could not have made a better choice. Fairman was a reserve officer, in civilian life a legal scholar and historian of great distinction. On October 16 he responded to Betts's inquiry, noting that Eisenhower could not have meant that the JAG's modest staff was to carry out J.C.S. 1023/10 "by its own proper means" but rather that the problem was "to propose a proper allocation of functions." Understandably aghast at the "enormous scope" of the crimes covered, including as they did "all the [atrocity-type] offenses committed in Germany since the Nazi regime came into power," Fairman also pointed to the charges against members of organizations subject to conviction of criminality at Nuremberg, whose numbers might well exceed 100,000 individuals. Accordingly:

> It is a matter of great urgency to prepare prosecution of cases within the mandate of J.S.C. 1023/10—other than those now before the International Military Tribunal and those now before the War Crimes Group. Considerations of continuity of effort, expert knowledge, and public responsibility already established point to the Office of the U.S. Chief of Counsel [Jackson] as the organization upon which reliance should be placed. . . . Perhaps the present Chief of Counsel could be prevailed upon to accept this extended responsibility; or some member of his staff might be designated Chief Prosecutor.

Fairman concluded his memorandum with a recommendation that Charles Fahy, as legal adviser to Clay, be brought into the picture and that Jackson be approached at once. Fahy came to Nuremberg, immediately sought out Shea (who had just returned from Berlin), and urged him to "take over the job of succeeding Jackson and clearing up the many trials which will have to succeed the first one." Shea was "very reluctant," but his response was inconclusive.

The following day Betts and Fairman arrived in Nuremberg, and for three days there were numerous conferences among Betts, Fairman, Fahy, Jackson, and Shea concerning the problems raised by J.C.S. 1023/10. Jackson made it clear from start to finish that he would return to the Supreme Court after the pending trial if not sooner and was not available to handle anything thereafter. Shea remained on the fence but had concluded that this was "a real call from the government" and that if he was wanted "badly enough" to meet his terms—a presidential appointment, passage to Nuremberg for his wife, Hilda, and guaranteed army support—he "wouldn't turn it down."

However, at a meeting on October 22, Shea's willingness evaporated when Jackson "suggested that taking on this job might have some disadvantages from my [Shea's] point of view in respect of participating in the first trial." Shea promptly replied that he "did not want to incapacitate myself in that regard in order to succeed him [Jackson] on the subsequent trials." Jackson made no move to relax that condition. Instead, that afternoon, he suggested to Betts and Fahy that General Donovan might be willing to take on the job. Betts immediately sought him out, and Donovan declared that he was "willing if it is cleared up and down the line." Fahy, unhappy with that outcome, called General Clay and thereafter told Shea that Clay would "much prefer" him to Donovan.

Fahy also told Shea that efforts would be made with Eisenhower and Clay to meet Shea's conditions, but nothing came of that, and in a letter of October 25 to Betts, Jackson reiterated that no one could take on this heavy new task and at the same time "carry any substantial part of the actual labor of the major trial." The very day that Jackson raised the factor that chilled Shea's interest, Jackson circulated the staff reorganization directive which put the two men at loggerheads and, ten days later, led to Shea's departure. At about the same time the Donovan-Jackson relationship froze, and a month later Donovan, too, was on his way home.

In view of the circumstance that these events coincided with Jackson's breaks with Shea and Donovan, it is hard to avoid the suspicion that the Justice viewed the possibility that one of them might agree to organize the subsequent trials as a means of removing him from the first one. It is clear that Fahy, who had worked closely and cordially with Shea in Washington, brought him into the picture on the merits. Jackson, however, had already been in sharp disagreement with Donovan with regard to the General Staff indictment and was well aware of Storey's and Amen's negative views of Shea and his "economic case." This suspicion is reinforced by the absolutism of Jackson's pronouncement that anyone on his staff who took on this new assignment would be obliged to abandon all participation in the first trial.

## 4

I knew nothing of these problems, proposals, and conferences until a month later, when the trial began. Fahy was one of the many who visited Nuremberg on the occasion of Jackson's opening statement, and while there he came to my office to raise and discuss the possibility of my taking leadership of the J.C.S. 1023/10 missions. He was fully aware of my obligations with regard to the General Staff–High Command charges, and when I stated that I wished to carry that assignment through to conclusion, he raised no objection. Neither did Jackson, when I discussed the matter with him, and indeed I did not until many years later learn that Shea had been offered the assignment and had rejected it because of Jackson's insistence that acceptance would end his participation in the "major trial."

Once again I was confronted with a wholly unexpected opportunity that would postpone repatriation and settling down to learn the ways of private law practice. Once again my weakness for the unusual venture prevailed. My acquiescence in Fahy's proposal was conditional, and I expressed considerable uncertainty that American lawyers and judges could be recruited in sufficient quantity for these further war crimes trials. For this reason I insisted that no public announcement of my acceptance be made. But I agreed to attack these problems as soon as I had presented the

General Staff case. That postponed any substantial work on the subsequent trials until the second week in January.

Meanwhile, however, Betts and Fahy pushed on with the legal and administrative bases for the fulfillment of J.C.S. 1023/10. Their efforts culminated in a letter dated December 1, 1945, to Jackson from General McNarney's Chief of Staff, General W. Bedell Smith. The gist of the letter was that (1) the Office of the United States Chief of Counsel (Jackson's organization) "should continue in existence beyond the present trial, and take control and general responsibility for all further war crimes proceedings against the leaders of the Axis powers . . . as well as against members of groups and organizations declared criminal," (2) the prosecution of those accused should be conducted consistently with the provisions of the London Charter, and (3) the presidential Executive Order appointing Jackson should be amended to authorize these projects. Attached to the letter was (1) a "Memorandum of Plan" envisaging my future appointment as Chief of Counsel and providing that I would be responsible to the Deputy Military Governor, General Clay, and (2) a proposed draft of an amended Executive Order.

On December 3, I met in Frankfurt with Generals Smith and Betts, and the next day Jackson, in a letter to Smith, expressed agreement with the program. Simultaneously, he wrote to the President, explaining the situation and recommending amendment of the Executive Order. On January 16, 1946, President Truman signed the necessary amendments.

Meanwhile Fahy's office in Berlin was working on a proposed law for adoption by the Control Council. The result was Control Council Law No. 10, signed on December 20, 1946, by the members of the Council: General McNarney, Field Marshal Bernard Montgomery, General Louis Koeltz for the absent General Pierre Koenig, and Marshal Georgi Zhukov.

The preamble to Law No. 10 declared that its purpose was "to give effect to the terms of the Moscow Declaration of 30 October 1943 and the London Agreement of 8 August 1945, and the Charter issued pursuant thereto." Otherwise, however, there was little similarity between the two documents. Law No. 10 established no tribunals or committees of prosecutors and therefore contained nothing corresponding to Parts I, III, and V of the Charter. There was a list of permissible punishments which, in addition to the usual items, included forfeiture of property. The greater part of the Law dealt with the interchange of suspects among the four occupying powers and with other nations. The Law contained no provision for the review by higher authority of judgments of conviction or sentences imposed, and the declared purpose of uniformity among the zones was ill served by providing that "The tribunal by which persons charged with offenses hereunder shall be tried and the rules and procedures thereof shall be determined or designated by each Zone Commander for his respective Zone."

As matters developed, Law No. 10 accomplished little by way of zonal uniformity on war crimes. The British proceeded under the Royal Warrant guidelines, and made no provision for crimes against peace. The French were chiefly interested in German crimes in France against Frenchmen and generally relied on French law rather than international law, even in war crimes cases. As for the Russians, only occasional scraps of war crimes information emerged from behind the Iron Curtain.

In the American Zone, however, Control Council Law No. 10, together with the amended Executive Order, laid the legal and administrative basis for the war crimes cases at Nuremberg which were to follow the pending trial before the International Military Tribunal.

## 5

In mid-January Storey resigned and returned to Texas. In his place as Executive Counsel, Jackson appointed Tom Dodd, who was more canny and a better lawyer than his predecessor. Calvocoressi returned to England for RAF demobilization, promising to return when General Staff matters again arose in court. Alderman returned about the time that Peter left, and rejoined me at the house in Dambach.

I was now in a position to devote most of my time to preparing for the trials that were to follow the current one, and for which I was expected to step into Jackson's shoes. The immediate and crucial problem was the recruitment of staff. This was my personal responsibility and the focus of my immediate and major efforts.

But there was another matter of great moment both to the current trial and those to come, and it was therefore of concern to both Jackson and me. That was the indictment of the accused organizations. The evidence against them had been presented to the Tribunal, but basic questions, both legal and practical, remained unresolved.

As Jackson had described the plan in his initial report to President Truman, once membership in a convicted organization had been proved, the "individual member would thereafter be allowed only personal defenses or extenuating circumstances, such as that he joined under duress. . . ." The London Charter, in empowering the Tribunal to "declare" that an indicted organization was "criminal," further provided that thereafter individuals might be brought to trial "for membership" therein and that the accused could not challenge "the criminal nature of the group or organization."

The members of the Tribunal had from the start been troubled by the nature of the organizational indictments and the vagueness of the Charter provisions in this connection. Most immediately, plans had to be made for selecting those members of organizations who would be allowed to give evidence in their defense. That was primarily an administrative matter, but difficult legal problems would be raised if, as was expected, some or all of the organizations were declared "criminal."

For example, if a member of an organization declared criminal was put on trial before a court competent to hear such cases, would proof that the defendant was unaware of the organization's criminal policies and activities be a defense? If evidence submitted to the Tribunal showed that its leaders deliberately employed criminal means, but most of the members were kept in ignorance of this, should the organization be declared criminal? Could the Tribunal exclude from a declaration of criminality particular parts of an organization, or all members below a specified rank?

The Tribunal's concern mounted as the time approached when such questions would have to be confronted, and early in December the judges decided to ventilate the problems by discussing them with the lawyers. On December 11, after the public session ended, the Tribunal gathered privately with the prosecution leaders and the lawyers representing the indicted organizations. Lord Lawrence asked the prosecution whether it planned to charge the organizations as a whole, or to propose excluding specified parts.

Jackson, in a "take-charge" mood, at once asserted that the case against the organizations was "an American responsibility" because "this was always a part of the American case beginning with the Yalta Conference where it was accepted."* In answer to Lawrence's question, Jackson pointed out that only those members of the Nazi Party constituting the Leadership Corps were charged and that the scope of the General Staff was specifically limited in the Indictment. He added that there would be "no objection if the judgment of this Court were stated to apply only to voluntary membership." Subsequently, Jackson was questioned:

> BIDDLE: What is the definition of a criminal organization? Is the knowledge of members regarding the purposes and acts of the organization relevant? . . . I mean if 75% did not know of any criminal acts was the organization criminal?
>
> JACKSON: Yes. In the intent of the Charter it would be up to the 75% to plead lack of knowledge as a personal defense. . . .
>
> BIDDLE: If 75% of the membership were conscripted is the organization still criminal?
>
> JACKSON: Yes. It is the same organization.
>
> PARKER: . . . Is his lack of knowledge a defense to the member in a subsequent trial?

---

*Charging the Nazi organizations had, indeed, been a part of the American planning from the beginning, but, as far as I know, there is no basis for the statement about the Yalta Conference.

JACKSON: Yes, it is a defense to the individual's guilt, but not to the criminality of the organization. . . .

Biddle was not pleased by Jackson's responses and noted: "Jackson takes a rigid position that knowledge has nothing to do with criminality, and that it is enough to show criminal acts by some to hold all—including charwomen apparently. Weakens a bit on questions from Birkett and me."

The Tribunal adjourned without reaching any conclusions, and thereafter the prosecution's evidence against the organizations was received without further discussion of these questions. In January, on the Tribunal's request, Judge Birkett drafted a statement, read in open court, that listed a number of questions which the prosecution should deal with when, at a later time, the Tribunal would "invite argument from the Counsel for the Prosecution and for the Defense." Later the chief prosecutors met and agreed that Jackson would prepare and present the principal statement for the prosecution.

## 6

The legal questions, controversial as they might be, could be resolved by argument, but truly mountainous practical problems would confront those who were charged with putting their decisions into effect. These difficulties would not significantly arise from convictions of the Reich Cabinet or General Staff, for the number of members of both together would be well under two hundred. But if any of the other three were convicted—and the SS and Party leadership were the most probable convicts—there would be hundreds of thousands of members implicated by the Tribunal's judgments.

Hardly a word had been addressed to this aspect of the situation during the discussions I have just described. But it must have been apparent to all the other participants, as it certainly was to me, that judicial proceedings, even giving full effect to Bernays's vision of summary process, could not possibly deal with such numbers without hundreds of courts and years of hearings. Furthermore, many defendants would confront capital and other serious charges, enmeshed in evidentiary problems, that could be fairly tried only with due deliberation and by competent judges.

Obviously, I could not contemplate with equanimity taking personal responsibility for such a mammoth and intractable undertaking. I was, therefore, greatly relieved when, in mid-January, I was visited by a deus ex machina in the form of a letter from Charles Fahy enclosing a document entitled "Draft Report of Denazification Policy Board."

Before the end of the war, the word "denazification" had come into official use to designate the occupation policy to destroy the Nazi Party and remove all "active" supporters of Nazism from official or important private employment. Only "minimal" party members were allowed to remain privately employed. Under General Clay's administration of OMGUS, denazification became one of the "four Ds"—together with demilitarization, democratization, and decartelization—which were the major elements of OMGUS's mission.

Efforts to enforce the denazification of public and managerial employment encountered obstacles, often because a former Nazi was an efficient employee who could not readily be replaced. In the American Zone of Occupation, enforcement was initially entrusted to the army, over the strong opposition of General George Patton and some others. During the second half of 1945 there were several declarations and regulations mandating compliance with denazification, but dissatisfaction with the results, particularly as expressed in the American press, increased.

Under these circumstances, Clay established in November a Denazification Policy Review Board, with Fahy as chairman, and gave it the task of drafting a "new comprehensive denazification law." In collaboration with Clay's two personal assistants, Robert Bowie and Donald S. McLean (both lawyers), and Lieutenant Colonel Fritz Oppenheimer (an able German-born lawyer), in mid-January 1946 the Board produced a draft. This was the document which I received from Fahy, the contents of which I promptly described in a memorandum to Jackson. There were several features of the draft that directly and importantly involved Nuremberg:

> The report is based on the assumption that the Office of Chief of Counsel will not be able to prosecute more than a few hundred, or at the outside, a few thousand major and sub-major war criminals. . . .
>
> The report therefore recommends that the vast majority of the so-called "organization cases" should be handled under the denazification program rather than separately. This program calls for the imposition of sanctions on a category basis, of course more severe against active or important Nazis than against minor people, and with appropriate administrative proceedings in German courts for application of these categories in individual cases and for appeals.

From my standpoint, these proposals were highly desirable, most of all because they would "bring the task of the Office of Chief of Counsel, after the present proceedings, into manageable proportions."

"Democratization" was another of Clay's "four Ds," and the general believed the Germans should learn by doing. To this end Clay had already approved the establishment of governing councils in the three provinces (*Länder*) of the American Zone: Hesse, Württemberg-Baden, and Bavaria. It was now Clay's intention that the new denazification law should be enacted, not by the Control Council or OMGUS, but by the joint councils of the three *Länder* (the Länderrat) at their "capital" in Stuttgart. The German officials would be responsible for enforcing the law by establishing the "tribunals" (a mix of lay "assessors" and lawyers) to try the individual cases. The "categories" I mentioned in my memorandum to Jackson were four: "major offenders," "offenders," "lesser offenders," and "followers," with specified sanctions for each. These included not only disqualification from various levels of employment (the original primary aim of denazification), but also incarceration in "labor camps," confiscation of property, and various other penalties.

The Board's drafting was perceptive and skillful. It had something for everyone. Clay was able to advance his concept of democratization by clothing the Germans with increased governmental responsibility. The Germans were given control of the denazification process—a gift which some of them may have regarded as Greek, but one which enabled them to imprint their own policies on the process. At Nuremberg, those who were to conduct the ensuing trials could now focus their efforts on (as the draft put it) "other major war criminals not yet indicted, key industrialists, bankers, etc., and . . . high officials in the Nazi party or in organizations which may be declared criminal."

There followed some six weeks of discussion of the draft between Clay's group and the Länderrat members, without any changes important to Nuremberg interests. On March 5, 1946, it was published by the Länderrat as the "Law for Liberation from National Socialism and Militarism."

It would be far too much to say that this law and its execution "resolved" the problem which had led Bernays eighteen months earlier to propose criminal indictment of the Nazi organizations. The prediction that Germans would not go far in punishing other Germans for their Nazi past was largely fulfilled, and it is probable that Bernays (like many others) regarded the whole proceedings as a whitewash. However that may be, it certainly took me "off the hook," and, short of mustering American judges and prosecutors far beyond the bounds of possibility,° there was no way that I or anyone else could have done better.

## 7

For Jackson, however, the main problem was to convince the Nuremberg Tribunal that its declarations of organizational criminality would not lead to arbitrary or unjust consequences. In mid-January he sent me, for my com-

---

°Some 3.5 million individuals (about one-quarter of the entire population in the American Zone) were listed as "chargeable cases" for trial before denazification tribunals in the American Zone. Many of these were subsequently amnestied without trial. The program involved 540 tribunals and a staff of 22,000, and it lasted until the spring of 1948.

ments, a draft of the statement he proposed to make before the Tribunal. Not unexpectedly, it was a fluent and forceful argument, but the concluding pages of his draft contained passages stating, at least by implication, that individual members of organizations declared criminal could themselves be convicted on the basis of voluntary membership without more. It was my strong opinion that the Tribunal would not accept that interpretation of the London Charter. Accordingly, in a memorandum I advocated taking the position that *knowledge* of an organization's criminal policies or participation in its criminal activities was a necessary element of individual guilt. I took no further part in Jackson's handling of these problems and returned to Washington early in February.

Howard Petersen, a young lawyer who had been a junior law partner of John J. McCloy's and personal assistant to Robert Patterson during and after the war, had succeeded McCloy as Assistant Secretary of War. On February 18, he sent a long letter to Jackson containing recommendations directly contrary to what I had urged in my memorandum.

Understandably concerned by the vast number of dwindling American manpower resources for war crimes activities, Petersen urged that Jackson argue, in line with the literal language of the Charter, that voluntary membership alone, regardless of knowledge or participation, be held criminal. Petersen's view was that trials in which proof of membership was all that was necessary for conviction could be expeditiously conducted, while the interjection of questions of knowledge and participation would inevitably complicate and greatly lengthen the trial proceedings.

At that time international mail into the American Zone of Germany was erratic, and by February 26 Petersen's letter had not yet reached Jackson. He had, however, received a cabled summary of the letter from Charles Horsky, a public-minded Washington lawyer who was assisting him on a part-time basis. In a cable to Horsky, Jackson responded to Petersen:

> My problem is first with the Tribunal and secondly with my associates. Our confidential information is that both British and American judges are not disposed to go along on a declaration of organization criminality which does not clearly leave open individual defenses or which applies to people who may have innocently gotten into these organizations. The background for this is a profound fear that the judgment of the Tribunal will be used in Russian and perhaps in French zones as basis for wholesale roundups and severe penalties and their fear and dislike of affording a basis of conviction of masses of persons. Much of my argument is addressed to overcoming these two fears. . . . I am not in a position to say that there is no merit in that fear.

Such was the situation on February 28 when Jackson rose to present his argument to the Tribunal. He was well aware that the judges entertained questions and misgivings about the organizational charges and that quite apart from the tactical and legal problems, specifying the defenses available to accused members raised moral issues relevant to the fairness and future repute of the Charter and the trial.

The subject before the Tribunal was not calculated to evoke the passionate eloquence of Jackson's opening statement. However, he at once reminded his listeners of the enormous quantity of evidence establishing the organizations' atrocious policies and actions: "These organizations indoctrinated and practiced violence and terrorism. They provided the systematized, aggressive, and disciplined execution throughout Germany and the occupied countries of the plan for crimes which we have proven. The flowering of this system is represented by the fanatical SS General Ohlendorf. . . ."

Jackson went on to buttress the concept of organizational guilt by pointing to precedents in statutes enacted in the United States (the Smith Act of 1940), Britain (sedition acts of 1817, 1846, and 1936), and Germany (criminal code of 1871). The argument suffered from the great age of several of the precedents and the fact that those of recent origin were not universally admired. Furthermore, there was the circumstance, subsequently stressed by defense counsel, that the cited statutes declared *membership* to be criminal rather than the organization itself, whereas the Charter called for a declaration against the abstract entity, which thereafter could be invoked against the members.

Turning to the issues most troubling to the judges, Jackson laid down five criteria which he declared to be essential to a finding of organizational criminality:

(1) The organization or group must comprise persons "associated in identifiable relationship with a collective, general purpose."

(2) Membership in the organization "must be generally voluntary."

(3) The aims of the organization must be criminal "in that it was designed to perform acts denounced as criminal in Article 6 of the Charter."

(4) The criminal aims of the organization must be "of such a character that its membership in general may properly be charged with knowledge of them."

(5) In accordance with Article 9 of the Charter, there must be a member of the organization on trial before the Tribunal whom the Tribunal convicts of a crime under the Charter.

Criteria (2) and (4) described limitations not mentioned in the Charter and were welcomed by most of the judges. Biddle recorded that "at the [morning] recess everyone most enthusiastic about Bob's argument . . ." But he added: "We still have difficulties." In criterion (4), for example,

Jackson had not made *actual* knowledge an element of the offense. In the trial of an individual member, Jackson declared, his lack of knowledge of the organization's criminality "might possibly be a factor in extenuation," but "the test would be not what the man actually knew, but what, as a person of common understanding he should have known." On that basis, if the Tribunal had already held that criterion (4) was proven, the defendant in a later trial would have to give very particular reasons to explain why he, as a reasonable man, did not also know.

Jackson concluded by suggesting that the members who wished to testify in defense of their organizations should be heard, not by the Tribunal itself, but by "a panel of masters" appointed in accordance with Section 17(e) of the Charter. Fyfe, who followed him, undertook to show that all five of the indicted organizations fulfilled the five criteria that Jackson had laid down. Auguste Champetier de Ribes, who had succeeded de Menthon as French Chief Prosecutor, confined himself to confirming the legitimacy under French law of charging organizations with crime.

General Rudenko's comments were brief but pointed and reflected his government's insistence on a free hand for the national tribunals. The IMT, he declared, had no power except to convict or acquit the indicted organizations. If convicted, the national tribunals had "the right, but not the obligation" to bring the members to trial. If they exercised the right, the only effect of the IMT's judgment would be that the national tribunals were bound to accept the finding of organizational guilt. Beyond that, all other trial matters, procedural or substantive, were no concern of the IMT and would be settled by the national tribunals in accordance with each nation's rules and policies.

The Tribunal then heard from the lawyers representing the indicted organizations. Their presentations, which occupied the rest of the day and part of the following morning, expectably included attacks on the legitimacy of charging organizations with criminality. More effective were their criticisms of Control Council Law No. 10, which, read literally, appeared to authorize capital punishment for mere membership in a convicted organization.

But most of all, the defense lawyers complained of the practical problems confronting them in locating and examining organization members who wished to testify before the Tribunal and were competent to confront the evidentiary issues. Dr. Martin Loeffler, representing the SA, was especially concerned because, in contrast to the SS and Party leaders, most of whom were assembled in internment camps, with few exceptions the SA members were free, and correspondingly difficult to assemble. Dr. Robert Servatius, representing Sauckel and the Nazi Party leadership, strongly opposed Jackson's proposal of court-appointed masters to take members' evidence: "In my opinion it is one of the main rights of a Defense Counsel to collect his own information. . . . My proposal is this: that each [intern-ment] camp should have a German lawyer who receives his information from the main Defense Counsel and instructs the members interned in the camp and collects information." That was certainly a straight road to a united front among the members.

When the defense lawyers finished, the Tribunal gave the chief prosecutors an opportunity to reply, and several of the judges put questions to them. Concerning Control Council Law No. 10, Jackson declared himself "frank enough to say I would not have drafted it in the language it is drafted in," but argued for reasonable interpretation of careless ambiguities. Law-rence asked Jackson whether "an individual who was being tried before a national court would be heard on the question whether, in fact, he knew of the criminal purpose of those groups?" Plainly, Lawrence regarded this as a crucial question. But Jackson, perhaps with Petersen's letter in mind, did not respond with a clear affirmation:

> Well, I think he would be heard on that subject, but I do not think it would be what we in the United States would call a complete defense. It perhaps would be a partial defense or mitigation. I should think that the . . . court . . . trying it might well have felt that he should have known under the circumstances . . . and that his denial, if believed, will weigh in mitigation rather than in complete defense.

Under Biddle's interrogation, Jackson remained adamant against ac-cepting individual pleas of ignorance if the tribunal was dealing with crimi-nal actions previously determined to be widely known. Fyfe supported Jackson's position: "the Prosecution's test is constructive knowledge. That is, ought a reasonable person in the position of a member to have known of these crimes."

Sir David, for his part, was prepared to go a long way to find guilt. Asked by Biddle whether a member of the SA who had joined in 1921 and resigned the next year was guilty of conspiring to wage aggressive war, Fyfe replied: "Yes, in this sense. . . . A man who took an active and voluntary part as a member of the SA in 1921 certainly, in supporting the Nazi Party, was supporting the published program of the Party which had the aims you have just put to me." Whatever the theoretical basis for such a reply, it was poorly calculated to win the judges over to the prosecution's position.

The Tribunal's hearing on organizations ended during a morning ses-sion on March 2, after a brief closing statement by General Rudenko, whose answers to questions by Biddle revealed him as surprisingly hospitable to the rights of individual member defendants:

> RUDENKO: . . . We are bearing in mind the fact that the national courts investigating the problem of the responsibility of individual members of the

organizations will, of course, proceed from the principle of individual guilt, since, naturally, we cannot exclude the possibility that . . . there might be individual members who might have been lured into the organization . . . and have been unaware of its criminal purpose.

BIDDLE: But that would not be any defense to him, would it? He could not say that he had no knowledge, because we would already have found that the knowledge was so open and notorious that he must have known.

RUDENKO: Why? I personally proceed from the standpoint that if the national court investigates the case of members who plead ignorance of the criminal purpose of the organization to which they belonged, the national court must examine these arguments submitted in their defense and estimate them accordingly.

These views were far more congenial than those of Jackson or Fyfe to Anglo-American legal principles.

It is noteworthy and somewhat surprising that virtually no mention was made of the denazification program and its relation to the organizational charges. It is true that the German-enacted law in the American Zone was not promulgated until a few days after these hearings, but the existence and probable passage of the law was widely known, and the Control Council had adopted what amounted to a denazification directive in January 1946.

The greatly diminished practical importance of the Nuremberg charges against the organizations was apparent to me and many others when I left Nuremberg in early February. Perhaps Jackson, having made so much of the organizational charges from the very beginning, was reluctant to introduce factors that might lead the judges to conclude that the organizational issues were not worth the time being spent on them.

According to Dr. von der Lippe, the general impression of the defense counsel was that the Tribunal had confronted the prosecution with "very critical questions." Biddle, he thought, had been sharp and "almost unfriendly" in his questions to Jackson. Inconclusive as the hearing was, it had certainly exposed and to some extent clarified the issues that confronted the Tribunal.

8

By the end of January I had thought and conferred enough about my proposed undertaking to have gained some comprehension of its scope and of the uncertainties and obstacles that had to be confronted. Mindful of the Gustav Krupp crisis during the preceding November, in the course of which Shawcross had assured the French that Britain would join with them in preparing for an international trial of Alfried Krupp and other German industrialists, I conferred with Patrick Dean, who represented the Foreign Office at Nuremberg, and Elwyn Jones, who warmly supported such a trial. I made the rounds of the American legal and administrative staffs, already greatly shrunken in numbers, to ascertain the possibility of recruiting them for the subsequent trials.

Finally, on January 30, I submitted to Jackson a memorandum entitled "Future Trials," embodying my general conclusions:

> Accordingly, my best guess at the shape of things to come is as follows:
>
> (a) One more international trial, at which the list of defendants will include a heavy concentration of industrialists and financiers.
>
> (b) Several or a series of trials of other major criminals to be tried in American courts in the American zone. . . .
>
> (c) A continuation of the trials of local criminals being conducted by the American theatre Judge Advocate.°
>
> (d) Trials of other major war criminals in the courts of the occupied countries or by one of the other allied powers.
>
> (e) Treatment of the general run of organizational cases under the denazification program.

Except for the first item, the conclusions proved to be valid.

Far more pessimistic, however, was my assessment of the manpower problem:

> It will be quite impossible to conduct the subsequent proceedings with the present legal staff of the Office Chiefs of Counsel. Indeed, it will even be impossible to form the bare nucleus of a staff for further proceedings from the personnel now in Nuremberg. This is so for two reasons:
>
> (a) With practically no exceptions the present staff has absolutely no interest in participating in further proceedings. The reasons for this are by now irrelevant; the fact is that almost without exception the lawyers now in Nuremberg want to finish their work here as quickly as possible and get home.
>
> (b) The legal staff has already diminished to such a point that there is no substantial personnel which can be diverted from work on the present trial to work on subsequent proceedings. Indeed, Mr. Dodd advises me that he is worried as to whether sufficient legal personnel remain to handle adequately the work on the present trial.

°The group under Colonel Straight, who reported to General Betts.

At most, there were six or eight lawyers who might stay on, but none were immediately available. If there were to be any "subsequent proceedings," the legal staff must be recruited anew. The only reservoir of talent was the United States, and it behooved me to return without delay. But it was several years since I had had any contact with American legal circles, and I had "no idea how successful my recruiting activities may be." Consequently, I advised Jackson: "That no announcement concerning the creation of any section or division of your staff to deal with further proceedings be made until we are in a position to move forward."

On February 5 Jackson replied, in a memorandum not in full accord with mine; in particular, he appeared to be still wedded to Allied prosecution of the criminal organization members rather than prosecution through the OMGUS-planned denazification proceedings:

> When this matter first came up, I suggested that G-2 [i.e., army intelligence] should immediately start classifying prisoners of war, obtaining their admissions so far as possible as to organizations to which they belonged, their ranks, places at which they served and other pertinent information. This would doubtless result in classifications in different categories with each member's classification admitted. Very few of them can advance any personal defense against that kind of classification. In fact, at the time their statements are taken, most of such defenses can be foreclosed by admission. They can then be dealt with in very rapid fashion and, perhaps, in substantial groups. I do not think we can abandon prosecution of members after asking the Tribunal to make the Declaration of Criminality.

As I had already stated my views, I did not respond. But I altogether disagreed with the idea that individuals accused of serious crimes could be dealt with on such an assembly-line basis, and if Jackson's proposals had prevailed, I am sure that I would not have accepted responsibility for their enforcement. Fortunately for me, the Control Council approved the Clay-Fahy denazification program so that I never had to confront the issue.

Jackson also took an attitude different from mine on the prospect of another four-party war crimes trial. From the outset he had made it clear that he himself would not be available, nor would he commit his country to participate in any additional international trials. In his memorandum to me, his stated reasons were:

> . . . first, I doubt that there will be public support for a repetition of the trial against less widely known and reprehended characters. Second, the Russians were almost certain to insist that any second trial be held in their territory and presided over by a Russian judge. This would present a difficult situation. Third, the agreement for interna-

tional trials expires on August 8th, and I see no reason to believe that the second trial could be completed by that time.

Except for the third reason,* I agreed with Jackson's concerns and felt it might well be the better part of wisdom not to risk a second walk on tenterhooks. But my inquiries had confirmed that the French and Russians were counting on an international trial of industrialists and that the British were bound to support that course. Under these circumstances it appeared to me that for the United States to play Achilles sulking in his tent would be harmful to the enduring value of the war crimes trials and that we should at least make an effort to see if an acceptable plan for a second trial could be agreed upon.

Jackson's negative attitude toward my recommendations on the second trial and the criminal organizations was disquieting, but not nearly so troubling as the recruitment problem. If Jackson was hard-pressed to hold a staff together for the first trial, how likely was it that a new contingent of American lawyers could be induced to leave their jobs and families and go abroad to prosecute less notorious Nazis? Jackson himself had warned me of the probable lack of public support for a second international trial. Was such support for "all-American" trials any more likely?

As the dimensions of the recruitment problem emerged, my outlook turned pessimistic. I had a good opinion of my own capacities and was confident that I could direct a prosecution, given a competent staff. But I was virtually unknown among American lawyers, in contrast to Jackson, whose name in the profession was a veritable lodestar. In this frame of mind, on February 6 I addressed a memorandum to Jackson and Fahy:

> I believe that you both should give careful consideration to finding someone of greater ability, reputation and rank to handle this matter and to take over when Mr. Justice Jackson returns to the Supreme Court. It does not matter who does this job, but it is most important that it be done by someone who can perform effectively.
>
> If, despite the above, or the lack of a more suitable appointee, you both feel that I should undertake this assignment, I shall be glad to do so if I can arrange my family affairs properly.
>
> If it is decided that I should undertake the assignment, I feel that I should be given the rank which the appointment needs. This should be done not in my interest, but in the interest of the successful accomplishment of the assignment and so that the United States may be more effectively represented in international negotiations on war

---

*On this third point, Jackson was entirely mistaken. Article 8 of the London Agreement provided that it should "remain in force for one year [which would fall on August 8, 1946] and shall continue thereafter, subject to the right of any Signatory . . . to terminate it" in accordance with due notice, and so forth. The trial then in process was not concluded until October 1, 1946.

crimes matters. I also believe that this should be done in the very near future, both to facilitate recruiting personnel and because some of the most important tasks, particularly in the international field, must be handled in the not too distant future. . . . The British are starting to move forward and prepare for a further trial, and we should not be in the position of being unable, for lack of staff, to do as much as the best interests of the United States require.

The next day, armed with a letter from Jackson to Secretary of War Robert Patterson, I departed Nuremberg and proceeded to Washington.

## 9

I reached Washington in mid-February and was delighted to find that recruitment of lawyers for my staff was already under way. One of my benefactors was Tom Harris, an old friend with whom I had worked at the Federal Communications Commission during the New Deal period. Since the end of the war Tom had been in Berlin on the OMGUS staff, and in January he visited me in Nuremberg to canvass the possibility of taking part in the later trials. He decided instead to return to law practice, but generously agreed to do some recruiting for me, and by the time I got home he had lined up several good prospects. Charles Horsky had also been helpful.

I presented Jackson's letter to Secretary Robert Patterson, who gave me introductions to some of his legal friends in New York. He also told me to take up policy problems with Assistant Secretary Petersen and administrative matters with the Civil Affairs Division of the War Department, headed by Major General John K. Hilldring.

As things worked out, I saw a great deal of Howard Petersen and very little of General Hilldring, who had delegated his division's war crimes responsibilities to his subordinate, Colonel David Marcus—well known as Mickey Marcus, who two years later achieved immortality in the annals of Israel when he was killed during the fighting in Jerusalem during the 1948 war.[*]

I was very lucky. Mickey was a heart-and-soul supporter of the war crimes trials, intelligent, energetic, and a skilled "operator," with many

[*] Mickey Marcus, born in Brooklyn in 1900, was a 1924 graduate of West Point who, after three years' service as a lieutenant, left the army and in 1928 graduated from Brooklyn Law School. After serving in the Department of Justice and on the staff of the United States Attorney in New York, he joined the New York City Department of Corrections, and in 1936 was appointed its Director by Mayor Fiorello LaGuardia, whom Mickey considerably resembled in physique and personality. After Pearl Harbor he rejoined the army and served first as a Judge Advocate and later as a legal assistant at several major international conferences, including Potsdam. After his service in the Civil Affairs Division he resigned from the army and joined in the struggle for Israeli independence. He is buried in the post cemetery at West Point.

contacts and friends in legal, military, and New York political circles. In recruiting and in ensuring a logistical base for our enterprise, Mickey played the leading part.

Shortly after my arrival I received a cable from Fahy stating that he and Jackson had carefully considered my memorandum and that he was "convinced you are the one to carry through the work," adding that he was writing to Patterson in support of my request for a promotion. Petersen assured me that the Secretary would support it and that there was every reason to expect favorable action when the next list of promotions was sent to the Senate. These statements were reassuring, but of course the principal uncertainty remained the question of whether a staff, large and competent enough to handle at least half a dozen cases, and preferably considerably more, could be assembled.

Nevertheless, on March 2, after I had been in the United States barely two weeks, I received a cable from Jackson declaring that he, Fahy, and General Betts all agreed that there could be no further delay in announcing my appointment. Much as I was distressed to oppose three gentlemen much senior to me for whom I had great respect, I could think of nothing worse than announcing a governmental policy that would soon have to be abandoned for lack of willing participants.

Accordingly, I did not respond, with the result that two weeks later Jackson sent Petersen an angrily worded cable that accused me of attaching conditions to my acceptance, which he had thought to be unconditional. In fact, my memorandum of January 30 had explicitly provided against any public mention of the project until the recruitment problem appeared to be in hand, and my memorandum of February 6 had conditioned my acceptance on my ability to "arrange my family affairs properly," which, as Jackson well knew, meant permission for my wife to join me in Germany.

Jackson was particularly disturbed by my insistence that Mary accompany me. He emphasized that he had "at all times taken the position that my organization is a temporary one that . . . does not justify requests by those here for those trials in any capacity to bring their wives." But I was to be employed to direct a series of later trials, which would certainly last at least a year, and probably longer, after the conclusion of the IMT trial.

Much more important than my personal situation was our speedy discovery that some of the lawyers we were seeking to recruit would accept if, but only if, their wives could also come. Thus the continuation of Jackson's rule and its application to the later trials was a direct hindrance to our recruitment efforts, on the success of which the whole venture depended.

Jackson and Fahy appeared not to grasp these factors, but fortunately Petersen and Marcus did; at no time did any of the Washington officials put me under pressure to commit myself. It was not until March 29 that Jackson made the public announcement of my appointment as Deputy Chief Counsel and of an order for the establishment of the "Subsequent Proceedings Division" within the Office of Chief of Counsel (OCC) in a press release.

By that time the "wife problem" had been resolved by General McNarney's decision to allow both military and civilian Americans stationed in Germany to be accompanied by their spouses. The first "shipment" of army "dependents" was scheduled to leave port on April 16, and Mary was assigned a berth.

During March the recruitment of prosecution staff had made good progress. Mickey Marcus had told OMGUS to prepare for the shipment of forty-five attorneys, and twenty to thirty each of administrators, court reporters, translators, stenographers, and typists.

Major Walter Rapp, who had been of great help on the General Staff case, returned to the United States for demobilization. He promptly accepted my proposal that in a civilian capacity he head the interrogation staff for the subsequent trials.

The army assigned as my executive officer Colonel Clarence Tomlinson, a regimental commander who had served in both the Far East and Italy during the war. Charles T. Malcolmson, who had been press officer at the Department of Justice and was highly regarded in the news fraternity, agreed to serve as our public relations director. A request to my friend Alfred McCormack at the Cravath firm led to the loan of their young associate Jack Robbins as my legal assistant.

American occupation facilities were not yet equipped for the needs of small children, so Mary and I had to leave our two daughters in the care of grandparents and, for part of the time, an institution that specialized in the temporary care of children. At the time we thought our stay abroad would not greatly exceed one year, but that estimate fell far short, and in 1947 we were able to bring the girls to Nuremberg.

On April 17 I drove Mary to Fort Hamilton, where she boarded the army transport *T. H. Barry* for the passage to Bremerhaven. Virtually all the passengers were regular army wives, and the ranking ladies were Mrs. Mark Clark and Mrs. Lucius Clay. They were, of course, much courted by their juniors, and Mary was amused by the gossip comparing the prestige of the four-star General Clark, commanding in little Austria, with the three-star General Clay, thought to be slated for the big command in Germany.

I spent another week in Washington before flying to Nuremberg via Paris, accompanied by Tomlinson and Malcolmson. My last day at the Pentagon Building was a pleasing one for me. In the morning I was asked to come to the office of General Hoyt Vandenberg (at that time the Chief of Army Intelligence), where I found Howard Petersen, Colonel Carter Clarke (my commanding officer during the war), and a number of other officers. I was awarded the Distinguished Service Medal for my wartime services. That afternoon, Walter Rapp came into my office with a pair of silver stars and informed me that the Senate had confirmed my appointment as brigadier general.

I reached Nuremberg on April 26 and learned that the *T. H. Barry* had just docked at Bremerhaven and that Mary would arrive in Nuremberg the next day. We stayed temporarily at the Grand Hotel, but shortly were assigned a comfortable small house in Erlenstegen.

Thus the second and much longer phase of my Nuremberg undertaking began.

# Chapter 12

# THE FRENCH AND
# SOVIET PROSECUTIONS

On January 17, 1946, François de Menthon, Chief Prosecutor for the Republic of France, had opened the French case before an audience of curious listeners. The French chief had spent much time in Paris and was little known to the participants in the trial. The French in general had been understaffed and reticent, and the audience did not know what to expect; to some it appeared unlikely that de Menthon could come up with anything new.

The French chief was equal to the occasion. Neither Britain nor America had suffered under the Nazi yoke; Shawcross and Jackson had spoken for the world. De Menthon, who had joined the Resistance and witnessed the brutalities and terrors of the German occupation, spoke for "the peoples who only yesterday were enslaved and tortured in both soul and body." He echoed the cry of the European governments in exile for "justice," first articulated in the St. James Declaration of January 1942. He called upon the Tribunal "to judge and to condemn the most monstrous attempt at domination and barbarism of all times."

De Menthon's opening was emotional but not mawkish; von der Lippe thought it "eloquent" in the "continental-European manner," and remarked that it was marked "above all by the beauty of the French language." There followed a deeply emotional paean to "France, invaded twice in 30 years . . . by German imperialism" and "temporarily crushed by superiority in numbers, matériel, and preparation," a country which "never gave up the battle for freedom and was at no time absent from the field." De Menthon was a strong Gaullist, and patriotism sang in every tone and turn of his utterance, as he hymned the France of which he was a part. But it failed, I fear, to drive from his listeners' minds that other France, the France of Vichy, and Pétain and Laval.

De Menthon then spoke briefly of the charges set forth in the London Charter and declared that "France sees fit to ask the Tribunal to qualify juridically as crimes both the war of aggression itself" (despite France's earlier opposition to this charge during the drafting of the Charter) "and those acts of violation . . . of the laws of all civilized countries which have been committed by Germany in the conduct of the war. . . ." Both crimes against peace and war crimes he viewed as "more precise" than crimes against humanity—the category which the French lawyers had never accepted as valid international law and which the French chief now suggested to be a mere duplication of "crimes that are provided for and punishable under the penal laws of all civilized states."

But legalisms were soon laid aside as de Menthon approached the core of his thesis. Jackson and Shawcross, he noted, had described the particular crimes committed by the Nazis. How and why had they happened? De Menthon's response included the most striking and memorable passages in his statement:

> I propose today to prove to you that all this organized and vast criminality springs from what I may be allowed to call a crime against the spirit. I mean a doctrine which, denying all spiritual, rational, and moral values by which the nations have tried, for thousands of years, to improve human conditions, aims to plunge humanity back into barbarism, no longer the natural and spontaneous barbarism of primitive nations, but into a diabolical barbarism, conscious of itself and utilizing for its ends all material means put at the disposal of mankind by contemporary science. This sin against the spirit is the original sin of National Socialism from which all crimes spring.
>
> This monstrous doctrine is that of racialism. The German race, composed in theory of Aryans, would be a fundamental and natural concept. . . . Race is the matrix of the German people; proceeding therefrom this people lives and develops as an organism. The German may consider himself only as a healthy and vigorous member of this body, fulfilling within the collectivity a definite technical function; his activity and his usefulness are the exact gauge and justification of his liberty. The national body must be "moulded" to prepare it for a permanent struggle. . . .
>
> The expression "blood" which appears so often in the writings of the Nazi theorists denotes this stream of real life, of red sap which flows through the circulatory system of every race and of all genuine culture as it flows through the human body. . . .
>
> National Socialism ends in the absorption of the personality of the citizen into that of the state and in the denial of any intrinsic value of the human person.
>
> We are brought back . . . to the most primitive idea of the savage tribes. All the values of civilization accumulated in the course of

centuries are rejected, all traditional ideas of morality, justice, and law give way to the primacy of race, its instincts, its needs and interests. The individual, his liberty, his rights and aspirations, no longer have any real existence of their own.

De Menthon asked rhetorically how this "sin against the spirit" had come to be nurtured in a Germany "fertilized through the centuries by classic antiquity and Christianity, by the ideals of liberty, equality, and social justice, [and] by the common heritage of western humanism." His response was hardly original; he mentioned Nietzsche, Fichte, and Hegel as progenitors of Hitler and traced the Fuehrer's course to war. It was lucid history, but he came no closer to answering the question than the many others who have tried.

In the course of the narrative, de Menthon quoted the language of the 1928 Kellogg-Briand Pact. He then declared: "War of aggression thus ceased to be lawful in 1928," and supported this statement on the basis that the signatories of the pact were mutually bound not to resort to war, that violation of the pact was a violation of international law, and that therefore the aggressors, by invading and waging war against other signatories, thereby committed crimes under international law.° Furthermore, on this basis the London Charter had created no new law, since the "crimes against peace" recognized in the Charter had already been so declared by agreement among the Pact of Paris signatories. This was a far cry from Judge Falco's rejection of "crimes against peace" at the London conference seven months earlier. The French prosecution, at least, had come a long way.

But de Menthon did not go on to apply his new peace thesis to the evidentiary case. For him, war crimes were the major and crucial charge against the defendants, and he now turned to the evidence establishing the commission of such crimes in the occupied countries of Western Europe. He divided them into four major categories: "Forced Labor, Economic Looting, Crimes against Persons, and Crimes against Mankind."

Sauckel, "acting together with" Goering and Speer, bore the heaviest burden of guilt for the forced labor program, which in Western Europe embraced France, Norway, and the Low Countries. "Economic Looting" included "both the taking away of goods of every type and the exploitation, on the spot, of the national resources for the benefit of Germany's war."

Under "Crimes against Persons," de Menthon discussed "executions of hostages, police crimes, deportations, crimes involving prisoners of war, terroristic activities against the Resistance, and the massacre of civilian populations." The Frenchman declared that *all* killing of hostages was

---

°De Menthon's legal analysis was substantially the same as the theory developed by Colonel William Chanler, which he presented to Secretary Stimson in the fall of 1944.

condemned by the Hague Conventions—a legal point of very dubious validity.* Beyond doubt, however, the magnitude and manner of the German Army's hostage-killings rendered them unlawful as well as horrifying.

Reading de Menthon's many passages on Nazi war crimes forty years later reveals a jarring omission of reference to Jews and the Holocaust. In part this is due to the division of evidence, on a West-East basis, between the French and Soviet delegations. True, the Holocaust reached its climax in Poland and the eastern reaches of the Soviet Union. Still, the *deportation* to those lands of Western Europe's Jews is not mentioned in de Menthon's account of "deportations," which deals only with "deportation and internment in the concentration camps of Germany." Auschwitz is mentioned, but only to observe that many of its inmates were "sterilized" and that "the most beautiful women were set apart, artificially sterilized, and then gassed."

There was more of the same when de Menthon came to his last war crimes category, "Crimes against Mankind *(la condition humaine)*." By this, he explained, he meant a racialist Germanization of occupied territories: "Racialism classifies occupied nations in two main categories; Germanization means for some a Nationalist Socialist assimilation, and for others disappearance or slavery." De Menthon described the Germanization that followed the German wartime annexations of Luxembourg, Eupen and Malmédy, Alsace and Lorraine. But despite his emphasis on "racialism" as the root of the Nazi evil, both at the beginning of his speech and here, near its end, he had only this to say about the Jews: "It is also known that racial discriminations were provoked against citizens of the occupied countries who were catalogued as Jews, measures particularly hateful, damaging to their personal rights and to their human dignity."

Indeed, that is the only explicit reference to Jewry in de Menthon's entire presentation. When hearing him, I did not mark this fact. Nor did I hear any discussion of it, nor have I noted any reference to the matter in the writings of those who have discussed the Nuremberg trials.

Toward the end of his statement, de Menthon dealt with the defendants individually, putting emphasis on those, including Goering, Frick, Keitel,† and Seyss-Inquart, whose depredations had borne particularly heavily

---

*De Menthon relied on Article 50 of the Hague Convention, which prohibits the imposition of a "general penalty" on "the population" of the particular occupied area. Plainly, this does not cover the *selection* of a number of individuals to be held as security against attacks or other offenses against the occupying troops. Hostages had been killed in reprisal for such attacks in prior wars, and in one of the subsequent Nuremberg trials the Tribunal held that hostage-killing was not intrinsically criminal, though it was subject to various limitations (*United States* v. *List*, XI TWC 766, esp. 1248–57. In 1949, the Geneva Convention was amended by adding a provision outlawing the taking of hostages.

†De Menthon mistakenly referred to Keitel as having "command over the occupation armies." In fact, Keitel commanded only his own small staff at OKW and was merely a conduit for the Fuehrer's orders as Commander in Chief of the Wehrmacht.

on Western Europe. He briefly discussed the Nazi organizations in a manner that would have greatly pleased the departed Bernays:

> But perhaps it will seem to you that the punishment of hundreds of thousands of men who belong to the SS, to the SD, to the Gestapo, to the SA, will give rise to some objection. I should like to try, should this be the case, to do away with that objection by showing you the dreadful responsibilities of these men. Without these organizations, without the spirit which animated them, one could not understand how so many atrocities could have been perpetrated. The systematic War Crimes could not have been carried out by Nazi Germany without these organizations, without the men who comprised them. It is they who not only executed but willed this body of crimes on behalf of Germany.

Parts of de Menthon's peroration were, I thought, the most sensitive and moving of his utterances:

> Who can say: "I have a clean conscience, I am without fault? To use different weights and measures is abhorred by God." This text from the Holy Scriptures (Proverbs XX, 9–10) has already been mentioned here and there; it will serve tomorrow as a theme of propaganda, but above all, it is profoundly written in our souls. Rising in the name of our martyred people as accusers of Nazi Germany, we have never for a moment repressed it as a distasteful reminder. . . .
> If this criminality had been accidental; if Germany had been forced into war, if war crimes had been committed only in the excitement of combat, we might question ourselves in the light of the Scriptures. But the war was prepared and deliberated long in advance, and upon the very last day it would have been easy to avoid it without sacrificing any of the legitimate interests of the German people. And the atrocities were perpetrated during the war, not under the influence of a mad passion nor of a warlike anger nor of an avenging resentment, but as a result of cold calculation, of perfectly conscious methods, of a pre-existing doctrine.

And then, addressing the Tribunal:

> Your judgment must be inscribed as a decisive act in the history of international law in order to prepare the establishment of a true international society excluding recourse to war and enlisting force permanently in the service of the justice of nations; it will be one of the foundations of the peaceful order in which nations aspire on the morrow of this frightful torment. The need for justice of the martyred people will be satisfied, and their suffering will not have been useless to the progress of mankind.

De Menthon's address was far more self-revealing than those of his predecessors. Jackson's speech, powerful and moving as it was, came down from the mountaintop. De Menthon was a personal presence; France's torture was his own blood and tears.

His speech was well received; Jackson, who had not admired him, pronounced his performance "very good." Hans Frank added an unctuous note, telling Dr. Gilbert: "Ah, that is stimulating! That is more like the European mentality. It will be a pleasure to argue with that man! But you know, it is ironic—it was the Frenchman de Gobineau who started racial ideology!"*

2

De Menthon immediately resigned as Chief Prosecutor and returned to Paris and politics. His successor, Auguste Champetier de Ribes, had been one of the few members of the French Cabinet who, in 1938, had opposed yielding to Hitler's demands which led to the Munich crisis and the crushing of Czechoslovakia; he had joined the Maquis during the Resistance. Unfortunately, he was in very poor health and only rarely took part in the court proceedings. M. Champetier de Ribes was very self-effacing. He was not formally introduced in open court, nor does the record contain any announcement of his replacement of de Menthon. Although his appointment became known within thirty-six hours after de Menthon completed his address, Champetier de Ribes did not appear at the lectern until February 28, when he made a short statement in support of the prosecution's charges against the Nazi organizations.

The French presentation of evidence began with Edgar Faure, who shared with Dubost the title of Deputy Chief Prosecutor.† Faure announced that the first and second parts of the French case would be "Forced Labor" and "Economic Looting" and that the evidence would cover Denmark, Norway, Holland, Belgium, and Luxembourg, as well as France. Throughout the French presentation these smaller countries were given their due by the speakers. Since many of the same sorts of things happened in each of these countries (except Denmark, which, prior to 1943, was less troubled), the procedure was inevitably repetitive, but necessarily so in view of the demands of pride and politics.

Faure spoke briefly, then turned over the presentation of "Forced

---

*Joseph Arthur, Comte de Gobineau (1816–1882), was a French diplomat and writer, whose *Essai sur l'Inégalité des Races Humaines* (1853–55) propounded the thesis that the races of humankind are inherently unequal in ability and cultural worth and that only white races are creative in cultural terms.

†It appears, however, that Dubost was the ranking Deputy, or at least he thought so, as he spoke to the Tribunal "in my capacity as representative of the French Prosecution."

Labor" to Assistant Prosecutor Jacques Herzog and "pillage of public and private property" to Assistant Prosecutor Charles Gerthoffer. In both cases, the legal bases for the charges were the sections of the Hague Conventions governing the obligations of occupying troops to the inhabitants of the occupied territory and the provisions of the 1940 Franco-German Armistice Convention. The conquering German military forces came in with soothing promises of compliance with these obligations, but soon established occupational practices that were increasingly harsh, grasping, and violent.

Certainly there was no lack of proof that the consequences of these policies were devastating. The statistics alone were mind-shattering. Herzog produced evidence that over 150,000 Belgians, 430,000 Dutch, and 2,600,000 French "were pressed into work serving the war effort of Nationalist Socialist Germany." Of the French, over 875,000 workers were deported to Germany, and nearly a million prisoners of war were used for military-supportive purposes, all in flagrant violation of laws to which Germany had been bound for many years.

Gerthoffer's evidence on "economic pillage" described the seizure and removal to Germany of factories, machinery, and other manufactures, but even more damaging was the seizure of foodstuffs. Under Article 52 of the Hague Conventions, requisitions by an occupying force are limited to "the necessities of the army of occupation." But the German seizures, on the black as well as the open markets, so far exceeded the permissible limits that the health of the inhabitants was seriously undermined. German seizures of foodstuffs and of forest and fossil fuels comprised substantial fractions of the entire French production, running in some cases as high as 50 percent for forest fuels, 29 percent for coal, 80 percent for petroleum and motor fuels, 75 percent for oats, and 60 percent for eggs. As a result of these purchases and confiscations, in the course of the war French food rations dropped from 1,800 to 1,300 calories or less per day, a level the German government itself recognized as a "regime of slow starvation, leading to death." In his conclusion, Gerthoffer told the Tribunal:

> Incurable sicknesses such as tuberculosis developed and will continue to extend their ravages for many years. The growth of children and adolescents is seriously impaired. The future of the race is a cause for great concern. The results of economic spoliation will be felt for an indefinite period. . . .
>
> Remember, gentlemen, the words of Goering when he said: 'If famine is to reign, it will not reign in Germany."

These were wounds that victory could not heal.

On January 24 Dubost took the lectern to present the second main segment of the French case. He defined it as his task (which was to occupy five full-day sessions of the Tribunal) to establish that the defendants "systematically pursued a policy of extermination" not primarily motivated by war aims, but rather by a "policy of domination, of expansion, beyond war itself." In fact, the greater part of Dubost's presentation related to the German concentration camps, while shorter portions dealt with hostages, assassinations, and prisoners of war. These matters were easier to grasp than problems of finance and commerce, but the scope and nature of the atrocities was, if anything, even harder to believe.

Following de Menthon's lead, Dubost treated all killings of hostages as war crimes. Weak as the legal basis for that view was, the quantity and scale of hostage executions far exceeded anything previously deemed lawful. In France nearly 30,000 hostages were killed. In the Netherlands the total was 3,000, and in the other Western European countries the toll was proportionate. But thousands more were imprisoned or deported to concentration camps simply because the Germans wanted them out of the way, and many such soon met their deaths, including 40,000 French who died in French prisons under German control. Dubost produced proof of many individual instances in which death was preceded by unspeakable torture.

Dubost chose to present the concentration camp evidence through the testimony of seven witnesses. Three of them had been prisoners at the Mauthausen camp in Austria, the atmosphere of which had earlier been briefly described by witness Alois Hoellriegel, a camp guard. Dubost's witnesses, Maurice Lampe, Jean-Frederick Vieth, and François Boix, had been longtime prisoners at Mauthausen; they spoke with passion and detail. Their accounts confirmed Hoellriegel's testimony that inmates were frequently killed by throwing them off a cliff into a quarry and that guards referred to the victims as "paratroopers." Mauthausen took in many prisoners of war whom the Germans removed from the regular prisoner-of-war camps and sent to Mauthausen for execution, often preceded by torture. These included forty-seven British, American, and Dutch air officers who had parachuted after their aircraft were hit. They had tried to make their way back to their own lines and, apparently because of their escape efforts, were sent to Mauthausen in September 1944. Lampe testified:

> I must mention that one of the American officers asked the commander that he be allowed to meet his death as a soldier. In reply he was bashed with a whip. The 47 were led barefoot to the quarry.
>
> For all the prisoners at Mauthausen the murder of these men has remained in their minds like a scene from Dante's Inferno. This is how it was done: At the bottom of the steps they loaded stone on the backs of these poor men and they had to carry them to the top. The first journey was made with stones weighing 25 to 30 kilos and was accompanied by blows. Then they were made to run down. For the

second journey the stones were still heavier; and when the poor wretches sank under their burden, they were kicked and hit with a bludgeon, even stones were hurled at them.

This went on for several days. In the evening when I returned from the gang with which I was then working, the road which led to the camp was a bath of blood. I almost stepped on the lower jaw of a man. Twenty-one bodies were strewn along the road. Twenty-one had died on the first day. The twenty-six others died the following morning. . . .

None of the defense counsel chose to cross-examine Lampe.

Among Dubost's other witnesses were Dr. Victor Dupont, who testified to the killings at Buchenwald concentration camp, and Dr. Alfred Balachowsky, a laboratory chief at the Pasteur Institute and an internee at Buchenwald, who described the atrocious medical experiments that were performed on the inmates with the approval of the highest German medical authorities, including Dr. Siegfried Handloser, Chief of the Wehrmacht Medical Services.

Dubost's most dramatic witness was a much-decorated member of the French Constituent Assembly, Mme Marie Claude Vaillant-Couturier—an odd name ("valiant dressmaker") for a very brave woman. A member of the Resistance, she had been arrested by the Germans in Paris early in 1942 and spent nearly a year in German custody. In March 1943 she was taken in a convoy of 230 Frenchwomen to Auschwitz and spent the rest of the war there and at the Ravensbrück camp. At Auschwitz the Frenchwomen were put to work, under such appalling conditions that only forty-nine survived a year. Mme. Vaillant-Couturier described the process of selecting those to be sent to the gas chambers and the medical experiments performed on inmates; in both activities the name of Dr. Josef Mengele appeared in the trial record for the first time.

In the summer of 1944 Mme. Vaillant-Couturier was moved to Ravensbrück, a camp primarily for women. Here she was put in the same block with a number of Polish women, known as "rabbits" because they had served as experimental guinea pigs. Serious wounds had been inflicted on their legs, and gas bacilli and other infectious agents were put into the wounds in order to determine the curative value of sulfanilamides. Some of the "rabbits" died, and the others were left with unsightly and hampering disabilities. Dr. Hanns Marx (Streicher's lawyer, but acting in behalf of Dr. Babel, representing the SS) most unwisely undertook to cross-examine, but Mme. Vaillant-Couturier's answers only made matters worse for the defendants, and he soon gave up.

When Dubost finished with his witnesses, he resumed documentary presentation, which now focused on war crimes against prisoners of war and civilians. His last submissions were official French reports describing the killing of civilians by SS units in June 1944, including the infamous massacre at Oradour-sur-Glane, a village about twenty-five miles northwest of Limoges. The killings were perpetrated by a company from the 2d SS Panzer Division Das Reich, which had fought for two years on the Russian front, where neither side had much regard for the Hague Conventions. In 1944 Das Reich was transferred to southern France, and after the Allied landings in Normandy it was ordered to move north to join the troops opposing the Allied forces. The landings had triggered widespread attacks on German soldiers by the Maquis, and Das Reich was suffering casualties on the way north, which provoked severe reprisals that were often visited on citizens who had no connection with the Maquis.

What happened at Oradour-sur-Glane differed from many comparable contemporary events only in the unbelievable cruelty and ferocity with which the raid was carried out. Led by the battalion commander, Major Otto Dickmann, the invaders rounded up all the inhabitants in the village square. Then the women and children, numbering over 400, were herded into the village church, while the men, some 240 strong, were divided into groups, each of which was marched into one of six barns. The Germans then shot all of the men and fired the barns. The church was closed, and old and young alike were attacked with guns and hand grenades, after which the church was set on fire. A group of twenty villagers returning from a shopping trip to Limoges were also shot. Most of the houses in the village were burned. There was a mere handful of survivors, who had played dead or fled into the woods. If such a thing is possible, Oradour-sur-Glane was worse than Lidice.[*]

Dubost had had his difficulties with the Tribunal during his many hours at the lectern, primarily because the French had not been able to translate the documents into all the other languages of the trial and because of technical failures in arranging and numbering the hundreds of documents that they introduced. One account of the trial declares that Dubost "reached an unparalleled level of incompetence"—an accusation I believe to be wholly unwarranted. As one of the leaders, Dubost of course shared responsibility for the technical failures, but there were clerical tasks which senior counsel could not personally perform, and some mistakes were inevitable considering the small size and slender resources of the French delegation. Dubost handled Lawrence's criticisms with aplomb and, in his

---

[*]The document read to the Tribunal by Dubost was, in all important respects, in line with the results of subsequent investigations. Major Dickmann was killed in action in Normandy three weeks after the massacre. Postwar efforts at retribution had sad results. Many of the SS soldiers at Oradour were Alsatians, and their trial on war crimes charges in 1951–1953 was loudly protested in Alsace, which had been returned to French sovereignty after the war. The light sentences imposed on the defendants enraged the non-Alsatian French.

conclusion, apologized handsomely for "errors of detail" which had "slipped into our work."

Dubost's presentation was well organized and sturdily spoken, but he was not widely admired. His personality was stark, and Jackson was not the only one who thought him to be a Communist and accordingly distrusted him. Lawrence was quick to confront Dubost with evidentiary problems and on at least two occasions accused him of documentary flaws which proved to be nonexistent.

Edgar Faure, who succeeded Dubost, was much more to the Tribunal's liking. He was personable, gracious, an able lawyer, a skilled speaker; all these qualities were abundantly confirmed by his subsequent political career, during which he became Premier. But the technical difficulties did not stop; Faure had been on his feet barely fifteen minutes when Dr. Stahmer rose to complain that the defendants had received no copies of the documents Faure was submitting to the Tribunal. However, these lapses did not subject Faure to any displeasure. Even the hard-to-please Biddle noted that "the lawyer, Faure, is doing a really first-rate job."

Faure's "job" was the third and last major part of the French case, embracing "Germanization" and "persecutions on political, racial and religious grounds" in line with Counts 3(j) and 4(b) of the Indictment. As it turned out, most of Faure's time—two and a half court days—was spent on Germanization.

Considering the past history of Alsace and Lorraine, it is easy to understand French sensitivity on this subject, especially since, despite all the written and spoken German promises that accompanied the June 1940 Armistice, the Nazis were in full control of those provinces barely two months later. Without formal annexation, both were put under the thumbs of *Gauleiters* (Josef Buerckel in Lorraine and Robert Wagner in Alsace). The French language was prohibited, and some 70,000 inhabitants who refused to acknowledge German origin were deported to the unoccupied portion of France.

Nevertheless, in the wake of all that had gone before, it was hard to make Germanization a gripping subject. Much of what had been done by the Nazi proconsuls was common knowledge. Victory cannot bring back the dead, but it can reestablish boundaries and governments and repeal laws. It is easy to understand, if not agree with, Biddle's complaint in a letter to his wife: "The French are still on this morning, proving such highly important materials as decrees in Alsace that the population must not wear berets, or hats that looked like berets, under penalty of going to a concentration camp!°I try to curb and shorten their endless zeal, but the Russians,

---

° In fact, the law did not prescribe "concentration camp," but fine or imprisonment. Faure was aware that he was walking a thin line: "In this regulation the ridiculous disputes supremacy

with an eye on their case which is to start next week, strenuously object to any interference."

But Faure's evidence contained much more serious matters, some even concerning Denmark, which, unlike the other German-occupied countries, had kept its King and government and a good part of its sovereignty. Really serious German oppression began in the summer of 1943, when the German police and SS arrived and disarmed the Danish police. These oppressive acts triggered efforts at resistance, including sabotage. On December 30, 1944, at a meeting with Hitler attended by Himmler, Keitel, Jodl, Kaltenbrunner, and three German officials in charge of the Denmark occupation, it was decided that reprisals should consist of "compensatory murders." Beginning early in 1945, there were 267 assassinations of Danes, most of them well known, accomplished by German Gestapo agents. Each of them received from Himmler a personal letter of congratulation for these accomplishments.

In Belgium, Faure focused attention on the famous library of the University of Louvain (now known by the city's Flemish name, Leuven), which had been virtually destroyed by the German Army in World War I and was severely damaged again, by German artillery fire, on May 16–17, 1940. The evidence of German responsibility was given by Van der Essen (the witness did not state his other name or names), a professor of history at the university and a member of the Belgian Commission for War Crimes. He testified that two German batteries were posted in villages adjacent to the city and that their fire was directed only at the library, which was hit eleven times. It was also hit by one or more bombs from German aircraft, and the resultant fire gutted the interior of the building.

Van der Essen testified on other matters, but his cross-examinations by Dr. Exner (for Jodl) and Dr. Stahmer (for Goering) dealt exclusively with the library. Asked by Exner what "motive might have induced the German Army" to attack the library a second time, Van der Essen replied:

> All the evidence seems to indicate . . . that the motive . . . for the destruction of the library was the German Army's desire to do away with a monument which commemorates the Treaty of Versailles. On the library building there was a virgin wearing a helmet crushing under her foot a dragon which symbolized the enemy. Certain conversations of German officers gave the very clear impression that the reason why they wished to set fire systematically to this building was their desire to get rid of a testimony of the defeat in the other war, and above all, a reminder of the Treaty of Versailles.

---

with the odious. I would almost like to ask the Tribunal to pardon me, but truly, nothing in this is invented by us."

Exner's response was a flat "I don't believe it." I, too, have my doubts. The Germans knew they were about to take Louvain, and the "monument" to Versailles could have been much more neatly and permanently done away with by a stick of dynamite than by artillery shells and aerial bombs. More probably the entire building, the destruction of which in 1914 had helped to label the Germans as "Huns," was put to the torch in 1940 to show Nazi scorn of foreign opinion and put fear into the Belgian populace.

After Faure finished, Gerthoffer returned to the lectern to report on "the pillage of works of art in the occupied countries of western Europe," relying on Article 56 of the Hague Convention, which protects both "historical monuments" and "works of art" from seizure or destruction. The Tribunal had already heard a great deal about this subject, and Lawrence directed that anything further must be "quite short because it must be cumulative." Gerthoffer took about two hours and was followed by two assistant counsel, Pierre Mounier and Constant Quatre, who assembled the French evidence against each of the defendants who was implicated by the French prosecution's evidence—Rosenberg, Sauckel, Speer, Goering, Seyss-Inquart, Keitel, and Jodl.

Such was the structure and such were some of the highlights of the French case. If the French had begun the trial, their evidence would have been sensational. That it was not was largely due to the fact that nearly all of their evidence concerned matters which had already been developed by the Americans, and even episodes described for the first time concerned the same subject matter and the same charges that the Americans had covered in presenting the conspiracy charge.

And so world press coverage was light, and the audiences in the courtroom dwindled. Dr. von der Lippe dutifully recorded the court developments, but called the French presentations on plundering "monotonous," and his entries reflect greater interest in what the famous Reverend Martin Niemoeller had to say in an evening lecture at the Fürth church, and in defense plans for his own courtroom sessions, the time for which was approaching.

The defendants' attention also lapsed. Dr. Gilbert's notes of his discussions with the defendants during the French case reveal no mention of the French presentations until the very last day (February 7, 1946), when the disclosure that Goering had not paid for the confiscated paintings that had been turned over to him was repeated. Gilbert's notes on the talk at lunch state:

> Fritzsche and Speer showed that Goering's stealing of art treasures was really the damaging accusation in German eyes. "They didn't even mention the worst part of it," Fritzsche pointed out, "—that he even *sold* the stuff he stole. But that Frenchman who

presented the case did a really good job—much more effective than name calling, and he cleverly left the word for it up to the court to decide."

"You see," said Speer, "how can there be any talk of a united front among the defendants when that man has disgraced himself like that?"

Goering came over after lunch while I was reading the paper to some of the others, looking over my shoulder. He started to wisecrack about having a grudge against the brain-doctor. The others walked away to avoid the pretense of joking with him, and Goering expressed great interest in the day's news.

Strange men, these Nazis—sitting quietly through descriptions of the wars and massacres for which Goering bore heavy responsibility and then sending him to Coventry for feathering his nest with the spoils of war.

The Tribunal's reaction to the French case was mixed. The judges had already sat through over six weeks of hearings when the French began. It was already apparent that there was more than enough evidence to convict most of the defendants, and the American and British judges were anxious to "get on with it" and hear what the defense would have to say. Lawrence was unfailingly courteous, but did his best to shorten the French presentations. Biddle and Birkett, who probably had the quickest minds on the bench, were the most impatient. Birkett recognized the force of the French evidence, but thought it unnecessary, as his diary notes disclose:

28 January. The evidence is building up a most terrible and convincing case of complete horror and inhumanity in the concentration camps. But from the point of view of this trial it is a complete waste of valuable time. The case has been proved over and over again.

From a purely forensic standpoint, no doubt Birkett was right, but the Nuremberg trial was more than a forensic undertaking. The French and Soviet participants recognized this more clearly than their British and American colleagues. As Biddle had noted, the French and Russian judges supported each other in their determination to create a trial record that would do full justice to their evidence of Nazi crimes throughout the full reach of Festung Europa.

The French on the bench had no reason to be ashamed of their countrymen at the lectern. Birkett complained of what he called the "toneless" voice of a French lawyer, and it is true that the language's lack of fixed syllabic accent can cause the reading of a document to sound sleepy. But the French evidence was, despite the administrative difficulties, well organized and forceful, and the presentation was both dignified and skillful.

*3*

Roman Rudenko was a familiar figure in the Nuremberg courtroom; he had argued points of law, questioned witnesses, and sat and listened. Nevertheless, the audience for his opening statement on February 8, 1946, was even larger than that for the rarely seen de Menthon. Apart from general curiosity, his listeners had several particular questions in mind: What, if anything, would he say about the Nazi-Soviet Pact of 1939? About the Nazi-Soviet division of Poland? About the Soviet attack against Finland?

Dr. Gilbert thought that the courtroom, crowded for the first time in weeks, depressed Goering. "Yes, they want to see the show," he told Gilbert. "You will see—this trial will be a disgrace in 15 years."

Physically and stylistically, the dumpy and plain-spoken Soviet chief was a far cry from the graceful and sophisticated de Menthon. But he had force, as his blunt, declarative statements filled the courtroom. The familiar Communist vocabulary was now heard, as "Hitlerites" and "fascist aggressors" (Rudenko very rarely used the word "Nazi") were excoriated for attacking the "peace-loving" countries of Europe.

Retreading the course of war previously covered in detail by Alderman and Fyfe, Rudenko described the invasions of Czechoslovakia, Poland, Yugoslavia, and then (for some reason omitting Greece) the Soviet Union. Certain events contemporaneous with the destruction of the Polish state seemed to have been erased from Rudenko's memory. "On 1 September 1939 the fascist aggressors invaded Polish territory in treacherous violation of existing treaties," he declaimed, and read from a document, already introduced by Alderman, to show "how the gangster assault of Hitler's Germany on Poland was prepared in advance." Of course, the crucial "preparation in advance" was the Nazi-Soviet treaty, which guaranteed Hitler against Soviet opposition.

Gilbert recorded that Goering and Hess, in disgust, took off their headphones. During the lunch break, Goering was scornful: "I did not think that they [the Russians] would be so shameless as to mention Poland." Had Goering listened more closely to Alderman he might have noticed that the American, presumably in deference to Soviet sensitivities, had also made no mention of the Nazi-Soviet Pact, or the Soviet seizure of eastern Poland, or the 1940 attack against Finland.

The rest of Rudenko's address—somewhat shorter than those of his fellow chief prosecutors—followed much the same course as that of de Menthon. Rudenko did, however, discuss the Holocaust (but not by that name) near the end of his discourse: "The fascist conspirators planned the extermination to the last man of the Jewish population of the world and carried out the extermination throughout the whole of their conspiratorial activity from 1933 onwards." And then, addressing the Tribunal, he concluded:

> If your honors please, I here appear as the representative of the Union of the Soviet Socialist Republics, which bore the main brunt of the blows of the fascist invaders. . . .
>
> In sacred memory of millions of innocent victims of the fascist terror, for the sake of the consolidation of peace throughout the world, for the sake of the future security of nations, we are presenting the defendants with a just and complete account which must be settled. This is an account on behalf of all mankind, an account backed by the will and the conscience of all freedom-loving nations.
>
> May justice be done!

## 4

The levels of hierarchy within the Soviet delegation were confusing to the other nationalities, partly because Pokrovsky, though only a colonel, was the Deputy Chief Prosecutor and partly because the civilian members of the Soviet prosecution staff wore brown military-style uniforms with insignia of rank corresponding to those of army officers. N. D. Zorya, for example, wore his brown uniform with the shoulder insignia of a major general and was so addressed, even though his actual title was State Counselor of Justice Third Class, clearly inferior in rank to L. R. Shenin and M. Y. Raginsky, who were State Counselors of Justice Second Class, but were not addressed as "General." Then there was L. N. Smirnov, who on the nonalphabetical published list was named immediately below Zorya, but whose title was Chief Counselor of Justice, which certainly sounds grander than any of the others. Smirnov was treated by his colleagues with great respect and had perhaps the most important evidentiary assignment. Rudenko himself, though introduced as a lieutenant general, wore the brown uniform and was a civilian official.

In this maze of insignia and titles, the only sure thing was that Pokrovsky, despite his modest rank, spoke for the Soviet prosecution when Rudenko was absent. And it was Pokrovsky who, after Rudenko finished his opening statement, commenced the presentation of evidence. His topic was crimes against peace, and his material, much of which Alderman and Fyfe had already dealt with, was limited to the German aggressions against Czechoslovakia, Poland, and Yugoslavia. In the course of his presentation, it became clear that Pokrovsky's primary aim was to show that these attacks—especially in Yugoslavia—were preparations for an invasion of the Soviet Union which was premeditated and in no respect a response to Soviet threats.

On the morning of February 11, Colonel Pokrovsky turned over to General Zorya the task of dealing with the attack against the Soviet Union. Declaring that documents should not be the only source of information and that "the testimony of people who participated" was desirable, Zorya read answers given by General Walter Warlimont, a former subordinate of Jodl's known to be in the Nuremberg jail, to questions put to him by a Russian interrogator in November 1945. Under rules previously laid down by the Tribunal, this required that Warlimont be made available for cross-examination in court if the defense lawyers so desired.

A few minutes later, Zorya indicated that he was about to read from an interrogation of the much better known Field Marshal Friedrich Paulus, who was not in the Nuremberg jail but was generally assumed to be held as a prisoner of war in Russia. Dr. Nelte (Keitel's attorney) at once raised a question about the propriety of reading Paulus's statement, taken by the Russians in January 1946. When Lord Lawrence asked Zorya to respond, the general declared that he would read extracts from Paulus's deposition and that "no later than this evening . . . Friedrich Paulus will be brought to the courtroom" to testify.

Except for the Russians, everyone in the courtroom was thunderstruck, and Lawrence adjourned the session until the afternoon. When the Tribunal returned, Zorya did not read from Paulus's interrogation but called him as a witness for the prosecution, to be questioned by General Rudenko. Paulus then appeared and took the witness stand.

Born in 1890, Friedrich Paulus° was one of the "bright" German officers who excelled at planning and strategy. Like others of comparable talent, Paulus was repeatedly assigned as Chief of Staff to older officers who were given the command because they were better in the field (and known as *Feldherrn*) than in the planning room. After a series of such assignments, in the spring of 1940 Paulus was appointed deputy (First Quartermaster) to General Franz Halder, Chief of the Army General Staff. While holding this assignment, on September 3, 1940, Halder gave Paulus the task of preparing the operational plan for an attack against the Soviet Union by a German army of some 140 divisions, with the aim of destroying the Soviet forces in the western part of that country and reaching a line running from Archangel southward along the Volga to the Caspian Sea. Paulus prepared such a plan and performed numerous follow-up tasks while serving under General Halder, and it was to testify about these activities that he had been brought to Nuremberg. But those circumstances do not explain why Paulus's appearance as a witness created such a sensation.

At the end of 1941 Paulus was appointed Commander in Chief of the

---

°Thanks to a prevailing assumption that every German general is entitled to a "von," Paulus is often and incorrectly referred to as "von Paulus."

Sixth Army, then fighting in southern Russia. There ensued the famous battle for Stalingrad, in the course of which the Sixth Army was encircled. Hitler ordered Paulus to hold out to the last man and promoted him to Field Marshal. But eventually, and to the utter disgust of Hitler, who had expected Paulus to commit suicide, Paulus surrendered the remnants of his command to the Soviet forces.

In captivity, Paulus's subordinate General Walter von Seydlitz–Kurzbach formed a group called the "Free Germany Committee," which comprised emigrant German Communists as well as a large number of German prisoners of war in the Soviet Union. Paulus himself publicly denounced the Hitler regime. However, the Seydlitz group had served the Russians' purpose as soon as Germany was defeated, and most of its military members, including Paulus and Seydlitz, remained prisoners until well into the 1950s.

Considering the career, actions, and notoriety of their erstwhile comrade in arms, it is easy to understand the curiosity, tension, and hostility with which the military defendants anticipated Paulus's arrival. "I always stuck up for him with the Fuehrer," Keitel declared. "It is a shame for him to be testifying against us." The curiosity was widely shared; Dr. von der Lippe described the scene as the afternoon session began:

> The press reporters were all there; supposedly they had been told of Paulus' appearance beforehand. The defense lawyers were more or less taken by surprise. The news of Paulus' presence spread through the courthouse like wild-fire. Everyone rushed to the hearing-room so as not to miss the spectacle.

But when Paulus presented his testimony, in a measured and highly professional way, his evidence was not sensationally new. Alderman's documents and explanations had already established beyond dispute that the German invasion of the Soviet Union was premeditated, intended to bring all of western Russian under German dominion, and in no way a defensive response to Soviet initiatives. But Zorya was right; a witness can convey meaning beyond the bare reading of documents. And it was fascinating to hear, from the lips of one of the few men who sowed the dragon's teeth from which developed the biggest and bloodiest war between two nations in human history, how and where the seeds were sown and how they grew.

Paulus's testimony was not all factual exposition; there was a sting in the tail:

> RUDENKO: Who of the defendants was an active participant in the initiation of a war of aggression against the Soviet Union?
>
> PAULUS: Of the defendants . . . the Chief of the Supreme Command of the Armed Forces, Keitel; Chief of the Operations Branch, Jodl; and Goering,

in his capacity as Reich Marshal, as Commander-in-Chief of the Air Forces and as Plenipotentiary for Armament Economy.

RUDENKO: . . . Have I rightly concluded from your testimony, that long before 22 June [the date of the German attack] the Hitlerite Government and the Supreme Command of the Armed Forces were planning an aggressive war against the Soviet Union for the purpose of colonizing the territory of the Soviet Union?

PAULUS: That is beyond doubt according to all the developments as I described them and also in connection with all the directives issued. . . .

Rudenko had no more questions, nor did any of the other prosecutors. Dr. Hans Laternser, representing the indicted General Staff, requested and received permission for a postponement of cross-examination until the following morning. Shortly thereafter, the Tribunal recessed. Dr. Gilbert described the ensuing scene in the dock:

> During the afternoon intermission, the military section blew up in an uproar, and they argued with heated invective with their attorneys and each other. "Ask that dirty pig if he's a traitor! Ask him if he has taken out Russian citizenship papers!" Goering shot at his attorney.
>
> Raeder saw me watching and shouted at Goering, "Careful! The enemy is listening!"
>
> Goering kept right on shouting to his attorney, and there was real bedlam around the prisoners' dock. "We've got to disgrace that traitor," he roared. Keitel was still arguing with his attorney, and Raeder passed him a note with the same warning.
>
> At the other end of the dock, the attitude was more sympathetic to von [sic] Paulus. "You see," said Fritzsche, "that is the tragedy of the German people. He was caught between the devil and the deep blue sea."

The following morning Dr. Nelte began Paulus's cross-examination. In answer to Nelte's questions, Paulus explained that until after Stalingrad he had not realized the criminal nature of the attack because, like most of the officers' corps, he "saw nothing unusual in basing the fate of a people and a nation on power politics" and thought he was doing his "duty to the fatherland." Asked whether he would "grant to others . . . that they in good faith only wanted what was best for the fatherland," Paulus readily assented.

Exner and Laternser made some headway by pressing Paulus with questions about the strength and deployment of the Soviet forces in the period before the German invasion, suggesting the possibility that the Russians were themselves contemplating an attack. Paulus was not sure-footed in handling some of these questions, too often professing ignorance or lack of memory. At the morning intermission Goering, using Hess as a foil, played for a laugh. "He doesn't remember—Hess, do you know you've got a competitor? The witness doesn't remember. Haha. . . . Why, he was the expert on Russian troop strength."

Questioning by other defense counsel and by Biddle and Nikitchenko produced no significant changes in Paulus's testimony. Dr. von der Lippe thought that the cross-examination was moderately effective (*"halbwegs gut"*) and that the prosecution had gained nothing by calling Paulus. But the witness had put flesh on the documentary bones, and the drama of the occasion had emphasized the proof that millions of lives had been lost in consequence of a brutally deliberate attack on a government which, whatever its faults, had done nothing to provoke or justify it.°

The next day (February 13) Colonel Pokrovsky returned to the lectern to present the evidence of German war crimes against prisoners of war. For the most part, this concerned the treatment of Soviet prisoners, and the documents (Pokrovsky called no witnesses) told an appalling story. An affidavit by General Curt von Oesterreich, Chief of the Prisoners of War Section in Poland, stated that he was ordered to "construct open air camps surrounded only by barbed wire," and that there were no roofed barracks for the Russian prisoners. It was in these open internment areas that Soviet prisoners, by the millions, starved and froze to death. As Field Marshal von Reichenau explained to his staff, "Supplying the . . . prisoners of war with food is mistaken humanitarianism." Thousands of other prisoners were killed in Sachsenhausen, Maidanek, and other concentration camps. Captured German soldiers testified that Generals Walter Model and Walther Nehring, both armored division commanders, gave orders that no prisoners should be taken—presumably to expedite the advance of their troops. Especially hideous was the Germans' establishment of *Grosslazaretten* (large hospitals) where deliberate overcrowding, filth, infectious disease, and hunger killed the "patients" daily by the hundreds.

Pokrovsky continued his presentation by describing an occurrence in which Polish soldiers were the victims. This was the infamous Katyn massacre, which Rudenko had insisted on including in the Indictment as a war crime committed by the Germans, despite warnings by the other chief prosecutors.

---

°The Russians had ruffled American security agents by bringing Paulus to Nuremberg without their knowledge. A few minutes after Paulus left the stand, Zorya produced General Erich Buschenhagen, another Soviet prisoner and a member of the Free Germany group. Buschenhagen, formerly Chief of Staff to General Falkenhorst (Commander of the German forces in Norway), described the circumstances leading to Finland's collaboration with Nazi Germany in attacking the Soviet forces along the Finnish-Soviet border. Like Paulus, Buschenhagen described the attack as an "aggressive war against the Soviet Union." Buschenhagen's testimony mentioned, for the first (and as far as I know the only) time during the trials, Soviet Russia's aggressive war against Finland in 1939–1940.

In support of the charge that the Germans, not the Russians, were responsible for this atrocity, Pokrovsky submitted and read extracts from a report by a Soviet special commission established to "investigate the circumstances that attended the executions" of the Polish officers. The commission's conclusions included the following:

> According to the estimates of medico-legal experts, the total number of bodies amount to over 11,000. . . .
>
> In the autumn of 1941, in Katyn Forest, the German occupational authorities carried out mass shootings of the Polish prisoners of war. . . .
>
> The conclusions reached after studying the affidavits and medico-legal examinations . . . fully confirmed the material evidence and documents discovered in the Katyn graves.
>
> By shooting the Polish prisoners of war in Katyn Forest, the German fascist invaders consistently realized their policy for the physical extermination of the Slav peoples.

On February 14 Pokrovsky relinquished the lectern to Chief Counsellor Smirnov, who presented evidence "testifying to the very grievous crimes committed by the Hitlerian conspirators against the peaceful population in the territories of the U.S.S.R., Yugoslavia, Poland, and Czechoslovakia." It was a task which was to occupy the Tribunal for four days.

To a large extent, Smirnov's evidence was based on depositions by eyewitnesses of German atrocities, submitted to the Extraordinary State Commission of the Soviet Union.° Considering the nature and quantity of the documents previously submitted by the American and French lawyers, it seemed that nothing could be worse, but in fact these earlier presentations paled in comparison to Smirnov's offerings. The reason, it became clear, was that the Nazi leaders, by order, fear, and example, succeeded in convincing their followers that Slavs were indeed subhuman and, except for those who could be put to useful slavery, should be killed in such atrocious fashion as to incite a country-wide reign of utter terror. This required both indoctrination and training; as Smirnov put it:

> And indeed, in order to murder millions of innocent and defenseless people, it was necessary not only to develop the technical formula of "Cyclone A" [poison gas], to construct gas chambers and crematory ovens, nor only to elaborate a procedure for mass shootings. It was also essential to educate many thousands who would carry out these policies "not in the letter but in the spirit"—as stated by

---

°Under Article 21 of the London Charter, the commission's reports were admissible in evidence. According to Smirnov, there were 54,784 depositions on war crimes committed against Soviet civilians. Like Pokrovsky, Smirnov called no witnesses on this subject.

Himmler in one of his speeches. It was necessary to train persons deprived both of heart and conscience, perverted creatures who had deliberately cut themselves off from the basic concepts of morality and law.

In support of his thesis, Smirnov produced a document entitled "The Twelve Commandments for the Behavior of Germans in the East and for Their Treatment of the Russians," signed by Herbert Backe, State Secretary of the Ministry for Food and Agriculture, which admonished its readers: "You must realize that you are the representatives of Greater Germany and of the New Europe for centuries to come. You must, therefore, carry out with dignity even the hardest and most ruthless measures required by the necessities of the state. Weakness on the part of an individual will, on principle, be considered as just cause for his recall."

Smirnov then pictured the results of such instructions in a long succession of eyewitness descriptions, some by prisoners, others by German soldiers or civilians. For example, a prisoner engaged in burning corpses testified:

> Yanov Camp was surrounded by a barbed wire entanglement.
> . . . A man would be thrown in and left there for several days on end.
> He could not extricate himself from the wire and he eventually perished. . . . A man would be strung up by the neck, hands, and feet.
> Dogs would be set upon him and would tear him to pieces. Human beings were used as targets for shooting practice. This was mostly done by the following members of the Gestapo: Heime, Müller, Blum, Camp Commandant Wilhaus, and others whose names escape me.
> . . . Men would be taken by the legs and torn in two. Infants from 1 month to 3 years old were thrown into buckets of water and left to drown. . . . Women were strung up by the hair, after having been stripped naked, and left to hang until they died.

For four days the courtroom was an echo chamber of unthinkable torture and uncountable killings throughout the German-occupied areas in the Soviet Union and in Poland, Yugoslavia, and Czechoslovakia. While dealing with the last-named country, Smirnov told the story of the destruction of Lidice (a village not far from Prague), an atrocity then well known throughout Europe and America. It is a sad story, but in the context of German-occupied Russia it was not remarkable. As Smirnov pointed out:

> The fate of Lidice was repeated in many Soviet villages. Many peaceful citizens perished in even greater torment. They were buried alive or died, victims of still more brutal forms of execution.

Smirnov went on to give figures of the death toll in several cities: 632,253 during the blockade of Leningrad; over 100,000 at Vilna; 70,000 at Kaunas; some 200,000 at the Yanov camp; 1.5 million at Maidanek.

Were the statistics inflated? Were the atrocities invented or overstated? Total reliance on official reports based on untested depositions by unseen witnesses is certainly not the most reliable road to factual accuracy. Furthermore, some of the numerical totals, such as those for Maidanek and the German-occupied cities, are plainly estimates, in contrast to Leningrad, where circumstances made exact counts possible. Considering the number of deponents and the play of emotional factors, not only faulty observation but deliberate exaggeration must have warped many of the reports. But granting all that, were the flaws so numerous and so deep as to undermine the general accuracy of the picture presented?

Except perhaps for Goering, neither judges, nor defense counsel, nor other onlookers appear to have concluded that the Soviet evidence was basically untrustworthy. Judge Birkett, who continued to deprecate both the French and the Soviet presentations on the ground that their showings were superfluous, took a reasoned position on the credibility of Smirnov's evidence:

> *15 February.* The presentation of the case dealing with crimes against the civilian population of various countries overrun by the German armies has been most detailed, and is contained for the most part in official documents which purport to record judicial hearings of the evidence. The impression created on my mind is that there has been a good deal of exaggeration, but I have no means of checking this. But no doubt can remain in any dispassionate mind that great horrors and cruelties were perpetrated.
>
> I think, also, that there is a good deal of evidence to show that the Nazi hierarchy used calculated cruelty and terror as their usual weapons. But it is impossible to convict an army generally, and no doubt many of the terrible excesses were those of a brutal and licentious soldiery, to quote Gibbon.
>
> The only importance of the evidence is to convict the members of the Cabinet and the military leaders of calculated cruelty as a policy.

I do not agree with the last two sentences. I do not believe that German soldiers are more "brutal and licentious" than those of other countries; indeed, their traditional obedience (*Befehl ist Befehl*) is such that *if ordered to behave* they are more likely than others to obey. But when it came to orders to commit atrocious war crimes, *Befehl ist Befehl* led to ready acquiescence. What Birkett disparages as the "only importance" appears to me as very important indeed. Furthermore, the capacity of Nazi indoctrination to turn ordinary humans into monsters is, to me, the most terrible feature of the Hitler years.

Troubled by the torrent of horror stories, Dr. von der Lippe could "only hope that at least some of the prosecution's claims are exaggerated." But even Goering acknowledged to Dr. Gilbert that "it is sufficient if only 5 per cent of it is true."

On February 19, Smirnov turned to the mass executions in the death camps found by the Soviet forces as they occupied Poland—Auschwitz, Maidanek, Chelmno, Treblinka, Sobibor, and Belsec. The credibility of the evidence was reinforced by captured German photographs. These were the photographs Rudenko had previously shown me. Since the source was German, and the pictures often portrayed identifiable locations or individuals—e.g., SS generals Arthur Gebauer and Karl Strock—their authenticity was solid. The scenes were in line with the content of the documentary evidence. There were also Soviet motion pictures of the captured camps and the sites of other Nazi atrocities.

Smirnov concluded this portion of the Soviet case by showing a documentary film entitled *The Atrocities by the German Fascist Invaders in the U.S.S.R.* I was in the United States at the time and did not see the film until some years later. Dr. Gilbert, who by this time was inured to atrocity revelations, described it as "even more terrible than the one presented by the Americans," as it showed "the acres of corpses of Russian PW's murdered or left to starve in the fields where they had been captured; the torture instruments, mutilated bodies, guillotines and baskets of heads; . . . the crematoria and gas chambers; the piles of clothes, the bales of women's hair at Auschwitz and Maidanek."

Goering alone brushed off the film as "no proof" because it could "easily" have been faked. Frank, despite his own bloody record in Poland, sought to lay the blame on Hitler and Himmler; Schacht called it "a disgrace not only for Germany but for all mankind that such atrocities could have taken place." Fritzsche broke down in tears and was unable to discuss his reaction until two days later, when Gilbert found him "pale and miserable." The Russian film had been the last straw. Among the other defendants there was much shifting of the blame, but little disposition to join in Goering's attack on the credibility of the film.

On February 20 Smirnov gave way to colleagues Shenin and Raginsky, who described Nazi plunder and destruction of property and art, including cultural and historic sites such as the palaces in and near Leningrad; the ancient churches of Novgorod, Pskov, and Kazan; and the homes of Tolstoy, Chekhov, Pushkin, and Rimsky-Korsakov.

Moving as these accounts were, they were almost a relief after the atrocity film. Soon the defendants' gloom was further alleviated by Winston Churchill's famous speech on March 5 at Fulton, Missouri, in which he declared that the Soviet government had lowered an "iron curtain" between Western and Eastern Europe. The next day Dr. von der Lippe recorded that the speech was "in everyone's mouth," and he copied into his diary a long extract from the report in *The Stars and Stripes,* which headlined Churchill's plea that the Western nations "unite to stop Russians." Goering was elated. "Naturally, I told you so," he crowed, as he went to lunch the next day. A rift between East and West fed the defendants' *Schadenfreude* and might even redound to their advantage.

On February 25 Smirnov presented the evidence in support of the third charge in the Indictment, entitled "Crimes against Humanity." As he acknowledged, there was little to distinguish crimes so charged from those already dealt with as war crimes against military and civilian victims. But most of the crimes now dealt with were pictured as directed against particular national or religious groups. However, these were very broad common denominators. Smirnov began by entitling the first part of his presentation "extermination of Slav people," which of course included Poles, Czechs, and Yugoslavs as well as Russian Slavs.

Of more significance was the fact that despite the Soviet government's reluctance to recognize Jewry as a primary and unique victim of Nazism, in the afternoon of February 26, Smirnov started presenting evidence on Nazi "persecution of the Jews," which continued through most of February 27. The English translation of the record is (I hope not deliberately) offensive, as Smirnov began by describing the "excessive anti-Semitism of the Hitlerite criminals" as presenting "a perfectly zoological aspect." Fortunately, nothing else was similarly disturbing.

Smirnov relied largely on American captured documents concerning the Einsatzgruppen and on reports of the Soviet and Polish governments describing the death camps. He then called four Jewish witnesses who described, from personal experience, the activities of the German Einsatz unit in Vilna, where the Jewish population was reduced from approximately 80,000 to 600 persons; the procedures at the Treblinka camp, where, with the use of thirteen gas chambers, several thousand Jews were killed each day within a few minutes of their arrival; and the treatment of Jewish children at the Birkenau section of the Auschwitz camp.

The woman who had been at Auschwitz, Severina Schmaglenskaya, gave unbearable testimony: Newborn children of Jewish mothers were killed immediately, and infants selected for extermination on their arrival were often thrown into the crematory ovens without prior asphyxiation in the gas chambers. "In the name of all the women of Europe who became mothers in concentration camps," she demanded, "I would like to ask German mothers, 'Where are our children now?' "

Dr. Gilbert saw defendants and their lawyers lowering their heads or biting their lips. At the end of the session, he overheard Kranzbuehler ask his client Doenitz: "Didn't anybody know anything about any of these things?" Doenitz "shook his head and shrugged sadly," but Jodl declared that "Of course somebody knew about it."

Jodl, of course, was right. If nobody had known about "these things," they would not have happened.

## Chapter 13

# THE DEFENDANTS:
# GOERING AND HESS

The French and Soviet prosecutors had finished, and the Tribunal had heard prosecution and defense lawyers discuss problems raised by the charges against the Nazi organizations. During the morning session on March 4, 1946, Sir David Maxwell-Fyfe informed the Tribunal that the case for the prosecution was concluded. Thereupon the case for the defense was formally begun.

In fact, however, plans and preparations for the defense had been under way even before the trial began. Since early November, the Tribunal's General Secretariat had been finding and procuring the documents and potential witnesses the defense lawyers wanted. In mid-January, as the British and American cases neared their close, the chief prosecutors' interest in the defendants' case quickened. At their meeting on January 16, Jackson brought up the matter:

> Mr. Justice Jackson referred to the case for the defense. It was important to curtail this as much as possible and he was thinking whether they [the prosecution] could take advantage of Article 20° and possibly make a motion to the Tribunal for a ruling that defense counsel should offer a statement of what they intended to prove, (a) by each witness, and (b) generally. . . . A ruling such as he proposed would enable them:
>> (i) To admit many of the facts the defense wish to prove.
>> (ii) In other cases to obtain a ruling that the facts were irrelevant.
>> (iii) To prepare to meet the defense.

°Article 20 of the Charter provided that "The Tribunal may require to be informed of the nature of any evidence before it is offered so that it may rule upon the relevance thereof."

If his colleagues agreed, he would prepare a motion.

De Menthon and Pokrovsky were doubtful about the possibility of limiting the defense submissions. No action was taken at the time, but at a prosecutors' meeting on February 5, a draft Jackson had prepared was accepted and it was agreed that it should be presented to the Tribunal shortly after Rudenko's opening speech.

But the defendants had stolen a march on the prosecution. On February 4 they had submitted to the Tribunal a "Proposal for the taking of defense evidence," prepared by Kranzbuehler but filed under Stahmer's name, with very reasonable provisions. Each defendant was to name the witnesses he planned to call; two weeks before a defense counsel's case was scheduled to begin, he must file his document books with the General Secretariat; the Tribunal was to facilitate consultation between defense counsel and witnesses. The defendants also requested a three-week recess between the close of the prosecution's case and the opening of the defense case.

The prosecution proposals, filed a week later, were characterized by von der Lippe as intended to restrict the scope of the defense case. The defense would be required to specify in advance whether it would concede or contest various general propositions, such as the aggressive character of the war and the Germans' abuse and killing of prisoners of war and civilians in German-occupied territory. The result was a conclave of defense counsel under the leadership of Kranzbuehler, who, according to von der Lippe, was able, *suaviter in modo, fortiter in re* (gently in manner, strongly in deed), to reconcile the many conflicting views.

After a long discussion on February 16 between prosecution and defense, the Tribunal was negatively inclined toward the prosecution's proposals and leaning toward approval of the defense motion. The Tribunal ordered that documentary and witness applications in behalf of the first four defendants (Goering, Hess, Ribbentrop, and Keitel) should be heard the following Saturday, February 23.

The defense's plea for a recess was heard on February 18. It was opposed by Fyfe, and denied by the Tribunal the following morning. The total rejection of any recess came as a shock to the defense counsel; at a conclave that evening their spirits were "at zero." Dr. Nelte (for Keitel) proposed a "united front" of the military defendants under his client's leadership, but none of the other military defendants would join him, for the very sensible reason that such a front might go far to convince the Tribunal that the General Staff was indeed an "organization."

The Tribunal continued on February 20 to consider the rival procedural proposals and related matters. At first, it dealt only with testimony by the defendants themselves and provided, in accordance with Anglo-American legal practice, that the defendants might testify under oath but could not be compelled to do so. Biddle recorded in his notes:

Terrific fight over whether a defendant can be called as a witness, i.e., under oath—the idea shocks the Russians. The opposite shocks Parker, who says he would resign if such a construction were given [to the] Charter. I reprove him and he withdraws remarks, and we vote N[ikitchenko] down.

On February 21 the Tribunal approved the defendants' proposals, adding various details of no great importance, and denied the prosecution's motion in its entirety. The decisions were publicly announced in court on Saturday, February 23. The defense counsel had ample grounds for self-congratulation. But it was short-lived, for when Lawrence announced that the court would now proceed to deal with Goering's applications for witnesses and documents, he went on to describe the appropriate procedure for defense counsel to follow:

> . . . the procedure which the Tribunal proposes to adopt is to ask counsel for the defendant whose case is being dealt with to deal, in the first instance, with his first witness, and then to ask Counsel for the Prosecution to reply upon that witness. . .; that is to say, to hear the defendant's counsel and the Prosecution Counsel upon each witness in turn.

Of course, no such strings had been attached to the prosecution's decision to call witnesses—no one had ever suggested that the defendants should have an opportunity, in advance of the appearance of a prosecution witness, to object on grounds of irrelevance or for any other reason. And when Lawrence called on Stahmer to proceed with naming Goering's proposed witnesses, Dr. Martin Horn (for Ribbentrop) was immediately at the lectern to protest: "I ask to be informed why the Court has the intention of treating the Defense in a fundamentally different manner from the Prosecution."

The protest was in vain. Lawrence justified the prescribed procedure on the ground that the defendants' witnesses and documents had to be procured for them by the Secretariat. That was well enough for justifying advance notice of the defendants' needs, but did not meet their objection to the Tribunal's authorizing the prosecution to intervene in the process by making objections before the witnesses were questioned. In all probability the Tribunal was desirous of holding down the number of defense witnesses in the interests of time and concluded (no doubt correctly) that the prosecution, with the benefit of advance information, would be better able than the Tribunal to point out the likelihood of irrelevant or cumulative requests.

*2*

The presentation of the defendants' evidence began the following morning. Their cases were to be heard in the order of their listing in the Indictment. Dr. Stahmer's beginning in no way resembled the opening statements of the chief prosecutors because the defense counsel were entitled to only one speech in behalf of each of their clients, to be delivered after their evidence had been submitted. Dr. Stahmer first made a few comments on the Treaty of Versailles and then called his first witness: General of the Air Force Karl Bodenschatz, who had been Goering's fellow member of the Richthofen Squadron in World War I and, during World War II, liaison officer between Goering as Commander in Chief of the Luftwaffe and Hitler's military headquarters. His choice as starter did not speak well for Stahmer's savvy, as Bodenschatz owed his status more to personal loyalty than to acuity. Furthermore, he had been with Hitler on July 20, 1944, when Klaus von Stauffenberg's bomb exploded in an assassination attempt, and he was still recuperating from serious wounds that had impaired his hearing and shattered his nerves.

Bodenschatz testified to Goering's help in resolving the Munich crisis of 1938 peacefully and his opposition to war with Britain in 1939 and with the Soviet Union in 1941. He described a few instances in which Goering had pulled old friends out of the Gestapo's clutches and, most inadvisedly, declared that Goering had sharply criticized the activities of Himmler's goons during the infamous Kristallnacht.

The general was in no shape to confront a tough cross-examiner, and cross-examination was to be the order of the day during the defense case. None of the prosecutors had occasion to cross-examine during their own cases; they had not called many witnesses, and Kranzbuehler was the only German lawyer who had shown much talent for the ungentle art. Now, painfully aware that the documentary tide had set heavily against them, the defendants were resting their main hope in their own and their witnesses' testimony. The trial had taken a turn in which much might depend on forensic skills.

However, the prosecution's abilities in this regard were largely confined to the British and American teams; the French and Russians were as inexperienced as their opponents. Consequently, when the chief prosecutors met early in March to distribute among them the task of dealing with the testimony of the twenty-one defendants and their witnesses, the Russians and French were given major responsibility for only two defendants each—respectively Keitel and Frank, and Sauckel and Seyss-Inquart. The rest were divided as evenly as prime seventeen permits: the Americans took Goering, Kaltenbrunner, Rosenberg, Frick, Funk, Schacht, Schirach, Speer, and Fritzsche; the British took Hess, Ribbentrop, Streicher, Doenitz, Raeder, Jodl, Papen, and Neurath. The prosecutors also decided that there should be a "back-up" counsel from another delegation for each of the principals. Ordinarily not more than two prosecutors would cross-examine a defendant or other witness, but there was no absolute barrier to other cross-examiners if circumstances so required.

Accordingly, it was Justice Jackson who rose to cross-examine Boden-schatz. The General was slow-witted and made heavy weather of it, especially at the end, when Jackson pointed out that Goering, although annoyed from an economic standpoint about the Kristallnacht's destruction of property, had joined in the decision to impose a fine of a billion Reichsmarks on the German Jews to recompense the state for the destruction the state itself had caused.

Overall it was a brief and run-of-the-mill cross-examination, but the defendants were mightily impressed: Steinbower (for Seyss-Inquart): "Your American attorneys have a good deal of experience in cross-examination, and it is obvious that Mr. Jackson is one of the best." Jodl: "Your man Jackson is a clever prosecutor." Schacht: "Your Prosecutor Jackson is certainly a brilliant cross-examiner." But Dr. Gilbert, who recorded this praise, added that these same defendants were not Goering-lovers, and were delighted to see his first witness come off badly.

Goering's next witness was less to be pitied. Before the war, Erhard Milch had made his mark in German civil aviation, and in 1933, at Goering's request, he accepted a commission and became the second-ranking officer in the air force. He had the rank of *Generalfeldmarschall* and the status of Inspector General of the Luftwaffe and State Secretary of the Reich Air Ministry. He was not a combat commander; his talents were administrative and organizational. During most of the war Milch was a member of the Central Planning Board, an interdepartmental agency that, as Milch described it, handled "the distribution of raw materials" among "the Army, the Navy, the Air Force" and civilian branches "such as industry, mining, industrial and private building, *et cetera.*" Like Goering, he straddled the military and civilian organs of war, and if he lacked Goering's public and political stature, he was far more capable of sustained concentration and hard work.

What did he have to say in defense of his former chief? Not much. Stahmer brought out only Milch's opinion that the Luftwaffe had been designed primarily for defense, that Goering was "against war" and opposed the attack against Soviet Russia, and that he knew nothing of the murderous medical experiments on inmates of the Dachau concentration camp. Stahmer's examination took barely fifteen minutes; its value was negligible and the risk enormous, as events were soon to prove.

Milch's versatility as a Nazi leader precipitated a flood of questions from other defense counsel. Dr. Laternser (for the General Staff) probed the Wehrmacht's state of readiness for war in 1939; Dr. Flächsner (for Speer) and Dr. Servatius (for Sauckel) asked many questions about the Central Planning Board (which Stahmer had not even mentioned) on which their clients had worked closely with Milch; Dr. Jahrreiss (for Jodl) and Dr. Siemers (for Raeder) asked military questions, and Dr. Kauffmann (Kaltenbrunner) inquired about Milch's visit to Dachau in 1935. Many of the questions from these lawyers had little to do with Goering.

The result was that when Jackson cross-examined Milch he had a wide range of subjects to deal with and was on his feet for some four hours. Milch was intelligent and very well informed, but these faculties did him little good because he was so deeply involved in the same crimes of which Sauckel and Speer stood accused. He had no escape from Jackson's relentless use of documents already put in evidence during the American case. Milch floundered from forgetting to lying and ended with a flat denial that he had ever had prisoners of war shot, in the face of his own report to the Central Planning Board that he had ordered the hanging of Russian officers who had tried to escape: "I wanted them to be hanged in the factory for the others to see." Milch left the witness chair utterly discredited.

It had taken two full days to deal with two witnesses. Milch had been questioned by six defense counsel in addition to Stahmer and briefly cross-examined by Roberts and Rudenko after Jackson had finished. The Tribunal was aghast at the slow pace, and the following morning (March 12), before the regular session, the judges met privately with the chief prosecutors and representative defense counsel to discuss a proposed rule that only one prosecution counsel might cross-examine a defendant or defense witness and that "when witnesses for an individual defendant are called, the other defense counsel must not do more than elicit from the witness specific matters they require for their case. . . ." There was strong opposition from the prosecution, and the Tribunal "decided to consider the matter further." No such rule was ever adopted, and drawn-out examinations and cross-examinations continued.

In fact, the next two witnesses testified very briefly, but Jackson's cross-examination was in each case thrice as long. Colonel Bernd von Brauchitsch (son of the Field Marshal and Commander in Chief of the army from 1938 to 1941) had served throughout the war as Goering's chief adjutant. His direct testimony established only that Goering instructed his staff to disregard Hitler's 1944 order that enemy airmen who landed by parachutes or crash-landed in Germany should be regarded as "terror-fliers" and lynched. Jackson made no real effort to confute that testimony, but asked questions about the attack against Russia, Goering's relations with Hitler and the SS, and Field Marshal von Brauchitsch's activities in retirement. The answers were of no account.

Personally, the young colonel had made a soldierly impression, but Paul Koerner, as von der Lippe put it, was "less appealing." Koerner had been an acolyte of Goering's since the late 1920s and had risen high in the Nazi government. Interrogated a few months earlier by Dr. Kempner, Koerner had declared that he "regarded Goering as the last big man of the Renaissance," that he had given Koerner "the biggest job of his life," and that it would be "unfaithful and disloyal to give any testimony against him." When Jackson read this to the Tribunal, everyone wondered why on earth Stahmer had put Koerner in the witness box. Furthermore, Koerner, like Milch, had been a member of the Central Planning Board and was as answerable as Sauckel, Milch, and Speer for the criminal forced labor program. Under cross-examination, Koerner fell back on the usual "admit nothing, and remember as little as possible" response.

Goering's last witness, before he took the stand himself, was a major military figure of World War II. Field Marshal Albert Kesselring was an army artillery officer who, without prior air experience, shifted his commission in 1933 to the new German Air Force, which badly needed able officers. Kesselring learned to fly and studied his new trade assiduously. By 1940 he was commander of the air fleet which, on the German side, bore the brunt of the fighting during the Battle of Britain. Later in the war he was given command of all Wehrmacht forces in Italy and North Africa, with the title Commander in Chief South. During the final weeks of the war he replaced Field Marshal Gerd von Rundstedt as Commander in Chief on the Western Front.

Although Kesselring's testimony took approximately a full day, Stahmer's questions lasted no more than fifteen minutes. Apart from procuring a repetition of earlier statements that the Luftwaffe was designed for defensive purposes, the questions were exclusively directed toward the aerial bombings of Warsaw in September 1939, Rotterdam in May 1940, and Coventry in November 1940. All those cities had been attacked by planes under Kesselring's command, and he strongly contended that all three had been directed at important military targets.

Stahmer's decision to focus on these events was wide of his mark. The Indictment contained no charge of unlawful aerial bombardment against either Goering or the defendants generally.* The prosecution had made no effort to build a war crimes case based on attack from the air.

As Kesselring correctly remarked in his testimony, "The Hague Conventions on land warfare did not provide for the requirements of air warfare." Furthermore, the great city air raids of the war—Hamburg, Berlin,

---

*The first paragraph of Count One of the Indictment charged that the conspiracy included a criminal plan to engage in "the indiscriminate destruction of cities, towns, and villages, and devastation not justified by military necessity." However, the specifications of this general charge in Count Three (g) made no reference to aerial bombardment. Neither did the paragraph in Indictment Appendix A describing Goering's crimes.

Dresden, Tokyo, Hiroshima, and Nagasaki—had been conducted by Britain and the United States, which made it most unlikely that the prosecution would make a big thing out of the Germans' earlier raids which, destructive as they were, paled by comparison. It is not surprising that Goering's responsibility for the German attacks, which Stahmer took such pains to justify, played no part in the Tribunal's judgment. Indeed, it might fairly be said that if Goering's role in the Third Reich had been restricted to his command of the Luftwaffe, he would have had much less to fear at Nuremberg.

The bombing in Rotterdam, however, raised an issue not pertinent to Warsaw or Coventry, which Fyfe pressed very sharply when he cross-examined Kesselring. On the morning of May 14, 1940, the fifth and last day of Dutch resistance to the German invasion, Dutch troops still held a line on the south side of Rotterdam and the north bank of the Lek River. On the opposite bank of the Lek were German air-landed troops commanded by General Kurt Student (an air force officer) and army troops of the 39th Panzer Corps commanded by General Rudolf Schmidt.

A bridge over the river was still standing, and during the morning General Schmidt sent the Dutch commander a demand for surrender, under the threat of an air attack on the Dutch Army positions in Rotterdam. During the ensuing negotiations, Student sent a radio message to the commander of the Luftwaffe bombing group designated to carry out the attack, stating "bomber attack suspended owing to surrender negotiations." Red flares were displayed over the Dutch positions to deflect any bombers approaching the target area. Despite Student's radio message, two bomber units were dispatched, one of which failed to see the flares. Its bombs devastated a large area in Rotterdam and caused over 800 deaths.

In an active state of war, the Dutch Army positions were certainly a legitimate target, even though their location in the city indicated that an aerial attack would probably cause heavy civilian casualties. But if the attack was ordered by the Luftwaffe command with full knowledge that surrender negotiations were progressing, customary international law, despite its lack of precision, would condemn such conduct as militarily unnecessary and dishonorable.

This was the charge that Fyfe sought to fasten on Kesselring and, through him, on Goering. There was ample documentary evidence that the High Command was eager to put an immediate end to Dutch resistance so that the German combat troops in Holland could be shifted south to reinforce the German troops fighting in Belgium and northern France. Fyfe tried to drive home the charge that the bomber attack had little to do with the Dutch resistance confronting Student and Schmidt and was intended to terrorize the Dutch and force a total capitulation. And, in fact, General H. G. Winkelmann, Commander in Chief of the Dutch Army, signed a proclamation of military capitulation late that afternoon.

However, there was insufficient proof that either Kesselring or Goering was personally aware of the surrender negotiations, and Kesselring vehemently denied that any such information reached him. The issue has been much discussed in later literature without conclusive solution, and the Tribunal made no mention of it.

The contention that the German Air Force "was purely a weapon of defense" (voiced by Milch as well as Kesselring) was intended to counter Counts One and Two of the Indictment on the theory that Goering and his staff could not have been planning to wage aggressive war if the air arm was intended only for defensive use. Milch based his argument on "the fact that principally fighters and antiaircraft artillery were provided." Kesselring stressed the light weight and short range of the German bombers and the lack of heavy four-engine bombers.

On cross-examination, Jackson challenged Kesselring's thesis with considerable effect by asking about the ratio of bombers to fighters in the Luftwaffe when the war began. Kesselring's reply revealed that there were at least as many bombers as fighters if not more, which greatly weakened the Germans' position. Kesselring, aware much more than Milch of the pitfalls in the "purely defensive" characterization of the Luftwaffe, promptly qualified his statement by declaring that "no matter whether defensive or offensive war is concerned, the task of the air force must be carried out on the offensive," prompting Jackson to ask: "In other words, the Luftwaffe was a defensive weapon if you were on the defensive, and an offensive weapon if you were on the attack?" That was pretty close to the truth, and Kesselring replied: "One could put it like that." Realizing that this concession had left little of his initial "purely defensive" claim, he added that "the essential of an offensive air force is the long-distance four-engine heavy bombers, and Germany had none of these."

Jackson dropped the issue, but in fact Kesselring's fallback position was insupportable. Heavy bombers can lift bigger bombloads and carry them farther than medium bombers, but a lack of them does not prove that an air force is "purely defensive" or that the heavy bomber is intrinsically "offensive." The idea that the types of airplanes automatically determine the offensive or defensive character of an air force is spurious. Before the war began, Britain's bomber force was built in large part to *deter* Germany from bombing Britain and to diminish the Luftwaffe's impact if deterrence failed. This was the then famous Trenchard-Weir theory of British air power. As the historians of the Royal Air Force during World War II wrote: "Positive aims, such as forcing the enemy to give ground . . . are strategically offensive. Negative aims, such as resisting his attacking forces or destroying their means of attack, are strategically defensive."

Medium and heavy alike, the bombers' purpose was, at the outset, defensive. Furthermore, an attack against an enemy's factories and airfields may be defensive, in that it may render the enemy less able to retaliate, and offensive, in that the enemy is rendered less able to resist offensive invasion.

But the facts of the Luftwaffe's history are even more compelling. When the Nazis came to power in 1933, with Germany still bound by the Versailles Treaty to limit its army to 100,000 men and to eschew airplanes and submarines entirely, no doubt the Nazis were eager to increase the nation's defensive armor. But it is clear beyond dispute that from the beginning, and openly after 1935, the Reich was aiming for military might that would bring about a great expansion of German sovereignty and domination, by aggressive war if necessary.

The Wehrmacht was intended for offensive warfare, and the Luftwaffe was part of that purpose. Its major role, for which it was well designed, was to cooperate with the army in winning on the ground and overrunning Poland, Belgium, France, or whatever other country was on the list of victims. Fighter planes to protect the ground troops from enemy aerial attack; dive bombers to terrorize and disperse enemy formations near the front; light and medium bombers to destroy enemy airfields, ammunition dumps, railway yards, troop columns on the move, and targets of opportunity of all sorts—these were some of the tasks of the Luftwaffe as it joined the army tanks and mobile forces that waged the Blitzkrieg and turned Poland, Norway, Denmark, the Netherlands, Belgium, France, Yugoslavia, and Greece into Nazi dominions in less than two years. To argue that the Luftwaffe was not designed, intended, and used offensively was ludicrous.°

Kesselring's testimony was in part more plausible and better governed than that of the other witnesses who preceded Goering to the witness box. But even he succumbed to the noxious mendacity of so many German witnesses in denying knowledge of what they must have known. Consider the following interchange:

> JACKSON: Do you want this Tribunal to understand that you never knew that there was a campaign by this state to persecute the Jews in Germany? Is that the way you want your testimony to be understood?
>
> KESSELRING: A persecution of the Jews as such was not known to me.
>
> JACKSON: Is it not a fact that Jewish officers were excluded from your army and from your command?
>
> KESSELRING: Jewish officers did not exist.

As von der Lippe noted, Stahmer was having no easy time. Certainly his witnesses had said little to help Goering, and perhaps there was little

---

°Neither the Luftwaffe nor the German Navy was well designed or equipped for a war which ultimately embraced Britain, the United States, and the Soviet Union as adversaries, as Kesselring rightly pointed out. But those circumstances in no way warrant describing the Luftwaffe as "purely a weapon of defense."

that witnesses could do, given Goering's status and his multiple activities as revealed in so many documents. It remained to be seen whether he could do any better speaking for himself.

3

Early in the afternoon session of March 13, Goering left the dock and entered the witness box. He was no longer *der Dicke* ("the fat one"), and his baggy trousers betrayed the recent thinning of their contents. Prison fare had honed not only his frame, but his mind and memory as well.

That evening he would complain that "I could not keep my hands from shaking," and he certainly had every right to be tense. He was convinced that the trial would be his life's last chapter and that what he would say, and how he would say it, would deeply mark his historical image. Goering had prepared carefully, and Dr. Stahmer had consulted at length with other counsel, including Siemers and von der Lippe.

The pattern of the testimony was that Stahmer asked a long series of short, specific questions to which Goering replied at whatever length the question appeared to him to require. For example, after Goering had described the Nazi Party's attainment of governmental power on January 30, 1933, Stahmer asked: "What measures were now taken to strengthen this power after Hitler's appointment?" Goering's reply lasted some twenty minutes and concluded with his proud avowal that he had done all he could to cement a Hitlerian dictatorship:

> In conclusion I wish to say: (1) It is correct that I . . . have done everything which was at all within my personal power to strengthen the National Socialist movement, to increase it, and have worked increasingly to bring it to power under all circumstances and as the one and only authority. (2) I have done everything to secure for the Führer the place as Reich Chancellor which rightfully belonged to him. (3) When I look back, I believe I have not failed to do anything to consolidate our power to such an extent that it would not have to yield to the chances of the political game or to violent actions, but would rather, in the further course of reconstruction, become the only factor of power, which would lead the Reich and lead it—as we hoped—to a great development.

In this manner Goering's interrogation by Stahmer continued for two and a half court days. It was a remarkable performance, and partly for that reason there were no interruptions by the Tribunal or complaints that too much time was being taken. Goering was lucid and impressive, and his description and explanation of how and why things happened during the rise of Nazism and the life of the Third Reich was interesting and at times fascinating.

Goering received general praise for his poise, skill, and candor, even among those for whom he was no favorite. "That is the Goering of the old days," said Papen, "when he was still reasonable." Doenitz was "surprised that Goering had shown such sober self-control" and observed that "Biddle is really paying attention. You can see that he really wants to hear the other side of the story." Even Schacht and Speer had words of praise mixed with criticism. And so, though from a quite different angle, did Judge Birkett:

> 18 March. Goering reveals himself as a very able man who perceives the intent of every question almost as soon as it is uttered. He has considerable knowledge, and has an advantage over the Prosecution in this respect, for he is always on familiar ground.

But the judge was alarmed by the possible consequences of allowing Goering to speak at such great length:

> If this procedure is followed in the case of all the defendants . . . then the time taken will be so great that the trial will be written down as a failure. It will have done more to restore German belief in their leaders, and the verdicts against the leaders will be regarded by the German people as excessively unjust.

Birkett's fears proved groundless. Goering might impress his auditors by speaking "fluently, calmly, confidently, and with a pleasant attitude" (von der Lippe's wording), but what sort of defense was he presenting? Frank avowal may be virtuous, but it does not wash away criminal guilt, especially when there is little sign of repentance.

Essentially, Goering contended that it was justifiable for Germany to rearm and accumulate sufficient military power to seize the territories it lost under the Versailles Treaty and other lands needed for the growth and greatness of the Reich. For these purposes, the ends justified the means. Accordingly, Goering acknowledged, inter alia, that he had set up concentration camps in which political opponents of Nazism were incarcerated; that in the 1934 Roehm purge he had participated in the execution without trial of persons whom Hitler distrusted; that he had authorized the huge financial penalty and the civic disabilities imposed on the Jews after the 1938 Kristallnacht; that he had joined in carrying out the decision that Austria, the Sudetenland, Danzig, and the Polish Corridor must be reunified with the Reich, by force if necessary; that in 1939 he had threatened to bomb Prague in order to force the capitulation and annexation of Bohemia and Moravia; that he had joined in authorizing the annexation of large portions of Poland in addition to the corridor and in the appointment of Himmler to control these territories; and that he had officially justified the invasion and occupation of the other countries overrun by Germany on the ground of military necessity.

Not all of these actions were war crimes. But Goering's own story of the 1933–1940 years certainly painted a vivid picture of a fulfilled governmental conspiracy to prepare for and wage aggressive wars. Goering subsequently urged Hitler "not to start a war against Russia at that moment," but made it quite clear that he was not moved "by considerations of international law or similar reasons," but "by political and military reasons only."

On the record of Goering's testimony, the conclusion is inescapable that he voluntarily furnished evidence more than sufficient for his conviction under Counts One and Two of the Indictment. It is puzzling, therefore, that his last witness (who testified four days later, interrupting Jackson's cross-examination) was called to picture Goering as an opponent of these wars. The witness was Birger Dahlerus, a Swedish civil engineer and businessman who was well connected and linguistically at home in both Britain and Germany, and who had known Goering since 1934. In his capacity as Minister of the Interior in Prussia, Goering had cleared administrative obstacles to Dahlerus's marriage to a German woman. The next year, Dahlerus reciprocated by giving Goering's stepson a job in Sweden. Thereafter Dahlerus saw Goering "once or twice a year."

Early in July 1939, during a visit to England, Dahlerus became convinced that Britain would go to war if, as seemed increasingly probable, Germany were to attack Poland. He and a group of British business friends, distressed by the prospect of a major European war, decided that a meeting between their group and Goering might lead to proposals for resolving the crisis peaceably. Apart from Dahlerus's prior acquaintance with Goering, this channel was selected because Goering's peacekeeping actions at the time of the 1938 Munich crisis encouraged the hope that he might now play a comparable role.

Dahlerus went to Berlin and was given audience by Goering on July 6, 1939. Goering discounted Britain's attitude on the Polish question as a "bluff," but after consulting Hitler he approved the idea of his meeting with Dahlerus's group. Such meeting (in which Goering was accompanied only by a few subordinates) was in fact held on August 7 at Dahlerus's wife's home in Schleswig-Holstein. The discussion was friendly but unyielding on both sides, and the participants agreed only "that it would be of the greatest value if a meeting could be arranged as soon as possible by representatives of England and Germany." Once again Hitler approved the proposal, but a few days later the Nazi-Soviet Pact was signed, and the planned meeting was forgotten as events rushed inexorably to war a week later.

During these seven weeks leading to war, Dahlerus was constantly shuttling back and forth between London and Berlin. In retrospect the scene is bizarre. Dahlerus was an able businessman and full of good intentions, but he represented only himself and was unknown to the public. Yet he was received and consulted, or used as a messenger, by, among others, Neville Chamberlain, Lord Halifax, and Sir Alexander Cadogan (who thought Dahlerus "might be rather stupid" and described him as "like a wasp at a picnic—you can't beat him off") and, on the German side, in addition to Goering, the Fuehrer himself, who received Dahlerus three times.

Dahlerus's testimony was drawn from a book recounting these activities which he published in Swedish in September 1945 and subsequently in English. There was also a German translation which was used by Fyfe in cross-examining Dahlerus. Dahlerus told a remarkable story, but what did his testimony do for Goering? It certainly showed that Goering was willing to spend much time discussing with the British the possibility of a peaceful settlement, but that alone tells nothing about his motives. At the meeting on August 7, Goering told his British auditors that "he would do anything in his power to prevent a war," and both Goering and Hitler repeatedly told Dahlerus that they wanted an "understanding" with England. But these are slim reeds on which to base an opinion of Goering's purpose.

Goering apparently laid great store by Dahlerus as a witness, and Stahmer, together with Siemers (who was a personal friend of Dahlerus), had long discussions with him prior to his testimony. These were experienced lawyers, and Goering was no dummy—factors which make it truly remarkable that none of them appear to have taken adequate account of the content of Dahlerus's book before deciding to call him as a witness. In addition, they seem to have neglected to call Dahlerus's attention to the documents put in evidence by Alderman that described Hitler's conferences with and speeches to his subordinates, including Goering, which led to the outbreak of the war.

As a result of these oversights, Fyfe's cross-examination of Dahlerus was a field day, for Dahlerus's book did not portray Goering favorably, as either a peacemaker or a person. At its outset the book states that the author first saw Goering embroiled in a "stormy interview" with Wilhelm Furtwaengler, the famous conductor of the Berlin Philharmonic, who was vainly seeking permission to keep his Jewish *Konzertmeister*. Fyfe read a number of extracts from the book, merely asking the witness to confirm their accuracy. These described Hitler as "shrieking" that if there were a war he would "build U-boats, U-boats, U-boats" and acting "more like a phantom from a story book than a real person," and Goering as receiving Dahlerus "clad in a poisonous green dressing-gown fastened around the middle with a jeweled buckle" while giving Dahlerus no support in the interviews with

Hitler and treating the Fuehrer with "obsequious humility." Goering sat fuming at the revelation of these indignities.

More to the point was Fyfe's use of the documents on Hitler's preparations for the attack against Poland—the conferences with the senior generals and other officials in which Hitler had declared that Danzig was not the subject of the war but "expanding our living span in the East," and that the pact with Stalin had made it possible to "isolate Poland." Had Goering ever informed Dahlerus of these avowals? To all such questions the witness answered that Goering had never disclosed any such matters to him.

In fact, there was good reason for Goering's reticence. As he later pointed out, he was under no obligation to disclose high state secrets to a volunteer negotiant. If Goering wished to keep the discussions alive, it would have been folly to disclose Hitler's intransigent utterances, which might well have discouraged Dahlerus from further efforts.

But Fyfe succeeded in giving the impression that Goering's conduct was nefarious duplicity. Dr. von der Lippe wrote: "Dahlerus's interrogation [by Fyfe] so developed that no one took him for a friend of Goering . . . To the contrary, many thought him a prosecution witness and had better not have been called [by Goering]."

Dahlerus's answer to Fyfe's last question was "Had I known what I know today, I would have realized that my efforts could not possibly succeed." When Goering returned to the witness box, he endeavored to put his witness's testimony in a better light. But he made the bad mistake of declaring that what he wanted was to solve the crisis "peaceably . . . along the lines of the Munich solution." Probably that was sincere, but of course the fate of Czechoslovakia after Munich was still fresh in every mind. And neither Dahlerus nor Goering himself ever suggested that he did not knowingly engage in aggressive war against Poland.

Thus Goering invested the greater part of both his own and his witness's testimony without making much headway before a Tribunal in duty bound to apply the Charter's condemnation of aggressive war. With respect to the charges of war crimes, his major effort was to justify the actions of the Luftwaffe, a relatively easy task in view of the lack of international rules limiting aerial warfare, and the destruction and death sown in Germany by British and American bombers.

There was, however, one action involving the Luftwaffe which plainly violated the laws of war, and to which Goering paid particular attention. In March 1944, seventy-five captured Royal Air Force officers at Sagan in Silesia (now Zagan in Poland) escaped from their prison known as Stalag Luft III. About a third of them were recaptured almost immediately by the prison guards, but the others, who remained longer at liberty and were captured by the German police, were shot. Apparently because there had recently been several large escapes by prisoners of war, Hitler had ordered Himmler to shoot the police captives.

Goering did not contest the illegality of these killings.° He testified, however, that he was away from his headquarters and on leave at the time of the escape and that when he learned what had happened, he told Hitler that the order was "completely impossible" and might cause the British to take reprisals against German prisoners of war. By that time, Goering's relations with Hitler were "extremely bad," and the Fuehrer had "violently" rejected Goering's objections.

As for war crimes committed in the civil context, Goering's testimony was brief and vague. He had established the first concentration camps, but they had been intended to sequester rather than punish political enemies of Nazism. After Himmler took control of the camps in 1934, Goering said he had nothing to do with and little knowledge of what was going on in them.

Goering acknowledged that in his capacity as Commissioner of the Four-Year Plan he had "general plenary authority over all matters concerning economy," including the deportation of foreign laborers to the Reich. But in 1942 Hitler "had already begun to intervene much more strongly and directly in such problems," and Sauckel, after his appointment as Plenipotentiary General for the Allocation of Labor, took his orders directly from the Fuehrer. Goering added that, in his opinion, the Hague and Geneva convention rules limiting the right of an occupying power to seize properties and displace workers were incompatible with "the technical expansion of modern war." Events were to prove that Goering and his lawyers had badly underestimated the legal and evidentiary importance of these matters.

Goering was then questioned by no less than sixteen defense counsel, most of whom hoped for responses that would cast their clients in a good light. In a number of instances, Goering was able and willing to give answers which were helpful insofar as they belittled the importance of the questioners' duties. Keitel's role was "a very thankless one" in which he "came between the millstones of stronger personalities"; the Army General Staff as a whole had an attitude "very reticent and timid for a general staff"; Ribbentrop "definitely had no influence in the sense that he could have steered Hitler in any one direction." In reply to a question whether there was any "conspiracy" among the Nazi leaders, Goering jauntily replied that:

°The right of prisoners of war to attempt escape was recognized in the Lieber Code, Section XXVII. At the time of the Nuremberg trials, the matter was governed by the 1929 Geneva Convention, which provided (Section L) that recaptured prisoners "shall be liable only to disciplinary punishment."

There was no one who could even approach working as closely with the Führer, who was as essentially familiar with his thoughts and who had the same influence as I. Therefore at best only the Führer and I could have conspired. There is definitely no question of the others.

## 4

Late in the morning session of March 18, the defendants' lawyers finished their questioning, and Jackson rose to cross-examine Goering. The first interchange was:

JACKSON: You are perhaps aware that you are the only man living who can expound to us the true purposes of the Nazi Party and the inner workings of its leadership?

GOERING: I am perfectly aware of that.

Why did Jackson begin that way? In his oral history memoirs, he described his preparations for the confrontation:

I had prepared a rather careful cross-examination of Goering because of the difficulties of the case with which the Americans were charged. . . .

As I had originally planned the cross-examination, I had thought to confront him first with the documents showing his criminal acts. Among other things he had signed some eighteen decrees which embodied the whole anti-Semitic program. We had evidence of his looting of art treasures, of his financial irregularities that he would not like to admit.

I had thought it might be wise to first confront him with these and rather to take the conceit out of him. Then I planned to turn to the political questions which I was obliged to go into because we had to sustain our charge of general conspiracy—that from the beginning it was the purpose of these men who got together in the top Nazi ranks to overthrow the Weimar Republic, to suppress the liberty of the German people, to force the preparation for war, and to conduct war without declaring it.

However, as the direct examination of Goering went, I became convinced that I should reverse the process and should start by flattering him and induce him to display his Nazi attitudes as much as possible, instead of humiliating him. So I started out with broad political questions. I asked him first if he was aware that he was the only man living who could explain the Nazi philosophy. He said he well understood that.

Jackson did not state why Goering's direct testimony moved him to change his original plan; presumably Goering's often lengthy replies to Stahmer's questions convinced Jackson that a soft approach and broad questions would produce damning admissions.° And so, according to plan, Jackson asked a long series of questions about Nazi policies and actions that lasted the rest of the day. These questions elicited statements or restatements of the reasons for the elimination of parliamentary government, adoption of the Leadership Principle; the suppression of political opposition; the purpose of the concentration camps; the wisdom of the attack against the Soviet Union; the significance of the Reichstag fire, the Roehm purge, and the Treaty of Versailles; the Anschluss with Austria; the relations between Goering and Schacht; and the Four-Year Plan.

Goering answered these questions—many of which he had already dealt with in direct examination—in some cases by ready and brief agreements, but in many by partial or complete disagreement with Jackson's apparent assumptions. Generally, Jackson was unable or unwilling to confute Goering's objections, and his handling of the questions soon created the impression that the defendant was dialectically superior to the prosecutor. For example, in discussing the concentration camps during the early period (1933–1934), when they were under Goering's control, Jackson asked: "Was it also necessary in operating this [concentration camp] system, that you must not have persons entitled to public trials in independent courts? And you immediately issued an order that your political police would not be subject to court review or to court orders, did you not?"

That question obviously could not be answered "yes" or "no," and required explication of several issues. Were all arrestees barred from public trials? Were all camp inmates so barred? If so, was it "necessary"? What orders did Goering issue and for what reasons?

Goering spoke a few sentences in reply to these inquiries but was cut off by Jackson, who by this time had probably received more enlightenment than he wanted, and denied Goering's request to make further explanation of his answer, saying: "Your counsel will see to that." Jackson started to ask another question but was interrupted by Lawrence, who told him that "the Tribunal thinks the witness ought to be allowed to make what explanation he thinks right in answer to this question." Jackson told Goering to proceed with his explanation, which he did. The questioning then proceeded much as before, but in fact Jackson was internally seething. He had seen Biddle whispering to Lawrence before the interruption and laid on Biddle the

---

°Jackson must have discussed his purpose with his biographer, Eugene Gerhart, who thus described Jackson's thinking: "During Sunday evening, March 17, Jackson mused over his opening question to Goering. . . . Various plans of attack tantalized him. Goering was arrogant and conceited—why not turn his weakness against him? That was it! Lead him on—make him hang himself. But how? Where to begin?"

blame for what Jackson regarded as an obstacle to the success of his cross-examination.

Jackson's mood was not improved as he became aware that his performance was widely criticized. In his report for the day to the British Foreign Office, Patrick Dean wrote:

> Justice Jackson began his cross-examination of Goering at noon today and continued all afternoon. It was very disappointing and unimpressive and has been severely criticized here. He never pressed Goering on any of the numerous matters on which the cross-examination touched even though Goering was frequently lying and good material for cross-examination exists. In consequence Goering indulged in much Nazi propaganda and showed everything in the most favorable light for himself.

The defendants' admiration, which Jackson had won for his cross-examinations of Goering's witnesses, rapidly dissipated. Von der Lippe found Jackson's opening questions only "medium good" and felt that in the afternoon Goering "controlled the situation." Jackson was "unable to follow" Goering, "much less to outmaneuver him." Goering "amazed everyone, prosecutors, defense lawyers, journalists, and many of the Tribunal's staff, by his mental dexterity and eloquence." Von der Lippe noted that many onlookers thought that Jackson had sustained a real fiasco and that he might in consequence seek "revenge."

But for Jackson there was no revenge, and worse to come. His cross-examination was interrupted by the Dahlerus testimony, which ended about a half hour before the end of the session on March 19. Resuming discussion of political and military prewar actions by the Nazi government, Jackson asked Goering whether the German remilitarization of the Rhineland, on March 7, 1936, had been planned long in advance. Goering replied "at most 2 to 3 weeks," whereupon Jackson produced the record of a meeting of the Reich Defense Council on June 26, 1935, which called for (as worded in the English translation) "preparation for the liberation of the Rhine."

Goering at once pointed out that the reference was to the Rhine River and not the Rhineland and that the German word had been erroneously translated "liberation," while its correct meaning was "clearing." The document, Goering explained, did not involve a plan to militarize the Rhineland, but comprised basic directions for military mobilization in the event of war and provided that the Rhine must be "cleared" of civil river traffic to clear the way for military shipping.

In a feeble effort to save face Jackson then asked: "But [these preparations] were of a character which had to be kept entirely secret from foreign powers?" To which Goering replied: "I do not think I can recall reading beforehand the publication of the mobilization preparations of the United States."

It must be observed that this was not a case wherein Goering had gone beyond the scope of the question or spoken at too great length. Furthermore, Jackson's question was answered, not directly but unmistakably: Goering had agreed that mobilization plans were kept secret. But the sting of sarcasm, coming on the heels of another technical defeat by Goering, led to an explosion:

> Well, I respectfully submit to the Tribunal that this witness is not being responsive, and has not been in his examination, and that it is perfectly futile to spend our time if we cannot have responsive answers to questions.
>
> We can strike these things out. I do not want to spend time doing that, but this witness, it seems to me, is adopting, and has adopted, in the witness box and in the dock, an arrogant and contemptuous attitude toward the Tribunal which is giving him the trial which he never gave a living soul, nor dead ones either.
>
> I respectfully submit that the witness be instructed to make notes if he wishes, of his explanations, but that he be required to answer my questions and reserve his explanations for his counsel to bring out.

Lawrence replied that he had already laid down the general rule "which is binding on this defendant as upon other witnesses." No doubt hoping that Jackson might profit by a night's sleep, Lawrence then stated: "Perhaps we had better adjourn now at this stage." And the Tribunal rose.

Anything but soothed, Jackson returned the following morning loaded for bear. After repeating the last interchange between himself and Goering, he stated:

> Now, representing the United States of America, I am confronted with these choices—to ignore that remark and allow it to stand for people who do not understand our system; or to develop, at considerable expense of time, its falsity; or to answer it in rebuttal. . . .
>
> The Charter in Article 18 provides that the Tribunal shall rule out irrelevant issues and statements. . . . I respectfully submit, if the ruling of the Tribunal that the defendant may volunteer questions of this kind is to prevail, the control of these proceedings is put in the hands of the defendant, and the United States has been substantially denied its right of cross-examination.

Lawrence interrupted to express agreement that Goering's reference to American mobilization plans was "irrelevant, and the answer ought not to have been made." But he reaffirmed the Tribunal's prior decision that the defendants should first answer questions directly and if possible with yes or no, but thereafter could "make such explanation as may be necessary," as long as they spoke briefly. Jackson acknowledged that he "must, of course, bow to the ruling of the Tribunal," but repeated at length his arguments already made and formally moved that the Tribunal reverse itself and require defendants' "explanations" to be handled by defense counsel on redirect examination. When he repeated his concern about Goering's reference to American mobilization plans, Lawrence, rather impatiently, answered:

> Surely it is making too much of a sentence the witness said, whether the United States makes its orders for mobilization public or not. . . . Every country keeps certain things secret. Certainly it would be much wiser to ignore a statement of that sort.

But Jackson would have none of this: "The point is, do we answer these things or leave them, apart from the control of the Trial? And it does seem to me that this is the beginning of this Trial's getting out of hand, if I may say so, if we do not have control of this situation. I trust the Tribunal will pardon my earnestness. . . ."

The Tribunal's members can hardly have welcomed being told to their faces that *they* were letting things get "out of hand," or that *we* (presumably the Tribunal and the prosecution) must "have control" of the trial. Almost fiercely Lawrence replied: "I have never heard it suggested that the Counsel for the Prosecution have to answer every irrelevant observation made in cross-examination." But Jackson, by now beyond taking advice, persisted:

> That would be true in a private litigation, but I trust the Court is not unaware that outside of this courtroom is a great social question of the revival of Nazism and that one of the purposes of the defendant Goering—I think he would be the first to admit—is to revive and perpetuate it by propaganda from this Trial now in process.

That brought Dr. Stahmer to his feet with an indignant denial of any intent "to make propaganda," and a defense of Goering's reply to Jackson's question, in which he cleverly suggested that if Goering had named any country other than the United States, "the remark would have been considered harmless." Lawrence had had more than enough of this exchange, and emphatically reiterated to Jackson that a defendant, after giving a direct answer to a question, might legitimately "make a short explanation."

Defeated and bitter, Jackson resumed the cross-examination. Defiantly, he asked a few more questions concerning the Reich Defense Council, but soon abandoned that unlucky subject and turned to Goering's participation in the Nazi government's treatment of Jews. Here he was on much stronger ground, for he was equipped with over a dozen decrees personally signed and promulgated by Goering, including the "Nuremberg Laws" of 1935; the laws for the registration of Jewish property (1938) which imposed a billion-mark fine on Jews after Kristallnacht, forbade Jews to own retail stores, and confiscated Jewish jewelry; the sequestration of Jewish property in Poland (September 1940); and exclusion of Jews from compensation for war damage (November 1940). The documents spoke for themselves, and Goering made no effort to mitigate his responsibility for brutal crimes against Jews. Those committed in Poland, of course, constituted war crimes.

Jackson concluded with brief attacks on Goering for looting art (which the French had covered effectively), the use of French and Soviet prisoners of war for unlawful military purposes, the bombing of Warsaw (which Goering dealt with very effectively), and the forced labor program. Jackson had survived the day's questioning without another debacle, but not very impressively; Dean coolly reported Jackson's handling as "better conducted than hitherto, though little use was made of the splendid material available."

In retrospect, it is obvious that many of the participants in the trial, including the press, greatly exaggerated the importance of Goering's cross-examination. The contents of the documents received in evidence during the months just passed were more than enough to convict him on all counts. Neither Goering nor his witnesses had shaken either their authenticity or their impact. Had it not been for the tensions and expectations which the trial had aroused, the prosecution might well have waived cross-examination, which could have little effect on the evidentiary case that had already been made.

But Goering's past status, and the domineering stance he had adopted, created an atmosphere that seemed to call for a confrontation between him and the prosecution. Many came to equate the outcome of that confrontation with the success or failure of the trial itself. Judge Birkett, barrister first and always, was swept away by this view:

> *18 March.* In this long drawn-out trial of the major war criminals at Nuremberg, intense expectation was centered on the moment when Goering . . . was cross-examined.
>
> It was, in a very real sense, the critical moment of the trial. If the leader of the surviving Nazis could be exposed and shattered, and the purposes and methods of the Nazi Government revealed in their horrible cruelty, then the whole free world would feel that this trial had served its supreme purpose; but if, for any reason, the design

should fail, then the fears of those who thought the holding of any trial to be a mistake would be in some measure justified. . . .

At 12:15 on the morning of March 18, Mr. Justice Jackson rose to begin the long-awaited cross-examination . . . but before the adjournment had been reached it was clear that all the high hopes were to be disappointed. . . .

The cross-examination had not proceeded more than ten minutes before it was seen that he [Goering] was the complete master of Mr. Justice Jackson . . . [who] despite his great abilities and charm and his great powers of exposition had never learnt the very first elements of cross-examination as it is understood in the English courts. He was overwhelmed by his documents, and there was no chance of the lightning questions following upon some careless or damaging answer, no quick parry and thrust, no leading the witness on to the prepared pitfall, and above all no clear over-riding conception of the great issues which could have been put with simplicity and power. . . .

*20 March.* The trial from now on is really outside the control of the Tribunal, and in the long months ahead the prestige of the trial will steadily diminish.

For all his experience and prowess, Judge Birkett was viewing the Nuremberg courtroom as if it were the Leeds Assizes, with two barristers jousting over the truth or falsity of a witness's testimony. The "purposes and methods of the Nazi Government" had already been "revealed in their horrible cruelty" beyond the power of Goering or anyone else to mitigate. Birkett's strictures on Jackson's cross-examination were well founded, but to imagine that the stature of the Nuremberg trials would stand or fall on Jackson's performance was ridiculous.

Another misconception, embraced particularly by the English and American lawyers, was that the defendants, especially Goering, might use the trial as a vehicle to spread "Nazi propaganda" and, as Birkett put it, "restore German belief in their leaders." In this connection, one must bear in mind that the defendants were accused of conspiring to initiate and wage aggressive war, and the prosecution had to prove that the defendants *intended* to do so. So charged, the defendants had every right to contend that they did not so intend, or initiate, or wage. In Goering's case especially, his testimony would inevitably include many explanations of why he did what he did. Thus the line between these "explanations" and what some might regard as "Nazi propaganda" was very thin.

If Goering intended to engage in Nazi propaganda, his best opportunity came during his direct interrogation by Stahmer. In fact, despite his numerous lengthy responses, there was little said that was not germane to the charges against him. He did not say that the Leadership Principle or any other element of Nazism should be restored in the future. Considering the state to which Germany had been reduced, Goering was smart enough to realize that any such harangue would make him a laughingstock, or worse, in the minds of his countrymen.

The chimerical fear of propaganda was thus no basis for Jackson's appeal to the Tribunal to confine Goering's responses to brief, direct replies. Even Birkett conceded that Goering's answers were not irrelevant. Nevertheless, Birkett strongly urged that Goering should be severely admonished to curtail his answers in order to expedite the proceedings and restore Jackson's confidence. When Biddle and Parker successfully objected, Birkett called the negative decision "a fatal mistake." Fyfe, however, thought Birkett's judgment "seriously at fault" because "If Goering—who, after all, was on trial for his life—could run rings around prosecuting counsel, that was a matter for counsel to put right without assistance from the Tribunal. Public opinion would not have tolerated—either at the time or subsequently—the constant interference of the judges on behalf of the Prosecution." Fyfe was right; what Jackson was requesting would have had the worst possible result for Jackson himself, as well as everyone else except the defendants.

Furthermore, Jackson was in no position to complain about Goering's answers. Jackson had opened his cross-examination by recognizing Goering as "the only man living who can expound to us the true purposes of the Nazi Party and the inner workings of its leadership." That was nothing other than an open-ended invitation to Goering to "expound" in answering the very broad questions of fact and purpose which followed. Goering was doing exactly what Jackson had asked him to do, and what broke Jackson's self-control was that his witness was answering too articulately and unashamedly. Jackson's strategy completely misfired, because he did not understand the nature of his opponent. Albert Speer, talking to Dr. Gilbert,° made what Jackson himself later called "the most penetrating observation" about the affair:

> You know, when Jackson cross-examines Goering, you can see that they just represent two entirely opposite worlds—they don't even understand each other. Jackson asks him if he didn't help plan the invasion of Holland and Belgium and Norway, expecting Goering to defend himself against a criminal accusation, but instead Goering says, Why yes, of course, it took place thus and so, as if it is the most

° It is remarkable that Gilbert's diary describes only Jackson's questions on Goering's anti-Semitic decrees and makes no mention of the general criticism of his cross-examination or of his appeal to the Tribunal. Gilbert was regularly informing Jackson about the personalities and statements of the defendants, and I suspect that he may have influenced Jackson to approach Goering in a flattering way. The results were so unfortunate that Gilbert may have thought it best to treat the affair with silence. The "legal details" of Gilbert's book were checked by Jackson's son prior to publication.

natural thing in the world to invade a neutral country if it suits your strategy.

Jackson continued to insist that his cross-examination had been useful because of Goering's admissions of actions which were criminal under the Charter and the laws of war, and he included excerpts from the cross-examination in a book he published in 1947.° But most of the admissions had already been made during Stahmer's direct examination, and in retrospect it is hard to see that Jackson accomplished much.

Jackson paid dearly for his tactical blunders, in both public prestige and his own discontent. He was unlucky in that his troubles were noted by two women with sharp and formidable reputations, who visited Nuremberg to report on the trial.

Rebecca West and Janet Flanner (who wrote for *The New Yorker* under the nom de plume Genêt), albeit with occasional misstatements, wrote beautifully and perceptively in 1946 about the denizens of the Palace of Justice.† West wrote that the defendants "were amused when Mr. Justice Jackson could not cross-examine Goering at all well, because he had a transatlantic prepossession that a rogue who had held high office would be a solemn and not a jolly rogue, and was disconcerted by his impudence." Flanner pursued the matter at greater length:

> As the trial moved out of its preparatory period of massive, static documentation and entered its period of skirmishing and battle in the open, where the brains and personalities of the opponents were what counted, Jackson began to show inadequacies as the leading Allied man. Up to then his main contribution to this very special legal scene had been the high humanitarianism which marked his fine opening address in November. Beneath that humanitarianism there lies his burning private conviction that the Nazi prisoners are mere common criminals. This, too logically, led to his treating them in a blustering police court manner, which was successful with the craven small fry but disastrous for him in cross-examining that uncommon criminal, Goering, himself accustomed to blustering in a grander way. Even physically, Jackson cut a poor figure. He unbuttoned his coat, whisked it back over his hips, and, with his hands in his back pockets, spraddled and teetered like a country lawyer. Not only did he seem to lack the background and wisdom of our Justice Holmes tradition, but his prepared European foreground was full of holes, which he fell into en route to setting traps for Goering.

---

°Jackson, *The Nuremberg Case* (Alfred A. Knopf, 1947). The selected excerpts do not include Jackson's colloquies with Lord Lawrence in the course of the cross-examination.

†West, *A Train of Powder* (Viking Press, 1955), p. 17, and *Janet Flanner's World: Uncollected Writings, 1932–1975* (Harcourt Brace Jovanovich, 1979), p. 118.

Jackson was well-nigh unhinged by the torrent of criticism. Fyfe reported to Birkett that Jackson was "in a terrific state," and Colonel Dostert, who had been upbraided by Jackson for the translation error on "liberating" the Rhine, took the same message to Biddle. It was a blow from which Jackson only gradually recovered.

When Fyfe took over the cross-examination, it was plain that his primary task was psychological; he must regain the initiative, be master of the colloquy, and if possible discredit Goering. For his initial subject he chose the killing of the air force fugitives from Stalag Luft III because they were British and because he had noticed gaps in Goering's explanation of the episode under Stahmer's questioning.

Fyfe had some good cards, and he played them well. He had thoroughly mastered the documentation on the Stalag Luft III escape, and it soon became apparent that he was better prepared and more knowledgeable than Goering. Some of the documents Goering had never seen before, and Fyfe used them to reveal the holes in Goering's earlier testimony. Goering soon sensed the danger of "expounding" on the subject for fear that Fyfe would catch him in a mistake. The witness became cautious; he was weak on names and dates and frequently pled no knowledge or memory. Fyfe was in the driver's seat, and there was a wave of relief at the prosecution tables.

Fyfe then tried to involve Goering in the actual killings. He was able to show that much more information about them had reached Goering's headquarters than he had mentioned on direct examination and that the killings had continued for some three weeks after Goering's return to duty. On this basis Fyfe charged that Goering "did nothing to prevent these men from being shot, but cooperated in this foul series of murders." He then changed to another subject, cutting off Goering's effort to reply.

However, Fyfe's evidence fell short of establishing Goering's complicity in the murders. None of the escaped prisoners whom the camp guards rounded up was harmed. Goering received no order from Hitler. The Fuehrer gave instructions directly to Himmler, under whose command the German police shot the fugitives they captured. Goering complained to Hitler and left with a wasp in his ear. A few of the fugitives succeeded in remaining at liberty long after Goering heard about Hitler's order, but he had neither the authority nor the force to stop Himmler from continuing the shootings. It is conceivable that a quick decision to send the camp guards out farther might have saved a few more lives, but the prosecution established no basis for a criminal charge against Goering in this unpardonable affair.

Von der Lippe recorded that "Goering found the cross-examinations by Maxwell-Fyfe and Rudenko considerably more unpleasant than Jackson's." The two "unpleasant" interrogations were of very different natures.

Rudenko did not engage in efforts to show that Goering had been lying or concealing facts, as Fyfe had done in the Stalag Luft III murders. The Soviet prosecutor's aim was much simpler; he showed Goering documents already in evidence and demanded that he acknowledge complicity in the crimes the documents disclosed. The two men understood each other well and fought with heavy clubs rather than rapiers. Their discussion of Rudenko's charge that the German attack against the Soviet Union had as its goal German annexation of most of the western U.S.S.R. is typical:

RUDENKO: Do you admit that the objectives of the war against the Soviet Union consisted of invading and seizing Soviet territory up to the Ural Mountains and joining it to the German Reich, including the Baltic territories, the Crimea, the Caucasus, also the subjugation by Germany of the Ukraine, of Bielorussia, and of other regions of the Soviet Union? Do you admit that such were the objectives of that plan?

GOERING: That I certainly do not admit.

RUDENKO: You do not admit that! Do you not remember that during the conferences at Hitler's headquarters on the 16th of June [actually July] 1941, at which you were present as well as Bormann, Keitel, Rosenberg, and others, Hitler stated the objectives of the attack against the Soviet Union exactly as I have stated them? This was shown by the document submitted to the Tribunal. Have you forgotten that document? Have you forgotten about that?

GOERING: I can remember the document exactly, and I have a fair recollection of the discussion at the conference. I said the first time that this document, as recorded by Bormann, appears to be greatly exaggerated. . . .

RUDENKO: I would like to draw just one conclusion. The facts bear witness that even before this conference, aims to annex foreign territory had been fixed in accordance with the plan prepared months ago. That is correct, is it not?

GOERING: Yes, that is correct, but I would like to emphasize that in these minutes, I steered away from these endless discussions. . . .

RUDENKO: Please read it once more and tell me just where you disagreed.

GOERING: "After the lengthy discussion about persons and matters concerning annexation, *et cetera*, opposing this the Reich Marshal stressed the main points that might be the decisive factors for us: Securing of food supplies to the extent necessary for economy, securing of roads, *et cetera*, communications."

RUDENKO: It is understandable that the securing of food plays an important part. However, the objection you just gave does not mean that you objected to the annexation of the Crimea or the annexation of other regions, is not that correct?

GOERING: If you spoke German, then, from the sentence that says, "opposing that the Reich Marshal emphasized. . . ." you would understand everything that is implied. In other words, I did not say here, "I protest against the annexation of the Crimea," or, "I protest against the annexation of the Baltic states." I had no reason to do so. Had we been victorious, then, after the signing of peace we would in any case have decided how far the annexation would serve our purposes. At the moment we had not finished the war. . . .

RUDENKO: I understand you. In that case, you considered the annexation of these regions a step to come later. As you said yourself, after the war was won you would have seized these provinces and annexed them. In principle you have not protested.

GOERING: Not in principle. As an old hunter, I acted according to the principle of not dividing the bear's skin before the bear was shot.

RUDENKO: I understand. And the bear's skin should be divided only when the territories were seized completely, is that correct?

GOERING: Just what to do with the skin could be decided definitely only after the bear was shot.

RUDENKO: Luckily, this did not happen.

GOERING: Luckily for you.

Patrick Dean informed the Foreign Office that Rudenko had "made little headway" against Goering, and it is true that toward the end the cross-examination fell apart, as the prosecutor implied guilt he could not prove and the witness denied knowledge of things he ought to have known. But, overall, Rudenko's success was greater than Dean allowed. Wisely, Rudenko put more emphasis on the forced labor program than had his predecessors. Goering had acknowledged responsibility in this area rather perfunctorily during Stahmer's questioning, but Rudenko drew very explicit admissions from him that, as head of the Four-Year Plan, he had "unlimited powers in the economic sphere" with "authority to issue directives and instructions to the highest Reich departments," that during the war "these powers were extended to the economic structures of the occupied countries," and that this responsibility extended to the forced labor program. These acknowledgments were to prove the foundation of the Tribunal's conviction of Goering under Counts Three and Four (war crimes and crimes against humanity) of the Indictment.

Champetier de Ribes declared that he saw nothing in the French interest that required further cross-examination, and Dr. Stahmer rose to conduct the redirect examination. This lasted only a few minutes, during which Goering testified that the then famous Hermann Goering Division was a ground division under army command and that his only connection with it was for "matters of personnel and equipment."

When Dr. Stahmer asked Goering to describe again the nature of his relation to Hitler, Jackson objected that the subject had already been covered. Lawrence agreed and cut Stahmer off from further discussion. Stahmer then asked Goering to elucidate the difference between his "formal" as opposed to his "actual" responsibility for the actions of his subordinates. The Tribunal had soon had enough, and Lawrence told Goering not to "make speeches." Stahmer then declared that he had "no further questions to ask," and Goering returned to his place in the dock. Stahmer continued for an hour or so offering in evidence his documents and sworn interrogatories from absentee witnesses, and so providing an anticlimactic end to Goering's Nuremberg case.

5

The Goering case had taken twelve days of court time, from March 8 to March 22, 1946. Had the other defendants' cases proceeded at the same pace, their trials would have lasted ten months, with the organization cases and closing statements still to be heard. The Tribunal took pains to crush any such expectations by announcing, on the afternoon of March 22:

> The Tribunal has allowed the Defendant Goering, who has given evidence first of the defendants and who has proclaimed himself to be responsible as the second leader of Nazi Germany, to give his evidence without any interruption whatever, and he has covered the whole history of the Nazi regime from its inception to the defeat of Germany.
>
> The Tribunal does not propose to allow any of the other defendants to go over the same ground in their evidence except insofar as it is necessary for their own defense.

As things worked out, the cases of the twenty defendants lasted until the end of June, requiring seventy-eight trial days—about four days for each defendant, about one-third of the time used on Goering's case. The Tribunal's pronouncement had what most of the trial participants regarded as a very salutary effect on the proceedings.

Rudolf Hess presented a unique and interesting case, but not a long one; the entire proceeding took only a day and a half. This was partly due to Hess's flight to Britain on May 10, 1941, which greatly shortened the possible period for the commission of war crimes, and even more to Hess's decision not to take the witness stand, with the result that he was not examined or cross-examined. Hess had been planning to testify, but on March 24, as a result of strong urging from his counsel, Dr. Seidl, and Goering, he told Gilbert that he had decided not to, "because he did not want to be subjected to the embarrassment of not being able to answer questions the prosecution would ask."

However, Seidl made no such announcement to the Tribunal until March 26, after he had called his two witnesses and offered his documents in evidence. He said: "I had then the further intention of calling the defendant himself as a witness." This was not true, for Seidl's decision not to call Hess to the stand had been reached two days earlier. Seidl went on: "In view of his attitude as to the competency of this Court, he has asked me, however, to dispense with this procedure. I therefore forego the testimony of the defendant as a witness and have no further evidence to put in at this point."

Seidl had announced at the outset of his presentation that "Hess contests the jurisdiction of the Tribunal when other than war crimes proper are the subject of the trial" (a futile contention in view of the Charter and the Tribunal's prior rulings), but this had nothing to do with Hess's decision not to testify, as his disclosure to Gilbert reveals. Seidl's declaration raised no question of Hess's mental competence. Dr. Gilbert had been monitoring Hess's condition, which had revealed that he had virtually no recollection of his own past or the events of the trial. These circumstances, and his unwillingness to testify in his own behalf, might well have justified questioning his competence to defend himself, but Seidl did not raise the issue.

The Hess case was further limited, and the selection of his witnesses explained, by another introductory statement to the Tribunal by Dr. Seidl. Hess, he declared, "assumes responsibility for all orders and directives which he issued in his capacity as Deputy of the Fuehrer and Minister of the Reich." Therefore, Hess "does not desire to be defended against any charges which refer to the internal affairs of Germany as a sovereign state." That, of course, covered a large part of Hess's activities as Deputy to the Fuehrer and administrative head of the Nazi Party. Accordingly, Seidl announced that he would "submit evidence only with reference to questions in the clarification of which other countries have a justified interest."

In line with that limitation, Hess's two witnesses were Ernst Bohle, formerly a State Secretary at the Foreign Ministry and Leader of the Auslandsorganisation (Foreign Organization) of the Nazi Party; and Karl Stroelin, formerly Lord Mayor of Stuttgart and ex officio Honorary President of the German Auslandsorganisation. Bohle's immediate superior was Hess, and both witnesses looked to Hess as the man whom Hitler had "entrusted with the supreme direction of all matters concerning Germans in foreign countries."

Instead of questioning these witnesses, Seidl read into the trial record their sworn affidavits. The burden of Bohle's was that the activities of the members of his organization were valid under the laws of the countries in which they resided, that the members never engaged in subversive or hostile activities against their host governments or functioned as a Fifth Column, and that neither Hess nor Hitler ever gave orders for any such hostile action. Stroelin's affidavit was to the same general effect. Apart from the affidavit, Stroelin, under questions from Neurath's counsel, Dr. von Lüdinghausen, spoke highly of the character and peaceful inclinations of Neurath.

Neither Hess nor Neurath was the better for the testimony. Griffith-Jones for the British and Colonel Amen for the American delegations were well supplied with documents and prior interrogations of the two witnesses that deprived their oral testimony and affidavits of most of their credibility. The Auslandsorganisation was not so innocent, nor Neurath so benign, as they had been pictured.

Schacht and Papen were vitriolic in their disgust with Bohle, and most of the defendants agreed that as a witness he was a failure. Dr. von der Lippe lamented that "methodical denigration of the defense witnesses by the prosecutors continues."

Among the few documents introduced by Seidl was the record of a meeting between Hess and Lord Simon that took place shortly after Hess's arrival in Britain. Hess's prime purpose was to end the state of war between Germany and Britain, and to this end Hess laid out a four-point basis for peace:

> 1. In order to prevent future wars between the Axis and England, the limits of the spheres of interest should be defined. The sphere of interest of the Axis is Europe, and England's sphere of interest is the Empire.
> 2. Return of German colonies.
> 3. Indemnification of German citizens who before or during the war had their residences within the British Empire, and who suffered damage to life and property; . . . indemnification of British subjects by Germany on the same basis.
> 4. Armistice and peace concluded with Italy at the same time.

That is interesting as history, but it is hard to see what benefit Seidl thought would accrue to Hess. Albion has sometimes been perfidious, but it was not to be expected that Britain would acquiesce in Hitler's retaining the fruits of all his aggressive wars and thus leave him suzerain of all Europe.

More to Seidl's purpose was his last document book, which contained a large collection of opinions about the Versailles Treaty, such as whether Germany signed it under duress, whether or not its economic consequences were disastrous, whether Germany may not have had the right to rearm since other countries had not disarmed. These issues opened the way for making a legal issue of the *causes* of World War II—the very issue which Jackson had warned against from the beginning.

Fyfe immediately challenged the relevancy of these documents, and there was a long argument before the Tribunal, in which Seidl was supported by Dr. Rudolf Dix (for Schacht) and Dr. Martin Horn (for Ribbentrop). Lawrence appeared to oppose Seidl's case on the ground that whatever the pros and cons of the Versailles Treaty, they would not affect the guilt or innocence of the defendants under the criminal charges in the Charter. Fyfe, while not denying that a defendant might seek to justify some of his own actions on the ground that he sincerely believed the Versailles Treaty to be unlawful, insisted that the opinions of the politicians, economists, and others cited in Seidl's documents were irrelevant. After a luncheon consultation, the Tribunal ruled the documents irrelevant and inadmissible.

Seidl's remaining document of special interest was a recently signed affidavit by Dr. Friedrich Gaus, formerly Chief of the Legal Department of the Foreign Ministry, pertaining to a "secret agreement" between Hitler and Stalin which had been made at the same time as the well-known Nazi-Soviet Nonaggression Treaty of August 23, 1939.

The temporary rapprochement between Nazi Germany and the Soviet Union was a matter of embarrassment to the Soviet delegation at Nuremberg, and when Seidl prepared to read part of the Gaus affidavit, General Rudenko was immediately on his feet insisting that "this document should not be read into the record." Seidl was out-of-bounds procedurally, for he had only a German copy of the Gaus affidavit, and Lawrence sternly informed him that no decision about admitting the document in evidence could be made until it had been translated in accordance with the Tribunal's rules.

The Gaus affidavit was finally translated and its contents read into the record (over Rudenko's objection) by Seidl on April 1 in the course of his examination of Ribbentrop. It included a description of the "secret agreement," which embodied a division of Polish territory between Germany and the Soviet Union and German recognition of the Soviet Union's "sphere of interest" as including the Baltic States.° The document was undoubtedly relevant to the Ribbentrop case, but bore no apparent relation to the Hess case.

Thus the Hess case was left essentially unchanged by Seidl's presentation. Plainly, the lawyer was more interested in exposing the seamy side of Allied and Soviet diplomacy than in helping Hess. One must allow that he got no help from his client, and there was little he could have done to brighten the picture of Hess the Nazi leader. The immediate question—whether Hess the relic would have been more appropriately confined in a mental institution than in the Nuremberg jail—was not raised.

---

°For the text of the "secret agreement," see *Nazi-Soviet Relations, 1939–1941,* published by the U.S. Department of State (1948), pp. 78–109.

# Chapter 14

# THE DEFENDANTS: "MURDERERS' ROW"

I n the case of the next seven defendants—Ribbentrop, Keitel, Kaltenbrunner, Rosenberg, Frank, Frick, and Streicher—the quantity, scope, and content of the prosecution's evidence were clearly sufficient to support a conviction under the charges in the Indictment. In no case except Streicher's was there substantial question about the sufficiency of the evidence to support a capital sentence. In all cases the sentences were reviewed and confirmed by the Control Council, and the defendants were hanged.

**Ribbentrop:** Joachim von Ribbentrop ran a close race against Kaltenbrunner and Streicher for the title "man most disliked by his fellow defendants." But the other two were Nazi thugs—Kaltenbrunner was hated with horror and Streicher with loathing—while Ribbentrop was regarded with utter scorn.

Ribbentrop had been a linguistically gifted and elegantly clad champagne salesman. He joined the Nazi Party in 1932 and came to Hitler's attention when he played a small part in the events leading to Hitler's selection as Chancellor in January 1933. Impressed by Ribbentrop's claim of extensive personal contacts in Britain and France, Hitler consulted him frequently on diplomatic matters. In 1936 Ribbentrop was appointed Ambassador to London, and two years later he replaced Neurath as Foreign Minister, a position he held until the end of the war.

Ribbentrop's continuing tenure at the Foreign Office was based solely on Hitler's support, not because of Ribbentrop's advice but for his servile obedience, and Hitler's exaggerated notion of Ribbentrop's reputation abroad. The professional staff at the Foreign Ministry could not abide

Ribbentrop, who was arrogant, overbearing, and inept. Genuine "vons," like von Neurath and von Papen, laughed at Ribbentrop's "von," which came from adoption rather than birth.

But scorn reached its apex at Nuremberg, where it soon became obvious that Ribbentrop was in a constant state of terror. True, he had plenty to worry about, but Ribbentrop was not the only defendant in that box, and he paraded his fears to a degree that none could tolerate. Gilbert's diary during the period of Ribbentrop's case (March 26 to April 3) quotes over a dozen of the other defendants' derisive comments on him and his defense efforts:

PAPEN: Now you see it! That was the Foreign Office.

FRITZSCHE: And just imagine German soldiers going to war, confidently thinking that there is a competent Foreign Office and a responsible administration. . . .

FUNK: Disgraceful! Disgraceful—the whole thing!

SCHACHT: Ugh! Such a washrag for a Foreign Minister—and look at the people he had working for him—Such a good-for-nothing, stupid weakling!

Under the law of the Charter and the laws of war, Ribbentrop's evidentiary situation was hopeless. If he did not instigate the decisions to wage aggressive war, there was in any case no hint of resistance to Hitler's initiations. Ribbentrop willingly furnished the diplomatic support for all the military actions from the occupation of Prague to the invasion of the Soviet Union, signed the law establishing the Protectorate over Bohemia and Moravia, publicly justified the attacks on Norway, the Low Countries, and Yugoslavia, and urged Japan to attack the Soviet Union.

Ribbentrop's record on war crimes was even more damning. He brought pressure to bear on Laval and Mussolini to expedite the deportation of French and Italian Jews to Eastern Europe and told Admiral Miklós Horthy, Regent of Hungary, that "Jews must either be exterminated or taken to concentration camps."

Given his reputation, it is not surprising that Ribbentrop got little help from others. His counsel, Dr. Martin Horn, was awkward and no favorite of the Tribunal, especially when he presented nine document books containing some 350 documents. His principal witness, Baron Gustav Steengracht von Moyland, former State Secretary at the Foreign Office, was dull and merely tried to shift the blame from Ribbentrop to Hitler.

Far worse for his defense was his last witness, Paul Otto Schmidt, who had interpreted at many of Hitler's conferences with foreigners and was bright and well informed. His direct testimony gave Ribbentrop no real help, and under cross-examination by Fyfe, Schmidt confirmed the veracity of an affidavit in which he stated: "The general objectives of the Nazi leadership were apparent from the start, namely, the domination of the European Continent, to be achieved, first, by the incorporation of all German-speaking groups in the Reich, and secondly, by territorial expansion under the slogan of 'Lebensraum.' " There could hardly be a better description of violations of the charges in Counts One and Two of the London Charter.

Ribbentrop's testimony was so tangled in lies and mistakes that devastating cross-examination was easy. In fact, it seemed hardly necessary, but Fyfe could not let such an opportunity pass, and the British had plenty of bones to pick with a former ambassador to London who had been despised there. Fyfe took nearly a full day, and Faure, Amen, and Rudenko another four hours of cross-examination.

Dr. Horn did not reexamine, and Ribbentrop returned to the dock, where the general feeling was that he was "finished." Gilbert overheard Goering tell Raeder that "Ribbentrop is all washed up."

**Keitel:** Wilhelm Keitel was the ranking officer of the German Army, but he was not a commander. His rise in rank had been chiefly due to his administrative pliancy and the marriage of his eldest son to Field Marshal von Blomberg's daughter. Hitler found him useful as a high-level amanuensis and promoted him so that the senior Field Marshal would be "his man."

Thus Keitel's role in the military hierarchy was comparable to Ribbentrop's among the diplomats. Both were Hitler's mouthpieces and not doers on their own. In contrast to Ribbentrop, however, Keitel was soldierly and carried himself with dignity at Nuremberg. But he was not highly regarded among his fellow officers, who had given him the sobriquet "Lakeitel," from *Lakai*, meaning lackey." When France capitulated in 1940 Keitel openly declared Hitler "the greatest field commander of all times." He was the sort of weak man whom Hitler could count on to follow his orders regardless of law or morals.

Keitel's counsel, Dr. Otto Nelte, began by calling his client to the witness stand. Nelte, whose case was well organized, went immediately to the crucial questions:

NELTE: The Prosecution, in presenting evidence regarding violations of the laws of war . . . repeatedly points to letters, orders, *et cetera*, which bear your name. . . . What do you say to this general accusation?

KEITEL: It is correct that there are a large number of orders with which my name is connected, and it must also be admitted that such orders often contain deviations from existing international law. . . . [Also] there are a group of directives and orders based not on military inspiration but on an ideological foundation and point of view. In this connection I am thinking of the group of directives which were issued before the campaign against the Soviet Union and also which were issued subsequently.

NELTE: What can you say in your defense in regard to those orders?

KEITEL: I can only say that fundamentally I bear the responsibility which arises from my position for all those things which resulted from these orders and which are connected with my name and signature.

That was a commendably frank admission of personal responsibility for war crimes, including the atrocities committed in consequence of the orders issued in connection with the invasion of the Soviet Union. Later on, Nelte turned to Counts One and Two of the Indictment:

NELTE: So that we can understand each other . . . we must be quite clear as to what is meant by way of aggression. Will you tell us your views on that subject?

KEITEL: As a soldier, I must say that the term "War of Aggression" as used here is meaningless as far as I am concerned . . . according to my own personal feelings, the concept "war of aggression" is a purely political concept and not a military one. . . . I think I can summarize my views by saying that military officers should not have authority to decide this question and are not in a position to do so; and that these decisions are not the task of the soldier, but solely that of the statesman. . . .

NELTE: But you are not only a soldier, you are also an individual with a life of your own. When facts brought to your notice in your professional capacity seemed to reveal that a projected operation was unjust, did you not give it consideration?

KEITEL: I believe I can truthfully say that throughout the whole of my military career I was brought up, so to speak, in the old traditional concept that we never discussed this question. Naturally, one has one's own opinion and a life of one's own, but in the exercise of one's professional functions as a soldier and an officer, one has given this life away, yielded it up. Therefore I could not say either at that time or later that I had misgivings about questions of a purely political discretion, for I took the stand that a soldier has a right to have confidence in his state leadership, and accordingly he is obliged to do his duty and to obey.

The difficulty with this response was that the "state leadership," Adolf Hitler, was equally indifferent to questions about "just wars," and Keitel knew it. His attitude was not far from that of Goering, who was not moved by "considerations of international law." No doubt there were, and still are, military men who embrace the same view, but it was not one leading to an acquittal of charges under Counts One and Two.

Nelte then took Keitel chronologically through the military events

The twenty-one defendants seated in the dock. *Left to right, lower tier:* Hermann Goering, Rudolf Hess, Joachim von Ribbentrop, Field Marshal Wilhelm Keitel, Ernst Kaltenbrunner, Alfred Rosenberg, Hans Frank, Wilhelm Frick, Julius Streicher, Walther Funk, and Hjalmar Schacht. *Left to right, upper tier*: Adm. Karl Doenitz, Adm. Erich Raeder, Baldur von Schirach, Fritz Sauckel, Gen. Alfred Jodl, Franz von Papen, Arthur Seyss-Inquart, Albert Speer, Constantin von Neurath, and Hans Fritzsche. Seated in front of the dock are several defense lawyers, including, at far left, Otto Kranzbuehler (in uniform) for Doenitz., and, sitting in front of him, Otto Stahmer for Goering. *National Archives*

The Lutheran pastor Charles Gerecke was an American from Missouri. His chapel, contrived from two cells, was frequented by a dozen Protestant and four Catholic defendants. Gerecke was much liked by the members of his congregation. *R. D'Addario*

During a break in the proceedings, Capt. G. M. Gilbert, the prison psychologist, is quizzed by the defendants (left to right) Speer, Neurath (partly hidden behind Speer), Funk, Fritzsche, and Schacht. Gilbert's published notes (*Nuremberg Diary*) present a valuable picture of the defendants' behavior at Nuremberg. He disliked most of them, especially Goering, and made some of his information about them available to Jackson. *National Archives*

Robert H. Jackson (right foreground) in the course of cross-examining Hermann Goering. Behind him is his secretary, Mrs. Elsie Douglas, and at her right Lt. Com. Whitney Harris, assisting Jackson. *R. D'Addario*

At the lectern is French Chief Prosecutor François de Menthon, whose opening speech in January 1946 was greatly admired. It was also his last appearance before the Tribunal, as he resigned the next day to resume his political career. He was succeeded by the frail Champetier de Ribes, seated at the left front corner of the French table, hand to face. On the right front corner is Charles Dubost, Deputy Chief Prosecutor and effectively the leader of the French team. To the left, at the Soviet table, the Chief Prosecutor, Gen. R. A. Rudenko, is seated at the right front corner, and opposite him is Deputy Chief Prosecutor Col. Yu. V. Pokrovsky. *National Archives*

A closeup of Rudolf Hess, accentuating his beetlebrows, sunken eyes, and grim expression. Behind him, Raeder is holding a barrier before his face to prevent his being photographed. On Hess's left, Ribbentrop as usual has his chin raised and eyes closed. Behind him, Schirach is attending to his own writing rather than the proceedings. *R. D'Addario*

LEFT: Rebecca West described Ernst Kaltenbrunner as looking like "a particularly vicious horse," and many agreed. Among the defendants he and Streicher were the ones most strongly disliked. His ominous aspect and direct responsibility to Himmler raised shivers, and his testimony was shot through with unbelievable claims of innocence. *R. D'Addario* RIGHT: Otto Kranzbuehler, German naval judge advocate representing Adm. Doenitz, was generally regarded as one of the two or three best defense lawyers at Nuremberg. His skill in securing from U.S. Adm. Chester W. Nimitz a statement that the U.S. navy followed the same rules as the Germans for submarine attacks against surface vessels, gave vital legal protection to Doenitz and Raeder. *R. D'Addario* BELOW: The author at the lectern, cross-examining Field Marshal von Manstein. *R. D'Addario*

Erwin Lahousen, a former Austrian army intelligence officer who transferred to German military intelligence after the Anschluss, was the first witness brought before the Tribunal. As a top aide to Adm. Wilhelm Canaris, chief of German military intelligence, Lahousen was kept well informed by Keitel and Ribbentrop about Nazi policies and actions in conquered Poland, many of which were atrocious and criminal. His testimony (November 30, 1945), together with an American film on the Nazi concentration camps (presented the day before), gave the defendants their first heavy shock of shame and fear. *National Archives*

Few of the defendants were as jovial as Arthur Seyss-Inquart, and Papen, who sat next to him, called him "the complete Austrian, cheerful, relaxed, often telling Viennese stories." But he was an ardent Nazi. At the end of the war Seyss-Inquart, like Speer, resisted Hitler's "scorched earth" orders, but he was nevertheless condemned to be hanged, a fate he accepted with great *sangfroid*.
*R. D'Addario*

LEFT: Erich von dem Bach-Zelewski, an SS general active in Poland and other parts of the Eastern Front, was regarded by many, including Goering and Jodl, as one of Himmler's bloodiest hatchetmen. But when the author brought him before the Tribunal to testify for the prosecution, Biddle declared that "he looked like a mild and rather serious accountant." Bach-Zelewski gave strong testimony about the German armies' atrocities on the Eastern Front, and so maddened the military defendants that when he left the witness box, Goering shouted "*Schweinehund!*" at him. *Charles W. Alexander* RIGHT: In mid-February 1946, the Soviets brought from Russia Field Marshal Friedrich Paulus, the German commander at Stalingrad whose surrender had ended the battle. The sudden appearance of their former comrade-in-arms was no blessing to Goering, Keitel, and Jodl, for Paulus testified that Germany, and not the Soviet Union, had been the aggressor. The mere presence of Paulus in Nuremberg was far more startling than anything he had to say. *National Archives*

On April 24, 1946, Hans Bernd Gisevius, a member of the wartime anti-Hitler resistance in Germany, appeared as a defense witness for Wilhelm Frick. He had previously been called in behalf of another defendant, Hjalmar Schacht. Gisevius had much to say, and leveled a devastating attack on Goering. Most observers felt that Gisevius did little for Frick and much for Schacht, and left Goering covered with mud. *National Archives*

August 30, 1946, was the prosecution's last day in court. At its close the five prosecutors who had presented charges of organizational criminality before the Tribunal, posed together. *Left to right:* Champetier de Ribes, Thomas Dodd, Sir David Maxwell-Fyfe, Roman Rudenko, and the author. *National Archives*

~ *Soeben aus einem Bunker hervorgeholt.* ~

In Poland, few photographers were on hand to produce pictures such as this. The German inscription in gothic script at the bottom reads, in translation: "Just brought out of a bunker." In or near the Warsaw Ghetto, the Jews lying on the ground have just been found by German soldiers and pulled out of a protective hole of some kind. At the left, a couple appear to be consoling each other. *National Archives*

On October 1, 1946, the last day of the trial, the Tribunal acquitted three of the defendants. After the others had been sentenced to hanging or imprisonment, an open meeting was called to greet the three who had been freed—left to right, Papen (with handkerchief in breast pocket), Schacht, and Fritzsche. It was not a dignified affair. Fritzsche reveled in wine and cigarettes, Schacht sold his autograph for chocolate to nourish his hungry family, and Papen played the gentleman. Their freedom was of brief duration—before long, all three were convicted under German law.
R. D'Addario

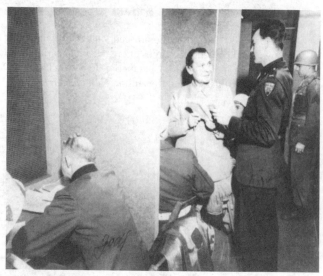

In one of the cubicles where the defendants were allowed to consult with their counsel (as Jodl is doing at left), Goering is charming a big American lieutenant, Jack Wheelis, known as "Tex." On the reverse side of the original of this picture, Goering wrote the inscription "To the great hunter from Texas." Goering also gave Tex several gifts, all of solid gold, among them a fountain pen and a cigarette case; Tex reciprocated by helping Goering's wife and daughter.
*Courtesy of Texas History Center, Austin*

Wheelis numbered among his friends yet another war crimes defendant. Walter Schellenberg, a young SS general and one of Heinrich Himmler's chosen aides, was on first-name terms with Tex. At a later Nuremberg trial, Schellenberg was convicted of war crimes and sentenced to six years' imprisonment. The nature of Wheelis's relations with Schellenberg and Goering, as well as with Goering's family, raises the possibility, if not the probability, that he helped Goering conceal the cyanide capsule with which he committed suicide.
*Courtesy of Texas History Center, Austin*

leading up to the invasion of the Soviet Union and read an affidavit, written and signed by Keitel, concerning what he had earlier called "ideological" directives and the joint roles of the army and SS in their execution:

> With the directives for the Barbarossa [code word for the plan to attack the Soviet Union] Plan for the administration and utilization of the conquered Eastern territories, the Wehrmacht was, against its intention and without knowledge of the conditions, drawn further and further into the subsequent developments and activities. . . .
>
> In reality it was not the Commander-in-Chief of the Army who had the executive power assigned to him and the power to decree and to maintain law in the occupied territories, but Himmler and Heydrich decided on their own authority the fate of the people and prisoners, including prisoners of war in whose camps they exercised the executive power.
>
> The traditional training and concept of duty of the German officers, which taught unquestioned obedience to superiors who bore responsibility, led to an attitude—regrettable in retrospect—which caused them to shrink from rebelling against these orders and these methods even when they recognized their illegality and inwardly refuted them.

As an explanation of the behavior of the Germans in Eastern Europe, Keitel's statement is helpful as far as it goes, but it overlooks the millions of German officers and men in their teens, twenties, and even thirties whose mental impressions of Slavs and Jews had been irreparably warped by Nazi doctrine. Keitel's apology, if such it may be called, did nothing to extenuate, let alone excuse, his miserable weakness.

Furthermore, the evidence showed that Keitel, even though he had tried to persuade Hitler to follow a lawful course, once he had failed, presented these orders to his subordinates forcefully and with no hint of his own inner doubts. For example, when the "ideological" orders (as Keitel called them) of September 8, 1941 (providing that "politically undesirable" Soviet civilians and prisoners of war should be turned over to Himmler's security "task forces" who would decide "their fate"), was shown to Admiral Wilhelm Canaris, the head of the OKW intelligence section, the Admiral sent Keitel a memorandum strongly criticizing the order as unlawful and based on "principles unknown to the Wehrmacht authorities." Keitel replied: "These objections arise from the military conception of chivalrous warfare. We are dealing here with the destruction of an ideology and therefore, I approve such measures and I sanction them." Thus Keitel did not merely sign the unlawful orders, he put his rank and authority behind them in order to drive unwilling subordinates into obedience.

There was plenty of material for cross-examination. Rudenko (who was supposed to take the lead) was brief and blunt. When Keitel disclosed that German troops had occupied parts of Moravia while President Emil Hácha was still on the way to Berlin to negotiate with Hitler, Rudenko barked: "This is treachery!" Keitel coolly replied: "I do not believe I need to add my judgment to the facts."

Fyfe was, as usual, thoroughly prepared and in no hurry. He took twice as long as Rudenko and again bore into the Stalag Luft III escapes, making more headway against Keitel than he had against Goering. Keitel, as Chief of OKW, had general responsibility in prisoner-of-war matters. Like Goering, he objected to Hitler's order that the fugitives captured by the police not be returned to the camp. But when Hitler insisted on the course of events which led to the murders, Keitel curtly overruled the objections of his subordinates in the prisoner-of-war section of OKW and directed that the camp authorities inform the inmates that their fellow prisoners had been shot as a warning against further escape attempts. Here again Keitel threw his authority behind Hitler's order with full knowledge of its criminal purpose.

Keitel's cross-examination ended with his admission that he had been "carrying out criminal orders in violation of one of the basic principles of our professional soldier's code," but that he "did not have any inner conviction of becoming criminal in so doing, since after all it was the head of the state who . . . held all the legislative power."

This seeming inconsistency led Nelte, in a brief redirect examination, to lay "the greatest importance" on Keitel's admission and again ask, "How was it possible and how do you explain that those orders and instructions were carried out and passed on by you and how it is that no effective resistance was met with?" Keitel replied:

> To find an explanation of this, I must say that you had to know the Führer. . . . I have often testified here that I wanted to give expression to my scruples, and that I did so. The Führer would then advance arguments which to him appeared decisive . . . stating the military and political necessities and making felt his concern for the welfare of his soldiers and . . . the future of our peoples. I must say that, because of that, but also because of the ever-increasing emergency, militarily speaking, in which we found ourselves, I convinced myself . . . of the necessity and the rightness of such measures. So I would transmit the orders that were given, and promulgated them without letting myself be deterred by any possible effects they might have.
>
> Perhaps this may be considered as weakness and perhaps I shall be accused of the same guilt. But at any rate, what I have told is the truth. . . . As far as I am concerned, and as a soldier, loyalty is sacred to me. I may be accused of having made mistakes, and also of having

shown weakness toward the Führer, Adolf Hitler, but never let it be said that I was cowardly, dishonorable, or faithless.

Lord Lawrence then asked Keitel whether he had ever put his protests to Hitler in writing. Keitel remembered only one such occasion. He had no copy and was unable to describe the nature of the issue. His testimony was finished, and he returned to the dock, where Goering scolded him for answering hard questions so frankly.

Nelte then called to the stand Hans Heinrich Lammers, Chief of the Reich Chancellery—an agency which stood in relation to Hitler as Chancellor somewhat the way OKW stood in relation to Hitler as Commander in Chief. Like Keitel, Lammers was an administrator and not a policymaker, but as a civil servant of long standing he knew every corner of governmental machinery, and as a Reich Minister he was a man of considerable prestige.

Nelte had called Lammers to confirm Keitel's statement of his limited authority as Chief of OKW, but when Lawrence realized this duplication he cut short Lammers's testimony, so it took only a few minutes. But under the Tribunal's practice, since Lammers had testified, counsel for the other accused were entitled to examine him. Nine defense counsel, representing defendants who held the rank of Reich Minister, did so. As Chief of the Reich Chancellery, Lammers had constant contact with the ministers, and their counsel were in most cases successful in drawing testimony from him to the general effect that the ministers were administrative officials who had little influence or even contact with Hitler in the formulation of state policy and thus small share in or responsibility for actions charged against them in the Indictment. This resulted in long cross-examinations by Elwyn Jones and Colonel Pokrovsky, who were armed with documents which cast these defendants and Lammers himself in a much more sinister light.

All of this took many hours that had nothing to do with Keitel, but the Tribunal on April 10 returned to his involvement in the Sagan case and called, as its own witness, General Adolf Westhoff, Keitel's subordinate (as a colonel) in the OKW prisoner-of-war section. Examined first by Fyfe and then by Nelte, Westhoff gave testimony that confirmed but added little to what Fyfe had established during his cross-examination of Keitel.

Colonel Pokrovsky, however, confronted with a senior German officer dealing with Soviet prisoners of war, was loaded for bear. Keitel and Westhoff had admitted that during the first year of the war (1941–1942) Soviet prisoners were not treated in accordance with the Hague and Geneva conventions, but they had not described the consequences. Pokrovsky now offered in evidence a memorandum dated February 19, 1942, from one Dr. Grotius of the OKW Economic and Armament Office, that discussed the shortage of manpower:

The present difficulties in the utilization of manpower would not have arisen had we decided in time to utilize the Russian prisoners-of-war on a larger scale. There were 3,900,000 Russians at our disposal, of which at present there are only 1,100,000 left. From November 1941 to January 1942 alone 500,000 Russians died. It will hardly be possible to increase the number of the Russian prisoners-of-war employed at present (400,000). If the typhus cases do decrease there may be a possibility of employing from 100,000 to 150,000 more for the economy.

In contrast with that, the employment of Russian civilians is constantly gaining greater importance. . . . The utilization of these Russians is exclusively a question of transportation. It is senseless to transport this manpower in open or unheated box cars and then to unload corpses at the place of destination.

Lawrence was openly shocked by this terrible accounting, but when the Tribunal rose for the lunch break Jodl was livid with rage, shouting that the winter of 1941–1942 had killed thousands of German soldiers. No doubt, too, many Russians were already half dead when captured. But thousands are not millions, and a considerable portion of the 2,800,000 dead Russian prisoners had been captured in the summer and fall of 1941. These deaths were clearly the result of Hitler's ideological orders. Besides, there is no parallel between a soldier who dies from lack of food or shelter while fighting and a prisoner of war who is deliberately left by his captors to die from cold or starvation.

Keitel's case had taken an unconscionably long time, and the strain on the participants was telling. On April 4, the Tribunal met in private with the chief prosecutors and representatives of the defense in an effort to reduce the volume of defense documents requiring translation. The meeting was amicable, but the next day, at a chief prosecutors' meeting, there was general dissatisfaction with the Tribunal's handling of the defense case, which all thought was taking much too long.

Jackson's criticism was especially sharp; he blamed the judges for not adopting the prosecution's earlier proposals, and added: "The Judges do not realize the atmosphere outside the court room and the political matters behind this case. . . . If the Court lets the defendants attack their [i.e., the Court's] country's policies it is rather hard for the Chief Prosecutors to laugh it off and forget, for after all we represent the authority of Nations."

Jackson was still angry at the Tribunal for not restraining Goering, and these new grievances were also festering in his mind. The result was that when the Tribunal opened the session on April 9, Jackson unexpectedly appeared at the lectern and announced that the printing of the defendants' documents "has proceeded in its abuses to such an extent that I must close the document room to printing documents for German counsel." Jackson's targets were the defendant Rosenberg and his counsel, Dr. Thoma, and his

complaint was that their Document Book I contained irrelevant philosophical "rubbish" and anti-Semitic statements describing Jews as a "bastard
population" and "arrogant in success, obsequious in failure."

There certainly was basis here for complaint, but Jackson's manner
and the absurdity of his taking so drastic a step on his own authority caused
Birkett to record: "The subject was unimportant, but the manner of Jackson's appearance was revealing and disturbing. He is a thoroughly upset
man because of his failure in cross-examining Goering."

Lawrence told Jackson that there must have been administrative mistakes, and this proved to be the case. The anti-Semitic statements had been
marked for elimination from the printing, and the documents should have
been reviewed by the prosecution before printing was ordered. But the
fracas took half the morning and left Jackson in an even angrier mood.
Biddle wrote:

> Bob Jackson came to see [Judge] Parker and me after lunch [the
> same day] in a very wild and uncontrolled mood. Apparently the
> criticism of his cross-examination of Goering has got way under his
> skin. He threatens to resign—this is not new; talks about refusing any
> printing of documents which he does not approve (irrespective, appar-
> ently, of what we order!); says Lawrence always rules against the
> Americans (this is absurd); says immense trouble has been caused to
> the morale of his organization by Katherine's [Biddle's wife] coming
> over (to which I say perhaps but that was authorized by the Presi-
> dent). . . . Bob still contends that the defendants are engaged in active
> propaganda, and the Tribunal is falling into disrepute, that Thoma
> violated an order (he doesn't know the facts). Parker and I tried to cool
> him off, said we'd help to prevent unnecessary printing, and agreed
> that Lawrence is too easy-going. Bob certainly has it in for me. He's
> very bitter. He seems to me very unfair and unhappy. I am sorry for
> him.

Certainly an unlovely picture of the relations between the leading
Americans at Nuremberg. The turn of the seasons from early March to
early April was a time of general malaise at the Palace of Justice, with
Jackson's crash, administrative difficulties, too many hours at the lectern
taken by Jackson and Fyfe as well as defense counsel, and Birkett moaning
into his diary that the caliber of the Tribunal "does not compare favorably
with the highest Courts in England and there has been much weakness and
vacillation. . . ." It had taken the Tribunal twenty-eight sessions to cover the
defenses of the first four accused.

**Kaltenbrunner:** Thus it was not until April 11 that the Ernst Kaltenbrunner case began. Tall and lantern-jawed, face pockmarked and scarred, the

defendant was the most ominous-looking man in the dock and had no friends there. Rebecca West wrote that he "looked like a vicious horse." But despite his sinister visage, Kaltenbrunner was, like his fellow Austrian Seyss-Inquart, a well-educated lawyer.

However, Gilbert's IQ examination tested Kaltenbrunner below all the other defendants except Streicher, though Kaltenbrunner's IQ was slightly above the "normal" range. He joined the Austrian Nazi party in 1932 and the SS a few months later. He became a strong supporter of Anschluss, and after it came was appointed a government official in the fields of intelligence and security. In January 1943, seven months after the assassination of Reinhard Heydrich, Kaltenbrunner replaced him as Chief of the Reich Security Main Office (RSHA), where he was immediately responsible to Heinrich Himmler, the Reichsfuehrer SS (Head of the SS).

As Chief of the RSHA, Kaltenbrunner, like Heydrich, had authority over both the SD (Security Service) and the Gestapo (Secret State Police), which was headed by Heinrich Mueller.° It was a basic part of Kaltenbrunner's defense, which his counsel, Dr. Kurt Kauffmann, developed early in his questioning, that Kaltenbrunner's authority over Mueller was only formal and that Himmler continued to deal directly with Mueller, whose direct authority extended to imprisonment and execution orders. The defendant also sought to distance himself from Adolf Eichmann (the two had known each other since their early years in Austria) and Oswald Pohl, Chief of the SS Economic and Administrative Office, which had administrative responsibility for the concentration camps. Kaltenbrunner thus endeavored to narrow his sphere of responsibility to the intelligence services of the SD.

Thereafter, Kauffmann followed the example of Dr. Nelte and Keitel by confronting Kaltenbrunner with one after another of the criminal events with which the prosecution had targeted his client. Relying heavily on the limits of his responsibility as he had described them, Kaltenbrunner denied guilt for each and every event. Of some, he had never heard; in others, he had not been involved; if the document bore his typed signature, someone else had put it there without his knowledge; if the signature was handwritten, it had been forged.

For example, Kauffmann put before his client a report from the adjutant of the Mauthausen concentration camp that in January 1945 some fifteen uniformed American soldiers of a military mission, captured behind the German lines in the Balkans, were brought to Mauthausen. The adjutant stated that the camp commandant then told him: "Now Kaltenbrunner has approved the executions." The letter to the commandant was secret and "signed, Kaltenbrunner." The defendant denied all knowledge of the event and declared that he could not possibly have signed the letter.

---

°"Gestapo" Mueller disappeared at the end of the war, and his fate is unknown.

Otto Ohlendorf, whom Kaltenbrunner described as "one of my chief collaborators," testified that after Kaltenbrunner became Chief of RSHA, he "had to concern himself" with the Einsatzgruppen and "consequently must have known the background of the Einsatzgruppen which were under his authority." When Dr. Kauffmann questioned Kaltenbrunner about this testimony, Kaltenbrunner replied that he had no idea of the existence of these Einsatzkommandos as described by Ohlendorf, that he first learned of them in 1943, that by then the Einsatzgruppen had been put under other command, and that he himself had no involvement with them.

In similar vein, Kaltenbrunner asserted that he had only once visited a concentration camp (Mauthausen), denied that he ever saw a gas chamber, and denied virtually everything else that Kauffmann put to him. His credibility was already at a low ebb when he was cross-examined by Colonel Amen, who soon produced testimony from three persons, one of whom had known Kaltenbrunner previously in Austria. All three testified that Kaltenbrunner had visited Mauthausen at least three times. Two of them testified that he examined the crematorium and one that he had gone into the gas chamber and witnessed executions. Kaltenbrunner denied all of these statements.

Later Amen called attention to Kaltenbrunner's earlier testimony that he had nothing to do with the Nazis' forced labor program. Kaltenbrunner now testified that he had had no correspondence with the burgomaster of Vienna, SS Brigadefuehrer Blaschke. Amen then read to him a letter signed by hand "Yours, Kaltenbrunner," replying to a letter of June 7, 1944, from the burgomaster and addressed by Kaltenbrunner's hand to "Dear Blaschke." The letter to Blaschke informed him that "four transports with approximately 12,000 Jews" would shortly reach Vienna, where workers were needed to construct military defenses south of that city. The letter continued:

> According to previous experience it is estimated that 30 per cent of the transport will consist of Jews able to work, approximately 3,600 in this case, who can be utilized for the work in question, it being understood that they are subject to removal at any time. . . .
> The women and children of these Jews who are unable to work, and who are all being kept in readiness for a special action and therefore one day will be removed again, must stay in the guarded camp also during the day.

The "special action" was, of course, extermination of the Jews, and the letter put the writer in the middle of slave labor and the "final solution." Kaltenbrunner insisted that he was not the writer, but could not explain the signature, which matched perfectly examples of his hand. Amen abandoned all pretense of questioning: "Is it not a fact that you are simply lying about your signature on this letter in the same way that you are lying to the Tribunal about almost everything else you have given testimony about?" Kaltenbrunner lost control and shouted that "for a whole year I have been submitted to this insult of being called a liar." He spoke incoherently, saying that his mother "who died in 1943 was called a whore and many other things were hurled at me." Lawrence told Kaltenbrunner to try to restrain himself, but would have done better to tell Amen to ask questions and not bully the witness.

Reactions to Kaltenbrunner's performance were mixed. Discussing his handling of Amen's cross-examination, Dr. von der Lippe wrote:

> Some of the audience are impressed by his intellectual capacity, and the Tribunal follows it with interest, even with a sort of appreciation of Kaltenbrunner's cold-blooded dialectic. Many viewers are of the opinion that Kaltenbrunner, who under all the circumstances is a lost man, is better off than Keitel, who in a like situation, did not have the angry strength to resist in the same way.

And an echo of these impressions came from Judge Birkett:

> Kaltenbrunner is making a vigorous defense, denying his signature to documents of a most incriminating nature, endeavoring to show that he was really without power or influence. He is a fluent speaker and speaks with great animation and uses much gesture. In some matters he is no doubt right and it is then that he grows animated. Some of the things attributed to him are no doubt exaggerated, but it is impossible to think of the position occupied by Kaltenbrunner and, at the same time, to believe that he was ignorant of so many matters.

The last clause of Birkett's diary entry was the principal theme of the defendants' comments at lunch and in their cells with Dr. Gilbert. There was much contempt for Kaltenbrunner, and of the nine defendants Gilbert mentioned—Goering, Doenitz, Fritzsche, Frank, Raeder, Seyss-Inquart, Speer, Schacht, and Papen—all thought Kaltenbrunner was lying.

After Kaltenbrunner had returned to the dock, Kauffmann called as a witness Rudolf Franz Ferdinand Hoess, who had been Commandant at Auschwitz from May 1940 to December 1943. For a lawyer defending Kaltenbrunner (or any of the other defendants), it was an extraordinary decision.

Without initially mentioning his client, Kauffmann drew from Hoess, without difficulty, testimony that while he was Commandant, "hundreds of thousands of human beings were sent to their deaths" at Auschwitz. Based on information given him by Adolf Eichmann, "the man who had the task of organizing and assembling these people," over 2 million Jewish "men, women, and children had been destroyed."

Subsequently, Hoess testified that Kaltenbrunner had never visited Auschwitz and that the two had met only once, in 1944 after Hoess had left Auschwitz. Orders for executions at Auschwitz were "practically all" signed by Herman Mueller, with a very few signed by Himmler or Kaltenbrunner.

Hoess had joined the Nazi Party in 1922 and the SS in 1934. Thereafter his profession was the management of concentration camps at Dachau and Sachsenhausen prior to Auschwitz. From December 1943 to the end of the war, Hoess was in Berlin as a section chief, under Oswald Pohl, in the Inspectorate of concentration camps. Hoess was accustomed to violence; in 1924 he had been involved in a "political murder" and was sentenced to a long prison term. But at Nuremberg, von der Lippe remarked his "weak, high voice" and thought that he "looked harmless, at least at a distance."

Colonel Amen, on cross-examination, encountered no difficulties. He at once destroyed Kauffmann's point that most of the execution orders were signed "Mueller," by getting from Hoess an admission that Mueller signed as representative of the Chief of RSHA who, after December 1942, was Kaltenbrunner.

After that Amen read an affidavit Hoess had previously signed that established more precisely the Auschwitz death toll. From the beginning in 1940 to December 1, 1943, "at least 2,500,000 victims were executed and exterminated there by gassing and burning, and at least another half million succumbed to starvation and disease, making about 3,000,000." Among them were "approximately 20,000 Russian prisoners-of-war . . . who were delivered at Auschwitz in Wehrmacht transports operated by regular Wehrmacht officers and men." The total was approximately the same number as that of the Soviet prisoners of war who died of exposure and starvation.

Dr. Gilbert, astonished by Hoess's apathy and matter-of-factness, questioned him several times in an effort to understand his indifference. Hoess responded:

> Don't you see, we SS men were not supposed to think about these things; it never even occurred to us. And besides, it was something already taken for granted that the Jews were to blame for everything. . . . It was not just newspapers like *Stürmer* but it was everything we ever heard. Even our military and ideological training took for granted that we had to protect Germany from the Jews. . . . We were all so trained to obey orders without even thinking that the thought of disobeying an order would never have occurred to anybody.

It is beyond understanding that Hoess was put on the witness stand not, like Ohlendorf or Bach-Zelewski, by prosecution counsel but by the defense. Considering the broad range of Kaltenbrunner's activities, there was little to be gained by attempting to prove that he was never at Auschwitz and never personally signed a death order there.

The consequences were not limited to Kaltenbrunner. The awful scale of the Nazi terror—produced by a Fuehrer to whom the defendants had pledged and given their allegiance, and by Himmler, Heydrich, Pohl, Mueller, and other leaders of the Nazi government—cast a pall of shame over the defendants and their counsel. No wonder Dr. von der Lippe described the effect of the Hoess testimony as "crushing" (niederschmetternd).

**Rosenberg:** Alfred Rosenberg was a Baltic German, born in Reval and educated in Riga and Moscow, who emigrated to Germany in 1918 and joined the Nazi Party a year later. He had started writing articles for a small Munich newspaper; its themes were congenial to Hitler, and Rosenberg became editor of the Nazi newspaper Voelkischer Beobachter (People's Observer). Later his books on Jews and Freemasons gave Rosenberg stature as a Nazi theoretician, and his The Myth of the Twentieth Century (1930) was deemed second only to Mein Kampf as a Nazi bible, even though many snickered at it. Rosenberg never made much headway with other Party leaders; as with Ribbentrop, his advancement was based almost solely on Hitler's continued good opinion.

Rosenberg's political ascent began when he was elected to the Reichstag in 1930. In 1934 Hitler appointed him head of the Nazi Party's Office of Foreign Affairs and Deputy for the "Spiritual and Ideological Training of the Nazi Party." None of these positions was of managerial or policymaking importance, but that was not true of his final appointment, in July 1941, as Reich Minister for the Occupied Eastern Territories.

Rosenberg was not a menacing figure like Kaltenbrunner, and there was nothing of the soldier, diplomat, or boss about him. Doenitz thought him "a man who would not hurt a fly," and in his manner of speech he certainly smelled of the lamp. As a witness he was maddeningly verbose and drove both his counsel (Dr. Alfred Thoma) and Lawrence to distraction with his insistence on treating every question as raising theoretical and historical matters. It was much easier to find him irritating than evil, and it was not until the evidence was forced onto the stage that one became aware of the atrocious consequences of this woolly and maundering man's activities.

Before the war, Rosenberg had become acquainted with Vidkun Quisling, a Norwegian politician and founder of a quasi-Nazi political party, the

Nasjonal Samling. In June 1939, Quisling came to Germany and, while visiting Rosenberg, spoke alarmingly of the danger of a British or Soviet occupation of Norway in the event of war. Rosenberg testified in detail about the ensuing consequences of the meeting, at which Quisling stressed the military value of a German occupation of Norway. Rosenberg persuaded Hitler to receive Quisling and hear his report and also spoke to Admiral Raeder about him. Thereafter Rosenberg passed on to Hitler Quisling's reports on developments in Norway, which were delivered by Quisling's associate, Viljam Hagelin. As a result of these reports and meetings, Raeder became a strong advocate of a German occupation of Norway, which eventually took place in April 1940. The defendant's own account clearly established his participation in bringing about the occupation.

Rosenberg next testified briefly with regard to the Einsatzstab Rosenberg, an organization set up in 1940 under the auspices of the Nazi Party to seize art objects and other valuable properties abandoned by or taken from Jews and other disfavored owners. There had been extensive documentary testimony about the Einsatzstab presented by the French and Soviet prosecutions. Rosenberg portrayed these unlawful seizures as intended to safeguard abandoned property and protect artworks from bomb damage. He admitted, however, that he "had the hope that at least a large part of these objects would remain in Germany."

The greater part of Rosenberg's testimony dealt with his role and actions as Minister of Occupied Eastern Territories, i.e., the German-occupied parts of the Soviet Union.* On April 2, 1941—nearly twelve weeks before the initial attack against the Soviet Union—Hitler told Rosenberg that he would be made "a political adviser in a decisive capacity" in the coming invasion. Rosenberg at once set to work on "the possible treatment of political problems and possible measures to be taken in the territories to be occupied in the East." On July 17, 1941, by which time there were already broad areas of "occupied" Soviet Union, Rosenberg was appointed Reich Minister, with primary authority over civil administration. These facts adequately established Rosenberg's participation in the aggressive war against the Soviet Union.

Rosenberg testified that he had friendly feelings for the Soviet people, especially the Ukrainians. To whatever extent these protestations were genuine, his hopes were dashed at the policy conference of July 16, 1941, attended by Hitler, Goering, Keitel, Bormann, Lammers, and Rosenberg, about which Goering had previously testified. Overriding, as usual, objections from any of the others, Hitler laid down the major policies and aims: ultimate annexation of the entire Baltic area, the Volga Germanic region,

---

*The German-occupied areas of Poland, not annexed to the Reich, were under Hans Frank as Governor-General.

the Crimea, and Transcaucasia; a general policy to dominate, administer, and exploit the captured areas; pacification to be achieved by the sternest methods, including the "eradication of everyone who opposes us."

Rosenberg's appointment as Minister was accompanied by a Hitler decree covering the entire administration of the occupied areas. It stated that the Minister should "coordinate . . . his wishes with those of the other supreme authorities . . . and in the event of differences of opinion to seek a decision by the Führer."

These "other supreme authorities" included the military commanders, Himmler as Chief of the German Police, Goering as head of the Four-Year Plan, and Sauckel as Plenipotentiary for Allocation of Labor. Naturally, Rosenberg's testimony stressed these many and important limits on his own authority as a means of shifting from himself responsibility for the many criminal aspects of the German occupation.

The rest of Rosenberg's direct testimony embodied his efforts to portray himself as a frequent investigator and reporter of German atrocities and an unsuccessful appellant to Hitler for less inhumane occupation policies. Dodd's cross-examination soon changed the picture. He asked Rosenberg: "Did you carry out the compulsory labor directives under your ministry, force people to leave their homes and their communities to go to Germany to work for the German state?" Confronted with his own order that "all inhabitants of the Occupied Eastern Territories are subject to the public liability for compulsory work," Rosenberg had to agree that the answer to Dodd's question was yes.

Later Rosenberg was confronted with a speech he had delivered on June 20, 1941 (just before the invasion of Russia), to a group of German government officials assigned to occupation duties. Some vacuous comments on the "Russian soul" aside, Rosenberg had declared:

> The job of feeding the German people stands this year, without doubt, at the top of the list of Germany's claims on the East. . . . We see absolutely no reason for any obligation on our part to feed also the Russian people with the products of that surplus-territory. We know that this is a harsh necessity, beyond feelings. A very extensive evacuation will be necessary, without any doubt, and it is sure that the future will hold very hard years in store for the Russians.

Seize the crops and send them to Germany, seize the Russians that are employable and drive the rest of them to the East—such was the fate of the Russian civilians as Rosenberg envisaged it.

Toward the end of his cross-examination Rosenberg's memorandum of his meeting with Hitler on December 14, 1941, was produced, showing that they discussed the text of a speech which Rosenberg was planning to deliver (he never did) in the Berlin Sportpalast. The second paragraph of the memorandum included the following:

> I [Rosenberg] took the view not to speak of the extermination [*Ausrottung*] of Jewry. The Führer affirmed this view and said that they had laid the burden of war on us and that they had brought the destruction; it is no wonder if the results would strike them first.

Rosenberg admitted that he knew that mass murders of Jews by the Einsatzgruppen were already taking place in the occupied areas. He made a weak argument that *Ausrottung* could have "various meanings," but the context and contemporary events showed clearly enough that *Ausrottung* meant just what the German dictionaries say: "eradication, extermination."

**Frank:** Hans Frank was no more attractive than most of his fellow defendants, but he was among the more interesting. A lawyer by profession, he joined the Nazi Party in 1927 and two years later, at the age of twenty-nine, became the Party's principal lawyer. In 1933 Hitler appointed him a minister and Reich Commissioner for Justice. Frank founded and was the first President of the Academy of German Law. He was a reserve officer and served in the army during the invasion of Poland. On October 26, 1939, Hitler appointed him Governor-General of the remnant of prewar Poland that became known as the "Government-General." This position he held until the end of the war.

Frank was intelligent (seventh man on Gilbert's IQ scale), well educated, sensitive to the arts, and a skilled pianist. Given these tastes, it is not surprising that Frank made his headquarters not in war-battered Warsaw, but in the beautiful and lightly damaged city of Cracow, in southern Poland.

The Italian journalist and writer Curzio Malaparte (author of the elegant, sardonic book *Kaputt*, an account of his wartime travels), who visited Poland during the winter of 1941–1942, spent considerable time dining and talking with Frank and his entourage. Malaparte paints a vivid word picture of Frank—"The German King of Poland," as he liked to be called:

> Before me sat Frank on his high stiff-backed chair in the old Polish royal palace of the Wawel in Cracow, as if he were sitting on the throne of the Jagellos and the Sobieskis. He appeared to be fully persuaded that the great Polish traditions of royalty and chivalry were being revived in him. There was a light of innocent pride on his face, with its pale, swollen cheeks and the hooked nose suggesting a will

both vainglorious and uncertain. His black glossy hair was brushed back revealing a high ivory-white forehead. There was something at once childish and senile in him in his dull, pouting lips of an angry child, in his prominent eyes with their thick, heavy eyelids that seemed to be too large for his eyes, and in his habit of keeping his eyelids lowered—thus cutting two deep, straight furrows across his temples.

The weaknesses perceived by Malaparte when Frank was in his glory emerged more vividly at the end of the war when Frank was arrested and brought to Nuremberg. Before he arrived there Frank had made an attempt (perhaps not genuine) to commit suicide. He converted (or reconverted°) to the Catholic faith. He professed feelings of remorse and guilt, but his moods fluctuated wildly from sullen silence to rhetorical pronouncements on whatever came into his flighty mind.

The day before Frank took the witness stand, he told Dr. Gilbert: "I will be the first to admit my guilt." Asked by Gilbert, "In what way do you feel guilt?" Frank replied: "Because I was an ardent Nazi and did not kill him [Hitler]."

Early in his testimony, Frank carried out his decision in a way that reflected both shrewdness and instability:

DR. SEIDL [Frank's counsel]: Witness, what do you have to say regarding the accusations which have been brought against you in the Indictment?

FRANK: . . . I myself, speaking from the depths of my feelings and having lived through the 5 months of this trial, want to say that now after I have gained a full insight into all the horrible atrocities which have been committed, I am possessed by a deep sense of guilt. . . .

SEIDL: Did you ever participate in the annihilation of the Jews?

FRANK: I say "yes," and the reason why I say "yes," is because, having lived through the 5 months of this trial, and particularly after having heard the testimony of the witness Hoess, my conscience does not allow me to throw the responsibility solely on these minor people. I myself never installed an extermination camp for Jews, or promoted the existence of such camps, but if Adolf Hitler personally has laid that dreadful responsibility on his people, then it is mine too, for we have fought against Jewry for years, and we have indulged in the most terrible utterances—my own diary bears witness against me. Therefore, it is no more than my duty to answer your question with "yes." A thousand years will pass and still this guilt of Germany will not have been erased.†

---

°It is said that Frank had early been an Old Catholic, but the religious sequence is vague.

†This last sentence has been repeatedly quoted in books and other publications about the Nazi period.

The reference to "my own diary" is to the forty-three volumes of Frank's diary of his Governor-Generalship, which he voluntarily turned over to the American soldiers who arrested him. Testifying, he explained that he did this because "when, on 30 April 1945, Adolf Hitler ended his life, I resolved to reveal that responsibility of mine to the world as clearly as possible."

Thus Frank's "confession" was shrouded in claims that he had not known of the worst atrocities while he was Governor-General, but only when informed of them at Nuremberg, and that he himself had not perpetrated the atrocities. He treated his own guilt as civic rather than personal. No wonder that Jodl, Fritzsche, Speer, and others questioned the reality of Frank's confession. Dr. von der Lippe was more explicit. He saw Frank as "cold, complacent, sometimes mawkish," and regarded the "confession" as provoking doubt of Frank's sincerity: "The hearers asked why Herr Frank, instead of an individual confession of guilt, gave us this remarkable confession in behalf of the entire German people?"

Frank described his decision not to destroy the diary as a contribution to knowledge of the truth about the Third Reich. But he lost sight of that purpose when confronted with passages that incriminated him. Tom Dodd, Executive Trial Counsel and now doing most of the cross-examination for the American prosecution, referred to some Polish professors at the University of Cracow whom the Germans had seized and transported to the Oranienburg concentration camp near Berlin. Frank recorded in his diary his own statement that the professors should be returned to Poland for either imprisonment or liquidation. He replied: "I did say all that merely to hoodwink my enemies; in reality I liberated the professors."

More generally, Frank declared:

> One has to take the diary as a whole. You cannot go through 43 volumes and pick out single sentences and separate them from the context. I would like to say that I do not want to argue or quibble about individual phrases. It was a wild and stormy period filled with terrible passions and when a whole country is on fire and a life and death struggle is going on, such words may easily be used.

Such was Frank's defense against the many passages in his diary which portray him as a participant in the forced labor program, the ghetto life of the Jews, the degradation of the Poles, and other atrocious features of the Nazi system in the Government-General. Apart from the diary, the main focus of Frank's defense was virtually identical with Rosenberg's: to stress the limits of his own authority, his subservience to Hitler's policies, and the overarching role of Himmler and the SS.

These limits were real, and efforts to restrain either Himmler or

Sauckel were generally futile. But these factors do not exculpate men like Frank who gave their allegiance to Hitler to the end and who signed the decrees and gave the orders for the criminal actions of the Nazis during the occupations of Poland and other countries.

Hans Frank admitted his guilt in his own way, but that was a long way from pleading guilty to the Indictment.

**Frick:** The trial was moving faster. Frank's case lasted only a little over two days. Wilhelm Frick decided to follow Hess's example and give no testimony. The presentation of documents by his counsel, Dr. Otto Pannenbecker, took barely an hour; their contents, by this time predictable, were intended to show that Frick, despite his many resounding titles, had very little authority over or involvement in actions that raised questions of criminality.

Like Frank, Frick was trained in the law. He entered the civil service and in the early 1920s was a police official in Bavaria. Frick became an ardent Nazi and marched with Hitler in the abortive 1923 putsch in Munich. During the early Nazi years Frick, partly because of his administrative experience, was a valued member of Hitler's staff. When Hitler became Chancellor in 1933, Frick, Goering, and the Fuehrer himself were the only Nazi members of the new Cabinet. Frick served as Minister of the Interior from 1933 until 1943, when he was appointed Reich Protector of Bohemia and Moravia and Reich Minister without Portfolio.

Frick was the consummate bureaucrat—stiff, orderly, taciturn, unimaginative—and the least interesting of all the defendants. Gilbert could get virtually nothing out of him, and Gilbert's published diary records no visit to Frick's cell until April 22, just before his case was called. Gilbert's first entry of any significance described a discussion on January 3, 1946, at the lunch break after Ohlendorf's testimony about the Einsatzgruppen killings of hundreds of thousands of Jews:

> Fritzsche was so depressed, he could not eat. Frick, however, remarked how nice it would be to be able to go skiing in this fine weather. Fritzsche stopped eating and looked at me [Gilbert] in desperation, then glared at Frick.

Frick was, indeed, a very cold fish.

Frick had drafted and signed so many laws and decrees, and devised so many governmental organizations and reorganizations dealing with occupied countries, annexations, anti-Jewish measures, and war agencies, that he had no hope of acquittal. But he thought he might escape the gallows if he could sufficiently distance himself from Himmler and shake off responsibility for Gestapo actions. He told Gilbert that "he would not take the stand himself, but would have one witness, Gisevius, one-time Gestapo official, who would also testify for Schacht."

In the summer of 1933 Hans Bernd Gisevius passed his law examinations and secured a junior position in the Prussian Secret Police, soon to be widely known as the Gestapo. He was anti-Nazi, rather fiercely righteous, and immediately became critical of the course of events. Soon he became an important figure in German resistance groups. Early in 1946 he published a book recounting these experiences entitled *Bis zum bittern Ende,* which was widely read and regarded as a sensational exposé of Nazism.°

Gisevius had held minor office under both Goering and Frick and was fully familiar with the various shifts in authority over the Gestapo during the years from 1933 to 1936. That was the evidence that Frick wanted from his witness. But Gisevius had much to say about other defendants. Before court opened on the morning of April 24, Gilbert overheard Streicher ask Frick whether Gisevius was really going to appear:

> Frick assured him he was. Streicher asked whether he would really say all those nasty things about Goering that people were saying he had written in his book. Frick said he supposed he would. To Streicher's question whether that would be bad for Goering, Frick answered coolly: "I should worry. I only care about staying alive myself."

Later on Gilbert overheard Rosenberg scolding Frick for bringing in a witness who would give testimony damaging to the defendants. Frick, cool as ever, retorted: "Will you please leave my defense to me? I didn't stick my neck into yours, just let me handle my own. If I hadn't called him, Schacht would have called him anyhow."

Gisevius testified that traditionally administration of the police was in the Ministry of the Interior, but Frick soon found that Goering, as Prime Minister of Prussia, and later Himmler, as head of the SS, were poaching in his domain. Dismissed from the Secret Police, Gisevius found employment in the Interior Ministry. Frick gave Gisevius some protection, and Gisevius informed Frick of illegal actions by the Gestapo under Goering's command. But these efforts to defeat Goering and Himmler were unsuccessful, and in 1936 Hitler officially gave Himmler full control of police and civil security matters. Gisevius's brief recital of the facts removed Frick from the direct responsibility for police atrocities, but this alone was of little

---

°Published in English in 1947 under its translated title, *To the Bitter End.* Many readers have questioned its accuracy, and perhaps Gisevius was gilding his own lily. But the general authenticity of his book is powerfully supported in an Introduction by Allen W. Dulles, who headed the OSS office in Zurich during the war and subsequently was Director of the CIA.

moment, considering the massive documentation harmful to Frick on other matters.

It soon became apparent that, for Gisevius, Frick's problems were of small moment and that his immediate target was Hermann Goering. The witness began by accusing Goering of turning the Secret Police into a "robbers' den" where unlawful arrests, murders, and protective warrants for murderers were common practice. Gisevius then declared that the so-called "Roehm Putsch" of June 30, 1934, was misnamed; that neither Roehm nor the SA which he led was planning anything subversive, and that the putsch was in fact a Goering-Himmler conspiracy to eliminate Roehm and destroy the SA as a force in German politics. Goering, in charge of the Berlin part of the conspiracy, was responsible for the murder of "a large number of innocent people."

No words were too derogatory to be applied to Goering. Gisevius's testimony describing Goering's actions during the Nazi government's early years was plainly calculated to confute Goering's version of that period in his own testimony.

But these jailings and murders, however criminal in German law, were not war crimes, nor easily seen as part of a conspiracy to initiate aggressive war. Their relevance to Frick's case was dubious, and under other circumstances the Tribunal, pushing as it was for brevity, would undoubtedly have cut Gisevius short. However, the testimony was dramatic and historically fascinating, and the Tribunal may also have felt that since Goering had been allowed to say his say without much interruption, his antagonist deserved the same.

Shortly before Pannenbecker finished his questioning, Gisevius raised the tension even higher by exposing a clumsy effort by Goering to prevent him from discussing the notorious "Blomberg-Fritsch affair." Gisevius asked the Tribunal for permission to discuss "an incident which occurred this morning" when he overheard a conversation between Stahmer and Dix (Schacht's counsel). Stahmer at once interrupted to challenge Gisevius's right to reveal a "personal discussion with Dr. Dix concerning the Blomberg case" which "was not intended to be heard by the witness."

Jackson, always eager to find fault with defense counsel, at once intervened: "The incident has been reported to me, and I think it is important that this Tribunal know the influence—the threats that were made at this witness in this courthouse while waiting to testify here, threats not only against him but against the defendant Schacht. . . . I ask that this Tribunal allow Dr. Gisevius, who is the one representative of democratic forces in Germany, to take this stand to tell his story."

In January 1938, Field Marshal Werner von Blomberg, then Commander in Chief of the Wehrmacht (the only army officer ever to hold that title), had married a young woman who had a police record of prostitution.

This fact did not become public, but was rumored in military circles and caused Hitler to relieve Blomberg of his post and from any further military service.

After the war, Blomberg had been confined at Nuremberg as a potential witness, but he was very infirm and soon died. Goering, claiming a wish to protect the deceased Blomberg's reputation from suffering public exposure of his wife's past history, told Stahmer that if Schacht's witness Gisevius testified about the affair, he (Goering) "would not spare Schacht," as Stahmer put it. Stahmer had passed this information to Dix during the conversation Gisevius overheard that morning.

Stahmer declared that he had spoken to Dix "as one colleague to another," presumably meaning that he was doing Dix a favor by warning him of Goering's intentions. Dix corroborated most of what Stahmer had stated, but added that Stahmer had quoted Goering as threatening that he would " 'disclose everything against Schacht'—and he knows lots of things about Schacht which may not be pleasant for Schacht." Not surprisingly, Dix interpreted Stahmer's message as more of a threat than a favor.

Lawrence then gave Gisevius the green light, but the witness declared he had nothing more to say about Blomberg's marriage; rather it was Goering's part in the affair, which he would expose later on. Pannenbecker had only a few more questions bearing on Frick, and then Dix started his questions dealing with the case for Schacht, which took much longer than Frick's.

The following morning, April 25, Dix asked his witness to describe the "Fritsch crisis," the reference being to General Werner von Fritsch, Commander in Chief of the German Army from 1934 until his forced retirement in early February 1938. Despite Gisevius's previous denial, his account of the crisis involved Blomberg as well as Fritsch, with Goering and Himmler as the villains of the piece.

The gist of the Blomberg-Fritsch affair, which Gisevius described at some length, was that Goering had shown the police file on the new Frau von Blomberg to Hitler in order to put an end to Blomberg's career. Himmler also had a file, which named an army officer named Fritsch or Frisch as sexually involved with one Schmidt, a male prostitute. In Hitler's presence, Goering confronted General Fritsch with Schmidt, who identified the general as the officer named in Himmler's file.

Despite Fritsch's denial, Hitler suspended him from his command and soon thereafter informed a group of senior generals about these developments. He then appointed General Walter von Brauchitsch to replace Fritsch as Commander in Chief of the army. Hitler himself replaced Blomberg as Commander in Chief of the Wehrmacht. Goering was promoted to Field Marshal and thus became the senior officer of the military establishment. Hitler also replaced Neurath with Ribbentrop as Foreign Minister, appointed Funk Minister of Economics, and made other governmental changes of less importance.

The result was a great strengthening of Hitler's dominance of the German government. Gisevius and his coconspirators had been counting on Blomberg, Fritsch, General Ludwig Beck, and like-minded officers and officials to check what they regarded as the criminal, reckless Nazi policies. Now Blomberg was out of the picture. Fritsch was tried before a military court of honor and fully acquitted of the charge,° but Brauchitsch remained Commander in Chief and Fritsch was given no new assignment. Beck remained Chief of Staff for only a few months. Neurath and Schacht were deprived of their positions of authority in diplomacy and economics and were replaced by yes-men. Hitler, flanked by Goering, Himmler, and Goebbels, held virtually absolute power.

The victory had been won by vile and treacherous means. Blomberg, guilty of nothing but a professionally injudicious marriage, was sacked, and his name was stricken from the army list. Fritsch, broken by the false charges of Goering and Himmler, died on the field of battle in Poland.† Goering's machinations were, of course, not war crimes, but insofar as their purpose was to remove officials who appeared as obstacles to aggressive military plans, these actions might plausibly be described as part of a conspiracy to prepare for war under Count One of the Indictment.

After defense counsel had finished questioning Gisevius, Jackson's inquiry was only nominally a cross-examination. The two men had met soon after the war; Jackson knew the witness's story and had already saluted him as a "representative of democratic Germany." But Jackson's forensic posture was uneasy, as he would soon be cross-examining Schacht, whom he regarded as the American prosecution's prime quarry, whereas Gisevius had just given strong testimony in support of Schacht.

Clearly, Jackson was in no position to challenge the sincerity or the intelligence of Gisevius's appraisal of Schacht. But to ask him no questions at all would have appeared like a surrender. Carefully avoiding questions that might lead to confrontation, Jackson elicited testimony that Schacht had thought well of both Hitler and Goering during the first five years of the Nazi regime and did not turn against them until the end of 1937.

Jackson then turned to easier game and undid whatever benefit Gisevius had brought to Frick. Gisevius readily agreed that despite the

°The individual named in Himmler's file turned out to be a retired Captain Frisch.

†After Fritsch was cleared of the charges, he was "rehabilitated" by being given the title of *Chef* of Artillery Regiment 12, which he had commanded years earlier. The appointment was purely honorary (the regular regimental commander was entitled *Kommandeur*), but Fritsch insisted on accompanying the regiment during the attack on Poland in August 1939. He was killed near Warsaw by a Polish bullet. It is doubtful that he committed suicide, but he certainly risked his life unnecessarily.

difficulties Frick had with Goering and Himmler, he had full knowledge of their criminal handling of the Gestapo and legal responsibility for the consequences. This was manifest, for example, from Frick's signature on the decree legitimizing the killings during the Roehm purge.

Frick and Schacht were then forgotten as Jackson, obviously knowing what answers he would get, swung the spotlight on other defendants. After Heydrich's death, did Kaltenbrunner's appointment cause any improvement in the behavior of the Gestapo? "Kaltenbrunner came and things became worse from day to day," Gisevius replied. "More and more we learned that the impulsive actions of a murderer like Heydrich were not so bad as the cold legal logic of a lawyer who took over the administration of such a dangerous instrument as the Gestapo." Kaltenbrunner had "an even more sadistic attitude than Himmler." Was the Foreign Office informed of the crimes of the Gestapo? Gisevius could speak only of the period when Neurath was Foreign Minister; during those years, reports from the Ministry of the Interior describing Gestapo crimes were sent to the Chief of Protocol, who "often submitted that material to Neurath."

Gisevius's testimony was especially damaging to Keitel, who had portrayed himself as a mere amanuensis to Hitler, with little power of his own. Asked by Jackson "whether Keitel occupied a position of real leadership and power in the Reich," the witness replied:

> Keitel occupied one of the most influential positions in the Third Reich. . . .
> It may be that Keitel did not influence Hitler to a great extent. But I must testify that Keitel influenced the OKW and the Army all the more. Keitel decided which documents were to be transmitted to Hitler. It was not possible for Admiral Canaris or one of the other . . . [OKW staff members] to submit an urgent report to Hitler of his own accord. Keitel took it over, and what he did not like he did not transmit, or he gave these men the official order to abstain from making such a report. Also, Keitel repeatedly threatened these men, telling them they were to limit themselves exclusively to their own special sectors, and that he would not protect them with respect to any political utterance which was critical of the Party and the Gestapo, of the persecution of the Jews, the murders in Russia, or the anti-Church campaign, and he said that he would not hesitate to dismiss these gentlemen from the Wehrmacht and turn them over to the Gestapo.

As Gisevius's testimony went on and on, strong disagreements were aroused among the listeners. Von der Lippe wrote that some found him self-righteous and unsympathetic, others intelligent and quick-witted. The anti-Goering defendants—Schacht, Papen, Neurath, Speer, Fritzsche—were delighted to see Goering's seamy side exposed. But according to

Gilbert all the defendants—even Schirach, Goering's greatest admirer—thought that he had been unmasked as a conniving and ruthless plotter. Gisevius, however, had lost the respect of the military defendants because of his condemnation of the generals for not having stood up to Hitler and restored traditional German values. Jodl was especially incensed by his revelations of the Roehm purge, shouting that "one pigsty was worse than the other! It is a disgrace for the decent people who followed in good faith into this dirty *Schweinerei.*"

Thus the "Frick case" was turned into what might better be called the "Gisevius intervention."


**Streicher:** Julius Streicher confronted the Tribunal with the first and only serious questions of criminal guilt arising among the defendants on "murderers' row." The legal issues were both narrowed and sharpened by the indictment against Streicher, the only important part of which was the charge under Count Four (crimes against humanity), "including particularly the incitement of the persecution of the Jews set forth in Count One° and Count Four of the Indictment." There was no accusation that Streicher himself had participated in any violence against Jews, so the sole (and difficult) legal issue was whether or not "incitement" was a sufficient basis for his conviction.

Streicher was born in 1885 in a small village in Bavarian Swabia. His father was an elementary schoolteacher, and the son followed the same profession. In 1909 he accepted a position in the municipal school in Nuremberg where, except for the war years, he spent the rest of his life. In 1914 he entered the army as a lance corporal and emerged from the war a lieutenant, decorated for gallantry. Back in Nuremberg he resumed teaching but was also drawn into politics and soon became an anti-Communist conservative and a fanatic anti-Semite.

Streicher was not well educated, and much has been made by commentators of his listing at the bottom of Dr. Gilbert's ladder of the defendants' IQs. But as Gilbert warned, IQs are only a partial test of overall ability, and Streicher's career after he returned from the war showed him to be a man of force and forensic skill. Despite his ill-favored physique—his short, stocky build, bald head, and coarse features gave him a porcine appearance—Streicher drew crowds and won a substantial group of followers. In 1921 he was mesmerized by a Hitler speech and soon thereafter

°Streicher was also charged under Count One of the Indictment, but the only action of which he was accused under Count One was that: "He promoted the accession to power of the Nazi conspirators and the consolidation of their control over Germany." There was no charge that he was involved in conspiracy to prepare for or bring about aggressive war or forcible domination of other nations, and acquittal under Count One was thus a foregone conclusion.

Streicher dissolved his own "movement" and turned the members over to the Nazis—a gift Hitler gratefully acknowledged in *Mein Kampf*. In 1923 he marched with Hitler in the Munich putsch, and that same year he founded the notorious anti-Semitic weekly, *Der Stuermer*. In 1925 Hitler appointed Streicher Gauleiter of Franconia (northern Bavaria, including Nuremberg), a position he held until 1940.

During the 1920s and the early 1930s Streicher, for all his crude and sometimes unlawful actions and the disgusting contents of *Der Stuermer*, did nothing that embarrassed Hitler or jeopardized his own position. For example, in the early 1930s Otto Wegener, a successful businessman and former army staff officer, whom Hitler was using as a consultant on economic and military policy, was with Hitler at a private meeting with Streicher in Nuremberg. In his memoirs Wegener wrote of Streicher:

> He did not seem to me unpleasant. He was a determined fellow, who happened to ride his hobby horse of anti-Semitism hard and who had made it his life's mission to unmask the Jew, as he put it. . . . Streicher is a fanatic. And in his fanaticism he sometimes goes too far. . . .
> Unlike some other gauleiter, Streicher did not, even after the seizure of power, live like a lord. . . . Nevertheless, he lacked the ethical balance that was essential for him and that Hitler expected of him.

Streicher's own "balance" got worse and worse, and there was little sign of ethics. He was often sued on money matters in the Palace of Justice itself. None of these actions triggered his fall from grace, but his public statements belittling Hermann Goering's sexual prowess were another matter. In 1940 the Nazi Party Supreme Court found Streicher guilty of financially corrupt practices and other unlawful acts. Hitler ordered Streicher to resign as Gauleiter but, still protective of his old supporter, put him under house arrest on his country estate in Franconia, expressly forbidden to set foot in Nuremberg. But Hitler did *not* forbid Streicher to continue publishing *Der Stuermer*. Indeed, the Fuehrer wanted the filthy rag to flourish. On January 25, 1942, Goebbels wrote in his diary:

> The Führer sent word to me that he does not desire the circulation of the *Stürmer* to be reduced or that it stop publishing all together. I am very happy about this decision. The Führer stands by his old Party members and fellow fighters. . . . I, too, believe that our propaganda on the Jewish question must continue undiminished.

And so Streicher, with Hitler's strong support, ran his paper by telephone, home conference, and personal contribution as author and continued to publish it until the closing months of the war.

I have covered Streicher's personal career in detail because the need is great in view of the unique charge against him. The other defendants all held important national governmental positions and operated on a national scale. Proof of the charges against them was written in the orders, decrees, and memoranda which they wrote, issued, and filed.

Except for his meaningless membership in the Reichstag, Streicher had no national governmental status, and he left no such trail of official documentary evidence. His speeches as *Gauleiter* in Franconia certainly invited hatred of Jews, but did not reach large areas, and in 1939, by Hitler's order, the speeches stopped. His evidentiary trail lay in the issues of *Der Stuermer*, and it was primarily that periodical which brought Streicher national—even international—notoriety. The coming of the war and his own political eclipse in 1940 removed Streicher from the public eye, and it was the general recollection of Streicher the *Gauleiter* of the 1930s that accounted for his being assigned a seat in the dock for this great international trial.

More than anyone in the dock, Streicher was his own man; *Der Stuermer* was his alone. Goebbels, Otto Dietrich, Fritzsche, and the entire Ministry of Propaganda meant nothing to Streicher. He was loyal to Hitler, but even though he knew that his idol thought he "went too far," he did not trim his sails.

*Der Stuermer* was not a governmental agency; it was a private newspaper owned and edited by Julius Streicher. The charges in the Indictment were brought against a private newspaper owner and journalist to punish him for publishing statements in which he believed.

Given the narrowness of the Indictment, Streicher's evidentiary trial was rightly brief. He was an obscene ruin of his prewar self; Rebecca West, as already noted, described him as "a dirty old man of the sort that gives trouble in parks." He had been giving his counsel, Dr. Hanns Marx, a hard time, and when Marx opened the case by calling his client to the witness stand and asking him for "a short statement of your career," Streicher responded by declaring that "my defense counsel has not conducted and was not in a position to conduct my defense in the way I wanted." The unhappy Marx asked the Tribunal whether, under these circumstances, he should continue to represent Streicher. Lawrence, in a fatherly way, told him to proceed. Streicher recited a brief autobiography, generally accurate but with occasional recollections of the supernatural—"inner voices" that told him what to do, a halo on Hitler's head the first time he heard the Fuehrer speak. But some of his answers were crisp and well phrased, as when Marx asked him about his "relations with Adolf Hitler":

> Anyone who had occasion to make Adolf Hitler's acquaintance knows that I am correct in saying that those who imagined that they could pave a way to his personal friendship were entirely mistaken.

Adolf Hitler was a little eccentric in every respect and I believe I can say that friendship between him and other men did not exist—a friendship that could be described as an intimate friendship.

Marx then questioned his client on the various charges that the prosecution had raised against him. Streicher denied that his actions had incited violence against Jews or that there was any evidence of such incitement; he declared that the mass killings of Jews first became known to him in 1945 when he was a prisoner in Mondorf; he acknowledged ordering the destruction of the main Nuremberg synagogue in 1938, but insisted that the purpose was architectural rather than anti-Semitic; he denied having taken any part in the events of Kristallnacht and stated that he had been opposed to what had happened, but admitted that "because of the atmosphere which prevailed" he had been forced to speak publicly against Jews the following morning; he disclosed that he had visited the Dachau concentration camp four times, but only for the purpose of selecting noncriminal inmates from Franconia, most of whom were Social Democrats or Communists, for an annual trip to the Hotel Deutscher Hof in Nuremberg for Christmas dinner! Finally, he stated that for the first ten years (1923–1933) the coverage of *Der Stuermer* had been limited to Franconia, during which time the circulation had risen from 2,000 to 25,000 per annum, that in 1935 an "expert" publisher had turned *Der Stuermer* into a nationwide organ with a circulation of from 600,000 to 800,000, and that during the war circulation dropped to some 150,000 per year.

Streicher's direct examination lasted little more than half a day, and Griffith-Jones's cross-examination even less. The prosecutor knew well enough that his task, under the Indictment, was to portray the defendant as one who incited the persecution of Jews, and the obvious—and perhaps the only—way to accomplish this was to inundate Streicher with suitable examples of what he had publicly written or said.

Griffith-Jones began with the defendant's speech on April 1, 1933—the day of the official boycott of all Jewish stores—in which Streicher referred to Jews as "a nation of blood-suckers and extortionists" and lauded the Nazis' determination "to expose the external Jew as a mass murderer." Streicher coolly denied that he had preached religious hatred because Judaism was a race but not a religion. The purpose of his anti-Semitism, he declared, was not to "persecute" but to "enlighten."

Griffith-Jones then told the witness frankly that the purpose of his questions was to show that Streicher had "set out to incite the German people to murder and to accept the fact of the murder of the Jewish race." A series of extracts from *Der Stuermer* was offered in evidence, including:

The Jewish problem is not yet solved. . . . Only when world Jewry has been annihilated will it have been solved. [January 1939].

The Jews in Russia must be killed. They must be utterly exterminated. [May 1939].

If the danger of the reproduction of that curse of God in the Jewish blood is finally to come to an end, then there is only one way open—the extermination of that people whose father is the devil [written by Streicher, early 1942].

Griffith-Jones then challenged Streicher on his statement to Marx that he learned of the extermination of Jews only in 1945. The prosecution produced what he called "a bundle of extracts from the *Israelitisches Wochenblatt* [published in Switzerland] from July 1941 until the end of the war." Streicher admitted that he and the staff of *Der Stuermer* received and read that periodical, and Griffith-Jones read into the record a series of extracts reporting and lamenting the killing of "many thousands" of Jews in various cities in the Ukraine. The later reports became more and more frantic and in late 1942 were speaking of "millions" of Jewish dead. Streicher's usual reply was that he could not remember reading the reports, "but I would not have believed them if I had." Griffith-Jones ended his cross-examination by reading from several of Streicher's own articles from a 1944 *Der Stuermer* that referred to "the most terrible germ of all times, the Jew," who "must be destroyed, root and branch" and expressed hope for the time when "Judaism will be annihilated down to the last man."

Marx called four witnesses in Streicher's behalf, only one of whom—Ernst Hiemer, the coeditor of *Der Stuermer*—added anything of value. He corroborated Streicher's unwillingness to believe the published reports of mass killings, but testified that by the middle of 1944 Streicher accepted their validity.

Some issues of *Der Stuermer* contained pornographic cartoons of Jewish sexual crimes. But when Marx pressed for detailed information, Lawrence neatly cut off further discussion by pointing out that the Indictment made no charge "with respect to this particular sort of books." Thus the proprieties were observed, and shortly thereafter the Streicher case was concluded. But neither direct nor cross-examination had resolved the difficulties of deciding Streicher's fate.

# Chapter 15

# THE DEFENDANTS:
# BANKERS AND ADMIRALS

I returned to Nuremberg as the Streicher case was finishing. May was just around the corner, and Nuremberg seemed less forlorn than when I had left in February. The Germans were no longer freezing, there was some lovely weather, and despite the boredom that afflicted the denizens of the Palace of Justice, they seemed more willing to accept the prospect of four or five more months in the spring and summer.

The Tribunal, the other three prosecution delegations, the defendants, and the Palace staff had changed very little, but the American delegation had markedly shrunk. Tom Dodd had succeeded Storey as Executive Counsel and was handling much of the court work, but Jackson was again active, preparing to cross-examine Schacht.

Sidney Alderman was still in Nuremberg, but Jackson had given him no new assignment, so Sidney was mostly enjoying himself. Francis Biddle and Herbert Wechsler had departed the house in Hebelstrasse and settled in the Villa Conradti, previously used as the VIP house, where they soon received their wives, whose travel to Nuremberg had been personally authorized by President Truman, to Jackson's great annoyance. As a result of Biddle's move, the Villa Schickedanz, a much larger place with a swimming pool, became the VIP house.

Socially, my attractive wife, plus my newly acquired star and decoration, spelled better lodging and transportation and many more invitations to parties and functions. These social gatherings brought us new friends, two of whom were to play important parts in my future Nuremberg career.

Brigadier General Leroy Watson, Commandant of the Nuremberg Enclave, was a West Pointer and classmate of Dwight Eisenhower who had commanded an armored division during the Normandy invasion. As a result of what in retrospect appears to have been a misunderstanding, his corps commander, General "Lightning Joe" Collins, removed Watson from his command and sent him back to Eisenhower's headquarters, a major general reduced to lieutenant colonel. Eisenhower gave Leroy command of a battalion, and he soon rose to head an infantry division, as a brigadier general.[*] After I succeeded Jackson as Chief of Counsel, I worked closely with Leroy on many administrative matters. He lived in Nuremberg with a good-looking Czech woman, Leba Barbanova, whom he subsequently married.

Another important new friend was Tom Hodges, who was Watson's one-man intelligence service in the Enclave. He was actually a lieutenant, but was directed to wear major's insignia to give him greater prestige and widen his ambit of social access. Tom spoke excellent German and passable French and had a pleasant high baritone singing voice which was in constant social demand. He and I became close friends, and when I took charge of the prosecution he became Chief of the Interpretation and Translation Division.

Once back at Nuremberg I could, of course, go to court and use my own eyes and ears to assess the defendants' cases. But except for occasional visits to the courtroom, I could not watch for long because of the many demands on my time in connection with preparations for the later trials, for which I had major responsibility.

I knew enough about the progress of the defendants' appearances, however, to be aware that important changes were about to take place. Streicher was the ninth defendant to be heard, and it appeared virtually certain that all nine would be convicted and most of them (perhaps excepting Hess or Streicher) given capital sentences. But the remaining twelve defendants promised no such smooth going for the prosecution. Schacht and Doenitz, soon to be heard, would be very difficult cases for the prosecution, and there were others for whom capital sentences seemed harsh. As things turned out, only four of the twelve (including the absent Bormann) were sentenced to death, and three were acquitted.

The two bankers, Funk and Schacht, were seated in that order at the end of the dock's front row. In ordinary course Funk would have been heard first, but most of the evidence involving Schacht concerned the prewar years, while Funk, who succeeded Schacht as both Minister of Economics and President of the Reichsbank, came to the fore later. It thus appeared that chronological clarity would be served by hearing Schacht's defense first, and that was done.

**Schacht:** Hjalmar Horace Greeley Schacht got his polyglot name because his parents were born as Danish citizens (before the German annexation of

---

[*]Eisenhower himself told the story in "What Is Leadership," *Reader's Digest* (June 1965), p. 52.

Schleswig-Holstein in the 1860s) and his father emigrated to the United States and lived there for some years before returning to Germany, where Hjalmar was born. He was educated in Hamburg and several universities in Germany and Paris. He worked for the Dresdner Bank and in 1923 went into government service as Commissioner for German Currency. Shortly thereafter he was appointed President of the Reichsbank, but resigned in 1930 because of disagreement with the Bruening government's fiscal policies.

Schacht then traveled extensively, lecturing on economic questions in Britain, the United States, and elsewhere. In December 1930 he met Goering, and the following month he met Hitler at Goering's home. Schacht became interested, though not immediately involved, in Hitler and the Nazi program.

Schacht was at the top of Dr. Gilbert's IQ ladder (though only marginally above Seyss-Inquart, Goering, and Doenitz), and Gilbert described him as having "a brilliant mentality, capable of creative originality." Certainly his education and linguistic skills were superior, and he was the most sophisticated in the ways of the world.

To those whom he respected, Schacht could be charming, but he did not suffer fools gladly and was arrogant, tough, sarcastic, and domineering. He was invariably convinced that he was both right and in the right, and from this opinion it followed that he was deeply convinced of his own innocence and of his ability to prove himself innocent. In the dock, he often sat with his body turned to the right and his back to the interpreters, thus giving him a view of the entire courtroom, which he scanned with vast and angry disapproval. For most of his colleagues in the dock he had no use, and they, understandably, found him most unlikable.

Schacht was a strong nationalist, and agreed readily with Hitler's views that the bonds of the "Versailles Diktat" should be broken and German military power revived. Hitler did not pretend to any expertise in economics or finance, and Schacht became a willing consultant in these fields. He also helped raise money for Hitler in the elections of 1932 and 1933.

On Hitler's suggestion, President von Hindenburg reappointed Schacht to the presidency of the Reichsbank. After Hindenburg's death in August 1934, Hitler added Ministry of Economics to Schacht's duties, and the following year he became Plenipotentiary for War Economy, under the Reich Defense Law. Schacht worked well with Blomberg, and for a time also with Goering, but by the end of 1935 he was already at sword's points with Goering, whom Hitler had appointed Coordinator for Raw Materials and Foreign Exchange.

Just as in 1930, this stiffnecked man would not yield to higher authority, and when, in October 1936, the Four-Year Plan was established with

Goering as Plenipotentiary, it became plain that Schacht was on the toboggan. He suspended his activities as Plenipotentiary in February 1937, and in August he bluntly told Goering that his fundamental policy was "unsound" and put his resignation as Minister of Economics into Hitler's hands.

At the Fuehrer's earnest request the resignation was not made public until February 1938, when Funk's appointment as Minister of Economics was announced. Also on request, Schacht stayed on as President of the Reichsbank, with the honorary title of Reich Minister without Portfolio. But barely a year later, when Schacht demanded a curtailment of armament expenditures in order to pay government debts, Hitler at once dismissed him as Reichsbank President and put Funk in his place.

Schacht retained his empty title as Reichsminister without Portfolio until 1943. With the war going badly for Germany, and Himmler and Bormann bearing down on disaffection, Schacht was deprived of his title and other honors. Then in July 1944, soon after the attempt on Hitler's life, Schacht was taken to the Ravensbrück concentration camp. He spent the rest of the war there and at other such camps, including Flossenburg and Dachau, and was first liberated, and then imprisoned, by American troops.

As this skeleton portrayal of Schacht's career indicates, neither the period of his involvement in Nazi governmental action nor the nature of his activities suggests the possibility of guilt under Counts Three or Four (war crimes and crimes against humanity) of the Indictment. He was indicted under Counts One and Two,° which charged that

> He promoted the accession to power of the Nazi conspirators and the consolidation of their control over Germany . . . ; he promoted the preparations for war set forth in Count One of the Indictment; and he participated in the military and economic plans and preparations of the Nazi conspirators for Wars of Aggression and Wars in Violation of International Treaties, Agreements, and Assurances set forth in Counts One and Two of the Indictment.

Beyond doubt Schacht had assisted the Nazis in violating international treaties such as Versailles. But violations of treaties are not necessarily war crimes, and Article 6(a) of the Charter charges "a war" in violation of treaties. No doubt Schacht greatly assisted in rearming Germany, but that alone was not a crime under the Charter.

---

°During a colloquy between Dix and Jackson, while Schacht was in the witness box, Jackson took the position that the Indictment charged *all* the defendants with conspiracy to commit war crimes and crimes against humanity. Jackson was correct with respect to the Indictment, but was still unaware that the final language of Article 6 of the Charter covered only conspiracies to commit crimes against peace. Since the Indictment could not exceed the scope of the Charter, the charge of conspiracy against Schacht in Count One embraced only conspiracy to commit crimes against peace and did not include war crimes or crimes against humanity.

What the prosecution had to prove was that Schacht *knew* that the arms he was helping to produce would be used to wage an aggressive war or a war in violation of international treaties or that he *intended* the arms to be so used. No doubt Schacht would have tried to kill anyone who dared to bracket his case with Streicher's. But even though the crimes of which they were accused were wholly different, the evidentiary features were analogous. In each case the prosecution had to prove that the defendant *knew* or *intended* that his actions would bring about results proscribed as criminal under the Charter.

And, of course, that was what Schacht's counsel, Drs. Rudolf Dix and Herbert Kraus, sought to prevent. Dix was unofficially the dean of the defense counsel; both he and Kraus were capable lawyers. But Dix was solemn and long-winded, and his direct examination of Schacht took almost two full days.

Schacht was predictably articulate, emphatic, and, for the most part, precise. He made no bones about his nationalist views and his abhorrence of the "Versailles Diktat." He strongly believed that Germany should rearm to the extent necessary for defense against other great powers and to support a strong voice in international negotiations. The annexation of Austria came as a surprise to him, but the Anschluss was inevitable; he deprecated some of its features, but said that "spiritually and culturally it was welcome."

Schacht's opinions on Versailles, rearmament, and the Anschluss were, of course, not crimes under the Charter. The question was whether these views suggested that his mind was hospitable to Hitler's policy of German aggrandizement by force of arms. The prosecution's task was to cast doubt on the credibility of Schacht's insistence that he was strongly opposed to war, that he had no foreknowledge of Hitler's plans to "wage wars of aggression," that as soon as he became aware that Hitler was set on aggressive military action he took steps to remove himself from his government positions, and that he then became involved in resistance to the Nazi government.

In support of these claims, Schacht had the benefit of Gisevius's testimony, given during the Frick case. Gisevius first met Schacht late in 1934 when, at Schacht's request, he provided an expert who located and eliminated Gestapo microphones planted in Schacht's home. Gisevius "did not understand how an intelligent man who was as capable in economics as he [Schacht] was could enter into a close relationship with Hitler" and was "all the more bewildered" because he "in a thousand small ways resisted the Nazis." Mutual trust developed slowly, but was strengthened during Schacht's problems with Goering in 1936 and 1937. After the Blomberg-Fritsch affair Schacht told Gisevius, "That means war," and Schacht soon became one of an anti-Nazi resistance group that included Admiral Canaris,

General Hans Oster, Gisevius, and Carl Goerdeler (former Mayor of Leipzig and recently dismissed as Reich Price Controller), who was regarded as the group's leader.

Gisevius's testimony supported the most important elements of Schacht's defense. The witness had often heard Schacht say that "such a large nation [as Germany] in the center of Europe should at least have means of self-defense," but Schacht himself had no information about the progress of rearmament and had to get such knowledge from the military members of the resistance group. In 1936 and 1937 Schacht had made efforts to limit armament expenses and thus slow the pace of rearmament. Was Schacht an active member of the resistance group? Yes, he had brought Goerdeler into the group, and in 1938 he had persuaded Field Marshal Erwin von Witzleben to join in preparations for a military revolt if Hitler ordered an attack against Czechoslovakia. He had made two trips with Gisevius and Goerdeler to Switzerland to warn the British and French of Hitler's aggressive designs on Poland and, in the later trip, of the likelihood of an attack against the Soviet Union. He had done many other things.

Gisevius's praise was not unqualified, but in general it was very positive. Dix's last question asked Gisevius to explain Schacht's seemingly contradictory actions. Gisevius replied:

> I would like to emphasize that the problem of Schacht was confusing not only to me but to my friends as well; Schacht was always a puzzle to us. Perhaps it was due to the contradictory nature of this man that he kept the position in the Hitler government so long. He undoubtedly entered the Hitler regime for patriotic reasons, and I would like to testify here that the moment his disappointment became obvious he decided for the same patriotic reasons to join the opposition. Despite Schacht's many contradictions and the puzzles he gave us to solve, my friends and I were strongly attracted to Schacht because of his exceptional personal courage and the fact that he was undoubtedly a man of strong moral character, and he did not think only of Germany but also of the ideals of humanity. That is why we went with him, why we considered him one of us; and if you ask me personally, I can say that the doubts which I often had about him were completely dispelled during the dramatic events of 1938 and 1939. At that time he really fought, and I will never forget that. It is a pleasure for me to be able to testify to this here.

Such words, from a man whom Jackson had publicly extolled, made his cross-examination of Schacht, difficult at best, much harder. Even Biddle, who had thought Gisevius "too facile a witness—fluent, detailed, oversure of himself, much too pat," nonetheless concluded that he was "in the main truthful."

The British had not listed Schacht as a proposed defendant, and their respected staff researcher, E. J. Passant, had presented a strong memorandum arguing that while Schacht might be "an unpleasant and unreliable character," he was not "a war criminal in the sense of the prosecution." No doubt Jackson was moved to insist on his inclusion for the same reason that caused him to push so strongly for trying Krupp—a belief that "public opinion in the United States" would insist on "joining industrialists" in the dock. Having failed to get a Krupp there, Jackson was all the more eager to convict Schacht and had listed himself to conduct the cross-examination.

The American prosecution's handling of the Schacht case had not fared well, in part because of Storey's and Amen's dislike for the "economic case," which would include Funk, Sauckel, and Speer as well as Schacht. Jackson had entrusted the economic case to Shea, but the Storey-Amen animosity had resulted in Shea's early departure from Nuremberg and demoralization of his staff. Ben Deinard had soon left. Perhaps for different reasons, Colonel Murray Gurfein, a very able advocate who had intensively interrogated Schacht, had left Nuremberg when General Donovan departed in late November.

Jackson's principal assistant in preparing his cross-examination was Captain Sam Harris, who in December had presented the evidence on enforced Germanization. He was bright and industrious and collected a large amount of information for Jackson, but he did not have the close knowledge of Schacht which Gurfein had developed.

I believe that Jackson never became sufficiently aware of Schacht's limited sphere of activity in the Nazi enterprises. At a chief prosecutors' meeting on April 5, 1946, Jackson told his colleagues that "If the Tribunal held that there was no case against Schacht he did not see how they could hope to make a case against any industrialists." Shawcross promptly agreed, but both men were either ignorant of the problem or speaking tactically. The idea that a man who had ceased to play any important part in Nazi affairs months before the war and who ended the war as a dissident concentration-camp inmate was the best possible candidate for conviction as a war criminal, was preposterous. A week later, at a meeting of the British prosecution staff, Elwyn Jones demolished Jackson's claim by pointing out that "Schacht was only in on preparation for war, whereas some of the industrialists were responsible for slave labour and preparation for aggressive war." And, he might have added, the industrialists did not end up in concentration camps.

Furthermore, Jackson's failure with Goering had blotted his copybook with the Tribunal, or at least its British and American members. During Schacht's direct examination Birkett wrote:

> Jackson has come to the microphone twice this morning to protest against some of the questions. He has done this in a most petulant and aggressive manner, and is obviously suffering from frayed nerves.

This is the result of his failure against Goering, and he seems to fear
a similar failure against Schacht and he is anxious to prepare the way.

In fact, Jackson intervened no less than twelve times during Dix's
questioning, and on the second occasion—when Dix raised the question of
whether or not Schacht was charged in the Indictment with war crimes—
Jackson spoke angrily: "I simply cannot be bound by silence after this
flagrant misstatement of our position in conjunction with this witness's
testimony. It is not true that we make no charges against Dr. Schacht with
reference to the Jews." But it should be added that most of Jackson's
objections were entirely legitimate and were upheld by the Tribunal.

Jackson started his cross-examination by having Schacht confirm his
private statement in 1938 that he had "fallen into the hands of criminals"
and then asked him to name the "criminals with Hitler." Schacht named
only Goering and Ribbentrop in the dock and Himmler, Bormann, and
Heydrich, who were dead or missing. He professed inability to name any
others. Considering Schacht's six years of high-ranking service in the Nazi
government and the type of information he was receiving from Gisevius and
others, it is hard to believe that his answer was truthful. But Jackson
weakened the effect by producing a number of photographs showing
Schacht in public company with Bormann, Ley, Streicher, Frick, Goebbels,
Papen, Goering, Hitler, and others. Of course, public officials frequently are
photographed in groups. Schacht's photographic proximity carried no evidence of involvement with anyone particular, and Jackson's ploy was a dud.

Thereafter, however, Jackson did better. Seeking to minimize his role
in Hitler's appointment as Chancellor, Schacht had previously declared that
although he had privately told his acquaintances that Hitler "must become
Chancellor," he had never expressed such a view to anyone in Hindenburg's circle who could influence the decision on whether or not Hitler
would be chosen. Jackson then referred to a statement by Papen that in July
or August 1932, when Papen was Chancellor, Schacht had urged Papen,
who was certainly in "Hindenburg's circle," to resign the Chancellorship so
Hitler, "the only man who can save Germany," might take his place.

Schacht acknowledged that he had told Papen that "Hitler must
become Chancellor" and now resorted to evasive and unconvincing arguments to escape from his dilemma. Jackson followed with Schacht's letter
to Hitler on November 12, 1932, that discussed "our attempt to collect a
number of signatures from business circles" supporting Hitler's claim to the
Chancellorship. It became plain that Schacht had done much more to
advance Hitler's cause than he had previously admitted.

The Indictment had described Schacht as a member of the Nazi Party.
Schacht had convincingly denied this, but admitted that he, like all other
Cabinet ministers, had been awarded the Nazi Party Golden Swastika.

Jackson now asked him whether he wore the decoration other than "on official occasions." Schacht replied: "Yes, it was very convenient on railroad journeys, when ordering a car, *et cetera.*" The sarcasm drew a few titters, but was unwise, both as a matter of decorum and as an admission that he had used the Nazi decoration for personal convenience. Jackson then drew the additional admission that after he received the Golden Swastika in 1937, and until 1942, Schacht contributed 1,000 marks each year to the Nazi Party.

Schacht was at times overconfident in his responses. Explaining his efforts to influence or "lead" Hitler, he remarked: "I think you can be much more successful in leading a person if you do not tell him the truth than if you do tell him the truth." Of course that is sometimes true, but it did not fit the occasion, and Jackson milked it: "I am very glad to have that frank statement of your philosophy, Dr. Schacht. I am greatly indebted to you."

During his direct examination, Schacht had read, from a speech he had made in Königsberg on August 18, 1935, a passage critical of many things going on under the Nazis, including "people . . . who brand every German who trades in a Jewish store as a traitor." Jackson now called Schacht's attention to the next paragraph, which the witness had not read on direct testimony. Its last sentence was: "The Jews must realize that their influence is gone for all time."

That was the beginning of Jackson's series of questions on Schacht's attitude toward the Jews under the Nazi regime, which proved more damaging to Schacht's personal image than anything else in the cross-examination. Schacht testified that he agreed with the Nazi government's intention to limit the number of Jews in governmental or cultural positions, that he had read *Mein Kampf* and knew Hitler's views "in the Jewish question," that he agreed with the statutes prohibiting all Jewish lawyers from practicing in the courts and "excluding all Jews from civil service positions," that as Reich Minister of Economics he signed a decree prohibiting Jews from "receiving licenses to deal in foreign currencies," that he had signed a law imposing the death penalty on Germans, including Jews, who transferred German property abroad, and that he signed a law "dismissing all Jewish officials and notaries public."

This wholesale acquiescence in the march of Jewish outlawry was sad enough, but worse was the indifference of Schacht's responses. Considering what came later, it would have been at least more gracious if Schacht had expressed some regret at the ultimate consequence of these steps.

Toward the end of his cross-examination Jackson made efforts to show that Schacht knew of and shared Hitler's expansive aims. Initially Schacht argued that his difficulties with Goering were simply a battle for power and had nothing to do with his views with respect to the amount and purpose of rearmament.

Jackson got nowhere with Schacht on this point, but he did considerably better when he turned to reading excerpts from Schacht's public speeches extolling Hitler, delivered months after the time when, according to Schacht, he had concluded that Hitler was bent on military aggrandizement. Jackson's implication, of course, was that if Schacht had concluded that Hitler was a threat to peace, he would not have lent his voice in praise of the Fuehrer. In reply, Schacht clung to his belief that as long as he should not or could not resign, he must act, at least minimally, the part of an official in Hitler's government.

Finally, Jackson pursued, I thought pointlessly, the amount of salaries and pensions that Schacht received from his official posts. In the course of the discussion, Schacht remarked that the regulation specifying his pension was still in effect: "I hope that I shall still receive my pension; how else should I pay my expenses?" Jackson replied: "Well, they may not be very heavy, Doctor." Laughter from the audience was quickly checked by Lawrence: "Just a moment; it is quite unnecessary for anyone present to show his amusement by laughter." I am sure that I was not the only person present who thought that to make a joke of anyone's liability to loss of life or liberty was most inappropriate.

A few moments later, Jackson ended the cross-examination. Dix called an additional witness: William Vocke, a fellow member of Schacht's on the Directorate of the Reichsbank.

A businesslike, non-Nazi banker who had been on the board from 1919 to 1939, Vocke had been dismissed a few days after Schacht. In a much narrower ambit Vocke, like Gisevius, confirmed Schacht's account of his aims and actions with respect to peace and rearmament:

> Schacht said a foreign policy without armament was impossible in the long run. Schacht also said that neutrality . . . must be an armed neutrality. Schacht considered armaments necessary, because otherwise Germany would always be defenseless in the midst of armed nations. . . . Finally, however, and principally, Schacht saw in armaments the only means of revitalizing and starting up German economy as a whole. Barracks would have to be built; the building industry, which is the backbone of economy, must be revitalized. Only in that way, he hoped, could unemployment be tackled.

Under Jackson's cross-examination, Vocke agreed that his relations with Schacht had not always been smooth and that he had heard various accusations against Schacht, but he in no way departed from his statements on direct examination.

Jackson's cross-examination of Schacht won him no praise among his colleagues. Biddle curtly called it "a weak cross-examination." Birkett, rightly proud of his own prowess in the art, filled many paragraphs of his diary with a disquisition on the elements of cross-examination in order to explain Jackson's weakness and his inability to cope with Schacht. He concluded that Schacht "most certainly held his own."

Despite my own limited experience in this field, I do not think that Jackson's showing with Schacht (much of which I observed) was nearly as bad as the judges declared. Both Goering and Schacht, in intelligence and knowledge, were formidable opponents, but otherwise the forensic situations were quite different. In Goering's case, the prosecution was armed to the teeth with damning documents and interrogations which Goering could not confute. But despite those weapons Jackson was unable to score off his opponent, and he lost control of himself.

In Schacht's case, however, the store of documents was both much scantier and far less lethal. Virtually none of them implicated Schacht in intrinsically criminal activity, and proof of criminal intentions—i.e., a purpose to prepare for aggressive war—was entirely circumstantial and suggestive. This left very little room for the type of questioning that Fyfe had used to score a few times off Goering.

Despite these difficulties, Jackson made some headway with Schacht. The apparent weakness of Schacht's position was the public appearance of his status and his pro-Hitler statements from 1938 to 1942, when by his own declaration he well knew that Hitler was on the road to war. Furthermore, Schacht retained his official membership in the government, gave money to the Nazi Party, and spoke well of Hitler's policies. However, his explanations that these actions were tactical, and necessary to his clandestine anti-Hitler activities, were strongly supported by Gisevius and others.

It is significant that most of the defendants did not agree with Biddle and Birkett, and were dubious of Schacht's veracity. Not only Goering and his followers but also Raeder, Doenitz, Jodl, Speer, Schirach, Fritzsche, Funk, Keitel, Frank, and Papen declared, with varying degrees of scorn, that Schacht's denials of acquiescence in Hitler's leadership were unbelievable and that he had not appeared then the way he now presented himself. During the lunch hour on May 3, Dr. Gilbert noted that "Several of the defendants commented that Jackson was doing a particularly good job on Schacht."

Of course, the outcome of the Schacht case would not be determined by the appraisals of Jackson's cross-examination. Dr. von der Lippe wrote that "The general impression is that because of Schacht's strong spirit, and the quality of his counsels, he is in a more favorable position than the other accused." Others would have added that thus far Schacht was the only defendant whose prospects of acquittal were substantial.

**Funk:** Walter Emanuel Funk was born in 1890 into a merchant family in Königsberg. He studied political science, literature, and music at the University of Berlin, went into journalism, and in 1922 became editor-in-chief of a leading German business periodical, the *Berliner Borsenzeitung* (Berlin Stock Exchange Times). This gave him some knowledge of economics and a wide range of acquaintance among businessmen and financiers.

In 1931, Funk relinquished his editorship, became a sort of free-lance commentator on economic and political news, and joined the Nazi Party. At first his two main contacts were Otto Wagener (then Hitler's economic adviser) and Gregor Strasser, head of the Berlin branch of the Nazi Party.* At that time Funk was a combination of shrewd business consultant and entertaining bon vivant. According to Strasser: "He plays the piano well, with a marvelous touch, he has a wonderful voice, he's a champion card player, and he goes along with the rest when it's time to tipple a bit."

By the time Funk entered the dock at the age of fifty-six, there was little left of this once gay blade. Pasty, pudgy, in poor health, blubbering when testimony or photographs illuminated the horrors of the Nazi record, and openly scared—a pitiful wreck of a man who had fallen beneath respect, and knew it. For the trial, Funk's greatest asset was that it was hard to think that anyone could be afraid of him.

But in 1932 and 1933, things were going well for Funk. He was a welcome visitor in President von Hindenburg's home and was growing in Hitler's good graces. The Nazi government needed a press representative—a role for which Funk had experience—and Hitler appointed him to his first government position as Reich Press Chief, attached to the Chancellery. Six weeks later, however, the Propaganda Ministry, headed by Joseph Goebbels as Minister of Public Enlightenment and Propaganda, was established. Funk's group was incorporated into the new ministry, where he was made State Secretary. In this capacity, which lasted until late 1937, Funk had nothing to do with propaganda, his duties being largely administrative.

In November 1937 Hitler told Funk that disagreements between Goering and Schacht required that Schacht be removed as Minister of Economics. Funk was to take Schacht's place, and Hitler referred him to Goering for the details. Goering told Funk that the activities of the Ministry of Economics were to be merged with the Four-Year Plan and that the Minister of Economics would work under the directives of Goering as Delegate for the Four-Year Plan. Funk's appointment was published early in February 1938. Less than a year later Schacht was again in disgrace with

---

*Gregor Strasser was killed in 1934 in the Roehm purge. Wagener and Hitler fell out in July 1933. Wagener returned to his private business activities, and rejoined the army during the war, which he ended as a Brigadier General and German Commandant on the island of Rhodes.

the Fuehrer, this time in his capacity as President of the Reichsbank, and Hitler appointed Funk to replace him. Funk held these positions until the end of the war, and it was his activities in them which largely accounted for the charges against him in the Indictment.

These charges included all four counts of the Indictment. The particulars included promotion and preparations for war; participation in "the military and economic planning and preparation" for wars of aggression; authorization, direction, and participation in war crimes and crimes against humanity, "including more particularly crimes against persons and property in connection with the economic exploitation of occupied territories."

Funk's counsel was Dr. Fritz Sauter, a tall, rather excitable man who prefaced his questions with explanatory remarks calculated to give witnesses more than a hint of the answers he expected. Sauter told the Tribunal that Funk was chronically ill, and therefore his examination would cover only "absolutely necessary questions." Dr. von der Lippe noted rather sourly that, anyhow, Funk "was able to give long and detailed answers" and that "he argued adroitly and spoke forceful German."

Funk convincingly established the continuing limits in his authority; his brief tenure as Press Chief had given way to a role as one of Goebbels's underlings, and his elevation to formal leadership at the ministry and the Reichsbank had put him under Goering's thumb. He became Minister but confronted a "higher ministry" and dolefully remarked: "But that has happened to me all my life. I arrived at the threshold, so to speak; but I was never permitted to cross it." This figure of speech was to stand Funk in good stead when the Tribunal pondered his case.

But ministers at the second or third level of command are not necessarily ciphers, and even before cross-examination, Funk could not avoid disclosing actions that involved him in preparations for aggressive wars and oppression of the Jews. Thus Funk testified that immediately before the attack against Poland, he "did everything to ensure that in the event of war, peacetime economy would without disturbance be converted into a war economy." Funk also testified that he had advance knowledge of Hitler's intention to attack the Soviet Union, had assisted Rosenberg in economic planning for the war, and participated, together with Goering and Rosenberg, in Hitler's conference of July 16, 1941, on Nazi civilian policy in the Eastern occupied areas.

Sauter then turned to Funk's attitude toward Jews and, in particular, his actions during and after Kristallnacht. Funk participated in the meeting immediately after Kristallnacht, which was called by Goering and attended by Goebbels and Heydrich, at which the Jews were subjected to a huge financial penalty and the decision to exclude them from economic life was approved. Funk admitted that he "issued directives for the execution of the basic orders and laws which were made," explaining that

In this matter I placed the will of the State before my conscience and my inner sense of duty because, after all, I was the servant of the State. I also considered myself obliged to act according to the will of the Führer, the supreme head of the State, especially since these measures were necessary for the protection of the Jews, in order to save them from absolute lack of legal protection, and from further arbitrary acts and violence.

Only at the end of his questioning did Sauter bring up the matter of Funk's membership, beginning in the fall of 1943, on the Central Planning Board. Funk declared that he took little interest in the procurement of foreign laborers from the occupied territories and was chiefly concerned with obtaining raw materials "for the administration of consumer goods and the export trade"—a matter in which Funk had the assistance of Otto Ohlendorf. According to Funk, he had no knowledge of Ohlendorf's macabre exploits on the Russian front in 1941–1942.

On cross-examination Dodd was, as usual, carefully prepared, but he did not have much ammunition. Funk's repeated and generally plausible insistence that he had little authority to determine policy was, of course, in itself no defense; Keitel had made the same claim. The difference was that the Wehrmacht was running the war, and though Keitel had no basic decision-making authority, he had to frame, distribute, and enforce a continuing flow of orders from Hitler. Funk bore no comparable burdens. Far from confronting Hitler's demands, Funk lost access to him and rarely saw him. Even the second level (i.e., immediately under Hitler) of Nazi leaders—Goering, Fritz Todt, Speer, Bormann—generally worked with their own staffs rather than through Funk's shrunken ministry. Funk simply had a worse case of what also afflicted Rosenberg and Frick.

Nevertheless, Dodd made some headway. He presented documents showing that Funk, despite his protestations of dismay after Kristallnacht, had made a speech picturing the episode as a spontaneous popular uprising, when he knew that Goebbels and others had instigated it. After the conquest of Poland, he made a speech boasting that he had been directing "war economic preparation" for over a year prior to the outbreak of war. In 1942, the Ministry of Economics had participated in looting French assets via the black market, paying for the goods out of funds extorted from the French themselves. These and other documentary assaults on Funk and his ministry revealed that his activities were by no means as trivial or harmless as he had pretended, and this evidence considerably tainted his credibility.

Finally, Dodd resorted to his one sharp new weapon:

DODD: When did you start to do business with the SS, Mr. Funk?

FUNK: Business with the SS? I have never done that.

DODD: Yes, sir, business with the SS. Are you sure about that? . . . I ask you again, when did you start business with the SS?

FUNK: I never started business with the SS. . . . [Emil] Puhl [Vice President of the Reichsbank, whom Sauter had called as a witness] one day informed me that a deposit had been received from the SS. First I assumed that it was a regular deposit, that is a deposit which remained locked and which was of no future concern to us, but then Puhl told me later that these deposits of the SS should be used by the Reichsbank [i.e., the contents were not a deposit but a delivery to the Reichsbank, as Funk later explained]. I assumed they consisted of gold coins, which every German citizen had to turn in as it was, and which were taken from inmates of concentration camps and turned over to the Reichsbank. . . .

DODD: Just a minute. Were you in the habit of having gold teeth deposited in the Reichsbank?

FUNK: No.

DODD: But you did have it from the SS, did you not?

FUNK: I do not know.

Dodd then told the Tribunal that he had an affidavit from Puhl, which he proposed to read. Sauter objected on the ground that Puhl himself should be required to testify. Dodd explained that the affidavit had been taken at Baden-Baden, three days earlier, on May 3. The Tribunal agreed that if the affidavit was read, Sauter could call Puhl as a witness, and then it adjourned until the following morning.

When the Tribunal reconvened, instead of immediately reading the affidavit, Dodd continued his cross-questioning, with the obvious purpose of obtaining answers from Funk that would be contradicted by Puhl's affidavit. Funk essentially repeated his prior testimony, adding that Puhl had "also told me—and he said it somewhat ironically—it would be better that we should not try to ascertain what this deposit was." Beyond that, Funk insisted that he knew nothing of the actual contents of the SS deliveries or what the Reichsbank had subsequently done with them.

Dodd then displayed a short film purporting to show Reichsbank vaults containing opened bags from which diverse gold and jeweled articles, including gold dentures, were spilling. Dodd then read Puhl's affidavit in part as follows:

> 2. In the spring of 1942 Walter Funk, President of the Reichsbank . . . had a conversation with me. . . . Funk told me that he had arranged with Reichsführer Himmler° to have the Reichsbank receive in safe custody gold

---

°In his last book, *Infiltration* (1981), Albert Speer described Funk as "shrewd and bright," but added: "Funk was always soft when it came to SS matters. It was rumored that the SS had a detailed dossier on Funk's dissolute love life. . . . Such a dossier must have existed in Heydrich's or Kaltenbrunner's filing cabinets".

and jewels for the SS. Funk directed that I should work out the arrangements with [Oswald] Pohl who, as head of the economic section of the SS, administered the economic side of the concentration camps.

3. I asked Funk what the source was of the gold, jewels, banknotes, and other articles to be delivered by the SS. Funk replied that it was confiscated property from the Eastern Occupied Territories, and that I should ask no further questions. I protested against the Reichsbank handling this material. Funk stated that we were going to go ahead with the arrangements for handling the material, and that we were to keep the matter absolutely secret. . . .

5. The material deposited by the SS included jewelry, watches, eyeglass frames, dental gold, and other gold articles in great abundance, taken by the SS from Jews, concentration camp victims, and other persons. This was brought to our knowledge by SS personnel who attempted to convert this material into cash and were helped in this by the Reichsbank personnel with Funk's approval and knowledge.

Subsequent paragraphs of the affidavit stated that Funk later told Puhl that Himmler and the Minister of Finance, Lutz Schwerin von Krosigk, had agreed that the cash proceeds would be held in the Reichsbank for the account of the State and that the proceeds were eventually turned back to Oswald Pohl's economic section of the SS "to finance production of materials by concentration camp labor in factories run by the SS."

The result was an almost hysterical explosion of anger and fear from Funk. He denounced the affidavit as "not true," accused Puhl of trying "to put the blame on me," ranted at length on these themes, and stonewalled all Dodd's questions by denying knowledge.

Dodd finished, and Counselor M. Y. Raginsky cross-examined for the Soviet Union. He put into the trial record one useful document—a Funk speech in 1939 wherein he stated: "As the Plenipotentiary for Economy appointed by the Führer, I must see to it that during the war all the forces of the nation should be secured also from the economic point of view. The contribution of economy to the great political aims of the Führer demands . . . above all careful co-ordination."

Raginsky's appearance was otherwise a vivid illustration of the difficulties that lawyers of totalitarian countries have in understanding cross-examination. In a society in which the State is always "right," defense lawyers are loath to encourage their clients to try to prove the State "wrong." These lawyers rarely confront combative witnesses. Such factors help to account for exchanges like the following:

RAGINSKY: I asked you if this company [of which Funk was President] had as object the exploitation of the Grozny and Baku oil fields. Did the oil wells of the Caucasus form the basic capital of the Continental Oil Company?

FUNK: No.

RAGINSKY: No? I am satisfied with your answer.

Sauter reexamined Funk only briefly and made no mention of the Reichsbank's golden horde. Nor did his one witness, Franz Hayler, a businessman who had close relations with the Ministry of Economics, whom von der Lippe thought made "a good impression." The Funk case then passed from the scene until May 15, when Puhl was brought to the witness stand.

Puhl's answers to Sauter's questions added considerable detail to the story, but not much of importance to Funk's degree of involvement. Puhl expressed the opinion that what was seen in the film "had been put there expressly for the purpose of taking the film." He declared that he and Funk occasionally visited the strong rooms where the SS valuables were kept, but he never saw them and had no knowledge of whether Funk had.

More important, Puhl now declared that the statement in his affidavit that the SS valuables had "been taken by the SS from Jews, concentration camp victims, and other persons" was based on information he had obtained from his American interrogators in Frankfurt and that he had no such awareness in 1942. Lawrence at once interrupted to point out that in the affidavit, the sentence immediately following stated: "This was brought to our knowledge by SS personnel" whom the Reichsbank staff were assisting. Sauter, alive to the damaging nature of Lawrence's reading, made Puhl repeat that the information came during his recent Baden-Baden interrogation.

Puhl, insofar as his affidavit was concerned, was Dodd's own witness, but Dodd examined him roughly, expressing disbelief in his responses and asking him: "Are you worried about your part in all this?" Dodd was now armed with another long affidavit, executed by one Albert Thoms, a Reichsbank employee who worked in the vaults. This led to the calling of Thoms as a witness. Thoms knew about the specific nature of the SS valuables and revealed that the gold teeth had been "melted down by the Prussian State Mint." By this time it was clear that both Puhl and Thoms were more interested in saving their own skins than in the truth about Funk's involvement.

So ended the evidentiary defense case for Walter Funk, on May 15, 1946. It appeared plain that he would be convicted, but far from clear how the Tribunal would assess his guilt. There was evidence of his participation in aggressive wars, but it was scanty, and he certainly was not in the inner group of leaders most likely to be found conspirators. He shared responsibility for the anti-Jewish laws resulting from Kristallnacht, but there was a genuine sound to his denunciation of Nazi anti-Semitism. Furthermore, Kristallnacht itself did not involve war crimes, and there was no proof that it was intended as a step toward the Holocaust.

The depth of Funk's involvement in the Reichsbank's handling of the SS's confiscated valuables remained unclear, but Funk was the President, and his direct involvement was deep enough to be criminal. The aid given to the SS by the Reichsbank would, in common-law terms, render the participants "accessories after the fact" in the crimes committed by the SS against the victims. That would be serious, but perhaps not a capital offense.

## 2

After the Schacht and Funk cases, there were several departures from the American delegation. Sam Harris and Bernhard Meltzner, both of whom had been working on these cases, headed for home. So did Walter Brudno, no longer in his private's uniform. Sidney Alderman pulled himself together, picked up his cherished Mariani violin, and returned to Washington to resume his position as Counsel to the Southern Railway. Herbert Wechsler, Biddle's most valued legal counselor, returned to New York to resume his professorship at the Columbia Law School. Fortunately for the Tribunal, Wechsler remained in touch with Biddle by letter.

On or about May 9, Catherine Biddle gave a large dinner party at the Villa Schickedanz in honor of her husband on his sixtieth birthday. The Tribunal judges and staff and all members of the four delegations were invited. It was a lovely evening, the food and drink were served outdoors around the large swimming pool, and Catherine (an accomplished poetess) spoke charmingly of enduring love.

It was the only large social gathering in Nuremberg that I remember in which the pervading spirit was warm and playful. The generally stone-faced Nikitchenko imbibed freely, flirted with Catherine, and made as if to throw her in the pool, drawing an immediate rebuke from the sharp-eyed Rasumov. After dinner the swimming pool was put to use. The first two in were Jenny Pradeau and Janine Herisson, among the prettiest and youngest of the French delegation, who appeared in what were soon to be known as bikinis. Few if any of us had previously seen these provocative garments, and the sides of the pool were soon crowded with ogling males.

At the Palace of Justice, mid-May was the time of the admirals. In the dock's upper row, Doenitz was at the extreme left, next to Raeder. As with the bankers, the admirals were seated in the wrong order chronologically, for in 1943 Doenitz had succeeded Raeder as Commander in Chief of the Navy. If the precedent of the bankers had been followed, Raeder's case would have been heard first, and in fact Doenitz's counsel, Otto Kranzbuehler, requested the Tribunal to change the sequence, but the judges refused, for reasons not stated in the record. The two cases each required a full week, and the British handled the cross-examinations.

**Doenitz:** Karl Doenitz, born in Berlin in 1891, had been a naval officer since 1910, and in the submarine service during the last two years of World War I. Germany was forbidden submarines under the Versailles Treaty, and Doenitz commanded destroyers and the cruiser *Emden* until after Hitler's denunciation of the Versailles limitations in the spring of 1935. Thereafter Doenitz was made commander (formal title "Flag Officer U-boats") of the embryonic submarine branch of the navy.

Expansion during the next few years was not rapid. Doenitz testified that when World War II began, there were between thirty and forty operational U-boats. By that time Doenitz held the naval rank of Captain, but a month later he was promoted to Rear Admiral and, during 1940, to Vice Admiral.

Both Doenitz and Raeder were intelligent, dignified, and neatly clad—the best-appearing men in the dock. The naval image was further enhanced by Kranzbuehler, who, "as was generally expected, cut a very good figure" (von der Lippe's description) in both uniforms and civvies.*
Doenitz rejoiced in "being represented by an upright example of a clean-cut young German naval officer," and Raeder also benefited from Kranzbuehler's expertise in naval law, a subject for which he represented both admirals.

Doenitz was indicted under Counts One, Two, and Three, and, in addition to the usual general charges, the Indictment referred "particularly" to "crimes against persons and property on the high seas." With regard to Count Three, Kranzbuehler knew, from his client's interrogations, that the prosecution intended to accuse Doenitz, on the basis of his ready admission that German submarines had frequently sunk British and other merchant ships without warning, of violating the London Submarine Protocol of 1936. That agreement, which Germany and most other naval powers had ratified, provided that a "merchant vessel" could not be sunk by either surface vessels or submarines without the attacking vessel first placing "passengers, crew, and ship's papers in a place of safety." On the face of things the German practice was a gross violation, causing many deaths at sea, and the charge could well lead to capital consequences for both admirals.

Kranzbuehler, however, apparently had reason to believe—whether on information from Germany's Japanese allies or, after the war, from friendly British or American naval officers—that the United States Navy had routinely sunk Japanese merchant ships without warning. On March 5, 1946, nearly two months before Doenitz took the witness stand, Kranz-

---

*The German Navy remained an entity for several months after the German surrender for removal of mines and other hazards. Thus Kranzbuehler rightly wore his uniform at Nuremberg until the navy's final dissolution.

buehler, in accordance with the Tribunal's procedural rules, requested permission to send an interrogatory to Admiral Chester W. Nimitz, wartime Commander in Chief of the American Naval Forces in the Pacific Ocean.

Fyfe immediately objected: "the question whether the United States broke the laws and usages of war is quite irrelevant; as the question before the Tribunal is whether the German High Command broke the laws and usages of war; it really raises the old problem of evidence directed to *tu quoque* [you too]." And as far as he went Fyfe was on sound ground; in general criminal law, if a defendant has committed a particular crime, the fact that others have also, even if the others are the accusers, is no defense.

But Kranzbuehler rejoined shrewdly and forcefully:

> The stand taken by the Prosecution differs entirely from the conception on which my application is based. I in no way wish to prove or even to maintain that the American Admiralty in its U-boat warfare against Japan broke international law. On the contrary, I am of the opinion that it acted strictly in accordance with international law. In the United States' sea war against Japan, the same question arises as in Germany's sea war against England, namely the scope and interpretation of the London Submarine Agreement of 1936. The United States and Japan were both signatories to this agreement.
>
> My point is that, because of the order to merchant vessels to offer resistance, the London Agreement is no longer applicable to such merchantmen. . . .
>
> Through the interrogatory to Admiral Nimitz I want to establish that the American Admiralty in practice interpreted the London Agreement in exactly the same way as the German Admiralty, and thus prove that the German sea war was perfectly legal.

Thus Kranzbuehler turned from the *tu quoque* to an issue of the interpretation of the London Agreement of 1936. Questions from Lawrence and Biddle led Kranzbuehler to specify the ambiguous words in the agreement as "merchant vessel," and the gist of his argument was that vessels which are armed and ordered to attack submarines, or (later) to travel in convoy with destroyers or other naval craft, are not "merchant vessels" within the meaning of the London Agreement. As a practical matter, of course, for a submarine to attempt to comply with the terms of that agreement under such circumstances would be suicidal.

As Biddle later wrote, he found Kranzbuehler's argument "convincing and from the large view, unanswerable. . . . We would look like fools if we refused [the interrogatory] and it later turned out that Nimitz had torpedoed without warning." But his colleagues were not easily persuaded. Biddle continued: "Whereupon I pleaded personal privilege; it was an American question. We had nothing to conceal." This appeal convinced Lawrence, and on April 10:

The Tribunal decided that this interrogatory is to be allowed as it now stands, but is to be accompanied by a statement in substance as follows:

> The International Military Tribunal have authorized the enclosed questionnaire formulated by counsel for Admiral Doenitz, to Admiral Nimitz. The basis of the Tribunal's decision in authorizing the questionnaire was that it was appropriate to construe the international law of submarine warfare by determining what actions were taken by the powers during the war.

This statement was not as lucid as Kranzbuehler's exposition, but the interrogatory served Kranzbuehler's purpose and proved to be the most important single factor in saving the two admirals' skins.

When Doenitz's case was heard, no reply from Nimitz had yet been received. Doenitz took the witness stand on the afternoon of May 8; Kranzbuehler's questions lasted only a little beyond the same time on the ninth. The colloquy was precise and highly professional.

Counts One and Two were soon dealt with. Doenitz had attended none of Hitler's meetings with the Wehrmacht's leaders that preceded the outbreak of war and said he had nothing to do with the plans. For both the Polish and the Norwegian campaigns, the Naval Operations Staff gave him orders for the deployment and the missions of his few submarines. He had given no attention to the question whether or not these were aggressive wars: "Whether the leadership of the state was thereby politically waging an aggressive war or not, or whether they were protective measures, was not for me to decide; it was none of my business."

Kranzbuehler then turned to the merchant ship sinkings. At the outbreak of war, Doenitz testified, his orders were to abide by the London Agreement, but he knew that the Naval Operations Staff expected that British tactics might necessitate a change. Within weeks it became apparent that British merchant ships were being armed and ordered to cooperate with the Royal Navy by attacking U-boats and sending radio reports of their sightings. On October 4, 1939, the U-boats were ordered to sink armed British merchant ships without warning. The sea war intensified rapidly as naval technology of both U-boats and their hunters on the sea and in the air improved. On May 14, 1942, Doenitz, accompanied by Raeder, reported to Hitler:

> Therefore it is necessary to improve the weapons of the submarines by all possible means, so that the submarines may keep pace with defense measures. The most important development is the torpedo with magnetic detonator which would . . . hasten considerably the sinking of torpedoed ships . . . and also have the great advantage that the crew will not be able to save themselves on account of the

quick sinking of the torpedoed ship. This greater loss of men will no doubt cause difficulties in the assignment of crews for the great American construction program.

Thus the crews as well as the ships were to be combat targets. In a military sense it was wholly logical; ships cannot sail without crews, and knowledge of increased casualties might well chill recruitment of crews. Questioned by Kranzbuehler, Doenitz coolly explained that it was important for him to have "a good magnetic detonator" so that "one torpedo, or a very few, would suffice to bring about a more speedy loss of the ship and the crew." It was becoming apparent that the neat, precise admiral was a very hard and ruthless man.

How far would he carry the war against the crews? Would he approve shooting shipwrecked crew members in their lifeboats? Doenitz drew a line between killing crewmen on their ship, who were able to fight the U-boats, and "shipwrecked" crew members, "who, after the sinking of their ship, are not able to fight any longer and are either in lifeboats or other means of rescue in the water. Firing upon these men is a matter concerned with the ethics of war and should be rejected under any and all circumstances."

That statement was fair and firm on its face, but in the preceding January, Colonel Phillimore had called two former U-boat captains who testified before the Tribunal that on September 17, 1942, Doenitz had issued an order to all U-boat officers that encouraged the killing of shipwrecked crew members. The order in question had been issued in consequence of events following the sinking, five days earlier, of the British ship *Laconia* off the southwest coast of Africa.

After the German occupation of Norway in the spring of 1940, the U-boats (especially larger ones of great range, which had by then become available) took to the high seas. Oceanic space and distances from land often made it reasonably safe for U-boats to help the crews of their victim ships.

Such was the situation when *U-156*, one of four large U-boats on their way to operate off Cape Town, encountered and sank the 19,700-ton *Laconia*, which was carrying 800 British crew and passengers and 1,800 Italian prisoners of war. Italy was then Germany's ally, and perhaps for that reason Doenitz, with Hitler's consent, ordered the German U-boats in the area to join *U-156* in helping the survivors.

Lifeboats were taken in tow toward the Ivory Coast. Many of the Italians had drowned during the *Laconia*'s sinking, but the operation ultimately accomplished the rescue of virtually all the Britons and 450 Italians.

On September 16, however, a four-engined aircraft with American markings (a B-24 Liberator bomber based on Ascension Island) appeared and, despite a Red Cross flag and other efforts to communicate, later returned and dropped bombs which capsized one of the lifeboats and damaged the *U-156*. The rescue efforts were soon broken off, and Doenitz, confronted with increasing use of airplanes against his submarines, circulated his much-discussed order of September 17, 1942:

> No attempt of any kind must be made at rescuing members of ships sunk, and this includes picking up persons in the water and putting them in lifeboats, righting capsized lifeboats and handing over food and water. Rescue runs counter to the elementary demands of warfare for the destruction of enemy ships and crews.

It was the last two words that the prosecution read as establishing that "deliberate action to annihilate survivors would be approved under that order." In answer to Kranzbuehler's questions, Doenitz sharply denied any such meaning and declared that Korvettenkapitän Karl Heinz Moehle "is the only person who had doubts about the meaning of that order."

The brief remainder of Kranzbuehler's interrogation concerned Doenitz's actions after he succeeded Raeder as Commander in Chief of the navy in January 1943. Nothing was explored in depth. Doenitz's statement that he "never received from the Führer an order which in any way violated the ethics of war" led Kranzbuehler to inquire whether his client had ever received the Commando Order. Doenitz replied that he had viewed it as a measure of reprisal against the killing of German prisoners by (presumably British) commandos. He denied that he had ever been involved in carrying out the order; when his attention was called to the 1943 shooting of British commandos in Norway, Doenitz "assumed" that this had been the work of the local police and Himmler's SD.

Other questions from Kranzbuehler revealed Doenitz as a strong supporter of the Nazi regime. Before the war he had "regarded Adolf Hitler's high authority with admiration and joyfully acknowledged it." As Commander in Chief of the Navy, he "accepted and agreed to the national and social ideas" of national socialism; his oath of allegiance to Hitler was "sacred" to him. When Kranzbuehler questioned him on speeches he had made to naval audiences in which he extolled Hitler and Nazism, Doenitz replied that it was his duty "to preserve unity and the feeling that we were the guarantors of this unity." He closed the subject with hard words for the "Putsch of 20 July," declaring that if it had been successful, "the firm structure of the state would gradually have been destroyed." It was an odd and inept comment, considering the evidence of German national disintegration which lay all around the country.

Doenitz got high marks from most of his fellow defendants. During an intermission, Dr. Gilbert recorded, Goering jumped up, rubbed his hands, and declared to those around him, "Ah, now I feel great for the first time in those weeks—Now we finally hear a decent German soldier speak for once." Encomia also came from Frick, Streicher, and Frank, who declared that "Doenitz makes a marvelous impression." However, Speer's nose was out of joint because of his friend Doenitz's condemnation of all who had turned against Hitler.

Gilbert remarked to Doenitz that "it is noticeable that military men still refuse to say anything against Hitler even if they know he was a murderer." Doenitz replied that the Tribunal "did not give me a chance to say anything about the black side of Hitler." It was a pretty weak response, since Kranzbuehler could easily have provided his client an opportunity.

The questions put to Doenitz by his fellow defendants' counsel were more interesting than usual. Seeking information with respect to the General Staff and High Command, Dr. Laternser drew a blank; Doenitz denied that he had "close personal contact" with the army or the air force, denied that he knew most of the General Staff members, denied knowledge of whether the army and air force commanders had a "common political aim," and begged Laternser to confine his questions to the navy.

Dr. Nelte (for Keitel) then asked a series of questions intended to discredit Gisevius's damaging testimony about Keitel's role as Chief of OKW. Doenitz supported every one of Nelte's points, testifying that Gisevius had "very much exaggerated" Keitel's importance, that, contrary to Gisevius's statements, Keitel never threatened his subordinates or kept officers or others from access to Hitler. "It was not possible for Field Marshal Keitel to keep anyone away," declared Doenitz, "and he would never have done so anyway." Considering Doenitz's previously avowed remoteness from army leaders, there was scant basis for his replies to Nelte. Undoubtedly Doenitz regarded Gisevius as a traitor and welcomed the opportunity to discredit him.

This assault against Gisevius, however, roused Dr. Dix, who explained to the Tribunal: "Schacht's defense is naturally interested in the credibility of the witness Gisevius." Dix attacked the accuracy of Doenitz's affirmative response to Nelte's statement that the SD and the police "had no jurisdiction over members of the armed forces," but Doenitz relapsed into inability to answer, and the controversy remained unresolved.

Fyfe then cross-examined Doenitz at what I thought was excessive length. For example, Fyfe at the outset spent much time tallying the number of Hitler conferences that Doenitz attended after he became Commander in Chief, the various individuals whom he met there, and the various matters discussed. He then challenged: "I put it to you, defendant, that you were taking as full a part in the government of Germany during those years as anyone, apart from Adolf Hitler himself."

Doenitz replied "that description is not correct," and he was right; it was a grossly exaggerated assessment. But even had it been more plausible factually, it was a feckless point. Assuming that some or many of the participants in Hitler's meetings were redolent with sin, attendance alone was not a war crime. True, it might have served (though insufficient standing alone) as circumstantial evidence of conspiracy to initiate aggressive war, but Germany's starting of such wars was many months in the past by the time Doenitz became Commander in Chief.

Fyfe was more successful in questioning Doenitz about the use of concentration-camp labor to work in Denmark on the building and repair of ships for use in the Baltic Sea. Doenitz's memorandum in December 1944 stated that "12,000 concentration camp prisoners" would be utilized, and when Fyfe asked whether they would be German or foreign workers, Doenitz replied, "I did not think about that at all," despite the fact that Germany's foreign labor was well known to be forced and thus in violation of the Hague Convention rules. In the same memorandum, Doenitz proposed the infliction of group punishments if sabotage occurred.

On an earlier occasion, when Doenitz informed the staff of the naval shipyard that there was a general strike in Copenhagen, he added the information that Hitler had told him that "the only way to deal with terror is by terror" and had advocated the infliction of severe punishment without trial. These documentary disclosures provoked one of the few occasions when Doenitz appeared weak and flustered.

Fyfe took Doenitz slowly over the issues that had already been covered in interrogations and in Kranzbuehler's questioning, without any marked success. He then felt obliged to resort to matters which portrayed Doenitz in an unfavorable rather than a criminal light. "Did it ever occur to you," he asked the defendant, "that in the case of a merchant ship, if it were sunk without warning, it meant either death or terrible suffering to the crew and to these merchant seamen?" The stony admiral shed no tears: "Of course, but if a merchant ship is sunk legally, that is just war, and there is suffering in other places, too, during the war." Turning to the sinking of the passenger liner *Athenia*, Fyfe asked if Doenitz had ordered the U-boat's log to be altered so as to conceal German responsibility. Doenitz readily acknowledged this, but observed that the highest authority had ordered complete secrecy. What else could the Flag Officer U-boats do but obey?

In conclusion, Fyfe read into the record an extract from Doenitz's nationwide radio speech on Hero's Day, March 12, 1944:

> What would have become of our country today, if the Führer had not united us under National Socialism! Split into parties, beset with the spreading poison of Jewry and vulnerable to it, and lacking, as a defense, our present uncompromising world outlook, we would long since have succumbed to the burdens of this war and been subject to the merciless destruction of our adversaries.

Fyfe, of course, asked what Doenitz meant by his reference to Jewry. It is surprising that his reply has been so little noted: "It shows that I was of the opinion that the endurance, the power to endure, of the people, as it was composed, could be better preserved than if there were Jewish elements in the nation." Thus Doenitz fixed his stamp of approval on the Nazis' expulsion of the Jews from Germany.

So ended the testimony of this intelligent and forceful but harsh and purblind man, whose character appears to have been even more hardened by the loss of his two sons, both U-boat officers, in the war.

Kranzbuehler broke the tension of cross-examination by introducing a number of documents helpful to the admirals' cause and then called three witnesses. In order they were Admiral Gerhard Wagner, who from the beginning of the war until 1944 had been a member of the Naval Operations Staff and from then to the end of the war a special assistant to Doenitz; Admiral Eberhard Godt, who, throughout the war, was Doenitz's chief of U-boat operations; and Commander Guenter Hessler, Doenitz's son-in-law and a U-boat staff officer whose duties included instructing U-boat commanders before they left port on the applicable combat rules. Thus all three witnesses were Doenitz's closely associated subordinates, a factor bound to diminish the credibility of their evidence given in his behalf. Colonel Phillimore cross-examined all three, more aggressively than Fyfe had handled Doenitz.

Kranzbuehler's principal purpose in calling these witnesses was to confute the testimony given earlier by Lieutenant Peter Heisig and Lieutenant Commander Moehle to the effect (in Heisig's case) that Doenitz, in a speech to a large group of U-boat officers in the fall of 1942 and (in Moehle's case) in the order of September 17, 1942, had approved shooting the survivors of ships sunk by U-boats. Wagner, Godt, and Hessler all denied that there was any basis for the charge and faced sharp cross-examination from Phillimore, who had previously called Heisig and Moehle as witnesses for the prosecution.

Heisig's testimony importantly involved the case of Lieutenant Heinz Eck, captain of a U-boat which sank the ship *Peleos*, who then ordered the shooting of crew members on rafts and other wreckage.° This was the only admittedly proven case of a U-boat crew's killing shipwrecked enemy crewmen. Eck and four others were convicted of murder by a British military court on October 20, 1945. Eck and two others were condemned to death by shooting; the sentences were confirmed on November 12 and were carried out on November 30, 1945.

The dates are important because Heisig's affidavit was given to the

---

°Eck testified that he wished to sink the rafts so that enemy aircraft would not detect the sinking. Since there were crewmen on the rafts, Eck knew that firing at the rafts would likewise kill the men.

prosecution on November 27, 1945. Under cross-examination by Kranz-buehler, Heisig stated, "I made the statement in defense of my comrades [meaning in particular Lieutenant August Hoffman, who was convicted and shot with Eck] who were put before a military court in Hamburg and sentenced to death for the murder of shipwrecked sailors." Heisig's sup-posed purpose was that his testimony on Doenitz's speech would give the Eck group an opportunity to raise the defense of superior orders.° Of course, as Kranzbuehler pointed out, by November 27 it was too late for any such help to the Eck group. Did Heisig know this when he made the affidavit, which could not help Eck but was potential poison to Doenitz?

Admiral Wagner was the next to get tangled in dates, when Kranz-buehler brought out that Wagner and Heisig had been together in the Nuremberg prison in early December 1945. Wagner testified that Heisig said he had been told that if he confirmed that Doenitz's speech had encouraged the killing of survivors of shipwrecks, he would save not only Eck and Hoffman but the other defendants as well and that "Of course, you will thus incriminate Grossadmiral Dönitz, but the material against Admiral Dönitz is of such tremendous weight that his life has been forfeited any-way." This, of course, was Wagner's effort to discredit Heisig.

Cross-examining Wagner the following day, Phillimore stated that Eck was executed on November 30, and therefore: "That is to say he was executed before you had this conversation [with Heisig]. Did you know that?" Wagner replied: "No. I just discovered that now." Did Heisig know it before he gave evidence? "Obviously not," said Wagner. Phillimore then pointed out that Kranzbuehler, cross-examining Heisig, had told him that the sentence on Eck had already been confirmed. "Then he [Heisig] told an untruth to me," said Wagner. Perhaps Heisig was lying, but either Wagner was, too or he had been very poorly briefed by Kranzbuehler.

Heisig and Wagner were not the only witnesses who were tripped by dates. Lieutenant Commander Moehle had testified that Doenitz's order of September 17, 1942, meant that "in the case of sinkings of merchantmen . . . there should be no survivors." He buttressed his testimony by describing his consultation on the meaning of the order with a Lieutenant Commander Herbert Kuppisch, "a specialist on the staff of the U-boat command," whose comments suggested that the order was intended to bring about the killing of shipwrecked crew members. Hessler, however, established that one of the episodes in November 1943 which, according to Moehle, Kup-pisch used as an illustration did not occur until after Kuppisch had been lost at sea in August 1943.

Thus both prosecution and defense overplayed their hands to the

---

°Eck himself did not invoke that defense. The other defendants relied on superior orders given them by Eck as captain. The defense was not accepted by the Military Court, which relied on the *Liandovery Castle* case.

detriment of truth. Certainly Doenitz's order of September 17 did not tell his readers to shoot the shipwrecked enemy in their lifeboats, but it left no doubt that the deaths of crewmen were greatly to be desired. But the prosecution's case would have been much stronger had it more to show, by way of action on the order, than the stupid and brutal bungling of Eck on his first combat mission.

The other topic, which engaged the witness Wagner, was the Commando Order, which Doenitz had sloughed off as a question of reprisal and with which he denied having any connection. The prosecution had introduced documents concerning the capture, on a Norwegian island in the summer of 1943, of the uniformed crew of a Norwegian torpedo boat. According to the documents, the crew members were interrogated by subordinates of Otto von Schrader, Commanding Admiral of the Norwegian West Coast. The Admiral turned them over to the SD, who shot them pursuant to the Commando Order.

Doenitz denied knowledge of the matter despite sharp and disbelieving pressure by Fyfe on cross-examination. Wagner emphatically corroborated Doenitz's lack of information and added that he himself had learned of the incident for the first time at Nuremberg. His reward was a protracted and accusatory cross-examination by Phillimore, who argued forcefully that such an episode must have been reported to Doenitz's headquarters, and this argument appeared to discredit Wagner's confused denials. But later developments cleared Doenitz of responsibility; Schrader was a naval officer, but he was a military area commander and therefore reported not to Doenitz but to General Nikolaus von Falkenhorst, Wehrmacht Commander of Norway.°

Godt's and Hessler's testimony added little to Wagner's. After Hessler had finished, Kranzbuehler closed his case. A few days later the admirals' "ship came in" in the form of Admiral Nimitz's answers to Kranzbuehler's interrogatory, and on July 2 it was read in court. The salient features of the answers were

2.Q. Did the U.S.A. in her sea warfare against Japan announce certain waters to be areas of operation, blockade, danger, restriction, warning, or the like?

°Admiral von Schrader shot himself in July 1945, apparently in fear that the British would try him for turning over the commandos to the SD. General von Falkenhorst was tried on July 29, 1946, in a British military court in Brunswick on nine charges covering his distribution of the Commando Order and responsibility for handing over to the SD a number of British and Norwegian commandos who were shot by the SD. These charges included the one which Fyfe and Phillimore endeavored to hang on Doenitz, but that charge was dropped, apparently on the ground that the commandos were from the beginning in the hands of the SD. On the other charges, Falkenhorst was convicted and sentenced to death, but his sentence was commuted to life imprisonment. He was freed after a few years.

A. Yes. For the purpose of command of operations against Japan the Pacific Ocean areas were declared a theater of operations.

3.Q. If yes, was it customary in such areas for submarines to attack merchantmen without warning, with the exception of her own and those of her Allies?

A. Yes, with the exception of hospital ships and other vessels under "safe conduct" voyages for humanitarian purposes.

4.Q. Were you under orders to do so?

A. The Chief of Naval Operations on 7 December 1941 ordered unrestricted submarine warfare against Japan. . . .

13.Q. Were, by order or on general principles, the U.S. submarines prohibited from carrying out rescue measures toward passengers and crews of ships sunk without warning in those cases where by doing so the safety of their own boat was endangered?

A. On general principles, the U.S. submarines did not rescue enemy survivors if undue additional hazard to the submarine resulted or the submarine would thereby be prevented from accomplishing its further mission. . . .

15.Q. In answering the above question, does the expression "merchantman" mean any other kind of ships than those which are not warships?

A. No. By "merchantmen" I mean all types of ships which were not combat ships.

It is noteworthy that the interrogatory made no reference to the 1936 London Agreement or to the meaning of "merchant ship" as used therein—issues which Kranzbuehler had emphasized in stating his position to the Tribunal. But Kranzbuehler had faithfully avoided asking Nimitz for his opinions; what he wanted was to be told *the practices* of the United States Navy, and he got them. To be sure, the line between *tu quoque* and the meaning of "merchant ship" in the London Charter was a very thin one. But it was as clear as clear could be that if Doenitz and Raeder deserved to hang for sinking ships without warning, so did Nimitz.

**Raeder:** Erich Raeder was the oldest defendant except for Neurath and had been a naval officer since 1897. During World War I he was chief of staff to the then famous Admiral Franz von Hipper, whose praise made Raeder a man marked for high office. In 1928 he was appointed Chief of the Naval Directorate (*Chef der Marineleitung*) the top naval commander, tantamount to Commander in Chief, and directly responsible to the Minister of Defense. In 1935 Hitler designated him Commander in Chief of the Navy. In the Indictment he was charged under Counts One, Two, and Three, "including particularly war crimes arising out of sea warfare."

As with Doenitz, the most serious war crimes accusations involved the German submarines. As Doenitz's direct superior, Raeder was equally responsible for sinking without warning and the efforts to increase the casualties among merchant seamen. Kranzbuehler had handled these matters for both admirals, and Raeder's counsel, Dr. Walter Siemers, did not refer to them during his questioning of Raeder.

Under these circumstances, one might have expected Raeder's case to be the shorter, but it was not, for two reasons. The first was evidentiary: Raeder was the only defendant who had held a top military command during the pre-Hitler years when the Weimar government engaged in various efforts to circumvent the Versailles military restrictions, to which the prosecution had pointed as precursors of the alleged conspiracy to initiate aggressive war. He was also one of the two defendants (with Goering) who held top military commands during the first ten (1933–1943) of the Hitler years. During this period, therefore, Raeder was a prime candidate for conviction under the conspiracy charge in Count One of the Indictment. Virtually all of Dr. Siemers's examination of his client concerned that charge.

The other time-consuming factor was the personality of the principals. Raeder was elderly and tended to ramble. Dr. Siemers was painstaking and intelligent, but had trouble adjusting to Anglo-American trial procedures. He continually inserted explanations and opinions between his questions and could not cure his habit of telling Raeder what to say. These foibles caused frequent admonitions from Lord Lawrence. The case was a week old when Birkett despairingly noted: "The trial has now got to a stage when nobody makes any effort to consider time. Siemers (for Raeder) goes on endlessly, repeating himself over and over again."

The direct examination was slow and dull. Siemers started by spending several hours on events prior to Hitler's appointment as Chancellor; this was technically warranted because the prosecution had raised these matters, but they were no part of any Nazi conspiracy, and Lawrence grew restive. When Siemers eventually reached Hitler's arrival on the military scene, Raeder emphasized that the Fuehrer had made a very strong and favorable impression on him and the other officers present.

As for the conspiracy charge, Raeder made no effort to deny that Hitler had waged aggressive war. His defense was that neither privately nor during military conferences had he become aware of Hitler's warlike intentions, and in support of this claim he focused his attack on the accuracy of the records of Hitler's military conferences and on the conclusions the prosecution drew from those documents. Describing the nature of Hitler's speeches, Raeder declared:

> Hitler spoke at great length, going very far in retrospect. Above
> all, in every speech he had a special purpose depending on the audi-

ence. Just as he was a master of dialectics, so he was also a master of bluff. He used strong expressions again according to the objectives he was pursuing. . . . He also contradicted himself frequently. . . . One never knew what his final goals and intentions were.

Anyone familiar with the Fuehrer's speeches would readily agree that much of this description is accurate. But, as Dr. Siemers admitted, in the well-known conference of November 5, 1937, with the four military chiefs and Neurath (at that time Foreign Minister), the record "contains serious references to a war of aggression . . . it says that, armament now being completed, the first goal is the overthrow of Czechoslovakia and Austria." Raeder replied that Goering had told him just before the meeting that "The Führer wanted to spur on the Army to carry out the rearmament somewhat faster" because "it was going too slowly for the Führer." But why did Hitler want to pick up speed, other than to carry out his aggressive plans? Raeder then said that, in his opinion, "the speech was specifically intended to force von Neurath out of the Cabinet." But the speech did not have that result,° and the idea that the man who four years earlier had disposed of numerous unwanted officials by murder would have taken so wimpish a way of firing Neurath was ridiculous.

Raeder tried the same minimizing of Hitler's purpose with regard to the somewhat larger military gathering on May 23, 1939, when Hitler announced his decision: "To attack Poland at the first suitable opportunity. We cannot expect a repetition of the Czech affair. There will be war." True, the speech was also full of inconsistencies about whether or not the attack would be launched if Britain kept her promise to join Poland against Germany, but the intention to plan and mobilize to crush Poland was unmistakable. Nevertheless, Raeder fastened on a statement near the end of the speech in which Hitler announced the formation of "a small planning staff† at OKW" and insisted that "it was the formation of a research staff which motivated the speech." How such a simple notice of appointment could have "motivated" a long speech covering a multitude of subjects and revealing intent to attack Poland Raeder did not explain.

Raeder truthfully asserted that Hitler, up to the last moments of peace, had assured him that there would be no war with Britain. That is not surprising, since Hitler himself, especially after securing the pact with the Soviet Union, had hoped that Britain would not come to Poland's aid. It is also true that Raeder strongly opposed the attack against the Soviet Union in 1941 and that he had no prior knowledge or part in the Nazi conquest of

---

°Hitler replaced Neurath with Ribbentrop as Foreign Minister in early February 1939, during the personnel shake-up triggered by the Blomberg-Fritsch affair.

†In the German record the word was *"Studienstab,"* but the context made clear that the staff's purpose was military planning.

Yugoslavia. But there is little by way of mitigation in these facts and certainly nothing that clears Raeder of the charge that he knowingly participated with Hitler in planning and waging aggressive war.

Only in the case of Norway, however, was there evidence that Raeder had taken the initiative in bringing about an aggressive war. Shawcross, in his opening statement, had described Raeder's role in bringing to Hitler's attention the military advantage to Germany that would accrue from an occupation of Norway's Atlantic coast. The Attorney General had also mentioned the Germans' contention that they had occupied Norway only to prevent the British and French from carrying out their own plans to invade Norway. Shawcross had vigorously denied that charge and argued that even if it were true, it would not justify the German attack—the by now familiar *tu quoque* response.

Of course, Raeder in his testimony and Siemers in presenting his documents stressed the probability of a British invasion of Norway and soft-pedaled the benefits to Germany of naval and air bases in Norway. The Germans certainly had reason for concern because their country imported large amounts of Swedish iron ore, much of which came by ship from Narvik to German ports, and because British control of Norway's coast would considerably tighten the British naval blockade.

However, warnings of an imminent British coup reached the Germans only from Norwegian sources and chiefly from Nazis and quasi Nazis such as Quisling, who opposed the Norwegian government and welcomed a German entry which might enable the Quislingites to ride to power on the backs of German soldiers. Raeder had no proof of British interference until a few hours before the ships of his armada—from Narvik in the north to Oslo and Christiansand in the south—were about to enter the ports, discharge their cargoes and passengers, and commence occupation of the Norwegian mainland.

Shawcross, calling the German charges "patently false," had not told the full truth. On March 28, 1940, the British government had decided to lay mines in Norwegian territorial waters at and south of Narvik to cut off the ore traffic to Germany. Anticipating German counteraction, the British had also decided to send an infantry brigade to Narvik and five battalions to ports farther south to deal with any German interference. There was no provision for air participation, and no landing in Norway would be attempted in the face of Norwegian resistance. Considering the size and determination of the German invaders, the British forces were ridiculously inadequate.

Early in the morning of April 8, British destroyers laid mines near Narvik, and simultaneously the government made a public announcement and delivered an explanatory note to the Norwegian government. Troops were embarked on transports at Scottish ports, readying for the crossing to

Norway. But by that time British aircraft had spotted and reported ships of the German fleet sailing from Germany northwesterly, the cruiser *Hipper* had met and sunk the British destroyer *Glowworm,* and the Polish submarine *Orzel* had sunk a German transport carrying troops and supplies to Bergen. Warned of the British ships' proximity, the German ships raced to their targeted ports to land their passengers and cargoes. The British, however, had not yet divined that Norway was the Germans' goal and anticipated a major naval engagement. They recalled the minelaying destroyers and disembarked the troops so that their naval forces would all be available for battle.°

Both prosecution and defense had some knowledge of these British plans and actions between March 28 and April 8, 1940, based on documents which the Germans had captured from the French archives after the French surrender. But the British records of those events had remained sealed; †Foreign Office and prosecutors were worried that their disclosure might be embarrassing, while Dr. Siemers nourished suspicion that the documents might be helpful to the defense. He submitted to the Tribunal a request for "the British Admiralty documents, May 1939 to April 1940," which was discussed in court on March 6, 1946. Fyfe, without taking a position, promised that he would "make inquiries."

The result was an answer from the Foreign Office giving "reasons why these records cannot be made public," which the Tribunal made available to Siemers but did not allow him to read into the record. On May 1, Siemers objected strongly but ineffectually to the refusal of his request.

Siemers had not played his cards well. It is virtually certain that if Kranzbuehler had handled the "sink without warning" issue by asking the Pentagon authorities to give him access to all the files on submarine operations against Japan, he would have been curtly refused. Siemers might better have followed Kranzbuehler's tactics and sent a carefully drawn interrogatory to the First Lord of the Admiralty. It might not have been answered, but even so the embarrassment to both Britain and the Tribunal would have been considerable. As it was, Siemers's protest attracted virtually no notice and a relieved Foreign Office staff member noted: "It looks as though the Norway issue will pass completely without undue attention being drawn to it."

Fyfe's cross-examination began unexcitedly with more discussion of events prior to 1933, which I thought quite unnecessary. He then went to

---

°Churchill ordered these measures. Had the British gone ahead with their plans, they could undoubtedly have knocked the Germans out of Narvik (where they were protected only by destroyers) with the brigade assigned to Narvik and a few cruisers and destroyers.

†To the best of my knowledge, the general content of the British records was not disclosed until the publication of Winston Churchill's *The Gathering Storm* in 1948.

the aggressive war charge, dealing with Czechoslovakia, Poland, Norway, and the Soviet Union. Even though it was primarily the Wehrmacht's newfound strength that caused the collapse of the Czechs, Fyfe was on slippery ground, since it was his own government that had in fact forced the Prague government to give in.

No such embarrassments arose in Poland's case, and Raeder's minimizing of the May 1939 conference was absurd. But Fyfe did not make the most of his opportunity; here and elsewhere, Fyfe's response to Raeder's evasions was to ask incredulously: "Do you really want the Tribunal to believe that? Is that your answer?" That was nothing but theatrics, unsupported by any effort to explode Raeder's positions by sharp factual questioning.

As for Norway, Fyfe drew Raeder's admission that he "was in favor of carrying out the landings in Norway at the earliest possible time." He continued to claim that his intent was to forestall the British, but he had no proof that they intended to invade Norway. Fyfe, turning from cross-examiner to spokesman, declared that "there was no British order for an invasion at all; there was an order for laying mines." The second clause was correct, the first was at best a half-truth.

Although the evidence about war crimes was scanty, Fyfe had some success. Raeder admitted that he had, without objection, distributed the Commando Order to subordinate naval headquarters and went so far as to say that he thought the order "justified." During the cross-examination of Admiral Wagner, Colonel Phillimore had produced evidence of the killing, by German naval troops, of British commandos captured in uniform near Bordeaux. The executions were in 1942, when Raeder was still Commander in Chief; Siemers made no effort to attack the evidence.

In addition, Fyfe introduced an affidavit by Walter Dittman, a German administrative official formerly stationed in Libau, Latvia, describing extensive killing of Jews in 1941–1942 by the Gestapo and the Latvian police. Some of the Jews had worked for the German Navy in Libau, and word of the killings reached administrative officials in Kiel, who refused to take any action. Raeder volunteered that he had been in Libau during the war, but denied any knowledge of such events.

Raeder's first two witnesses were men of some eminence who, overall, did him more harm than good. Karl Severing was a German Social Democratic politician who had been Minister of the Interior from 1928 to 1930 and Minister of Prussia from 1930 to 1933. Most of his testimony merely bolstered Raeder's plausible contention that naval violations of the Versailles Treaty prior to 1935 were of minor importance. Ernst von Weizsaecker was a diplomat who had been State Secretary of the German Foreign Office. He was questioned principally about the sinking of the *Athenia*, concerning which he had little to add to previous testimony.

On cross-examination, Elwyn Jones asked each of these witnesses at what point they, or responsible officials generally, anticipated that the Hitler regime would lead their country into aggressive wars. Having just heard Admiral Raeder insist on his total unawareness of any such likelihood until World War II was on top of him, it was refreshing to hear Severing say that "From January 30, 1933, on . . . the choice and appointment of Hitler as Chancellor of the Reich meant war, not in the least doubted by me and my political friends." Weizsaecker, in turn, replied: "That the foreign policy of Hitler's government was a dangerous one I realized clearly for the first time in May 1933; the fact that an aggressive war was planned, perhaps, in the summer of 1938, or at least the course pursued in foreign policy might very likely lead to war."

The third and last witness, Raeder's Chief of Staff Admiral Erich Schulte-Monting, also did little to help his former superior. Aware that Raeder's version of Hitler's May 23, 1939, speech on Poland was weak, Schulte-Monting testified that Raeder had told him that after that speech Hitler, in a private conference with Raeder, had "reassured him and had told him that politically he had things firmly under control" and that "solution of the Polish Corridor" would not involve "a war with England." That was interesting if true, but why had Siemers not had Raeder himself give this testimony instead of getting it secondhand from Schulte-Monting?

In fact, as Elwyn Jones brought out on cross-examination, ambiguities in Hitler's speech were of little moment compared to the scope and detail of the Wehrmacht's preparation for the attack. In this, the navy had a part to play on Poland's Baltic seacoast. All the military leaders must have been aware that only Poland's capitulation would prevent fighting, and Hitler had already warned them that such a development was not to be expected, and that "there will be war."

Raeder won no high marks from his fellow defendants; even those inclined to support him, such as Keitel and Ribbentrop, gave him only "perfunctory comments of encouragement," according to Dr. Gilbert. Whatever sympathy he might otherwise have won melted when Colonel Pokrovsky, cross-examining, put into the record a memorandum which Raeder had written while a prisoner in Moscow.* The contents were particularly hard on Goering ("unimaginable vanity and immeasurable ambition" and "untruthfulness, impracticability and selfishness"), Doenitz ("conceited and not always tactful nature"), Speer ("flattered Doenitz's vanity and vice versa" and "hardly qualified" for command of the navy), and Keitel ("a man of unimaginable weakness").

---

*Pokrovsky read only a few excerpts, and the Tribunal decided not to have any more read into the verbal record, but admitted the entire document as evidence and gave copies to all the defendants.

Doenitz did his best to conceal his annoyance, but privately described Raeder to Dr. Gilbert as a "jealous old fogey." All semblance of unity among those in the dock was breaking down, much to the glee of Schacht, whose reaction to Raeder's case was: "He disapproved of aggressive war and was deceived by Hitler, but he planned and began war just the same. That's a militarist for you."

# Chapter 16

# THE DEFENDANTS:
# THE LAST NINE

As May 1946 reached its final week, there remained eight men in the dock, and the absent Bormann, whose defenses were yet to be presented. Except that all nine, in one way or another, served the Nazi regime before and during the war, these men had no common denominator. Three of the defendants—Sauckel, Speer, and Bormann—were Nazis who had held prominent and highly important positions in the government during the greater part of the war. Three—Schirach, Seyss-Inquart, and Fritzsche—held important but less noteworthy posts. Two—Papen and Neurath—were non-Nazis who had held high office before Hitler came to power and who stayed on as German diplomats, tolerated by the Fuehrer despite their political nonconformity. General Alfred Jodl, though inferior in rank to the other four military men in the dock, had been Hitler's principal assistant in operational planning and military decisionmaking.

The presentation of these nine cases took the remainder of May and the entire month of June, encompassing twenty trial days. Good weather was often interrupted by spring rains, and the dark, wet streets of shattered Nuremberg dampened the spirits.

The denizens of the Palace of Justice suffered casualties. On May 23, the Soviet prosecutor N. D. Zorya died from a gunshot wound at the headquarters of the Russian delegation. General Rudenko informed General Gill that the death was due to "the incautious usage of the fire-arm by General Zorya."

For the American delegation, a much sadder blow was Charles Malcolmson's death from a heart attack on May 31, only one month after his arrival in Nuremberg. He was only thirty-nine, had made a fine reputation as press representative for the Department of Justice, and was admired and liked by Biddle and the other Justice Department alumni. Funeral services were at the Church of the Resurrection in Nuremberg; the pallbearers from the press included Walter Cronkite and Richard L. Stokes. Biddle wrote to his wife that he was "much depressed" after the ceremonies in "raining, dreary weather."

Among the judges, Birkett was the most upset by the long-drawn-out hearings and the prospect of months yet to go. He was so wedded to the crisp, no-nonsense procedures of his beloved English courts that he could not abide the stumbling slowness of the German lawyers. Throughout May and June his notes and letters are chiefly diatribes against these lawyers, the interpreters, and occasionally his more patient colleagues:

> *May 23:* When I consider the utter uselessness of acres of paper and thousands of words and that life's slipping away, I moan for the shocking waste of time.
>
> I used to protest vigorously and suggest matters to save time, but I have now got completely dispirited and can only chafe in impotent despair. . . .
>
> *June 20:* When Flächsner [Speer's counsel] succeeded Kubuschok [Papen's] at the microphone, it became clear that there were lower depths of advocacy to be reached, unbelievable as it sounds. . . .
>
> *June 21:* Oscar Wilde began *De Profundis* by asserting that "suffering is one long moment" and the truth of that assertion cannot be better exemplified than in this awful cross-examination, which the Tribunal is compelled to suffer and endure.

Fortunately, the German lawyers were blissfully ignorant of what was going through Birkett's mind, and they were fortunate, too, that his colleagues were better aware of the difficulties and tensions of defending a client against a capital charge before a tribunal following unfamiliar procedures. Lord Lawrence was aware that fairness required patience and firmness rather than lectures on the merits of Anglo-American criminal procedure.

During this period, except for his cross-examination of Speer, Justice Jackson seldom appeared at the lectern, and general guidance of the prosecution's court actions was primarily in the hands of Maxwell-Fyfe. In May and early June, however, Jackson's name was often in the American newspapers on matters having no connection with the Nuremberg trial. These events culminated in a public statement by Jackson which was widely discussed and which, in some quarters, affected his personal standing.

The matter had its origin in Chief Justice Charles Evans Hughes's retirement from the bench on July 1, 1941, when Jackson was Attorney General. President Roosevelt seriously considered nominating Jackson as

Chief Justice, but decided instead to name Harlan F. Stone and nominate Jackson as Associate Justice in the vacancy left by Stone's ascendance. According to Jackson's later statements, Roosevelt had in mind that should Stone subsequently retire, Jackson would be chosen to succeed him as Chief Justice.

President Truman, of course, had no part in these considerations, and when Chief Justice Stone died of a sudden heart attack on April 22, 1946, there was no indication that Truman would favor Jackson or, indeed, anyone in particular for appointment as Chief Justice. Those in the know, however, had not forgotten Roosevelt's favorable view of Jackson as a possible Chief Justice.

During the time he was on the bench, Jackson had often differed sharply with the views of Justices Hugo Black and William Douglas. Early in May 1945, at the very time Jackson accepted his appointment as Chief Prosecutor, he had written an opinion which had deeply angered Black.

The details of the case, an important one,° need not concern us, beyond noting that it was decided in the Supreme Court by a vote of five to four, that Justice Black was in the majority and Justice Jackson in the minority, that the lawyer representing the winning claimants had been Black's law partner before Black's appointment to the Supreme Court, and that Black had not recused himself despite the involvement of this former partner, and instead had cast a vote necessary to his former partner's success. Over Black's stormy objection, Jackson had filed an opinion, for himself and Justice Felix Frankfurter, which drew attention to these circumstances and which by inference cast doubt on the propriety of Black's actions.

While Truman was still considering whom to nominate as Chief Justice, two well-known newspaper columnists, Drew Pearson and Doris Fleeson, published stories that Justices Black and Douglas would resign if Jackson became Chief Justice. Miss Fleeson's article, published on May 16, 1946, included a description of Jackson's opinion which had so antagonized Justice Black, and details which she could have obtained only through someone with inside knowledge of the Court's closed meetings. The tenor of both Pearson's and Fleeson's article was strongly positive for Black and negative for Jackson.

In Nuremberg, Jackson was kept abreast of developments by friends in the United States. He strongly suspected that either Black or Douglas had given the two columnists the information they had used in order to put Jackson in a poor light at a time when he undoubtedly was under consideration for the Chief-Justiceship. Whether or not Jackson took any steps to advance his own fortunes, I do not know. At all events, he kept his peace

°*Jewell Ridge Coal Corp.* v. *United Mine Workers*, 325 U.S. 161 (1945).

publicly until after Truman, on June 6, announced his nomination of Fred M. Vinson as Chief Justice. Vinson, then Secretary of the Treasury, had served briefly as a federal circuit judge, but much more notably as a top administrative official during the war.

Jackson, without consulting anyone except perhaps his son Bill, at once prepared a statement to negate and counteract the Fleeson column and to castigate Black's conduct in the case which had precipitated their quarrel. On June 8 he cabled the President the substance of what he was about to make public. Truman, in reply, suggested that the disagreement with Black should not be made public, but Jackson paid no heed. On June 10, he distributed copies of his statement to the press and immediately left Nuremberg for a trip to Scandinavia.

Jackson's statement was addressed to the Senate and House Judiciary Committees. At the outset, Jackson insisted that the argument was not "a mere personal vendetta among lawyers," but rather a controversy that "goes to the reputation of the Court for nonpartisan and unbiased decision." He then described the legal controversy in detail, including the events at the Court's closed meeting at which he had insisted on filing an opinion that raised question of Black's participation in the controversial case, and also in another case in which Black's ex-partner had represented the winning party. Jackson concluded:

> However innocent the coincidence of these two victories. . . . by Justice Black's former law partner, I wanted that practice stopped. If it is ever repeated while I am on the bench, I will make my . . . opinion look like a letter of recommendation by comparison.

Jackson, enjoying a pleasant trip through Norway and Sweden, escaped the thunderous crash of opinion pro and con that immediately erupted, both in the United States and at Nuremberg. All declared themselves "stunned," but there were such diverse views and reactions that it took some days to assess the results.

At Nuremberg, Biddle's reaction was scathing; Jackson's statement was "vulgar, silly, immature, and venomous"; Jackson was "like a child annoyed at his not getting the candy." Parker, whose own ambition to reach the Supreme Court had been frustrated when the Senate refused to confirm his nomination, was sympathetic: "I think . . . [Vinson's] is a fine appointment but I feel sorry for Bob Jackson. . . . Black is responsible for defeating him, and the only comfort to him is that Black did not get the chief's place. That would have created an intolerable situation for Jackson. . . . My sympathies are all with Jackson, but if he had asked me I would have advised him not to make this attack. Everybody will think he was motivated by pique."

Among the Americans at Nuremberg, there were all manner of opinions, while the British preserved a gentlemanly reserve and the Continental Europeans had difficulty understanding what the excitement was all about. Dr. von der Lippe recorded the comments in *The Stars and Stripes:*

> In Nuremberg, internationally prominent jurists, who have worked with Jackson since the inception of the war crimes trials, were quoted as saying that they feared his public involvement in controversy in the U.S. had damaged the prestige of the International Military Tribunal.

In Washington, at his news conference on June 14, the President, by manner rather than words, indicated dissatisfaction with Jackson's failure to telephone him before releasing his statement to the press. In Congress, there were some who took sides between the gladiators, but more who thought that both Jackson and Black had been hurt—indeed, a few thought both should resign. The *New York Times* editorialized more calmly:

> It seems to us that Justice Jackson has committed an error in taste and that Justice Black has committed the worse offensive [*sic*] of lowering judicial standards. . . . Justice Jackson does not question Justice Black's honor. He does question, and rightly, his judgment. . . . Faced with a similar situation the late Chief Justice Stone unhesitatingly disqualified himself. Can any impartial person doubt that Justice Black should have done the same?

Time heals wounds in part if not wholly, and when Jackson returned to the Court he and Black were able to sit on the same bench without throwing knives. But the important question was the effect in Nuremberg. I saw little evidence that the stature of the Tribunal had been lowered, but certainly Jackson's prestige within the Tribunal, already tainted by the failure of his Goering cross-examination, was worsened. The gentle Parker had no vote, but Biddle did, and another black mark for Jackson was bound to diminish his weight. Beyond question, the levers of control in the Palace of Justice were slipping from Jackson's hands and moving toward those of Sir David Maxwell-Fyfe and Francis Biddle.

**Schirach:** Baldur von Schirach, at thirty-nine, was the youngest and, except perhaps for Ribbentrop and Fritzsche, the weakest of the defendants. If wimps had then been spoken of, Schirach would have been so styled.

Educated in Weimar where his father was director of the court theater, Schirach was attracted to Nazism in 1924, when he heard speeches by

Rosenberg, Sauckel, and Streicher. He also became anti-Semitic, but testified that his "decisive" source was not Nazism but Henry Ford's *The International Jew*.

In 1925 Schirach heard Hitler speak in Weimar, and the following year he moved to Munich, where he became active in the Nazi Students League. In 1929 he became its leader. Hitler was pleased with his work and in 1931 installed Schirach as Reich Youth Leader, with the Party title of Reichsleiter, directly responsible to the Fuehrer. When Hitler came to power in 1933, Schirach became head of the Hitler Jugend, which rapidly absorbed all other youth organizations in Germany. In that capacity he became a government official. In 1940 Schirach was replaced as Hitler Jugend leader and made *Gauleiter* and Reich Governor in Vienna, where he remained until the end of the war. Like Streicher, Schirach was indicted only under Counts One and Four of the Indictment.

By the time Schirach's case was reached on May 23, 1946, he had been sitting in the dock for over five months, and events in both the dock and the prison had a profound effect on the testimony he ultimately gave. His discussions with Dr. Gilbert and the other defendants reflected the flabby and fluctuating course of his mind and motives.

In late October 1945, a few weeks before the trial began, Gilbert found Schirach handsome, articulate (he stood midway in Gilbert's IQ list of defendants), deeply remorseful, and resigned to death. By 1938, Schirach declared, Hitler had become "inhumane and a tyrant." In December, after a few weeks of the trial, Schirach was consorting with Speer and Fritzsche (the leading anti-Hitlerites), insisting that the Fuehrer "had gone crazy in 1943." Schirach had enjoyed considerable social contact with Hitler, through marriage to Henriette Hoffmann, the pretty daughter of Heinrich Hoffmann, Hitler's official photographer, who also served as chauffeur and a sort of court jester.

On February 9, 1946, however, Dr. Gilbert recorded a sharp change:

> Von Schirach's attitude of remorse before the trial has completely disappeared since he came under Goering's influence again in the first weeks of the trial. The essential moral weakness of this narcissist has been clearly shown in the manner in which he has subdued his indignation at the "betrayal" of German Youth by Hitler, under the influence of Goering's aggressive cynicism, nationalism, and pose of romantic heroism. . . . His original intention to write a denunciation of "Hitler's betrayal" to leave behind with me after he is executed, fizzled out, in spite of efforts by Major Kelley and myself to encourage him to write it. He has acted as Goering's messenger to lay down the "Party Line" to recalcitrant defendants like Speer. . . . After yesterday's argument in which Goering impatiently attacked both Fritzsche and von Schirach as "young weaklings" while he was by

implication a more heroic nationalist, I decided the time was ripe to make another attempt to draw out von Schirach.

These efforts by Gilbert and his medical colleague Douglas M. Kelley to keep Schirach remorseful did not have much effect, and in mid-March, when Goering took the witness stand, Schirach was delighted with his performance. Gilbert wrote:

> Von Schirach was very pleased with his hero. He thought it would be political madness to sentence him, because he was so popular, even in America, "and now you can see why he was so popular." He thought that Ribbentrop was far more guilty for the war.

Schirach was certainly malleable, which was hardly surprising in one who took his lessons in race relations from such as Henry Ford and Julius Streicher. Gilbert's next move was to require Goering to eat his lunch alone and to seat Schirach at a table with Speer, Fritzsche, and Funk. Within a month Gilbert noticed Schirach's repentant attitude, which was also affected by Hans Frank's confession. But the turning point, later in April, was Gisevius's disclosure of Goering's murderous conduct in the Roehm purge and his malicious conniving in the Blomberg-Fritsch affair.

Schirach was so upset by the unmasking of his hero that for some time he would not discuss the matter, and he retained to the end some admiration for Goering. But with his own case less than three weeks off, he declared to Gilbert that Goering "is a big man, but he belongs to an outworn, medieval tradition. . . . I am thinking of the future of German Youth." He began to draw psychic sustenance from the thought that "the future of anti-Semitism lay in his hands" and that "German Youth is listening for a word from their former leader." Gilbert then told him that "the only way he could make up in a small measure for what he had done was to come right out, speaking to and for German youth, and declare flatly that Hitler had betrayed them." These ideas fed both ego and motivation, and Schirach appears not to have sensed that few of his listeners would stomach the idea of Baldur von Schirach as the postwar spokesman of German youth.

Schirach was represented by Dr. Sauter, whose earlier appearance in behalf of Funk had not endeared him to the Tribunal.° After Schirach had given his presumed history, Sauter and he dwelt at great length with the Hitler Jugend (HJ), and Schirach's actions and policies during the years of his leadership.

In view of the charge in the Indictment that Schirach had "promoted

---

°Sauter's reputation does not suggest that he would have encouraged his client to come out against the Nazi regime.

the psychological and educational preparations for war and the militarization of Nazi organizations," Schirach's purpose was to distance the HJ from
the Wehrmacht and military matters in general. He testified that the uniforms of the HJ were not military and were intended only as uniform garb
for rich and poor alike, that he was involved in no conspiracy with the
Wehrmacht leaders or others, that there was no military training in the HJ
and no military officers among its leaders, that the only HJ use of rifles was
for marksmanship competition, as in other countries' youth organizations,
that he himself was the only Party official in the HJ's leadership, and that
he had no personal or official contacts with the Wehrmacht leaders and
received no information from them.

All of this was relevant to Schirach's charge under Count One, but it
was presented so ponderously by Sauter, and Schirach was so unctuous in
explaining how to train young men, that Lawrence became unusually caustic. When Sauter requested the Tribunal members to look at pictures of the
Foreign House of the Hitler Youth near Berlin, Lawrence sarcastically
refused: "We are quite prepared to take it from you without looking at the
house. The particular style of architecture will not affect us." At lunch,
Biddle strongly urged Lawrence to "stop this hogwash," but de Vabres
wanted Schirach's "psychological" background, and Parker was fearful of
"stopping freedom of speech."

The proceedings were livelier when Sauter turned to Count Four,
crimes against humanity, in connection with Schirach's tenure as *Gauleiter*
in Vienna. At the very meeting in which Hitler had assigned him to this
post, Schirach testified, Hitler said "that he was sending the Jewish population away from Vienna, and that he had already informed Himmler or
Heydrich . . . of his intention. . . . Vienna had to become a German city."

Hitler also told Schirach that the Viennese Jews would be sent to Hans
Frank's Government-General. Schirach admitted that "this plan of resettlement sounded perfectly reasonable to me." The deportation of some 60,000
Vienna Jews was actually carried out by Anton Brunner, an SS officer and
subordinate of Adolf Eichmann's. No doubt Schirach was correct in stating
that "it was entirely impossible for me to stop the deportation," but he also
declared, "I was of the opinion that the deportation was really in the
interest of Jewry" and explained that since the events of Kristallnacht in
November 1938, he had thought that deportation was the only way Jews
could escape the hatred and violence against them under the Nazi regime.
Schirach admitted, however, that in a public speech he made in Vienna in
September 1942, he had said:

> Every Jew who operates in Europe is a danger to European
> culture. If I were to be accused of having deported tens of thousands
> of Jews from this city, once the European metropolis of Jewry, to the

Eastern ghetto, I would have to reply, "I see in that an active contribution to European culture."

When Dr. Sauter asked Schirach when he had learned that "Hitler's plan aimed at extermination . . . of Jews," he replied that in 1944 his friend Colin Ross° "had told me that mass murders of Jews had been perpetrated on a large scale in the East." Schirach himself was able to verify that "executions of Jews were carried out by gas vans" in western Poland.†

These revelations led to Sauter's next question: "What, today, does the name of Auschwitz convey to you?" Schirach used the question as a springboard for his long-contemplated personal confession and his "acquittal" of German youth:

> It [Auschwitz] is the greatest, the most devilish mass murder known to history. But that murder was not committed by Hoess [Rudolf Hoess, the Commandant]. Hoess was merely the executioner. The murder was ordered by Adolf Hitler, as is obvious from his last will and testament. . . .
>
> The youth of Germany is guiltless. Our youth was anti-Semitic, but it did not call for the extermination of Jewry. . . .
>
> I have educated this generation in faith and loyalty to Hitler. The Youth Organization which I built up bore his name. I believed that I was serving a leader who would make our people and the youth of our country great and happy and free. . . . I believed in this man, that is all I can say for my excuse and for the characterization of my attitude. That is my own personal guilt. I was responsible for the youth of our country. I was placed in authority over the young people, and the guilt is mine alone.

At the luncheon break, Schirach's demarche was generally applauded by his fellow defendants. Goering was ill and not in court, Streicher was scornful, and Frank jealous, but there were accolades from Fritzsche, Speer, Funk, Papen, Neurath, Schacht, and even Doenitz. The wide approval went to Schirach's head, and he declared to Gilbert that what he had said "ends the Hitler myth" and "will no longer leave any doubts in the minds of German Youth." Then he turned dramatic: "Well, now I have made my statement and ended my life. I hope the world will realize that I only meant well."

On cross-examination, Tom Dodd spent nearly an entire afternoon

---

°Dr. Colin Ross was a much-traveled writer and close friend of Schirach's who had introduced him to Hitler. Ross committed suicide near the end of the war.

†Schirach testified that the gas van killings took place in the Warthegau, an administrative division comprising western portions of prewar Poland which were annexed by Germany in 1939 after the conquest and collapse of Poland as a nation.

trying to breathe some life into the charge that Schirach had conspired to initiate aggressive war. He was able to show from songs, books, and other sources that the HJ was much more militant, anti-Jew, and antichurch than Schirach had described it. For example, in 1938 the *HJ Year Book* contained an article entitled "Education for War of German Youth."

But with regard to Count One of the Indictment, all this was wasted effort. There was no evidence involving Schirach in plans or intentions of starting or waging aggressive war. He attended none of the meetings in which such plans were discussed and had only minimal contacts with military and diplomatic officials. He testified that in 1939 he was "firmly convinced that Hitler would not allow a war to break out," and the prosecution had no evidence to the contrary. Under these circumstances, even if the HJ had engaged in extensive military training under military supervision, such factors would have provided no basis for Schirach's conviction on Count One.

Schirach's admissions had left him on much shakier ground on Count Four, especially in the light of his public support for the expulsion of Jews from Vienna to Poland. Dodd had evidence which further strengthened the prosecution's case. In 1942, reports describing the activities of the Einsatzgruppen operating in the Soviet Union, including accounts of the massacres of many thousands of Jews, were sent regularly to Schirach in Vienna, marked for the attention of Dr. Fischer, a member of Schirach's staff. The defendant denied that he had ever seen them, but Dodd pointed to details that cast doubt on Schirach's credibility.

The reports were received at a time when Vienna Jews, with Schirach's approval, were still being sent to Poland. The allegations of Schirach's involvement in the expulsion of Jews from Vienna was further strengthened by Dodd's use of a document, previously introduced by Colonel Pokrovsky, which described a conference in October 1940 at Hitler's apartment that was attended by Bormann, Hans Frank, and Schirach, who had remarked "that he still had 50,000 Jews in Vienna whom Dr. Frank would have to take over." Later Hitler described his policy toward the Poles:

> The standard of living in Poland has to be and to remain low. . . . It is indispensable to keep in mind that there must be no Polish landowners. However cruel this may sound, wherever they are, they must be exterminated. . . . All representatives of the Polish intelligentsia are to be exterminated. This sounds cruel, but such is the law of life.

Even hearing such murderous plans from Hitler's mouth appears not to have weakened Schirach's loyalty to and admiration for his Fuehrer.

Perhaps the best example of Schirach's lack of sensitivity was his reply to Dodd's concluding question, which was directed at his asserted lack of prior knowledge of the Einsatzgruppen reports that had been sent to Schirach's office and were filed by his principal assistant, Dr. Dellbrugge. Schirach's explanation was:

> I can understand perfectly well why the Government President, since he was overburdened with work, did not submit to me material which had no connection at all with Vienna or my activities, but which were merely informative and concerned events in Russia, mostly guerrilla fighting in Russia.

By the time Dodd asked the question, Schirach knew that the reports showed the massacre by German SS troops of hundreds of thousands of Jews in areas ranging from the Crimea to Estonia. His description of the reports as "merely informative" was, to say the least, very cool.

**Sauckel:** Ernst Friedrich Christoph Sauckel, better known as Fritz Sauckel, was small and apparently inoffensive. Born in 1887, at the age of fifteen he became a sailor in the merchant marine and after the outbreak of World War I was captured by the French and was for five years a prisoner of war. After the war he worked in a factory in Schweinfurt, where he became politicized, and in 1925 he joined the Nazi Party. He met Hitler, and though Sauckel then had no close connection, in 1927 he was appointed *Gauleiter* in Thuringia, a former province in mid-Germany whose capital was Weimar. In 1933 he was appointed to the official position of Reich Regent of Thuringia.

By that time it was plain that Sauckel was much bigger than he looked and much abler than one might conclude on finding his name near the bottom of Dr. Gilbert's IQ list. He gave hundreds of public speeches and published articles and a couple of books. He was both the party and the governmental leader of Thuringia. The eminent Berlin journalist Louis Lochner regarded him as "one of the toughest of the Old Guard Nazis." Still, Sauckel was a regional potentate, and if he had remained only the boss of Thuringia there would have been little likelihood of finding him in the dock at Nuremberg.

Sauckel was charged on all four counts of the Indictment, but he had virtually no military or diplomatic connections, and there was literally no basis for conviction under Counts One and Two. He had considerable experience with labor problems, and by the end of 1941 the drain of manpower into the Wehrmacht was threatening a crisis in both manufacture and agriculture. And when Hitler called on Sauckel to deal with the labor shortage, Joseph Goebbels noted in his diary:

> Sauckel has been appointed Reich Plenipotentiary for man-power.... Undoubtedly his strong National Socialist hand will achieve miracles. It should not be difficult to mobilize at least a million additional workers from among the German people.

Accordingly, the Sauckel case involved exclusively the conduct of his office as Plenipotentiary General for the Allocation of Labor, a position to which he was appointed on March 21, 1942. His counsel, Dr. Robert Servatius, wisely spent only a few minutes on events prior to that date, and nothing was said about Counts One and Two.

Servatius was a much better lawyer than Sauter, and Lawrence found little fault with his questions.° But the defendant himself caused some problems, partly because of his odd habit of pausing "between each word," as Lawrence put it,† and partly because, as Dr. von der Lippe noted: "Sauckel speaks such vile German that the listener is in pain. Through the translation into English, grammar and composition are greatly improved, so the Tribunal doesn't hear the defective language."

Sauckel was unable to answer Servatius's question "Why were you chosen for this office?" but said that Bormann's official decree stated that Speer (who only a few weeks earlier had been appointed Reich Minister for Armaments and Munitions) had proposed him. But Speer (writing twenty-five years later) declared that Hitler, on Bormann's recommendation, had chosen Sauckel.

Thus the sailor turned workman turned local politician was elevated to the upper reaches, where he rubbed elbows with Goering of the Four-Year Plan, Speer the munitions maker, Field Marshal Erhard Milch of the Central Planning Board, Himmler and Heydrich of the Secret Police and Einsatzgruppen, Hitler's sinister confidant Bormann, and others whose names were then household words. Heady stuff but dangerous, a world of treachery, deceit, and slander, where life was like swimming in a tank of barracuda. It would not be long before Sauckel was on bad terms with Speer, and Goebbels, who had touted him as a miracle maker, would deride him as "one of the dullest of the dull."

There were other, less immediate but greater dangers. Goebbels had envisaged Sauckel's finding the new workers among the German people; however harshly that might be done, it was no war crime. Nor (subject to some restrictions) was it a war crime if foreigners came voluntarily to work in the Reich. But deportation—forced removals of foreigners in German-occupied areas from their habitats—was a crime under the provisions of the

°Dr. Servatius represented Adolf Eichmann at his trial in Jerusalem in 1962.

†Lawrence: "Defendant . . . it appears to me that if you would not make pauses between each word it . . . would be much more convenient for the interpreter."

Hague Conventions. The state of worker recruitment in France, in March 1944, is vividly portrayed in the discussion of "labor supply" at a meeting of the Central Planning Board:

> HANS KEHRL° (sitting in for Funk): Up to the beginning of 1943 . . . a great number of Frenchmen were recruited and voluntarily went to Germany.
>
> SAUCKEL (interrupting): Not only voluntarily, some were recruited forcibly.
>
> KEHRL: The calling-up [mandatory recruitment] started after the recruitment did no longer yield enough results.
>
> SAUCKEL: Out of the 5 million foreign workers who arrived in Germany, not even 200,000 came voluntarily.
>
> KEHRL: Let us forget for the moment whether some slight pressure was used. Formally, at least, they were volunteers. After the recruitment did no longer yield satisfactory results, we started calling-up according to age groups, and with regard to the first age group the success was rather good. Up to 80% of the age group were caught and sent to Germany. . . . Following developments in the Russian war and the hopes raised thereby in the Western nations, the results of this calling-up of age groups became considerably worse . . . the men tried to dodge the call-up. . . . Therefore relatively small percentages were caught . . . these men took to the mountains where they found company and assistance from the small partisan groups existing there.

No doubt, as Sauckel protested when his statement was read to the Tribunal, his "200,000" figure was an "utterly impossible proportion." But the colloquy reveals the forces that led to forced labor on a huge scale and the uneasiness of those, like Sauckel, who engineered it.

In mid-December 1945 Tom Dodd, in the course of the American presentation, had inundated Sauckel (and Speer, too) with incontestable documentary proof of Sauckel's management of the forced as well as the "voluntary" recruitment† of foreign workers and of the brutalities and deprivations suffered by the workers. Sauckel was a proletarian and contended, with some show of sincerity, that he did his best in behalf of the workers, but the bulk of them came from Eastern Europe and, considering the Nazi attitude toward Slavs, general good treatment was not to be expected. Dodd's evidence had had a crushing effect on Sauckel, Dr. Gilbert reported:

> Sauckel was trembling as if I had come in to torture him. He immediately began to defend himself with trembling voice and wring-

---

°Kehrl was a high official of both the Economics Ministry and the Central Planning Board.

†There was no reliable way to establish the percentage of voluntary recruits, some of whom may have appeared to be such, but who had consented without complaint because of fear of the consequences of objection.

ing hands: "I want to tell you that I know absolutely nothing of these things, and I certainly had absolutely nothing to do with it! It was just the opposite. I wanted to make conditions as good as possible for the foreign workers."

Servatius could do little for him but follow Kaltenbrunner's line and push responsibility onto others. Did Sauckel have authority over recruitment in military operational areas? No; in the East and in France and Belgium he could only ask the military authorities to take recruitment action. What about in the Occupied Eastern Territories? Sauckel's recruitment agents were assimilated with Rosenberg's staff. Who had authority over transport of the workers to Germany? The Reichsbahn, i.e., the Reich Minister of Transport, Dr. Julius Dorpmueller. Responsibility for working conditions was held by the *Gauleiters*, and Sauckel had authority only in his own Thuringia.

Determined to make this jerry-built system work, on January 6, 1943, Sauckel summoned some 800 officials to a meeting in Weimar and told them:

> Where the voluntary method fails (and experience shows that it fails everywhere) compulsory service takes its place. . . .
>
> We are going to discard the last remnant of our soft talk about humanitarian ideals. Every additional gun which we procure brings us a moment closer to victory. It is bitter to tear people from their homes, from their children. But we did not want the war. The German child who loses his father at the front, the German wife who mourns her husband killed in battle, suffers far more. Let us disclaim every sentiment now. . . .
>
> This is the iron law for the Allocation of Labor for 1943. In a few weeks from now there must no longer be any occupied territory in which compulsory service for Germany is not the most natural thing in the world.

The first cross-examination was handled by Jacques Herzog, a French junior prosecutor. It was well organized, but lasted the equivalent of a full day, to no sufficient purpose. Herzog, like his colleagues, was chiefly interested in damage or insults to La France, and most of his time was spent on mandatory call-ups of French workers—a crime already proved many times over.

Herzog was followed by General Alexandrov, who took nearly as long, partly because, in the Soviet fashion, he mixed his questions with pejoratives. For example, in asking whether foreign workers were used primarily in war industries, Alexandrov's question was: "Then the utilization of imported manpower was subordinated entirely to the conduct of the war of aggression by Germany? Do you admit that?" This, of course, caused Sauckel to deny that Germany's wars were aggressive, instead of agreeing, as he would have, that the foreign workers were used in war manufactures. Tired of these delays, Lawrence told Alexandrov not to mix in allegations of crime, but the habit was so ingrained that the General immediately did it again.

Nothing of moment emerged from Alexandrov's efforts. After Servatius finished a brief redirect, a new figure entered the cross-examining arena: Judge Francis Biddle. For close to an hour he rode Sauckel, insisting on short answers to direct questions. This style was a great relief to the listeners, and one commentator has labeled Biddle's the "deftest cross-examination" of the entire trial. Biddle himself thought it good, writing to his wife: "The French and the Russians had been quite inadequate and I decided to go to town on him [Sauckel]. . . . I really got him. He was frightened, brief, and totally responsive." But another commentator thought it "doubtful whether the Sauckel case had been at all advanced," and I share the doubt.

Sauckel's first three witnesses, all former subordinates, added nothing to his case. More interesting was the fourth and last witness, Dr. Wilhelm Jaeger, who had been retained in Essen by the Krupp firm to supervise the health of Krupp's foreign workers. Jaeger had given an affidavit to the prosecution but was called as a witness by Servatius, some of whose questions were thus in the nature of cross-examination. According to Jaeger's affidavit, when he started his work with Krupp in October 1942, the Krupp camps for foreign workers were surrounded by barbed wire and were grossly inadequate in food, clothes, shelter, and medical supplies. He testified, however, that under Sauckel's orders, early in 1943 the barbed wire was removed and the food situation improved. Unfortunately for the record, Jaeger's recollections were very imprecise, and since there was much other evidence about the situation of foreign workers, his testimony was not of great importance.

As a last question, Servatius asked his client "whether today you consider your activity justified or not." Sauckel answered: "From the point of view of the war situation and of German economy, and as I saw and tried to carry out my allocation of labor, I consider it justified." It was a frank answer, but not likely to promote an acquittal.

**Jodl:** Generaloberst° Alfred Jodl's father and several other forebears were Bavarian Army officers, and his younger brother Felix was a field com-

---

°The equivalent of an American four-star general and the highest German rank before Field Marshal.

mander who ended the war as a General of Mountain Troops. The army was, above all, the *fons et origo* of Alfred Jodl's outlook on the world and its problems.

Bald and of modest stature, Jodl was not a dashing figure, but by his middle forties his intellectual gifts for military planning and administration had greatly impressed his senior officers, and in 1935 he was marked and chosen for high-level staff work. Despite his brilliant staff faculties, Jodl was only in the middle of Dr. Gilbert's IQ list.

Professional soldiers generally look down on politicians, and Jodl's initial opinion of Hitler was negative. His attitude changed very rapidly in 1937 and 1938, when he was serving under Blomberg and Keitel as Chief of the Operations Section of the Wehrmacht command. Personal diary notes which Jodl kept until May 1940 (and which were entered in the Nuremberg trial record) are replete with laudatory comments on the Fuehrer and his triumphs, and criticism of older generals unwilling to see him as a genius.

Jodl did not meet Hitler until September 1939, at the beginning of the war. From then until near its end, except for a few short gaps, Jodl reported on the military situation at all the daily staff conferences and was frequently involved in colloquy, and not infrequently controversy, with the Fuehrer. It cannot have been a very happy life, for Jodl described Hitler's headquarters as "a cross between a cloister and a concentration camp."[*]

The relationship remained impersonal and, as time went on, increasingly frosty. Within these limits, however, it is safe to say that during the war Jodl saw and talked with Hitler more than any other Nuremberg defendant. It is, no doubt, the military and businesslike nature of the Fuehrer-Jodl relation, together with Jodl's capital sentence, that has made his conviction more controversial than any other. Especially in comparison to Keitel's dismal weakness, the picture of an exceptionally able officer doing a necessary and difficult military task and standing by his guns in the face of Hitler's criticism is appealing, particularly to military people, who see him as "just doing the job that he was told to do."

Jodl's indictment under all four counts was based on very generally phrased charges. It was alleged that Jodl used "his personal influence" and "close connection with the Führer" to promote "the accession to power of the Nazi conspirators," promoted "preparations for war" and "planning and preparation of the Nazi conspirators for Wars of Aggression and Wars in Violation of International Treaties," and "authorized, directed, and participated in . . . War Crimes and Crimes against Humanity." There was no further specification; the indictment was inexcusably vague. But long before Jodl's case was presented, the prosecution's evidence had disclosed clearly enough the relevant, and serious, accusations against him.

---

[*]Jodl's use of this comparison suggests that he knew more about concentration camps than he subsequently admitted.

Jodl was well represented. His lead counsel, Prof.Dr. Franz Exner, and supporting counsel, Prof. Dr. Hermann Jahrreiss, were both excellent, the first a specialist in criminal law and the second in international law. Exner was a Jodl family friend, and rapport between client and counsel was good. Dr. von der Lippe wrote: "The Jodl defense team was especially ceremonious because both professors wore violet university robes, and Frau Jahrreiss [assisting the lawyers] completed the color symphony with a violet gown."

The Jodl team decided to deal first with the murder accusations and began with the Commissar Decree. Hitler's order, issued before the conflict with Russia began, provided that all Soviet military commissars—fighting soldiers in uniform who also had political responsibilities for the loyalty and spirit of the troops—when captured should be killed.

Jodl had been asked to review a draft of the order, which he well knew was a capital violation of the laws of war. His reaction was to write, in the margins of the draft, a suggestion that the order should be redrawn as a reprisal declaration. That, of course, would have required postponement of the order until after the conflict had begun so that an accusation of Soviet atrocities could furnish a plausible basis for reprisals. Whether by oversight or intent, Exner dropped the matter at this point, leaving the clear implication that Jodl proposed reprisals, whether or not soundly based, in order to camouflage an undeniably murderous violation of the Hague Conventions.

Exner then turned to the much-discussed Commando Order, which I had previously dealt with at some length in my presentation against the General Staff. Jodl brought out that Hitler himself had drafted the order and that his own responsibility had been to distribute it. On the legal validity of the Commando Order, Jodl was, and remained, ambivalent. In reply to Exner's question, he said: "I was not at all sure that this decree, either in its entirety or in part, actually violated the law, and I still do not know that today." He suggested, however, that sabotage commandos ought to be examined to determine "whether they were carrying the famous armpit guns, which go off automatically when the arms are lifted in the act of surrender, or whether they used other despicable methods during the fighting."

Of course, the use of such weapons, blocking as it does the right to surrender, violates the laws of war whether or not the users are commandos. Such treacherous acts might be the basis of court-martial, or, if widely used, support reprisals. But that was far from validating death to *all* commandos, regardless of their conduct, without benefit of court-martial.

Exner then turned to more general questions. The extermination of the Jews? "I never heard, either by hint or by written or spoken word, of an extermination of Jews." The concentration camps? "I knew there were concentration camps at Dachau and Oranienburg. Some divisional officers visited Oranienburg once in 1937 and gave me very enthusiastic accounts of it." Attitude toward international law? "I recognized and valued international law with which I was well acquainted, as a prerequisite for the decent and humane conduct of war." All these matters and more went very smoothly, and Exner then turned to Counts One and Two and the matter of aggressive wars.

Here Jodl's handling of the questions continued to go smoothly through discussion of the Rhineland militarization and the annexation of Austria. Both these actions were military events of great strategic importance, but neither resulted in war, and both were of such a nature that Jodl could plausibly describe them as nonaggressive actions, carried out with the strong support of the people in those lands. The conquest of Czechoslovakia, in which Jodl was deeply involved, also fell short of being a war, but most of the inhabitants certainly did not welcome the German conquerors and there was planned aggression in abundance. It was in his discussion of the events leading up to the Munich Agreement of September 30, 1938, and the dismemberment of Bohemia and Moravia that Jodl overplayed his hand and so badly distorted the course of events that his credibility suffered irretrievably.

As pictured to the Tribunal by Jodl, Germany made few military preparations for war against Czechoslovakia until September 14, 1938, when Czechoslovakia partially mobilized. Germany, he said, had no intention of using force unless Britain and France did not intervene militarily and unless Czechoslovakia refused to submit to agreements made between Germany and "the Western Powers." It is remarkable that Jodl essayed so ridiculous a presentation, especially since his own diary and other well-known German documents on the Czech crisis which Alderman had put in evidence early in the trial tell so different a story.

The sequence of events began on May 19, 1938, when the British, French, and Czech governments all received intelligence reports of German troop concentrations near the Czech borders. There was already tension in the Sudetenland, where municipal elections were to take place on May 22. On May 20 the Czech government had called up one class of reservists and a few specialist troops to reinforce the police in the Sudetenland. The Germans hotly denied that there had been any threatening German troop movements, and in fact there was no evidence of hostile intent. There was, however, ample basis for Czech concern about the Sudetenland since the Sudeten leaders had broken off political negotiations with Prague and their chief, Konrad Henlein, was even then in Berlin for what Jodl described in his diary as a "basic conference between the Führer and K. Henlein."

To the Tribunal, Jodl described the Czech call-up as "a monstrous incident . . . Czechoslovakia not only mobilized but even marched up to our borders." The idea of a Czech attack against Germany was ludicrous, and since the Czech soldiers were there to keep the peace in the towns of the

Sudetenland, their presence near the German border was necessary and certainly not threatening. But Hitler was furious and recast the first sentence of Case Green (the secret name of the plan for military operations against Czechoslovakia) so as to read: "It is my unalterable decision that Czechoslovakia must be destroyed within a reasonable period of time by military action." Jodl showed no awareness of the absurd cruelty of planning the destruction of a nation because of a dictator's pique.

Jodl next laid great stress on the fact that "no date existed in any of the orders for the starting of a war against Czechoslovakia." But if the Czechs had been listening to the German plans they would not have been much relieved since the plans did call for an attack "on the first favorable occasion" after October 1, 1938. That certainly meant that all necessary preparations for an attack should be completed by October 1. Jodl nevertheless told the Tribunal that "actually before 14 September, as far as the military forces were concerned, nothing happened."

That can only be labeled a barefaced lie. Jodl's own diary notes for May 30, 1938, state: "The Führer signs Directive Green wherein he decides to destroy Czechoslovakia in the near future, and thus starts military preparations all along the line. The previous intentions of the Army must be considerably changed so as to envisage an immediate breakthrough into Czechoslovakia on X-day together with an attack by the Luftwaffe."

Thereafter, as document after document showed, preparation for the military destruction of Czechoslovakia went on apace. From May to July, Hitler himself was pressing the army and the Todt construction organization to expedite fortifications of all kinds along the Franco-German border to discourage the French Army from interfering with Hitler's aims. Plans were made for a "pincer" attack across Moravia, from the southern German to the northern Austrian borders, to cut the country in two. Hitler was asserting his authority to review and alter the army's decisions, and Jodl's diary reflected his faith in Hitler and impatience with the older generals "who no longer believe or obey because they do not recognize the genius of the Führer, in whom some of them still see the corporal of the World War and not the greatest statesman since Bismarck."

In concluding his discussion, Jodl portrayed the Czechs as the real villains because of their partial mobilization on September 14 and full mobilization on September 23. He, of course, made no mention of the fact that on September 12 Hitler had closed the Nuremberg Party Rally with a speech brutally denouncing President Eduard Beneš and describing the Czechs as "irreconcilable enemies" of Germany or that by September 24 the German assault units were on the way to their deployment positions. To preserve the secrecy of German preparations, there was no announcement of a Wehrmacht mobilization.

It was becoming increasingly apparent that Jodl would press his points beyond reason and decline to acknowledge fault in any actions of his own. Some problems he brushed away by labeling them "political" matters which were none of his business. This did not fool Judge Birkett, who wrote on June 4: "Jodl, in his explanations, gives the impression that he was much more than a mere soldier. He shows considerable political knowledge, much ingenuity and remarkable shrewdness."

There was yet another side of Jodl's mind which also emerged in 1938 in the course of a hot argument about military leadership and whether it should reside primarily in the army Commander in Chief (as in the Hindenburg-Ludendorff days of World War I) or in Hitler as Fuehrer. Arguing for the second solution, Jodl wrote on April 19:

> War in its total form is a power conflict between two or more states using all means. . . . It serves the preservation of the State and Folk and the assurance of their historical future. These high goals give war its total character and ethical justification. It lifts war above the purely political act, or a mere military duel for economic advantage. . . . Only the singleness and unity of State, Armed Forces, and People can assure success in war.

In short, Jodl not only liked war but also thought it good for mankind. His attitude toward an international prohibition of aggressive warfare can readily be imagined. These had been the views of the German officer corps for many years, and Jodl might have stated them frankly to the Tribunal since they adequately explained why he had never boggled at any of Hitler's numerous sudden military attacks against other countries. But Jodl did not do that. Instead, he endeavored to avoid the application of Counts One and Two by contending that none of these attacks were "aggressive." Thus, when Exner brought up the German occupation of Norway,* Jodl declared: "I did use all my strength to contribute to the success of an operation [Norway-Denmark] which I considered absolutely necessary to forestall a similar action on the part of the English."

This was plausible, but it was only the first of a line of comparable pleas. When Exner asked what was to be said about "violating the neutrality of Holland, Luxembourg, and Belgium," Jodl described the serious dangers to Germany if Britain and France might be "thrusting through Belgium and Holland" toward the Ruhr industrial area and stated that "the decisive factor was that owing to the many reports that reached us, the Führer and we ourselves, the soldiers, were definitely under the impression that neutrality of Belgium and Holland was really only pretended and

---

*Jodl was in Vienna as an artillery officer in March of 1939 when the Germans occupied Bohemia and Moravia, and during the preparation of plans for the attack against Poland. He returned to the OKW late in August 1939, a few days before the attack.

deceptive." Jodl had little to support this accusation other than British night flights over Dutch and Belgian territory, which those countries had little power to prevent and which certainly did not constitute an abandonment of neutrality. Jodl then fell back on the same basis that Keitel had used: "And as for the ethical code of my action, I must say it was obedience—for obedience is really the ethical basis of the military profession."

When Exner shifted to the German occupation of Greece, Jodl released long-pent-up rage at Italy which, as he said, "was beaten as usual" in its war with Greece and came to Jodl "crying for help." It was the "result of Italy's madness" that opened the way for Britain to come into the Greek picture, and "during the whole of the war Italy was no help to us, only a burden." All these blunders caused Hitler to occupy "the whole of Greece as an operational area, since we could not possibly tolerate a Royal Air Force base in the vicinity of the Rumanian oil fields." So once again Germany waged war on a country to keep the British out.

Yugoslavia was crushed as the result of a domestic political change in late March 1941, at a time when preparations for the attack against the Soviet Union were well advanced and the occupation of Greece was imminent because of British landings there. Jodl's justification was based on Hitler's conclusion that the political change in the Yugoslav government had turned that country into an enemy of Germany. Thus the reason for the attack was to protect Germany against Yugoslavia's interference with Germany's wars against Greece and the Soviet Union.

As for the great war in the East, Jodl argued that the Soviet Union had amassed strong forces on Germany's western borders and that the German attack was "undeniably a purely preventive war." In support of this thesis—which I and many wiser men than I find preposterous—Jodl painted a picture of an uncertain Fuehrer confronting a formidable array of Soviet divisions and eventually concluding that there was danger of a Soviet attack. Accordingly, said Jodl, "If, therefore, the political premise was correct, namely that we were threatened by this attack, then from a military point of view also the preventive attack was justified."

A "purely preventive war" must mean that the attacker is safer by attacking than he would be by not attacking. This is not the place for extensive military argument, but I cannot avoid noting Jodl's supporting declaration that the German forces in Russia "were never enough" to defend themselves because "this front of 2,000 kilometers . . . needed 300 divisions at least, and we never had them."

The front of 2,000 kilometers ran from the Black Sea to the Arctic Ocean at Murmansk, and a German Army advancing to occupy Russia was bound to spread out to about that length. But the supposedly feared attack by the Soviet Union against Germany would have had a front from the Black Sea to the south end of the Baltic Sea, a distance of about 1,000 kilometers. Considering also the enormous advantages in transportation, concentration, and other factors which would accrue to a seasoned Wehrmacht fighting at its own boundaries, it is hard to imagine a Soviet decision to put its head in the lion's mouth. In the 1940s as in 1812, the Russians won by first retreating. To me, Jodl's "preventive war" has never made sense.

Essentially, Jodl tried to turn all of Hitler's attacks into "preventive" instead of "aggressive" wars. But, with the possible exception of Norway, his efforts failed. Jodl showed that Hitler had reasons for doing what he did, but governments that begin wars always have reasons, and reasons alone do not prevent a war from being aggressive. Jodl, with regard to Count Two, was confronting the same evidentiary circumstances as did Goering, Ribbentrop, Keitel and others.

Khaki Roberts's cross-examination of Jodl has not been much praised, and it is true that his Old Bailey training caused him to approach Jodl as if he were a safecracker. Furthermore, Lord Lawrence had appeared not to like him, and when Lawrence cut off some of Roberts's questions, the big lawyer remarked that he had "a very extensive experience in cross-examination in many courts," which did not improve the judges' attitude.

But in my view Roberts made some headway. Jodl had pictured the Norway occupation as solely for the prevention of British intervention. But Roberts brought out Jodl's own 1943 speech, which hailed the Norway seizure as "the realization of our own maritime necessities, which made it necessary for us to secure free access to the Atlantic by a number of air and naval bases." These "necessities" were, in fact, the initial motivations of the Wehrmacht's Norway venture.

Roberts pushed Jodl hard on his involvement in the October 1943 deportation of 232 Danish Jews[*] to German concentration camps. Jodl persisted in treating this as a "political matter" and had written from OKW that it was "a matter of complete indifference to us." These insensitive features of Jodl's personality came out more than once, as when his verbal picture of the German march into Austria was entirely a matter of bands and flowers, with no awareness of the much less joyful feelings of Jews and other anti-Nazi Austrians.

Roberts also read, with good effect, the forced labor portion of Jodl's 1943 speech, in which he said: "The time has come to take steps with remorseless vigor and resolution in Denmark, Holland, France, and Belgium to compel thousands of idlers to carry out the fortification work which is more important than any other work. The necessary orders for this have already been given." Jodl admitted drafting this passage, but added, "That does not prove that I said it." This caution was understandable, coming as the words did from an avowed expert on international law.

---

[*]Most of the some 2,000 Danish Jews were enabled by other Danes to escape across the Kattegat channel to Sweden.

None of the other questioners, or the four witnesses called in Jodl's behalf, added much to the state of Jodl's case. But Jodl made several comments to Dr. Gilbert that he would never have made in court. He had decided that Hitler's asserted fear of a Russian attack was feigned, simply to get the generals to go along with a war that he wanted. Jodl also had come to the conclusion that none of the wars Hitler had brought about were really necessary from the German standpoint.

Despite his mastery of subject matter and forceful statement, Jodl did not draw unanimous praise from his fellow defendants. Goering and Doenitz gave him high marks, but Jodl had stayed with the Fuehrer to the bitter end, and now that Hitler had been shown for what he was, Jodl appeared to Schacht and others as a fool.

Near the end of Roberts's cross-examination, Jodl coined his own professional epitaph: "It is not the task of a soldier to be the judge of his Commander in Chief. May history or the Almighty do that."

**Seyss-Inquart:** When the Tribunal assembled on June 10, 1946, Franz von Papen, seated at Jodl's left, would normally have been the next defendant to be heard. But both Papen and Seyss-Inquart, who was sitting at Papen's left, had been involved in the German annexation of Austria, and at Papen's request Seyss-Inquart was heard first.

Arthur Seyss-Inquart, born in 1892 in Moravia but a Viennese resident since 1915, was a successful lawyer who, like his fellow Austrian Kaltenbrunner, became politically active and in 1936 was made a State Counselor. He deeply desired the Anschluss of Germany and Austria to be accomplished, despite its prohibition by the post–World War I Treaty of St. Germain. Seyss-Inquart admired Hitler, but was not a member of the Austrian Nazi Party. His somewhat neutral political status and generally good repute cast him in the role of an intermediary. In February 1938, as Hitler's pressure on Chancellor Kurt von Schuschnigg increased, Seyss-Inquart was appointed Minister of the Interior. By then he was conferring with Papen (then Ambassador to Austria), Hitler's personal envoy Wilhelm Keppler, and, on February 17, with Hitler in Berlin. Seyss-Inquart thus came to function as an intermediary in the events which led to the resignation of Schuschnigg, the German Army's parade from the German border to Vienna, and Germany's annexation of Austria. These events in February and March constituted nearly half of Seyss-Inquart's presentation to the Tribunal.

Limping slightly and peering through thick spectacles, Seyss-Inquart was the least scrutable of the defendants. He shared with Schacht, Goering, and Doenitz the top rungs on Dr. Gilbert's intelligence ladder, but lacked those men's personal force. Fritzsche, who during the war had found Seyss-Inquart a "courageous critic of various abuses in the Third Reich," now reported that "he refused to countenance the slightest criticism of the past" and "permitted no interrogator, no psychologist, and only very few of his fellows to penetrate the mask that he assumed in Nuremberg." And indeed Dr. Gilbert's book records only one discussion with Seyss-Inquart, whom he found "very cagey about making any remarks about any of the other defendants." On the other hand, his immediate neighbors in the dock found him congenial; Papen described him as "the complete Austrian, cheerful, relaxed, often telling Viennese stories," while Speer singled him out as one of the few defendants who "showed some understanding" of the "principle of responsibility."

Seyss-Inquart was indicted under all four counts of the Indictment. The particular charges were that he had "promoted the seizure and the consolidation of control over Austria by the Nazi conspirators," participated "in the political planning and preparation of the Nazi conspirators for Wars of Aggression," and "authorized, directed, and participated in 'war crimes and crimes against humanity' . . . including a wide variety of crimes against persons and property."

As a defendant, Seyss-Inquart was the antithesis of Jodl, who, while admitting a few violations of law by the Wehrmacht, had fought savagely against confessing any crimes for which he was responsible. Seyss-Inquart, in contrast, freely admitted responsibility for various violations of the laws of war in the course of his activities in the Netherlands. His lawyer, Dr. Gustav Steinbauer, made no visible effort to stimulate his client to fight his way through the rough spots.

Despite his own legal skills, Seyss-Inquart did not present a forceful defense. In particular, his extensive description of his conduct leading to the Anschluss was aimed at political accusations which would not support a criminal conviction, let alone a capital sentence. Of course there was a treaty violation when Germany entered Austria, but the Charter condemned "a war in violation of international treaties," and there had been neither war nor any evidence that Seyss-Inquart wanted one. As Fritzsche put it, Seyss-Inquart was "preoccupied with his record in Austria" to the detriment of attention to his wartime activities.

After the Anschluss, Seyss-Inquart began to encounter political and moral problems of a much more serious nature. Austria became a province of the Reich, and Hitler appointed him its *Reichsstatthalter* or Governor. But shortly thereafter, Hitler approved a hard-line Nazi, Josef Buerckel, as Reich Commissioner for the Reunion of Austria with the Reich, which gave him general control over the Nazi Party and political questions. There followed a shower of decrees to turn Austria into a fully Nazified province that included, of course, rigorous anti-Jewish provisions.

Seyss-Inquart could have endeavored to lay the whole responsibility on Buerckel but when asked by Steinbauer whether he had "participated in the grievous treatment of the Jewish population," he replied: "I cannot at all deny it, for certainly, as chief of the civil administration, I issued orders in that line in my field of authority." Although these prewar atrocities were probably not punishable under the language of the Charter,* they were harbingers of the actions that Seyss-Inquart would soon confront in wartime.

Shortly after the conquest and occupation of Poland, Seyss-Inquart was sent there with the rank of Reich Minister and subsequently was appointed Deputy to Hans Frank, the Governor-General. In November 1939, Seyss-Inquart made a tour of inspection in the areas of Warsaw, Lublin, and Radom, on which he made written report. Steinbauer referred to it, but slid rapidly over the contents, and one can well understand why. In Warsaw, and again in Lublin, Seyss-Inquart instructed the German staffs that "the chief guiding rule of carrying out the German administration must be solely the interests of the German Reich" by a "stern and flexible administration" and that "the resources and inhabitants of this country would have to be made of service to the Reich." He added that "independent political thought should no longer be allowed to develop." Later the report stated: "Near the frontier we saw the countless Jews and similar rabble who were on the 200 meters of no-man's-land between the German and the Russian frontier posts waiting to cross over into Russian territory in the darkness."

Seyss-Inquart was learning the facts of Nazi conquest in Eastern Europe, and his report contains no hint of disenchantment. Steinbauer did not call the Tribunal's attention to any of these passages, nor was there any mention of these flagrant violations of the Hague Conventions.

The Netherlands, under Nazi occupation, was sorely pressed, but Seyss-Inquart, not a brutal man, must have been pleased when Hitler, in the spring of 1940, appointed him Reich Commissioner of the occupied Netherlands. The gentler human climate there was largely because Nazi ideology did not regard the Western Europeans as *Untermenschen* like the Slavs. As Seyss-Inquart described his mission:

> I was responsible for the civil administration, and, within this administrative task, I had to look after the interests of the Reich. Apart from this I had a political task. I was to see to it that while Dutch independence was maintained, the Netherlands should be persuaded to change their pro-British attitude for a pro-German one and enter into a close economic collaboration.

---

*In fact, since the Jews were Austrians, these "grievous" orders were not war crimes. Nor, under the language of Article 6 of the Charter, were they crimes against humanity, for they were not part of a conspiracy to commit crimes against peace and were committed before the outbreak of the war. See the Tribunal's analysis of crimes against humanity, I TMWC 254, pp. 132-33.

Not surprisingly, independence and pro-Germanism did not mix well, and the gulf between people and occupiers widened as the war went on.

But Seyss-Inquart certainly tried. He brought in a number of Nazi officials to man his staff, but left a large number of Dutch administrators in their positions. He urged Dutch-German collaboration, but did not force it. Whereas his opposite number in Norway, Joseph Terboven,° had given Quisling a high position, Seyss-Inquart gave no preference to the Dutch Nazi leader, Anton Mussert.

Matters went reasonably smoothly for the first year or so, and Seyss-Inquart's superiors were delighted with his work. In February 1942, Hitler was looking for a "man for Belgium" who should be "an extraordinarily clever man, as supple as an eel, amiable—and at the same time thick-skinned and tough." Hitler then added: "For Holland, I have in Seyss-Inquart a man who has these qualities." And seven months later Goebbels noted in his diary: "The Führer is full of praise for Seyss-Inquart. He governs the Netherlands very cleverly; he alternates wisely between gentleness and severity. . . . In contrast to him is Terboven, who knows only the hard-fisted way, and on the other is Best in Denmark [Werner Best, Hitler's representative] who knows only the velvet glove."

Although Seyss-Inquart was the ruling figure in the Netherlands, he was not omnipotent. The military commander, General Friedrich Christiansen, had his own sphere of responsibility. Of greater practical importance was the fact that his nominally subordinate Commissioner of Security, SS General Hans Rauter, chief of the Security Police, had been selected by Himmler and received orders directly from Himmler's headquarters.

Other defendants would certainly have endeavored to push off on Rauter responsibility for the Nazi crimes, especially since Rauter had been the chief executant of the deportation of Dutch Jews to Auschwitz and other concentration camps. Not so Seyss-Inquart. Asked by Steinbauer, "What did you, as Reich Commissioner, do about the Jewish question?" he replied:

> I will say quite openly that since the first World War and the post-war period, I was an anti-Semite and went to Holland as such. . . . I had the impression, which will be confirmed everywhere, that the Jews, of course, had to be against National Socialist Germany. There was no discussion of the question of guilt as far as I was concerned. I had only to deal with the facts. I had to realize that particularly from the Jewish circles, I had to reckon with resistance, defeatism, and so on.

°Hitler put Reich Commissioners in charge of civil affairs in the Netherlands and Norway because in both countries the heads of government (Queen Wilhelmina and King Haakon) had escaped to England. In Denmark, Belgium, and France there were no German officials in immediate charge of civil affairs and German policy was exercised through the army.

After several visits from Reinhard Heydrich, Seyss-Inquart received orders from Hitler for the evacuation of all Dutch Jews to the Reich and ultimately to Poland. In answer to Steinbauer's question, Seyss-Inquart stated: "Since the evacuation was a fact, I considered it proper to concern myself with it to the extent that was possible for me as Reich Minister." The Jews were collected in Westerborg concentration camp, from where they were taken in criminally overloaded trains to the East. Seyss-Inquart asked the Tribunal "to consider that the most important and most decisive motive for me was always the fact that the German people were engaged in a life-and-death struggle." For most of the unfortunate Jews evacuated, it was a death struggle.

The other major criminal matter that confronted Seyss-Inquart was the Reich's demand for Dutch laborers. His testimony on direct examination was that up to mid-1942 some 250,000 Dutch workers had gone to Germany voluntarily and thereafter a slightly larger number of labor conscripts had gone. Debenet, a French prosecutor who later cross-examined Seyss-Inquart, had been left befuddled, leading to a colloquy that again reflects the defendant's frankness:

M. DEBENET: Defendant, do you claim that you forced no one to go and work in Germany?

SEYSS-INQUART: On the contrary, I believe I enrolled 250,000 Dutch people to work in Germany, and I testified to that yesterday.

M. DEBENET: Good. I shall dwell no more on that point.

When Steinbauer asked his client, "Who confiscated raw materials and machinery in the Netherlands?," Seyss-Inquart replied that "My offices" had done the bulk of it. However, Seyss-Inquart contended that the contrary provision of the Hague Convention* was "obsolete and could not be applied to a modern war because the labor potential of the civilian population is at least as important as the war potential of the soldiers at the front."

Most of the crucial proof against Seyss-Inquart came from his own direct testimony. But so did much evidence of his actions intended to avoid excessive prohibitions, penalties, and destructions, such as reductions in the number of hostage shootings wanted by General Christiansen or Himmler; promotion of a food drive early in 1945 for the benefit of Dutch children and, near the end of the war, blocking scorched-earth and flooding actions that would have laid waste much of Holland.

This last matter required Seyss-Inquart to go from Holland to Kiel by

---

*Article LII: "Requisitions in kind . . . shall not be demanded from municipalities or inhabitants except for the needs of the army of occupation."

speedboat to secure Admiral Doenitz's cancellation of Hitler's demolition orders. Although he was urged to remain in the safety of Kiel, Seyss-Inquart tried to return to Holland by land, but was captured by the British in Hamburg. When Steinbauer asked him why he had insisted on returning to the Netherlands, he replied: "I wanted to take care of my co-workers . . . and, finally, I was of the opinion that since we had been out in front in the hour of triumph we could lay claim to being out in front in the hour of disaster as well." Such sentiments go far to explain why, as Fritzsche put it, "He refused to countenance the slightest criticism of the past."

The cross-examinations revealed little that Seyss-Inquart had not already acknowledged. Nor did the testimony of the six German witnesses called in his support. More remarkable was the appearance of Seyss-Inquart's remaining witness, the Dutchman Heinz Hirshfeld, who had throughout the war been Secretary General of the Economic and Agricultural ministries. Hirshfeld (whom von der Lippe thought made a very good impression) in no way condoned Germany's occupation of the Netherlands and under cross-examination by Dubost gave several answers damaging to Seyss-Inquart. But the bulk of his testimony confirmed the defendant's description of his efforts to mitigate the pressures of the occupation.

When Seyss-Inquart's presentation ended, it was clear that he bore a heavy burden of negative evidence. The question remained: What, if any, weight would the Tribunal give to mitigating factors? It certainly did Seyss-Inquart no good that Hitler went to his death with a good opinion of him and in his "will" picked not Ribbentrop but Seyss-Inquart as Foreign Minister—a choice no doubt unpleasant for both, though for different reasons.


**Papen:**  Franz von Papen's first statement, in reply to his counsel's request for "a picture of your life," was that he "was born on soil which has been in the possession of my family for 900 years"—a ready guide to his measure of social values. He inherited his nobility and married his money, which was provided by the daughter of a wealthy Saar industrialist. He became a General Staff officer and in 1913 was appointed military attaché in Washington. There his clumsy activities (he blandly wrote in his autobiography that he was "a soldier, not a diplomat, and had therefore paid little attention to what the personal consequences of my activities might be") angered the American government, and in December 1915 he was declared persona non grata.

After returning to Germany, Papen served on the Western Front and later in Turkey. After Germany's defeat, he resigned from the army, acquired an estate in his native Westphalia, and interested himself in politics. He joined the Center Party, bought a dominant interest in the party newspaper (*Germania*), and was elected to a seat in the Prussian State Parliament. This was a perfectly respectable debut in politics, but there was no rapid ascent; Papen did not even become a member of the Reichstag. But he cut a far wider swath than his elective status suggests. He was charming, witty, a magnificent horseman, and had a wide range of friends and acquaintances in political, military, and social circles. But as a politician Papen was not taken seriously, and he had no political following of any consequence. And so when, on June 1, 1932, President von Hindenburg appointed him as Reich Chancellor, the public was bemused, and there was much laughter and scorn.

Papen told the Tribunal that he did not know why Hindenburg had appointed him. But both his testimony and the account in his autobiography indicate that General Kurt von Schleicher, the Minister of Defense and more politician than soldier, thought Papen would be malleable and "sold" him to the old President.

However that may be, it is on June 1, 1932, that the Indictment's charges against Papen begin.° The Indictment refers particularly to Papen's positions as Reich Chancellor, "Vice Chancellor under Hitler," and as Ambassador in Vienna and later in Turkey. It charges that Papen used these positions "and his close connection with the Führer" to promote "the accession to power of the Nazi conspirators" and the "preparation of the Nazi conspirators for Wars of Aggression and Wars in Violation of International Treaties."

The lack of precision in these charges is palpable, and the reason is obvious. Evidence in support of the charges was, to say the least, flimsy, and some of it appeared inconsistent with the accusations. Papen's counsel, Dr. Egon Kubuschok (assisted by Papen's son Friedrich), spent nearly two days on their defense, while Lawrence pushed them on and Birkett ground his teeth. Goering and others had written about and described to the Tribunal Hitler's rise to power in the early thirties, and it was a more than twice-told tale. Goering, Keitel, Jodl, and Seyss-Inquart had all discussed the events leading to the Anschluss. Papen's ambassadorship in Turkey yielded nothing pertinent to the Indictment.

The negative evidence was that Papen had played a part in Hitler's selection as Chancellor and had supported him politically, and publicly heaped lavish praise on him, notwithstanding even the suppression of Papen's speech in Marburg calling for reform in Nazi social and religious policies. Even after the Roehm purge in which Hitler and Goering had had hundreds killed without trial, including many having no connection with

---

°Papen was the only defendant other than Hess and Schacht who was not accused under Counts Three or Four. The Indictment refers to Papen as a Nazi Party member, which he was not, and a member of the Reichstag, which he was not at the time he became Reich Chancellor.

Roehm, and after Papen himself had been held in confinement for several days, and even after the murder of his close friend Edgar Jung and his press secretary, Herbert von Bose, Papen had continued to write fawningly to Hitler. He had resigned as Vice Chancellor, but a few weeks later he accepted Hitler's request that he become Ambassador in Vienna. There, as Papen acknowledged, he pursued a policy "of union of the two states" (Germany and Austria). On February 4, 1938, during the Blomberg-Fritsch affair, Papen was one of the diplomats dismissed from his post, but Hitler requested Papen to remain temporarily to bring about the now well known meeting on February 12 at Berchtesgaden, where Hitler lectured and threatened Schuschnigg unmercifully and insisted on further inroads on Austrian independence. Papen left the embassy on February 26, 1938, two weeks before the Wehrmacht's march into Austria and the Anschluss.

Late in April 1939, Papen accepted Hitler's request that he become Ambassador to Turkey, where he remained until August 1944, when Turkey severed diplomatic relations with Germany. He returned to Germany and had no further political activities.

During his direct testimony, Papen had naturally spread the gloss of innocence on all the evidence. But Major Barrington's presentation against Papen the previous January had been so limited and tentative that the prosecution's difficulties were already manifest. Fyfe now undertook the cross-examination, and the question was whether he could accomplish anything to revitalize the charges.

Fyfe's cross-examination has been greatly praised; *The Times* of London described it as his "most brilliant effort" with "subtle texture and silken innuendo," and two authors of praiseworthy books on the Nuremberg trials also gave him high marks. Sir David certainly gave a good demonstration of British barristers' skills, but the results retaught the lesson that the cleverest lawyers cannot grow evidence in the courtroom; they must have something in hand.

Under the terms of the Charter and the specifications of the Indictment, the prosecution had to prove that Papen had promoted German wars of aggression or in violation of international treaties. There was no such evidence. The best that Fyfe could do was to reproach Papen, in a very accusatory manner, for what Papen had already admitted: that he had supported Hitler's policies from January 30, 1933, until the Roehm purge on June 30, 1934, and that as Ambassador to Austria he had promoted Hitler's purpose to bring about the Anschluss. These activities could well be regarded as mistaken and dangerous, and put Papen in a bad light. But Fyfe did not ask Papen a single question with regard to the promotion of war.

Surely the British prosecutors were aware that under the Charter there was no case against Papen, and purists might argue that the case should have been voluntarily dismissed. Such a move would certainly have triggered widespread indignation. Thus leaving decision of the case to the Tribunal was no doubt a prudent procedure.

Twice Fyfe attacked Papen as a coward, at first by putting in evidence letters from Papen to Hitler, written in the wake of the Roehm massacres and the murder of Papen's friends and subordinates. In his first letter of complaint about his own "loss of honor," Papen wrote, "I remain loyally devoted to you and to your work for our Germany." In a later letter he described Hitler's "crushing of the SA revolt" as "manly and humanly great" and "courageous and firm." And still later, Papen wrote:

> After you have given the nation and the world last night your great account of the internal developments which led up to 30 June, I feel the need to shake your hand, as I did on 30 January 1933, and to thank you for all you have given anew to the German nation by crushing the intended second revolution and by announcing irrevocable and statesmanlike principles.

These letters certainly provoke scorn, and Fyfe did well to ask Papen, "Why did you write stuff like that to the head of a gang of murderers who had murdered your collaborators?" Among the other defendants there was much sneering and snickering at Papen's discomfort.

Fyfe's other attack was less acceptable. At the very end of his cross-examination, referring to the Nazi murder of Baron Wilhelm von Ketteler (another of Papen's assistants), Fyfe asked: "Why didn't you after this series of murders which had gone on over a period of years, why didn't you break with these people [Nazis] and stand up like General Yorck° or any other people that you may think of from history, stand up for your own views and oppose these murders? Why didn't you do it?"

The British prosecutor hurled this challenge while representing a nation which had refused to "stand up" and "break with" Hitler from 1933 to 1939, even though the British knew well enough what had happened during the Roehm purge. Furthermore, Papen had been virtually imprisoned and found his close associates murdered when he was released. That a high rank was no protection was plain from the simultaneous murder of Papen's successor as Reich Chancellor, General von Schleicher. Papen might well have responded to Fyfe that it is easy for A to tell B that B ought to have been a hero.

Thus Fyfe, with no evidence of crime, turned to showing up Papen as a cad. And in indicting Papen, the prosecution had incautiously relied on his unsavory public record, without thought for the legal necessity of proven crime.

---

°Yorck von Wartenburg was a Prussian general (1759–1830) chiefly remembered by his disobedient, but eventually successful, turning of the Prussian Army against Napoleon in 1812.

**Speer:** Albert Speer was the last of the "big" defendants—those few (Goering, Schacht, perhaps Doenitz) who had great ability and had risen to the top of the Nazi hierarchy. Schacht's leadership had been limited to the Third Reich's first five years; Speer's covered a little more than the last three. Both in the period of high authority and the nature of the criminal charges, Speer's case most resembled Sauckel's.

Unlike Sauckel, however, Speer had been closely associated with Hitler for some eight years before the Fuehrer appointed him to high office. In recent years Speer's autobiographical writings have been so widely read that many people know the story of the young German architect whose dreams of gigantic buildings so fascinated the Fuehrer that he entrusted Speer with task after task and in 1934 gave him commissions and titles which established him as the leading official architect of the Reich. Speer had joined the Nazi Party in 1931 (before meeting Hitler), and among his earliest creations were the Nuremberg Party Rally and the new Reichschancellery in Berlin. Undertakings of such magnitude required managerial as well as technical and artistic skills. In 1937 Speer was made Inspector General for the rebuilding of Berlin. In the modern idiom, he was seen as both "take-charge" and "gung-ho."

When the war began, Hitler did not abandon his architectural plans, but after the invasion of Russia and Hitler's departure to his East Prussian headquarters in Rastenburg, Speer turned to military construction, under the leadership of Dr. Fritz Todt, Chief of the Organization Todt and Reich Minister for Armaments and Munitions. Before the war, Todt had made an enviable reputation, particularly in the design and production of the famous German superhighways (*Autobahnen*). After the German conquest and occupation of France and the Low Countries, Todt, among other tasks, was in charge of building the so-called Atlantic Wall as a defense against enemy invasion.

On February 8, 1942, at a time when Hitler, Todt, and Speer were all in Rastenburg, Todt was killed in the crash of his plane taking off to Berlin. Hitler immediately summoned Speer and appointed him as Todt's successor.

At the time Speer was thirty-six years old, and had had few contacts with military or political leaders. As he told the Tribunal, "It was a complete surprise to everyone when I was called to office as a Minister." But in fact Speer possessed extensive and successful experience in building construction and had been working with Todt for months. The Fuehrer distrusted the generals, Speer was right at his elbow, and Hitler chose the trusted civilian whose talents he highly regarded.

Speer was well aware that he was about to enter the same political jungle that Sauckel would encounter six weeks later. Even before Speer left Hitler's office, Goering appeared and told Hitler: "Best if I take over Dr.

Todt's assignments." Goering had quarreled endlessly with Todt, and when Hitler rebuffed Goering with the information that Speer was taking over "all of Dr. Todt's offices as of this moment," Goering was stunned and disgruntled, and Speer well knew that he could expect no help from that corner.

Speer soon realized that building construction was no longer the main purpose of his ministry; his major task was to provide weapons and equipment of all kinds for the army. But his responsibilities soon widened. He testified that

> In 1942 I took over the armaments and production programs with altogether 2.6 million workers. In the spring of 1943 Dönitz gave me the responsibility of naval armament as well, and at this point I had 3.2 million workers. In September of 1943, through an agreement with the Minister of Economy, Herr Funk, the production task of the Ministry of Economy was transferred to me. With that I had 12 million workers working for me.
>
> Finally, I took over the air armament from Goering on 1 August 1944. With that the total production was marshalled under me with 14 million workers. The number of workers applies to the Greater German Reich not including the occupied countries.

Speer proved a good politician and, except in Goering's case, the transfers of responsibility went smoothly.

Such was the empire within which the crimes attributed to Speer were committed. In the Indictment he was charged on all four counts, but since Speer did not get involved in war matters until after the Soviet-German war was under way, the conspiracy charge in Count One was out of the question and Count Two's crimes against peace at best dubious. The basis of Counts Three and Four included "particularly the abuse and exploitation of human beings for forced labor in the conduct of aggressive war."[*]

Speer came to his trial exceedingly well prepared. Apart from his basic intelligence (though only middling on Dr. Gilbert's IQ ladder) and fresh recollection of the preceding three years, he had been interrogated almost unceasingly, not only by the prosecution, but also by a string of military, administrative, engineering, and other visitors greedy for full information on the nature and workings of the German war machine. For example, the United States Strategic Bombings Survey, whose members included such operatives as John Kenneth Galbraith, Paul Nitze, and George Ball, could not get enough of Speer's opinions and disclosures. Thoughtful defendants

---

[*]Note the narrower wording of the final clause of Sauckel's comparable charge: "forcing the inhabitants of occupied countries to work as slave laborers in occupied countries and in Germany."

can often profit from the questions and reactions of their interrogators, and in all probability this experience aided Speer in framing his strategy for the trial.

That strategy went beyond Speer's plans for the nature of his own testimony. Just as Goering sought to establish his leadership of the defendants and a united front to justify Hitler and Nazism, so did Speer take the lead in acknowledging the failure of Nazism, the evilness of Hitler, and the defendants' own responsibility for the debacle. In all probability, Speer had no desire to be a lone soldier and hoped that bringing other defendants to his side would improve his general standing with the Tribunal and the prosecution.°

To accomplish this, Speer sought to split some of the defendants away from the forceful Goering. In January, lamenting Goering's influence, Speer remarked to Gilbert: "You know, it is not a very good idea to let the defendants eat and walk together. That is how Goering keeps whipping them into line." A month later, Speer's remark bore fruit when the defendants' luncheon tables were separated, with Goering isolated. The apparent results have already been remarked in the case of Schirach.

The previous week, Speer had essayed a more complicated ploy. His lawyer, Dr. Hans Flächsner, being absent, Speer requested Dr. Kubuschok to speak for him during the defense counsels' interrogations of Ohlendorf and to ask him: "Do you know that the defendant Speer prepared an attempt on Hitler's life in the middle of February of last year?"† Ohlendorf answered in the negative, both this question and Kubuschok's next and last question: "Do you know that Speer undertook to turn Himmler over to the Allies so that he could be called to account and possibly clear others who were innocent?"

Since Speer would later testify, and could (and did) testify about his assassination effort, it is clear that Speer had Kubuschok break the news ahead of time in order to emphasize the cleft between himself and Goering. He certainly succeeded insofar as Goering, at the next intermission, accosted Speer very angrily, and a heated argument took place in the presence of the other defendants. That evening Speer told Gilbert that "I spoiled his united front." However, it appeared doubtful that Speer had won any new members for his side of the "front."

Speer's direct testimony required more than a full day. The first half was a description of how he had managed his ministry. For the general

---

°Concerning the prosecution, I remember many comments favorable to Speer. It was said that Speer had declared that he wanted to be convicted and sent to Alaska to serve his sentence by improving its commerce and industry.

†The printed record reads "of this year," which is wrong since the date of this interchange was January 3, 1946, and February "of this year" lay ahead.

listener it was not a great success, as it was technical, full of figures, hard for the layman to follow, and largely irrelevant to the charges in the Indictment. Dr. Flächsner became Birkett's pet aversion, and Lawrence was impatient. To some it appeared that Speer was more interested in showing how ably he had handled his mammoth task and in explaining how, in some activities, he had been able to greatly increase production while at the same time reducing the number of workers.

From a legal standpoint, the case was not complicated. Sauckel's had involved the procurement of foreign workers, while Speer's involved their use. Speer readily admitted his knowledge that many of the workers supplied to him had come to Germany against their will. Indeed, Speer's admission was somewhat cavalier:

> I had no influence on the method by which workers were recruited. If the workers were being brought to Germany against their will that means, as I see it, that they were obliged by law to work for Germany. Whether the laws were justified or not, that was a matter I did not check at the time. Besides, this was no concern of mine.

It was true that Speer had no *authority* over the recruitments. But his constant pressure on Sauckel to produce millions of workers, knowing as he did that Sauckel had found it necessary to use force in order to meet Speer's demands, was certainly "influence." At no time did Speer suggest that he was not *responsible* for these actions, which in fact were massive violations of the laws of war.

During the later part of his testimony, Speer discussed such questions as the effect of Allied bombing in Germany and the German-occupied countries, his changing attitude toward Hitler, the factors that brought about Germany's military collapse in the spring of 1945, and his efforts to thwart Hitler's scorched-earth orders and others for the destruction of Germany's industries and other national resources.

Even though these subjects were irrelevant to the major charges against Speer, the Tribunal found them interesting and was more attentive. Speer's description of Hitler's desire to punish the German people for their failure to win the war by destroying the nation's resources made a deep impression on the defendants both for and against Speer. Schacht called it a "masterful defense," while Rosenberg cursed Speer for denouncing Hitler.

Near the end of the testimony, Flächsner asked his client about his plan to assassinate Hitler. Speer acknowledged his intention, but coyly declined to give details. Lawrence, like a small boy asking to be told an adventure story, declared that the Tribunal "would like to hear the particulars."

The story, as Speer told it, was more psychodrama than melodrama. Speer was tormented with self-reproach about whether to kill the man who had done so much for him or fail to kill the man who was trying to destroy Germany. Sadly choosing the first alternative, he procured poison gas with the intention of putting it down the ventilation shaft of the famous Berlin bunker where Hitler ultimately committed suicide and where Hitler, in March 1945, was having daily conferences with his military and personal staffs. But when Speer approached the bunker to reconnoiter, he found that someone had prudently encased the above-ground portion of the ventilation shaft in a chimney twelve feet high and that the area was patrolled by SS guards. So his plan fell through, thus relieving Speer from the pangs of indecision.

Considerably more relevant to the criminal charges was Speer's reply to Flächsner's question of whether he wished "to limit his responsibilities" to his personal sphere of work:

> No, I should like to say something of fundamental importance here. This war has brought an inconceivable catastrophe, and indeed started a world catastrophe. Therefore it is my unquestionable duty to assume my share of responsibility for the disaster before the German people. . . . I, as an important member of the leadership of the Reich, therefore, share in the total responsibility, beginning with 1942.

But what was "responsibility"? That question was to arise again later in Speer's case.

Jackson's cross-examination was unaggressive, probably because Speer appeared contrite and might respond more usefully to a mild than to a fierce approach. However that may be, Jackson's approach was fruitful. Under his questioning Speer admitted that he "did use and encourage the use of forced labor from the concentration camps," that he saw no objection to sending "slackers" to concentration camps, that he knew the concentration camps "had a very bad reputation" and were "much more severe than the labor camps," and that with his own approval 100,000 Jews had been brought, against their will, from Hungary to Germany to work in subterranean airplane factories. Speer claimed that all these actions were legally valid "in view of the whole war situation and our views in general on this question." Speer's answer, of course, took no account of the contrary provisions of the Hague Convention.

In the remainder of the cross-examination, Jackson questioned Speer on a number of photographs and documents showing or describing bad living conditions of workers at the Krupp plants in Essen. He did not accuse Speer of personal responsibility for what was described, but rather sought to have Speer acknowledge the existence of unacceptable treatment of the workers. Speer answered that he "had no time to worry about such things on his visits," grew angry, and declared that some of the documents were "the result of British bombing" or "lies."

In conclusion, Jackson asked Speer to explain what he had meant by "responsibility" in his reply to Flächsner's earlier question on the scope of Speer's "responsibility." After several interchanges, Jackson said: "Well, your point is, I take it, that you as a member of the Government and a leader in this period of time acknowledge a responsibility for its large policies, but not for all the details that occurred in their execution. Is that a fair statement of your position?" Speer answered: "Yes, indeed."

Jackson and Speer were satisfied, but Dr. Flächsner (whom I thought brighter than Judge Birkett allowed) was not. In his brief redirect examination he asked:

> I refer once more to the answer you gave to Justice Jackson at the end of the cross-examination, and to clarify that answer I would like to ask you this: in assuming a common responsibility, did you want to acknowledge measurable guilt or corresponsibility under the penal law, or did you want to record a historical responsibility before your own people and before history?

Speer replied:

> That question is a very difficult one to answer; it is actually one which the Tribunal will decide in its verdict. I only wanted to say that . . . the leaders must accept a common responsibility . . . after the catastrophe, for if the war had been won the leaders would also presumably have laid claim to common responsibility. But to what extent that is punishable under law or ethics I cannot decide, and it was not my purpose to decide.

Speer left the witness box and Flächsner, instead of calling any witnesses, introduced into the record interrogatories from Hans Kehrl and other former associates of Speer.

Despite his acknowledgment of "responsibility" for his government's policies which had brought about a "world catastrophe," Speer had not pled guilty; his not guilty plea still stood. As with Sauckel and Seyss-Inquart, however, his innocence could not be established except on the basis that the applicable laws of war were obsolete. But the Charter left no room for such a decision.

Speer had stepped into the witness stand holding the best reputation of any of the defendants with both the judges and the prosecutors. His appearance, presence, and handling of interrogations led Biddle to declare him "the most humane and decent of the defendants" and Fyfe to describe him as "by far the most attractive personality among the defendants."

On the whole Speer left the stand with his reputation still intact, largely due to his denunciation of Hitler and prevention of his scorched-earth efforts. Yet the testimonial record left him as loaded with crime as Sauckel, and those who followed closely would not forget his callous reference to the use of force as "no concern of mine" and the treatment of workers as something that he "had no time to worry about." At such times he reminded me of Doenitz, with whom he had gotten along very well during the war. I can well understand an episode related by Fyfe in his autobiography:

> My wife was one of many people who were profoundly impressed by Speer's evidence and manner, and remarked to Griffith-Jones that he would be the sort of man Germany would need in the future. Griffith-Jones replied by producing a length of blood-stained telephone wire, about ten feet long, which had been picked up at Krupp's, and which had been used to flog workers.

When Speer was shown the steel switches, he replied they were "nothing but replacements for rubber truncheons. We had no rubber, and for that reason the guards probably used something like this."

As the Speer case closed, I was reminded of Seyss-Inquart. Speer had a far greater impact on the course of events, but in both cases the defendants left the stand with a heavy burden of unlawful action, yet, at the end, substantial efforts to prevent further death and destruction. Would mitigation play a part in the judgments?

**Neurath:** Constantin von Neurath, white-haired and visually impressive, was carrying his seventy-four years with enough difficulty so that his counsel equipped him with written questions and answers. The lawyer, Dr. Otto Freiherr von Lüdinghausen, would have done better had he asked fewer questions and shortened the answers. His failure to do so earned him a place in Judge Birkett's growing rogues' gallery, where Lüdinghausen was portrayed as "tall, aristocratic, aloof, insensible to affront, with an extraordinary droning voice, and bearded like a poet." As for his ability, the judge wrote: "He loses himself in the maze of events, and produces an effect of complete and utter stupefaction."

Like Papen's first words, Neurath's told too much about himself:

> I was born on 2 February 1873. On my father's side I come from an old family of civil servants. My grandfather, my great-grandfather,

and my great-great-grandfather were Ministers of Justice and Foreign
Affairs in Württemberg. On my mother's side I come from a noble
Swabian family whose ancestors were mostly officers in the Imperial
Austrian Army.

Until my twelfth year I was brought up in the country in extreme simplicity, with particular emphasis laid on the duty of truthful-
ness, responsibility, patriotism, and a Christian way of life, along with
Christian tolerance of other religions.

After this burst of fireworks, Lüdinghausen took his client through a
long recital of his positions and actions during the course of German political history, larded with readings of excerpts from affidavits of a bishop, a
baroness, and a former ambassador, all of whom extolled the defendant's
wisdom and morals. The presentation went so slowly that Lawrence intervened repeatedly to stop irrelevancies and repetitions. Eventually he complained that "we have been the whole morning at this and we haven't yet
really got up to 1933." He ended the session by admonishing Lüdinghausen
that "the Tribunal hopes that on Monday, when you resume, you will be
able to deal in less detail with this political history, which, of course, is very
well known to everyone who has lived through it, and particularly to the
Tribunal who have heard it all gone into before here." But on Monday
(June 24), despite constant pressure from Lawrence, most of the morning
passed before Lüdinghausen reached 1938 which, as Lawrence remarked,
was the beginning of "the time with which we have to deal."

Up to that point, Neurath had declared that he was not a Nazi and
"had no close connection of any kind with Hitler." He had approved most
of Hitler's major actions. Neurath defended Germany's withdrawal from
the League of Nations; he accepted Hitler's explanation of the killings that
accompanied the Roehm purge, remarking that "in such revolutions innocent people very often have to suffer"; he denounced the Versailles Treaty
and approved rearmament to obtain "equality" for Germany; he approved
remilitarization of the Rhineland. Apparently, for Neurath, Hitler's only
dreadful mistake was introducing his fellow defendant Ribbentrop into the
field of foreign affairs.

A few of Neurath's answers displayed moral or mental shortcomings.
Lüdinghausen asked his client's attitude not "toward Jews" but "toward
the Jewish problem," and Neurath replied: "I have never been anti-Semitic. My Christian and humanitarian convictions prevented that. A repres-
sion of the undue Jewish influence in all spheres of public and cultural life,
as it had developed after the first World War in Germany, however, I
regarded as desirable."

Asked about the Rhineland reoccupation, Neurath declared it to have
"no military, but only political significance," apparently unaware that the

purpose of the Rhineland demilitarization was to open the Rhineland, including the Ruhr, to a hostile French invasion. Yet less than an hour later, Neurath was explaining that German fortification of the Rhineland's western boundaries would decrease the feasibility and hence likelihood of a French invasion.

Those first four or five hours shed some light on the defendant as a person, but virtually nothing had been relevant to the charges in the Indictment. No evidence emerged suggesting that Neurath had supported plans for aggressive war, or that he had reason to believe that Hitler had such intentions. Neurath claimed throughout his testimony that the Hitler conference of November 5, 1937, at which Goering and Raeder were also present, was "the first time" that he became aware of Hitler's aggressive plans: " . . . it was quite obvious to me that the whole tendency of his plan was of an aggressive nature. . . . It was evident that I could not assume responsibility for such a policy."

Neurath testified that he was unable to meet with Hitler until mid-January. After protestations which Neurath thought insincere, Hitler accepted his resignation. On February 4, 1938, as part of that day's major shuffling of high officials, Neurath was replaced as Foreign Minister by Ribbentrop. In order to conceal the fact that Neurath had resigned in disagreement, Hitler directed, and Neurath agreed, that he would retain the title of Reich Minister and become President of the Secret Cabinet Council, a paper entity which never met.

Neurath remained in Berlin for some weeks. On March 11, when the actions leading to the Anschluss occurred, Ribbentrop was in London, and Hitler asked Neurath to come to the Reich Chancellery for consultation. When the German military entry into Austria became known, the British Foreign Office sent a note of protest. On March 12, Neurath drafted and, at Goering's request, signed a note in response. Neurath admitted that the note was in part incorrect, a circumstance which he attributed to inaccurate information given him by Hitler.

The same day Minister Vojtech Mastny, the Czech envoy in Berlin, visited Neurath and asked whether Hitler, after the Austrian occupation, "would now undertake something against Czechoslovakia as well." Neurath testified that he had told Mastny "that he could set his mind at rest, that Hitler had told me the previous evening . . . that he had no thoughts of undertaking anything against Czechoslovakia" and that the 1925 Locarno Arbitration Treaty between Germany and Czechoslovakia remained in effect.

Lüdinghausen then asked how Neurath could justify reliance on Hitler's word in view of his statements about Czechoslovakia which Neurath had heard at the Hossbach conference. Neurath replied:

> In this discussion [i.e., the Hossbach conference], Hitler talked about
> war plans only in a general way. There was no talk of an aggressive

plan against Czechoslovakia.° Hitler said that if events led to a war, Czechoslovakia and Austria would have to be occupied first so that our right flank be kept free. The form of this or any other attack on Czechoslovakia, and whether there would be any conflict at all in the East, was doubtful and open to discussion.

Since only a few minutes earlier Neurath had described the Hossbach conference as so upsetting that he had suffered a heart attack and presented his resignation, this milk-and-water description of the same event disclosed his testimony as governed by expediency, and was ridiculous.

Neurath then retired to his estate, but emerged briefly in late September 1938 to participate unofficially in the negotiations that led to the Munich settlement and to the German annexation of the Czech Sudetenland. Less than six months thereafter Germany, by threat of military force, annexed Bohemia and Moravia as a Protectorate of the Reich. Slovakia became an autonomous German appendage.

Hitler soon summoned Neurath to Vienna and requested him to accept appointment as Reich Protector of Bohemia and Moravia. Unbelievable as it seems, Neurath testified that he believed Hitler's assurances that he had acted in accordance with "a firm decision by the Czech Government" and that he wished Neurath to "win over the Czechs by a conciliatory and moderate policy."

Of course it was all lies. Hitler installed the Czech Nazi Karl Hermann Frank as Neurath's Secretary of State and gave Himmler full authority over police and security matters. Neurath had to carry out orders from national agencies in Germany, many of which were intended to align Czech social and economic policies with those of the Reich. Thus the Nuremberg Laws and other anti-Semitic policies were introduced under Neurath's local authority.

When Germany attacked Poland and World War II developed, restrictions on the Czechs grew ever harsher. In November 1939, Hitler ordered the universities and other institutions of higher learning closed; Neurath testified that he urged Hitler to reopen them, but "due to the dominating position of Himmler I had no success." By late 1940 Neurath was involved with Himmler's proposals for Germanization or even resettlement of the Czech population.

Although decisions and policies went increasingly against Neurath, he made no effort to resign. He testified that he was able to accomplish some things that mitigated "the definite domination of the SS" and that "in time of war, especially, I should leave such a difficult and responsible office only

---

°This statement was groundless. Hitler's presentation dealt explicitly with the circumstances under which the forcible annexations of Austria and Czechoslovakia could most readily be accomplished, with the military and economic benefits which these annexations would bring to Germany.

in case of the utmost necessity." But in September 1941, Hitler made the problem easier for Neurath, who testified:

> I received a telephone call from Hitler asking me to come to headquarters immediately. There he told me that I was being too mild with the Czechs and that this state of affairs could not be continued. He told me that he had decided to adopt severe measures against the Czech resistance movement and that for this purpose the notorious Obergruppenführer Heydrich would be sent to Prague.

Stupid as Neurath had been to take on this brutal and thankless job, he knew better than to hang around with the ruthless Heydrich in real command. He immediately asked permission to resign, which Hitler refused, allowing him instead to go on indefinite leave. Neurath returned to Germany and remained at home, but he was not officially relieved from office until October 1943.

His appointment had been a mismatch from the beginning, as Goebbels had foreseen. At lunch with Hitler he declared: "Everybody knows von Neurath as a weak sneak. But what is needed in the Protectorate is a strong hand to keep order. This man has nothing in common with us; he belongs to an entirely different world." Hitler replied that "von Neurath was the only man for the job" because he was "considered a man of distinction" and his appointment would be "reassuring" to the Czechs that they would not be mistreated. But from a professional standpoint, Goebbels was right. After Neurath left Prague, Hitler explained that he had "let himself be completely diddled [sic] by the Czech nobility."

On cross-examination, it was immediately apparent that Fyfe had it in for Neurath and that the old man was no match for him. Neurath's earlier denial of anti-Semitism, already somewhat tainted, was wholly discredited when Fyfe read into the record Neurath's statement to the *Voelkischer Beobachter* of September 17, 1933:

> The Minister [Neurath] had no doubt that the stupid talk abroad about purely internal German affairs, as for example the Jewish problem, will quickly be silenced if one realizes that the necessary cleaning up of public life must temporarily entail individual cases of personal hardship but that nevertheless it served only to establish all the more firmly the authority of justice and law in Germany.

Neurath could only answer that this was still his view, but "it should have been carried out by different methods." Fyfe then showed that Neurath had succeeded in buying his home in Berlin at a very low price because the selling owner's wife was Jewish.

As in Papen's case, Fyfe's questions based on Counts One and Two were of doubtful relevance to the Charter. But whereas Fyfe had attacked Papen as a cad, he exposed Neurath as a prevaricator or worse and effectively weakened his credibility. This was very damaging to Neurath's case, as he had endeavored to cast responsibility for almost every dubious or criminal German action in the Protectorate on Karl Hermann Frank or Himmler.

In fact, the judges' disenchantment with Neurath became manifest at the end of his testimony, when Biddle, Nikitchenko, and Lawrence all put questions to him. Biddle pushed Neurath to admit that he knew what kind of man Himmler was before he went to Prague. Nikitchenko trapped Neurath into testifying that he had been opposed to all of Hitler's "aggressions," from Austria to the Soviet Union, and had repeatedly told Hitler his views. Neurath agreed that Hitler "made short work of his political opponents." Why, then, had nothing happened to Neurath? "I always expected it" was the lame reply. Lawrence referred to Neurath's reply to Britain's protest at the Anschluss, which had stated that "the Reich had used no forceful pressure" and that the idea of any ultimatum was "pure invention." He led Neurath to admit that he had made no effort to check the accuracy of these falsehoods, despite abundant opportunity to get information from participants other than Hitler. Dr. von der Lippe wrote that "many listeners got the impression that these questions from the Tribunal betrayed a very negative attitude toward Neurath."

Considering all that Neurath knew about Hitler and his Nazis by March 1939, his willingness to become Reich Protector was an act of pure folly. Had he declined, it appears unlikely that he would have been invited to Nuremberg. On the other hand, Neurath may have been much less anti-Nazi and more ambitious than he ever admitted. Some six months after he returned home from Prague, Neurath paid a visit to Goebbels, who wrote in his diary:

> Herr von Neurath visited me and told me how he is now living. He feels rather shelved at a time when he enjoys the best of health. His attitude toward the Fuehrer is most loyal. All in all Herr von Neurath is a gentleman, who has never been guilty of any incorrectness or disloyalty toward the Fuehrer. The next time I report to the Fuehrer I shall tell him about this visit. Maybe the Fuehrer will see a new possibility for making use of Herr von Neurath.

Luckily for Neurath, the call from Hitler never came, and Goebbels's diary entry surfaced too late to be entered in the Nuremberg records.

**Fritzsche:** Hans Fritzsche, seated at the far end of the upper tier, was of all defendants the least conspicuous and, except for Sauckel, the most ordinary looking. He was slight of build and appeared young, but was several years older than Schirach and Speer. Born in 1900, he had been a soldier in World War I. There was, however, nothing martial about him, and of all the defendants he was the most susceptible to the trials' shocking moments. In November 1945, after the first showing of an atrocity film, Fritzsche "burst into tears and sobbed bitterly." He remained prone to emotional distress from both testimonial and visual descriptions of atrocious events. Socially, Fritzsche was friendly, generous, and popular with the other defendants. They all knew that he was in the dock only because of his capture by the Russians who, except for Raeder, had secured no well-known defendants.

In 1923 Fritzsche had taken an editorial position, and thereafter his entire career was devoted to editorial and other journalistic work, including radio broadcasting. After Hitler came to power, Goebbels established the Ministry for Peoples Enlightenment and Propaganda, and in May 1933, at Goebbels's invitation, Fritzsche entered the press section of the ministry and joined the Nazi Party. He was several times promoted, and during the last two years of the war was Chief of the Radio Section of the ministry, with the title of Ministerial Director. Fritzsche was an important member of the ministry, and his successful radio program, "Hans Fritzsche Speaks," made him well known to the German public. But within the ministry he was a third-level employee, subordinated to Reich Press Chief Otto Dietrich, who in turn reported directly to Goebbels.

Fritzsche had never met Hitler and was previously unknown to most of the defendants. He had worked briefly with Funk and had single brief contacts with Doenitz, Seyss-Inquart, and Papen. Despite Goebbels's sincere regard for Fritzsche's ability, their relations were impersonal. Goebbels's diary contains very few references to Fritzsche, and his only personal remark was "Unfortunately, Fritzsche is altogether too much on the side of the press"—a comment more interesting about the relation between Goebbels and the press than about Fritzsche.

The charges against Fritzsche in the Indictment comprised Counts One, Three, and Four. Under the first count he was accused of having used his positions and influence "to disseminate and exploit the principal doctrines of the Nazi conspirators." Counts Three and Four were targeted at advocacy and incitement of "anti-Jewish measures and the ruthless exploitation of occupied territories." In essence, this all came down to a charge of using the facilities of the Propaganda Ministry to foment aggressive war and to commit crimes against Jews and the inhabitants of German-occupied countries.

Fritzsche and his lawyer, Dr. Heinz Fritz, were less heavy-footed than their immediate predecessors, and their presentation went smoothly, with virtually no interjections from Lawrence. With respect to Count One,

Fritzsche testified that he had no advance notice of Hitler's wars, that he never heard Goebbels or anyone else "speak of any intention to wage aggressive war," and that "at every moment from the Anschluss of Austria on to the attack on Russia, information given to me and through me to the German public left no doubt of the legality or the urgent necessity of the German action." Referring to Sprecher's case against him presented in January, Fritzsche categorically denied Sprecher's charge that he had used propaganda to arouse Germans to hatred of the enemy peoples: "I did speak strongly against governments . . . but I never preached hatred generally or attempted to awaken it indirectly." What, then, did Fritzsche preach? "During the war I conducted the propaganda almost exclusively with the concept of the necessity to fight. I repeatedly painted the results of defeat very dark. . . . I quoted repeatedly the enemy demands for unconditional surrender."

Fritzsche naturally stressed that the slant and purpose of German propaganda was not determined by him. The organization of the Nazi press was created by Dr. Goebbels, Dr. Dietrich, and Reichsleiter Max Amann, who had been Hitler's company sergeant during World War I and was chief of the Nazi Party Press. Government press policy was prescribed by Dietrich, who stayed at the Fuehrer's headquarters and "received his instructions directly from Hitler." Military news came by radio from General Kurt Dittmar of OKW.

Thus Fritzsche's influence on policy was only interstitial. Furthermore, he believed the news that was given him, which at times was maliciously false—for example, Hitler's charge that Winston Churchill had deliberately caused the sinking of the British liner *Athenia* in order to blame the disaster on the Germans. Fritzsche testified that he had firmly believed the official German report, and not until he encountered Raeder at Nuremberg did he learn that a German submarine had sunk the *Athenia*.

Fritzsche's testimony with respect to war crimes charges was more complex. In July 1941, a few weeks after Germany attacked the Soviet Union, Fritzsche delivered two radio speeches which were certainly capable of causing hatred against people:

> Even worse than the marks of the mental, economic, and social terror exercised by the Jewish commissars were those of physical terror which the German army encountered along the roads of victory. . . . Intoxicated with blood and lust, it seems, these monsters in human shape fell upon their victims. . . .
> Wherever the German soldiers went in the country which the Soviet leaders had dominated . . . they encountered the traces of deeds which a normal human being . . . refuses to see because they are too despicable. . . .

> The evidence of letters reaching us from the front . . . demon-
> strates that, in this struggle in the East . . . culture, civilization, and
> human decency make a stand against the diabolical principle of a
> subhuman world.

Fritzsche insisted (unconvincingly to me) that these speeches attacked the
Soviet "system" but not the "people." He then added that their content

> shows clearly, as I understand it, the absolute cleanliness and honesty
> of the whole German conduct of the war. I still believe today that
> murder and violence and *Sondercommandos*° only hung like a foreign
> body, like a boil, to the morally sound body of the German people and
> the armed forces.

Considering the millions of Jews and others killed by the "foreign
body" and the millions of Soviet prisoners killed by regular German troops,
Fritzsche's description is hard to stomach. I concluded it was the product of
his militant patriotism and of his desire to get under the skins of the Russian
prosecutors, whose compatriots in Moscow had given him several months
of solitary confinement.

In May 1942, as a result of a falling-out with Dietrich, Fritzsche
resigned and joined the propaganda company of a German infantry division
attached to General Friedrich Paulus's Sixth Army, stationed near Stalingrad. According to Fritzsche, he cut a wide swath there, opposing the
Commissar Order and eventually getting it rescinded.†

Shortly before going to the Sixth Army, Fritzsche received a letter
from an SS officer in the Ukraine who stated that "he had received an order
to kill the Jews and Ukrainian intelligentsia of his area." Fritzsche inquired
of Heydrich, who assured him that there was no basis for the letter he had
received. When Fritzsche went to the Sixth Army, he undertook a personal
investigation covering Kiev, Poltava, Kharkov, and smaller places en route.
According to his account, Fritzsche found that there had been some shootings of Jews and others for specific offenses and after courts-martial, but
nothing comparable to mass shootings of Jews.‡

Like several of the defendants, Fritzsche stated that he was anti-

---

°The German name for a "special" or "separate" military unit, customarily used to
identify a unit of the Einsatzgruppen.

†Dr. Fritz had questioned Paulus when he testified at Nuremberg. Paulus remembered
Fritzsche, but not his actions against the Commissar Order. Paulus testified that he thought the
order had not been "operative" when he took command of the Sixth Army in January 1942.

‡Fritzsche went to the Sixth Army a few weeks after the largest Einsatzgruppen massacres
of Jews were coming to an end. He did not mention inquiring to the staff of the Sixth Army, to
which had been attached the Sondercommando led by the notorious Paul Blobel, which in
November killed over 33,000 Jews near Kiev, in the massacre known as Babi Yar. Unfortunately,
Fritzsche was not cross-examined closely on his contacts and activities in the Ukraine.

Semitic in the sense that he "wanted a restriction on the predominant influence of Jewry in German politics, economy, and culture." But some of his speeches went well beyond these concerns, particularly after the German-Soviet war was underway. In October 1941, for example, Fritzsche spoke of "a new wave of international Jewish-democratic-bolshevistic agitation" in opposition to Germany, which Fritzsche admitted was "quite in accord with the knowledge and opinion I held at that date."

The Soviet prosecutors included no sailors, and they had been glad to turn over to Fyfe the main cross-examination of Raeder. For Fritzsche, however, Rudenko himself took the lectern.° It was not a success, for Rudenko's method, as usual for the Soviet prosecutors, was a series of barking accusations utilizing familiar Communist clichés. Often it appeared that Rudenko thought his questions more important than the answers. Fritzsche, bright and accustomed to dialectics, readily turned the questions back on Rudenko, with obvious pleasure.

When the General produced the interrogatory which Fritzsche had signed in September 1945 at Moscow, he readily acknowledged his signature, but reiterated that he had not made the statements therein. "Why did you do that?" Rudenko asked. "I gave that signature after very severe solitary confinement which had lasted for several months" was the reply. Playing tough, Rudenko countered: "Of course you never thought . . . that after all you had done you would be sent to a sanitarium? It is obvious that you had to end in a prison and a prison is always a prison." It was a glimpse of what Rudenko regarded as commonplace.

Later Rudenko incautiously asked Fritzsche if he had believed that the German attack against Poland was "unavoidable." Still needling the General, Fritzsche replied: "At that time it was a matter of great satisfaction to me that in the week that followed I could see from the Soviet press that Soviet Russia and its Government shared the German opinion of the question of war guilt in this case."

No lawyer from the other delegations rose to attempt improvement on Rudenko's effort, and nothing of moment transpired thereafter. It appeared to me that Fritzsche did not emerge from his ordeal as young and innocent as when he began and that he knew much more about German atrocities than he let on. Fritzsche himself expected to be convicted, because he viewed himself as a stand-in for the deceased Goebbels. But if the Tribunal had faults, such chicanery was not among them.

**Bormann:** Martin Bormann was probably dead, but nobody was sure. After Hitler's suicide, he and other denizens of the Fuehrer's subterranean

---

°On April 29, 1946, at a chief prosecutors' meeting, Jackson had "given" Fritzsche to the Soviet delegation and withdrawn from the case.

retreat had fled westward through Berlin, hoping to avoid capture by the oncoming Russians. Two or three of them who survived were sure that Bormann had been killed en route, but no one had actually seen him killed or lying dead.

After Hess had flown to Britain, Bormann had taken his place. He had clung tight and made himself indispensable to the Fuehrer and ultimately reached a degree of power unexcelled by any of the other leading Nazis. But only Goebbels had had a good word for him, and most of the others abominated him. Speer wrote of Bormann: "Even among so many ruthless men, he stood out by his brutality and coarseness. He had no culture, which might have put some restraint on him, and in every case he carried out whatever Hitler ordered. . . . A subordinate by nature, he treated his own subordinates as if he were dealing with cows and horses. He was a peasant. I avoided Bormann; from the beginning we could not abide each other."

Reminiscent of Roehm, Bormann hated and was hated by the army. Near the end of the war, horrified by Hitler's order to arrest Goering, Keitel blamed this action on Bormann: "He alone could have had his infamous fingers in this; he had exploited the Führer's frame of mind to bring his protracted feud with Goering to such a victorious conclusion." General Heinz Guderian, Army Chief of Staff late in the war, wrote:

> Next to Himmler the most sinister member of Hitler's entourage was Martin Bormann. He was a thick-set, heavy-jowled, disagreeable, conceited and bad-mannered man. He hated the Army, which he regarded as the eternal barrier to the limitless supremacy of the Party, and he attempted, with success, to do it harm whenever he could, to sow distrust, . . . to drive all decent persons away from Hitler's entourage and from positions of authority, and to replace them with his creatures.

Bormann's general reputation was best summed up by Fritzsche:

> The vanished defendant had no friends. Neither in court nor in private talks did I ever hear a single friendly word spoken of this man whose good will had once been so avidly sought. I myself remembered him as the exponent of all the harshest measures in the conduct of the war as well as in domestic and party affairs. Often enough I had to cope with the complaints from his office because, for instance, hymns had been broadcast or a religious service introduced into a Sunday programme: at least half of the more unpleasant instructions which came to me from Goebbels were either directly or indirectly inspired by the Propaganda Minister's fear of Bormann.

Now as he was tried *in absentia* it was shown that this stocky dark-haired man with the face of a peasant had always been regarded as a tyrant; his subordinates, even down to the typists, had been full of resentment against him, and he had been on bad terms with his family and closest relations.

There was, however, room for compassion in Bormann's case, well deserved by "his" assigned counsel, Dr. Friedrich Bergold, for never has a lawyer been given so thankless a task. He had no client in the flesh, and no one wanted to help him. Immediately after he embarked on the case, he confronted a mountain of documentary evidence against Bormann offered in Lieutenant Tom Lambert's presentation for the prosecution in January.

There is no need to repeat Lambert's evidence other than to say that it included documents signed or issued by Bormann directing, in October 1942, complete expulsion of "the millions of European Jews" far into the East, endowing the Nazi Party units in Germany with partial control over prisoners -of war in order to assure harsher treatment and directing that no coffins should be utilized for the burial of Soviet prisoners, directing that no police or other criminal proceedings should be taken against civilians who participated in lynching Allied aviators who were obliged to land in German territory, and establishing (January 1942) Bormann, Sauckel, and Himmler as a group to procure the importation of some 500,000 female domestic Eastern workers from the Ukraine to be brought to Germany as "female housekeepers." There are examples of many other documents attributable to Bormann, ordering or encouraging atrocious criminal activity.

It is more than doubtful that Bormann's presence in court would have altered the judgment, for the documents were unanswerable. But his presence might have helped Dr. Bergold in finding witnesses or documents of which Bergold knew nothing. As it was, Bergold had fewer than a dozen documents for which the best one could say was that Bormann had written some letters that did not incriminate him.

Under these circumstances, Dr. Bergold turned to the only thing that would prevent a conviction, and that was to prove that Bormann was indeed dead. But here again Bergold had no success. He had asked for permission to call about five named individuals, most of them to testify about the probability of Bormann's death, but only one had been located. He (a Dr. Klopfer) did not arrive in Nuremberg until the very time that Bergold was due to present his case, and he was not expected to testify about Bormann's supposed death. When Bergold requested a short delay to give him time to confer with Klopfer, Lawrence admonished Bergold that he had had "many months to prepare your case," refused a postponement, and directed him to speak with Klopfer immediately and then examine him in court. This was too much for Dr. Bergold:

> Mr. President, it is quite correct I have had months at my disposal; but if I can obtain no witnesses and no information—I ask the Tribunal to put themselves in my place. . . . The witnesses were

not here, nobody could tell me where the witness Klopfer could be found. He was only found at the very last moment. I cannot discuss the entire case with him in 15 minutes. . . . It is not my fault that I have been assigned such an unusual defendant, one who is not present.

Despite this lament Lawrence stuck to his ruling, but all turned out smoothly because Bergold soon discovered that Dr. Klopfer knew nothing of value to his case and could be dispensed with. Thereupon Dr. Bergold read an inconclusive affidavit on Bormann's flight from the bunker, and then put into the record his sad little handful of documents.

A few days later Bergold was able to bring to the stand Erich Kempka, previously Hitler's chauffeur, who had met Bormann while both were fleeing from the Reichschancellery after Hitler's death. Kempka had been only a few yards from Bormann when a projectile hit a tank next to which Bormann was running. He saw Bormann collapse, but Kempka himself was knocked unconscious, and when he revived he saw no sign of Bormann. Kempka's testimony made it more probable, but not certain, that Bormann was dead.

The presentation of the Bormann case had taken little more than an hour.

2

When the Tribunal was convened for its morning meeting on July 1, 1946, it still confronted one more issue involving the defendants' evidence: the question of guilt for the massacre of thousands of Poles in the Katyn Forest near Smolensk. This was the atrocity which the Soviet prosecutors had insisted on charging against the Nazi government when the Indictment was signed and delivered to the Tribunal in Berlin.

Since the dead had all been shot in the back of the head and buried in long deep trenches in their Polish uniforms or other garb, it was clear enough that they had been murdered rather than killed in battle. The existence of this terrible cemetery had first been made public by Goebbels in a Radio Berlin broadcast on April 13, 1943, which blamed the Russians for the massacre. Four days earlier he had written in his diary that "these executions became known from hints given by the inhabitants" to German troops occupying the area. Before the broadcast, Goebbels had sent "neutral journalists" and "Polish intellectuals" to view the scene.

Two days later, Radio Moscow accused the Germans of concocting their accusations in order to "cover up the bloody crimes of the Hitlerite gangsters" who themselves had killed the Polish prisoners. Simultaneously General Wladyslaw Anders, commander of Polish forces raised in the Soviet Union and then operating in the Middle East, sent a telegram to the Polish government-in-exile in London, giving reasons for concluding that the Russians, and not the Germans, were guilty. The Polish government then publicly requested the International Red Cross to investigate the matter, and the German Red Cross joined in the request. The International Red Cross was willing to serve if "all other parties" complied. However, no agreement was forthcoming from Moscow, and on April 26 the Kremlin severed relations with the Polish government in London and established a Polish Committee, largely composed of Polish Communists, in Moscow.

The world was at war, and the involved governments were less concerned with the truth than with the politics of this situation. Goebbels's propaganda had succeeded in splitting the Soviet and Polish governments, which was just what the British had hoped to avoid. When General Wladyslaw Sikorski (Prime Minister of the Polish government) visited Churchill with "a wealth of evidence" of Russian guilt in the Katyn massacre, Churchill replied: "If they are dead, nothing you can do will bring them back" and counseled, unsuccessfully, against "provoking" Moscow.°

In May 1943 the German authorities organized a team of medical doctors from nearly all the countries allied with or occupied by Germany, which concluded that the killings had taken place in March and April of 1940, when the Russians were still occupying the Smolensk area. After the Soviet forces reoccupied Smolensk in September 1943, the government created a Special Commission for Ascertaining and Investigating the Circumstances of the Shooting of Polish Officers by the German-Fascist Invaders in the Katyn Forest. The title sufficiently indicates the outcome of the commission's work.

Such was the pattern of controversy which the Soviet Union insisted on placing before the Tribunal. Although each country was accusing the other, this was not a *tu quoque* argument, in which a belligerent seeks to justify its otherwise unlawful acts on the ground that the enemy is engaging in the same conduct. In the Katyn case, the circumstances were such that only the Soviet Union *or* Germany could have perpetrated the atrocity. The only way either of them could vindicate its innocence was by proving that the other was guilty.

On February 14, 1946, in the course of the Soviet prosecution's presentation of evidence, Colonel Pokrovsky referred to the Indictment's accusation that "the German fascist invaders" of the Soviet Union were responsible for the Katyn "mass execution of Polish prisoners of war." However, the only evidence he offered was the 1944 report of the Soviet

---

°The British were soon convinced that the Russians were the guilty ones and were supported by what Sir Alexander Cadogan called "an extremely well done dispatch" by Sir Owen O'Malley, Ambassador to the Polish government in London. Cadogan wondered, "How can *we* discuss with Russians execution of German 'war criminals,' when we have condoned this?"

Special Commission, presented "in accordance with a directive of the Extraordinary State Commission" of the Soviet Union. Pokrovsky read a few extracts from the report, which stated that the Polish prisoners had been held by the Russians in three camps west of Smolensk until September 1941, when the area was occupied by German forces, that the shootings were promptly carried out "by German military organizations disguised under the specific name 'Staff 537, Engineer Construction Battalion,' commanded by Lieutenant Colonel Friedrich Ahrens and his cohorts Lieutenant Rex and Lieutenant Hott," and that in 1943, fearing that Soviet forces would retake the Smolensk area, the Germans took various steps to alter the terrain and engage false witnesses in order to fix the blame on the Soviet Union. Pokrovsky himself added nothing, thus treating the Special Commission's report as all-sufficient to establish the truth.

The legal situation with respect to the Katyn issue was unusual. All but a few (Hess, Streicher, Schacht, and Papen) of the defendants and each of the indicted organizations had been charged with war crimes under Count Three, which contained the accusation of the Katyn massacre. However, the Soviet prosecution (the only one supporting the Katyn accusation) had not presented a shred of evidence dealing with Katyn against any defendant. It was clear that the Soviet prosecutors were primarily interested in getting the Tribunal to exonerate the Soviets of guilt for Katyn rather than in pinning the guilt on individuals.

It soon became apparent that the German defendants were equally determined to clear the Wehrmacht of the shame of Katyn, and Goering, as the ranking defendant, made his counsel available to handle the issue. Dr. Stahmer then applied to the Tribunal for permission to call six witnesses, five of whom were officers who had been stationed near the Katyn woods. On March 12, 1946, the request was considered in camera by the Tribunal and granted by the votes of Lawrence, Biddle, and de Vabres. The Tribunal's record states:

> General Nikitchenko declined to vote and desired that his reasons, as stated below, be recorded in the Minutes:
> "I cannot participate in this vote as the discussion and putting to vote by the Tribunal of a question as to whether an official Government act may be contested is a flagrant contradiction of Article 21 of the Charter."°

It is clear that under Article 21 the "committees set up . . . for the investigation of war crimes" would include the 1944 report of the Soviet

---

° Article 21: "The Tribunal shall not require proof of facts of common knowledge but shall take judicial notice thereof. It shall also take judicial notice of official governmental documents and reports of the United Nations, including the acts and documents of the committees set up by the various allied countries for the investigation of war crimes, and the records and findings of military or other Tribunals of any of the United Nations."

Union's Special Commission, which was thus entitled to the Tribunal's "judicial notice" of its contents and which would be given such evidentiary weight as the Tribunal saw fit. But Nikitchenko's angry complaint was that Article 21 should be interpreted as giving *binding weight* to such documents so that contrary evidence could not be heard by the Tribunal. On that basis, the defendants would be barred from attacking the Soviet commission's conclusion that the Germans were guilty of the Katyn massacre.

That was a ridiculous interpretation of Article 21, and for the second time Katyn had created a very delicate situation within the Tribunal. In Berlin, when Nikitchenko had insisted on a postponement while the Kremlin changed the number of the Poles slain at Katyn, the other judges had given in because Biddle feared that Nikitchenko would withdraw (see pp. 124–25). Now the Russians appeared equally intransigent, but Biddle rightly saw that he and the others *could not* yield because to allow the Soviet prosecution to declare the Germans guilty at Katyn and bar any argument from the Germans would stultify the trial. The approval of Stahmer's witnesses was then voted and announced, Nikitchenko dissenting. Rudenko, however, filed with the Tribunal a petition for rehearing of the question, in language which Biddle described as "intemperate" and which accused the Tribunal of violation of its duty and "gross error." On April 6, when the Tribunal considered the petition, Biddle came to the conference armed with an opinion drafted by Herbert Wechsler which, in dignified but forceful language, made mincemeat of Rudenko's petition.

When the conference began, Biddle declared that Rudenko's petition was so slanderous and arrogant that in the United States "the author of such an outrage would be cited for contempt" and that perhaps Rudenko should be "sent to prison immediately." Turning to Nikitchenko, he asked what he proposed should be done. The astonished General had no intelligible answer. Biddle then read the opinion to his audience, saying that it "could be read in open court before General Rudenko is arrested."

Nikitchenko turned his intention to preventing publication of the opinion, and the Tribunal members "cut a deal" by deciding that Rudenko's petition "should be denied and that no reasons for denial would be given." Biddle's opinion was not published, but was "placed on record" in the Tribunal's files. Nikitchenko dissented, but fought no more for his interpretation of Article 21 of the Charter.

On May 11 and June 2 the defendants in open court requested several more witnesses. The first time Pokrovsky, and the second time Rudenko, ignored the Tribunal's dismissal of Rudenko's petition and objected on the same grounds as before. Lawrence paid no attention. Pokrovsky was shrewd enough to say that he had confined his February presentation to the Soviet 1944 report, and indicated that if the defendants called witnesses, he, too, would want some. The Russians were clearly scared to meet the defense openly, for on June 19, 1946, Nikitchenko suggested to his fellow judges "that the evidence on the Katyn Forest incident be presented in written form rather than by witnesses." Nothing came of this idea. By the end of June the Tribunal had ruled that prosecution and defense might each call three witnesses and that the evidence on the Katyn massacre would be heard immediately after the individual defendants' cases had all been heard.

When the Tribunal convened on July 1, Stahmer called his first witness, Lieutenant Colonel Friedrich Ahrens, one of those accused as the murderers in the Soviets' 1944 report. He had commanded Signal Regiment 537, which had the task of maintaining communications between the Army Group, to which the regiment was attached, and all the Army Group's many subordinate units, covering a very large area. His headquarters was not far from the Katyn Forest, where he had observed a mound topped by a cross. But he was constantly on the move around his duty area and paid it little attention until learning that an animal had pulled bones out of the mound which a doctor told him were human bones. Thinking it well might be a soldier's grave, he informed an officer of what Americans would call the "Graves Registration Service." Subsequently a Doctor Butz, on orders from the Army Group, examined the area, and exhumations of the Polish corpses followed in the spring of 1943.

Ahrens denied any personal knowledge of when the killing of these Poles had occurred, but recalled that Dr. Butz had once told him that it had been in the spring of 1940. Under cross-examination by Smirnov, Ahrens stated that he had joined his regiment in mid-November 1941. The Germans had overrun Smolensk in July, so there was a four-month period in which the Germans might have killed the Poles without Ahrens's knowledge. Otherwise, Smirnov made virtually no effort to break Ahrens's testimony.

Stahmer next called Lieutenant Reinhard von Eichhorn, telephone expert on the staff of Army Group Center, who had been stationed near the Katyn Forest since mid-September. He testified that it would have been impossible for prisoners, Polish or not, to have been shot in or near Katyn without his knowledge. Smirnov's cross-examination ended by reading a portion of the Soviet 1944 report showing that the SS's Einsatzgruppe B, in October 1941, was stationed in Smolensk and was "evacuating" Soviet prisoners. Obviously, Smirnov was giving up on the German Army as the killer of the Poles. Informed listeners well knew that the SD was killing Jews and other victims, but that was a long way from killing Polish officers in the Katyn Forest.

Stahmer's last witness was Lieutenant General Eugen Oberhauser, Chief Signals Officer of the Army Group and Ahrens's commanding officer. He confirmed his subordinates' general testimony and stated that a signals regiment was neither equipped nor expected to perform a task such as mass executions. Smirnov accomplished nothing.

It was now the Russians' turn, and Smirnov first called the former deputy mayor of Smolensk during the German occupation, Professor of Astronomy Boris Barzilevsky. The witness testified that in September 1941 he had been told by the mayor, who had been told by one von Schwetz (a member of the German Kommandatur) that the Poles "have already died." All this was at least double hearsay, and there was no information about von Schwetz's source of information. Stahmer must have learned something about cross-examination from watching Fyfe, for he very effectively showed that Barzilevsky knew absolutely nothing about the Katyn issue or why the mayor and he were told these things.

Smirnov's second witness was Antonov Markov, a Bulgarian professor who testified through an interpreter and who had been one of a number of European doctors whom the Germans had organized and brought to Katyn late in April 1943. Markov, along with the others, had signed a "protocol" stating that the Poles' corpses had been in the ground no less than three years. Markov's testimony at Nuremberg was to the effect that the inquiry was superficial and rushed and that in the view of most of the members the corpses had not been buried more than one and a half years.

Smirnov's last witness was Victor I. Proserovski, a high-ranking doctor from the Ministry of Public Health of the Soviet Union. In January 1944 he had worked with other physicians in exhuming and examining 925 Polish corpses in the Katyn area. He shared the general conclusion that the corpses had been buried two years ago, in the autumn of 1941. The year 1940, according to the witness, was "completely excluded." Proserovski was very precise about the autumn of 1941—which of course covered the period while Army Group Center and Ahrens's regiment were moving into the Katyn area—and Stahmer could not shake him.

Smirnov and Stahmer both raised the question of additional evidence, but Lawrence briskly stated that the Tribunal "does not propose to hear further evidence" and turned to other matters. As an effort to determine whether the Soviet or the Nazi forces had killed the Polish prisoners, the Tribunal's trial was a travesty. All they got were three disagreeing opinions on the time of interment of the corpses and strong evidence from the German officers that the killings did not take place while Ahrens's regiment was headquartered near the forest.

Nothing went into the record about other highly important circumstances. What were the Russians doing with these Polish prisoners after they took them in 1939? When Germany attacked in June 1941, General Anders was released from prison and the Russians encouraged him to assemble a Polish legion to join in fighting the Germans. Why did not the 900 or 11,000 (as the case may be) join the legion? Anders could not find them, and the Russians gave no answer to his inquiries. There was evidence that all letters and other communications to Poland from the Polish prisoners eventually interred at Katyn had abruptly ceased in the spring of 1940.

Circumstantially, the guilt for Katyn leaned heavily on the Soviet Union, but it is well to remember that the SD, under Hitler's declared policy and Himmler's and Hans Frank's execution, was to exterminate "the Polish intelligentsia, the nobility, the clergy, and in fact all elements which could be regarded as leaders of a national resistance." Katyn was right in line with such purposes.

Three witnesses on each side were wholly insufficient to wrestle with these issues. The Tribunal's stiff refusal to allow the lawyers to go any further suggested that the Tribunal itself might leave to others the final resolution of Katyn.

# Chapter 17

# THE CLOSING ARGUMENTS

A rticle 24 of the London Charter governed the order of the trial's proceedings, and by July 3, 1946, the Tribunal had completed, with respect to the individual defendants, items (a) through (g) in the Charter's listing. The next two were (h) "The Defendants shall address the Court" and (i) "The Prosecution shall address the Court." These "addresses" were to be the lawyers' final arguments.

However, although the prosecution's evidence against the accused organizations had been completed in January, preparation for the organizations' defense witnesses had not been begun until mid-March 1946. The Tribunal delegated control of this activity to Lieutenant Colonel Airey Neave. Testimony for the organizations was begun before commissioners appointed by the Tribunal in order to select a few witnesses from each organization who would testify before the Tribunal.

The lawyers for the individual defendants had been hoping that the organizations' witnesses would be heard before the final arguments, as this would give the defendants more time for their lawyers to prepare their addresses. The Tribunal decided otherwise, partly because it preferred to go directly to a conclusion with the individual defendants and partly because it became apparent that Neave would not be ready to report on the witnesses for the organizations until at least ten days after the Tribunal would be finished with individual defendants' evidence. The defendants also requested a three-week recess for preparation of their arguments, which the Tribunal promptly vetoed.

Discussion then turned to the length of time that would be allowed for the individual arguments. The Tribunal first suggested a maximum of fourteen trial days for all the arguments. The defendants thought that much too little, and polled themselves on their individual necessities. On June 21 they reported to the Tribunal that their individual requirements ran from three (Bormann) to eight hours each and totaled 103 hours. With six-hour days and five days per week, that would have required nearly four weeks.

Although both Biddle and Nikitchenko dissented, on June 25 the Tribunal issued an order, more hopeful than firm:

> Except as to a few of the defendants whose cases are of very wide scope, the Tribunal is of the opinion that half a day to each defendant is ample time for the presentation of the defense, and the Tribunal hopes that counsel will condense their arguments and limit themselves voluntarily to this time. The Tribunal, however, will not permit counsel for any defendant to deal with irrelevant matters or to speak for more than one day in any case.

As matters worked out, the defendants' closing arguments took sixteen trial days and those of the chief prosecutors over three days, the whole requiring most of July. For the general viewer, July was by all odds the dullest month of the trial. The main burden was borne by the judges, who now had to listen once more to the same lawyers, talking about the same issues, that the court had been listening to during the preceding four months. Furthermore, the lawyers' speeches were bound to be highly repetitive of the past and of each other. What more was there to say? The judges girded themselves for a long, slow July.

For the prosecutors, things were not so bad. More of the American delegations' members were free to go home. Those remaining worked on the speeches their chiefs would make at the end of July and on the organizations. My own new arrivals for the "subsequent proceedings" were getting the hang of things and preparing for the new trials that would begin in October. We were all busy, but there was no great strain, and July was a lovely month, with enough leisure for weekend visits to Garmisch or Salzburg.

Needless to say, the defense counsel did not share in the boredom, for this was their last chance to speak in their clients' behalf. Their seriousness of purpose was immediately felt during the opening address by Dr. Hermann Jahrreiss, who had been chosen to speak for all the defendants on "general questions of law and fact."

Jahrreiss began by stating that "the main general and fundamental problem of this trial concerns war as a function forbidden by international law; the breach of peace as treason perpetrated upon the world constitution. This problem dwarfs all other juridical questions." In thus putting the validity of "crimes against peace" at the forefront of debate, Jahrreiss was in tune with Jackson's emphasis on waging aggressive war as the core of the Indictment.

Intrinsically, Jahrreiss's presentation was an expanded and greatly strengthened version of the motion, signed by Stahmer but "adopted by all defense counsel," which had been submitted to the Tribunal on November 19, 1945, the day before the Tribunal's opening session. That, too, had denied the validity of the Charter's "crimes against peace." Two days later the Tribunal had denied the motion on the ground that under Article 3 of the Charter, the jurisdiction of the Tribunal could not be challenged by either prosecution or defense. Jahrreiss referred to that ruling and remarked that, whatever the effect of Article 3, the question of validity of crimes against peace "nevertheless continues to exist" and indeed had been discussed at great length by "the British Chief Prosecutor" in his opening statement.

Surely neither Jahrreiss nor any informed person expected that his argument would cause the Tribunal to reverse its prior decision. One may, I think, safely surmise that Jahrreiss was hoping that his attack might shake one or more of the judges enough to make them more cautious about convicting on this basis and also that he was looking toward future legal opinion in the hope of undermining public and scholarly acceptance of the Tribunal's decisions.

Most of the factors and arguments discussed by Jahrreiss had been raised at the United Nations War Crimes Commission (UNWCC) in 1944, when the members of that body found themselves so evenly divided that they could reach no decision. But if there was little room for originality, Jahrreiss made up for that by his dignity, skill with words, and genuine passion. Especially telling was his handling of the ex post facto argument that whether or not "crimes against peace" were intrinsically valid, "not one of the defendants" could have known about any such principle at the time he committed the offenses charged against him.

Insofar as the validity of Counts One and Two of the Indictment were concerned, the defendants could hardly have had a better spokesman.

## 2

The defendants' lawyers were called in approximately the same order in which they were seated in the dock. Dr. Stahmer, as counsel to Goering, the most prominent and highest-ranking defendant, had thereby acquired some prestige among his fellows. But he was dominated by his brighter and more forceful client and did not share in the high regard of his fellows for Dix, Kranzbuehler, and a few other outstanding counsel.

Stahmer put his foot in his mouth immediately by complaining about "unequal distribution of strength between the Prosecution and the Defense" and the prosecution's failure to "submit evidence exonerating the accused." He was sharply admonished by Lawrence, who declared his complaint "entirely inaccurate" and pointed out that nearly all the documents offered in evidence by the defendants "had been procured for them . . . by the Prosecution." It soon became apparent that the Tribunal's warning against discussion of "irrelevant matters" was seriously intended.

If it may truly be said that no lawyer, however brilliant, could have done much to exculpate Goering, it may likewise be observed that a more sensitive writer could have made the script more palatable. How could even Stahmer have declared that "in the beginning [of the war] every endeavor was made to wage war with decency and chivalry" when everyone knew that the Germans had stomped into Poland intent on exterminating all "upper-class" individuals and reducing the population to virtual serfdom? How could anyone, other than tongue-in-cheek, have opined that Poland should have "appealed to the League of Nations"? Why did Stahmer carefully repeat Goering's testimony that he was entitled to "acquire" artworks of French Jews because "they had been previously confiscated by Führer decree?"

Except for Stahmer's satisfactory argument that the Germans could not plausibly be convicted of the Katyn massacre, there was nothing new or helpful to Goering in his presentation.

Dr. Seidl's appearance for Hess was a disaster. He had not procured translations of his German speech into the judges' languages. Lawrence testily told him to proceed under the "very inconvenient circumstances." Seidl began by attacking the Versailles Treaty, but Lawrence immediately told him that this subject had previously been declared irrelevant and the Tribunal was "not going to listen to it." Seidl several times skipped ahead in his text, but each time the Versailles Treaty was soon mentioned, and Lawrence, increasingly feisty, soon told Seidl that he would not be heard any further. He was told to recast his speech and was sent to the end of the line for its delivery.

Dr. Horn did no more for his client than had Stahmer for his. Ribbentrop was an ungracious and apparently ungrateful client, but there was no sign that, even if fired with zeal, Dr. Horn could have done any better. He argued that Ribbentrop was not given advance information of Hitler's warlike intentions, but that certainly was not the case with either Poland or the Soviet Union. Horn also insisted that Hitler's sole control of decision-making "can hardly be reconciled with the thought of a Common Plan or Conspiracy." But many, if not most, conspiracies are run by an individual who lays down a plan that all members must follow. Very little attention was given to the accusations of war crimes, and there was no mention of Ribbentrop's pressure on the French and Italian authorities to hasten the deportation of Jews to the East.

Dr. Nelte, for Keitel, was abler than his predecessors and not easily put down. Despite Lawrence's "correction" of Stahmer, Nelte declared that the prosecution had "made clear their definitely one-sided standpoint in an Indictment" in contrast to "the principle of objective accusation which dominates the German criminal proceedings." Lawrence at once repeated the gist of his lecture to Stahmer. Thereupon Nelte replied: "Mr. President, on this very spot Mr. Justice Jackson stated, 'We cannot serve two masters,' when he replied to the statement that according to German criminal law the Prosecution would also have to produce material in favor of the defendants." After further colloquy Lawrence rather lamely suggested a confusion of translation and dropped the matter.

Before long, however, Nelte complained about the French delegation's failure to provide him with some documents which Nelte was entitled to under the Tribunal's ruling. When Lawrence inquired why Nelte had not asked the Tribunal for assistance, Nelte replied that he was attempting "to show you that . . . the Prosecution did not want to help me. . . ." Annoyed, and prodded by Biddle (as von der Lippe noticed), Lawrence declared: "Dr. Nelte, I think that is a most unfair and a most improper thing for a responsible counsel to say. I think the mention of such a complaint is . . . simply an effort on your part to create prejudice against the French Prosecution and against the fair conduct of this Trial." Nelte coolly replied: "Mr. President, in my view it was merely meant to show how difficult it has been to find material in favor of our clients." That was certainly no apology,° but Lawrence simply admonished Nelte to get on with "something that is really material for the Tribunal to consider."

Nelte's main argument was that despite Keitel's rank (the highest in the army), impressive designation as Chief of the Wehrmacht, and personal signatures on Hitler's orders, he was not legally responsible for them. Keitel himself had made the same point in his testimony, but Nelte endeavored to reinforce it by picturing Keitel as a tragic figure doomed by fate, rather than guilt, to be "linked" with Hitler's crimes. This was true in the sense that if Hitler had not ordered the criminal acts, Keitel had neither the power nor, so far as the evidence indicated, the inclination to violate law or morals. But the weakness of Keitel's position was that he had hitched his own wagon to Hitler's star. Keitel's signature was more than a clerk's stamp. As Nelte, perhaps incautiously, admitted, Keitel was responsible for "carrying out the Führer's orders." Thus he put his own high rank and administrative authority behind Hitler's decisions.

Nelte was a strong advocate, and his peroration was not lacking in the "tragic" side of Keitel's failure:

> The defendant Keitel did not hear the warning voice of the universal conscience. The principles of his soldierly life were so deeply rooted, and governed his thoughts and actions so exclusively, that he

---

°Later that day Dubost clarified the matter of the French documents. Nelte then made apologies to Dubost, but not to the Tribunal.

was deaf to all considerations which might deflect him from the path of obedience and faithfulness, as he understood them. This is the really tragic role played by the defendant Keitel in this most terrible drama of all times.

Ernst Kaltenbrunner's counsel, Dr. Kauffmann, had submitted to the Tribunal the text of his address, from which the judges could see that it would be unusually short. One might have expected that they would have welcomed Kauffmann happily, but Lawrence had no mercy on him.

The judges can hardly be blamed. Kauffmann began with a rambling discussion of guilt and punishment in which his client was not mentioned. After about a half hour Lawrence interrupted the flow and suggested that Kauffmann come to his client's case, commenting that the text indicated that the lawyer was about to read a section entitled "The Development of the History of the Intellectual Pursuit in England." Kauffmann was reluctant to drop the subject, but agreed to skip some portions of his script. However, Kaltenbrunner remained unmentioned, and Lawrence increasingly irritated, until time for the luncheon recess. Before adjourning, Lawrence caustically remarked that according to the script, the next matters to be discussed were "Renaissance, Subjectivism, French Revolution, Liberalism, National Socialism." As the defendants filed out of the courtroom, Kaltenbrunner said to Dr. Gilbert: "I saw Colonel Amen holding his sides with laughter. You can tell him that I congratulate him on his victory over me in getting me such a stupid attorney." It was a bitter remark, but not without reason.

Perhaps because of strong advice, after lunch Kauffmann turned immediately to Kaltenbrunner's case. In structure and conclusion, it resembled Nelte's with Keitel. Despite Kaltenbrunner's high office as Chief of the Reich Security Main Office (RSHA) and immediate subordination to Himmler, said Kauffmann, Kaltenbrunner did not really control the Gestapo or its chief, Heinrich Mueller; Kaltenbrunner was primarily concerned with intelligence work. Of course Kaltenbrunner learned of criminal actions within the RSHA, but he did his best to limit them. For the most part the argument was little more than a replay of Kaltenbrunner's testimony, and Kauffmann made no effort to deal with John Amen's wounding cross-examination of his client.

Like Nelte, Kauffmann made no effort to call for an acquittal: "Kaltenbrunner is guilty, but he is less guilty than he appears to the eyes of the Prosecution."

After the two preceding and rather apologetic presentations, Rosenberg's counsel, Dr. Thoma, approached the lectern apparently full of faith in Rosenberg's innocence of anything that either of them regarded as criminal. Rosenberg was an avowed devotee of Hitler and an acknowledged anti-Semite, and had played a minor part in the decision to occupy Norway. But Thoma rightly concluded that nothing in his client's record, prior to Hitler's decision to attack the Soviet Union, would matter very much. Rosenberg's fate depended on the Tribunal's assessment of his conduct as Reich Minister of the Occupied Eastern Territories—the highest German civil authority east of Poland.

So Thoma plunged right into Rosenberg's Eastern administration, taking more than half of his long presentation. Despite its length, Lawrence did not even once interject a request for shortening the argument, which was well organized and, throughout, clearly relevant, with no Rosenberg in the witness box to muddy the waters. Lawrence's sole interruption came when Thoma, discussing forced labor, declared that "The Rules of Land Warfare contain no stipulation as to whether labor service may be demanded only in the home country or whether the conscript may be transported into the native land of the occupying power for the purpose of rendering labor service there." Lawrence then asked "whether it is your contention that the Hague rules authorize the deportation of men, women, and children to another country for the purpose of labor service?" Excluding children from his opinion, Thoma replied in the affirmative and, answering Lawrence's next question, cited a German writer in support of his position.

Thoma next undertook an explanation of the source and limits of Rosenberg's anti-Semitism, which aroused Rudenko to accuse him of "Fascist propaganda" and ask the Tribunal to "take appropriate action." Lawrence brushed aside Rudenko's complaint and told Thoma to proceed in his argument. The gist of it was that Rosenberg himself was never the instigator of anti-Jewish actions, but that he was "a true follower of Hitler, who took up Hitler's [anti-Semitic] slogans and passed them on."

All in all, Thoma's script was a remarkable combination of boldness and frankness. Acknowledging most of Rosenberg's most damning statements, Thoma made it at least plausible that Rosenberg was not anti-Russian, that he was in fact pro-Ukrainian, and that he had had no intention of treating brutally the inhabitants of his enormous domain. But at the outset Rosenberg had heard Hitler describe his own truly murderous program, and with full knowledge Rosenberg had taken the plunge. His situation was rather like, but far more dangerous than, Neurath's in Prague. Both men had found themselves with impressive titles and heavy responsibilities, without the power to fulfill them.

Ever faithful to the Fuehrer, Rosenberg did not even try to resign until October 1944. Hitler ignored the request. At Nuremberg Rosenberg, like Goering, refused to attack Hitler or Nazism. Dr. Thoma, who defended Rosenberg so stoutly, portrayed his client to Dr. Gilbert as an "arrogant heathen" and a "vicious anti-Semite."

The morning of July 11, 1946, found Dr. Seidl back at the lectern presenting the final argument for his other client, Hans Frank. Seidl made only a passing reference to Versailles, was all business, and began with a well-written and entirely convincing showing that before the war Frank's official positions were entirely concerned with legal matters, remote from the conspiracy charged against him in the Indictment. As a practical matter, Frank's case involved only his activities as Governor-General in Poland.

Seidl's argument was essentially the same as Frank's testimonial defense; police, labor recruitment, the treatment of Jews, and other important powers were not in the Governor-General's hands. Most of the notorious "Hans Frank Diary" had not been written by him. Frank had attempted to prevent the atrocities spread by Himmler's men.

Seidl's presentation was well organized and compact (it was completed in the morning session) and was far more forceful than Frank's answers to questions and, of course, Seidl was not cross-examined. However, his script owed a great deal to its omissions. It was all very well to urge caution in using the diary, but Seidl discussed none of the passages most harmful to his client. Seidl handled his points skillfully, but there was too much evidence against Frank to which there was no answer.

Dr. Pannenbecker's argument for Frick was even shorter than Seidl's, as befitted the thinnest record of all the defendants' cases. Frick had not testified, so there was no cross-examination; Pannenbecker's presentation of documents was brief, as had been Dr. Kempner's offer of prosecution evidence; and Frick's only witness, Gisevius, had spent most of his time on Schacht, Goering, and Keitel rather than Frick.

Thus Pannenbecker's script was the first systematic, chronological statement of the Frick case. It was very effective in distancing Frick from involvement in aggressive wars and shifting the blame for atrocities to Himmler and his minions. As in Frank's case, however, there was much prosecution evidence damaging to Frick which Pannenbecker ignored or could not confute.

## 3

The seven defendants dealt with above all confronted evidence so damaging to them that few people familiar with the Tribunal's proceedings had much doubt about their conviction and severe punishment. Their lawyers had struggled manfully and several of them admirably, but they must have felt the apparent hopelessness of their goal.

However, with only one or two possible exceptions, the remaining fourteen defendants did not confront wholly vain prospects. A few of them could reasonably cherish hopes of acquittal, and for all there was at least a possibility of escaping a death sentence. These prospects, however dim, stimulated the lawyers to sharpen their skills in search of mitigation or even exoneration. The tension, already high, was increased by rumors (recorded by von der Lippe) that the final arguments counted for little and the evidence was all that mattered. A wilder story was that the Tribunal had already decided that Schacht, Papen, and Fritzsche would be condemned to death, and Neurath as well, but, because of his age, he would not be hanged.

Julius Streicher was the next defendant in the sequence, and Dr. Marx's task was easy to state. To save Streicher from a capital sentence, Marx needed to do two things: persuade the Tribunal that there was insufficient evidence that Streicher had incited the killing of Jews, and prevent hateful reputation and repulsive appearance from crucially influencing the Tribunal's decision.

But what did "incitement" mean? Before the war Streicher and many other Germans "incited the persecution of Jews," but under the Charter these acts were not international crimes. Most German Jews were expelled to Poland shortly before the war, and soon after the Germans occupied that country. Within a year or so the Germans were sending Jews from other countries to the East for extermination or forced labor; that was certainly criminal persecution. But in the meantime the German government had rusticated Streicher, and his voice was heard only in *Der Stuermer*. It was a small newspaper (some 15,000 subscribers), and Streicher had no connections with Himmler or his subordinates, who were actually carrying out the Holocaust.

Marx traced Streicher's record in the Party and his activities with *Der Stuermer* during the war, and made a very strong argument that the defendant could have had little or no impact on the situation and fate of the Jews. A few issues of *Der Stuermer* contained articles calling for extermination of Jews, but its "incitement" was surely imperceptible, especially when Field Marshal von Reichenau and other military leaders were issuing instructions to their troops that were just as rabid against Jews as was Streicher's rag.

Marx made little effort to rehabilitate Streicher as a human being worthy of the law's protection. Indeed, at the end of his argument Marx declared that he had had "a difficult and thankless task" as defense counsel (which no doubt was true) and left Streicher's guilt or innocence "in the hands of the High Tribunal," thus seeming to wash his own hands of his client.

Representing Funk, Dr. Sauter began by announcing that his task was "especially dry and prosaic." He was right, but a large part of the cause was Sauter himself, whose dense and unorganized presentation was well nigh incomprehensible. Funk's own testimony and his cross-examination by Dodd had left him vulnerable on a number of scores, culminating in the Reichsbank's receipt of gold teeth and other mementos of their shocking source. Sauter's argument accomplished nothing in Funk's behalf. His best card was that Funk was so flabby and scared that it was hard for anyone to take him for a murderer.

Dr. Dix began his argument with emotion, effective for the audience but not for some of Schacht's fellow defendants. There in the dock sat Kaltenbrunner, chief of the RSHA, and here sat Schacht, who ended the war in a concentration camp, a prisoner of the RSHA. Dix himself had represented Schacht in 1944 and 1945 against charges of treason to the Reich, and now Dix was defending him against a charge of state conspiracy to wage aggressive war.

Dix invoked the shades of Nero who had executed Seneca, later sainted; Dix dryly noted that Schacht did not "indulge in any such expectations." It was a tribute to Dix's standing with the Tribunal that Lawrence allowed him to continue in such grandiloquent irrelevancies, but, unlike Stahmer, Dix had taken the precaution of frequently mentioning his client's name.

It was clear that Schacht's fate would be influenced by the Tribunal's impression of his genuineness as a conspirator against Hitler, to which Gisevius had testified. Gisevius had also attacked Keitel, and Nelte, in his final argument, had effectively demolished some of Gisevius's statements about Keitel. As Dix now saw the matter: "Dr. Nelte has also attacked the subjective credibility of Gisevius in the personal character of this witness and thus also indirectly the reliability of his testimony concerning Dr. Schacht."

Dix reacted fiercely:

> Your honors, it is here that minds part company. A gap that cannot be bridged opens up between Schacht's standpoint of all those who adopt that train of thought with which Dr. Nelte attempts to discredit the character of Gisevius. . . .
>
> Patriotism means loyalty to one's fatherland and people, and fight without question against anyone who criminally leads one's fatherland and people into misery and destruction. Such a leader is an enemy of the fatherland. . . . Every method is justified against such a criminal State leadership. . . .
>
> High treason against such leadership is true and genuine patriotism and as such highly moral, even during war. . . . Adolf Hitler was the greatest enemy of his people, in short, a criminal toward his people and . . . to remove him any means were justified and any, literally any, deed was patriotic. All those on the defendants' bench who do not recognize this are worlds apart from Schacht.

Dix ended his argument by requesting the Tribunal to find that "Schacht is not guilty of the accusation which has been raised against him and that he be acquitted." No other defense counsel had as yet flatly demanded an acquittal.

Kranzbuehler began his *Plädoyer* (as the Germans called the "address") by stating that the prosecution's accusations involving German naval warfare "are divided into two main groups: unlawful sinking of ships, and deliberate killing of shipwrecked personnel." The first of these was much the more complicated, involving interpretation of the London Agreement of 1936, the rights of neutrals, the treatment of blacked-out ships, zones of operations, and most particularly the circumstances in which merchant ships could be sunk without warning. The second group, not covered by naval treaties, involved the customary protective rules relating to ships crews, especially when shipwrecked.

All these and related matters were presented and analyzed by Kranzbuehler with dignity and skillful organization of the material. But it was not an important argument because most of it had been covered during Doenitz's evidentiary case. Doenitz and Kranzbuehler were both highly intelligent and professionally skilled. There was little to be added, and nearly all of Kranzbuehler's excellent script was a replay. The Nimitz interrogatory had previously been read to the Tribunal. It had supported, perhaps decisively, Kranzbuehler's argument that armed merchant ships were not "merchant vessels" within the meaning and protection of the 1936 Agreement and therefore could lawfully be sunk without warning.

Kranzbuehler did not overlook his client's indictment under Count Two, but merely called attention to his junior rank and limited range of authority early in the war. That was all very well, but I was surprised that Kranzbuehler did not point out that Doenitz's military situation when the aggressive wars were started was in no way different from that of a Luftwaffe commander dispatching a squadron of bombers over Poland or an army field commander ordering his corps to attack the enemy forces. If the war in question was aggressive, would all such commanders be guilty under Count Two?

For me, the most interesting feature of Kranzbuehler's argument was that he revealed himself to be just as hard and intransigent as Doenitz. No word of criticism of Hitler passed his lips: "I feel neither called upon nor able to judge a personality like Adolf Hitler." Kranzbuehler was prepared to condone "the resettlement in the Government General of Jews living in Germany" (note that he did not refer to them as "German Jews") on the ground that "expulsions of Germans on a much larger scale" were then taking place as a result of postwar changes in Central Europe's national borders. But, although these actions, too, can certainly be considered inhumane, "expulsion" is something more when the expellers accompany the expelled to ensure that they are kept in ghettos and then either kill them or use them as forced labor. Of course, it is not a war crime to be either a Nazi or an anti-Semite. But those who publicly use the expression "spreading poison of Jewry" (see p. 405) have themselves been infected by some kind of poison.

"After the brilliant advocatory-rhetorical performance of Dix, and the excellent, business-like performance of Kranzbuehler," wrote Dr. von der Lippe, "it was of course not easy for Siemers to begin a third brilliant *Plädoyer*." Siemers was a good lawyer, but lacked the presence of his two predecessors and was not a favorite of the judges, who sometimes found him too argumentative. However, on this occasion Siemers's argument went smoothly and was adequately delivered. Like Kranzbuehler's, however, the greater part of Siemers's address was just a second edition of Raeder's testimony. This did not much strengthen his case.

In fact, the principal flaw in Siemers's presentation was his failure to deal at all with damaging pieces of evidence presented by the British prosecution. For example, in dealing with the German occupation of Norway, Siemers made a good argument in support of Germany's right to occupy Norway if Britain was about to take that step herself. But he made no mention of the evidence which clearly showed that Raeder had initially approached Hitler, not with fear that Britain might occupy Norway, but on the basis that German naval and air bases on Norway's west coast would bring them great military advantages. Nor did Siemers discuss Germany's occupation of Denmark, where there had been no concern about a British invasion. Another oversight was Siemers's failure to deal adequately with the prosecution's charge that German naval units in Bordeaux had executed, pursuant to the Commando Order, two British prisoners. Subsequently, the Tribunal cited that episode as proof of Raeder's guilt of war crimes.

As for conspiracy to wage aggressive wars, Siemers continued to advance the spurious idea that his client could not have been a conspirator with Hitler because the Fuehrer made all the decisions. Siemers also insisted that Raeder had believed Hitler's private assurance that he would not resort to war. But Raeder not only was present at Hitler's "lectures" to the assembled military leaders in 1939 in which he decisively ordered them to prepare for wars that were patently aggressive, but Raeder had also willingly directed the naval preparations necessary to carry out those orders.

Siemers's argument had not been "brilliant" but, from the viewpoint of the defendants, his client's case was much more difficult than Schacht's or Doenitz's. Nevertheless, Siemers ended with a brave request to the Tribunal that Raeder be acquitted "on all points of the Indictment." Raeder, well pleased, had tears in his eyes as he thanked Siemers.

Dr. Sauter's argument for Schirach was much better than his previous appearance for Funk, perhaps because the prosecution's case against Schirach was not impressive. The prosecution's idea that the Hitler Jugend was a prep school for the Wehrmacht had proved to be a mirage. Schirach was impressionable, weak, and malleable, as his fluctuating attitude in the prison had shown, and he was not the man to break away from Hitler. So Schirach, like Neurath, accepted one of Hitler's proconsul positions, in which he was obliged to administer Nazi laws and the Fuehrer's orders. Avoiding violations of the laws of war was virtually impossible.

Sauter, recasting the content of the evidentiary hearing, was able to improve the appearance of his client's record. It was not, however, sufficient to support Sauter's claim that "the defendant von Schirach is not guilty . . . and cannot be punished because he did not commit a punishable act."

Representing Fritz Sauckel, Dr. Robert Servatius, scholar of law and languages, told the Tribunal that "The Charter does not say what is to be understood by 'slave labor' or by 'deportation' "—both words that are used in Articles 6(b)and 6(c) of the Charter. He then informed his listeners that in the Russian text of the Charter, "deportation" in 6(b) used the word *uvod*, "which means only removal from a place," while in 6(c) "deportation" was translated as *ssylka*, meaning "deportation in the sense of a penal deportation."

The meaning of these words was certainly relevant to the case at hand, for "deportation" and "slave labor" (or "forced labor") were at the root of the accusations against Sauckel. Unlike the other defense counsel, but for good reason, Servatius devoted the first half of his address to the discussion of legal problems involving the Charter and the Hague Convention on Land Warfare before coming to the evidentiary features of his case.

"The Charter cannot prohibit what international law permits in wartime," rightly declared Servatius, adding: "If the Hague Convention on Land Warfare is examined for a definite rule concerning deportation and forced labor, it will be realized that no such regulation exists." That, too, was correct, but it followed that there was no explicit rule *permitting* deportation and forced labor. Servatius had to resort to "military necessity" to reach his goal, arguing that the war had become so all-embracing that Germany could not have continued without utilizing foreign labor, by force if necessary.

But this simple answer left untouched other factors which Servatius did not address. Acknowledging the incompleteness of the written rules, the prologue to the Hague Convention specified that "unconcluded" cases should be decided by "the usages established among civilized people, from the laws of humanity, and the dictates of the public conscience." Within these general provisions, Article 46 of the convention, which protected from the occupying power "Family honor and rights, the lives of persons, and private property," is impossible to reconcile with "deporting" families or pieces of families hundreds or even thousands of miles away for indeterminate periods of forced labor. The nervous comments of Sauckel and others when discussing forced labor disclosed their awareness of the criminality of the mass deportations.

Servatius's contrary arguments were forcefully presented, and the nature of the evidence left him no other avenue. The rest of his argument followed the lines of Sauckel's testimony and ended with the curious plea that he should be acquitted because of his "good intentions".

Dr. Exner was an eminent professor and devoted to Jodl's interests, but he was not a court lawyer, and his speech was neither interesting nor persuasive. Furthermore, his argument so closely tracked Jodl's testimony as to become painfully repetitive. Every point his client had made was made again, while nothing that should have been previously discussed, but had not been, was dealt with in this last chance.

Jodl's own tendency to overstate things came through again. For example, Lawrence was obviously scornful of Exner's argument that Germany was within her rights in attacking Belgium and Holland even without prior notice, because they had not prevented British war planes from flying over them at night, and therefore these small countries had lost their neutrality, and could be treated as enemies.°

At the end of Exner's argument, just before he asked for Jodl's acquittal, Exner told the Tribunal that he had warned Jodl of his own lack of court experience, whereupon Jodl replied: "If I felt a spark of guilt in me, I would not choose you as my defense counsel." It was a gracious way to end the *Plädoyer*, but few are those who can truly make such a claim, and Jodl was not among them.

Seyss-Inquart's counsel, Dr. Steinbauer, was well aware that his client had left the witness stand shouldering a substantial burden of admitted violations of the Charter and of the laws of war. Seyss-Inquart's plight was no doubt intensified by his own refusal to denounce Hitler or the Nazi government. Under these circumstances it was apparent that the only possibility of less than a very heavy sentence depended on showing important grounds for mitigation.

In my opinion, Steinbauer followed this avenue to a degree, but insufficiently. To begin with, he devoted the first half of his nearly daylong argument to the years culminating in the Anschluss, in which Seyss-Inquart played an important part but did nothing criminal. Steinbauer then paid no attention to his client's positions in Austria after the Anschluss, or in Poland, although in both capacities he had engaged in anti-Semitic statements and actions. Steinbauer failed to make plausible arguments that since Austria had become part of the Reich, the defendant's acts there, even if culpable,

---

°During the months before Germany attacked France, British flights over the Low Countries to Germany were largely for the purpose of dropping propaganda leaflets. Exner did not say whether or not the Luftwaffe had also flown over Belgium and Holland at that time.

were not war crimes. Nor did he point out that in Poland, Seyss-Inquart's statements were not shown to have had any criminal consequences.

The prime area of decision on Seyss-Inquart's case and fate, in any event, lay in his conduct as Reich Commissioner in Holland throughout the years of the Netherlands' occupation by the Germans. There was no denying that Seyss-Inquart had violated the laws of war with respect to treatment of the Dutch Jews and deportation of forced labor. Steinbauer, like many of his colleagues, argued strenuously that "crimes against peace" had no legal basis, that the rules of the Hague Convention were obsolete, and that obedience to orders and military necessity justified everything the defendant had done. But months before Steinbauer's argument it had become apparent that these arguments were not likely to prevail with the Tribunal. A defendant's proven actions for the benefit of public safety and welfare might, however, have positive results.

Steinbauer had included a number of such actions in his address, but it had not been assembled and described in such a way as to impress the listener the way Speer's description of his own prevention of Hitler's scorched-earth policy had been presented. Steinbauer had testimonial evidence from Dr. Hirshfeld, a high Dutch administrative official, from Doenitz, from General Philipp Kleffel (Commander of the German troops in Holland), and from British and American generals, which confirmed Seyss-Inquart's vital role in preventing the inundation of large areas in Holland by German-planned destruction of dikes and locks. Steinbauer made brief mention of these matters near the end of his address, but neither he nor his client had much skill as a press agent.

Lawrence next called upon Bormann's appointed spokesman, Dr. Bergold, who, without expressing any opinion as to Bormann's guilt or innocence, declared that the prosecution's documents did not establish that Bormann had any influence on Hitler's decisions. After a brief argument, Bergold recommended that the Tribunal either suspend the proceedings on the ground that it had been proved that Bormann was dead or postpone them until such time as Bormann could be heard. To me, this appeared to make good sense.

The case against Franz von Papen had been in trouble ever since the prosecution's case had been presented. Dr. Kubuschok, despite Judge Birkett's strictures on his examination of his client, wrote a very good brief, and his argument was uninterrupted. He asked for nothing, but in conclusion stated that it was "obvious" that Papen was "not guilty."

Dr. Flächsner, for Speer, spent most of his argument, in line with the efforts of Sauckel's and Seyss-Inquart's lawyers, to discredit the Hague Convention's provisions relevant to the deportation of forced labor. Relying, like his predecessors, primarily on alleged military necessity and obsolescence of the Hague rules and an argument that others than Speer (presumably including Sauckel) were responsible for the deportations, Flächsner concluded that "Speer is not responsible for the means employed for the procurement of foreign labor, nor for its removal to Germany."

During the course of the argument, Lawrence asked Flächsner whether there had been "any communication between states, either at the League of Nations or elsewhere, since the war of 1914–1918, which suggests that the Hague Rules of Land Warfare were no longer applicable?" Flächsner admitted that there had been none, and Lawrence's question certainly suggested that he was not buying Flächsner's argument against application of the rules.

Earlier in the address Lawrence had asked Flächsner to deal with the meaning of the words "waging of a war of aggression" in Article 6(a) of the Charter. It was a difficult question, and Flächsner can hardly be blamed for postponing his reply until near the end of his speech. His response was that the words applied only to "the person who has supreme command" and that "all others are only led, even if their participation may mean a considerable contribution to the war." This interpretation would, of course, exclude not only Speer from liability under the clause, but also everyone except the deceased Hitler. That can hardly have been the intent of the Charter's framers.

Flächsner devoted the last portion of his address to a recapitulation of Speer's blocking of Hitler's "policy of destruction." His last sentences were plainly a plea for mitigation: "Speer had to betray Hitler in order to remain loyal to his people. One cannot but respect the tragedy which lies in this fate."

Except for Nelte's argument for Keitel, Lüdinghausen's for Neurath was the longest of all these *Plädoyers*. It was also the most tedious, as Lüdinghausen carefully went over virtually everything that Neurath had testified about, except the embarrassing matters that Fyfe had brought up on cross-examination. Even von der Lippe, usually kind to his colleagues, thought Lüdinghausen took too long. Lawrence, who had berated Lüdinghausen for his slowness while questioning Neurath, must have gone to sleep during the argument, for he said not a word from start to finish of more than a full day of Lüdinghausen argument, none of which was to any purpose.

Fritzsche's evidentiary hearing had gone very well, and general opinion in the courthouse was that he would be acquitted or, at worst, given a light sentence. However, these encouraging signs by no means relaxed his counsel, and Dr. Fritz produced a very insightful and professional *Plädoyer*.

Unlikely as it was that the inconspicuous Fritzsche would be convicted of conspiracy, he had been charged under Count One of the Indictment. Conspiracy under the Charter related only to "crimes against peace," and since Fritzsche admittedly had no part in "planning, preparation, or initiation" of Hitler's wars, the only theoretical possibility was that the defendant had used his "positions" and supposed "influence" in conspiring to "wage" aggressive wars. This issue raised the same question that Lawrence had asked Dr. Flächsner: What was the meaning of "wage"?

Responding much more reasonably than Flächsner had, Fritz declared: "Only those persons can be considered as waging a war of aggression who planned it themselves." This reading might be criticized on the ground that those who "planned" were already guilty regardless of the "waging." But Fritz's interpretation was sensible in that it marked out a group tainted with "war guilt." Furthermore, if "waging" alone were punishable, as Fritz pointed out: "In such a case, hardly one citizen of a country which had started a war of aggression would be guiltless." Needless to say, Fritz's principle would also shield his client from any guilt for "waging."

Fritz had sharp eyes and had noticed that Drexel Sprecher, presenting the prosecution's evidence, had referred to Fritzsche as an "accomplice" of the "master planners" of aggressive wars and declared him "quite as culpable" as they. In order to provide a "cushion" if Fritzsche were convicted, Fritz took pains to tell the Tribunal that in German criminal law, an "accomplice" is "punished less severely than the perpetrator himself."

Fritz was not an intransigent like Kranzbuehler and very sensitively assured the Tribunal that he was not contending that his client was white as snow: "Of course, it was a sin, indeed the grievous sin against the spirit [de Menthon's phrase] to have continued to serve the [Nazi] system." But though a sinner, said Fritz, Fritzsche "is not guilty in the sense of the Indictment brought against him before the Tribunal. I ask for his acquittal."

And so, on the afternoon of July 25, 1946, the Tribunal came back to Dr. Seidl, to present his rewritten *Plädoyer*. That morning Lawrence had announced in court:

> The argument as rewritten by Dr. Seidl has been carefully examined by the Tribunal. It still contains many allusions to the unfairness of the Versailles Treaty, irrelevant material, quotations not authorized by the Tribunal, and other matters which have nothing to do with the issues before the Tribunal. The Tribunal have, therefore, deleted the objectionable passages and have directed the General Secretary to hand a marked copy containing the deletions to Dr. Seidl.

Seidl's address was remarkable, among other things, in that there was so little mention of Hess. Seidl did not deign to deal with the documents introduced by the prosecution in February. Instead of arguing that his client was innocent of the charges in the Indictment, Seidl insisted that the Nazi government's foreign policies and military actions were entirely legal and that Article 6 of the Charter and Counts One and Two of the Indictment were legally invalid: "Article 6, Paragraph 2a of the Charter does not exist."

Furthermore, Article 9 of the Charter, dealing with "criminal organizations," was declared equally invalid under international law. These views were stated with skill and force, but were very unlikely to help Seidl's client. Only at the end of the address was Hess as a person discussed and then only for the purpose of arguing that his flight to Britain and proposals to the British Cabinet showed him to be a peaceful man.

Dr. von der Lippe had obtained, and copied in his diary the parts of Seidl's speech which the Tribunal had deleted. They proved to be passages the public reading of which would have embarrassed the Russians. For example, Seidl had quoted, from a book written by British Ambassador Nevile Henderson: "Russia and Germany play cat and mouse with each other. . . . Russia's hope is a war between Germany and the West, while Russia will play the laughing third."

The last stricken passage was more serious, for in it Seidl referred to the Soviet Union's secret pact of 1939 with Germany dividing Poland between them and establishing their respective "spheres of influence" in the Baltic States and Bucovina, as well as Russia's 1940 attack on Finland. These actions, argued Seidl, were aggressive wars just as much as Hitler's conquest of Poland, and therefore the Russian judges' participation in the trial rendered questionable the Tribunal's jurisdiction over the prosecution's charge against the German defendants with respect to Poland.

By asking the Tribunal's permission to read this material, Seidl managed, while asking, to mention the essential features of the secret agreement. Lawrence, with visible exasperation, declared: "The Tribunal has fully considered this matter and does not desire to hear your point."

Dr. von der Lippe acknowledged Seidl's cleverness, but opined that his teasing would have "little effect." But journalists and others came crowding up asking for unabridged copies of Seidl's *Plädoyer*, and the diminutive Seidl, who had become the trial's gadfly, was "very pleased with his popularity."

## 4

The following morning, July 26, 1946, Robert Jackson approached the lectern to deliver the final argument for the American prosecution. For the defendants, the atmosphere was tense. For nearly five months they had pled their various defenses against the prosecution's charges. Had they made any dent on their accusers? Would the chief prosecutors acknowledge any merit in their arguments? The tension in the dock was not eased by news that the military judges at the Dachau trial of the SS soldiers responsible for the murder of American prisoners at Malmédy° had found all

---

°Many of the judgments were later commuted by General Clay. The Malmédy trial led to hearings by a U.S. Senate committee, in the course of which Senator Joseph McCarthy of Wisconsin became a rising and controversial political figure.

seventy-three defendants guilty and sentenced forty-three of them to death.

The chief prosecutors had had some difficulty in determining the order in which they would proceed. When they had first met in Berlin, and again in early December, they had discussed the closing arguments inconclusively. There were suggestions that only one prosecutor should speak for all, but there was more support for giving Shawcross the major role, with shorter speeches by the other three. Early in April there was a long discussion wherein it was agreed that Shawcross would make the main legal argument in behalf of all and that the other three would make shorter statements in accord with their particular needs for home consumption.

Final decisions were reached in a long meeting on July 1, 1946. Rudenko's suggestion that they speak in the same order as in the opening statements was accepted. Jackson, as the first speaker, would focus on Count One and the proof of conspiracy. Shawcross, replying to Jahrreiss, would support the legal validity of "crimes against peace" as stated in Count Two and present an overview of the entire case. The French and Russian prosecutors would deal primarily with war crimes and crimes against humanity.

Jackson had shaken off the malaise contracted in his encounter with Goering. He was most comfortable, and skilled beyond his fellows, in the preparation and presentation of courtroom arguments. At the lectern he was the picture of confidence. In his first paragraph he described the evidence before the Tribunal as embracing a "vast and varied" panorama and the trial record as "mad and melancholy," foretelling an alliterative address.

After commendably brief general observations, Jackson turned to "the conspiracy count which was the duty of the United States to argue." He then declared: "The pillars which sustain the conspiracy charge may be found in five groups of overt acts,* whose character and magnitude are important considerations in appraising the proof of conspiracy."

The first such group Jackson labeled "The Seizure of Power and Subjugation of Germany to a Police State." I thought this a weak selection. The crimes listed in the Charter mentioned no such actions. There was virtually no evidence (other than Hitler's *Mein Kampf*) that the civil or military leaders, during the early Nazi years, were planning aggressive wars, while there were abundant reasons why German leaders would want to rearm for defensive or negotiating purposes.

Jackson's second group, "The Preparation and Waging of Wars of Aggression", was plainly suited to his purpose, and by 1938, if not sooner,

---

*In the United States, laws defining the elements of conspiracy commonly require not only intent to join others in committing crimes, but also "overt acts" that are committed as part of the conspiracy.

the likelihood of planned aggressive war was obvious. It was covered by both Article 6(a) of the Charter and Count Two of the Indictment.

Groups three, four, and five all involved Article 6(b) and (c) of the Charter and Counts Three and Four of the Indictment. Jackson was still assuming that Section 6 of the Charter covered conspiracies to violate 6(b) and (c), whereas, as the Tribunal eventually ruled, only conspiracies to violate 6(a) were declared criminal.

Essentially, therefore, proof of conspiracy hung on Jackson's second group, but that was quite enough to support Jackson's case if he could prove that some or all of the defendants were parties to the conspiracy as described in Article 6(a) of the Charter, including particularly "planning, preparation, initiation or waging a war of aggression."

Prove it Jackson could and did, but for some, not all. He outlined the willingness of Goering, Ribbentrop, Keitel, Raeder, and Jodl to follow Hitler's every decision and order for the preparation and waging of wars which they knew to be in fact aggressive.

Later in his address, Jackson dealt with the arguments of many of the defendants that they could not have been conspirators because they disagreed among themselves and with some of Hitler's decisions. But in very few cases did they refuse to follow orders, and the mere fact of different opinions was no breach of the conspiracy. As Jackson put it:

> Of course it is not necessary that men should agree on everything in order to agree on enough things to make them liable for a criminal conspiracy. Unquestionably there were conspiracies within the conspiracy and intrigues and rivalries and battles for power. . . . Wherever they differed, their differences were as to method or disputes over jurisdiction, but always within the framework of the common plan.

Moving away from legal issues and toward the defendants individually, Jackson mixed accusation with scornful humor:

> The large and varied role of Goering was half militarist and half gangster. He stuck his pudgy thumb in every pie. He used his SA musclemen to help bring the gang into power. In order to entrench that power he contrived to have the Reichstag burned, established the Gestapo, and created the concentration camps. He was equally adept at massacring opponents and at framing scandals to get rid of stubborn generals. He built up the Luftwaffe and hurled it at his defenseless neighbors. . . . He was, next to Hitler, the man who tied the activities of all the defendants together in a common effort.

Shorter and equally derogatory paragraphs, only occasionally inaccurate, were attached to "the zealot Hess," "the duplicitous Ribbentrop," "Keitel, the weak and willing tool," "Kaltenbrunner, the grand inquisitor,"

Rosenberg, the intellectual high priest of the "master race," "the fanatical Frank," and then "Streicher, the venomous vulgarian," which was too much for me. Fortunately, the remaining defendants were dealt with in a more matter-of-fact way, except for Sauckel, who was "the greatest and cruelest slaver since the Pharaohs of Egypt."

Near the end of his address, Jackson turned to the defense so often pled by the defendants when confronted with infernal crimes: "Nobody knew about what was going on. Time after time we have heard the chorus from the dock: 'I only heard about these things here for the first time.'" In reply, Jackson took this chant with mock seriousness:

> If we combine only the stories of the front bench, this is the ridiculous composite picture of Hitler's government which emerges. It was composed of:
>
> A Number 2 man who knew nothing of the excesses of the Gestapo which he created, and never suspected the Jewish extermination program although he was the signer of over a score of decrees which instituted the persecutions of that race;
>
> A Number 3 man who was merely an innocent middleman transmitting Hitler's orders without ever reading them, like a postman or delivery boy;
>
> A foreign minister who knew little of foreign affairs and nothing of foreign policy;
>
> A field marshal who issued orders to the Armed Forces but had no idea of the results they would have in practice;
>
> A Party philosopher who was interested in historical research and had no idea of the violence which his philosophy was inciting in the twentieth century;
>
> A governor general of Poland who reigned but did not rule;
>
> A Gauleiter of Franconia whose occupation was to pour forth filthy writings about Jews, but who had no idea that anybody would read them;
>
> A minister of interior who knew not even what went on in the interior of his own office, much less the interior of his own department, and nothing at all about the interior of Germany;
>
> A Reichsbank president who was totally ignorant of what went in and out of the vaults of his bank;
>
> And a plenipotentiary for the war economy who secretly marshaled the entire economy for armament, but had no idea it had anything to do with war.

It was overdrawn and crude, but fiercely effective. And Jackson capped his address with a deeply moving last paragraph that matched the best writing of his opening statement:

It is against this background that these defendants now ask this Tribunal to say that they are not guilty of planning, executing, or conspiring to commit this long list of crimes and wrongs. They stand before the record of this trial as blood-stained Gloucester stood by the body of his slain king. He begged of the widow, as they beg of you: "Say I slew them not." And the Queen replied, "Then say they were not slain. But dead they are. . . ." If you were to say of these men that they are not guilty, it would be as true to say that there has been no war, there are no slain, there has been no crime.

## 5

The defendants reacted with indignation at the names Jackson had called them and anger at his disregard of their own arguments. Papen declared: "That was more the speech of a demagogue than of a leading representative of American jurisprudence. . . . What have we been sitting here eight months for? The prosecution isn't paying the slightest attention to our defense. They still insist on calling us liars and murderers." Doenitz and Schacht agreed, and so did Goering, except that he was pleased with Jackson's scorn for Schacht.

Goering also suggested that "the British prosecutor would probably be more dignified." He was right in that Shawcross, who immediately followed Jackson, was more stiffly disdainful and engaged in no scornful humor. But any defendants who expected a more comfortable session had their hopes soon dashed when Shawcross, in his very first paragraph, declared that "each of these defendants is legally guilty" and that "the people of Germany" share the guilt "in large measure." From start to finish Shawcross's message was that each of the defendants was a murderer.

Shawcross's lesson was a long one, three times longer than Jackson's. In discussion with the other chief prosecutors, Shawcross had portrayed his reply to Jahrreiss's attack on "crimes against peace" as his main point, but in length it was less than a tenth of his address, which lasted more than a full day's session. What Shawcross did was to describe the course and content of the prosecution's case, from Versailles to Nazi Germany's collapse a quarter of a century later. It was well organized and excellently delivered by Shawcross. But as I listened, I could not help wondering, as many others in the audience must have, "Why now?" By that time most of the evidence was familiar to the audience and certainly to the Tribunal. At this late stage of the trial, the copious repetition tended to muffle the parts that were intended to answer the defendants' arguments and were what the judges would most want to hear.

Shawcross approached his reply to Jahrreiss by listing Nazi Germany's aggressive actions and wars from the Rhineland reentry in 1936 to the attack against the Soviet Union in 1941. At the beginning and the end of this sequence, he dropped a thought "by the way" that gave the defendants cause to shiver. At the beginning Shawcross stated:

> But let it be said plainly now that these defendants are charged also as common murderers. That charge alone merits the imposition of the supreme penalty and the joinder in the Indictment of this Crime against Peace can add nothing to the penalty which may be imposed on these individuals.

In other words, since all the defendants were charged as "common murderers" under Counts Three and Four, which were not subject to the arguments that Jahrreiss had brought against the validity of Counts One and Two, the defendants would gain nothing by way of penalties even if Counts One and Two should be invalidated. The plain implication was that Shawcross expected all the defendants to be convicted under Counts Three and Four and be liable to the "supreme penalty."

After discussing Germany's attack against the Soviet Union, Shawcross castigated the defendants because no warning had been given in any of Hitler's wars:

> In no single case did a declaration of war precede military action. . . . In every single case, as the documents make clear, that was the common plan. . . . Every one of these men acquiesced in this technique, knowing full well what it must represent in terms of human life. How can any one of them now say he was not a party to common murder in its most ruthless form?[*]

Shawcross politely saluted Jahrreiss's "distinguished speech," but both of their contending arguments were well worn. Since both of the contenders also knew that, in all probability, the Tribunal would abide by the Charter's mandate, there was a certain unreality about the debate. Shawcross's purposes were to supply material that might be used in the press or by the Tribunal if it decided to deal with the issue in its opinion. His rebuttal to Jahrreiss was well written and forcefully spoken, but political and legal disagreements on this issue, among lawyers everywhere, ran too deep to be settled by mere skill in advocacy.

Most of the rest of Shawcross's address was devoted to Counts Three and Four. He spoke with a force befitting the magnitude and horror of the

---

[*]Shawcross did not mention Hague III 1907: "The contracting Powers recognize that hostilities between themselves must not commence without previous and explicit warning, in the form either of a reasoned declaration of war or of an ultimatum with conditional declaration of war."

crimes and conceded no doubt, nor partial acquittal nor mitigation, to anyone in the dock. In tune with this attitude, Shawcross did not argue against troublesome points made by the defendants; he either blew them away without discussion or omitted them altogether.

For example, the evidentiary record made it clear that the German Navy, initially and briefly, directed its submarines to give warning before sinking, but ended that policy when it became clear that British merchant ships were being armed and directed to attack U-boats by shooting and ramming. On this point, Shawcross cavalierly stated: "We need not concern ourselves with the niceties of argument whether the practice of arming merchantmen affects the position." He cited the *Laconia* as if it were a brutal sinking, when the German submarines had spent two days towing the lifeboats to a place of safety for them. And Shawcross did not even mention Admiral Nimitz's interrogatory.

So, too, the record shows that Raeder had called Hitler's attention to the military advantages of German naval bases on the Norwegian coasts and also to the disadvantages of finding that the British had beaten them to it. Shawcross's comment was that "a strenuous attempt has been made in the course of this Trial to suggest that Norway was invaded only because the Germans believed that the Allies were about to take a similar step. Even if it were true, it would be no answer." That was certainly cutting both the truth and the law very fine, since Britain was in fact planning an occupation of the Norwegian coast at that very time, and if that had happened it is by no means clear that Germany would not have had the right of counter-attack. That is exactly what the British did (unsuccessfully) when they saw that the Germans had been quicker.

Shawcross ended his address with "brief comments" on each of the "guilty men." He raised nothing new, but it is worth a comment that he said: "Of Streicher, one need say nothing," although I (and many others) thought his case one of the most debatable. So, too, I noted with wonder that Shawcross castigated Schacht for becoming Plenipotentiary for War Economy in May 1935, when a few weeks later Shawcross's own government entered into the Anglo-German Naval Agreement, which virtually ended the Versailles limits on German militarization and gave Hitler specific approval of his building a submarine fleet.

As part of his peroration, Shawcross quoted a passage which he attributed to Goethe,° saying that some day fate would strike the German people

> because they betrayed themselves and did not want to be what they are. It is sad that they do not know the charm of truth; that mist,

---

°It subsequently was established that these were not the words of Goethe, but were attributed to Goethe by Thomas Mann in his novel *Lotte in Weimar* (1939).

smoke, and berserk immoderation are so dear to them; pathetic that they ingenuously submit to any mad scoundrel who appeals to their lowest instincts, who confirms them in their vices and teaches them to conceive nationalism as insolence and brutality.

Shawcross then declared: "With what a voice of prophesy he spoke—for these are the mad scoundrels who did these very things."

Whether or not these sentiments were an apt appraisal of the German people was debatable, but it appears to me a strange way to end a long address which had made no mention of the question of the German people's responsibility for the events of the Nazi years.

## 6

Shawcross fared even worse than Jackson with the defendants. Ribbentrop: "Compared to him, even Jackson was a charming fellow." Goering: "Compared to Shawcross, Jackson was downright chivalrous." Schacht told Dr. Gilbert that "both Jackson and Shawcross had made miserable speeches, so biased and so unfair." Only Speer said he "was delighted" with Shawcross, "after listening to all the stupid nonsense of the defense attorneys." After Shawcross finished, Frank was loudly cursing "that damn Englishman."

The defendants gained a small measure of relief when the French prosecutors took the lectern. Their conclusions about the deserved fate of the defendants were just as dire as those of their predecessors, but there was less heavy denunciation and gentler accents.

Gallant old Champetier de Ribes, despite his frailty the epitome of a French gentleman, was able to read the introduction of the address, but could not carry it further. The task was then passed to Dubost, who gave what Birkett described as a "robust and vigorous" presentation. The reading of most of the script was low-keyed and almost contemplative. De Menthon, in his opening, had at times seemed more interested in the legal and moral structure of the case than the crimes of the individual defendants; and, until near the end, Dubost's delivery had the same tone.

Perhaps, for lawyers, the most interesting passages were those in which Dubost dealt with the same factors that Jackson had encased in the conspiracy concept. Dubost stated:

> The conquest of living space, that is, of territories emptied of their populations by every means including extermination—that was the great idea of the Party, the system, the State, and consequently of all those at the head of the main administration of both State and Party.
>
> That is the main idea, in the pursuit of which they united and for which they worked. They stopped for nothing to achieve their end.

Dubost also remarked that "The defendants did not actually commit the crimes; they were content to decree them. According to our French law, they are therefore *accomplices* in the technical sense of the term . . . the perpetrators of serious offenses and their accomplices are subject in most countries to capital punishment or to very severe penalties, such as forced labor or solitary confinement."

But, said Dubost, to avoid these conclusions the defendants "have tried to establish the existence of watertight partitions between the different elements of the German State. However, this is false":

> The aim pursued by the Party was . . . the advancement of an increasingly complete union between the State and the Party. This is the reason for the legislation which makes it compulsory for the head of the Party Chancellory to be consulted in the appointment of high-ranking officials, which incorporates Party chiefs into municipal administration, integrates the SS into the Police, and converts the SS to police officers, makes the direction of the Hitler Youth a State department, brings the direction to Party headquarters abroad into the Foreign Office, and merges the military personnel of the Party [SS] to an ever increasing degree with those of the Army.

Dubost then spent some time, with references to individual defendants and to the Party and State agencies, showing their interlockings, interdependences, and mutual activities in support of the common goal of living space. "All the crimes of the defendants lie in their political life," said Dubost and capped his argument:

> In this way, gentlemen, by presenting the facts, apart from any legal conception of conspiracy or complicity which might be debatable according to the varying opinions of the jurists, we furnish proof of solidarity and of the equal culpability of all in the crime.

In other words, there is no need to resort to esoteric or unfamiliar doctrines such as "conspiracy" if there is proof that the defendants as accomplices holding high positions in the Party and State complied with Hitler's goal of the conquest of living space. All such accomplices would be guilty of the group's actions as a whole.

In the later part of the address, Dubost undertook to prove that each of the defendants complied with those requisites. In a few cases—Streicher, Doenitz, Papen—the "proof" was thin, and Dubost acknowledged that Schacht's case (which he left to the end and dealt with at much greater length) was "peculiar in itself." It appeared to me that Dubost was very troubled, but was bound to get his man: "The measure of his guilt is full, his responsibility complete."

In conclusion, Dubost admitted that there were degrees of guilt among the defendants, but he insisted that all should be executed. "You must hit hard, without pity," he urged the Tribunal. "It is enough that the verdict be just!" Dubost and his colleagues would be prosecuting lesser defendants before French courts. "How could we demand the death penalty for . . . the camp commandants who have on their conscience the death of millions of human creatures whom they killed by order, if we hesitated today to demand the supreme penalty for those who were the driving force of the criminal State which gave the orders?"

## 7

General Rudenko's address was like his own physique—squarely built, stocky, and tough. He voiced no speculations, doubts, or literary allusions. His address contained only a few pages on legal issues, such as conspiracy and crimes against peace, and the rest of his long argument dealt with the crimes of the individual defendants, with a very brief hortatory conclusion.

Considering that his three colleagues had spoken and that Shawcross had spent some nine hours laying out the entire case, Rudenko could hardly be expected to break much new ground. He appeared untroubled by his situation and produced a forceful speech in which he made good use of many shocking statements by the defendants in their days of power, impossible to deny or defend plausibly.

As might have been expected, Rudenko spoke with particular hostility against Hess who, because of his flight to Britain and efforts to persuade his surprised hosts to join with the Nazis against the Soviet Union, the Kremlin regarded as an especially evil enemy. Rudenko also dedicated a full page to Bormann, of whom he spoke as if Bormann were still alive, possibly because there had been sporadic rumors of links between Bormann and the Kremlin, and therefore Rudenko wished to speak in a way that would negate any such possibility.

Those of us who had followed Rudenko's unchanging way of conducting cross-examinations were amused that he proudly quoted from his own cross-examination of Keitel:

> You, Defendant Keitel, called a Field Marshall, repeatedly referred to yourself as a soldier before this Tribunal, and you, by your bloodthirsty resolution of September 1941 approved and sanctioned the murder, in cold blood, of thousands of unarmed soldiers. Do you confirm this?*

*Rudenko added: "Keitel was forced to admit this fact." Keitel, in fact, admitted, as he had already several times before, that he had signed the documents that Rudenko referred to, but he continued to defend their legitimacy.

Like Shawcross, Rudenko did not mention his own government's more plentiful skeletons in the closet. Denouncing Ribbentrop for his "criminal plan against peace—the attack on Poland" and his "hypocritical declarations" about Germany's peaceful plans, Rudenko made no reference to Russia's simultaneous conquest and annexation of eastern Poland.

Turning to the "military group" (Keitel, Jodl, Doenitz, and Raeder), Rudenko scoffed at them as "noble-minded simpletons" because they followed Hitler's commands even when they thought his orders unlawful. Surely Rudenko knew well enough that many officers in many countries would do likewise.

Rudenko's last advice to the Tribunal was brief and to the point: "I appeal to the Tribunal to sentence all the defendants without exception to the supreme penalty—death. Such a verdict will be greeted with satisfaction by all progressive mankind."

Thus the French and Soviet prosecutors explicitly demanded death sentences for all, Shawcross repeatedly stressed the legitimacy of such a decision,° and Jackson, for all of his denunciation, made no explicit recommendation. The chief prosecutors, at a meeting prior to delivery of the addresses, had discussed whether, and if so when, they should raise with the Tribunal the matter of penalties. At that time only Fyfe had expressed a personal opinion (that Streicher should be hanged, but Speer might be allowed some mitigation). The discussion as a whole was inconclusive, with some suggestions that each Chief Prosecutor should consult his own country's Tribunal members. Whether that was done I do not know.

Objection might have been made to the British, French, and Soviet demands on the ground that they were premature. The defendants' evidence and final arguments regarding the indicted organizations had yet to be heard by the Tribunal, and since most of the defendants had been members of one or more of the organizations, these proceedings might cast further light on their actions. Furthermore, in line with Continental legal practice, Article 24(j) of the Charter provided that the last act before delivery of judgment was that "Each defendant may make a statement to the Tribunal." That, too, was to be taken account of by the Tribunal before coming to its decisions.

---

°Shawcross, however, had told his fellow chief prosecutors, at their meeting on July 1, 1946, that "at this stage" he would have to ask for "the death penalty for everyone," but that he really hoped "that the Court will discriminate among the defendants and not the same sentence for all of them."

# Chapter 18

# THE INDICTED
# ORGANIZATIONS

On July 30, 1946, when the Tribunal commenced receiving evidence dealing with the German organizations indicted under Article 9 of the Charter,* it was only six weeks short of two years since Colonel Murray Bernays had first proposed such a procedure. It was about one year since Bernays had resigned from the American prosecution staff.

Bernays's motivation had been his (generally shared) belief that in the SS and other large Nazi organizations, there were hundreds of thousands of war criminals—so many that individual trials were impossible—who could only be punished on the basis of their proven membership in an organization declared criminal as an entity.

I have already described the problems and disagreements that Bernays's brainchild precipitated: doubts and objections, within the Tribunal and elsewhere, concerning punishments based only on membership in proceedings lacking the customary elements of criminal justice; strong support for Bernays's proposal in the United States War Department and by the American and British chief prosecutors; General Clay's overlapping projection of the Denazification Program, to be undertaken by the Germans, which the American authorities in Berlin and I myself thought preferable to the Bernays plan.

In December and January, my colleagues and I had presented evidence against the several organizations named in the Indictment without undertaking to deal fully with these and other controversial legal and ad-

---

*"At the trial of any individual member of any group or organization the Tribunal may declare (in connection with any act of which the individual may be convicted) that the group or organization of which the individual was a member was a criminal organization."

ministrative issues. The Tribunal then called upon prosecution and defense counsel to state their views, and, from February 28 to March 2, 1946, the Tribunal heard arguments, which were helpful, but far from conclusive on the issues.

In accordance with Article 9 of the Charter, in October 1945 the Tribunal had ordered that notices of the impending trials of the organizations should be sent throughout occupied Germany. Notices were sent to the press, to the internment and prisoner-of-war camps where many of the organization members were to be found, and to others, through suitable channels. A mass of letters, affidavits, and applications to be heard in support of the organizations was received. The SS members alone sent 136,000 affidavits, confronting the Tribunal's Secretariat with staggering problems of interpretation and examination.

The arguments of the lawyers and the march of the calendar galvanized the Tribunal, and on March 12, 1946, the judges adopted an order "with respect to further proceedings on the charge against organizations and the applications of members thereof to be heard." The document's main points were:

(1) Defense counsel were given permission to visit the camps for the purpose "of selecting witnesses to be brought to Nürnberg to give evidence on the criminal or non-criminal character of the accused Organizations" to which they belonged. . . .

(4) Whenever persons have been brought to Nürnberg, Counsel shall have free access to them for the purpose of ascertaining which, if any of them, Counsel desire to call as witnesses before the Tribunal and which . . . to examine before a Commissioner. . . . Counsel for the Defense and for the Prosecution shall have the usual rights of examination, cross-examination and reexamination and evidence taken shall be recorded by the Commissioner. The Commissioner shall be Lt. Colonel Neave and he . . . shall recommend to the Tribunal suitable persons to be appointed Assistant Commissioners if the necessity should arise. This Order shall be carried out under the direction of Lt. Colonel A.M.S. Neave,° in collaboration with the Office of the General Secretary and subject to necessary security regulations. . . .

(6) In this proceeding, evidence is considered to be relevant which bears upon the following issues:

(a) Whether the organization or group charged consisted substantially of an aggregation of persons sharing a general common purpose to engage in activity defined as criminal under Article 6 of the Charter. . . .

(b) Whether membership in the Organization or group was

---

°Colonel Neave had been in immediate charge of organization matters since January 1946, and was in very good standing with the judges.

generally voluntary or the result of physical compulsion or legal decree;

(c) Whether the purposes and activities of the Organization or group, defined as criminal under Article 6 of the Charter, were generally known to the members, so that its membership in general . . . may justly be held to have had knowledge of them at some relevant time."

Neave set to work with his usual efficiency and on May 20 was able to begin hearing witnesses for the organizations, conducting the hearings himself. Soon realizing that one person could not proceed fast enough, he had the Tribunal appoint several assistant commissioners and later secured a second hearing room so that two witnesses could be examined at the same time. The Tribunal had previously retained eight lawyers to represent the defendants. Cross-examination by the prosecution was handled mainly by Kempner for the United States, Griffith-Jones for the British, and Pokrovsky for the Soviet Union.

Legal questions could not, of course, be settled except by ruling of the Tribunal, but nevertheless there were lengthy arguments concerning the meaning of "physical compulsion" in clause 6(b) of the Tribunal's distinction between "voluntary" and "compelled" membership in the organizations, particularly the SS and Gestapo. Defense counsel sought to broaden "physical compulsion" so as to cover "psychological" and "economic" compulsion, but Neave, as he later put it, "had no difficulty in rejecting the arguments of the defense" so that only "evidence of physical intimidation" would be regarded as relevant.

Lieutenant Colonel Neave, a decorated British officer whose escapes from the German Stalags were well known, was at first a bit awed by the German Field Marshals who came to testify before him. In his book about the Nuremberg trial he gave a separate chapter to his impressions of these witnesses, in which he rightly praised their defense by Dr. Laternser, but found much to criticize about the attitude and credibility of his clients.

By late July 1946, Neave and his commissioners had conducted hearings for 101 witnesses, from among whom those to testify before the Tribunal would be selected. On July 25, Lawrence read in court an "order of the procedure to be followed on the cases against the organizations." Each defense counsel should first offer whatever parts of the evidence taken by the commission he wished to be made part of the Tribunal's record. Defense counsel should then call a selection of their witnesses who had testified in the commission hearings for examination and cross-examination before the Tribunal. Finally, each defense counsel should make his "closing speech," and the prosecution counsel would reply.

On the morning of July 30, 1946, after Rudenko had finished his final speech against the individual defendants, Lawrence dealt briskly with the selection of witnesses to be heard and then told Dr. Servatius to call his witnesses in defense of the first of the organizations to be tried, the "Corps of Political Leaders of the Nazi Party."

## 2

In November 1945, on the third day of the trial, Ralph Albrecht had given the Tribunal a short lecture on the organizational structure of the Nazi Party, with emphasis on its Leadership Corps, from Hitler at the top down to the lowly *Block* and *Zellen* officials who had no real authority and were generally unpaid, part-time, nonuniformed helpers. Not much more was heard about these matters until December 17, when Colonel Storey began presenting the prosecution's evidence against the indicted organizations, beginning with the Leadership Corps.

The Indictment described the Corps as "a distinctive and elite group within the Nazi Party" and "the central core of the common plan or conspiracy" described in Count One. The concluding paragraph of the Indictment provided:

> The prosecution expressly reserves the right to request . . . that Political Leaders of subordinate grades or ranks or of other types or classes, to be specified by the Prosecution, be excepted from further proceedings in this Case, but without prejudice to other proceedings or actions against them.

Plainly the purpose of the last provision came from awareness that charging *all* Nazi members with criminality would be both ridiculous and unmanageable. But while there was no denying that the *whole* Nazi Party was an "organization," could the same be said if the lower branches of the organizational tree were severed? Was a part of the Party an "organization"? This was the same problem that concerned Calvocoressi and me when we charged specified military commanders with comprising an "organization" or "group" within the meaning of Article 9 of the Charter.

Storey had argued that the Leadership Corps was the "directing arm" of the Party and therefore could be treated as a "group" or "organization," but he carried the problem no further. When Jackson argued before the Tribunal on February 28, 1946, he adopted the position that the Leadership Corps included all Nazi Party officials from the Fuehrer down to the *Zellenleiter*, "but not members of the staff" of the three lowest categories. However sensible, this action highlighted the assumed power of the prosecution to select and vary the indicted portions of the Nazi Party.

Storey's evidence was by no means devoid of documentary material implicating some members of the Nazi Party in crimes against Jews, mistreatment of enemy airmen forced to land in Germany, and other wartime offenses against the Geneva Conventions. But the amount of solidly proven crimes committed by Party officials was small indeed compared to the testimony and documentation implicating the denizens of Himmler's evil empire, and this relative paucity of Party crimes raised questions of the extent of the members' knowledge of crimes committed in their own ranks. And when Servatius called his witnesses, it soon became clear that he was shooting at this target in particular.

Going from the high to the low ranks, Servatius called a *Gauleiter* from Hamburg, a *Kreisleiter* from Oldenburg, an *Ortsgruppenleiter* from the Allgäu, and a *Blockleiter* from Nuremberg. Of course all of them minimized the pernicious aspects of the Party's actions and their ignorance of concentration camps and the massacre of Jews. As for international affairs, they had wanted the Anschluss with Austria and recovery of the former German colonies, but had not expected to go to war for these aims.

The prosecution was able to make a few dents in this bland presentation. When Fyfe, cross-examining Gauleiter Kaufmann, asked him about Kristallnacht, Kaufmann replied that he had been able to prevent most of the excesses in Hamburg and that in the other *Gaue*, "with exceptions, the men responsible for these actions had in no case been Political Leaders." Kaufmann's reply to Fyfe was thoroughly discredited when Fyfe produced a report by the Supreme Court of the Nazi Party which stated: "it was understood by all the Party Leaders present, from the oral instructions of the Reich Propaganda Minister [Goebbels] that the Party should not appear outwardly as the instigator of the demonstrations, but in reality should organize and execute them."

But overall the cross-examination of Servatius's witnesses was not profitable. Servatius called as a witness Hans Wegscheider, blacksmith, veterinarian, Mayor of Hirschdorf, and *Ortsgruppenleiter* in Kreis Kempten Land, population 40,000, in the very rural Allgäu:

s: What was the attitude of the Political Leaders toward the [Jewish] question?

w: Since there were no Jewish businessmen in our district . . . no Jewish people lived there and this question was not a burning one.

s: Were there no Jewish cattle dealers?

w: Only in the town of Kempten there was a wholesale firm of cattledealers, Loew Brothers, and our peasants sold and exchanged cattle there.

s: Were not steps taken against this and voices of protest raised?

w: No, for a long time after the assumption of power our farmers traded with this wholesale firm. . . .

s: Did not trouble arise with the Church because of the Party's attitude?

w: No, not in the country. . . . We went to Church and in my particular Ortsgruppe, I and my eight Political Leaders sang in the Church choir. The other church musicians and singers, about 30 in all, were all Party members. . . . I believe more or less it was the same in the other districts as well. . . .

s: Did aviators make emergency landings in your territory and were they lynched?

w: No.

s: What happened to them?

w: I myself had the opportunity to take in an American flyer who had landed about 100 meters behind my home. I took him into the house and fed him, and after perhaps a quarter of an hour he was sent for by the Kempten police in an auto. . . .

s: In your Ortsgruppe . . . foreign workers were employed. . . . Did you not hear about the fact that these workers were to sleep in a barn and were to receive their food there too?

w: . . . The Labor Office only gave each Polish worker a note which was to be turned over to the farmer and which said the Polish workers should not eat at the farm table and that they must be at home at a certain hour. In discussing this matter with the *Bauernführer* [farm manager] at that time, I told him that this could not be done with our peasants in the Algäu. If the foreign worker behaved decently . . . he was to enjoy the same rights as the German worker.

It was the kind of testimony that rings true, but Griffith-Jones could not understand rules that were not followed:

> GJ: You see on that document that Poles are not allowed to complain, they have . . . no form of entertainment, no restaurants, no sexual intercourse, no use of public transport. . . . In no case may he be granted permission to leave his village, and in no case may permission be granted to visit a public agency on his own whether it is a labor office or the district peasant association. Why shouldn't he be allowed to visit the district peasant association?
>
> w: I see here that this letter comes from Karlsruhe. That is an entirely different Gau. These measures were not decreed in our region, or at any rate, not to such a large extent. . . .
>
> GJ: Are you telling us that the care of foreign workers was different in your Gau, to the Gau at Baden or Karlsruhe?
>
> w: Yes.

Griffith-Jones soon gave up, but both Nikitchenko and Lawrence had further questions for the imperturbable Wegscheider. Servatius's witnesses had shown that while the Nazi Party or part of it might be an "organization," it was not an organization like the quasi-military agencies in the Himmler complex. The Nazi Party officials were closer to the German people, whose varied habits and opinions were reflected in differing rules and reactions among both the rulers and the ruled.

Servatius began his final argument, presented on August 22, in accordance with the Tribunal's procedure, after all the defense counsel for the indicted organizations had called their witnesses and offered their documents. It was a forceful analysis of the legal basis of the prosecution's case against his organizational clients. He pointed out, quite rightly, that many of the prosecution's accusations—establishment of a dictatorship, dissolution of the trade unions, Kristallnacht and other anti-Jewish laws, and antichurch actions—were not war crimes and not within the Tribunal's jurisdiction unless they could be tied into preparation for aggressive war, which was unlikely. He questioned the "group" or "organization" status of the slice of the Nazi Party selected by the prosecution. And he criticized, as had all his colleagues, the juridical validity of inflicting criminal penalties on individual members without giving them all the rights of defendants.

As for the crimes attributed by the prosecution to the Party leaders, Servatius contended that there was no evidence to connect them with initiating aggressive war, that they had no responsibility for the concentration camps or the atrocities committed under Himmler's auspices, that there was no proof that lynching captured enemy aviators was "tolerated and approved of by the Political Leaders," that service in the Party was only nominally voluntary, and that much of the prosecution's evidence concerned matters, such as anti-Semitic and antichurch activities, which were not crimes within the reach of the Charter.

In these contentions, Servatius was not seeking to prove that war crimes had not been committed by Political Leaders, but to question the prosecution's assumption that most of the Political Leaders, numbering some 600,000 members, were aware of or implicated in the Party's crimes.

Probably believing that his clients' receipt of a clean bill of health from the Tribunal was unlikely, Servatius in his conclusion drew attention to several matters which he urged the Tribunal to consider. Among other things, he called attention to "the bulk of the little Political Leaders, who are made responsible . . . only indirectly through their leaders." He also observed that:

> the degree of punishment is uncertain. The scope of the penalties fixed in Law Number 10 of the Control Council, which includes the death penalty, offers no protection if their interpretation is left to the free decision of the various national tribunals which may subsequently sit

in judgment.* The judgment of the Tribunal might cause new harm.
. . . The punishment must not be a revenge.

Lord Lawrence thanked Servatius for having "kept within the limit of time." In my opinion he had done about all he could have done for his clients.

### 3

The Tribunal next turned to what might well be called the "Himmler Organization of Groups," comprising both civil and military groups. According to the Indictment, the charges were brought against the Schutzstaffel (Protection Squad) of the Nazi Party, which Himmler had commanded since 1929 and which included the Waffen (armed) SS, which fought with and under the command of the army, but remained administratively under Himmler, and "all other offices and departments" of the SS, including the RSHA (Reich Security Main Office), originally led by Heydrich and after his death by Kaltenbrunner. This included among its numerous departments the Sicherheitsdienst (SD, Security Service), the Sicherheitspolizei (SIPO), and the Gestapo (Secret State Police). The last-named had been in existence since 1933, several years before it was made a part of the RSHA, and for that reason was described in the Indictment separately from the other SS agencies. From 1935 until the end of the war it was headed by Heinrich Mueller, commonly called "Gestapo" Mueller.

Storey had presented the case against the Gestapo, and it certainly contained much evidence of terrible atrocities, especially in the German-occupied Eastern regions. In fact, many of the atrocities described by the prosecution involved a mingling of Gestapo, SD, and SIPO participants, and Storey's presentation did not always indicate the Gestapo's role in the crime.

There was little that the lawyer for the Gestapo, Dr. Rudolf Merkel, could do against the mass of really hellish evidence. He called as a witness Dr. Werner Best, a lawyer and civil servant who had been an administrative chief in the Gestapo from 1936 to 1940 and in 1942 had been appointed Reich Plenipotentiary in Denmark. Dr. Best tried to portray the Gestapo members as professional police for the prevention of "political crimes." But he then referred to their part in the arrest of 20,000 Jews during Kristallnacht and declared that the Gestapo members were "misused and abused" by higher authority. Cross-examining, Whitney Harris brought up other crimes, such as the surreptitious killing of prominent Danes to counteract Danish sabotage, in which the Gestapo had been directly involved. An odd

---

*Under Article 10 of the Charter, it was envisaged that members of an organization declared criminal by the Tribunal might be brought to trial before national or occupation courts.

feature of the cross-examination was that virtually no mention of Gestapo Mueller occurred, despite Kaltenbrunner's frantic efforts to pin many of the crimes charged against him on Mueller. If the Gestapo was in fact an "organization," presumably its Chief's crimes would be valuable in criminalizing the organization.

In his final argument, Dr. Merkel spent little time on legal arguments and had the good sense not to dispute Gestapo crimes that were proven and notorious. He had some success in showing that there were many Gestapo members who had no part in the crimes. But Merkel put major emphasis on his final pages, pointing out particular sections of the Gestapo, including office employees, telephone operators, and other such categories, whom Justice Jackson had previously proposed to exempt from the Indictment. Merkel also mentioned administrative officials and technical employees whose work had nothing to do with police activities. Merkel concluded: "I have not considered it my duty to excuse crimes and evil deeds or to whitewash those who disregarded the laws of humanity. But I desire to save those who are innocent; I desire to clear the way for a sentence which will dethrone the powers of darkness and reconstitute the moral order of the world."

The Indictment, in identifying the SS as a criminal organization, had a final clause: "including Der Sicherheitsdienst (Commonly Known as the SD)." This verbal coupling of the SD with the SS caused endless confusion, as may be seen from the fact that Storey, in presenting evidence against the Gestapo, had repeatedly linked the SD not with the SS but with the Gestapo. And other misunderstandings arose from the structure of the RSHA, which was divided into seven departments (*Amten*)° and was not part of the SS. On December 20, 1945, Storey, undertaking to present the evidence against both Gestapo and SD, had told the Tribunal that the SD had four sections, as follows: "Section A dealt with questions of legal order and structure of the Reich. B dealt with national questions, including minorities, race, and health of the people. C dealt with culture, including science, education, religion, press, folk culture, and art; and D with economics, including food, commerce, industry, labor, colonial economics, and occupied regions."

This range of activities was certainly wide, but far from bloodthirsty. Furthermore, Storey continually described events as perpetrated by "Gestapo and SD" so that one could not be sure that the SD proper—i.e., Amts III and VI—were involved. An affidavit by Walter Schellenberg, Chief of Amt VI, gives a good picture of the loose usage of the initials "SD" and also the small size of the "real" SD as compared to the Gestapo and the Kripo (Criminal Police):

---

°A department was called an *Amt*, and the seven were I and II administration, III SD, IV Gestapo, V Criminal Police, VI SD offices outside of Germany, and VII ideological research.

The "Sipo and SD" were composed of the Gestapo, Kripo, and SD. In 1943-45 the Gestapo had a membership of about 40,000 to 50,000, the Kripo had a membership of about 15,000, and the SD had a membership of about 3,000. In common usage and even in orders and decrees the term "SD" was used as an abbreviation for the term "SIPO and SD." In most such cases actual executive action was carried out by personnel of the Gestapo rather than of the SD or the Kripo. In occupied territories members of the Gestapo frequently wore SS uniforms with SD insignia.

The upshot of Storey's presentation of the SD was that he had very little evidence of crime that was undeniably perpetrated by the SD. And later, when Dr. Hans Gawlik called his two witnesses in defense of the SD, he soon undertook to capitalize on that situation.

Gawlik turned to the prosecution's evidence and cited half a dozen criminal episodes where better-informed individuals—Jodl, Kaltenbrunner—had corrected Keitel and others by pointing out that the SD had no executive power and that the executions in question had been performed by the Gestapo.° Gawlik further explained that in German-occupied areas, "All members of the RSHA, including . . . even those who were not members of the SS . . . wore the SS uniform with SD insignia" on the sleeve, and "measures carried out by the Security Police were considered to be SD measures."

As for the Einsatzgruppen, Gawlik referred to an SS officer, Brigade Fuehrer Franz Stahlecker, who was Chief of Einsatzgruppe A and whose report on the actions of his command up to October 1941 included a breakdown showing the affiliations of the 990 members of the Einsatzgruppen. The SD numbered 35 men comprising 3.5 percent of the whole, compared to 340 Waffen-SS, 133 Order Police, 89 Gestapo, and 41 Kripo. The remainder were motorcycle riders, interpreters, and other supporting staff.

Gawlik reminded the Tribunal of evidence that Himmler had ordered the creation of the Einsatzgruppen with the agreement of the German Army High Command. Accordingly, Gawlik concluded, the SD Amt III as an entity was not involved in the activities of the Einsatzgruppen.

Lawrence had had enough and intervened sharply:

L.: Dr. Gawlik, the Tribunal understands that the SS, the Gestapo, and the SD all disclaim responsibility for the Einsatzgruppen. Could you tell the Tribunal who is responsible for the Einsatzgruppen?

G.:The Einsatzgruppen were subordinated to—the responsibility may be seen from my statement on Page 61. I should like to refer you to the testimony of Dr. Best, Schellenberg, Ohlendorf, and to the document. . . .

---

°I must confess that I was not among the well-informed on this subject when I presented the case against the General Staff in early January, and I used Storey's statement that the Einsatzgruppen were formed by "the SIPO and SD."

L.: Dr. Gawlik, the Tribunal would like to know who you say was responsible for the Einsatzgruppen. They do not want to be referred to a crowd of documents and a crowd of witnesses. They want to know what your contention is.

G.: The Einsatzgruppen, in my opinion, were organizations of a special kind which were directly under Himmler, and for the rest, the testimony of the witnesses diverges as to how far they were subordinate to the [army] commanders-in-chief.

Dr. Gawlik had missed his chance. Instead of puttering around, he should have at once answered, as he surely knew, that Himmler and Heydrich° were the responsible parties. Of course, they could not have proceeded without the acquiescence and cooperation of the Germany Army. Gawlik's assertion that Ohlendorf and the other SD members who joined the Einsatzgruppen did not go in their capacity as members of Amts III or VI appears to be solid, but of course they were liable as individuals for their participation in the Einsatzgruppen's atrocities.

Taking the SD in the strict sense of the members of Amts III and VI, it does not appear to me that the prosecution's evidence was sufficient to support a declaration of organizational criminality. But the presence of Ohlendorf as Chief, the presence of SD members among the Einsatzgruppen, the proximity of Amt III to Amt IV, and the general confusion in which the SD was bracketed with the police were too much for Gawlik's arguments. Perhaps he pushed the Tribunal too hard; Dr. von der Lippe recorded his opinion that Gawlik had overplayed his hand. However, Gawlik closed his speech with a careful assemblage of various occupations and situations of SD employees who should be excluded from the organizational accusation. Such a solution might help to satisfy Gawlik's closing plea that "the number of persons affected by this decision ought to be strictly limited."

The SS comprised virtually all the rest of Himmler's empire.† It had many mansions, of which the two largest were the Allgemeine (General) SS, the first and only embodiment of the SS until 1939, and the Waffen-SS, the fighting arm of the SS, so named in 1940. There were some ten other branches, of which the more important included the RSHA and the SS Economic and Administrative Main Office (WVHA), which, among other activities, administered the concentration camps.

In December 1945 Major Warren Farr had delivered a well-organized and forceful presentation of the prosecution's evidence against the SS, covering the concentration camps, persecution and extermination of the

---

°It is altogether probable that Hitler had approved the Einsatzgruppen project, but I know of no evidence on that question.

†In July 1944 Himmler succeeded General Fritz Fromm (shot because of his implication in the abortive effort to kill Hitler) as Commander of the Home Army, and in February 1945 he was made Commander in Chief of Army Group Vistula on the Eastern Front.

Jews, and involvement in preparations for aggressive war. This had taken less than a full day's session. But when, seven months later, Horst Pelckmann presented his defense of the SS against the charge that it was a criminal organization, the issues and evidence were so numerous and varied that more than five full days' sessions were required to complete the oral evidence, much to the Tribunal's annoyance.

Pelckmann's first witness was a nobleman, Friedrich Karl Freiherr von Eberstein, appearing in behalf of the General SS. Farr had described this organization as "the backbone" of the SS, but this was true only until the outbreak of war in 1939. The chief responsibilities of these early SS men were to escort and protect officials and guests at Nazi public meetings. The members were otherwise employed, and their part-time SS duties were unpaid. After the Nazi seizure of power, and particularly in 1934 after the downfall of Roehm and the SA leaders, the General SS grew rapidly, and by 1939 it had reached a strength of 240,000 men. But when war came in 1939, virtually all the able-bodied members went into military service or other war work. Eberstein testified that "The General SS had practically ceased to exist during the war."

During its years of strength, Farr had charged, the General SS had participated in anti-Jewish actions during Kristallnacht, an accusation which Eberstein rejected. Whatever the truth of the matter, Kristallnacht was not a war crime, and Eberstein acknowledged no such crimes committed by the General SS.

In 1934 Eberstein became Police Chief in Munich and later was appointed Higher SS and Police Leader in that area. Cross-examining him, Elwyn Jones asked him questions about conditions in the Dachau concentration camp near Munich, about the actions of Oswald Pohl and other SS potentates to appropriate the properties of murdered Polish Jews, and about the use of concentration-camp inmates for atrocious medical experiments. Jones used newly available captured documents to lay the basis for his questions, most of which Eberstein declared himself unable to answer.

Elwyn Jones thus accumulated damning criminal evidence against various unscrupulous and murderous SS individuals. However, none of these documents, or Eberstein's answers to these questions, related to the General SS. So as regards the General SS, the prosecution produced no evidence to support a finding of organizational criminality.

Pelckmann next turned his attention to the Waffen-SS, a fighting force which by the end of the war comprised some thirty-five divisions and approximately 550,000 men. It embodied from two-thirds to three-quarters of all members of the SS. Rightly or wrongly, the Waffen-SS acquired the reputation of spreading terror, not only among enemy troops but also among civilians. It was, surely, the horror spread by these half a million soldiers which moved Colonel Bernays to propose criminalization of the Nazi organizations, among which the Waffen-SS was the prime target.

The lawyers at Nuremberg were in general agreement that Article 9 of the Charter should not be applied to an organization unless most of its members had joined voluntarily. The prosecution had been proceeding on the basis that this was true of the Waffen-SS, although it was known that toward the end of the war some recruits had been forced to join. Pelckmann's second witness, Robert Brill, was a junior Waffen-SS officer whose task it had been to register the source and flow of recruits. Based on records, Brill now showed that drafting for the Waffen-SS had been going on since its very beginnings, when its first 100,000 included 36,000 who had been drafted into the police and then combined with 64,000 Waffen-SS volunteers. Drafting continued during the following years. During the war 320,-000 casualties were suffered, the majority of whom were volunteers, and by the end of the war the Waffen-SS draftees somewhat outnumbered the surviving volunteers.

Pelckmann's principal Waffen-SS witness was Paul Hausser (incorrectly spelled "Hauser" in the trial record), who, as an army general, had retired in 1932 and two years later joined the SS to train its military units. By the end of the war he was a *Generaloberst*, commanding an Army Group. Hausser interestingly described the background and development of the Waffen-SS but, despite his high rank and experience, contributed little on war crimes issues. He stated that his troops were "instructed on the rules of the . . . Hague Rules of Land Warfare" and insisted that the Waffen-SS, under the operational command of the army as it was, complied with the regular rules of warfare. But Hausser completely ignored the fact that Himmler retained control of all administrative, financial, and legal matters concerning the Waffen-SS and that the army commanders had no authority to try SS members for serious offenses.

Cross-examining Hausser, Jones confronted him with numerous documents describing SS atrocities in Poland, Yugoslavia, and the Soviet Union. These were strong evidence against the SS, but Hausser was quick to point out that with two exceptions (one of which was the notorious Prinz Eugen Division, operating in Yugoslavia) the troops in question were not of the Waffen-SS. Later Jones drew attention to the infamous atrocity at Oradour-sur-Glane in southern France, where troops of the Waffen-SS Das Reich division (which Hausser had formerly commanded) drove several hundred women and children into the town church and burned them alive. Jones could have made his point even sharper had he brought out that all the major military atrocities in Western Europe were committed by Waffen-SS—for further example, the Malmédy massacre of American troops in Belgium and the shooting of sixty-four British and American troops by the Waffen-SS Hitlerjugend Division.°

Pelckmann's last two witnesses were lawyers; Gunther Reinecke had

---

°This was the atrocity that so angered General Eisenhower. See p. 110.

been the Chief Judge of the Supreme SS and Police Courts, and George Konrad Morgen had been drafted into the SS and became a criminal investigator detailed to the Kripo. The witnesses sought to put all the blame on a few SS leaders—especially Oswald Pohl, Gestapo Mueller, Dr. Ernst Grawitz, and Himmler himself—who selected men like Hoess and Karl Koch (of Buchenwald) as concentration-camp chiefs.

Reinicke and Morgen, in their legal and investigative capacities, testified that they both had endeavored to expose the villains and bring them to trial. At first they believed that Himmler would support them, and Koch was tried, convicted, and hanged, but in mid-1944 Himmler moved to render their efforts ineffective.

To establish that Waffen-SS men were not separated from but were engaged in all the other SS agencies, Jones, cross-examining Reinecke, produced a German report entitled "Total Strength of the SS on June 30, 1944." That strength was stated at 794,941 persons and the Waffen-SS at 594,443, of whom 368,654 were members of the combat divisions; most of the others were occupied in training, recruiting, and other combat-supportive activities. However, 39,415 Waffen-SS were engaged in other SS occupations, including 24,091 of the WVHA guarding concentration camps. The remainder were at the SS main office and lesser SS enterprises.

Jones seized on these tabulations as proof that the Waffen-SS was linked with and part of the entire SS establishment. Reinicke, however, retorted that these were only "nominal SS," who were labeled "Waffen-SS" but performed nonmilitary duties and had nothing to do with the Waffen-SS troops. To this Jones answered: "All these men were carried on the strength of the SS; they were members of the Waffen-SS; they wore Waffen-SS uniforms, and they were paid by the Waffen-SS." Reinecke replied that the 24,000 "Waffen-SS" at the WVHA were nothing but camp guards having nothing to do with the Waffen-SS. Elwyn declared that the "document speaks for itself" and ended his cross-examination of Reinecke. After Morgen's brief testimony, Pelckmann had completed his case.

Thereafter Elwyn Jones cross-examined Wolfram Sievers, who had testified in support of the SS. Sievers was Reich Manager of the Ahnenerbe (Ancestral Heritage Society), a small and little-known branch of the SS engaged in scientific research of various types. Before the commission, Sievers had mentioned the close relation between Himmler and Dr. Sigmund Rascher, known to have used concentration-camp inmates for painful and often lethal medical experiments. Sievers had claimed to know nothing of the details, but immediately after his testimony Alexander Hardy, a young Boston lawyer who had joined my staff for the subsequent trials and was collecting evidence for a trial of Nazi doctors, came to Jones's office with a file of documents on Sievers that had been sent to Nuremberg from the Berlin Document Center. After reading them, Elwyn successfully applied for permission to cross-examine Sievers before the Tribunal.

The Sievers file proved revolting beyond all imagining. It began with a letter from Sievers to Himmler's personal assistant, Rudolf Brandt, enclosing a report, dated February 9, 1942, by Dr. August Hirt, of the Reich University of Strasbourg,° as follows:

> Subject: Securing of skulls of Jewish-Bolshevik commissars for the purpose of scientific research. . . .
>
> We have large collections of skulls of almost all races and peoples at our disposal. Of the Jewish race, however, only very few specimens of skulls are available, with the result that it is impossible to arrive at precise conclusions from examination. The war in the East now presents us with the opportunity to overcome this deficiency. By procuring the skulls of the Jewish-Bolshevik commissars, who represent the prototype of the repulsive, but characteristic, subhuman, we have the chance to obtain scientific material.
>
> The best practical method for obtaining and collecting this skull material could be followed by directing the Wehrmacht to turn over alive all captured Jewish-Bolshevik commissars to the Feldpolizei. The Feldpolizei, in turn, would be given special directives to inform a certain office at regular intervals of the numbers and places of detention of these captured Jews, and to give them close attention and care until a special delegate arrives. This special delegate, who will be in charge of securing the material . . . will be required to take a previously stipulated series of photographs, make anthropological measurements, and, in addition, determine as far as possible descent, date of birth, and other personal data.
>
> Following the subsequently induced death of the Jew, whose head should not be damaged, the physician will sever the head from the body and will forward it to the proper point of destination in a hermetically sealed tin can especially made for this purpose and filled with a conserving fluid. Having arrived at the laboratory, the comparison tests and anatomical research on the skull, as well as determination of the race membership and of pathological features of the skull form, the form and size of the brain, *et cetera*, can be undertaken by photos, measurements, and other data supplied on the head and the skull itself.

According to the report, there were 150 victims of this process. Further "research" at Strasbourg called for the assemblage of the dead bodies of 109 Jewesses. In September 1944, as the Allied armies were approaching Strasbourg, there was much discussion about what to do with Dr. Hirt's "Collection of Jewish Skeletons." Writing to Rudolf Brandt, Sievers explained:

°At that time, Alsace had been virtually annexed by Germany.

The corpses càn be stripped of the flesh and thereby rendered unidentifiable. This, however, would mean that at least part of the whole work had been done for nothing and that this unique collection would be lost to science, since it would be impossible to make plaster casts afterward. The skeleton collection as such is inconspicuous. The flesh parts could be declared as having been left by the French at the time we took over the Anatomical Institute and would be turned over for cremating. Please advise me which of the following three proposals is to be carried out: (1) The collection as a whole to be preserved; (2) The collection to be dissolved in part; (3) The collection to be completely dissolved.

Elwyn Jones clinched the legal relevance of these appalling documents by reading Himmler's certification that the "*Ahnenerbestiftung* are parts of my personal staff and thus departments of the SS."

Pelckmann's closing argument was not a success. It is true that he had met the hardest task of all the lawyers dealing with the organization cases, for the size and spread of the SS and its activities were enormous. This feature might well have justified giving him more time than the half day to which Lawrence was limiting everyone. But no exception was made for Pelckmann, and he did his own cause no good by speaking in generalities during the first part of his speech, after which Lawrence rode herd on him mercilessly.

But perhaps more time would not have helped Pelckmann. He was dealing with over 700,000 members of the SS. The evidence clearly showed that many thousands of them had known of and been involved in war crimes, some of appalling evil. But could one say the same of hundreds of thousands? Pelckmann and his witnesses had raised the issue, and, in his way, he stated it in his conclusion:

> I indict every one of the murderers and criminals who belonged to that organization or one of its units—and there are more than a few of them.
>
> I acquit the thousands and hundreds of thousands of those who served in good faith, and who therefore share only morally and metaphysically, not criminally, the guilt which the German people must bitterly bear.
>
> But I warn the world and its judges against the commitment of mass injustice in legal form, against the creation of a mass of condemned and outlawed individuals in the heart of Europe; I warn so that the longing of all peoples and men may be fulfilled.

## 4

On August 9, 1946, Dr. Hans Laternser began his defense of the General Staff and High Command of the German Armed Forces, described in the Indictment as "Functioning . . . in association as a group at a highest level in the German Armed Forces Organization" in violation of all four counts in the Indictment.

My own attitude toward the effort to bring this "group" within the ambit of Article 9 of the Charter had changed since I had stated the prosecution's case early in January. Up to that time, despite my doubts about the sufficiency of the "group's" definition and the legal validity of Article 9, I had proceeded on the basis that there was merit in Bernays's concern about the great multitude of probable war criminals, and my superiors had chosen this way of dealing with the problem—an attitude supported by the great volume of documentary material revealing much criminal activity by Germany's military leaders.

As previously described, for me the whole picture had been changed when General Clay launched the Denazification Program, under which the vast majority of Nazi organization members would be dealt with in German administrative proceedings or courts. Even more immediately important, it had become clear that the purpose Bernays had had in mind did not apply to the German Staff–High Command case (or the Reich Cabinet as well), which numbered only some 135 members who could best be dealt with in regular court proceedings. For enforcement of international penal law against the German military leaders the "organizational" procedure was quite unnecessary.

It now appeared to me, however, that Jackson wished (although he never said this to me) to fix the stigma of criminality on the German military leadership as a whole by the Tribunal's declaration. I had no right to abandon the course that Jackson had assigned me to take, and, furthermore, to drop the project would be regarded by many as a whitewash of the German leaders, which, in my view, they ill deserved. It was up to me to carry on, although I was by no means sanguine that the Tribunal would find that the General Staff as defined in the Indictment was a "group" within the meaning of Article 9 of the Charter.* To me, the most important objective was to ensure that the result did not appear to be an exoneration of German military leadership.

---

*Although I did not read the records of the Tribunal's meetings until many years later, I was not surprised to find that at the meeting of May 14, 1946, "The President [Lawrence] asked the members of the Tribunal to give thought to the question of the trying of the High Command, i.e., is there or is there not a case against it."

As witnesses, Laternser called three field marshals: Walter von Brauchitsch, who had been Commander in Chief of the army from 1938 to his retirement late in 1941, and Erich von Manstein and Gerd von Rundstedt, both renowned commanders of Army Groups. Brauchitsch was of particular importance to me in that he was one of three generals who signed affidavits (which I had put into evidence in January) stating in substance that the officers described in the Indictment were those in whose hands "lay the actual direction of the Armed Forces." In my view, the signature of these affidavits by Brauchitsch and two other generals gave the strongest available support to the reality of the "group" described in the Indictment.

Consequently, I kept a sharp lookout for signs that Brauchitsch might try to back away from his affidavits, but this did not occur until the very end of Laternser's direct examination. The bulk of Brauchitsch's testimony was muddled and unimpressive. He declared again and again that there were "no plans" for the Wehrmacht's aggressive movements, which was ridiculous since no one can maneuver large masses without a plan, good or bad, and anyhow Sidney Alderman and the British delegation had put into the record abundant documentary evidence of the planning that preceded the Wehrmacht's many invasions. Time and again Brauchitsch declared that he "had no idea" of coming events and that he "received no report" of things of which he clearly should have been aware. The impression was that he knew as little as possible in order to avoid trouble.

When Laternser finally turned to his client's affidavits which I had put in evidence, Brauchitsch was anything but lucid. He did not say that there was anything "wrong" with the affidavits, but that they "might lead to misunderstanding." Lawrence was annoyed by the foggy answers to Laternser's questions and demanded that Brauchitsch say "whether or not there is anything wrong in your affidavits . . . which is inaccurate or untrue?" The answer was: "No, nothing which is untrue, but something which can be misunderstood." What was that? Brauchitsch mentioned an error in the sketch accompanying the affidavit and the use of the word *gruppe* meaning "group," which of course was a key word in the Charter and the Indictment.° Lawrence rattled him to the point that he declared: "no connection whatever existed between the various branches of the Armed Forces"—a statement which, if true, would go far to explain Germany's eventual military collapse.

When I cross-examined Brauchitsch, I only asked him whether he "had had full opportunity to make changes in those affidavits," whether he

---

°There was an error in the chart in that the chiefs of staff had been put in a column indicating them as having order-giving instead of consulting powers. *Gruppe* is a common word in military usage, for instance, *Herresgruppe* for "Army group," used to indicate more than one subordinate military entity.

did make changes, and whether he had written the last and crucial sentence in his own handwriting. To all these questions he said yes. His only subsequent qualifications had nothing to do with the crucial sentence, so I decided to leave well enough alone and asked no more questions.

Peter Calvocoressi and I had agreed that I would cross-examine Manstein and he Rundstedt. We were both aware that as cross-examiners we were neophytes. Peter was an equity barrister who had had little court work, and I, although I had argued a number of important appellate cases, had never examined a witness in court—a lack of experience which I had not revealed to my colleagues at Nuremberg. The results were a lesson in the superiority of a good bridge hand over mere skill, and I was the lucky one.

Manstein was younger and brighter than Brauchitsch, and he began with a well-reasoned attack on the prosecution's effort to create a "group" out of the General Staff–High Command as described in the Indictment. The officers listed were indeed "the holders of the highest positions in the military hierarchy," but they never functioned as a group. That was essentially true, and I had no good answer.

On other matters, Manstein was less surefooted. Contrary to the views of many of his colleagues, Manstein opined that when, after the German victory over Poland, Britain would not make peace, Germany had "no other way out than to attack in the West" and "thus end the war," which of course the victory over France did not accomplish. Manstein also stated that once Germany had drawn back from attacking Britain, Germany was forced to wage a "preventive" war against Russia, thus running Germany directly into a "two-front" war," which, up to that time, it was generally agreed, would be the worst possible strategy.

Near the end of his testimony Manstein spoke of the Einsatzgruppen, no doubt because in January Otto Ohlendorf had testified to a conference he had had with Manstein at Simferopol in the Crimea and other meetings at Nikolaev and elsewhere he had had with Manstein's staff officers. Answering Laternser's questions, Manstein admitted that he might have once met Ohlendorf at the Eleventh Army headquarters, but he denied all knowledge of exterminations of Jews. He knew only that the Einsatzgruppen "were organized to prepare for the political administration; that is to say, to carry out the political screening of the population in the occupied territories of the East." What this "screening" involved, Manstein did not specify.

When I cross-examined Manstein, I had concluded that fencing with him about the "group" would be playing from weakness and that his vulnerable spot was the Einsatzgruppen, redolent as they were with atrocious murders on a vast scale. I did not for a moment believe Manstein's claim that he knew nothing of the massacres. I did not expect to make him confess his knowledge, but rather to show how absurd it was to suppose that murder groups moved through the army's front and rear lines without being noticed or that an alert commander would not want to know what these unusual armed units sponsored by Himmler were doing.

I thought I made some headway, but my "luck" consisted of a new document which Bob Kempner had put into my hands in which Manstein was shown to have distributed to his troops an anti-Jewish manifesto that closely resembled one which Field Marshal von Reichenau had issued on October 10, 1941, and which I had offered in evidence in January. I asked Manstein what he had done when Hitler had sent him the Reichenau manifesto "as a model." He replied: "I did nothing about it and I considered such an order as quite beside the point, because I wanted to conduct the fight in a military manner and in no other way."

I then offered in evidence the new document of November 20, 1941, signed by Manstein, which read in part:

> Since 22 June the German people have been engaged in a life-and-death struggle against the Bolshevist system.
>
> This struggle is not being carried out against the Soviet Armed forces alone in the established form laid down by European rules of warfare. . . .
>
> The Jewish-Bolshevist system must be exterminated once and for all. Never again must it encroach on our European living space.
>
> The German soldier has not only the task of crushing the military potential of this system. He comes also as the bearer of a racial concept and as the avenger of all the cruelties which have been perpetrated on him and on the German people. . . .
>
> The soldier must appreciate the necessity for the harsh punishment of Jewry, the spiritual bearer of the Bolshevist-terror. This is also necessary in order to nip in the bud all uprisings which are mostly plotted by Jews.

Manstein feebly insisted that he could not remember this document, but admitted that he had signed it. His credibility was shattered, and Laternser told my associate Walter Rapp that if he had known of this document he would never have called Manstein as a witness. Von der Lippe wrote that Manstein's efforts to explain "made the situation no better" and that the session ended in "an unsympathetic atmosphere." Manstein's debacle triggered several laudatory newspaper articles, but I was well aware that my success was entirely due to Kempner's production of Manstein's order.*

---

*Manstein's letter was an important basis for his subsequent trial and conviction before a British military court.

Gerd von Rundstedt had been the doyen of the German Army officers' corps since 1934, and when he took the witness stand he was in his early seventies. He looked and was the very model of a Feldherr; Hitler treated him with great respect and gave him the top field commands, except for two brief retirements, until March 1945. He was greatly admired by his colleagues, but mainly as a field commander rather than a general staff genius like Manstein.

With Germany's collapse and the dissolution of the army, Rundstedt's world was no more, and he was an angry old man. He contradicted his colleagues freely and declared, with absolute assurance, knowledge of things he could not possibly know, like his assertion that the Commissar Order was "simply not carried out." Later he told Peter Calvocoressi that "There was not a single person in the West who lost his life on the strength of the Commando Order," oblivious of or indifferent to the fact that in 1944 fifteen American soldiers in uniform had been shot as commandos in northern Italy by order of General Anton Dostler, who later met the same fate for his obedience to the order. This episode had been repeatedly mentioned in the Tribunal's proceedings, as had other shootings of British naval commandos.

Cross-examining Rundstedt, Calvocoressi endeavored to bolster the "group" by forcing Rundstedt to acknowledge a gathering of the leading generals in August 1938 seeking to unite in opposition to making war against Czechoslovakia. But Peter had no such potent document as Kempner had given me.*

As was to be expected, Laternser's closing argument was excellent with regard to the "group" issue. But his handling of the criminal aspects of the prosecution's charges was seriously marred by his repeated disregard of the defense's difficulties. For example, while Laternser was able to declare with considerable validity that the annexation of Austria and the Sudetenland had not been aggressive wars and would not necessarily have alerted the generals to Hitler's aggrandizing intentions, the same could certainly not be said of the domination and virtual annexation of the rest of Czechoslovakia in March 1939. Laternser brushed it off as a "purely political action" and, to be sure, there was no fighting. But to call this a "peaceful entry" was no way to describe a bitter yielding to the mandate of vastly superior forces and threats to destroy the country. Here was no ethnic factor such as gave some shred of validity to the Sudeten claims; here was only a crass seizure of the lands and peoples of another country in flagrant viola-

---

*The lack of such documents was due to the fact that the captured German military documents had not yet been fully examined. Subsequent research disclosed documents showing that both Rundstedt and Brauchitsch had distributed the Reichenau order and that Rundstedt, in his distribution, had written on the document: "I thoroughly concur with its contents."

tion of agreements freshly made with Britain, France, and Italy. This was the trigger of Neville Chamberlain's final awakening to Hitler's real intentions, and what he saw, the German generals could also see.

It appeared to me that Laternser had been ill served by the inflexibility and stonewalling of the elderly generals whom he had called as witnesses and on whom, presumably, he had relied. Younger and fresher minds might have prevented him from, for example, exhorting his listeners to gaze at his "three Field Marshals" and ask whether "anyone can gain the impression that these men were criminals and had committed crimes against the laws of war and humanity." Manstein had, only two weeks earlier, been shown up as a liar and an advocate of the "hardest measures" against Jews, which the Einsatzgruppen were even then providing—an exposure which Laternser did not see fit to deal with in his final argument.

5

The last two organizations charged were the Reich Cabinet (Reichsregierung) and the Sturmabteilung of the Nazi Party, commonly known as the SA. The Reich Cabinet had at least as frail a claim as the General Staff to be accredited as an Article 9 "organization" or "group." The SA, on the other hand, had less difficulty on that score, but its loss of prestige in consequence of the 1934 Roehm purge and its very secondary status during the war raised doubt of its sufficient importance to warrant the charges.

Defending the Reich Cabinet, Dr. Egon Kubuschok (who was also Papen's lawyer) called but one witness: Franz Schlegelberger, State Secretary in the Ministry of Justice since 1931 and acting Minister from January 1941 to August 1942, when he was dismissed by Hitler. His testimony was very brief, and it is not clear why Kubuschok called him; Lawrence complained that the witness's testimony did not appear to "bear on the Reich Cabinet," and Kubuschok himself, in his final argument, barely mentioned Schlegelberger.

Kubuschok's argument, however, was crisp and effective. His major attack was against the Reich Cabinet's status under Article 9 of the Charter. Normal Cabinet procedure had declined after the Roehm purge in June 1934, and its last meeting was in February 1938. Thereafter proposed bills were handled by circulation among the members, and there was no cohesion among them. The number of Reich Cabinet members during the years 1933 to 1945, apart from the sixteen under Indictment at Nuremberg and eight believed to be dead, totaled only about twenty-two.

As for the criminal charges, the formation of the Reich Cabinet had occurred many years earlier and plainly was not criminal. Most of the state's questionable activities had been vested in new agencies such as the Four-Year Plan. Prewar anti-Jewish legislation had not been targeted at launching aggressive wars. The wartime criminal actions against Jews were the work of the Himmler organizations, and the Cabinet members were given no information about them. Under all these circumstances, Kuboschok concluded, any charges against individual members should be handled in regular judicial proceedings.

In contrast to the brief Reich Cabinet proceedings, the SA case took from Monday, August 12, to the following Friday. But not all the time was well spent because much of the discussion dealt with events in the prewar years, and there were no indications that they concerned preparations for aggressive wars. The crimes charged, therefore, were not war crimes and thus were not covered by Article 6 of the Charter.

Better remembered in America and England as the "Brownshirts," the SA was highly visible, in press and film, as the Nazi street gangs who fought Communists and other rival parties and factions and harassed Jews. It was, no doubt, these recollections and unawareness of what had followed that led the chief prosecutors to include the SA among the indicted organizations. But that aspect of the Nazi scene faded away as Hitler succeeded in crushing organized opposition and then destroyed the SA's leadership in the Roehm purge. As with the General SS, the outbreak of war drew many SA men to the Wehrmacht.

Representing the SA, George Boehm called three short-winded witnesses, of whom only the third gave evidence important to the case. Theodor Gruss, a corporal in World War I, had thereafter joined the Stahlhelm (the largest of the war veterans' associations) and subsequently became the organization's Chief Treasurer.

Gruss described the process by which, in 1933, Franz Seldte, Stahlhelm leader and Reich Labor Minister, carried out Hitler's orders and transferred all members of the Stahlhelm over the age of forty-five to membership in the SA. According to Gruss's testimony, many if not most of the Stahlhelm members went to the SA with reluctance and only under great pressure. They numbered well over a million (compared to some 300,000 SA men), and generally insuperable obstacles prevented resignations. These statements, of course, laid the basis for a contention that, after 1933, a majority of the SA men had not joined voluntarily.

Boehm's last and principal witness was Max Juettner, a former official in the Stahlhelm who made a highly successful transfer to the SA and became Deputy Chief of Staff and Chief of the SA's main office. He proceeded to contradict almost everything Gruss had said about the difficulties the ex-Stahlhelmers had encountered in the SA. That was passing strange, and soon Lawrence told Boehm: "The Tribunal would like to know whether your case is that the SA, after the incorporation of the Stahlhelm, was a voluntary organization or was involuntary, so far as the Stahlhelm was concerned."

Several interchanges between Lawrence and Boehm failed to elicit a clear response, and Boehm complained that the question "was not supposed to be the subject of my presentation of evidence, Mr. President." Lawrence replied: "At some stage no doubt you will be able to tell us which of the witnesses you adopt."

Fyfe cross-examined Juettner for a full day's session. Discussing the organization problems with the Tribunal early in March, Fyfe had taken a very broad view of guilt in answer to a hypothetical question based on the SA, and now he kept after Juettner, hour after hour, with great force.

Fyfe began with accusations that the SA had been involved in atrocities against the people of the German-occupied Eastern areas. Juettner admitted that an SA unit had "on instructions from the Wehrmacht, transported prisoners of war to the rear during the Polish campaign" and that the SA had established bases in the Polish areas annexed by Germany and in the Government-General. These facts might be of use to the prosecution as showing the SA engaging in aggressive war, but were not in themselves criminal. And Juettner vehemently denied Fyfe's accusations that the SA had any bases or activities in Lithuania or had participated in atrocities there or anywhere else. The cross-examination soon turned into a running battle between accusation and denial in which it was hard for the listener to form an opinion.

Boehm, like Seidl, took pleasure in needling the Tribunal by complaining that the defense lawyers were not fairly treated. Early in his final argument, Boehm stated that he had been unable to canvass the prisoner camps in the Soviet Zone and that this situation was "one of the most serious objections against the Trial which will always remain in history." Lawrence declared this "a most improper observation" and said it was groundless since Dr. Servatius had been in the Soviet Zone and had "made no complaint to the Tribunal." In a most unusual development, Servatius rose and confirmed Lawrence's statement, leaving Boehm's complaint in shambles. Undaunted, Boehm later declared that the Secretary General had not produced two witnesses whom he had requested, again arousing Lawrence's ire.

Boehm never explicitly resolved the evidentiary clash between Gruss and Juettner over the amalgamation of the Stahlhelm and the SA, but he followed the Gruss testimony that the Stahlhelm accepted the merger under orders and unwillingly and argued that forced members were excluded from criminal liability as SA members.

Boehm ended his argument with a quotation from Pope Pius XII's speech of February 20, 1946:

> Erroneous ideas are circulating in the world which declare a
> man guilty and responsible solely because he was a member of or

belonged to a specific community, without making any effort to examine or to investigate whether there really exists a personal responsibility on his part for such acts of commission or omission.

## 6

And so, near the end of the Tribunal's session on August 28, 1946, the defense lawyers finished their last pleas. It was now time for the prosecution's final arguments, and Fyfe led off with what was to be much the longest of these efforts.

Fyfe informed the Tribunal that he would cover the Party Political Leaders, the SA, and the SS; these were, of course, the largest chunks of the prosecution's case against the organizations. He began with a short attack on Dr. Klefisch's speech against Article 9 of the Charter. However, instead of using legal arguments, Fyfe resorted to political and evidentiary factors. Many of the organizational criminals were still at large in Germany, said Fyfe, and they should not "be set loose among the German people and amongst the people of Europe."

Fyfe then leveled an almost brutal attack on the defendants' evidence:

> On the face of it, the evidence which has been given by almost all the witnesses called before your Commissioners is untrue. You yourselves [i.e., the Tribunal] have seen and heard some of these witnesses, selected by defense counsel presumably because they were thought to be the most reliable. . . . Their evidence is no better.

Fyfe then named Sievers, Morgen, Brill, Hausser, Schneider, and Best as especially fork-tongued and concluded:

> The evidence of all of them is the same. They are asked if they knew of the persecution and annihilation of the Jews, of the dread works of the Gestapo, of the atrocities within the concentration camps, of the ill-treatment of slave labor, of the intention and preparation to wage aggressive war, of the murder of brave soldiers, sailors, and airmen. And they reply with "the everlasting No."

The effect on the Tribunal of this frontal attack is not clear. No doubt there was a lot of mendacity among the witnesses, but I saw no basis for such an across-the-board attack and, judging by the results, neither did the Tribunal.°

---

°Indeed, Fyfe's words suggested that the defense counsel must have known that their witnesses were committing perjury. Fyfe, who had always treated defense counsel with old-fashioned courtesy, made no such explicit statement.

Fyfe then turned to the Political Leaders and, I thought, greatly strengthened the prosecution's case. He did not have unusual grace of speech, but his text was well constructed, he spoke with great force, and he was, as always, so well prepared that he almost never was caught off guard. To incriminate the Leadership Corps, Fyfe had put together documents and selections of testimony involving the leaders in wartime atrocities against Jews, slave labor, euthanasia, mass mistreatment and killing of Soviet prisoners of war, and unlawful treatment of enemy aviators forced down in German-occupied territory.

Although he made no admission of difficulty, Fyfe was well aware that the SA posed much more difficult problems than the Leadership Corps, and he immediately tackled the defense's contention of involuntary membership. During his long cross-examination of Juettner, Fyfe had repeatedly branded Juettner a liar, but on this question Juettner's testimony that the Stahlhelm men were well received in the SA and that resignation was easily obtained served Fyfe's argument that the SA was a voluntary organization. Fyfe quoted several paragraphs of Juettner's testimony as settling the issue and made no mention of Gruss, whom Boehm had relied on to support the contrary view.

Fyfe succeeded admirably in portraying the SA as riddled with violent crime on the streets and in the early concentration camps such as Oranienburg, where the SA officer Werner Schaefer had been the first Commandant. After the Roehm purge, little street fighting remained for the SA, but, as Fyfe put it: "The Church and the Jews remained an ever present problem." All this helped to paint the SA as an evil enterprise, but the prosecution's legal difficulty was that prewar sins, however criminal and disgusting, were not war crimes, and were thus outside the reach of Article 6 of the Charter.

Fyfe made an effort to show SA "preparation for war and wartime activities," but he had pitifully little evidence to cite. Ingenuously, Fyfe declared: "The crimes of the SA did not end with the outbreak of war." He might more accurately have said that the SA's crimes began with the coming of war, for the international laws of war then came into play. Then, at least, the SA's activities in German-annexed and -occupied Poland appeared to have produced a small but shocking body of evidence. Whatever exaggerations or mistakes might be found in the affidavits on which Fyfe relied, he made no mention of them.

The SS, the last of Fyfe's group, posed no such problems, and he informed the Tribunal that he "did not conceive to be necessary to deal at any length with the evidence against the SS." But there was a voluntary problem here, too, about which the defense witness Brill had testified. Fyfe quarreled with Brill's conclusion that by the end of the war the Waffen-SS was more conscript than volunteer, but he appears to have disregarded

Brill's inexact but probably valid argument that the deaths were greater among volunteers, who had served at the front three to four years more than the recently drafted conscripts. Obviously, exact calculation was impossible, but the conscripts were a very large portion if not a majority of the total surviving muster. These circumstances might well move the Tribunal to provide in its decision for the exclusion of the conscripts on some suitable basis of proof.

Fyfe had covered the Organization charges so completely that Tom Dodd, who presented the major argument for the United States, had very little fresh ground left for him. I had expected Dodd to focus on the Reich Cabinet, Gestapo, and SD, which Fyfe had handled only cursorily. Instead, Dodd proceeded to cover all of the organizations except the General Staff–High Command.°

Dodd's text was well put together, but it was really a compendium of the prosecution's evidence, all of which was by that time well known to the Tribunal and the court lawyers and staff. It therefore appeared to me that Dodd was offering his swan song not so much to the Tribunal as to the world outside, and especially to the American public. Only at the end did Dodd turn to the legal questions about Article 9, and then he swept away the defendants' arguments rather cavalierly, and extolled the importance of the case against the organizations:

> By a declaration of criminality against these organizations, this Tribunal will put on notice not only the people of Germany but the people of the whole world. Mankind will know that no crime will go unpunished because it was committed in the name of a political party or of a state; that no crime will be passed by because it is too big; that no criminal will avoid punishment because there are too many.

The last clause did indeed embody the purpose which had moved Murray Bernays to propose the organization charges. But by the end of the trial it had become apparent to most of us that such thorough police and court work was most unlikely.

---

°Fyfe, speaking for the British government, had explicitly supported the charge against the General Staff–High Command. Dodd did not; he stated: "I shall not discuss the High Command since it is to be the subject of a special argument by a member of the American staff," meaning me. The charge against the General Staff–High Command was still a subject of great controversy, and I believe Dodd, who had political ambitions, did not wish to endorse its prosecution.

7

On Friday, August 30, 1946, the prosecution's last day at the lectern, it was my turn to present, against the General Staff and High Command, the final argument which Peter Calvocoressi and I had prepared. We had decided in favor of brevity, and the reading, which elicited no interruption from the Tribunal, took only some two hours.

Although we had concluded that the Tribunal was likely to dismiss the charges against the General Staff on the ground that it did not constitute an "organization" or "group" within the meaning of Article 9, it was obvious that since the chief prosecutors had brought the charge, it was up to us to argue the contrary as best we could. But there was very little to say that had not been said already. The defense lawyers had made some weak arguments—such as the silly contention that the generals were not "voluntary" officers—which we could knock down. But our best evidence remained the affidavits that Brauchitsch, Halder, and Blaskowitz had signed, and which included the statement that the generals listed in the charge had "the actual direction of the Armed Forces" and "were in effect the General Staff and High Command."

I then turned to the criminal charges of planning and waging aggressive wars. Dr. Laternser had argued that there was not enough agreement among the generals or between the generals and Hitler to prove a common plan or conspiracy. Arguments among conspirators are probably the rule rather than the exception, and in any case a conspiracy is established among those who knowingly and willingly join in criminal conduct. The further argument that Hitler made all the decisions without consultation was similarly irrelevant and not supported by the evidence. Voluminous documentation, including Jodl's diary, described many discussions of strategy or tactics between Hitler and the generals. A good illustration was Hitler's directive to the Wehrmacht leaders on November 12, 1940, discussing several alternative military actions such as the invasion of Spain, assistance to the Italians in North Africa, and an action in Greece:

> I shall expect the commanders-in-chief to express their opinions
> on the measures anticipated in this directive. I shall then give orders
> regarding the method of execution and synchronization of the individ-
> ual actions.

For obvious reasons, the Wehrmacht was more vulnerable to the aggressive war charge than any of the other organizations. But for my purpose, which was to build so strong and shocking a criminal case against the Wehrmacht that the judges would be moved to denounce its conduct of the war even if the Tribunal found the General Staff–High Command not covered by Article 9, the charges of war crimes would, I believed, have the greatest effect. There certainly was an abundance of such evidence, including the Commissar Order, the Commando Order, the orders withdrawing Soviet soldiers and citizens from the protection of the laws of war, and the Einsatzgruppen.

I chose to put initial and primary emphasis on the Commando Order because the others of these organized atrocities, ghastly as they were, were ordered and chiefly applied on the Russian front. The Commando Order, in contrast, involved British and (later) American troops who were landed by boat or plane along the Atlantic and Mediterranean shores. Furthermore, we had documentary or sworn proof of the shooting of some fifty-five British and American troops pursuant to the Commando Order.

Laternser and some of the generals suggested that the order might be supported as a reprisal for British mistreatment of German troops, but it was a halfhearted effort, and the German government never claimed a reprisal. The generals' main argument was that although they had distributed the order as OKW had required, unspecified "steps were taken" and "military leaders found ways and means to prevent the carrying out" of the Commando Order.

This handling of the matter I described as "shameful" and "murderous" and attacked it with full sincerity:

> When Hitler directed the issuance of this order, the leaders of the Wehrmacht knew that it required the commission of murder. The responsibility for handling this question lay squarely on the group defined in the Indictment. The chiefs at OKW, OKH, OKL, and OKM had to decide whether to refuse to issue a criminal order or whether to pass it on to the commanders-in-chief in the field. . . . There is no evidence that a single member of the group openly protested or announced his refusal to execute it. The general result was that the order was distributed throughout a large part of the Wehrmacht. This put the subordinate commanders in the same position as their superiors. We are told that some of the generals tacitly agreed not to carry out the order. If so, it was a miserable and worthless compromise. By distributing the order with "secret" or "tacit" understandings, the commanders-in-chief merely spread the responsibility and deprived themselves of any effective control over the situation.
> Because he was responsible for enforcing the Commando Order, General Dostler was tried, convicted, and shot to death. For the same reason, General Falkenhorst now stands condemned to die. But responsibility for these murders is shared by Falkenhorst and Dostler with every German commander-in-chief at home or in the

field who allowed this order to become the official law of the Wehr-macht and participated in its distribution. On this charge alone, I submit, the General Staff and High Command group is proved to have participated directly, effectively, and knowingly in the commission of war crimes.

The Commissar Order, and those directives withdrawing the protec-tion of the laws of war, were dealt with by Laternser and his clients in much the same way as the Commando Order. No generals openly rejected them, but according to Brauchitsch, Manstein, and Rundstedt, discreet hints not to enforce the orders were given to lower-ranking field commanders. To the extent that these hints were followed, the commissars' fate was only slightly delayed since all prisoners were screened in the camps by Himmler's min-ions and the commissars were soon put away.

As for the asserted preservation of the laws of war by the German Army, Laternser and his witnesses gave no evidence in support of their claim. The OKW orders greatly increased the power of junior officers, many of whom were thoroughly Nazified. I called the Tribunal's attention to the case of an SS officer who was on trial in 1939 for shooting fifty Jews in a Polish synagogue. The German military judge granted the defendant "ex-tenuating circumstances" because "as an SS man, particularly sensitive to the sight of Jews, and to the hostile attitude of Jewry to the Germans, he therefore acted quite thoughtlessly in youthful rashness."

What an obscure military judge may do or say was more than matched by the brilliant Manstein, caught in lies, and shown to have been willing to "stand sponsor for Nazi ideology." Thus "The German Army was demoral-ized by its own leaders." I quoted the report of a young German lieutenant, finding his efforts to pacify and exploit the Ukraine frustrated because Russian prisoners

> were shot when they could not march any more right in the middle of villages and some of the biggest hamlets, and the corpses were left lying about, and the population saw in these facts what they did not understand and which confirmed the worst distortions of enemy propaganda.

Toward the end of our presentation, I sought to draw the Tribunal's attention to the present and the possible future as seen by witnesses such as Manstein and Rundstedt:

> The first steps toward the revival of German militarism have been taken right here in this courtroom. The German General Staff has had plenty of time to think since the spring of 1945, and it well knows what is at stake here. The German militarists know that their

future strength depends on re-establishing the faith of the German people in their military powers and in disassociating themselves from the atrocities which they committed in the service of the Third Reich. . . . The documents and testimony show that theirs are transparent fabrications. But here, in embryo, are the myths and legends which the German militarists will seek to propagate in the German mind. These lies must be stamped and labeled for what they are now while the proof is fresh.

For some of the generals, war was ingrained. Manstein "considered the glory of the war as something great." Jodl, in a memorandum embodying the "considered opinion" of OKW, had written in 1939:

> Despite all attempts to outlaw it, war is still a law of nature which may be challenged but not eliminated. It serves the survival of the race and state and the assurance of its historical future.
> This high moral purpose gives war its total character and its ethical justification.

I concluded with a denunciation of militarism and pointed to its destructive worldwide consequences:

> The truth is spread on the record before us, and all we have to do is state the truth plainly. The German militarists joined forces with Hitler and with him created the Third Reich; with him they deliberately made a world in which might was all that mattered; with him they plunged the world into war, and spread terror and devastation over the continent of Europe. They dealt a blow at all mankind; a blow so savage and foul that the conscience of the world will reel for years to come. This was not war; it was crime. This was not soldiering; it was savagery. We cannot here make history over again, but we can see that it is written true.

I sat down and faced a dark scowl from Goering and a stony glare from Jodl. Champetier de Ribes rose painfully and walked slowly to the lectern to deliver the final argument for France.

In keeping with his frail health, Champetier de Ribes spoke for barely half an hour. But within a narrow compass the speech was excellent. Dr. von der Lippe wrote: "His short, pleasing [*erfreulich*] presentation was, like all French address at Nuremberg, philosophically colored." After my denunciatory passages, the audience was ready for a gentle voice that spoke not so much of crime as of morality and quoted "our great Bergson": "Humanity groans, half crushed by the weight of the progress it has made. . . . The increased body awaits the addition of a soul, and the machine requires a mystic faith." And he went on to speak of Cato the Elder, the Magna Carta, and more recent moral landmarks such as the Charter of the United Nations and (perhaps a bit slyly) the Constitution of the Union of Soviet Socialist Republics, which proclaims "the fundamental rights and duties of citizens of the USSR . . . without distinction as to the nationality or race."

As for the case against the defendants, Champetier de Ribes picked two arguments made by defense counsel relating to the Gestapo, SD, and High Command. The first was the defense's effort to draw a line between the officially announced purposes of these organizations, which were blameless, and the conduct of the members, which were criminal. On this basis, it was argued that the miscreants were not acting for the organization; they could be charged as individuals, but no blame would attach to the organization. Champetier de Ribes had several answers, but most conclusively that Hitler drew no such line and that under the Fuehrerprinzip: "There is no other legality than the good pleasure of the chief, whose orders must be executed without any possible dissension all the way down the scale."

The defendants' second argument was that the various organizations were independent of each other, as were also the various sections within a single organization, and that "defense counsel are trying to clear from responsibility the greatest possible number of their supposedly isolated groups." But, said the speaker, this separatist view was contrary to all the evidence by which Dubost had "showed that the close collaboration of the organizations and the services is beyond discussion. . . . In fact all the departments of the Gestapo, the SD, the SS and the High Command, are jointly responsible for the crimes committed in common," a good showing that the Wehrmacht shared responsibility with the Einsatzgruppen for the massacre of Jews and other victims of Himmler's selection.

Champetier de Ribes's strong sense of righteousness and his love of peace were reflected in his concluding words addressed to the Tribunal:

> In declaring the collective organizations criminal in order to enable the competent authorities to punish the guilty, but only the guilty, . . . your sentence will contribute greatly to the great work of universal peace which is being undertaken in the organization of the United Nations as well as at the Peace Conference in New York as in Paris, by the representations of the free peoples, "anxiously awaited by sincere men of upright heart."

General Rudenko, the last prosecutor to address the Tribunal, spoke almost as long as had Fyfe. In its organization also his speech resembled Fyfe's in covering the several organizations one after another. In content, however, it was much less analytic than Fyfe's and, like Dodd's, was largely repetitive of well-known documents. However, Rudenko began by under-lining a legal position which he had put forward during the organization discussions on February 28. His purpose was to restrict the Tribunal's power to deciding whether or not an organization should be held criminal. All other questions "remain within the competence of the national courts." Thus in every nation, the authorities might indict organization members or not, impose heavy or light penalties, and deal with individual defenses as they thought best.

Rudenko could be rough. Denouncing the SA as the "ringleader of German Fascism," he declared: "Essentially, the plea of Herr Böhm [repre-senting the SA] was, generally speaking, devoid of any legal argument that would render it worthy of attention. It was a statement made from the viewpoint of a convinced Nazi, repeating . . . the worst instances of Hitlerite propaganda, which counsel had carefully extracted from the SA press."

Boehm was not present, but his associate Dr. Martin Loeffler inter-vened to excoriate "this very severe personal attack" and assure the Tribu-nal that Boehm "had never been a member of the National Socialist Party." Lawrence cooled the antagonists by interpreting Rudenko's comment as not accusing Boehm of Nazi membership but only portraying "the viewpoint of the convinced Nazi," and on that rather weak explanation, the dispute sputtered to an end.

In Moscow, Stalin was still in command, and Rudenko's reference to the Gestapo's "widely known and notoriously terrible concentration camps" rang hollow in company with the widely known Gulags and Siberian penal colonies. But it was reassuring that Rudenko did not, like so many of his fellow officials, make little mention of the Germans' extermination of the Jews. For some minutes, Rudenko discussed "the special mass extermination centers for the Jewish population of Poland," the "secret extermination camp in Chelmno where over 340,000 Jews were done away with by means of murder vans," and the "Eichmann plan for the extermination of the Jews of Europe." He also spent much time on the Einsatzgruppen, especially in connection with the OKW and the German generals in the Soviet Union.

Rudenko's concluding words were the last spoken by the prosecution before the Tribunal:

> The Prosecution have fulfilled their duty towards this Tribunal, towards the sacred memory of the innocent victims, towards the con-science of the nations, as well as toward their own.
> May the Judgment of the Nations—severe but just—fall upon these Fascist hangmen.

It might have been a better ending if Champetier de Ribes had spoken last.

# Chapter 19

# THE DEFENDANTS'
# LAST WORDS

I n Anglo-American criminal law, as has been pointed out previously, defendants may decide or refuse to testify under oath, whereas, in Continental practice, defendants may not testify on oath, but may, at the end of the trial, make an unsworn statement to the court. In the procedure set forth in the Charter, the defendants were allowed to testify under oath *and* to make a final unsworn statement. Accordingly, when on August 31, 1946, the Tribunal assembled, Lord Lawrence stated:

> Article 24 D(j) provides that each defendant may make a statement to the Tribunal. I now call upon the defendants who wish— whether they wish to make statements. Defendant Hermann Wilhelm Goering.

Lawrence had earlier taken steps to ensure that the proceedings would be brisk. On August 15 he had read in open court the following:

> The Tribunal have been informed that some of the defendants have deposited long statements for translation with the Translation Division.
> There is no necessity for the defendants' statements to be translated, and they will not be translated by the Translation Division. The Tribunal draws the attention of the defendants and their counsel to the order of 23 July, which was in the following terms: ". . . The defendants . . . will be limited to short statements of a few minutes each to cover matters not already covered by their testimony or the arguments of counsel." The Tribunal will adhere strictly to this order, and the defendants will not be allowed to make statements which last longer than, as the order says, "a few minutes." These statements will be made by the defendants from their places in the dock.

Fritzsche recorded that some of the defendants "who had prepared drafts of sixty or seventy pages felt deeply shocked by the limitations," but "in the end we almost all realized that it was best for these last words to be reasonably short and significant; they would not make any difference to the verdict." Perhaps that was underrating the possible effect of the statements, but brevity was certainly desirable. Arguments about law and evidence were not in keeping with the occasion, which was intended as an opportunity for the defendants' apologias.

The courtroom was packed—though Rudenko was the only Chief Prosecutor present—as befitted the last day of the trial, and proceedings unfamiliar to the British and American lawyers. But there were other reasons for the intense curiosity of the audience. For the first and only time the defendants would not be answering questions thrown at them by the prosecution and defense lawyers; they would be speaking for themselves. They had been sitting in the dock for ten months watching and hearing their own and their fellow defendants' lives revealed and torn open by witnesses, lawyers, and judges and had learned much about their country and themselves. What effect had all this had on the men in the dock? Were they perceptibly different from when they first came to Nuremberg? How would they comport themselves now, with months of tension behind them and the Tribunal's measurement facing them?

A guard holding a pole with a microphone moved it within Goering's reach, and he rose to speak:

> The Prosecution, in the final speeches, has treated the defendants and their testimony as completely worthless. The statements made under oath by the defendants were accepted as absolutely true when they could serve to support the Indictment, but conversely the statements were characterized as perjury when they refuted the Indictment. That is very elementary, but it is not a convincing basis for demonstration of proof.

Those who may have expected that Goering would say something remarkable were surely disappointed. The flat denial that he had any knowledge of the "terrible mass murders" which he condemned and "cannot understand" was followed with claims that he "did not want a war" and did not "bring it about." Only at the end of a short and very dull speech did Goering speak of his country: "The only motive which guided me was my ardent love for my people, its happiness, its freedom, and its life. And for this I call on the Almighty and my German people to witness."

But such words from such a man did not ring true. Papen was beside himself and at the luncheon break furiously attacked Goering: "Who in the world is responsible for all this destruction if not you? . . . You haven't taken the responsibility for anything! All you do is make bombastic speeches. It is disgraceful!" Goering laughed at him, but nobody joined in, and Goering won no praise for his effort.

The defendants were to speak in the order of their seating in the dock, and Rudolf Hess was next. According to Fritzsche, Hess had told his lawyer (Seidl) and Goering that he would not make a statement. But after Goering sat down, Hess rose and took from a pocket several sheets of paper, from which he proceeded to read into the microphone.

The result was a ghoulish and sad fiasco. Actually, Hess spoke intelligently for some minutes, insisting (no doubt accurately) that some witnesses had testified untruthfully and others had signed false affidavits. But Hess soon moved into a long discussion of people who had "strange eyes" that were "glassy . . . like eyes in a dream," which had (apparently) a connection with untruthful or abnormal behavior.

Goering tried to persuade Hess to stop, but Hess ignored him. Lawrence apparently decided that it would be best not to interrupt in the hope that Hess would soon stop of his own accord. But after reading for twenty minutes or more, Hess lapsed into incoherent repetition, for example: "However, at that time the world was confronted with an insoluble riddle, the same riddle which confronts it today with regard to the happenings in the German concentration camps. At that time the English people were confronted with an incomprehensible riddle, the same riddle which today confronts the German people with regard to the happenings in the German concentration camps." That last sentence was then repeated, substituting "South African" concentration camps, and then again, substituting "Reich Cabinet" for "English people."

Eventually, Lawrence gently told Hess that his time was up, but Hess protested that since he had not testified, he ought to be allowed time for his statement. Lawrence refused to argue and repeated his order; Hess replied that he would not make the statement that he had intended, but would make a few "concluding remarks." His conclusion was in part as follows:

> I was permitted to work for many years of my life under the greatest son whom my people has brought forth in its thousand-year history. Even if I could, I would not want to erase this period of time from my existence. I am happy to know that I have done my duty to my people, to my duty as a German, as a National Socialist, as a loyal follower of my Führer. I do not regret anything. . . . No matter what human beings may do, I shall some day stand before the judgment seat of the Eternal. I shall answer to him, and I know he will judge me innocent.

Mad as Hess was, there was deep sincerity in his voice and carriage, and certainly he was the only defendant, other than Seyss-Inquart, whose last bow to Hitler was honest. But his principal effect on me was to reinforce my belief that he was quite unable to defend himself and should not have been tried.

Joachim von Ribbentrop's statement was angry and stupid, but it is hard to see what he could have said to better his position. "I am held responsible," said he, "for the conduct of a foreign policy which was determined by another." True, but not enough to mitigate the willing support of Hitler's policies from the annexation of Austria to the eventual collapse of the Thousand-Year Reich. Ribbentrop purported to "deplore the atrocious crimes which became known to me here," but was silent about his own full participation in the deportation of Jews from France and the other German-occupied countries to the extermination camps in Eastern Europe. With a final snarl, Ribbentrop declared: "The only thing of which I consider myself guilty before my people—and before this Tribunal—is that my aspirations in foreign policy remained without success." To which the listener can only reply: "Thank God!"

Wilhelm Keitel began his apologies by reminding the Tribunal that he had "acknowledged on the witness stand my responsibility in connection with my official position" and telling his listeners that "It is far from my intention to minimize my part in what took place." He then, "In the interest of historical truth," spoke to correct five "errors" made in the final arguments of the chief prosecutors. Keitel's criticisms appeared to be correct, and his anxiety to straighten things out was in keeping with the character of a careful staff officer. But after what appeared to many of his listeners as nitpicking, Keitel concluded with what was, in my opinion, the bravest and most thoughtful statement made that day:

> Now, at the end of this Trial I want to present equally frankly the avowal and confession I have to make today.
>
> In the course of the trial my defense counsel submitted two fundamental questions to me, the first one . . . was: "In case of a victory, would you have refused to participate in any part of the success?" I answered: "No, I should certainly have been proud of it."
>
> The second question was: "How would you act if you were in the same position again?" My answer: "Then I should rather choose death than to let myself be drawn into the net of such pernicious methods."
>
> From these two answers the High Tribunal may see my viewpoint. I believed, but I erred, and I was not in a position to prevent what ought to have been prevented. That is my guilt.
>
> It is tragic to have to realize that the best I had to give as a soldier, obedience and loyalty, was exploited for purposes that could not be recognized at the time, and that I did not see that there is a limit even for a soldier's performance of his duty. That is my fate.

From the clear recognition of the causes, the pernicious methods, and the terrible consequences of this war, may there arise the
hope for a new future in the community of nations for the German
people.

Keitel blamed nobody but himself and had acknowledged his own
weakness and blindness. As I sat at the American prosecution's table and
heard those balanced words *"meine Schuld"* (my guilt) and *"mein
Schicksal"* (my fate), I was much moved. The trial had at least enriched his
self-perceptions.

Like Ribbentrop, Kaltenbrunner was an angry man, whom nobody
liked, in a hopeless situation. He was much brighter than Ribbentrop, and
on trial he had wriggled and squirmed in countless maneuvers to fend off
the piles of documents that were his nemesis and to put all the blame on
Himmler and Gestapo Mueller. Now he replayed all the denials and explanations that he had previously offered, but this time there was little attention. In conclusion, Kaltenbrunner referred ominously to unnamed forces
(obviously the Russians) "threatening the world" and charged that "I am
accused here because substitutes are needed for the missing Himmler."

Alfred Rosenberg's statement was less frenetic than Kaltenbrunner's,
but otherwise the two were much alike in that they spent most of their time
rehashing well-worn issues and accusations. Considering that Rosenberg
had been part of the Hitler ménage since early times, it was notable that
he had little to say about Nazism and mentioned the Fuehrer only to
deplore that increasingly he "drew persons to himself who were not my
comrades, but my opponents." Otherwise Rosenberg's eyes were in his own
shoes; he never mentioned a single other individual by name. Nor did he
leave any thoughts for the future other than a brief expression of hope for
"a new, mutual understanding among nations, without prejudice, without
ill-feeling, and without hatred."

Hans Frank's apologia could hardly have been more different from
those of the prior two defendants. He began by denigrating Hitler's decision
to commit suicide and leave "no final statement to the German people and
the world"; therefore Frank and those of like mind should send the message.° Germans had come to this pass, said Frank, because they had turned
away from God, and that was the root of the message: "I beg of our people
not to continue in this direction be it even a single space, because Hitler's
road was the way without God, the way of turning from Christ, and, in the
last analysis, the way of political foolishness, the way of disaster, the way
of death."

---

°Obviously, Hitler's so-called will was not the sort of "final statement" that Frank had in
mind.

Frank had converted to Catholicism during the trial and no doubt thought he was speaking from the heart, but his tone and pose suggested that he enjoyed sermonizing from his imagined pulpit in the dock.

Frank then made an abrupt shift in the tenor of his statement. When testifying, Frank, supposedly speaking as a penitent, had said that "a thousand years would not suffice to erase the guilt brought upon our people because of Hitler's conduct in this war." Now, said Frank, that statement must be rectified because:

> Every possible guilt incurred by our nation has already been completely wiped out today, not only by the conduct of our wartime enemies toward our nation, and its soldiers, which has been carefully kept out of this trial, but also by the tremendous mass crimes of the most frightful sort which—as I have now learned—have been and still are being committed against Germans by Russians, Poles, and Czechs, especially in East Prussia, Silesia, Pomerania, and Sudetenland. Who shall ever judge these crimes against the German people?

If Frank's question has not gone completely unanswered, certainly the response has not been loud. When delivered, the passage caused no stir in the courtroom.

Wilhelm Frick, in consonance with his almost belligerent silence, spoke only three short paragraphs. He declared that he had a clear conscience and that "to have acted any differently would have been a breach of my oath of allegiance and high treason."

Julius Streicher had more to say, which was accomplished with dignity and dispatch, in part as follows:

> The prosecution had asserted that mass killings [of Jews] could not have been possible without Streicher and his *Stürmer*. The prosecution neither offered nor submitted any proof of this assertion. . . .
>
> These actions of the leader of the State against the Jews can be explained by the attitude toward the Jewish question, which was thoroughly different from mine. Hitler wanted to punish the Jews because he held them responsible for unleashing the war and for the bombing of the German civilian population. . . . I repudiate the mass killings . . . in the same way as they are repudiated by every decent German.
>
> Your Honors! Neither in my capacity as Gauleiter nor as political author have I committed a crime, and I therefore look forward to your judgment with a good conscience.
>
> I have no request to make for myself. I have one for the German people from whom I come. Your Honors, fate has given you the power

to pronounce any judgment. Do not pronounce a judgment which would imprint the stamp of dishonor upon the forehead of an entire nation.

Funk had been greatly upset at the discovery in his own Reichsbank of gold teeth and other valuables taken from concentration-camp inmates. He spent most of his apologia talking of nothing else and bemoaned the failure of others to tell him what was involved. His panic led him to absurd statements, for instance: "The fact that the confiscation of these assets was taking place through the SS agencies subordinate to Himmler could not arouse any suspicions in me." Even the proof of his meeting with Oswald Pohl and his admission that he had "assumed that some of the gold and foreign currencies which was deposited with the Reichsbank came from concentration camps," he claimed, gave him no idea that he should examine the contents.

Funk acknowledged that he had "let myself be deceived all too easily," but insisted: "I consider myself free from any criminal guilt which I am supposed to have incurred in discharge of my duties."

Schacht was self-righteous, boastful, and arrogant. He declared: "I did not stain my hands with one single illegal or immoral act" and the "terrorism of the Gestapo did not frighten me." He mentioned his fellow defendants only to describe the plainly guilty ones as "pitiful and broken characters." He boasted of the skill with which he had wiped out unemployment and raised the state revenues.

But there was no denying that Schacht was one of those people who are painfully right. Schacht admitted only that he had "erred politically" and had not realized "the extent of Hitler's criminal nature at an early enough date." But in that he was certainly not alone, and the mistake was no crime. Schacht concluded: "Therefore my head is upright and I am unshaken in the belief that the world will recover, not through the power of violence, but only through the strength of the spirit and morality of actions."

Doenitz went Schacht one better; he not only denied any criminality, but also any mistake. If the same set of facts in the submarine warfare had been repeated, he said, "I would have to do exactly the same all over again."

Dr. von der Lippe called Doenitz's statement "short and dull." The defendant essayed only three points: first, German submarine warfare had been lawfully and honorably conducted; second, the prosecution's accusation of a Nazi criminal "conspiracy" was only "political dogma" and of no value in assessing guilt, while the "Führer principle" had seemed to be proven right, but since "no other result has been achieved through the Führer principle than the misfortune of this people, then this principle as such must be wrong" (really a double point); third, "as the last Commander-in-Chief of the German Navy and the last Head of State, I bear the responsibility for everything which I have done and left undone."

With no mercy for his own client, von der Lippe described Raeder's apologia as "not brilliant, and even pedantic." In fact, there was little Raeder could add to Doenitz's points, except in regard to the invasion of Norway. But Raeder chose to ignore that issue, except indirectly. His conclusion was reminiscent of Keitel's:

> If I have incurred guilt in any way, then this was chiefly in the sense that in spite of my purely military position I should perhaps have been not only a soldier, but also up to a certain point a politician, which, however, was in contradiction to my entire career and the tradition of the German Armed Forces.

Although Schirach had been examined and cross-examined extensively on his actions as *Gauleiter* in Austria, he did not mention this part of his Nazi career. His statement was entirely given over to the Hitler Jugend and his activities as its leader. He spoke furiously against the British prosecution's accusation that he had "corrupted millions of German children" and skillfully answered it, not in terms of exonerating himself, but to "remove the distorted picture of German youth." Schirach concluded: "May you, Gentlemen of the Tribunal, contribute through your judgment towards creating an atmosphere of mutual respect among the younger generation, an atmosphere which is free of hatred and revenge."

Von der Lippe wrote that "Sauckel delivered an unusually good and thoughtful 'last performance.'" Others were not so favorable. Sauckel's statement was one of the longest, and much of it was intended to picture himself as a simple and humble family man, obedient to Church and State. One could excuse Sauckel for not thinking in legal terms about World War II, but as a sensible person he must have known that Germany had attacked most of its neighboring countries. As one of the top government administrators and Plenipotentiary in the labor field, he surely knew that forced labor was a violation of international law, and in his statement he said: "The necessity for this [i.e., bringing conscript labor] was our emergency." Necessity may be the mother of invention, but it may also be the mother of crime.

Referring to the leaders of the Wehrmacht, Alfred Jodl stated: "They did not serve the powers of Hell and they did not serve a criminal, but rather their people and their fatherland." He then invoked his "goals":

> As far as I am concerned, I believe that no man can do more than to try to reach the highest of the goals which appear attainable

to him. That and nothing else has always been the guiding principle for my actions, and for that reason, Gentlemen of the Tribunal, no matter what verdict you may pass upon me, I shall leave this court-room with my head held as high as when I entered it many months ago.

But which "highest" of the attainable goals did Jodl reach? Was it high rank? Yes, but not the highest, and rank alone may not be a worthy goal. Was it victory? That was not attained, and the failed effort reduced much of his country to desolation. Was it loyalty to a superior? That was achieved, but loyalty is a selective rather than an absolute goal, and loyalty to a man whose criminality had become apparent is itself a crime. It appears to me that Keitel had analyzed the nature of his goals much more acutely than had Jodl.

Franz von Papen, who had attacked Goering so angrily, had recovered his composure when he faced his audience. Now Justice Jackson and Sir Hartley Shawcross were his immediate targets; both of them had dealt scornfully with Papen. Jackson had called him "nothing but the hypocritical agent of a godless government," and Shawcross had joked that Papen "preferred to reign in Hell rather than serve in Heaven."

Papen treated the other defendants with utter indifference; from Goering to Fritzsche, not one was named, nor did Papen touch any issues in which any of them were involved. With circumspection, Papen did not explicitly deny his guilt: "When I examine my conscience, I do not find any guilt where the Prosecution has looked for it and claims to have found it. But where is the man without guilt and without fault?" Papen was still the old fox.

To me Arthur Seyss-Inquart was, of all the defendants, the most individual and complicated. There was about him more than a touch of ancien régime, and if the Austro-Hungarian Empire had not been broken up after World War I, I am sure Seyss-Inquart would have preferred that to an Austro-German Anschluss. In his apologia, Seyss-Inquart attacked the prosecution's efforts to show him as planning for future aggressive wars. On the basis of his public statements, following the Anschluss, Seyss-Inquart explained:

> As long as the Danube area was incorporated in the Austro-Hungarian monarchy its development was beneficial to all, and the German element did not display any imperial activity, but only fur-thered and contributed to culture and industry. Ever since this area was broken up by the integral success of the nationalistic principle, it has never achieved peace. Remembering this, I thought of reorganiz-ing a common Lebensraum, which, as I openly declared, gives . . . such a social order to all, namely, Germans, Czechs, Slovaks, Hungarians,

and Rumanians, as would make life worth living for every individual.
. . . These statements can no more serve as evidence of the intention
to wage a war of aggression than the decision of Teheran concerning
the German eastern territories. °

Seyss-Inquart then restated several of his basic points of view with
regard to the issues at hand. With regard to World War II:

> Then the war broke out, which I immediately recognized . . . as
> a life-and-death struggle for the German people. To the [Allies']
> demand for an unconditional surrender I could only oppose an uncon-
> ditional "no" and my unconditional service to my country. I believe in
> the words of Rathenau: "Courageous nations can be broken but never
> bent."

On his attitude toward the Dutch:

> Could I be the friend of the Dutch, the overwhelming majority
> of whom were against my people which, in turn, was fighting for its
> existence? Besides, I have only regretted that I did not come to the
> country as a friend. But I was never a hangman nor, of my own will,
> a plunderer. . . . My conscience is untroubled to the extent that the
> biological condition of the Dutch people during the period of my full
> responsibility . . . was better than in the first World War, when it was
> neither occupied nor blockaded. . . . Finally, I did not carry out the
> order [of Hitler] to destroy the country . . . and on my own initiative
> I put an end to the occupation for defense purposes when resistance
> in Holland had become senseless.

Finally:

> And now I probably still owe an explanation regarding my atti-
> tude to Adolf Hitler. Since he saw the measure of all things in himself,
> did he prove himself incapable of fulfilling a decisive task for the
> German people, indeed for Europe itself, or was he a man who strug-
> gled, although in vain, even to the point of committing unimaginable
> excesses, against the course of an inexorable fate? To me he remains
> the man who made greater Germany a fact in German history. I
> served this man. And now? I cannot today cry "Crucify him," since
> yesterday I cried "Hosanna."

Only a brave man could have spoken those words.
In the audience, there was much anticipation and curiosity about

°I.e., the decision at the Teheran Conference of 1945 to give some of eastern Poland to
the Soviet Union and part of eastern Germany to Poland.

Albert Speer's statement. There was a general belief that the evidence against him was heavy—as heavy, for example, as Sauckel's. Speer could not help himself by arguing his innocence; his cards were his defiance of Hitler's scorched-earth orders and his own personality. How would he portray himself in this last opportunity?

Speer's entire speech was a lecture on the rapidity of "modern technical development" and the great danger to mankind if these new discoveries were applied to weaponry. He did not mention questions of evidence or law and referred to himself only once, near the end: "Of what importance is my own fate, after everything that has happened, in comparison with this high goal"—by which he meant the goal of the Tribunal in "preventing such degenerate wars in the future."

At the time, the world was full of not only the debris and horror of the war but also the new engineering of which Speer had been speaking—jet airplanes, snorkel submarines, rockets, and, of course, the atomic bomb. It was a timely moment for Speer's lecture and, to the audience, he appeared as a wise prophet of future needs and dangers. Rereading it today, his words to me seem less impressive and Speer's grand indifference to his own fate too studied.

Constantin von Neurath's statement was so brief that I will simply quote it:

> Firm in the conviction that truth and justice will prevail before this High Tribunal over all hatred, slander, and misrepresentation, I believe that I should add only this one to the words of my defense counsel: My life was consecrated to truth and honor, to the maintenance of peace and the reconciliation of nations, to humanity and justice. I stand with a clear conscience not only before myself, but before history and the German people.
>
> If, in spite of this, the Tribunal should find me guilty, I shall be able to bear even this and take upon myself as a last sacrifice on behalf of my people, to serve whom was the substance and purpose of my life.

Hans Fritzsche alone submitted to the Tribunal, in writing, a memorandum concerning the evidence in his case. At the beginning of his apologia he explained that the memorandum was a reply to a number of accusations which the chief prosecutors had made against him in their final speeches. In order to save the Tribunal's time, he would not read the memorandum, but submit it for the Tribunal's judicial notice.

The burden of Fritzsche's statement was to criticize the prosecution because it had pictured the admitted atrocities "in such a way as if all of Germany had been a tremendous den of iniquity." Fritzsche acknowledged that "It is quite possible, perhaps even understandable, that the storm of indignation which swept the world because of the atrocities . . . should obliterate the borders of individual responsibility." And in his conclusion he said:

> It may be difficult to separate German crime from German idealism. It is not impossible. If this distinction is made, much suffering will be avoided for Germany and for the world.

To me, the most remarkable and gripping statements were those of Keitel and Seyss-Inquart. Schacht spoke very professionally, but he was too arrogant and had little to say that he had not said before. Streicher spoke crudely but to the point and left me in a continuing quandary about the legal basis of the charges against him.

Both sides of the case were pleased with the conduct of the occasion. Fritzsche wrote: "To me these speeches seemed the most dignified made by any of the accused during the whole trial, and to judge by the respectful silence in which they were received in that crowded hall, the court and the public were of the same opinion. Their attitude, indeed, seemed to me no less dignified than our own." Birkett wrote: "This was a morning when the dignity of the Trial might have been impaired by unseemly scenes. As it turned out, the dignity of the Trial was enhanced by the defendants themselves."

After Fritzsche had finished, Lord Lawrence thanked both prosecution and defense for the way in which their members had performed their duties and stated: "In the opinion of the Tribunal, Defense Counsel have performed an important public duty in accordance with the highest traditions of the legal profession, and the Tribunal thanks them for their assistance."

Lawrence then announced that the Tribunal "will now adjourn until 23 September in order to consider the judgment." Later there was a further postponement until September 30, 1946.

# Chapter 20

# THE JUDGMENTS
# OF SOLOMONS

D
uring the summer and early fall of 1946, the life-styles of the
members of the Nuremberg war crimes community were a very
mixed bag. The only thing that no one could fault was the glorious
weather, particularly relished by the encaged defendants, whose daily walk
in the prison yard was their only touch of nature.

But fine weather, even for those able to enjoy its amenities, could not
dispel the terrible boredom. The Tribunal, like the Apocalypse, was supposed to drive out evil and enthrone good, but the goal was not attained on
four horses. For nearly a year the inmates and workers of the courthouse
had been fairly drowned in documents, arguments, speeches, witnesses,
translators, reporters, and other judicial whatnot. In the nature of things,
these ingredients of the proceedings became more and more repetitive as
time went on. In August the trial of the organizations had been especially
wearisome, enlivened only occasionally by surprises such as the ghastly
Sievers explosion or Judge Biddle's unintentional public lecture on broth-
els.° Rebecca West, who visited the Trial in its closing weeks, later wrote:

> The trial was then in its eleventh month, and the courtroom was
> a citadel of boredom. Every person within its walk was in the grip of
> extreme tedium. This is not to say that the work in hand was being
> performed languidly. An iron discipline met the tedium head on and
> did not yield an inch to it. . . .
> It might seem that this is only to say that at Nuremberg people

---

°Lord Lawrence, who had been a little inattentive, suddenly heard a witness utter the
word "brothel." Unsure of what he had heard, Lawrence turned to Biddle for enlightenment.
Biddle, unaware that his own voice was plugged into the line for the earphones in use throughout
the hall, replied: "Brothel, Geoffrey, bordello, brothel, whorehouse." "I see," replied Lawrence
as a wave of laughter swept the room.

were bored. But this was boredom on a huge historic scale. A machine was running down, a great machine, by which mankind, in spite of its infirmity of purpose and its frequent desire for death, has defended its life.

But with the defendants, boredom fought with tension. In the fall of 1945, when they realized that the trial would last for many months, their fate did not loom as imminent. But in July, when the chief prosecutors had their last say and nothing but the organizations stood between the defendants and the answers to what might be their own last questions, continued boredom seemed, at least to some, not so bad.

When the trial finished at the end of August and the judges withdrew to consult on the judgment, the defendants received from Colonel Andrus a brief but marvelous bounty which relieved the boredom and for some the tension as well. Aroused by the report of Lieutenant Colonel Dunn, a new psychiatrist, which described a high general level of tension, especially apparent with Kaltenbrunner, Andrus relaxed the bonds of solitary confinement by providing the defendants with a room for cards and other games and much desired conversation. Even more welcome to the prisoners was the grant of permission to see and talk with their wives and children, albeit through a grill.

Keitel and Papen, declaring their situation too distressing, refused to see their wives. But most of the others wanted to see their loved ones, fearing the worst from the judges' decisions. Emmy Goering came with their daughter Edda, Schacht's second wife with two young daughters. Ribbentrop and Frick had family visitors. Frau Adele Streicher was still in the prison as a witness for her husband and came daily. Raeder had the solace of a son and a daughter, but the poor man could not see his wife because the Russians would not bring her to Nuremberg, despite Lawrence's request and a plea to Rudenko from Siemers and von der Lippe. The last visits were on September 28, two days before the Tribunal announced its judgment.

Despite Rebecca West's accurate perception that the atmosphere of the Palace of Justice smelt of boredom, most of the lawyers and at least one of the judges were doing pretty well outside the edifice. Miss West's arrival had been expected by Judge Biddle, who had previously met her in the United States. On July 21, 1946, his notes read: "Tomorrow dinner will meet Rebecca West and will make English love if she hasn't grown too fat." Apparently she had not, and soon she joined Biddle, at that time the solitary tenant of the Villa Conradti. On July 30 (the same day that Rudenko finished his closing argument and the Tribunal began dealing with the organizations) Justice Jackson gave a large farewell dinner party at the Villa Schickedanz.

Biddle and his guest attended; the judge recorded that he had sat next to the interpreter known as the "Passionate Haystack," but found her rather stiff, and that Dr. Gilbert informed him that among the defendants were three "homos": Frank, Schirach, and Fritzsche. But the affair did nothing to ease the relations between Biddle and Jackson. Biddle wrote in his notes: "Jackson snubbed Rebecca, which made her very angry—she used nice clean short Saxon words."

Soon the two were off to the Salzburg Festival and then a four-day vacation in Prague—"the most beautiful town I have ever seen," Rebecca wrote. Both were married, and it was, to steal the name of a then famous motion picture, a "brief encounter." If there was pain, it was well compensated for by West's beautifully written articles from Nuremberg, initially published in *The New Yorker*.°

The times called for other good-bye parties, and the Soviet judges complied on July 25. Jackson himself left on July 31, uncertain whether he would return when the Tribunal read its judgment. On August 21 the French delegation hosted a delightful party and dance in honor of their Minister of Justice, M. Tetjens, and on August 31 there was a huge party at the Press Club.

But the great sign of reviving artistic life in those days was the reopening of the Salzburger Festspiele, last presented in 1939. On September 23, Mary and Peter Calvocoressi accompanied me to the Festival, where we heard *Don Giovanni* and *Der Rosenkavalier*. The casts included not only well-known prewar singers like Rosette Anday, but also new young artists developed during the war, whom we were hearing for the first time—wonderful singers, in particular, Irmgard Seefried and Elisabeth Schwarzkopf.

The end of the trip to Salzburg by car was most unpleasant—militarism at its worst. When we reached the Austrian border two motorcyclists from the American forces in Austria signaled us to follow them to the Fuschlsee, where we would be staying. To reach it we had to drive right through the center of Salzburg. The motorcycle escort set off at a crazy speed with its sirens screaming and, without slowing, roared right through the city with the inhabitants jumping madly to escape destruction. "Pardon my mailed glove," Rebecca West had written to describe the utter indifference of the American soldiers to the inhabitants.

During late August and September, apart from the judges, the busiest people in the Palace of Justice were the young lawyers and others on my staff preparing new cases to be launched for the "subsequent proceedings" as soon as the International Military Tribunal had finished its work.

---

°See *Greenhouse with Cyclamens*, in *A Train of Powder*. With the end of the trial, relations between Jackson and Biddle soon mended; in a letter to Biddle, Jackson wrote on September 13: "I suppose you have seen Rebecca West's article in the *New Yorker*: It has created a good deal of interest here as it gives a good impression of the atmosphere of Nuremberg."

2

On September 1, 1946, when the Tribunal went to work on its opinion, free from the interferences of public court sessions, the judges did not start from scratch. Since May the judges' aides—"Butch" Fisher, Jim Rowe, and Bob Stewart—had been working both on legal questions relating to the Charter and the Indictment and on analyses of the evidence for and against individual defendants. In April, Herbert Wechsler had returned to New York and Columbia Law School, but Biddle greatly trusted Wechsler's legal skills and sound judgment and continued to call on him for advice.

Two of the four pairs of judges were English-speaking, and both Charter and Indictment showed the marks of Anglo-American legal practice. The French and Soviet judges appear to have taken it for granted that the British and Americans would have the major share in producing the Tribunal's opinion. Established custom put the responsibility in the hands of the President, but Lawrence made no bones of his distaste for voluminous paperwork. He could not gracefully request Biddle or Parker to do the work, and it had already become the practice that Birkett, a skilled legal draftsman, would produce drafts of the Tribunal's important documents.

On June 27 the Tribunal held its first formal meeting° to discuss the problems and progress of the opinion. There were twenty-two such meetings during the approximately two months between this date and the publication of the opinion at the end of September. Eight of these occurred while the Tribunal was still in session and the others during September. The first eight gatherings were entirely devoted to questions of law and the structure of the opinion; judgments on the individual defendants and the organizations were not discussed until the ninth sitting, on September 2, 1946.†

The judges initially met to consider Birkett's draft of a "long preliminary opinion," which had already been reviewed by Lawrence, Biddle, and Parker. This was the first time the Russians and French saw what the English-speaking judges had produced. Nikitchenko politely called it "excellent" but then criticized it as much too long and as containing many passages—history of the Charter, analysis of the Indictment, and so forth—which were unnecessary. The Soviet judges had always regarded the trial as a much less complicated, cut-and-dried task than did their Western colleagues.

---

°Of course, I had no idea what was going on with respect to the Tribunal's opinion and remained in a state of ignorance until many years later, when I obtained and read copies of Biddle's notes from their resting place at Syracuse University.

†Information on the course of events during these meetings is virtually all derived from Biddle's personal notes (written in the first person) and the aides' memoranda.

Lawrence was eager to ensure that the opinion would be "the work of one hand," which would preserve unity of style and guarantee Birkett's continuing employment. Both Lawrence and Biddle thought that "aggressive war" should be handled more strongly, and Biddle called attention to his own memorandum on international law questions.

Throughout the trial, Donnedieu de Vabres had been the quietest of the judges, but now, like Jason throwing the rock among the soldiers born of dragons' teeth to get them fighting each other, the Frenchman produced a memorandum declaring that the introduction of the concept of conspiracy (in both Charter and Indictment) brought in a theory "unknown even to French law," which therefore would be "ex post facto." His memorandum was drawn as a part of the opinion, dealing with Count One of the Indictment, and stated: "The International Military Tribunal, after detailed consideration, rejects this first count."

De Vabres's exposition of his view brought the discussion to a stop. No one appeared to be ready for argument on this very basic issue. Biddle's notes contained the statement that de Vabres "particularly makes the persuasive argument that conspiracy in the truest sense is not known to international law." But he was cautious and on July 10 wrote to Wechsler explaining the situation and asking for advice.

Over the course of some weeks, de Vabres received several memoranda critical of his position from fellow judges. But the Tribunal did not formally assemble to discuss the issue until the sixth meeting, on August 14.° Lawrence invited de Vabres to "develop his idea," but de Vabres passed the task to Judge Falco, who described himself as "generally in agreement" with de Vabres, but proved to be considerably more flexible. He began by supporting the "rejection" of Count One, but in the spirit of compromise urged that the members "abandon our respective national ideas of criminal law and place ourselves on the facts." Unlike de Vabres, Falco thought that the Charter's language prevented Count One's rejection on legal grounds; that could better be done for lack of proof of the fact of conspiracy. But Falco personally thought it had been proved. Having thus both pleased and displeased both sides of the controversy, Falco suggested "as a compromise to limit conspiracy to crimes against peace and reject it as to the other two"—a proposal for which there was strong support in the language of the Charter and which was to provide the core of the ultimate agreement.

De Vabres then spoke at length, and nearly to the end of the meeting. He lightly referred to his "wounds from the bombardment of memoranda." He relied heavily on the contrast between the four counts in the Indictment

°The judges had no regular schedule of issues for discussion. To describe the meetings chronologically would therefore be confusing, and accordingly the text proceeds by subjects.

and the three (a)(b)(c) paragraphs in Article 6 of the Charter to argue that the Indictment had added a fourth crime entitled "conspiracy," which was not part of Continental law and therefore was ex post facto as applied to the defendants. He said little that had not been covered in his memorandum, submitted at the first meeting, and he concluded by pleading for concession to an issue of great moral moment to *la France*.

Parker then asked de Vabres if he would hold the defendants "not guilty under the first count," and de Vabres said yes. Lawrence declared that the Charter might be retroactive and that "we must follow it" and then adjourned the meeting. Biddle wrote: "British at their worst."

The following day the opposition to de Vabres's proposal exploded. Nikitchenko sneeringly declared that "We are practical, not a discussion club." He effectively attacked de Vabres's argument that there was no conspiracy because Hitler decided everything: "In any criminal group there is a leader. Silent agreement is as good as open support. . . . There never is equality in a conspiracy." Time and again he insisted that this was a practical and not just a legal problem, arguing that the conspiracy element tied the defendants together so that Fritzsche was guilty of the crimes of the conspirators, even though his own speeches were not criminal. He brushed aside de Vabres's ex post facto argument that the Charter "introduced many new things in the field of international law" and said the Tribunal was "not an institution to protect old law and to shield old principles from violation."

Nikitchenko spoke for nearly two hours, and Birkett succeeded him for still another. He was even more violent than Nikitchenko: "If Count One is rejected, the whole value of the trial will go. . . . Heart will be torn out if we reject Count One. . . . Do you want to acquit the Nazi regime? You would do grievous harm to the world and infinite harm to the Tribunal."

Three days later (August 19, eighth meeting) it was Parker's turn. He was calmer than Birkett but just as strongly opposed to de Vabres's arguments. Conspiracy was defined in the Charter, alleged in the Indictment, and proven in the evidence. There were half a dozen defendants proven guilty under Count One, but not under Count Two. He said in closing: "Conspiracy is tremendously important in international law. . . . If we knock out conspiracy we must knock out the organizations as well."

After Lawrence had read his memorandum opposing de Vabres, the turn finally came to Biddle, who had initially called de Vabres's views "persuasive" and then sought help from Wechsler. Whether Wechsler's wisdom had reached Biddle is not clear, but his initial remarks showed that he did not want to deadlock the Tribunal by siding with de Vabres or wholly defeat the French by joining with Lawrence and Nikitchenko. According to his notes, Biddle "pleaded for understanding" and "pointed out the extremes to which both sides had gone." He "suggested the difficulty of finding certain defendants guilty—such as Schacht—if we rely solely on Count Two." Biddle then suggested that "we write an opinion emphasizing the separate plans rather than a single great loose conspiracy, and that planning is part of waging war." The Tribunal then agreed to Biddle's offer to "write out a form" for the treatment of "conspiracy" in the opinion, and the problem thus passed temporarily into Biddle's hands.

On September 4 (eleventh sitting) the judges discussed the draft which Biddle had distributed two days earlier and which, in all probability, he had prepared with the aid of Wechsler's suggestions. Overriding Nikitchenko's contrary view, the three other voting judges agreed that the Charter did not apply the conspiracy provision to war crimes or crimes against humanity.

As for conspiracy to plan or wage aggressive war, de Vabres welcomed Biddle's treating the matter as involving several conspiracies rather than a single big one, but the French judge was still endeavoring to cross out Count One by treating the conspiracies as tantamount to plans for aggressive war and therefore already covered by Count Two. Two days earlier, when the Tribunal held its first meeting on the individual defendants, de Vabres had voted against convicting any defendant under Count One.

But Lawrence, Nikitchenko, and Biddle himself would not agree to de Vabres's ploy and insisted on a Count One covering conspiracies to engage in crimes against peace as defined in Article 6(a) of the Charter. Seeking to palliate de Vabres's doubts, Biddle offered to work into his own draft some of the contents of de Vabres's memorandum of late June. As Biddle put it in his note, the Frenchman "backs down a good deal under pressure." It is not clear just when de Vabres finally succumbed and accepted Count One,° but within a week or so he began to vote for conviction of some of the defendants under Count One.

The "conspiracy issue" was argued longer and more sharply than any other matter that arose during these deliberations. In retrospect, it appears to me that de Vabres raised the wrong issue at the wrong time.

Birkett had begun his statement by deploring that the issue "arose so late—ten months of trial." Right he was; de Vabres had attacked conspiracy on the ground that its legal nature was unknown to and incompatible with French criminal procedure. If he had raised the issue at once and was unsuccessful, the matter would have been immediately disposed of, as had been the case with the defendants' attack against crimes against peace; if successful, much time and expense would have been saved. Furthermore, an immediate success for de Vabres would have plainly been only a legal ruling, not a factual decision on whether or not there had actually been a

---

°Biddle's notes on the meeting of September 4 end "with one foot in the air" and are obviously incomplete. His notes on the subsequent Tribunal meetings do not refer to conspiracy.

conspiracy. But after the entire evidentiary trial and ten months of court battling, the decision de Vabres called for would inevitably be regarded as vindicating the defendants and the Nazis generally from the charge of being conspirators—the factor which firmly set Birkett and Parker against de Vabres's proposal.

Furthermore, in calling conspiracy an "additional" crime, de Vabres was misled or misleading. Conspiracy as a crime does not stand on its own feet. Conspiracy is the crime of two or more persons planning or acting together to commit a crime *other than* the coming together itself; in the case at hand, planning with knowledge and intent to commit crimes against peace as defined in the Indictment. Without the crime against peace as a goal, there was no conspiracy.

In addition, unlike war crimes and crimes against humanity, which can be accomplished by individuals, planning or waging aggressive wars can only be accomplished by a group—a conspiratorial group including individuals whose acts may not be intrinsically criminal, but which, if accomplished with knowledge and purpose to aid the conspirators, are a part of the criminal conspiracy. Therefore it was entirely justifiable that the Charter should include conspiracy as a means of committing crimes against peace.

However, overbroad application of the conspiracy principle may drag innocent people into the prosecution's net. It was to forestall such abuses that Wechsler and Biddle were limiting the scope of conspiracy vis-à-vis the defendants.

## 3

During July and the first half of August, the Tribunal held four meetings to continue the review, which had begun with the initial meeting on June 27, of Birkett's drafts of the opinion. Much of the discussion was just what would be expected from a group of lawyers poring over the work of one of their number: "Shouldn't we say more about this and less about that?" "Hasn't this been left out?" "We ought to cut out these emotional expressions like 'shocked the conscience of mankind.'" The notes of such talk are of little value today.

But the judges did confront some real problems of substance, and one of these again involved conspiracy, on the evidentiary rather than the legal side. The defendants could not be convicted of conspiracy without proof that they knew of and supported their group's intention to plan and wage aggressive war. Was there such proof? And if so, when did such a group come into existence?

On June 22, Butch Fisher had submitted a memorandum on this very question, covering the period from 1920 to November 1937. Biddle gave it good marks, but questioned Fisher's statement that the pace of rearmament under Hitler showed that the Germans "were developing an economic system which was sensible only if there should be a war." In the margin Biddle penciled "also as a big stick," echoing Theodore Roosevelt's well-known advice.

Fisher's conclusion was that "the evidence does establish that the common plan to wage aggressive war began at the end of 1933, when the Nazis had acquired complete control of the German Government and had begun a vigorous program of rearmament." He added that the members of the common plan "were at least the leading members of the government concerned with diplomacy and rearmament."

As a scholar's formal conclusion, Fisher's draft had merit. But quite sensibly, the judges were not keen to become the target of historians. To several of them, the Hossbach memorandum on the high-level meeting of November 5, 1937, seemed a good bench mark, and it was agreed to rewrite Birkett's draft, using much of Fisher's groundwork and indicating that at some time before that date, one or more conspiracies against peace were in process.

There were other puzzling problems, including some relating to individual countries. The German occupations of Austria and Czechoslovakia had occurred before the attack against Poland, generally regarded as the "beginning" of World War II. Austria had been annexed with the support of a large fraction of the population, and this could hardly be called a "war," even though it was the German Army that brought this about. If it was not a war and the annexation was peaceful, German atrocities in Austria were not war crimes. How about crimes against humanity? Did the Austrian annexation have nothing to do with aggressive war? Except for the Sudetenland, Czechoslovakia had not been annexed. But Slovakia had declared itself independent of Czechia, and Bohemia and Moravia had been forcibly put under German rule. Were the German actions crimes against peace? Were the German atrocities in Bohemia and Moravia war crimes?

Then there were German conquests with regard to which full disclosure of all factors would be embarrassing to one or more of the accusers. It was difficult to criticize the Munich settlement of the Sudetenland dispute when both Britain and France had sponsored it. It was impossible to discuss the death and division of Poland without grievously embarrassing the Soviet Union. It proved impossible to secure all the evidence bearing on the German conquest of Norway, because the British knew it would be embarrassing to them if all the evidence in their possession was made public. There was little embarrassment, but considerable puzzlement, about whether Germany's invasion of Greece was a crime against peace, when Britain already had troops in Greece before the German invasion. Initially, Biddle was opposed to treating the German invasion of Greece as an aggressive war, but Nikitchenko and Parker took the opposite view, and ultimately the judges decided to include Greece as a victim of Germany's aggressive invasion, in violation of Count Two of the Indictment.

The embarrassing circumstances described above were handled by the judges in a variety of ways. The judges decided that Germany had used "aggressive methods" to bring about the Anschluss and that Czechoslovakia had been "seized" and forced to capitulate. But neither of them was to be described as an "aggressive war." At Nikitchenko's earnest request, no mention was to be made of the "secret pacts" between Germany and the Soviet Union with which Dr. Seidl had so annoyed the Tribunal. Nor would there be any talk of the British documents pertaining to Norway, which the Foreign Office had withheld from Dr. Siemers. On these matters the Tribunal was engaging in half-truths, if there are such things.

4

At their tenth meeting, on September 3, 1946, the Tribunal turned to a discussion of the accused organizations. The final evidence on this subject had not become available to the judges until the end of August, so there had been little time for them to reflect on these issues, but the Tribunal had the benefit of memoranda from their aides dealing with each of the accused "organizations or groups," including a long paper by Jim Rowe on the General Staff and High Command.

Biddle opened the discussion by referring to the language in Article 9 of the Charter ("the Tribunal may declare . . . that the group or organization . . . was a criminal organization") and declaring: "We have complete discretion since 'may' is used in the Charter. We could therefore consider matters of policy, of conscience, of effect on international law, of guiding subsequent proceedings." Since Biddle's first days on the Tribunal, he had had a jaundiced view of the organizational feature of the trial. His opening remarks plainly showed that he would at least work to narrow the reach of Article 9, if not to eliminate it from the proceedings.

Falco, de Vabres, Parker, and Birkett all agreed generally with Biddle's view that the Tribunal had the power and, indeed, the duty to limit the application of Article 9 to those whose guilt under the Charter was clear. Parker had already drafted limiting proposals, and de Vabres wanted an international agreement to "create the same practice" in the different national zones of Germany.

But Nikitchenko would have none of these limitations. He was not worried that the Tribunal's decisions "might be used against the innocent." In his view, in line with Rudenko's argument before the Tribunal in February, the Tribunal's only power was to declare whether or not the indicted organizations were criminal. What happened thereafter was entirely in the hands of the national tribunals.

At the conclusion of the meeting Biddle, whether sensing a hoped-for opportunity or irritated by so much inconclusive talk, proposed to blow up the ship. In his notes he wrote: "I suggest throwing them all out—a shocking thing, this group crime. I got Parker almost on my side." But there were no other takers, though de Vabres was moved to suggest that "this is protective work, not penal, and we should emphasize this." It was a good thing that Murray Bernays was not present to hear his brainchild so described.

For the next ten days the Tribunal was primarily concerned with the fates of the individual defendants, and it did not return to the organizations until its twentieth meeting, on September 13, 1946. Near the beginning, Falco raised a most important question which had not been mentioned at the September 3 meeting. Which, if any, organizations should the Tribunal declare to be "criminal"? Falco named three—the Gestapo, SS, and Political Leaders.

The ensuing colloquy was primarily devoted to proposals for limiting the range of Article 9, but in its course, two of the judges expressed views very similar to Falco's listing of the three criminal organizations: Parker, "SS, Gestapo, and SD . . . leave out Reich Cabinet, SA, and General Staff"; Birkett, "Gestapo, SD, and SS though very troublesome" because of many facets. As to the High Command and Reich Cabinet, it "would be very hard to say they were groups."

Nikitchenko, however, argued that all six of the indicted organizations should be declared criminal. The Charter, he said, "had in mind 'groups' as part of organizations." Therefore, he stated, "Gestapo and General Staff, of course, can't be considered 'organizations,' but fall under category of 'groups.' "

Biddle, meanwhile, made two separate efforts to whip up sentiment for his proposal at the earlier meeting: "Drop organizations. It is shocking to convict men without trial, which is what we are doing." He argued that since the Denazification Program had been put into effect there was no need for the organization trials because "the job has already been done."[*] But Biddle found no takers and turned back to his efforts to limit Article 9.

Lawrence made a rather vague statement (thus triggering disrespectful remarks in Biddle's notes), the only definite revelations being his opinions that the Reich Cabinet should be included "as they must have been well aware of what was going on" and that the General Staff should not be held guilty.

Parker finished with comments prompted by Biddle's desire to put aside the organizations: "If we refused to declare criminal the Gestapo and SD, it would create a good deal of surprise in France as well as in Germany.

---

[*]It is probable that Biddle either forgot or was unaware that the OMGUS Denazification Program was in force only in the American Occupation Zone.

Should exclude General Staff and Reich Cabinet, without saying they were not criminal. Give practical reasons—they are small groups and can be individually tried."

Biddle then called for voting on the organizations. His notes state: "*Lawrence, Biddle, De Vabres* vote criminal Gestapo, S.S. and S.D., Political Leadership, and declare not criminal, S.A., General Staff and Political Leadership. *General* [Nikitchenko] votes them all in." Plainly, Biddle meant to write "Reich Cabinet" instead of the repetition of "Political Leadership." Furthermore, his inclusion of "declare not criminal" is in conflict with Parker's explicit advice that those words *not* be included. Biddle was not operating at his peak of precision.

The judges' aides had previously recommended these results with one exception: Rowe's memorandum on the General Staff had strongly recommended that it be declared a criminal organization. He found no difficulty in perceiving a "group" measured by military rank and level of authority, and once past that hurdle he saw the top military men as undeniably planning and waging wars, which they must have known to be aggressive. But I had come to think that the real difficulty with the "group" problem was that the line drawn did not enclose an *institutional entity*, like *the* Gestapo or *the* Reich Cabinet. On top of this, the Tribunal had no reason to wrestle with such problems of verbiage, since it was under no mandate to indict every organization and the size of the General Staff–High Command, as defined, could easily be dealt with on an individual basis, like the Reich Cabinet.

The exclusion of the General Staff and the Reich Cabinet from designations of criminality put nothing in the way of trials for whatever members of them appeared to warrant such treatment. The SA, of course, was another matter since it was, or had been, a huge organization. But because of its shrinkage of size and importance after the Roehm purge, the Tribunal brushed it aside with very little discussion, and even Nikitchenko was not much upset.

Much more difficult than selecting which organizations to convict was the matter of conceiving and stating rules to ensure fair proceedings against the members. Biddle and Parker did most of the work on these problems, with the aid of a memorandum which Herbert Wechsler had sent to Biddle. Essentially, the judges wished to get away from the original idea that proven membership alone was sufficient for conviction. The prosecution had agreed that the membership had to be voluntary, but the judges wished to move much closer to the necessary elements of proof generally required in criminal law.

Judge Parker, at the September 13 meeting, stated the test that was eventually adopted. Conviction of a defendant, prosecuted for membership in an organization declared criminal, required proof that the defendant had joined voluntarily *and* that the defendant knew that the organization engaged in crime as defined in Article 6 of the Charter. Failing that proof, the defendant could be convicted only upon proof that the defendant had personally participated in such crimes.

This test, requiring as it does voluntariness and knowledge, with no requirement of participating action on the part of the defendant, was unusual but not unique. In the United States the 1940 Smith Act had a virtually identical provision, and it is interesting that, in 1955, Judge Parker upheld a conviction under it.° At all events, the test greatly improved the rights of members of criminal organizations to prove their own innocence of any violation of the Charter.

After the meeting of September 13, the Tribunal met only three more times. Biddle's notes became fragmentary, in part because he spent two or three days in Paris and then arrived late at the meeting of September 16. The Tribunal was discussing Birkett's draft of the law applicable to the Tribunal, which Biddle "thought very loose, and which I criticized vigorously." The judges then fell into an argument on whether or not they should postpone the date for publication of the opinion from September 23 to September 30. Biddle "urged postponement with everything I had," but the disagreement between Biddle with the French and Parker with the British was so sharp that the judges adjourned, "very tired," without finding agreement. The next morning the British capitulated, and the week's postponement was agreed.

The Tribunal's last meeting, on September 26, was devoted to the organizations. In addition to the "voluntary-knowledge" requirement for conviction, the British and Americans were cutting off various portions of the three convicted organizations. They also were recommending uniformity of treatment in the four occupation zones and suggesting that the Control Council should amend its Law No. 10 in order to limit penalties to those prescribed in the Denazification Law.

Most of these provisions were anathema to Nikitchenko, who still believed that the Tribunal had no proper function other than the declarations of criminality. The meeting began with his strong demand that all these recommendations be abandoned. He found nothing in the Charter

---

°The relevant provision of the Smith Act, which penalizes efforts by "any society, group, or assembly" to destroy the government of the United States by force and violence, states: "Whoever . . . becomes or is a member of, or affiliates with, any such society, group, or assembly of persons, knowing the purposes thereof . . . shall be fined not more than $10,000 or imprisoned for not more than ten years, or both."

Judge Parker's opinion confirmed the conviction of Junius Irving Scales for violation of this provision of the Smith Act. In his opinion he stated: "Certainly it is within the power of Congress to forbid . . . membership in an organization having such destruction in its purpose, where there is knowledge of such purpose on the part of one accepting or retaining such membership"—*Scales v. United States of America*, 227 F.2d 581 (1955).

that limited the jurisdiction or power of the national courts. There was no support from the other members of the Tribunal, and when it came to a clutch, the Russians were repeatedly voted down three to one, though more formally three to nothing, as Nikitchenko refused to vote at all on the ground that the judges "had no authority" in the matters at hand. The increasing number of three to one votes against the Soviet members was pushing Nikitchenko toward his ultimate decision to publish a dissenting opinion.

## 5

On September 2, 1946, at its ninth sitting, the judges began to review the cases of the individual defendants and vote on the convictions and penalties to be applied. Although Article 4(c) of the Charter provided that "convictions and sentences shall only be imposed by the affirmative votes of at least three members of the Tribunal," Nikitchenko boggled at the idea of acquitting defendants on the basis of a two-two tie vote. But the Charter language was clear, and the General was unable to state any plausible alternative.

There was frequent disagreement about the method of carrying out death sentences. The military defendants were especially desirous that the capital sentences should be carried out by shooting rather than hanging—the latter deemed dishonorable for a soldier. De Vabres was much concerned and wanted to distinguish between "honorable" (for Jodl) or "dishonorable" confinement for those not given capital punishment. On September 9, de Vabres offered a resolution "that sentence for imprisonment for a term of years indicate the type of imprisonment—i.e., political, or imprisonment in the same manner as for ordinary criminals." But it was rejected by a vote of three to one. In fact, Article 29 of the Charter provided: "In case of guilt, sentences shall be carried out in accordance with the orders of the Control Council for Germany," which had informally indicated that sentences should be executed according to German practice. This prescribed the guillotine or hanging as the appropriate methods. As matters worked out, all the Tribunal's capital sentences called for "death by hanging."

Strong opinions of some of the judges soon developed. Nikitchenko, in line with the concluding statements of Dubost and Rudenko, voted for the death sentence right down the line. De Vabres believed that none of the defendants should be acquitted, but was the most softhearted of the judges in fixing penalties. Both of them, not surprisingly, found occasions to depart from their normal attitudes in order to avoid unwelcome splits and combinations.

Tentative voting started in the afternoon, as the judges went down the list of the defendants according to their usual seating. Except for Hess and until Funk there was little disagreement about guilty verdicts but some argument over the number of counts for which the defendants should be convicted. The judges generally dropped or postponed the decisions on defendants whose cases were recognized as difficult and controversial and bound to require long discussion.

The Tribunal, without need of discussion, voted Hermann Goering guilty on all four counts of the Indictment. De Vabres, however, voted him not guilty on Count One because of his rejection of the conspiracy accusation. When his case came up again on September 10, the Tribunal unanimously voted for capital punishment. De Vabres, in a maudlin mood, declared that Goering had "a certain nobility" and went off on his differentiation of "honorable" and "dishonorable" penalties. Nikitchenko, utterly disgusted, snarled, "Don't let us get into such ridiculous trifles!" At least the French judge was now willing to swallow the conspiracy, and the final vote for hanging was unanimous except for de Vabres's preference for shooting.

All of the judges agreed that Hess was guilty under Counts One and Two, but this was all that found unanimity. Biddle wrote: "Nikitchenko says probably we should hold him for [Counts] Three and Four. Volchkov thinks [Hess's] signing of the Nuremberg decrees made Hess guilty of the killing of millions of Jews"—an attitude which caused Biddle to note, as an aside: "Russians are going to be very extreme."

Bob Stewart (Parker's aide) had distributed a useful memorandum on the evidence against Hess. With regard to Counts One and Two, Stewart concluded that there was evidence "sufficient to connect Hess specifically with a conspiracy to wage aggressive war and with the actual waging of aggressive war, and to find him guilty under Article 6(a) of the Charter." Stewart went no further than to say that there also "may be" enough evidence to find Hess guilty on Counts Three and Four.

Stewart's careful study was not on the lips of the judges when they met on September 10. Lawrence and Nikitchenko thought Hess guilty on all four counts, Biddle and de Vabres voted for only Counts One and Two; since there was equal division on Counts Three and Four and unanimity on Counts One and Two, the latter prevailed. This result was of small account compared to the votes on the penalty—de Vabres for twenty years' imprisonment, Biddle and Lawrence for a life sentence, Nikitchenko for death. De Vabres stuck to his guns, so the impasse could be rectified only if Biddle and Lawrence joined de Vabres or if they and Nikitchenko joined forces. Biddle wrote: "We finally—except French—agree on life sentence." Presumably Nikitchenko feared that Biddle and Lawrence might join de Vabres, producing only a twenty-year penalty for the Russians' most hated bugaboo.

Why did not Biddle and Lawrence join Nikitchenko for a death sentence? The records do not shed light. But after watching the crazy behavior of a man plainly unable to defend himself, it would take an ice-cold judge to send him to the gallows.

The cases of Ribbentrop and Keitel provoked no argument. All four judges voted to convict them of all four counts and sentence them to death, and, for all but de Vabres in Keitel's case, the death was to be by hanging.

On September 2, the judges fell into disagreement on the counts against Kaltenbrunner. As listed in the Appendix to the Indictment, he was charged with Counts One, Three, and Four, but Biddle, de Vabres, and Nikitchenko all thought that passages in the body of the Indictment supported Count Two as well. Lawrence and all four of the nonvoting judges thought that the Tribunal was bound by the Appendix. It was a wasted argument, because there was very little evidence tying Kaltenbrunner into either Count One or Count Two. By September 10, opinions had changed; all the judges approved Counts Three and Four, but only two votes, by Lawrence and Nikitchenko, were cast for Count One. The result, according to Biddle's notes: "Guilty on III and IV, Hanging." It was ridiculous that so much time was spent on this matter since the judges were, from the beginning, voting for death by hanging.

On September 2, Biddle was not prepared to discuss Rosenberg's case, and the others were in disagreement on the number of counts. By September 10, all agreed that Rosenberg should be convicted on all four counts. Lawrence and Nikitchenko voted for hanging, and Biddle was leaning that way. De Vabres voted for life imprisonment, but the following morning Biddle provided the third vote for hanging.

Hans Frank was indicted under Counts One, Three, and Four and Wilhelm Frick under all four counts. But in both cases their guilt under Counts Three and Four was immediately voted, while there was disagreement about their guilt of crimes against peace. At the first meeting, Nikitchenko voted both defendants guilty of all four counts, even though Frank had not been charged under Count Two. De Vabres voted Frank guilty under all three of his counts and Frick guilty of only Counts Three and Four, which was odd since there was much more evidence implicating Frick than Frank in crimes against peace. Also odd was Lawrence's silence in Frank's case and Biddle's in both.

In the final voting on September 10, the Americans, British, and Russians voted Frank guilty under Counts Three and Four, and Frick guilty under Two, Three, and Four. Both were then condemned to death by hanging. De Vabres voted life imprisonment for Frank and reserved his opinion on Frick, leading Biddle to remark in his notes that de Vabres was "curiously tender."

In the initial discussions of Streicher, indicted only under Counts One and Four, the judges' selections of counts were all over the lot. All but Lawrence named Count Four; Lawrence, Biddle, de Vabres, and Nikitchenko all named Count Three, although Streicher had not been so indicted. Falco and the Russians also named Count One. There was no discussion of the penalty. But on September 10, with no sign of doubt or need for discussion, Streicher, by four votes, was condemned to death by hanging. There was no "curious tenderness" from de Vabres.

The Tribunal's hasty and unthinking treatment of the Streicher case was not an episode to be proud of. Unfortunately, Bob Stewart's memorandum on Streicher did nothing to awaken the Tribunal to the realization that even an unappetizing, fanatical old Nazi is entitled to careful judgment before being hanged. All the judges, but especially Biddle and Parker, nurtured in constitutional guarantees of liberty unfamiliar to their colleagues, were to blame. Biddle was perhaps too patrician to be sensitive to the situation, and fifteen years later, in his memoirs, made no reference to the hanging of Streicher. The carefree way in which the Tribunal members sent him to the gallows, as if they were stamping on a worm, is especially hard to condone.

Streicher's name immediately cropped up again when Volchkov incautiously suggested to his colleagues that Streicher's personal contacts with Hitler were important to his case. Biddle's notes read: "I blurt out that I think its preposterous to hold a little Jew-baiter as a conspirator° because he was a friend of Hitler, or a Gauleiter, or a Nazi. Lawrence bridles and says I have bad manners. Parker pours oil on the water, and says that . . . Streicher has nothing to do with planning or conspiracy."

Walter Funk was next. All the judges called him guilty under Counts Two, Three, and Four, and the British and Russians added Count One. On September 10, tentative votes by de Vabres and Parker called for life imprisonment, but all the others were for hanging. However, the final vote on the penalty was postponed.

Butch Fisher's memorandum on Funk was well turned: "It does not appear that Funk was a vicious man. . . . But Funk did not act on what he claims were his own ideas. . . . He cannot plead that he did not know better; he can only plead that he was a weak man." Those views were congenial to the judges, and the upshot was that on September 12 Funk, against whom there was far more evidence than against Streicher, was sentenced to life imprisonment by a three to one vote, Nikitchenko dissenting.

Rightly anticipating that discussions regarding Schacht, the admirals, and Schirach would be difficult and probably long, the judges jumped to Sauckel, whose case was regarded as both simple and serious. He was accused under the Indictment on all four counts, but Falco, de Vabres, Parker, Biddle, and Lawrence voted for his conviction only under Counts Three and Four. The Russians wished to convict Sauckel under all four counts, and Birkett leaned in that direction.

On September 10, with virtually no discussion, Sauckel was condemned to death by hanging. Initially, according to Biddle's notes, he was

---

°The Russians had just voted to declare Streicher criminal under Count One.

convicted only under Counts Two and Four, but the voting tabulation clearly shows four votes for Count Three, and only two for Count Two.

The initial discussion of Speer brought proposals of conviction on Counts Three and Four from the French, Americans, and British, with no record of the Russians' view. The voting judges cast two votes for guilt under Counts Three and Four, one vote to add Count Two, and of course the Russians wanted all four. But the voting on the penalty was at an impasse, for Nikitchenko and Biddle voted for death by hanging, while Lawrence and de Vabres proposed a term of years, so the case had to go over for later consideration.

Constantin von Neurath was the last defendant scrutinized on September 2. There was no discussion of a penalty and no progress with regard to the counts, suggestions for which ran from only Count One to all four. Thus the case, like Speer's, had to go over until a later meeting.

The Speer and Neurath cases were taken up again at the meeting of September 11, and Neurath's was soon disposed of, with convictions under all four counts and a penalty of fifteen years in prison. The Speer case, however, had been deadlocked, with the French and British strongly inclined in favor of Speer because of his poise and anti-Hitler activities near the end of the war. But Biddle was agreeing with Nikitchenko that Speer should be hanged.

Eventually, Biddle capitulated to his Western allies and broke the deadlock. He wrote in his notes that Speer's penalty would be fifteen years of imprisonment, but in fact the three-way agreement was fixed at twenty years. Nikitchenko, again, was left standing alone.

Toward the end of September 10 there were two more defendants whom the Tribunal hoped to handle briefly. In the case of Jodl these expectations were soon abandoned. The Tribunal was divided, and the defendant was anything but a weak man, so the judges decided "to reconsider Jodl."

The other defendant, Arthur Seyss-Inquart, gave the Tribunal very little trouble. Fisher's memorandum was evidentially sound, and some of his material was used in the Tribunal's opinion. The defendant's proven efforts to ameliorate the lot of the Dutch did not impress Fisher: "It is not a defense that Seyss-Inquart was less brutal than Himmler." But this remark was more smart than solid, for much might depend on *how much* less brutal the defendant's conduct had been. Furthermore, there was unimpeachable testimony that Seyss-Inquart had displayed both skill and courage near the end of the war in preventing further death and destruction, regardless of Hitler's orders. In contrast to the admittedly greater actions of Speer, in Seyss-Inquart's case none of these factors aroused much interest among the judges, largely because he was very laid-back and refused to turn away from his loyalty to Hitler.

So, with little or no doubts except on the part of de Vabres, Seyss-Inquart was convicted under Counts Two, Three, and Four and sentenced to death by hanging.

6

On September 6, 1946, the Tribunal opened its discussion on the fate of the defendant whose record gave the judges the most difficulty reaching a conclusion. In a preliminary vote, Lawrence thought Hjalmar Schacht should be acquitted. De Vabres "doesn't want to acquit anybody, but would suggest a light sentence for several defendants such as Schacht and Papen. . . . On moral values de Vabres would be shocked to see Keitel condemned to death and Schacht acquitted."

Biddle, lecturing rather than voting, spoke of prudence and moderation, but did Schacht no good by declaring that "Everyone knew when Schacht came to power that there was danger of an offensive policy" and that Schacht "shook hands with Hitler after the conquest of France." Parker naively remarked that Schacht "was a banker, therefore a man of character," but the rest of his statement was forceful and led to his conclusion that Schacht's innocence was "conclusive."

Falco was closer to Biddle's doubts of Schacht's sincerity, but stupidly laid weight on Schacht's "congratulating" Hitler after his aggressive intentions were clear. Birkett unhelpfully declared that Schacht should be "acquitted or severely punished," but then raised the sensible question of whether there was a "reasonable doubt" of Schacht's guilt, and concluded that he should be acquitted. Nikitchenko and Volchkov were unusually circumspect, but left no doubt that they would hold Schacht guilty.

The apparent situation was that the British were strongly behind Schacht, that de Vabres would convict but go easy on Schacht, that Parker and Biddle were at odds and Biddle might join with Nikitchenko, and that if he did there was going to be an impasse and a fight.

Biddle had had the benefit since July of a workmanlike memorandum from Fisher, the gist of which was that while Schacht probably did not want war, he had remained at his position after he had realized that Hitler's intentions involved aggression, had publicly praised the Fuehrer after the defeat of France, and had retained his Ministry without Portfolio until 1943. These, of course, were well-worn attacks by the prosecution, which Schacht had endeavored to explain.

The second round of discussion, on September 12, merely stiffened the impasse. Backed by Falco, de Vabres found Schacht guilty on Counts One and Two, but felt his subsequent mitigating actions required a prison sentence of only five years. Lawrence was still strong for acquittal, as were both Birkett and Parker, but Biddle would convict Schacht on Count One and put him in prison for life. Nikitchenko was still for the death penalty, but now saw that Schacht would go free unless something broke. He consulted Biddle on "how much we have to go down" in order to join with de Vabres. Finally, a deal was made for a penalty of eight years, to be calculated from the day of Schacht's arrest.

The next morning Lawrence called Biddle aside and told him that de Vabres had decided that Schacht should be acquitted, which of course put the judges back in the impasse. The reason? The previous day (September 12) Papen had been acquitted by a two to two impasse between Biddle and Lawrence for acquittal versus de Vabres and Nikitchenko for conviction and a light penalty. Fritzsche was then acquitted by three votes, with Nikitchenko dissenting.

Biddle described de Vabres's reasons vis-à-vis Schacht: "His reasons are that he would have voted to convict all defendants, since in some measure all are responsible, and since Papen and Fritzsche are acquitted, Schacht, who is far less responsible than Papen, should be acquitted. Unity of judgment demands acquittal of all three, and there will no longer be a contradiction."

Thus, in the end, it was Biddle who broke the impasse. He wrote: "FB decided only after long consideration. Schacht's fault was only serious imprudence. Can't bear responsibility of a sentence imposed on an old man." But it was a rather feeble cover-up, and Biddle was angry: "I say de Vabres is sentimental, is using his tender heart, not his mind. That it is shocking to say that the fate of other defendants should affect Schacht's fate."

One must answer that if these events were shocking, such shock waves are commonly running over the courts worldwide. Biddle had himself done the very same thing as de Vabres, and once more Nikitchenko was left alone.

The adventures of the other two defendants who were acquitted were not so strongly fought among the judges as was Schacht's. But for the most part both Papen and Fritzsche followed the same tracks, except that Biddle from the beginning shared Lawrence's support for acquittals. Fisher wrote memoranda on both defendants. In Fritzsche's case, he came out flatly for acquittal, while with Papen, after considerable effort, he was able to propose a finding of guilt under Count One.

It was becoming more and more apparent that de Vabres's approach to the adjudication of criminal accusations was wholly different from that of his colleagues. The British and American judges, despite some wanderings, proceeded on the basis of legal principles and evidence, and even Nikitchenko, despite his usual guilty votes, sounded like a lawyer and sometimes a very good one. But de Vabres's process of reaching a conclusion was often baffling. However strong the defendant's case, de Vabres did not wish to acquit; however weak, except rarely, he did not want to impose a severe sentence. He ended his argument for convicting Papen as follows: "He was constantly intervening, by trickery, in favor of Anschluss. His moral, or rather immoral, attitude is very important. Look at the way he behaved in the United States, playing the role of a spy. A corrupting creature . . . we are here to apply morals." No wonder the polite Parker could not resist sarcasm: "We are not trying him for being a *persona non grata* in the United States."

And so on September 12, immediately after Biddle and Nikitchenko had made their eight-year deal with de Vabres on Schacht, Papen was acquitted by a tie vote, and that in turn led to Schacht's acquittal.

Hans Fritzsche was first discussed by the judges on September 10 and 11. Falco declared that the defendant had been using propaganda in support of a criminal war and proposed imprisonment for two to five years, subtracting time already served. At the foot of the defendants' list, de Vabres for the first time spoke at once for an acquittal, adding: "A pity to inflict a very light sentence." Parker agreed, asking, "Why use a cannon to shoot a sparrow?" and adding a little explanation of freedom of speech, which would better have been used earlier, when the judges were sentencing Streicher. Birkett differed, saying that the case raised "no question of freedom of speech," and proposed to convict Fritzsche on Counts One, Three, and Four. Biddle was for acquittal, but the Russian judges (whose prisoner Fritzsche had been) complained that two years was not enough and proposed the three counts and ten years. Lawrence, surprisingly, declared that Fritzsche was "a propagandist working for the war" and knew "that the wars were illegal."

However, the following morning (September 12) de Vabres button-holed Biddle to say that "he was weakening on Fritzsche and thinks he will vote against acquittal." The other judges argued back and forth, and de Vabres, in a real quandary, "asked a postponement until we consider von Papen, saying he will never convict Fritzsche if Papen is acquitted."

And so, after the Papen "acquittal by impasse," Lawrence decided to vote acquittal for Fritzsche, and the next morning de Vabres did the same, thus making three votes for the acquittal of Fritzsche.

## 7

Next to Schacht, Admiral Karl Doenitz presented the Tribunal with its most difficult problem of penalty. There were several reasons for this, some embedded in legal or evidentiary problems, others in personal or political bias.

The principal memorandum on the Doenitz case was written by Jim Rowe, whose wartime naval intelligence duties, including service during the war in aircraft-carrier battles, had honed his knowledge and sense of naval realities. His memorandum was perceptive and detailed.° In his conclusion, Rowe found that Doenitz had not planned or waged aggressive war any more than many other German military officers not engaged in high-level staff work, that he had not "waged unrestricted submarine warfare contrary to international law," and that he should be found not guilty of the charges against him, to wit, Counts One, Two, and Three.

Rowe's analysis made a considerable impression on Biddle, but there was another reason for his decision to vote for Doenitz's acquittal. Biddle himself had been primarily responsible for Kranzbuehler's interrogatory to Admiral Nimitz. The result was public revelation that Nimitz's submarines had used the same methods at sea that the prosecution was presenting as serious crimes ordered by Doenitz, with the approval of Raeder, his superior until January 1943. Biddle, quite understandably, had no desire to be the judge who sentenced a German admiral for doing nothing more than had the greatly admired Nimitz. So Biddle was prepared to and did argue forcibly for Doenitz's acquittal. However, he proved to be the only judge who did.

The British view of Doenitz underwent a sea change. In June 1945, during the drafting of the Charter, when the Americans proposed Doenitz as a defendant, the British Admiralty expressed doubt that there was any evidence incriminating Doenitz and spoke well of the German Navy's "rules of chivalry." In August 1945, after the Churchill Conservative government had given way to Labour, the Americans proposed additions to the list of defendants, including Doenitz. The new British officials (Lord Jowitt and Shawcross) had no objection, but E. J. Passant, of the Foreign Office, submitted a memorandum advising against indicting Doenitz, reiterating the Admiralty's good words for the German Navy and reminding his readers that "most of the measures adopted by the Germans were also adopted by ourselves and the Americans, so that the defense could be in a position to throw a good deal of mud back at the prosecutor."

But now there were whispers from Labour sources that the Admiralty was opposing the Doenitz case in order to hide its own dirty linen. Most Britons had not so soon forgotten that those German submarines had come close to starving out Britannia and had sent many a British sailor to the bottom of the sea. And so Fyfe and his colleagues had, with great determination, taken charge of the cases against Doenitz and Raeder, and when, on September 9, the Tribunal began its preliminary discussion of the Doenitz case, Biddle and Lawrence found themselves on opposite sides of the case.

Furthermore, there was no one else on Biddle's side. Doenitz was accused under the first three counts; Falco wanted him convicted under

---

°As a legal scholar Rowe was no match for Fisher, let alone Wechsler. But he was a shrewd, practical, and forceful man and wrote very well.

Counts Two and Three, de Vabres only under Three. Falco was more truculent than de Vabres, who found the international law of the sea so puzzling that doubts should be resolved in Doenitz's favor and was prepared to explain Nimitz's practices by the "Japs' unjustified aggression."

Arguing for acquittal, Biddle went so far as to declare, "Germany waged a much cleaner war than we did," but this won him no followers. Parker regarded the Treaty of London as still gospel and hardly tipped his hat to Nimitz. The Russians voted conviction on all three counts. Lawrence voted guilty on Counts Two and Three. Considering Nimitz's practices, Lawrence was ready "to give Doenitz the benefit of the doubt on survivors." But he said the Admiral should be held guilty on Count Two for "waging aggressive war," and because so much that he did "was typically national socialist—harsh and inhumane."

The second meeting (September 11) settled the penalty and was brief but remarkable in its outcome. All were agreed that whatever Raeder's punishment was, Doenitz should suffer less. Falco suggested ten years; de Vabres said five to ten; Birkett (who had been absent at the previous meeting) voted for twenty; the Russians rumbled ominously but did not specify; Lawrence voted for ten years. Nikitchenko then voted for ten years. That settled the penalty, and the members then agreed to convict on Counts Two and Three.

Biddle had made no further protest on the conviction and penalty, but now "urged strongly the view that we should not convict on submarine warfare." There was much discussion, but no resolution, and the Tribunal finally adjourned, *subject to Biddle's drafting the opinion.* Thus the only judge who thought Doenitz should be acquitted and who had prepared a dissenting opinion in the event that he was *not* acquitted was selected to explain why he was to be convicted on Counts Two and Three and sent to jail for ten years.

Erich Raeder's case was much less complicated since Doenitz had been Raeder's subordinate until January 1943. Whatever Doenitz did with Raeder's knowledge and approval was also Raeder's responsibility. As has been seen earlier, Kranzbuehler was the lawyer representing both admirals on Doenitz's submarine activities, so Raeder also benefited from the Nimitz connection.

Biddle's notes on Raeder are extraordinarily brief considering the defendant's status and importance from 1928 to his retirement fifteen years later. Like Doenitz, he was charged under Counts One, Two, and Three. At the Tribunal's first and brisk discussion, six of the seven judges (Birkett was absent) voted to convict the defendant on all three counts, with de Vabres including only Counts Two and Three.

The major matters (other than the submarines) particularly charged to Raeder were his involvement in the German occupations of Norway and

Denmark, his liability under Counts One and Two relative to Hitler's other wars, in view of his rank and personal connections with Hitler, and his distribution and one exercise of the Commando Order.

On September 11, without much discussion, de Vabres voted for twenty years' imprisonment, Biddle and Lawrence for life imprisonment, and Nikitchenko for death. De Vabres came up and Nikitchenko came down, and Raeder was condemned to life imprisonment.

# 8

The three cases remaining for decision included Martin Bormann, the probability of whose death had continued to increase since his disappearance during his flight through Berlin just before the fighting ended. The pressure of other matters had kept this phantom in the Indictment and armed it with a lawyer. On September 2, 1946, his case was reached by the Tribunal.

In the discussion, Biddle alone argued that the case should be dropped. But the French and Russians did not want to, and so a tentative vote was taken in which all of the judges voted to find him guilty on Counts One, Three, and Four. On September 11 his case was again brought up, and the judges again found him guilty under Counts Three and Four and sentenced him to death by hanging.

Baldur von Schirach was indicted only on Counts One and Four, and when he was first discussed by the Tribunal on September 9, the Russians alone wanted to convict him on both counts, while the others named only Count Four. At the second meeting on Schirach, Falco opened with a severe attack on the defendant and proposed "life imprisonment, perhaps even death." De Vabres gave a brief lecture to his junior colleague: "Afraid we get an error of perspective, since we think so differently about Hitler's policies, the consequences of which we know today. Put ourselves in his [Schirach's] position at that time—suggest life to 20 years."

Biddle commented that Schirach "as Gauleiter . . . was seriously involved," but did not immediately state a penalty. Birkett suggested twenty years, but Lawrence then went for death on the extraordinary ground that Schirach had proposed that the Luftwaffe should bomb British towns to avenge the killing of Heydrich. Nikitchenko also proposed death. De Vabres then declared for twenty years. Biddle's notes accurately state that the decision was made for twenty years' imprisonment, but do not name the voting individuals, who must have comprised de Vabres and two others, undoubtedly Biddle and Lawrence.

Alfred Jodl, during his consideration on September 10, was voted by Lawrence, Biddle, and Nikitchenko to be hanged. But Falco and de Vabres were opposed, and a further discussion was called on September 12. However, the session was occupied entirely with the question of whether Keitel and Jodl should be shot or hanged. The French wanted to shoot both, Biddle wanted to hang Keitel and shoot Jodl, and the Russians and Birkett voted to hang both. Biddle finally agreed to hang both and, in conformity with all the other capital sentences, that was Jodl's fate.

At the very end of the Tribunal's last opinion session, on September 26, the judges once more discussed their decisions on Frick, Seyss-Inquart, and Doenitz. Biddle's notes do not reveal the nature of the discussion, other than that the Tribunal's written opinions in those cases were reviewed. Biddle rather carelessly stated that "since dinner is approaching," there were no suggestions on the first two defendants and "almost none" on Doenitz.

And so ended Biddle's notes. They were not, of course, written primarily for the benefit of posterity, but for Biddle's own better recollection as the days and decisions went by. The notes are, I believe, more revealing about the members as judges than any other surviving records, but they fall far short of setting forth the nature of the final opinion itself since they are primarily directed to the votes on convictions and penalties.

The opinion and judgment were the end of the Tribunal's responsibilities and will now be examined.

# Chapter 21

# JUDGMENT: LAW, CRIME, AND PUNISHMENT

Although Robert Jackson had been the central figure in the creation of the Nuremberg trials, in mid-September 1946 he was in Washington, drowned in the work of the United States Supreme Court and unsure whether or not he should return to Nuremberg to be present at the Tribunal's judgment on the charges against the defendants. In Washington, Jackson had piles of important work to do, while at Nuremberg he would have nothing to do but to sit, listen, and be seen. But there were other factors, discussed in his letter to Tom Dodd (in charge of the American prosecution staff in Jackson's absence), which Jackson sent on September 13, 1946:

> If you get any confidential dope that things are likely to go wrong on decision day, or that any particular necessity for my being present exists, I would appreciate your letting me know. It has occurred to me if there is ever to be a demonstration by the defendants it would occur at the time of sentencing. I do not know whether sentences will provoke the defendants or the prosecution.° If I were managing the court on that day, I think I would not have them all [i.e., the defendants] present when the individual sentences are pronounced. . . .
>
> I mentioned this matter at one time to Judge Parker, and I think to Francis Biddle. I do not know whether they have given any consideration to it and maybe it will seem overcautious to you. The world's eye will be focussed on the courtroom on that day and if these defendants should burst out in angry demonstrations, that will be the thing that will get the newspaper play.

°This probably sarcastic sentence was a good indication that Jackson had little faith that the judgment would conform to his own ideas of what it should contain.

Still indecisive, Jackson sent his son Bill to Nuremberg to enquire and report. On September 17, the day the Tribunal announced the postponement of the judgment until September 30, Bill sent his father a four-page single-spaced report on his informational gleanings. From Biddle he gathered only that "he hoped you would return," but "it was unlikely" that anything would "require your presence."

Judge Parker, however, who could and loved to talk longer than the next man, was full of thoughts, beginning with a "vociferous" denunciation of the Tribunal's decision to postpone the judgment. Curiously, he put the blame on Rowe and Fisher, who thought more time was needed to perfect the opinion and had "communicated their nervousness to Biddle, and as a result came the delay." It then developed, however, that Parker "had planned to make the principal speech at the Federal Bar Association meeting" on October 3 in Washington. The delay in Nuremberg required cancellation of Parker's address. Parker added, however, that no postponement would have been necessary "if everyone had worked as hard as he had," to which Bill attached "a nasty personal footnote . . . that Biddle spent three days of last week in Paris."

Parker then declared that the Tribunal had had to reject Jackson's "Krupp motion" in order to show that the Tribunal was not "a plaintiff's court." He also praised Lawrence as a presiding officer of "great grace and ability." Bill received such news silently, and his letter makes clear that these were not the views of the Jackson family. Much more disturbing to Bill was Parker's revelation that the Tribunal's decision on the indicted organizations would be treated so as to "avoid a wholesale condemnation," a position which Bill criticized as "anomalous" and based on "Wechsler's peculiar theories."

Finally, Bill succeeded in getting Parker to discuss the question of his father's return to Nuremberg for the judgment:

> He felt that you had an obligation to "see things through," and that the country felt the same and would expect you here even if you were a few days late in getting back on the bench. After all, he said, you started this thing, without you it never would have been, and you should be here to stand up in court and hear the result. . . . I do not hesitate to say that what he [also] had in mind was a fear that there would be a school, fed perhaps by your vengeful brethren, that you had run away. Perhaps implicit in this feeling was his [Parker's] expectation that the verdict on the organizations would not be what we of the prosecution had demanded.

Though differently put and less definite, Bill's own advice was to the same purpose: "I am not now firmly convinced that you ought to drop everything and come over, but I go to the extent that it would be a good thing if you did. . . . So I have changed my former view that you should come only for reasons of the case, to my present feeling that you should come because of yourself."

At the time I knew nothing of these uncertainties. Had I known, surely I would have thought it virtually unbelievable that Jackson might voluntarily absent himself from the Tribunal's final and decisive acts and the declaration of the defendants' fates. Such absence would have been an insult to the Tribunal, to Jackson's colleagues and subordinates, and to the entire legal and political fabric of which Jackson had been the master builder.

The Justice took the advice from Nuremberg, and on September 24 *The Stars and Stripes* reported that "Jackson returns to Nuremberg trials." Things were moving rapidly toward the climax. The newspaper also reported:

> The Control Council approved final plans for handling the Nazi war guilt criminals, including "strictly private executions" for those condemned to death, and imprisonment in Berlin for those sentenced to prison terms.
>
> News photographers, newsreel camera men and general public will be barred from the execution. Only official photographs will be taken.

The Control Council would be taking over the Nuremberg reins as soon as the Tribunal had rendered judgment.

The last few days before judgment were fraught with demands, last-ditch efforts, events mostly sad, and everywhere the shadow of death. In Berlin a Soviet-backed newspaper demanded "death for all Nuremberg defendants." Dr. von der Lippe described the spirit of the defendants as "very depressed." *The Stars and Stripes* published a dreadful bouquet of news: "Czechoslovakia sends 2,600,000 Germans *home.*° Berliners use Tiergarten as potato patch. Vienna rats equal population." From Berlin came personal news for the defendants:

> The Allied Control Council has ordered that any of the defendants sentenced to death by the International Military Tribunal shall be executed on the fifteenth day after the pronouncement of sentence in open court. Executions will be carried out without publicity by hanging or the guillotine. Defendants will be given four days to appeal the sentence to the Control Council.

---

°I.e., Sudetenland Germans deported to Germany.

Even though the public could not, as in days of yore, see the hangings, people came from far and wide to see and hear the judgment. As Bill Jackson put it: "More damn straphangers to get seats for Judgment Day, as it is called. . . . Biddle has asked the Kirks, Dodd has asked the Hornbecks and about 8 generals, and how the hell it will work out I have no idea."

## 2

The next morning, September 30, elaborate security measures and inexperienced guards produced a turbulent crush at the single open entrance at the Palace of Justice. Von der Lippe complained that within the building people could hardly move; some of the military police were excitable, and Rebecca West heard a shout at one of the judges: "And how the hell did you get in here?" Colonel Andrus was at his most absurd, ordering ladies not to cross their ankles and telling his guards to wake up elderly gentlemen dozing in the heat and boredom.

Jackson had not only returned, but had brought with him several former staff members who had gone home many months earlier, including Storey and, to my surprise, Francis Shea. Jackson and Dodd headed the American prosecution table, and the others included General Gill and myself, Albrecht and Amen, Whitney Harris and Bob Kempner, Drexel Sprecher, Bill Jackson, and a few others. I was seated behind Jackson, with an excellent view of the proceedings.

It had previously been announced that the reading would require two days. In fact, the judgment consisted of four principal parts: description of the rise of Nazism and the evidence against the defendants took the morning and part of the afternoon of September 30; the charges against the organizations took the rest of that afternoon; the decisions on the guilt or innocence of the individual defendants took the morning of October 1; the penalties to be inflicted on the guilty defendants were announced that afternoon.

The judges took their seats, and Lord Lawrence stated: "The judgment of the International Military Tribunal will now be read. I shall not read the title and the formal parts." Lawrence himself began the reading, and the task was thereafter passed to the other judges at intervals of about three-quarters of an hour.

The text began with short descriptions of the London Charter and the Indictment, together with statistical data of such things as the number of Tribunal open sittings (453) and witnesses heard (thirty-three for the prosecution, sixty-one for the defendants). The text, however, soon turned to an account of the origin (1919) and development of the Nazi Party, Hitler's acquisition of the Chancellorship (1933), the Nazis' seizure of virtually all governmental power during the next two years, and the course of rearmament, leading up to the initial exercise of military power in 1938.

The events so described were, of course, well known to Tribunal, prosecutors, and defendants alike and, indeed, generally familiar to the reading public. These included actions and episodes, such as the establishment of the dictatorship, the Roehm purge, concentration camps, persecution of the Jews, all of which had been widely criticized. There are some overtones of disapproval in these early parts of the judgment, which mentions a number of the defendants—Goering, Ribbentrop, Funk, Schacht, Raeder, Papen, Schirach, Neurath, and Gustav Krupp— who played parts in these events. But on the whole the Tribunal's presentation was matter-of-fact, and there was no effort to attach international crime to the defendants.

But the atmosphere changed abruptly when the judges reached the section entitled "The Common Plan or Conspiracy and Aggressive War," referring explicitly to Counts One and Two of the Indictment. The text stated:

> The charges in the Indictment that the defendants planned and waged aggressive war are charges of the utmost gravity. War is essentially an evil thing. Its consequences are not confined to the belligerent states alone, but affect the whole world.
>
> To initiate a war of aggression, therefore, is not only an international crime, it is the supreme international crime, differing only from other war crimes in that it contains within itself the accumulated evil of the whole.
>
> The first acts of aggression referred to in the Indictment are the seizure of Austria and Czechoslovakia; and the first war of aggression charged in the Indictment is the war against Poland begun on 1 September 1939.

Here there was unnecessary confusion. It was erroneous to speak of "other war crimes" when the Charter had explicitly separated "crimes against peace" (Article 6(a)) from "war crimes" (Article 6(b)). It was erroneous to state that "acts of aggression" (i.e., Article 6(a)) differed from "other war crimes" (Article 6(b)) only in its greater evil, when, in fact, "crimes against peace" can be committed without committing "war crimes" and vice versa.

If those errors are harmless, that cannot be said of the Tribunal's differentiating the "seizures" of Austria and Czechoslovakia from the "aggression" against Poland by calling the first two "acts of aggression" and the third "war of aggression." That there was "war" only in the case of Poland is of course clear. But what was the legal effect of the difference? In the Charter, Article 6(a) as well as 6(b) speak only of "war." Did that mean that the Austrian and Czechoslovakian "acts" were not covered by the Charter? The Tribunal did not here confront the question.

To establish the intention of Hitler and the defendants to prepare and plan to wage aggressive war, the Tribunal relied primarily on Hitler's book *Mein Kampf* and on his four meetings with his principal military and diplomatic subordinates, held on November 5, 1937, May 23, 1939, August 22, 1939, and November 23, 1939. These documents had been read and discussed repeatedly during the trial, and their inclusion in the opinion, as well as the Tribunal's discussion of the defendants' negative arguments, came as no surprise.

The judges next turned to an important part of their task: analysis of the several countries named in Counts One and Two of the Indictment as having been militarily conquered or otherwise attacked by Germany to determine whether or not, in each case, there had been violation of Article 6(a) or 6(b) of the Charter. Proceeding in chronological order, the Tribunal again encountered Austria and Czechoslovakia and thus the legal issue of nonwar annexations or occupations.

The Tribunal's opinion traced the events leading up to the German annexation of Austria in March 1938, stressing the prior German promises to respect Austrian independence and the activities of Hitler, Goering, and Seyss-Inquart in bringing about the Anschluss. The text referred to Germany's action as an "aggressive step" and met the defendants' arguments that Anschluss was favored by many Austrians, as follows:

> These matters, even if true, are really immaterial, for the facts plainly prove that the methods employed to achieve the objective were those of an aggressor. The ultimate factor was the armed might of Germany ready to be used if any resistance was encountered.

In all probability a majority of Austrians preferred to remain independent,\* but there was real division of opinion, and this circumstance, pace the Tribunal, was by no means "immaterial." If all Austrians had been filled with patriotic zeal, Hitler might not have found Anschluss so easy. And once again the Tribunal had not squarely confronted the legal issue. Under the Charter, "aggression" without "war" was not a crime, as recognized in Count Two of the Indictment, which does not accuse either Austria or Czechoslovakia and begins its list of "wars" with Poland. However, the events leading to the Anschluss were certainly evidence of a conspiracy to wage aggressive war at a later date, and the Tribunal's opinion would have been much clearer if these factors had been noticed.

Hitler made no prior preparations for the use of military force against Austria, and the decision in March to force the Anschluss was the result of what Hitler rightly saw as propitious circumstances. He was all but certain

---

\*Schuschnigg's effort to conduct a plebiscite was stopped by Hitler's threats.

that there would be no military resistance by the Austrians, and the German entry was more of a parade than a forceful invasion.

But the seizure of Czechoslovakia was quite a different story. Shortly after the Anschluss, Jodl was revising the existing plans for an invasion of Czechoslovakia so as to take account of "the changed strategic position because of the annexation of Austria." On May 20, 1938, Hitler secretly told his military subordinates that it was "his unalterable decision to smash Czechoslovakia by military action in the near future." The Tribunal's text recounted many of these preparations and the plans to be ready for an invasion of Czechoslovakia by October 1, 1938. The Munich settlement among Britain, France, Italy, and Germany ended the immediate prospect of war by ceding the Sudetenland to Germany, which effectively rendered Czechoslovakia undefendable. On March 14, 1939, Hitler and Goering told Czech President Hácha that Bohemia and Moravia must be put under German authority, that German troops were already on the march, and that any objections would result in the destruction of Prague by the Luftwaffe.

The last sentence of the Tribunal's discussion of these matters was "on 15 March German troops occupied Bohemia and Moravia and on 16 March the German decree was issued incorporating Bohemia and Moravia into the Reich as a protectorate, and this decree was signed by the defendants Von Ribbentrop and Frick."

To my surprise, the judges had made no effort to state the legal significance of the seizure of Bohemia and Moravia.° Obviously the German actions vis-à-vis Czechoslovakia were, like those in Austria, evidence of conspiracy to wage aggressive war in the future. But could a case be made that the seizure of Bohemia and Movaria was a violation of Article 6(a) even though "war" in the usual sense did not "break out"? Unlike the events in Austria, here the Germans without warning sent army and air forces in and over Bohemia and Moravia, with threats to flatten Prague if there was any resistance. With armed forces so menacing and superior that the leaders in Prague capitulated, could not this be called a "war" that brought immediate surrender? The Tribunal did not consider such an argument.

Next a longer section entitled "The Aggression Against Poland," in which there was little room for argument, was read. The Tribunal concluded:

> With the ever increasing evidence before him that [t]his intention would lead to war with Great Britain and France as well,† the

---

°Slovakia was left with its own government, but was put under German suzerainty.

†The Indictment in Count Two listed both Britain and France, between Poland and Denmark and Norway, among the aggressive wars. The Tribunal's judgment, however, contained no such direct accusation.

Tribunal is fully satisfied by the evidence that the war initiated by Germany against Poland on 1 September 1939 was most plainly an aggressive war, which was to develop in due course into a war which embraced almost the whole world, and resulted in the commission of countless crimes against the laws and customs of war, and against humanity.

The invasions of Denmark and Norway were bracketed together, and in both cases Germany had signed treaties of nonaggression on May 31, 1939. The two countries had been attacked by Germany less than a year later. As regards Denmark, the Tribunal stated: "No suggestion is made by the defendants that there was any plan by any belligerent, other than Germany, to occupy Denmark. No excuse for that aggression has been offered." The events leading up to the German invasion of Norway were accurately set forth, and the Tribunal concluded: "In the light of the available evidence it is impossible to accept the [defendants'] contention that the invasions of Denmark and Norway were defensive, and in the opinion of the Tribunal they were acts of aggressive war."

The Tribunal's reference to the defendants was, of course, to their contention that the German invasion of Norway was necessary to forestall plans similarly entertained by Britain and France, especially the former. Documents in support of such plans fell into German hands in France after the French surrender. The Tribunal did not attack the authenticity of the documents, but responded to the defendants' argument: "But these plans were not the cause of the German invasion of Norway. Norway was occupied by Germany to afford her bases from which a more effective attack on England and France might be made, pursuant to plans prepared long in advance of the Allied plans which are now relied on to support the argument of self-defense."

The Tribunal was correct in stating that the initial purpose of the German Navy's interest in Norway was to secure better bases for operations against Britain. But military plans often have multiple purposes, and it is unquestionable that the Germans also developed fears that Britain might seek Norwegian bases to cut off the flow of Swedish iron ore, much of which came to Germany by sea along the Norwegian west coast. Had Britain done so, it would be hard to argue that Germany could not rightfully seek to root out the British or prevent a British landing from succeeding.

It was to procure evidence of British plans that Dr. Siemers had requested the relevant documents from the Admiralty, and, as we have seen, the British refused to grant the request. The Tribunal's opinion made no mention of this refusal to give the defendant Raeder access to documents clearly relevant to his case as well as to the question of whether the invasion of Norway was an aggressive war.

In a very brief statement, the Tribunal read Hitler's repeated assurances to his military commanders that the occupation of the Low Countries was necessary for the war against Britain, that "declarations of neutrality must be ignored" and are "meaningless," and that the simultaneous neutrality assurances given to Holland and Belgium would not be honored. The Tribunal concluded:

> The invasion of Belgium, Holland, and Luxembourg was entirely without justification.
>
> It was carried out in pursuance of policies long considered and prepared, and was plainly an act of aggressive war. The resolve to invade was without any other consideration than the advancement of the aggressive policies of Germany.

The Tribunal also dealt summarily with Germany's conquests of Yugoslavia and Greece, invaded simultaneously on April 6, 1941. As portrayed in the Tribunal's opinion, both actions were the result of Mussolini's misguided invasion of Greece in October 1940, which pulled both Britain and Germany into the Balkans. Fearing the appearance of British troops in Greece to aid their hosts against the Italians, as early as mid-December Hitler laid plans to overrun the mainland of Greece the following spring. During the intervening months German troops were assembled in southern Romania and Bulgaria. On February 19, 1941, British forces arrived in Greece.

During these months the relations between Germany and Yugoslavia remained apparently equable, and on March 25, 1941, Yugoslavia joined the German-Italian-Japanese Tripartite Pact. But the very next day there was a political overturn in the Yugoslavian Government, and the new government repudiated the Pact. Hitler took umbrage and decided that Yugoslavia might be a poor neighbor when Germany carried out the planned invasion of Russia. Accordingly, he ordered that Yugoslavia and Greece be attacked simultaneously and without warning. In the Tribunal's opinion:

> It is clear from this narrative that aggressive war against Greece and Yugoslavia had long been in contemplation, certainly as early as August of 1939. The fact that Great Britain had come to the assistance of the Greeks, and might thereby be in a position to inflict great damage upon German interests was made the occasion for the occupation of both countries.

The account of the background and development of Hitler's decision to make war against the Soviet Union, in company with Finland, Rumania, and Hungary, was presented in the Tribunal's opinion in rather cursory form. The Tribunal's response to the defense and its own conclusions of law were even more curt:

> It was contended for the defendants that the attack upon the U.S.S.R. was justified because the Soviet Union was contemplating an attack upon Germany, and making preparations to that end. It is impossible to believe that this view was ever honestly entertained.
>
> The plans for the economic exploitation of the U.S.S.R., for the removal of masses of the population, for the murder of Commissars and political leaders, were all part of the carefully prepared scheme launched on 22 June without warning of any kind, and without the shadow of legal excuse. It was plain aggression.

The last country listed in the Indictment was the United States of America. The Tribunal described the relations between Germany and Japan and Ribbentrop's efforts to persuade the Japanese to attack Britain. Pursuant to the Tripartite Pact, its members were bound to come to each other's support if attacked by a nonmember country, but in the course of the German-Japanese discussions, both Hitler and Ribbentrop had deviated from their basic policy of avoiding warfare with the United States by telling Foreign Minister Mutsuoka that if Japan "became involved" in war with the United States, Germany would support Japan. Accordingly, four days after December 7, 1941, when Japan attacked the fleet and base at Pearl Harbor, Germany declared war on the United States. The Indictment declared this to be an aggressive attack and a crime against peace, and the Tribunal's opinion confirmed the charge.

It is beyond question that Germany declared and waged war against the United States, and legally the conviction of Germany's crime against peace is supportable. But to me it has a spurious air. During the first two years of the war, the attitude of the American Government toward Nazi Germany had been so unfriendly and its support for Britain so close to the line between neutrality and hostility that Germany and the United States each seemed to be marching toward war against the other. But this matter had no perceptible effect on the Tribunal's judgments.*

## 3

After brief mention of the legal importance of international peace treaties, the Hague Conventions, the Versailles Treaty, and the Kellogg-Briand Pact

---

*I have often wondered what the result would have been had Hitler not declared war on the United States at that time. Whether or not there was ever a declaration, I am sure that before long there would have been outright hostilities, but Hitler's decision certainly made it easier for the United States to declare war against Germany.

(the Treaty of Paris), the judges turned to an analysis of two important legal issues confronting them.

The Tribunal discussed first the issue which had been on virtually everyone's mind since the trial began and had already been argued and reargued by both prosecution and defense: Could perpetrating aggressive war be validly held against these defendants? The Charter declared this to be so, and the opinion repeated what the judges had already declared several times: that they were bound by the Charter, but "in view of the great importance of the questions of law involved . . . the Tribunal will express its view of the matter."

The answer, to no one's surprise, was affirmative. The court dealt first with the defense's argument that whatever might be the case under the Charter, the defendants had committed the acts in question years earlier, and since no such law was in existence at that time, they were protected by the principle against ex post facto laws. The court's opinion sought to negate this argument on the ground that the defendants "in defiance of treaties and assurances have attacked neighboring states without warning." All of the Nazi German attacks on other countries were commenced by these methods, long condemned as treacherous and prohibited in the Hague Conventions of 1899 and 1907. There was, therefore, no doubt of the criminality of the defendants' methods.

But this did not establish the criminality of aggressive wars, since they can be commenced with due warning and without violating treaties. To establish the criminality of aggressive wars no matter how begun, the judges relied primarily on the Pact of Paris and other pre–World War II international pronouncements declaring aggressive war to be an "international crime." The weakness of all these agreements is that neither the language of the Pact of Paris nor the phrase "international crime" necessarily applies to the actions of individuals.

The Tribunal's opinion sought to close this gap by pointing out that the Hague Conventions nowhere label violations of their rules as "criminal" or prescribe any penalties, and nevertheless have been enforced by punishments prescribed by courts-martial. Violations of the laws of war had been penally enforced for many years before the Hague Conventions were adopted, and their draftsmen left the imposition of penalties to the unwritten practices already followed. But the Tribunal's reliance on customary law was endangered by the fact that for centuries and at least until after World War I, customary law did not regard aggressive war as unlawful.

As far as I could see, the court's opinion brought no new arguments to the long-contested problem. But the treacherous nature of the German attacks was undoubtedly criminal so that punishments imposed under Counts One and Two, assuming sufficient evidence, were abundantly justified.

The judges then turned to conspiracy, the matter which Donnedieu de

Vabres had unsuccessfully endeavored to expunge and which Biddle had ultimately drafted. The main point of the court's opinion had to do with the fact that Count One of the Indictment provided that the charge of conspiracy could be applied to any of the three basic crimes stated in the Charter. Contrary to this feature of the Indictment and to the views of the prosecution, the court's opinion declared that conspiracy could be applicable only to crimes against peace and not to war crimes or crimes against humanity.

Originally, this reading had been proposed primarily to placate de Vabres, but the opinion showed that this was in any event the correct interpretation of the Charter. The availability of conspiracy was provided for only in Article 6(a) of the Charter, dealing with crimes against peace, and not in Articles 6(b) and 6(c). The paragraph following Article 6(c) referred to "conspiracy to commit any of the foregoing crimes," but the only "foregoing" conspiratorial crime remained conspiracy to commit crimes against peace.

The discussion of conspiracy in the Tribunal's opinion also took account of the distaste for the conspiracy principle felt by Continental lawyers (such as de Vabres) by refusing the broad range of conspiracy advocated by the prosecution: "But in the opinion of the Tribunal the conspiracy must be clearly outlined in the criminal purpose. It must not be too far removed from the time of decision and action."

During their private discussions, the judges had difficulty in determining when the conspiracy began and boggled at the view of some of the prosecution (notably Fyfe) that it began with the creation of the Nazi Party in 1919. Now the Tribunal's opinion declared that "it is not necessary to decide whether a single master conspiracy between the defendants has been established by the prosecution. . . . That plans were made to wage war, as early as 5 November 1937, and probably before that, is apparent. . . . But the evidence establishes with certainty the existence of many separate plans rather than a single conspiracy embracing them all."

At this point the opinion shifted from problems of the crimes against peace to war crimes and crimes against humanity. This was the last extensive description of evidentiary material in the opinion. In what seemed to me a very well written part of the opinion, the judges described evidence concerning murder and ill treatment of prisoners of war, murder and ill treatment of civilian populations, pillage of public and private property, slave labor policy, and persecution of Jews.

Following this evidence, the Tribunal dealt with three related legal issues. The first of the defense arguments was that some of the countries involved in these wars were not signatories of the Hague Conventions and that therefore the Germans were not bound by those Conventions vis-à-vis the nonsigners. The Tribunal brushed aside this contention on the ground that "by 1939 those rules laid down in the Conventions were recognized by all civilized nations, and were regarded as being declaratory of the laws and customs of wars which are referred to in Article 6(b) of the Charter."

The second contention was that since the laws of war apply only to hostilities between belligerents, they were not applicable to countries which "Germany had completely subjugated and incorporated into the German Reich." In reply, the opinion stated:

> The doctrine was never considered to be applicable so long as there was an army in the field attempting to restore the occupied countries to their true owners, and in this case, therefore, the doctrine could not apply to any territories occupied after 1 September 1939. As to the War Crimes committed in Bohemia and Moravia, it is a sufficient answer that these territories were never added to the Reich, but a mere protectorate was established over them.

This wording by implication recognized that the defense's position would be applicable to Austria, which had been annexed into the German Reich.

The third and most important issue related to crimes against humanity, and the prosecution's contention that Nazi atrocities in Germany (especially those against Jews) prior to the war with Poland would be punishable under the Charter's definition of crimes against humanity in Article 6(c). The Tribunal, however, read Article 6 very strictly so that the atrocities listed in 6(c) were punishable only if perpetrated "in connection with any crime within the jurisdiction of the Tribunal." That meant, of course, clauses 6(a) and 6(b), but the latter's coverage began on September 1, 1939. Prior to that date, crimes against humanity "were punishable only" in connection with crimes against peace in clause 6(a). In the Tribunal's opinion, the prewar Nazi atrocities "had not been satisfactorily proven that they were done in execution of, or in connection with" the provisions of Article 6(a) and therefore: "The Tribunal cannot make a general declaration that the acts before 1939 were Crimes Against Humanity within the meaning of the Charter."

The Tribunal's interpretation of Article 6 was legally accurate, and thus, as a practical matter, the Tribunal was deemed to have no jurisdiction over the Nazi atrocities in Germany prior to the war against Poland.

## 4

By this time the afternoon session was about half over, and the first day's remaining time was devoted to the accused organizations. The Tribunal's opinion closely followed the evidence taken in August and the decisions reached at the Tribunal's closed meetings in September.

Before dealing with the individual organizations, the judges' opinion stressed their concern over the death sentences authorized by the Control Council in Law No. 10 and stated that they should "make such declaration of criminality so far as possible in a manner to insure that innocent people will not be punished." And as had been planned, the Tribunal, over Nikitchenko's strong objection, had some recommendations for the Control Council: uniformity of treatment of members of convicted organizations, as among the four zones, and limitations on punishments imposed under Control Council Law No. 10 so as not to exceed the punishments imposed under the American Zone's Denazification Law.

The Tribunal took first the Leadership Corps and, after an ample description of its structure, aims, and activities, found the organization to have been guilty of violations of the laws of war by Germanizing citizens of German-occupied countries, persecuting the Jews of Europe, participating in the slave labor program, and mistreating prisoners of war. The Tribunal excluded from its decision leaders below the level of *Ortsgruppenleiter*, staff members other than office chiefs, and all who had left the Leadership Corps before September 1, 1939. Those within criminal groups would be personally incriminated if they remained in the organization "with knowledge that it was being used for the commission of acts declared criminal by Article 6 of the Charter, or were personally implicated as members . . . in the commission of crimes."

The Tribunal dealt next with members of the "Gestapo and SD," a linkage which has already been shown to breed confusion. Considering the evidence received at that time, I had concluded that the prosecution had not proven that the SD, limited to its own offices (i.e., Amts III, V, and VII), had substantially violated the laws of war. The Tribunal read the record differently and held that the SD had been "involved in the administration of the Slave Labor Program." However, members of the SD, Gestapo, and other units frequently were also SS members or wore SS uniforms even if they were not SS members. The volume of Gestapo atrocities was so great that the Tribunal had ample basis for declaring it a criminal organization, but it appeared impossible to thread the administrative maze with any assurance of accuracy. The Tribunal exempted from liability numerous clerical, routine, and honorary members of these organizations.

The SS itself was the last and largest of the convicted organizations. With its Waffen-SS army of over half a million soldiers and twelve main offices including police, concentration camps, and odd but frightful enterprises such as Ahnenerbe, the Tribunal had plenty to write about the SS's "structure and component parts" and a long list of "criminal activities." With such a range of atrocities, including the as yet unnamed Holocaust, a declaration of criminality for the SS was a foregone conclusion.

A large number of men had been drafted into the Waffen-SS and as they had not come voluntarily were excepted from the criminal group.

Otherwise, in all but a few special cases, the group included "all persons who had been officially accepted as members of the SS," including the Waffen-SS.

Of the three charged organizations that were not held to be criminal, the only large one was the SA. Except for Nikitchenko, who argued that all six of the organizations should be held criminal, there was no support for such a charge among the other judges. As the Tribunal put the matter:

> Until the purge beginning on 30 June 1934, the SA was a group composed in large part of ruffians and bullies who participated in the Nazi outrages of that period. It has not been shown, however, that these atrocities were part of a specific plan to wage aggressive war, and the Tribunal therefore cannot hold that these activities were criminal under the Charter. After the purge, the SA was reduced to the status of a group of unimportant Nazi hangers-on. Although in specific instances some units of the SA were used for the commission of War Crimes and Crimes against Humanity, it cannot be said that the members generally participated in or even knew of the criminal acts. For these reasons the Tribunal does not declare the SA to be a criminal organization within the meaning of Article 9 of the Charter.

The Reich Cabinet withered even more than the SA. Cabinet government, although dominated by Hitler, lasted for several years but, as the Tribunal found, after 1937 the Reich Cabinet never "acted as a group or organization." The Tribunal noted that none of Hitler's conferences on aggressive war plans took place in the presence of the Cabinet.

The Tribunal found, therefore, that there was no basis for declaring the Reich Cabinet a criminal organization. Additionally, there was no need for such action since, of the forty-eight members of the Cabinet, eight were dead and seventeen were already on trial as individuals before the Tribunal. There remained only twenty-three others available for trial, and the Tribunal concluded that "Any others who are guilty should also be brought to trial; but nothing would be accomplished to expedite or facilitate their trials by declaring the Reich Cabinet to be a criminal organization."

Last came the General Staff and High Command with Lord Lawrence reading the opinion. He stated immediately that "The Tribunal believes that no declaration of criminality should be made with respect to the General Staff and High Command." He then gave the same reason that had just been applied to the Reich Cabinet: "The number of persons charged, while larger than that of the Reich Cabinet, is still so small that individual trials of these officers would accomplish the purpose here sought better than a declaration such as requested." He then added, however: "But a more compelling reason is that in the opinion of the Tribunal the General Staff and High Command is neither an organization nor a group within the meaning of these terms as used in Article 9 of the Charter."

The Tribunal's opinion accurately stated the Indictment's description of the alleged "group" and then gave the reason why it could not be regarded as a "group" within the meaning of the Charter. The point was essentially the same as my private conclusion that the Indictment failed to describe an entity like "*the* SS" or "*the* Navy." As the Tribunal put it more clearly:

> For this alleged criminal organization has one characteristic, a controlling one, which sharply distinguishes it from the other five indicted. When an individual becomes a member of the SS for instance, he did so . . . certainly with the knowledge that he was joining something. In the case of the General Staff and High Command, however, he could not know he was in a group or organization for such organization did not exist except in the charge of the Indictment. He knew only that he had achieved a certain high rank in one of the three services, and could not be conscious of the fact that he was becoming a member of anything so tangible as a "group," as that word is commonly used.

I thought that this was correct, and so far as future military trials were concerned, I could see nothing in the Tribunal's conclusion that would obstruct trials of individual generals and admirals, or lesser officers, criminally implicated by the evidence. What had worried me was that the Tribunal's opinion might be misconceived, sincerely or mischievously, as an acquittal of the German military establishment.

This fear was immediately quieted, however, when I heard Lawrence continue to speak. In part, he said:

> Although the Tribunal is of the opinion that the term "group" in Article 9 must mean something more than this collection of military officers, it has heard much evidence as to the participation of these officers in planning and waging aggressive war, and in committing war crimes and crimes against humanity. This evidence is, as to many of them, clear and convincing.
>
> They have been responsible in large measure for the miseries and suffering that have fallen on millions of men, women and children. They have been a disgrace to the honorable profession of arms. . . . Although they were not a group falling within the words of the Charter, they were certainly a ruthless military caste. . . .
>
> Many of these men have made a mockery of the soldier's oath of obedience to military orders. When it suits their defense they say they had to obey; when confronted with Hitler's brutal crimes . . . they say they disobeyed. The truth is that they actively participated in all these crimes, or sat silent or acquiescent, witnessing the commission

of crimes on a scale larger and more shocking than the world has ever had the misfortune to know. This must be said.

Where the facts warrant it, these men should be brought to trial so that those among them who are guilty of these crimes should not escape punishment.

I could hardly have been better satisfied than with the Tribunal's denunciation and its call for justice against those whose crimes were evidentially proven.

The day's proceedings were finished, and Lawrence adjourned the Tribunal until the morrow. The day had been a heavy one for everybody, especially for the defendants. During the afternoon, Hess had fallen into a fit; Rebecca West wrote:

> On Monday afternoon the darkened mind of Hess passed some dreadful crisis. . . . All humanity left his face; it became an agonized muddle. He began to sway backward and forward on his seat with the regularity of a pendulum. His head swung forward almost to his knees. His skin became blue. . . . He was taken away soon, but it was as if the door of hell had swung ajar. It was apparent now, as on so many occasions during the trial, that the judges found it repulsive to try a man in such a state; but the majority of the psychiatrists consulted by the court had pronounced him sane.

At the end of the day, when the Tribunal refused to criminalize three of the organizations, some of the defendants' spirits rose. Von der Lippe pronounced this "a great success for the defense"—and indeed it might have been if the convicted organizations had ever been handled the way Bernays had planned. But von der Lippe found Lawrence's conclusion "a very bitter ending" to what he wrongly called "the acquittal." Von der Lippe had reason, however, to claim that "The enemy No. 1, the collective guilt idea embodied in the Indictment, is practically eliminated!" As Bill Jackson had feared, the prosecution's hopes had been dashed. Personally, I found that a very good thing.

## 5

October 1, 1946, was the real Judgment Day, which the defense, and not a few judges and prosecutors, had been dreading. In the morning, the Tribunal would announce, for each defendant, which, if any, of the four counts he had criminally violated. In the afternoon, the Tribunal would announce, for each convicted defendant, the penalty to be imposed.

During the morning, the convictions and acquittals of the defendants were read by the four voting judges, beginning with Lawrence. The individual decisions were uniformly constructed: an initial paragraph descriptive of the individual in question, then two sections covering crimes against peace and war crimes and crimes against humanity, in that order, and finally a single sentence entitled "Conclusion." The Tribunal reached its decisions primarily by the breadth and evidentiary strength of the Indictment's violations, modified at times by extraneous factors. The reading of twenty-one consecutive decisions was tiring and for the staff somewhat dull, but the decisions were not lacking in surprises.

Not, however, in the case of Hermann Goering. Lawrence read of his aggressive plans and actions from Austria to Russia and his war crimes from slave labor to extermination of the Jews. Some of his prewar activities were not crimes under the Charter, but they furnished part of the base for the conspiracy charge. The Tribunal found Goering guilty on all four counts; the concluding passage, for which Jim Rowe was part author, read:

> There is nothing to be said in mitigation. For Göring was often, indeed almost always, the moving force, second only to his leader. He was the leading war aggressor, both as political and as military leader; he was the director of the slave labor program and the creator of the oppressive program against the Jews and other races at home and abroad. All of these crimes he has frankly admitted. On some specific cases there may be a conflict of testimony, but in terms of the broad outline, his own admissions are more than sufficiently wide to be conclusive of his guilt. His guilt is unique in its enormity. The record discloses no excuses for this man.

While Goering's case was read, Hess had been scribbling, for the Lord knows what purpose. At the end of his own case, Goering told Hess that he had been convicted on Counts One and Two. Hess showed no interest.

There was little need for prolonged discussion of the evidence against this benighted man. Lawrence pointed to his close personal connections with Hitler, his involvement in the occupation of Bohemia and Moravia and the conquest of Poland, and his administrative support for rearmament and for Hitler's later conquests of Norway, the Low Countries, and France. All this was sufficient to warrant convictions on Counts One and Two.

The Tribunal had confirmed Hess's status as a defendant on the basis of psychiatric assurances and Hess's own demand to be tried with the others. But since then the judges had for nine months seen Hess and his gyrations in the dock. Whether sane or insane, he had thoroughly convinced me of his inability to defend himself adequately. Seidl, Hess's lawyer, had requested a new medical examination, but the Tribunal was adamant. Speaking of Seidl's motions, the Tribunal wrote:

These the Tribunal denied, after having had a report from the prison psychologist.° That Hess acts in an abnormal manner, suffers from loss of memory, and has mental deterioration during the Trial, may be true. But there is nothing to show that he does not realize the nature of the charges against him, or is incapable of defending himself. He was ably represented at the Trial by counsel appointed for that purpose by the Tribunal. There is no suggestion that he was not completely sane when the acts charged against him were committed.

In fact, Seidl's representation of Hess had seemed to me routine at best, and anyhow skilled lawyering is no substitute for a defendant's own capacities. Nor does sanity in the past eliminate the question of the defendant's incapacity when charged.

Von der Lippe called Hess's case "A thicket through which man only sees darkly." I cannot help suspecting that the Russians' implacable enmity toward Hess played a part, as it certainly did in much later years, when the other nations wanted to commute his life sentence.

The Tribunal's decisions on the next six defendants require little comment. Ribbentrop's diplomatic actions covered not only aggressions but also war crimes, especially in the deportation of French and Hungarian Jews. He was convicted on all four counts, as was also Keitel, whom the Tribunal declared to have, like Goering, "nothing in mitigation." Kaltenbrunner had succeeded Heydrich as chief of Himmler's RSHA, the entity housing the Gestapo, the Einsatzgruppen, and other prolific sources of atrocities. The Tribunal rejected Kaltenbrunner's claim that by private agreement with Himmler he would be responsible only for foreign intelligence, and found him guilty of Counts Three and Four.

General Nikitchenko took over the reading and dealt with Rosenberg, whose involvement in aggressive war concerned Norway and the Soviet Union, primarily the latter. As Reich Minister for the Occupied Eastern Territories, Rosenberg had knowledge of and responsibility for the atrocious policies that Hitler and Himmler laid upon the people of the German-occupied East. Despite Rosenberg's efforts to lay the blame on his superiors, the Tribunal found him guilty on all four counts.

Francis Biddle read the decision on Hans Frank, who had been indicted on Counts One, Three, and Four, but acquitted on the first count for lack of sufficient connection with the conspiracy. On war crimes, his situation was not unlike Rosenberg's; he had been Governor-General of German-occupied Poland and was pleading lack of responsibility for the full-scale atrocities against Jews and deportation of Poles. The Tribunal concluded that Frank had been a "willing and knowing participant" in the atrocities and found him guilty under Counts Three and Four.

°Presumably Gilbert.

De Vabres read the opinion on Frick, describing him as "the chief nazi administrative specialist and bureaucrat." He called attention to Frick's broad administrative authority, involving a host of violations of the Charter. The Tribunal convicted this colorless, competent, and ruthless man of violating Counts Two, Three, and Four of the Indictment.

Lord Lawrence read the case against Streicher, indicted on Counts One and Four. He immediately dismissed Count One, for lack of evidence implicating Streicher in any conspiracy to wage aggressive war. Turning to Count Four, Lawrence initially read much evidence dealing with Streicher's anti-Semitic activities prior to the outbreak of World War II, which, as the Tribunal itself had ruled, could not be treated as crimes against humanity.

Accordingly, the entire basis of Streicher's guilt rested on his actions from September 1, 1939, until the end of the war, which Lawrence discussed in the later part of the opinion. The evidence unquestionably proved that Streicher continued to utilize *Der Stuermer* as a vehicle to stir up hatred against Jews and applauded their extermination. The Tribunal concluded:

> Streicher's incitement to murder and extermination at the time when Jews in the East were being killed under the most horrible conditions clearly constitutes persecution on political and racial grounds in connection with War Crimes, as defined by the Charter, and constitutes a Crime against Humanity.

Thus Streicher was convicted under Count Four. That seemed to me legally defensible, but I cannot justify the Tribunal's failure to mention other facts, such as that from 1940 until the end of the war, Streicher was living on his farm in forced seclusion and his connection with *Der Stuermer* was his only "outside" source of information, that the paper's circulation had dwindled to about 15,000 copies during most of the war, that he had no connection with Himmler or any contact with those in Poland or the Soviet Union who were perpetrating the atrocities, and that publication of a newspaper, however maddening and unconscionable it may be, should be touched with criminal accusations only with the greatest caution.

Funk's case was read by Nikitchenko, but it is hard to believe that he agreed with its conclusions. Funk was charged under all four counts, and the evidence against him was voluminous, serious, and largely uncontested. As Minister of Economics and Plenipotentiary General for War Economy, he was involved in the economic and financial planning of aggressive wars against both Poland and the Soviet Union.

The Tribunal said of that: "Funk was not one of the leading figures in organizing the Nazi plans for aggressive war. His activity in the economic sphere was under the supervision of Goering. . . . He did, however, participate in the economic preparation for certain of the aggressive wars . . . but his guilt can be adequately dealt with under Count Two of the Indictment."

Members of a conspiracy do not all have to be top leaders, and the evidence was plainly sufficient to warrant a conviction under Count One as well. Why was this not done? Presumably by "dealt with" the Tribunal meant its decision on the penalty, and on that basis Goering and the other defendants convicted on Counts One and Two could also have been "adequately dealt with" under Count Two without Count One. The Tribunal's statement was very odd.

As for Counts Three and Four, both as President of the Reichsbank and a member of the Central Planning Board, Funk was involved in the slave labor program; he engaged in unlawful seizures of properties in France and in the East; the Reichsbank became the custodian of money and valuables seized from prisoners in concentration camps. The Tribunal found Funk guilty on Counts Two, Three, and Four, but the last paragraph of the opinion stated:

> In spite of the fact that he occupied important official positions, Funk was never a dominant figure in the various programs in which he participated. This is a mitigating fact of which the Tribunal takes notice.

The last sentence was taken by all as a signal that Funk would not be hanged.* But I have never understood why Funk's failure to reach the top rung of the Nazi hierarchy should be regarded as a "mitigation." After all, Funk occupied all the positions Schacht had held and more as well. This was certainly not "mitigation" in the sense of Speer's and Seyss-Inquart's risk of life and limb to stem the war's final torrent of death and destruction. Funk's deliverance from the hangman can only be explained by his cringing personality, suggesting that he was wholly incapable of doing physical harm.

Next came Schacht's case, read by Biddle, who had initially wanted to send Schacht to prison for the rest of his life. The redoubtable banker was charged only on Counts One and Two, and the Tribunal's opinion described at length Schacht's governmental career and his prominent role in German rearmament. "But rearmament of itself is not criminal under the Charter," Biddle read. "To be a Crime against Peace under Article 6 of the Charter it must be shown that Schacht carried out this rearmament as part of the Nazi plans to wage aggressive wars."

---

*On September 10, when the Tribunal voted on Funk, Lawrence and Nikitchenko voted for hanging, while Biddle and de Vabres were uncertain. Biddle's notes do not cover the final vote, but in all probability Lawrence joined with Biddle and de Vabres to make three for life imprisonment.

Schacht had remained President of the Reichsbank until he was dismissed by Hitler on January 19, 1939; he had thus participated in some phases of the Austrian and Sudeten annexations, in the course of which he had publicly extolled Hitler's successes. The opinion then read: "The case against Schacht therefore depends on the inference that Schacht did in fact know of the Nazi aggressive plans."

I knew that Jackson had set his heart on convicting Schacht, and it was obvious that Biddle was equally aware of this. He turned in his chair and looked squarely at Jackson as he read the last two sentences:

> On this all-important question evidence has been given for the Prosecution, and a considerable volume of evidence for the Defense. The Tribunal has considered the whole of this evidence with great care, and comes to the conclusion that this necessary evidence has not been established beyond a reasonable doubt.
>
> The Tribunal finds that Schacht is not guilty on this Indictment, and directs that he shall be discharged by the Marshal, when the Tribunal presently adjourns.

Up to this point the audience had heard ten of the defendants convicted of charges in the Indictment, and the sudden turn to an acquittal raised a rustle of surprised motion and whispering. Schacht retained his ramrod position, with his eyes fastened on the judges—vindicated, as he had always predicted, and unaware that he had escaped by the skin of his teeth.

## 6

Half of the morning's ordeal was over, and the onlookers shifted their gaze to the dock's upper tier. De Vabres was reading the case of Admiral Doenitz, but the words were chiefly those of Francis Biddle. Outvoted on his arguments for acquittal, Biddle had then pleaded for an opinion that would not rest the conviction on a charge of unlawful submarine warfare so that the Tribunal would not be in the position of penalizing Doenitz and Raeder for using the same tactics that Nimitz (as well as the British) had employed. Unless this was done, Biddle was prepared to issue a public dissent, and to avoid this, Biddle agreed to a ten-year incarceration for Doenitz and the Tribunal decided that Biddle himself should write the opinion.

Doenitz was charged on Counts One, Two, and Three. The Tribunal's opinion described the course of German submarine warfare at considerable length and concluded:

> In view of all of the facts proved, and in particular of an order of the British Admiralty announced on 8 May 1940, according to

which all vessels should be sunk at night in the Skagerrak, and the answer to interrogations by Admiral Nimitz that unrestricted submarine warfare was carried out in the Pacific Ocean by the United States from the first day that nation entered the war, the sentence of Dönitz is not assessed on the ground of his breaches of the international law of submarine warfare.

That decision satisfied Biddle on the submarine dispute under Count One, but the opinion contained other accusations under Counts Two and Three. Doenitz had permitted the Commando Order "to remain in full force," although no instance of his responsibility for its use was shown; Hitler in 1945 requested opinions from Doenitz and Jodl on the wisdom of denouncing the Geneva Convention, and Doenitz replied: "It would be better to carry out the measures considered necessary without warning, and at all costs to save face with the outerworld." Since the Convention was not denounced and no specific violations were ordered, this was at worst a callous remark. It had been proved that Doenitz had treated British prisoners of war in strict accordance with the Geneva Convention, and the opinion stated that the Tribunal "takes this fact into consideration and regards it as a mitigating factor." Nevertheless Doenitz was convicted on Count Three, obviously on very thin footing.

As for Count One, Doenitz was found not guilty because

> Although Doenitz built and trained the German U-boat arm, the evidence does not show he was privy to the conspiracy to wage aggressive wars or that he prepared and initiated such wars. He was a line officer performing strictly tactical duties. He was not present at the important conferences when plans for aggressive war were announced, and there was no evidence he was informed about the decisions reached there.

But a surprise, or even a shock, came with respect to Count Two:

> Doenitz did, however, wage aggressive war within the meaning of the word as used by the Charter. Submarine warfare which began immediately upon the outbreak of war, was fully co-ordinated with the other branches of the Wehrmacht. It is clear that his U-boats, few in number at that time, were fully prepared to wage war.

Immediately following came several paragraphs describing the importance of Doenitz's positions and then: "In the view of the Tribunal, the evidence shows that Doenitz was active in waging aggressive wars." On this basis, the Tribunal found Doenitz guilty on Count Two.

Quite apart from the fact that the Tribunal had absolved Doenitz from foreknowledge of the outbreak of war and that he was not a "planner" but a "line officer performing strictly tactical duties," Doenitz was not charged in the Indictment with "waging" aggressive war.° Of much more general importance, however, was that this decision raised the basic question of when to draw the line on the reach of Article 6(a). Virtually every commanding officer in the field was also "fully coordinated" within the Wehrmacht and "fully prepared to wage war." To be sure, Doenitz's command was a very important one, but hundreds if not thousands of officers had highly important responsibilities, and even within the relatively small navy there were some whose responsibilities were broader than those of Doenitz. Taken on its face the Tribunal's decision to criminalize Doenitz for doing what virtually all commanding officers were doing would equally criminalize all the others.† In my opinion, there was no principled basis for convicting Doenitz on Count Two.

The Tribunal's opinion on Admiral Raeder's case brought nothing new. He had sometimes disagreed with Hitler, but had supported him through all the Fuehrer's aggressive wars and actions from 1933 to his own retirement in 1943, and his conviction on Counts One and Two was inevitable. Raeder made no objection to distribution of the Commando Order to the various naval commands, and two British commandos were put to death at Bordeaux in December 1942. These were the bases of Raeder's conviction under Count Three.

Baldur von Schirach was charged only under Counts One and Four, and the Tribunal dismissed Count One for lack of proof that Schirach's Hitler Jugend was much involved in preparations for aggressive war. Since charges of crimes against humanity were inapplicable to Schirach's prewar activities, his guilt or innocence depended on the evidence of Schirach's activities as *Gauleiter* and Reich Governor in Vienna and certain adjacent parts of Austria. In December 1940, Hitler ordered the deportation to Poland of some 60,000 Jews from Vienna, and Schirach became involved in carrying out Hitler's orders. This, of course, was a serious crime under Article 6(c) of the Charter and a sufficient base for the Tribunal's convicting Schirach under Count Four of the Indictment.

The Tribunal, with Biddle reading, found the Sauckel case equally uncomplicated. Charged on all four counts, the Tribunal, in a single sentence, absolved Sauckel under Counts One and Two for lack of evidence. In a few paragraphs, the Tribunal convicted Sauckel under Counts Three

---

° Although both the Charter in Article 6(a) and the Indictment in Counts One and Two use the word "waging," none of the defendants was charged in the Indictment with "waging" aggressive war. Doenitz and Raeder were the only defendants convicted of "waging" aggressive war.

† Although I did not know this until many years later, Jim Rowe had made this same point in his memorandum on Doenitz.

and Four, based on his activities as Plenipotentiary General for the Utilization of Labor.

De Vabres read the opinion on Alfred Jodl, charged and convicted under all four counts. The brief text is largely based on Jim Rowe's likewise brief memorandum. The crux of the matter was that Jodl was aware of and signed numerous Hitler orders which violated the laws of war and defended himself by invoking the principle of absolute obedience to orders (*Befehl ist Befehl*). That principle has for many years had both opponents and defenders,* but was in fact contrary to Article 8 of the Charter.

Jodl insisted, and perhaps believed, that he would be acquitted and was visibly furious, like Goering, at the attacks that I had made against the unlawful actions of many German Army officers. Support for Jodl from military quarters is still heard from time to time. But the Tribunal had no division of opinion on the conviction and, indeed, declared that there was "nothing in mitigation," a sure signal of a capital sentence.

Franz von Papen, like Schacht, was indicted only on Counts One and Two. He was also the second defendant to be acquitted, but this had been more generally expected. However, the Tribunal was sharply divided, and the acquittal came on a two-to-two vote.

Those who wanted Papen convicted responded to the pressure of his reputation as a conniver and his support for Hitler's appointment as Chancellor. No doubt the ultimate consequences of Hitler's accession to power were catastrophic, but Papen's actions were not war crimes. No doubt, too, his actions as Minister to Austria were tilted toward Anschluss, but here, too, that was no war crime. Proof of knowledge and support of Hitler's plans for ultimate aggressive wars was lacking.

Fyfe had done his best to blacken Papen as a person, and Nikitchenko and de Vabres had voted for conviction. But, at least in my opinion, the Tribunal was right in concluding: "The Tribunal finds that Von Papen is not guilty under this Indictment and directs that he shall be discharged by the Marshal, when the Tribunal presently adjourns."

The case against Seyss-Inquart, indicted on all four counts, was next read by Nikitchenko. By his own doing, Seyss-Inquart remained the least visible of all the defendants and made the least effort to protect himself. The prosecution introduced evidence against Seyss-Inquart's activities as Reich Governor of annexed Austria and Deputy Governor of the Government-General of Poland, but in its decision the Tribunal rested the conviction on actions "which were committed in the occupation of the Netherlands." There was no evidentiary doubt, and the defendant did not deny that many of his decisions and enforcement of Hitler and Himmler's

---

*The principle of absolute obedience is contrary to the German law of 1871, but had British support until about 1940.

orders violated Article 6 of the Charter. Furthermore, Seyss-Inquart's unwillingness to criticize the activities of Hitler and his top associates probably gave the judges the impression that the defendant did not disapprove of, or was indifferent to, the Nazi policies. He was, in fact, though an Austrian, an almost fanatical German nationalist and patriot, and the needs of Germany, Nazi or not, were his first priority as an administrator.

However, repressive as his administry was, it was far better than those of Frank and Rosenberg or of Josef Terboven in Norway. Seyss-Inquart had no use for unnecessary brutality or destruction, and at the end of the war he, in his smaller area of management, pursued the same course as Speer in putting an end to Hitler's efforts to destroy everything about to be overrun by the Allies. Seyss-Inquart's efforts elicited the following from the Tribunal:

> It is also true that in certain cases Seyss-Inquart opposed the extreme measures used by . . . other agencies, as when he was largely successful in preventing the [German] Army from carrying out a scorched earth policy. . . . But the fact remains that Seyss-Inquart was a knowing and voluntary participant in War Crimes and Crimes against Humanity which were committed in the occupation of the Netherlands.

The last sentence could be, and in substance was, said of Speer. But he, and even Funk, won acknowledgments of mitigation. Seyss-Inquart drew only the Tribunal's conclusion that he "is guilty under Counts Two, Three, and Four" and "not guilty on Count One."

Albert Speer was indicted on all four counts, but he did not enter the Nazi Government in a war capacity until February 1942, and the Tribunal briefly dismissed the charges under Counts One and Two. Reading the opinion, Biddle started the discussion on Counts Three and Four as follows: "The evidence against Speer under Counts Three and Four relates entirely to his participation in the slave labor program." Biddle read from the opinion a compendium of the evidence of Speer's guilt on this issue, about which there never had been much doubt. In its last paragraph, the opinion stated:

> In mitigation, it must be recognized that . . . he was one of the few men who had the courage to tell Hitler that the war was lost and to take steps to prevent the senseless destruction of production facilities, both in occupied territories and in Germany. He carried out his opposition to Hitler's scorched earth program in some of the Western countries and in Germany by deliberately sabotaging it at considerable personal risk.

Constantin von Neurath, oldest of the defendants, was charged and convicted on all four counts. The Tribunal's opinion initially stressed his activities as Minister of Foreign Affairs, including his involvement in the 1936 occupation of the Rhineland; his knowledge of Hitler's aggressive plans in consequence of his presence at the 1937 Hossbach conference; his diplomatic activities during the Anschluss; and his negotiations in support of the Munich Pact of 1938. These matters might reasonably support a conviction under Count One, but I had difficulty in finding any basis for a conviction on planning or waging a war of aggression. Neurath's guilt under Counts Three and Four, based on his actions as Reich Protector of Bohemia and Moravia, is more solid, as the Tribunal had previously held that these territories were not annexed by Germany, and therefore the laws of war were applicable. The defendant's involvement in such crimes was amply proven. In conclusion, the Tribunal stated:

> In mitigation it must be remembered that he did intervene with the Security Police and SD for the release of many of the Czechoslovaks who were arrested on 1 September 1939, and for the release of students arrested later in the fall.

Lawrence read the opinion on Fritzsche, who was indicted under Counts One, Three, and Four. In none of these counts could the Tribunal find a sufficient basis for conviction, and in conclusion the judges stated:

> It appears that Fritzsche sometimes made strong statements of a propagandist nature in his broadcasts. But the Tribunal is not prepared to hold that they were intended to incite the German people to commit atrocities on conquered peoples, and he cannot be held to have been a participant in the crimes charged. His aim was rather to arouse popular sentiment in support of Hitler and the German war effort.
>
> The Tribunal finds that Fritzsche is not guilty under this Indictment.

General Nikitchenko was given the thankless duty of announcing that the absent and probably dead Bormann, accused as guilty under Counts One, Three, and Four, was not guilty under Count One, but guilty under Counts Three and Four. Lawrence then, at 1:45, adjourned the session until 2:50.

7

As the defendants left the dock, the three acquitted men were separated from the others and offered immediate liberty, but they chose to remain and were given separate luncheons and new cells on the top floor of the jail. Fritzsche was the most overcome by the acquittal: "I am entirely overwhelmed," he whispered to Dr. Gilbert, "to be set free here, and not even sent back to Russia—that was more than I had hoped for."

In the courtroom, the dock was empty when the judges returned to the bench. One by one, the convicted defendants were brought up from the jail in the elevator that opened into the courtroom, immediately behind the center of the dock. There they were given earphones to hear the German translation of Lawrence's announcement of their sentences.

Tension in the court was very high; Biddle wrote that he "felt sick and miserable," and I, who had done my best to convict the defendants, was glad indeed that I did not have to speak their fates. The session took only forty-five minutes, which meant less than two minutes per defendant. The spaces between seemed intolerable, but Lawrence spoke evenly and firmly, as did the interpreter, Wolfe Frank.

The elevator door opened, and Goering stepped out and put on the earphones. Lawrence started to speak, but at once Goering took them off and made motions to indicate that the earphones were not working. It was the worst possible moment for what otherwise would have been trivial. Fortunately, a repairman fixed them in a few seconds, and Lawrence began again:

> Defendant Hermann Wilhelm Goering, on the Counts of the Indictment on which you have been convicted, the International Military Tribunal sentences you to death by hanging.

Goering took the earphones, bowed slightly to the Tribunal, turned, and disappeared into the elevator. Hess came in, pushed away the earphones, looked around the courtroom while Lawrence was talking, and had to be turned around to go out, seemingly oblivious to the fact that he had been sentenced to "imprisonment for life."

The next six defendants—Ribbentrop, Keitel, Kaltenbrunner, Rosenberg, Frank, and Frick—were all sentenced to death by hanging. I shed no tears for any of them, but gave a thought to Keitel, who had finally seen and acknowledged the reasons for his fate in a dignified way.

Streicher was also sentenced to death by hanging and reacted angrily, stamping noisily out of the door to the elevator. I could hardly blame him for this show of temper, for I thought the Tribunal's opinion had been superficial, perhaps influenced both by his repulsive appearance and by the likelihood of a negative public reaction if Streicher got anything less than the worst.

I could not be sorry that anyone had escaped the gallows, but I saw no basis for Funk's "mitigating facts" which spared his life. Certainly Funk's range of crimes was far wider than Streicher's, and it was annoying to see Funk profiting by his own cowardice when others were facing death bravely.

As I had thought that the conviction of Doenitz on Count Two was not supportable and flimsy enough on Count Three, I was not surprised that the Tribunal gave him the lightest sentence—ten years—of all the convicts. But Doenitz's hard face suggested that he was not at all mollified. Raeder was even more distressed by his escape from the gallows and made it clear that he would have preferred a death sentence to imprisonment for life.

Schirach was given a twenty-year penalty, which, considering the limits of his responsibilities, seemed in keeping with the Tribunal's other penalties. Schirach appeared to take Lawrence's sentence without flinching. Sauckel, on the other hand, was bowled over by his death sentence and left the courtroom in great dismay.

Alfred Jodl had been well represented and had argued his case strongly. It was known to many that he expected to be acquitted. When he heard Lawrence sentence him to "death by hanging," he stiffened visibly, turned, and fixed his eyes on me for a second or two before going out.

Seyss-Inquart was the last to be sentenced to death. He appeared to take the punishment calmly, as he always had during the trial. I have continued to think that he and his lawyer could have pressed his case more forcefully, as Speer had his, with the result that his "mitigation" led to a prison sentence of twenty years. Neurath undoubtedly benefited by his age as well as "mitigation," as his conviction on all four counts drew a sentence of fifteen years.

Anticlimactically, Lawrence declared that the Tribunal was sentencing Martin Bormann to death. He then announced that the "Soviet Member" had dissented from the decisions in the cases of Schacht, Papen, and ⸱Fritzsche and from the decisions on the General Staff and High Command and the Reich Cabinet, and that he was of the opinion that the Defendant Hess should have been condemned to death. Lawrence further announced that "this dissenting opinion will be put into writing and annexed to the Judgment, and will be published as soon as possible."

Without another word, the Tribunal rose and left the courtroom. The trial was over.

8

After lunch, Fritzsche stood near the foot of the elevator shaft and saw Goering emerge from the lift, manacled, as all the convicts were after their sentences had been read. Goering noticed Fritzsche, and his guard allowed him to shake hands as well as the shackles allowed. With no mention of his own so recently stated fate, Goering said: "Very glad you've been acquitted. We had a bit of a bad conscience as far as you are concerned."

Goering went on to his cell, where Dr. Gilbert was observing the convicts as they came down from the courtroom. "Death," said Goering, and asked Gilbert "to leave him alone for a while." Hess came in, saying (and perhaps pretending) that "he did not know what the sentence was, and what was more, he didn't care."

Dr. Gilbert had a few words to record about the effects of the sentences on each of the convicts. His interest in them had been deep but strictly professional; he had never liked them, and now he pictured them as weaklings more than they deserved. Thus not only Ribbentrop and Kaltenbrunner were described as utterly broken, but Keitel as horror-stricken and begging Dr. Gilbert to "visit me sometime in these last days." Maybe so, but I have my doubts, and Keitel was soon to prove again his self-command.

Even Dr. Gilbert's accounts were not all derogatory. Rosenberg and Funk appeared more angry than scared, and Frank said softly: "Death by hanging. I deserve it and I expected it, as I have always told you. I am glad that I had a chance to defend myself and to think things over in the last few months."

Doenitz was (quite understandably) puzzled by his sentence, but said: "Ten years. . . . Well, anyway, I cleared U-boat warfare—Your own Admiral Nimitz said—you heard it." Doenitz said he was sure Admiral Nimitz understood him perfectly.

Sauckel cried, while Jodl was deeply angered and facing Gilbert said: "Death by hanging—that, at least, I did not deserve. The death part—all right—but *that*—That I did not deserve."

Frick was callous, Neurath upset, and Speer unobjecting to his sentence, which he called "fair enough." By far the most sturdy recipient of a capital sentence was Seyss-Inquart, who smiled at Dr. Gilbert and said: "Well, in view of the whole situation, I never expected anything different. It's all right." He asked if they would still get tobacco and then apologized for being "so trivial at a time like this."

The eleven who were to be hanged remained in their old cells until the appointed time to face the hangman. The seven convicts who were not to be hanged were moved to cells on the top floor to await preparation of Spandau Prison, in the British Zone of Allied-occupied Germany, which was to be their expiation home.

After the convicts were settled in their old or new quarters, the three acquitted were taken to a press conference in the Palace of Justice. It is not clear who called this meeting, which turned out to be a rather raucous occasion, one that Bob Cooper of *The Times* of London called "nauseous." Photographs show Fritzsche apparently enjoying tobacco and drinks as well as talk, and it was credibly reported that businessman Schacht traded his autograph for chocolate to succor the Schacht family. There were no reports of anything legally or historically useful being said.

Things quieted down after Dr. Dix appeared on the scene and told the three ex-defendants that German resentment at their acquittals was bubbling over outside the courthouse and that German police were ringing the building to take them into custody. Dr. Wilhelm Hoegner, the Bavarian Minister President, had sent to the courthouse a warrant for their arrest. Colonel Andrus offered them the hospitality of the jail as a "safe house," and they decided to accept. All three were to remain there for several days and Papen for longer.

Meanwhile the condemned eleven were having no such adventures. It is hard to think of anything more fearful and dismal than waiting in a small cell for the hangman to arrive. Most of them, however, would at least not be idle during the next four days, which was all the time that they had available to prepare their petitions for clemency and for their timely transmission to the Control Council in Berlin. The four-day limit applied only to those condemned to death, but most of the other convicts also filed pleas at the same time.

Petitions were filed in behalf of all the convicts except Kaltenbrunner and Speer. The former (himself a lawyer) was on bad terms with his counsel, and in very poor control of his own thoughts. Speer wrote that his own penalty "weighed little compared to the misery we had brought upon the world." Therefore he "waived the right to an appeal to the four powers."

Three of those condemned to death—Goering, Frank, and Streicher— declared that they did not wish petitions to be filed in their behalf, but their lawyers nonetheless submitted petitions. For Goering, Dr. Stahmer asked that either the sentence should be commuted to life imprisonment or the mode of execution changed to shooting. In support of the plea, the lawyer referred to Goering's bravery and chivalry in World War I. Frank's lawyer merely submitted a plea from Frank's family to commute the penalty to life imprisonment. Streicher's counsel contended that his client's alleged crimes were not sufficiently related to aggressive war, an argument which did not cover Streicher's behavior after the war had begun.

In all probability Hess's petition was not submitted by his own wish. But his lawyer, Seidl, characteristically but hardly effectively argued that it was Stalin, rather than Hess, who had conspired with Hitler against Poland. Bormann's lawyer argued only that despite the Charter's explicit provision, the Tribunal had no authority to try Bormann in absentia.

Two convicts—Keitel and Raeder—sought only death by shooting. Keitel referred to his "tragic mistake which had led to his downfall" and for which he wished to atone "by a death which is granted to a soldier in all armies in the world should he incur the supreme penalty—death by shooting." Raeder's sentence was life imprisonment, and he requested the Control Council "to commute this sentence to death by shooting, by way of mercy."

The remaining ten convicts, six of whom were sentenced to death and four to prison terms of varying lengths, all filed petitions requesting commutation of various kinds. The lawyers for Ribbentrop, Rosenberg, Frick, Sauckel, and Seyss-Inquart had only lame excuses, supported in some cases by pleas for mercy from their wives asking that their death sentences be commuted to life imprisonment. Seyss-Inquart had a last chance to plead for mitigation, but his counsel stupidly "claimed that Seyss-Inquart deserved mercy because he had forced ninety-thousand Austrian Jews to emigrate prior to the war, all of whom were saved from a terrible fate."

Jodl's petition had been prepared by his excellent lawyers, but they had already been excellent when the trial began, and there was little more to be said. Furthermore, these arguments were essentially legal in character, and the Control Council was not a court. Jodl asked that his death sentence be set aside or that he be executed by shooting.

The seven convicts who received prison sentences had already been "commuted" by the Tribunal and had correspondingly little force in their pleas, which sounded like Oliver Twist asking for "more." Funk had been lucky to escape hanging. His plea that he had "only carried out measures which Schacht had for years introduced" was absurd, considering that Schacht had been fired by Hitler before the war, while Funk had followed the Fuehrer to the end. Schirach filed a letter "purporting to reserve his right to petition for clemency . . . at a later date." This was within the language of Article 29 of the Charter, which empowered the Control Council "at any time to reduce or otherwise alter the sentences." Neurath's petition asked for "annulment of the judgment pronounced or at least postponement of the sentence in view of the advanced age of the accused, seventy-four years, and his poor health."

If the Control Council had been a judicial appellate court, Doenitz would have had much the best claim to a reversal of the judgment against him. Kranzbuehler, his counsel, asked instead that the ten-year sentence be commuted entirely or reduced by the time that Doenitz had already spent in jail.

The prosecution also had an interest in the Control Council's handling of the powers given it by the Charter. In mid-September, Jackson had sent a letter to Assistant Secretary of War Howard Petersen expressing his views about the defendants' petitions. The Control Council, he wrote, was not a court; its role was like that of a state governor or the President, who can pardon or commute the sentences of convicts but cannot alter or annul the decisions of the courts.° Jackson took the odd position that since none of the defendants had "rendered any service whatever to the prosecution," there were no grounds for clemency—a view which, for example, would have rendered Speer's anti-Hitler activities irrelevant. On September 17, 1946, Petersen sent Jackson's letter to the American authorities in Berlin.

Some of the convicts received support from other sources, especially in the case of Jodl. His wife, Luise Jodl, was an attractive and determined woman who sent messages to Field Marshal Montgomery, Field Marshal Juin, and General Eisenhower, as well as to Churchill, Stalin, and Prime Minister Attlee. All were informed of Jodl's plight and his reputation as an honorable soldier. Field Marshal von Brauchitsch sent to the British Foreign Office a letter on behalf of himself and other high-ranking German officers urging mercy for Jodl, in part on the ground that Jodl's "influence and position, to my knowledge, have been valued too highly."

## 9

In October 1946, the four members of the Allied Control Council comprised General Joseph T. McNarney, Air Chief Marshal Sir Sholto Douglas, General Joseph Pierre Koenig, and General Vassily Sokolovsky. Each of these officers was the commander of one of the four zones into which occupied Germany was divided. None of them was educated in law. Sholto Douglas included in his published autobiography a chapter entitled "A Matter of Conscience"† in which he described his experience as a member reviewing the petitions received from or respecting the Nuremberg convicts.

Douglas had taken over command of the British Zone from Field Marshal Montgomery in May 1946 quite unaware of this impending duty and when he first learned of it was much distressed at being burdened with so unfamiliar a task. His reaction, however, was not to shirk but to seek information and enlightenment on the Nuremberg trial and the sort of questions he might confront. To that end, Douglas left Berlin, ensconced himself in his office at the British zonal headquarters in Lubbece, and

---

°Under Article 29 of the Charter, the Control Council might "reduce or alter the sentences, but not increase the severity thereof."

†*Combat and Command: The Story of an Airman in Two World Wars*, by Marshal of the Royal Air Force Lord Douglas of Kirtleside, G.C.B., N.C., D.E.C., with Robert Wright (New York: Simon and Schuster, 1963), pp. 736–55.

ordered his subordinates to bring him "only the papers having to do with Nuremberg" so that he "could concentrate on this onerous task."

On September 7 the Control Council ordered that the official record of the Nuremberg proceedings should be sent to the legal directorate of the Control Council, and three days later, at the scheduled meeting of the Council, the members for the first time considered a few procedural problems raised by their approaching Nuremberg task. Then, a few days later, Douglas received from the British Foreign Office "a signal stating that it was thought that any review by the Control Council of the findings of the Nuremberg Tribunal should be primarily 'on grounds of policy.'"

The Council met next on September 20 and was initially in disagreement. McNarney wanted to turn everything over to its law department, and General Noiret (representing Koenig) proposed to set up a commission to advise them. Sokolovsky would have none of such "involved processes" and wanted the Council itself to pass on the petitions as soon as they arrived. Although Douglas suspected that the Russian general already had his orders to "reject all appeals," he sided with Sokolovsky because he, too, thought the Council needed no preliminary commissions, stating that "The Council should consider these pleas of clemency not as legal experts but as men of the world." McNarney and Noiret eventually agreed with Douglas's view.

A few days later Douglas learned, through London, that Justice Jackson had originated the view that the Council should deal with the petitions "as a matter of policy" and that Jackson also stressed that "there should be no review on legal grounds."

Early in October, after the Tribunal sentenced the defendants and while the documents and petitions were arriving in Berlin, Douglas's real troubles began. On October 4 he "received from the last quarter that I ever expected, an instruction that involved me deeply in what I considered a matter of conscience, and was very disturbing in its implications." The missive came from no less a person than Ernest Bevin, the Secretary of State for Foreign Affairs. As Douglas described it:

> It came in the form of a personal signal to me from London marked top secret, and it stated that Ernest Bevin . . . held strong views about the way to which the results of the Nuremberg Trials should be handled. I was asked to consult him before the Control Council reached any decision about confirmation of the Nuremberg sentences, and it was stressed that Bevin was particularly concerned about any measures of clemency which might be decided upon.

Douglas knew and admired Bevin, but he took "the strongest exception" to this directive. Douglas was an outspoken and somewhat explosive man and replied with a personal letter to Bevin and an official reply to the

Foreign Office, in both of which he stated that the handling of the petitions was a matter for "my conscience alone." In both missives he declared that his function with the petitions was "judicial° rather than political" and suggested that "the Secretary of State [Foreign Secretary] should let me have immediately his views on the commutation or reduction of the sentences, and I would take these views into account when it came to making up my own mind."

Douglas described the results of his letter as follows:

> This drew from London, as a result of a Cabinet meeting, further instructions to me, in a long, personal signal which I received in Berlin on the morning of October 8. . . . I was told that it was considered that there was some misapprehension on my part as to my exact position in this matter, and that it was not considered that I was in the position of a Commander-in-Chief reviewing a court-martial sentence, or filling the role of a Colonial Governor or the Home Secretary. . . . It was further stressed to me that it was not for the representatives on the Control Council to decide about the reduction or mitigation of sentence, and that it was the view of His Majesty's Government that from a political point of view it would be an advantage if there were no alterations in the sentences. . . . Finally, I was told that if there was any disposition among my colleagues on the Control Council to make any alterations in the sentences I was to refer to London for further instructions.

It may well have been Douglas's proposal that the Secretary make suggestions which Douglas might accept or reject that triggered the Foreign Office's decision to remind Douglas of the comparatively lowly status of chief air marshals. Whatever the reason, the London writer had made it painfully clear to Douglas that it was "his not to reason why" and that he should vote for no changes in the Tribunal's decisions without prior approval from London.

When Douglas realized that under London's directive he would "fill a role that would be nothing more than that of a puppet," he was furious. "The officials in London had not yet even seen the petitions for clemency, and yet they were already making up their minds, from political points of view, about what I was to do." The more Douglas thought, the more his outrage, and he reflected "that I might be placed in very much the same position as that occupied by Sokolovsky in his relation with the Russian government." That evening, over a drink with his personal aide Robert Wright, Douglas concluded: "The action that I planned to take . . . was that

---

°Judicial" was certainly the wrong word to use, for the Control Council was not a judicial organ. It was an "executive" power with which the Control Council was temporarily vested.

I would do as I was told unless—as Wright recorded in our talk—the issue was very clear cut, in which case I would make decisions of my own and to the devil with H.M.G."

On the next two days, October 9 and 10, 1946, the four members of the Control Council sat together in Berlin discussing the appeals for clemency. According to Douglas he did most of the talking, but that made little difference in the outcome. Douglas was too wise a soldier to cross swords with the Foreign Office, and as he wrote: "Eventually we rejected all the appeals and all the sentences were confirmed."

Some of the discussion and ratiocination, however, is enlightening. Raeder's request for death by shooting instead of life imprisonment was rejected by the Council on the ground that whatever Raeder's personal feeling, this would constitute an increase in the severity of the sentence, which Article 29 of the Charter forbade. The Council also rejected the petitions filed with respect to the convicted organizations, as well as Schirach's objection that these matters were beyond the scope of the Charter. These were the Council's only "legal" decisions.

Douglas's description of the colloquies among the members dealt exclusively with the requests on behalf of the three generals—Goering, Keitel, and Jodl—to be shot rather than hanged. As an airman, Douglas was fascinated with Goering, because, he recalled, "Twenty-eight years before, Goering and I, as young fighter pilots, had fought each other in the cleaner atmosphere of the air." Douglas felt "the strongest revulsion" to confirm Goering's sentence, but decided that Goering must hang because Fyfe's cross-examination of Goering convinced Douglas that Goering knew of the Germans' shooting of escaped British airmen at Stalag Luft III.

For Douglas, Keitel was far from the glamorous recollection of Goering in 1917–1918. But once again, he capped the reasons why Keitel should be hanged with a reference to Fyfe's cross-examination of Keitel on the Stalag Luft III murders.

Apparently the many pleas for Jodl's commutation or at least for a soldier's death aroused the only sharp division of opinion among the Council members. According to Douglas, "Koenig and McNarney were of the opinion that, being a general, he [Jodl] should at least be given the privilege of being shot." The reader may well wonder why, if general's rank is the criterion of a shooting rather than a hanging, Goering and Keitel, whose ranks exceeded Jodl's, should not have been similarly honored. Sokolovsky "spoke out very strongly against that. He said that Jodl deserved to be hanged just as much as any of the other criminals."

Douglas's reason for adhering to the Tribunal's decision was succinctly stated, if not wholly to the point:

I believed that the German generals had betrayed themselves. What had happened after the mass escape from Stalag Luft III, and the way in which fifty of our airmen were shot after they were captured, was proof enough of that for me. . . . It became all too clear to me as I studied the evidence that these two high ranking officers [Keitel and Jodl] were being tried, as [Robert] Cooper has pointed out, for "their responsibility in abominable crimes," and not for being soldiers.

And so for Douglas, Stalag Luft III was the touchstone of his insistence on death by hanging for each of the three military men. Most of the victims of these murders were Britons, as were Douglas and Cooper. It detracts from the force of Douglas's argument that while Keitel was deeply implicated in this crime, Goering's responsibility was arguable and Jodl, the focus of the dispute, had virtually no connection with the atrocity. In the Tribunal's opinion, Stalag Luft III was mentioned among the other atrocities against prisoners of war, but not in the Tribunal's summation against any of these three men.

At the conclusion of the Control Council's meetings on the Nuremberg petitions, Marshal Sokolovsky read a statement expressing his complete agreement with General Nikitchenko's dissenting opinion. Jackson had been disappointed by the acquittal of Schacht, and the other three chief prosecutors had called for death sentences for all the defendants. The Tribunal, however, had acquitted three defendants and spared the lives of seven more. It is no wonder that the four governments called a halt on leniency.

## 10

The lawyers for the condemned convicts were notified on October 11 that all the petitions had been denied, and they informed the clients and their families. The condemned then knew that the end was imminent, but were given no exact information; in fact, only five days remained.

Far from easing their plight for the last few days, most of the few amenities were eliminated. No longer could they exercise in the prison yard; outside their cells they were always handcuffed, and their only exercise was brief manacled walks in the cell block. The last talks with their families were guarded by military police.

On October 12, it was announced that the day's meetings with their families would be the last. The meetings were wrenching, and afterward most of the condemned fell into utter despair. Only Frank and Seyss-Inquart were somewhat reconciled to their fates.

Up to that time, Keitel had held up remarkably well. He had, in fact, given an extraordinary exhibition of concentration on matters other than death. On September 1, immediately after the evidentiary trial was finished, Keitel had begun writing his memoirs, covering the years 1933 to his imprisonment on May 13, 1945. What is most remarkable is that he continued to work on this project until October 10, 1946, when he wrote the last sentence: "I was transferred to a prison cell in Nuremberg on the 13th August [1945], and am awaiting my execution on 13th October, 1946. Finis, 10th October, 1946. [Signed] Keitel." No wonder his editor, Walter Goerlitz, wrote: "In general, it is astonishing that despite the great mental strain of the weeks between his sentencing and execution the field-marshal should have been capable of writing such a coherent account of his life and description of his *modus operanda* during these decisive years of German history."*

On October 13, Speer was taken for a walk, and the guard led him along the corridor of the condemned men's cells. As Speer later wrote, all of them except Frank, who was writing, were lying on their beds—idle and silent; Speer called it a "ghastly sight." Gilbert and the prison chaplains were paying frequent visits to the men in their cells, trying to ease the tension.

Schacht and Fritzsche had left the prison after a few days, but Papen, having heard that the other two had already been taken into custody by the German police, was still in the prison, moaning to Gilbert: "I am a hunted animal, and they will never leave me in peace." Frank overheard the conversation and burst into hysterical laughter: "Ha-ha-ha they thought they were free—Don't they know there is no freedom from Hitlerism! Only we are free of it! We got the best deal after all! Ha-ha!" But Frank was the only one who could laugh.

During the last few days prior to the executions, representatives of the Control Council appeared to manage the preparations and conduct the proceedings. The four-man committee in charge of the executions were Generals Roy V. Rickard (United States), Paton Walsh (Great Britain), Morel (France), and Molkov (U.S.S.R.). The committee had laid down a rule that no member of the prosecution should be allowed to witness the executions, and apparently the motive was vindictive.†

Against strong British opposition, the Control Council decided that representatives of the press might be present at the hangings; after considerable flurry, two members of the press from each of the four zonal governments were permitted. One member of the American press was admitted to inspect the eleven prisoners in their cells. The operation of the hanging

---

* *The Memoirs of Field-Marshal Keitel* (London: William Kimber, 1965).

† In a letter to Whitney Harris from Jackson dated November 18, 1946, Jackson wrote: "Apparently the military crowd were a little vindictive. They were very sore, I understand, because those who were sent to take charge of the executions were not put in prominent places at the rendering of the verdict. The impropriety of playing up the executioners before the judgment of guilt had been rendered or sentence imposed does not seem to occur to such mentalities, if that is what they can be called by courtesy."

was under the charge of Master Sergeant John C. Woods (a professional executioner with fifteen years' experience), assisted by two GIs. Apart from Colonel Andrus, such of his staff as he needed, and clerical and medical assistants, two German officials were admitted—Dr. Wilhelm Hoegner, Minister President of Bavaria, and Dr. Jakob Meistner, General Prosecutor of the High Court of Nuremberg.

The executions were to take place in the prison gymnasium. Speer, the architect, readily concluded that timbers being brought into the prison courtyard were to be used to set up the gallows, of which there were three. The executions were to begin very early in the morning of October 16, 1946.

The press correspondent admitted at about 9:30 p.m. found Jodl writing a letter, Ribbentrop talking to a chaplain, Sauckel nervously pacing the floor, and Goering apparently asleep on his bed. At about 11:40, Goering's guard looked into his cell and found him groaning and moving jerkily. The guard shouted, and in rapid succession Pastor Gerecke, Andrus, and Dr. Pfluecker reached the room.

In a few moments Goering was pronounced dead. There were glass fragments in his mouth, and it was apparent that Goering had smashed in his jaws and swallowed a cyanide capsule. He had left a small envelope containing a few notes, one of which was addressed to Colonel Andrus. To this day there has been no official statement or public proof of the means by which Goering obtained the cyanide capsule.

Despite the sensational nature of Goering's coup, time was closing in rapidly on the ten remaining condemned prisoners. The chaplains were visiting the condemned, the traditional "last supper" was offered but had few takers, and the inmates were ordered to dress in their court clothes—a task which Streicher loudly refused to undertake, and he was forced into them by the struggling guards. On the upper floor the other convicts were wakened by the noise, and Speer heard Hess shout, "Bravo, Streicher." At about 1 a.m. Andrus with an official party visited each of the condemned to read the official death sentence.

A few minutes later Ribbentrop, held by two guards, was led out of the prison and across to the gymnasium to confront the gallows, the hangman, and the small gathering of those admitted to witness the event.° He was unmanacled, but his hands were bound behind him. He walked to the foot of the gallows and was assisted by two guards to climb to the platform

---

°Most published accounts of the hangings were written by the members of the press. Whitney Harris, who had previously left Nuremberg and was working in the American legal section in Berlin, was asked by General Clay (who had unsuccessfully attempted to obtain permission for Harris to be present at the hangings) to report on the event. Harris, in a letter to Justice Jackson on October 19, 1946, stated that his "familiarity with the scene and close contact with the newspaper men who were present was quite sufficient to enable me to report on the details." I have relied principally on his account. See Harris, *Tyranny on Trial* (Southern Methodist University Press, 1954), pp. 485-88.

at the top. He stood on the trap, his feet were bound, and he was asked if he had any last words. He replied, very firmly: "God protect Germany. God have mercy on my soul. My last wish is that German unity be maintained, that understanding between East and West be realized, and that there be peace in the world." Sergeant Woods put the noose over him, and a black hood was dropped over his head. At 1:14 Woods pulled the lever, and Ribbentrop soundlessly vanished from sight. He died at 1:29.

Keitel, leaving his cell neat as a pin, was the next to climb the ladder to the second gallows (since Ribbentrop was not yet dead). He said: "I call on the Almighty to be considerate of the German people, provide tenderness and mercy. Over two million German soldiers went to their death for their Fatherland. I now follow my sons."* And then, when the noose and hood were over his head, Keitel shouted: "Alles für Deutschland! Deutschland über Alles!"

Kaltenbrunner was directed to climb the third gallows. Much steadier than had been expected, he said: "I served the German people and my fatherland with willing heart. I did my duty according to its laws. I am sorry that in her trying hour she was not led only by soldiers. I regret that crimes were committed in which I had no part. Good luck Germany." Rosenberg looked very shaky, and this wordiest of all Nazis, unlike all the others, did not speak. Frank, quiet and polite, on the way in thanked Andrus "for the kindness which I received in this incarceration" and, after mounting the gallows, said: "I pray God to receive me mercifully." Frick, terse as ever, said: "Let live the eternal Germany."

Streicher came into the building "blazing defiance." He refused to give his name, spat at Sergeant Woods and told him that "the Bolsheviks will hang you one day," and shouted "Heil Hitler" as he climbed to the platform. Once there he yelled, "Purim festival, 1946" and, as the hood was put over him: "I am now by God my father! Adele my dear wife." Sauckel angrily protested: "I die innocently. The verdict was wrong. God protect Germany and make Germany great again. Let Germany live and God protect my family."

Jodl, like Keitel, cleaned up his cell before leaving it to meet his Maker. He said only: "I salute you, my Germany." Seyss-Inquart, during his two-hour wait, marked "X" on "October 16" of the calendar he kept in his cell. His final words were selfless: "I hope that this execution is the last act of the tragedy of the Second World War, and that a lesson will be learned so that peace and understanding will be realized among the nations. I believe in Germany." Whitney Harris noted: "He died at 2:57, less than two hours after Ribbentrop had entered the execution chamber."

When the bodies of all the men had been cut down, they were placed,

---

*Keitel's youngest son was killed in action in Russia.

faces up, in wooden coffins. Goering's corpse was brought in and placed in the coffin intended for him. All of the corpses were next photographed individually, both clothed and unclothed. They were then carried in trucks to a crematory in or near Munich.° Whitney Harris wrote that "it was reported that . . . the ashes were taken away to be emptied in the river Isar."

Sergeant Woods, for all his experience, came under sharp criticism, some of which appeared to be borne out by the corpses' photographs, which had been made available to the press. Cecil Catling of the London *Star*, a veteran crime reporter, declared that the drop was not long enough and that the men had not been properly tied, all with the result that their heads struck the platform as they fell and they "died of slow strangulation." Woods had answers to these attacks, but clear proof was lacking. Judge Birkett was disgusted that the public had been given general access to the pictures, which indeed were distressing.

And so, Hermann Goering and the ten others condemned to death were gone. Gone also were the International Military Tribunal and the first Nuremberg trial. On the day before the hangings, Justice Jackson had submitted to President Truman his Final Report on the extraordinary mission that the President had asked him to undertake.

Justice Jackson, back on the United States Supreme Court, had also resigned his position as Chief of Counsel for the United States and sent to me a letter of encouragement in my new duties as Chief of Counsel for War Crimes. Thus, Nuremberg remained for three years the site of twelve more trials, involving some 190 defendants. But that, to quote Rudyard Kipling, "is another story."

---

°Other writers have said that the crematory was or may have been at Dachau in the former concentration camp, but I know of no proof of this.

# Chapter 22

# EPILOGUE AND ASSESSMENT

For several years, the three acquitted defendants were not much better off than the seven sentenced by the International Military Tribunal to long prison terms. Indeed, for the first four days, all ten of them were bedded in the Nuremberg prison cells, where the three were better off only in their freedom to move around in the Palace of Justice and to look through the windows at the German police waiting to pounce on them if they went outside.

After four days, however, Fritzsche and Schacht had had enough of protective incarceration and asked to be let out. At midnight they were put separately into vans, which sped away in different directions. Fritzsche was taken to the house where his counsel, Dr. Fritz, was lodged. The American major who had accompanied him got Fritzsche safely to his room, but the press soon ran him down, closely followed by the Nuremberg Chief of Police. An American colonel came next and saved Fritzsche from immediate arrest. The following day, the German authorities allowed Fritzsche to move freely in Nuremberg in return for his promise not to leave the city.

This limited liberty lasted four months, but Fritzsche was then called before the Spruchkammer (Denazification Court) in Nuremberg. This action was entirely legal, for Fritzsche's acquittal by the International Military Tribunal covered only the charges under Article 6 of the London Charter. The Spruchkammer had before it all of Fritzsche's broadcasts and his other Nazi activities, and he was sentenced, as a "major offender," to nine years of hard labor, plus loss of voting, pension, and public office rights.

Fritzsche was pardoned and freed in September 1950. Unhappily, he had little time to enjoy his freedom, for he died of cancer in September 1953, a few weeks before his brief autobiography, *The Sword in the Scales*, was published.

When Schacht left the Palace of Justice, he was taken to the house where his wife lived when in Nuremberg. He found the German security police waiting for him. The Chief of Police then arrived, took Schacht to the police station, and ordered him put in prison. By his own account, Schacht then "raised such hell" that the Chief got in touch with the Americans, with the result (as in Fritzsche's case) that Schacht was taken back to his wife's house for a good night's sleep.

The next day Dr. Dix appeared on the scene, and at his urging the Bavarian government "agreed," Schacht later wrote, "to allow me complete freedom of action throughout Germany, on condition that I reported to the police from time to time", while denazification proceedings were started in Nuremberg.

Schacht and his wife borrowed a car and set off to his wife's permanent home in the British Zone. Unfortunately, they went via Württemberg, where Bavaria's writ did not run, to visit a friend. Near Backnang the Stuttgart police arrested Schacht and put him in jail, where he remained until April 1947, when denazification proceedings were held. The court labeled Schacht an "arch-criminal" and sentenced him to eight years in the Ludwigsburg labor camp. Schacht's lawyers launched an appeal, and on September 2, 1948, Schacht was acquitted. His arrival in the British Zone, however, led to further denazification proceedings in Lüneburg, and final acquittal did not come until the end of 1950.

When Schacht arrived in the British Zone he was virtually penniless; the Reichsbank had lost most of his liquid assets, other properties were in Communist hands or requisitioned, and he was heavily in debt to his lawyers. He was seventy-one years old and had to support a wife and two children. So he contracted with the Hamburg publisher Rowahlt for a book, later published in English as *Account Settled*, which he had written during the trial. The book sold some 250,000 copies.°

In 1952 Schacht was invited by the Indonesian government to come for consultation on economic and financial matters. This turned into a sort of triumphal tour to Rome, Cairo (where the government treated him as its guest), India, and Indonesia. After returning home,† there was a second trip, to Egypt and Teheran. In December 1952 he was invited to Damascus for consultation on founding a central bank for Syria.

---

°Originally entitled *Abrechnung mit Hitler* (1948), English publication (1949). To my surprise and amusement, he included a long quotation from passages of Speer's and my concluding speeches (*Account Settled*, pp. 237-41; see also pp. 863-64).

†On the return flight to Rome, Schacht's plane unexpectedly landed at Tel Aviv. By good luck he was not challenged before the plane took off to Rome, but when his brief presence was made known, Israeli Prime Minister Ben Gurion said: "Had I known that Dr. Schacht was at the air field I should have arrested him at once." Had this happened, it should have made a very interesting war crimes case.

Home for Christmas 1952, Schacht (now seventy-five) busied himself with the proofs of his second book *(Confessions of "The Old Wizard"—The Autobiography of Hjalmar Horace Greeley Schacht)*. With increasing age his reputation faded, but, true to his determination to win, he had certainly "done better" than any other Nuremberg defendant. He died in 1970 at the age of ninety-two.

Franz von Papen was more cautious than the other two and did not leave the prison until shortly after the hangings had taken place. But his patience did him little good. He was initially given shelter in Nuremberg by an old friend, but he was in poor health and spent most of his days in hospitals in and near Nuremberg. In January 1947 he was called before the denazification court, put in the top category of Nazi activists, and sentenced to ten years in a labor camp.

Papen lived in one labor camp hospital after another for two years, in the course of which he was badly beaten by a crazed inmate. In January 1949 a denazification court heard Papen's appeal. His sentence was reduced to a lower category, and he was freed, but remained deprived of civil rights. He published his autobiography, *Memoirs*, in English, in 1953 and lived quietly with his family until his death in 1969.

It had been expected that the seven surviving convicts would be sent to Spandau Prison in Berlin before the end of the year. But for some reason there were several delays, and the move was not made until more than nine months after the end of their trial. Colonel Andrus had departed, and his second in command, Major F. C. Teich, took over and somewhat loosened the reins. Restrictions on mail were abolished. The chaplains were allowed to mail large packages of Speer's narrative manuscript to his family home.° There was more time available for walking and working in the prison yard and for conversation among themselves now that there were no more court sessions.

The conversation, however, was not always amiable. During the trial and since, Speer had advanced the view that regardless of individual criminality, those who continued to serve Hitler were responsible for the results of Hitler's acts. In principle, that was accusing his fellow defendants of the same responsibility—a view that they, especially the admirals, rejected. Schirach, who in the latter part of the trial had broken from Goering and turned to Speer's views, was still the wimp and was now leaning on the admirals. As Speer wrote, in December 1946 Schirach approached him "in a deliberate challenging manner" and said: " 'You and your total responsibility! The Court itself rejected the charge, as you may have noticed. There is not a word about it in the verdict.' " Speer held his ground, but the other

---

°Speer's second book—*Spandau: The Secret Diaries* (Macmillan, 1976)—is the best and only major work on the Spandau prisoners.

prisoners nodded approvingly of Schirach's statement and walked away silently, leaving Speer alone.

Thus Speer became and remained alienated from Schirach and the two admirals and somewhat less so from Funk and Neurath. Hess, for quite other factors, was "the cat that walked by himself," though Speer occasionally walked with him when Hess "seemed transformed" and talked freely.

On July 18, 1947, the seven prisoners were finally flown to Berlin and incarcerated in Spandau—seven men in a prison made for hundreds, in the extreme west end of Berlin in the British sector. With the arrival of the prisoners it became an international penitentiary, ultimately under the Control Council, but administered in monthly sequence by Russian, American, British, and French military officers.

Whichever country was in charge, the prison was well run; Speer called the treatment "irreproachable" but "cold and aloof." The major complaint was that they received only "the German rations precisely to the dram," whereas "in Nuremberg we had plenty to eat." If not enough to eat, there was plenty to do. When the British took over, the Director allowed and urged the prisoners to work in the large garden; all seven accepted, though Funk was a frequent malingerer.

The staff of the prison was polyglot and polytypic, and their initial coldness diminished. Less than three months after his arrival at Spandau, Speer recorded: "I can hardly believe it. A prison employee has offered to smuggle letters out for me." Anton Vlaer, a young Dutchman, was conscripted for forced labor during the war and worked in a Berlin armament factory. The prospect of "un-censored communication with the outside world" threw Speer into raptures: "That could mean transforming prison cell into scholar's den." Several years later Speer secured a second secret carrier.

Friction among the seven prisoners continued, and indeed increased, arising not only from events in the jail, but also from clashes during the war and at Nuremberg. Speer wrote that "Raeder's hate complex against Hess, so fierce it is almost grotesque, is outlasting all changes of time and place." Both admirals were competitive in their pride. Raeder, at seventy-two still vigorous, "treats Doenitz with the condescension of a superior officer, which particularly irritates him." Doenitz blamed Raeder for not having built up the U-boat arm rapidly enough before the war, thus preventing Doenitz from spreading havoc on the British merchant fleet during the war's early months. As Speer pictured the characteristics of the seven:

> Among us are passive types who pass the time by endless talk-
> ing. Among these are Funk, Schirach, and—a taciturn and absurd
> variant of the type—Hess. The active types who go to pieces without
> occupation are Raeder, Neurath, Doenitz, and I. We have at any rate

got rid of titles. Raeder is no longer the grand admiral and Neurath no longer foreign minister. But from fear of going down hill, we are careful to maintain a certain degree of formal manners. . . . We still address each other as "Herr," continue to respect precedence, and politely wish each other good-morning and good night.

All except Hess were, of course, primarily concerned with getting their sentences reduced; Hess throughout felt or feigned indifference. Although Kranzbuehler, after "talking with importance personages" in December 1952, had sent a clandestine message to Doenitz recommending that the prisoners should "count on serving out full time," in April 1954 he "sent word that the old and sick will come first." Neurath and Raeder were the oldest, and Neurath, Raeder, and Funk were by then the sickest.

None of the prisoners could be released ahead of time without the concurrence of all four members of the Control Council. Many thought that the Russians would never agree to any such concessions to their erstwhile enemies. But as matters worked out, except in the case of Hess, the Soviet government was not implacable. Kranzbuehler had been right the second time, and on November 6, 1954, the weak and ailing Neurath, who had suffered a severe heart attack in 1952, was released from Spandau. He died in 1956.

By September 1954 Raeder's health was fading rapidly, and by the spring of the following year he was no longer allowed to work and ceased trying to mask his illness. In September 1955 he was released. This was a much more surprising action, for Raeder had been sentenced to life imprisonment and also had been a Soviet prisoner. But his lawyer, Dr. Siemers, had crusaded shrewdly in Raeder's behalf, and eventually the Russians gave their consent. Raeder had enough energy left to publish his autobiography, translated as *My Life* in 1960, which was particularly useful for its coverage of the prewar years. He died in 1960.

Raeder had served for nine years, and Doenitz was sentenced for only ten. He was fifty-five years old, in good health, and there was no basis for a commutation. On September 30, 1956, the day for Doenitz's departure arrived.

During the war Doenitz and Speer had collaborated with mutual respect, but since Speer's repudiation of Hitler and Nazism, Doenitz had had nothing good to say about him. On this last day, Doenitz launched a bitter attack, triggered by the fact that Speer had spoken favorably of Doenitz to Hitler when the Fuehrer was considering the appointment of the admiral as his successor: "Because of you I've lost these last eleven years. You're to blame for it all. . . . But for you Hitler would never have had the idea of making me chief of state. . . . My career is wrecked." Speer replied: "For ten years you have slandered, disparaged, and ostracized me. . . . You and the others have endlessly talked about honor. Every other word you and Schirach utter is honor, bearing. This war has killed fifty million people. More millions were murdered in the camps of those criminals. But your ten years here perturb you more than the fifty million dead. And your last words here in Spandau are your career!"

So parted the two strongest men in Spandau, and so departed the hardest man in the former German Navy. Doenitz wrote an autobiography, *Ten Years and Twenty Days*, naturally focused on the U-boat war and his brief tenure as Chief of State. Despite their quarrels in Spandau, the two admirals' books were gentle with each other. Doenitz died in 1980.

Funk never took care of his health and was not a well man when he was taken to Spandau. He was a good raconteur and jokester, but very lazy, and his opinions counted for little. During his last three years in the prison he was bedridden much of the time. A diabetic who would not obey the medical rules, he was hospitalized in January 1947 and operated on in October 1949 and September 1954. Like Raeder he had been sentenced to life imprisonment, but he was much younger, about Doenitz's age. Funk was finally released in May 1957. Speer wrote: "I am happy for Funk, but also depressed. Now months will pass before people [meaning the authorities] again become concerned about Spandau." Funk died three years later.

In fact, it was not months, it was over nine years. Schirach and Speer were the two youngest defendants and in good health; Hess was sixty-three and had his ups and downs, but it appeared that he would never get by the Soviet "nyet." Speer wrote: "Now there are only three of us. I am really alone. Schirach and Hess do not count. What I dreaded has now come about."

But Speer was an extraordinarily well organized man. Reading, writing, and thoughts for the mind and working and walking for the body were his recipes against the decay of health and morale. He had started in 1954 to measure and record the length of his walks and his imaginary arrivals at distant cities. Two days before his release in 1966, he had walked some 20,000 miles and was approaching Guadalajara, Mexico.

Schirach had no such self-control. He was perennially out of sorts, partly because of a divorce. During the last two years he suffered an embolism in the leg and later a detached retina. Political disagreements and Speer's low opinion prevented any rapport between him and his fellow prisoners, but Schirach had been friendly with Funk, who kept in touch until his death. Speer, however, was much encouraged by a visit to Spandau by United States Ambassador David Bruce, who encountered Speer in the garden, shook hands, and "said that he wished to convey regards from McCloy." Speer recalled that Bruce "explained that the difficulty of achieving anything in my case was due to the obstinate attitude of the Russians" and declared with emphasis, 'You are not forgotten.' "°

---

°A few months before his release, Speer was shown a statement in *Stern* by Shawcross: "Herr Speer . . . should have been released long ago. Together with John McCloy . . . I have more

When time came (September 30, 1966) for the release of both Schirach and Speer, relations remained cool. Hess entrusted Schirach with messages to be delivered to Hess's family. When Speer offered to ensure delivery, Hess angrily pushed him away. But Hess was entirely calm watching his colleagues pack their possessions for the trip, and Speer described Hess's morale as "amazing."

Once at home after twenty-one years, Speer produced three books dealing with the Third Reich, Spandau, and Himmler. Schirach also produced a book centered on Hitler, *Ich Glaubte an Hitler* (*I Believed in Hitler*). Schirach died in 1974, and Speer in 1981.

Hess's sentence of life imprisonment was never commuted. He committed suicide in 1987 at the age of ninety-three, having spent over forty years in prison. Immediately after his death, Spandau Prison was torn down so that it would not become a historical attraction. The British planned to turn the space over to a supergrocery.

Hess was utterly devoted to Hitler and, if he had remained in Germany, there is no doubt that he would have followed his Fuehrer to the end. There is little reason to be sorry for his conviction. But common sense and humanity have their places. Until nearly the end of his life Hess was not "sick" in the usual sense, but he was a man bedeviled by fears and fantasies that tore him in mind and body. When he arrived at Nuremberg he was already no threat to mankind, and if there were any doubts about that, they were settled many years before his end. A commutation after ten or so years would not have suggested that crime was being dealt with too lightly.

As time went by, on panel discussions and television confrontations I was asked whether I thought that Hess should be released to his family. I generally replied that such long-continued incarceration, especially in a huge prison where he was the sole inmate, was a crime against humanity.

2

Hermann Goering was dead, but how did he die? Of course he died from swallowing cyanide, but how did he get the capsule of poison? The truth has not yet been proven.

An official inquiry into the matter was submitted to the Control Council and discussed on October 30, 1946. Sholto Douglas described the results:

> On this occasion, because of what we were going to discuss, it was
> decided to restrict the number of those present to the numbers of each

---

than once made efforts to obtain his release." Speer commented: "A dismal satisfaction that comes too late." In his final speech at Nuremberg, Shawcross had called upon the Tribunal to sentence all the defendants as murderers.

delegation who were most directly concerned. . . . Only just before the meeting I had received my copy of the report on the way in which Goering had committed suicide, along with copies of the last letter he wrote to his wife and a statement that could be regarded as his final testament.

It was agreed at our meeting that all of the copies of these documents which were in existence should be gathered up, and that all of them, except one—which should be preserved in the archives of the Control Commission—should be destroyed. It was further agreed that no information should ever be made public about the contents of any of these documents, that nothing more need be said by any of us, and that we should forever remain silent about what had already been said that day.

Douglas's book contains no explanation of why such secrecy was called for.

In 1990, West and East Germany were amalgamated; Germany was freed from all remaining Allied controls, and the Control Council was abolished. Goering's letters, written just before his suicide, still reposed in the Control Council archives, and by the kindness of Dr. David G. Marwell, Director of the Berlin Document Center, and Robert Wolfe, Director of the Captured German Records Staff in the National Archives, copies of Goering's letters and of the "Report of the Board of Proceedings in the Case of Hermann Goering (Suicide)," conducted by three U.S. Army officers and deposited in the Control Council archives, were furnished to me in November 1990.

There proved to be four letters, three dated October 11, 1946, and one undated. They were addressed respectively to the Allied Control Council, Pastor Gerecke, Goering's wife, and the prison Commandant, Colonel Andrus. October 11 was the day on which Goering learned that his plea to the Control Council, that he be shot rather than hanged, had been rejected. This event was discussed in each of Goering's letters.°

At least a part of the text of the letter to Andrus is in the possession of Robert Kempner and was published in 1977 in Werner Maser's *Nuremberg: A Nation on Trial*, pp. 251–52. A better rendering of the same part of the letter is Exhibit AM in the "Report of the Board of Proceedings." The letter to Goering's wife, Emmy, was delivered to her, but (as described hereafter) she did not agree with her husband's account in his letter to Andrus. A copy of the letter to Emmy was included in the material sent to the Control Council.

The letter to the Control Council, in two parts, is written on the letterhead of *Der Reichsmarschall des Grossdeutschen Reiches*:

---

°The translation of these letters into English was done by Bernard Kaiser and Douglas Cardwell, students at the Columbia Law School.

**I.**

*To the Control Council:*

Would that I might be shot! However, executing the German *Reichs-marschall* by hanging cannot be countenanced. I cannot permit this for Germany's sake. Besides, I have no more obligation to subject myself to punishment from my enemies. Therefore I elect to die as the great Hannibal did.

HERMANN GOERING

**II.**

I knew from the beginning that a death sentence would fall on me, having viewed the trial as a purely political act of the victors, but for my people's sake I wanted to stand trial and I expected that at least I would not be denied the death of a soldier. Before God, my people and my conscience I feel free from the reprehension that my enemies put on me.

HERMANN GOERING

The letter to "Dear Pastor Gerecke" was briefer:

Forgive me, but I had to do it in this way for political reasons. I have prayed for a long time to God and feel that I am acting correctly. Would that I might be shot. Please console my wife and tell her that mine was *no ordinary suicide* and that she should be certain that God will take me into his grace. . . . God bless you, dear Pastor.

YOURS,

HERMANN GOERING

The third letter asked the pastor to deliver Goering's last letter to his wife. Parts of it should remain private, but the following portion may be presented:

Upon mature reflection and intimate prayer to God I decided to take my own life and not to allow my enemies to execute me in that way. I would have consented anytime to be shot. But the *Reichsmarshall* of Germany cannot be hanged. Furthermore the execution would be presented as a spectacle in the press, in the movies, etc. (for the newsreels, I assume). Sensation is the main thing. But I wish to die peacefully and without publicity. . . . I take it a sign from God that through all the months of imprisonment he left me with the means to free me from earthly worry and that it was never discovered.

This last sentence, of course, is the one that bears most importantly on Goering's means of suicide. A longer discussion of that question is the subject of Goering's letter to Andrus:

*To the Commandant*

Since my imprisonment I have always kept the poison capsule on my person. I had *three* capsules when I was committed to prison in Mondorf.° The first one I left in my clothing, so that it would be found in the search. The *second* I left under the coatstand while undressing and took it again when I dressed. I hid this in Mondorf and here in the cell so well that, in spite of the frequent and very thorough searches, it could not be found. During the trial I kept it in my high riding boots. The *third* capsule is *still* in my little toilet case in the round container of skin cream (hidden in the cream). I had two opportunities to take the capsule in Mondorf, had I needed it. No one in charge of the searches was at fault, since it was almost *impossible* to find the capsule. It would have been purely *by chance*.

HERMANN GOERING

Doctor Gilbert told me that the Control Council rejected the change in the manner of execution to death by the firing squad.

GOERING

There was an additional page, signed by "Hermann Goering," but not dated or addressed, which was a twelve-sentence tirade against the "tasteless" manner of the executions, which was intended for "sensation-seeking reporters." Goering also expressed regret that he had been unable to help Keitel and Jodl to "escape this public death spectacle" and in conclusion declared that the victors' efforts to prevent suicides "was not worry for our lives, but only to have everything ready for the great sensation. But without me!"

I see no reason, after reading the first three letters, to question the Control Council's insistence on hanging as the prime, and indeed the only, motive of Goering's suicide. But the fourth letter, dealing with the cyanide suicide, is not convincing.

For one thing, it is vaguely written, whether or not purposely. For example, at Mondorf Goering presumably left one of his three capsules in his coat so that the authorities would find it and conclude that Goering had no more (a jejune conclusion). But Goering fails to tell us whether or not the authorities *did* find the capsule in his coat. If not, presumably Goering came to Nuremberg with three capsules; otherwise, only two. Then Goering absolves from any "fault" anyone "in charge of the searches," which, of course, fails to absolve anyone *not* so charged, which was most people.†

°The Luxembourg town where Goering and many other high-ranking Nazis were held, prior to transfer to Nuremberg.

†During the years since Goering's suicide there have been many suggestions of how he dealt with the capsule and even claims of having been the source. Bach-Zelewski so claimed. But no one gave him credence, especially since the two men loathed each other.

Goering's main purpose in this letter appears to be to crow over Andrus and his men by boasting of his own ability to hide the capsule in his cell "so well that . . . it could not be found" and that the capsule "was almost *impossible* to find." His secondary and avowed purpose was to protect those "in charge of the searches." But Goering's examples of his skills—putting the capsule "under the coatstand" (presumably at Mondorf and later "here in the cell") and in his riding boots "during the trial"—were utterly puerile. Granted that Andrus may not have been the sharpest of searchers, the suicide of Robert Ley in October 1945 had given Andrus due warning, and thus the guards would surely have looked in boots and under movables. Furthermore, there was a guard looking through the door window into the cell most of the time, and moving the capsule within the cell from one place to another would be about the quickest way to have it discovered.

On October 19 the Board of Officers searched the contents of Goering's effects in the prison storeroom and found the capsule in the skin-cream container, just as Goering had predicted. Throughout their investigation the members paid great attention to the possibility of places where a capsule might have been concealed for long periods, particularly at the toilet, where the seat was not within the sight of the guards' view through the door's window.

Under questioning, Dr. Pfluecker told the Board that the capsule might have been hidden in the "border" of the toilet seat. The Board's report stated: "The small brass container containing the poison could have been hidden under the rim of the toilet. . . . This was tested by the Board, who found that the container was difficult to locate when inserted in the recess of the toilet, even though they knew where it had been placed." The Board concluded that "Goering had the poison in his possession when apprehended and retained it until he employed it on the night of 15 October 1946." This was supported by a wide variety of factors and possibilities, without any conclusion of *how* he did it, except that Goering was a "subtle individual" who "outwitted his guards." Even so, the Board declared that there was no "dereliction on the part of any group of individuals connected with the administration of the prison in which he had been confined."

Thus the authorities were found responsible but innocent. As for Goering, some of his letter to Andrus was plainly true (e.g., the capsule in the skin cream), some of it was plausible, and some (e.g., the riding boots) very hard to believe.

More important, the letter completely fails to prove either that Goering was as clever as he claimed or to exonerate the guards or others from assisting Goering in enabling his suicide. Those claims could have been proved only by Goering's revealing *how* he hid the capsule "so well that . . . it could not be found," and he did not divulge that crucial matter. Goering could have lost nothing by the revelation after his death, *unless* someone else was involved. Indeed, unless Goering was prepared to explain his success, he would have done much better not to send the letter to Andrus and to leave the whole matter a mystery. Characteristically, though, he could not resist the temptation to crow.

We know from Goering's letter to his wife that she had known of the capsule since sometime before October 11, 1946. In a letter written November 28, 1975, Robert Kempner stated that Emmy Goering had told him that "a friend whose name she would not give, had passed the poison to her husband in Nuremberg." Frau Goering stated to Kempner that: "visiting the prison, she used the code 'Have you got the comb?' to make certain that Goering still had access to the cyanide" and that she also said that Goering "had not intended to use the poison unless his application to be shot was refused." Obviously, she knew what was in her husband's mind, which suggests that her statement about a secret friend is probably correct.

The friend may have been a tall, burly American first lieutenant, Jack George Wheelis by name, one of ten junior army officers who had custody of the keys to the baggage room. Wheelis appears in a photograph° showing him and Goering facing each other and apparently discussing an object which both are holding.

I myself have a pretty clear recollection of "Tex" Wheelis. My secretary, Betty Stark, was then going with another young lieutenant of the Palace of Justice guards, and on a few occasions I saw Tex at gatherings I attended. He was physically impressive and had a pleasant demeanor, but there was something about him that suggested lack of judgment, especially when he showed us a watch given him by Goering.†

For present purposes, Wheelis (who died in 1954) is important because he had access to the prison baggage room and had formed a friendship with Goering.‡ On the back of the photograph referred to above, Goering wrote: "To the great hunter from Texas."

When author Ben Swearingen visited Wheelis's widow in 1976, she showed him "a solid gold Mont Blanc fountain pen with Goering's name inscribed on the cap, a large and elaborate Swiss wristwatch bearing his name in facsimile signature, a solid gold cigarette case, and a handsome pair of gloves." Mrs. Wheelis stated that "All these gifts . . . were given to her husband for favors done on behalf of Frau Goering and her little daughter."

Swearingen subsequently perused the inventory of Goering's items

---

°See the last page of the photo insert following text page 354.

†Although I did not know it at the time, Wheelis also had his picture taken with Walter Schellenberg, an SS general subsequently indicted for war crimes and convicted. Wheelis referred to him as "Walter" and admired his promotion to general when still in his thirties.

‡Much of the rest of this account is based on Ben E. Swearingen's book *The Mystery of Hermann Goering's Suicide* (New York: Harcourt Brace Jovanovich, 1985).

that had been stored in the baggage room, and found both the pen and wristwatch listed in the inventory. Obviously, Wheelis had removed these articles from the baggage room and, if his widow's information was accurate, Emmy Goering would have regarded him as a "friend."

Like his nine fellow guardians of the baggage room, Wheelis signed identical prepared oaths stating: "I have had in my possession the key to the baggage room of the Prison during the period 1 October 1946 to 15 October 1946 and can state positively that Goering received nothing from, nor had acces [sic] to, the baggage room during that period." Assuming that Tex would have had compunctions about falsifying his oath, the reach of the oath is so limited that probably he would have had nothing to fear. In all likelihood, whatever access to the baggage room had been necessary was handled before October. This extraordinary limiting of the oath certainly was no credit to the Board of Officers.

Swearingen, despite the remarkable evidence he has amassed, makes no claim of positive proof that Wheelis aided Goering in procuring or keeping the cyanide. Neither do I, but I think it probable that if Goering had such assistance, it was provided by Tex Wheelis.

### 3

The leading participants in the first Nuremberg trial have generally fared well professionally, but few have achieved notable renown. Perhaps the most famous was Edgar Faure, who served with great distinction as Premier of the French Government. Of the other senior French prosecutors, Champetier de Ribes died within two or three years, de Menthon was appointed to the Cabinet, Gerthoffer stayed on in Nuremberg as the French representative and later returned to private practice in Paris. General Rudenko, on his return, was appointed Chief Prosecutor of the U.S.S.R., and held that position until the 1980s. Counselor Smirnov later became Chief Judge of the U.S.S.R. Supreme Court. Colonel Pokrovsky was stationed in Vienna, where I lost track of him.

Sir Hartley Shawcross left his parliamentary career and turned, highly successfully, to the corporate bar; at this writing he is still alive and sometimes heard from in the press. Maxwell-Fyfe returned to Parliament, became Conservative Lord Chancellor, published an autobiography in which he paid off some old scores, and died some years ago. Khaki Roberts returned to the bar, as did Griffith-Jones, who later became a judge at the Old Bailey. Elwyn-Jones became a Labour Lord Chancellor, was ousted by Mrs. Thatcher's roller coaster, and then became the Labour Party's principal voice in the House of Lords. He died in 1991. Airey Neave became a prominent Conservative member of the Commons. In 1978 he was killed by a bomb planted in his automobile by the Irish Republican Army. To the best of my knowledge, all the British Nuremberg prosecutors, except Lord Shaw-cross, have died.

Justice Jackson, after returning to the Supreme Court, suffered two heart attacks and died in October 1954. Earlier that year he had written the introduction to *Tyranny on Trial*, Whitney Harris's book about Nuremberg; in his last sentence, the Justice described his Nuremberg work as "the most important, enduring, and constructive work of my life." Of his senior associates, Storey, Dodd, Alderman, Shea, Amen, and Albrecht, none has survived, though many of the associate counsel are still active. Peter Calvocoressi, British but at Nuremberg working mainly for the Americans, is well known for his writings on historical and political subjects.

All but two of the Tribunal members were professional judges and returned to their judicial seats when the trial was over. The Soviet judges, however, passed out of contact with us. Their fellow members on the Tribunal sent letters and made other efforts to communicate with General Nikitchenko, but no reply ever came. Some years ago, however, the Soviet government issued a notice that Nikitchenko had died.

Professor Donnedieu de Vabres returned to his academic work and published an article about Nuremberg, stressing the Tribunal's refusal to adopt some of the prosecution's proposals. Francis Biddle, neither judge (except for a very short time) nor professor, came out the worst. He had been hoping for an ambassadorship—perhaps in Paris—but Truman had never really liked Biddle, and nothing was forthcoming. Biddle retired to live in Washington. He published two volumes of autobiography and died some years past. Of his assistants, Rowe and Fisher died several years ago, while Wechsler (who wrote a short reminiscence of Nuremberg) is still teaching and writing law with great distinction.

In strong contrast to the flight back home of all but a very few prosecution counsel, the German defense counsel, by a large majority, remained in Nuremberg to participate in the "subsequent proceedings." Only ten of the IMT defense counsel (including Stahmer, Nelte, and Exner) departed. Dix, Kranzbuehler, Seidl, Siemers, Servatius, Sauter, and von der Lippe were among the twenty-three veterans of the first trial who decided to stay on.

*4*

The events which culminated in the judgment by the International Military Tribunal began in the late summer of 1944 at the United States War Department in Washington and ended in the Tribunal's judgment in October 1946. The twenty-one defendants who were thus judged were a mere handful compared to the thousands who have been charged with crimes perpetrated in connection with World War II. To chronicle and assess the significance of all these cases would spread a huge canvas of memory and misery over virtually the whole of Eurasia.

But the International Military Tribunal, though small in the number of defendants, was and has remained the most striking and important trial of them all, and that is why it has become known as "Nuremberg"—a name which conjures up the moral and legal issues raised by applying judicial methods and decisions to challenged wartime acts.

Nuremberg was in part "revolutionary" in the sense that its makers adopted several novel criminal principles. In assessing Nuremberg I see three major questions: "How necessary was it?" "How well was it done?" "How successful was it?"

My answer to the first question is: "Absolutely." Other methods for bringing the Nazi criminals to book, from letting the Germans take care of their own malefactors to watching the British shoot them without trial, drew little support. Early in 1942 the newly formed Inter-Allied Commission on the Punishment of War Criminals had insisted on punishment "through the channels of organized justice"; those speaking for the millions of Hitler's victims wanted "vindication and retribution by law, applied through judicial process." Except in Whitehall the proposals to establish an international court to try war crimes charges spread, and early in 1945, thanks to Henry Stimson, the decision to establish an international tribunal blossomed in the War Department. Stimson and his colleagues saw that trials by military courts-martial, with lay judges, would not meet the demands of the situation, and so the establishment of a high-level tribunal, with jurists of distinction, was fixed.

Nothing less would have met the worldwide demand; the Tribunal, wherever it might have been established, was indeed "necessary." If agreement from a quite different source is desired, consider an article on Nuremberg by Otto Kranzbuehler, who, on other subjects, has differed with me often and forcefully:

> It was clear that after the obvious crimes committed under Hitler's leadership, particularly the annihilation process against the Jews, something had to happen to discharge the tension between victors and vanquished. . . . It was the United States who insisted that expiation must be sought and found by way of a judicial trial. The International Military Tribunal proceedings did, in my opinion, perform this function. It was the painful starting point for building the relations that exist today [1965] between Germany and her Western Allies.

If, then, the International Military Tribunal was necessary, how well was it made and utilized? It was a creation of the victors; were the defense lawyers given a fair opportunity to present their evidence and arguments?

Were the lawyers and the judges sufficiently intelligent and impartial? Remember Jackson's early shaft of light: "We must never forget that the record on which we judge these defendants is the record on which history will judge us tomorrow. To pass these defendants a poisoned chalice is to put it to our own lips as well." Those were beautiful words, but did the results match the aspiration?

Germany was in dire straits, struggling for food and shelter, but Nuremberg judges and prosecutors lived in comfort in commandeered houses with supplies available at the American PX. Defense counsel did not fare as well, but did much better than most of the Germans, with money and other assistance from the General Secretariat. From outside the Palace of Justice, there were angry accusations that the Americans were "coddling those Nazi lawyers" defending Goering and other rascals; it was one of those situations where there was no way to please everyone.

But the defense counsel were much more concerned with what they needed to ply their trade—especially adequate distribution to them of the bushels of documents that the American prosecutors were throwing in as evidence. Storey's egregious miscalculations of the needs of a *trial* were a low point in the Nuremberg saga, particularly since Jackson had not understood the necessities any better than Storey. It took nearly a month to straighten out the document distributions, but with the staff's Herculean efforts to raise the level of production, in the long run these errors caused no lasting harm.

Kranzbuehler understandably raised objections to the exclusion of the defense counsel from the prosecution's evidentiary archives. In normal circumstances, they would have been open to all counsel. But conditions were decidedly not normal. When the trial began, only a few months had passed since the end of a terrible war in which Germany had been a mortal enemy and had killed millions of Slavs and Jews outside the limits of war. None of the defense counsel were previously known to Tribunal or prosecution, and among the approximately thirty-five defense counsel were at least fourteen who had acknowledged past membership in the Nazi Party, most of them from 1933 or 1937 to 1945. No wonder the prosecution was slow in opening its stores of evidence to its opponents, as ultimately was done.

Kranzbuehler also argued that the use of non-German documents should have been permitted in the interests of history, and he pointed to the Soviet involvement in the occupation of Poland. In fact, the clever Seidl succeeded in getting some of these documents into the record, and indeed they were interesting historically. But I am unable to see that this matter in any way diminished the Nazis' guilt for the destruction of Poland.

More than anything else, however, the defense counsel were interested in and critical of the *law* as applied to the trial by prosecution and Tribunal. Since crime against peace was a new criminal concept, of which all the defendants had been accused, of course they were violently opposed. Furthermore, as the French judges' reaction showed, European Continental lawyers in general, bound as they are to statutory law, were virtually unanimous in their rejection of the crime against peace. I will discuss subsequently the posttrial *effect* of the Tribunal's acceptance and use of the crime against peace.

The other dimension of the trial that was likewise rejected by the defense lawyers was the "Organizations" undertaking. Although I was sensitive to the facts and factors that caused Bernays to launch this ill-favored vessel, I had been puzzled and doubtful from the start, and by 1946 I saw the enterprise much the way the defendants did. In effect, General Clay and Charles Fahy resolved the "mass" problem with denazification, and the Tribunal—especially Biddle—turned the "Organizations" into a constitutional, if impractical, entity. What might have been harmful was rendered harmless, and the "Organizations" played no significant part in the consequences of the Nuremberg trials.

Otto Kranzbuehler, in a later writing, sharply attacked the Tribunal and the prosecution for their handling of war crimes and took positions about them which would have greatly curtailed the ambit of the laws of war and which appear to me entirely wrong. In brief, he wrote that war crimes are limited to "(1) violations of the rules of war by members of the armed forces, or (2) armed hostilities by non-members of the armed forces." In other words, unless you are a regular soldier, you can commit a war crime only by engaging in "armed hostilities." [*]

As I read these words, it appears to me that, under Kranzbuehler's rules, war crimes charges could not have been brought against Hitler, Himmler, Goebbels, Eichmann, or any of the Nuremberg defendants except the five military men, for none of the others was a soldier or engaged in "armed hostilities." Thus a railroad engineer, driving a train full of Jews from Paris to Auschwitz, with knowledge of their fate, could be accused of war crimes if he was a soldier, but not if he was a civilian.

It is true that, until Nuremberg, most of the trials based on the laws of war (or on domestic legislation embodying the laws of war) were trials of military defendants. But I know of nothing in the laws of war that excludes unarmed civilians who violate laws of war from criminal liability.

Despite Kranzbuehler's great skill as a court lawyer, it appears to me that he, like his client, Doenitz, passed the war years looking out to sea,

---

[*]Kranzbuehler continued with a curious passage in which he declared that war crimes would not cover "statesmen or public officers for a policy leading to war," "generals for the military preparation for war," "members of the legal professions on account of their preparation for certain legislation," or "industrialists on account of the participation in the war economy." The statement is meaningless because none of the acts charged against the several types of individuals are necessarily criminal, whoever the actors may be.

oblivious of what was going on in the great areas of Hitler's conquests. When the war ended, Kranzbuehler apparently expected everything to fall back at once into the same niches it had occupied in 1939, or even 1933. Thus Kranzbuehler marvels at "the enormous step that was taken at Nuremberg" and adds that he "does not wish to criticize as it was a step forward." But he then doubts that these "steps" will have "authority as a precedent for the future." He insists that international law may never be "binding on the individual citizen."

There are other passages in Kranzbuehler's writing on the laws of war which appear retrograde to me. I have dwelt on his views because it is plain that Kranzbuehler is not writing just for his own satisfaction. He is a remarkably able lawyer, respected in law and business, whose views are undoubtedly influential.

## 5

Let us turn to the decisions which were made by the framers of the Charter and the Indictment and by the members of the International Military Tribunal. As for the Charter, the nodal point was the inclusion of the crime against peace, the gist of which had been sparked by Colonel Chanler and adopted by President Roosevelt himself. It embodied principles that Jackson had turned to while Attorney General, early in the war, and it gained momentum when the Labour government replaced the Conservatives and Shawcross became Attorney General. The Russians saw it only as directed against Nazis and Fascists, and the French never really accepted it. But with strong British support Jackson was able to put it through, and its presence in the Charter was approved by nineteen "adhering" members of the United Nations.

Arguments in support of punishing individuals ex post facto for violation of the crime against peace can be made, but, if conducted on a plane devoid of political and emotional factors, will be won by the defense. But in 1945 those very factors were overwhelming. Peoples whose nations had been attacked and dismembered without warning wanted legal retribution, whether or not this was "a first time." The inclusion of the crime against peace vastly enhanced the world's interest in and support for the trials at Nuremberg.

The other controversial aspect of the crime against peace was the inclusion of "conspiracy" as a basis for conviction. This matter has already been discussed, and I wish to add only that all eight defendants convicted of conspiracy were also convicted under Count Two of the Indictment and all but Hess under Count Three as well, which contains no reference to conspiracy. Frick and Seyss-Inquart were convicted of the crime against peace *only* under Count Two and nevertheless were condemned to death.

And this suggests that the presence or absence of conspiracy may not have been as important a factor in the eyes of the judges as in those of the American and British prosecutors.

As for Article 8 of the Charter, providing that obedience to a superior's command to commit a crime should be considered only in mitigation, I am in agreement with Kranzbuehler that the Article is flawed. If the defendant did not know, and had no basis for knowing, that the order he had obeyed was unlawful, the defendant should not be held liable at all. If he knew that the order called for unlawful acts, the defendant should be found guilty and allowed to rely on duress or other factors only as a matter of mitigation.

I also regret the inclusion in the Charter of Article 12, giving the Tribunal power to hear proceedings against an unavailable defendant in absentia. The aimless discussions of Bormann's state of health should have been dealt with summarily, as was done eventually in the Gustav Krupp case, by suspending the indictment until the defendant recovered or was found or proven dead. To utilize Article 12 in order to base a judgment of death against Bormann was wholly unnecessary and undignified.

Despite these several criticisms, however, it appears to me that the Charter served its purpose. Especially considering the divergence of the initial opinions in the opening discussions in London, and Jackson's sometimes overbearing tactics, he and the British were able to lay out a basis for the trial which proved adequate to the tortuous road ahead.

The Indictment contained some very good initial passages describing the political, economic, and military development of the Nazi Party and the Wehrmacht. In line with Jackson's conception of the prosecution's case, these opening sections were heavily laden with "Nazi conspirators" and the growth of a huge "conspiracy." The result was that the "conspiracy" pictured in Count One completely dwarfed Count Two, crimes against peace, which merely listed the several "wars of aggression" that had already been described in Count One. This, as we have seen, was part of Jackson's strategy to bring the entire case within the ambit of Count One and consequently of the American prosecution. Since Counts Three and Four (war crimes and crimes against humanity) were drawn in the Continental style, with extensive evidentiary itemization, the Indictment had little homogeneity, but that was of small consequence.

On the whole the Indictment was satisfactory, with the important exception of the selection of the defendants. The failure of the British to check the health of Gustav Krupp was a catastrophic blunder. It resulted in a totally unnecessary and unseemly argument among the chief prosecutors before the Tribunal. It prevented the trial of Alfried Krupp before the International Military Tribunal, which would probably have resulted in a capital sentence or a long prison term. Such a trial would also have had a strong effect on the judges at the later Nuremberg trials, in which Alfried Krupp and many other industrialists were convicted but soon released.

The whole process of selecting the defendants was badly managed by the British and American prosecutors, who had most of the major surviving Nazis in their hands. Neither Shawcross nor Jackson paid enough attention to their better-informed lawyers and German experts. Jackson was in Rome when the final decisions were made. Otto Dietrich, Goebbels's immediate subordinate, was in our hands and would have made a far more important defendant than Fritzsche.

What shall be said about the caliber of the Tribunal judges? Writing home, Biddle had belittled their capacity (despite his friendship with Birkett) and portrayed himself as the "man who ran the show." He had a sharp and critical mind and often succeeded in putting across his views, but in the "business of judging" he was a neophyte. Indeed, of the four voting judges, Biddle had only a few months on the bench and de Vabres none at all, Nikitchenko was an experienced military judge, and Lawrence alone had risen to high judicial office. Lawrence was neither brilliant nor a "great" judge, but experience, firmness, and common sense made him a great presiding judge. No other member of the bench could match Lawrence for that essential contribution. In the Tribunal's novel and difficult task, confronting fifty-odd enemies, many of whom were very able, and prosecutors eager to dominate the scene, Lawrence won and held the respect of all for the Tribunal. On that score, the performance of the Tribunal could hardly have been better.

Another positive aspect of the Tribunal was that despite the members' disagreements and profound differences, they were bent on bringing their enterprise to a successful conclusion. In conference, opinions were forcefully stated, but all realized that in some situations personal opinions must be suppressed in order to reach a votable conclusion. Nikitchenko was well aware of this necessity, and his dissenting opinion was not savagely written. Fortunately, his objections did not pierce the fundamentals of the case, as they involved only the penalties for a few individual defendants or organizations.

It was, however, in that very area that the Tribunal proved most prone to stumble. De Vabres's capricious insistence that all the defendants should be convicted, coupled with his dislike of heavy sentences, would have been laughable if his votes had not been often skewed.

It is hard to condone the Tribunal's unthinking and callous handling of the Streicher case. I agreed with Biddle that Doenitz should have been acquitted, but the opinion he devised to create a majority was absurd and should never have been accepted by the Tribunal.

From the beginning, it appeared to me that there was no sufficient case against Schacht to warrant a conviction, let alone a hanging. To counter the fact that Schacht had ceased to be involved in Hitler's enterprises even before the war had begun, Jackson, Fyfe, and Biddle (as well as others) had argued that Schacht had remained Reich Minister without Portfolio until

1943, had publicly complimented Hitler on his war successes, and had otherwise been a "good boy" in public. But there was uncontroverted testimony that Schacht had connived with the resistance as early as 1938. Any prominent government figure who had decided to hook up with the resistance would surely conclude that such a dangerous course could succeed only by appearing to be loyal to the regime. At any moment Hitler could have blown Schacht away like a fly, and it would have been the sheerest folly for Schacht to have taken a truculent attitude toward the Fuehrer. Yet Biddle, even after much discussion, still advocated sending Schacht to prison for life. I was astounded when I learned that Schacht had escaped conviction so narrowly.

As judges, the nonvoting members of the Tribunal seemed to me more level-headed than their seniors. This was not surprising, as Parker and Falco had much more judicial experience than either Biddle or de Vabres, and Birkett was far more of a lawyer than Lawrence. Parker, indeed, had been nominated for a seat on the Supreme Court of the United States, and only bad political luck had thwarted his confirmation. He was garrulous and told too many Southern jokes, but in conference he had the wisest head in the room.

All in all, I would agree with Biddle that, as judges, the Tribunal was not a brilliant group. But their work was professional, honest, and did no discredit to the heavy task that was set before them. Administratively the report is even better; with the aid of Airey Neave and other bright assistants, the Tribunal resolved problems such as the Organizations' witnesses with surprising fairness and dispatch.

Finally, we come to the lawyers for both the prosecution and the defense. Without the latter there never would have been either court or case, and the Tribunal was sensitive to this mutual interdependence. A plainly incompetent group of defense lawyers would have made a farce of the case; a rowdy contingent could have shattered the court's dignity. At the same time, the Tribunal could not dictate or even appear to guide the individual selections of defense counsel.

Again, thanks largely to Neave, the results were essentially satisfactory. Lawyers like Birkett, who appeared to think that cross-examination was the be-all and end-all of litigation, complained bitterly about the clumsiness and boredom perpetrated by defense counsel unaccustomed to common law procedures. But Dix and Kranzbuehler were not the only first-rate lawyers among the defense counsel, and particularly considering the ravages of Hitler, war, and defeat within the German professions as a whole, the performance of defense counsel was highly commendable.

The four groups of prosecutors teamed surprisingly well, but their motivations and outlooks differed sharply, and only between the British and some of the Americans was there warmth and camaraderie. The French, still pulling themselves together after the shock of German occupation and the Resistance, were the most reticent and least effective. De Menthon delivered an elegant opening statement but departed immediately, more interested in French politics than in Nuremberg. Dubost, able and tough, became the strong man only nominally subject to Champetier de Ribes. I liked Dubost, but few other Americans did, and of the other French, only Edgar Faure and Gerthoffer made any dent.

The Soviet lawyers understood the functions and interpretation of statutes well enough, but in the significance and handling of defendants and witnesses, the Russians came from a world wholly different from that of the Western countries. Just as Nikitchenko had arrived in London viewing Stalin's pronouncements as preestablishing the guilt of the defendants and leaving little but the penalties still to be determined, so Rudenko and his staff came viewing defendants' and witnesses' denials of guilt as lies. This explains the Soviet lawyers' frequent habit of calmly dropping the issue if a witness refused to accept the lawyer's accusation. The denials did not mean that the defendant was innocent, but that he was intransigent and thus all the more deserving of a speedy death.

After watching a cross-examiner such as Fyfe, the Soviet lawyers made some forays into these unfamiliar fields, but it came hard, and they certainly did nothing to strengthen the evidence produced by the Western powers. But Moscow did produce a mass of orally recorded and photographed evidence of German activities in the conquered areas of Poland and the Soviet Union, including Auschwitz and the other death camps in Poland, all of which were overrun by the Soviet armies.

General Rudenko himself was a powerful speaker, and his opening and closing statements were effective. On administrative matters, Colonel Pokrovsky was much the most sophisticated and cooperative of the Soviet prosecutors.

Excluding Attorney General Sir Hartley Shawcross, who was rarely in Nuremberg, the British prosecution comprised exactly six barristers. However, such economy of manpower would not have been possible had not the responsibility of the British in presenting the prosecution's case been initially limited to Count Two of the Indictment—a task far briefer and simpler than that of Count One, presented by the Americans. But as the case went on, the British contingent assumed a much greater importance in the conduct of the trial. The Court increasingly relied on Fyfe for guidance and assistance as the case moved into the French and Soviet presentations and when the defendants and their witnesses took over the lectern. Fyfe was a much better organized man than Jackson, and after the latter's debacle with Goering, Fyfe became the leading prosecution spokesman on the floor of the Tribunal.

But the core and focus of the Nuremberg enterprise was, from the beginning to the end, the American prosecution. The Charter had been drawn in general accordance with Jackson's proposals. Jackson and his staff had been primarily responsible for most of the Indictment. Jackson opened the prosecution's case. American lawyers dominated the first two months of the trial. At the outset Storey made horrendous administrative errors which slowed the trial's progress, but after some weeks the obstacles were overcome. Twenty-three American lawyers addressed the Tribunal—more than twice the combined British and French delegations and more than twice the Soviet delegation.

The American lawyers were as "bright" as the British barristers. The difficulties encountered by some of them were the result of prior law practice (such as I had experienced) which had not included court work with defendants and witnesses. The British press played up the superiority of the barristers, but no harm was done to the prosecution's case.

In concluding this discussion, I must recur to the unique and vital role played by Justice Jackson. He made mistakes and some bad ones, but there was much more to the Nuremberg case than legal disquisition or cross-examination. Two other things were vital: passion and eloquence. More than any other man of that period, Jackson worked and wrote with deep passion and spoke in winged words. There was no one else who could have done that half as well as he.

## 6

And so, the final question: Was the International Military Tribunal a success? Its creation raised many different desires, and there are many different tests of success. The best I can do is to deal with a few of the most apparent goals for which various groups were hoping and the several actions of the Tribunal and the prosecutors which were denounced by the defendants.

At the beginning of this assessment, I brought out that during the closing months of World War II there was a worldwide desire that the leading Nazis be tried by law and suffer condign punishment. The world was not devoid of opponents of this procedure, such as the late Senator Robert Taft, but the negative voices were all but drowned in the chorus of "yeas."

Furthermore, there were good reasons for not letting the fate of the Nazis take an unguided course, and once the British had abandoned their proposal to shoot some of the most hated out of hand, the world leaders agreed on a trial. A scattering of small trials would have carried no weight, whereas the world's eyes and ears would be fastened on a big international trial.

So the International Military Tribunal began and finished, with general approval and little criticism from the world public. There were no charges that the defendants were being railroaded, the disclosures of Nazi atrocities were appalling, and the judges appeared to be fair and humane men. Thus the Tribunal accomplished what it had been established for. The world public was satisfied, and even Dr. Kranzbuehler approved its general purpose. In short, the International Military Tribunal was a success.

But my second touchstone of success is much more complicated and controversial. Jackson had made crimes against peace—the criminalization of initiating aggressive war—the foremost feature of the Nuremberg trial, and the defense counsel had focused their biggest guns against this part of the case. The Tribunal had stood firm in accordance with the Charter and had convicted twelve of the defendants of crimes against peace. Rudolf Hess had been convicted *only* of crimes against peace and for that offense spent the rest of his long life behind bars. But many lawyers in many countries condemned these punishments, and there were only a few more convictions for crimes against peace, at Nuremberg or elsewhere.°

We must now take account of the distinction between the principle of crimes against peace and the use of that principle to punish individuals for actions committed several years before the principle was first applied. Defense counsel at Nuremberg were, of course, primarily concerned with the second matter.

People might well differ about the wisdom of declaring that initiation of aggressive war is an offense under international law, but surely there would be nothing unlawful about creating such a principle *for the future*. However, the Charter drew no such distinction, and unquestionably the Charter and the Tribunal's judgment applied Counts One and Two to prior actions of the defendants and thus inflicted ex post facto punishments. From the beginning this had been Jackson's purpose, in order to establish a *precedent* for punishing crimes against peace in the future. The Tribunal's judgment accomplished this but, of course, not to the satisfaction of the many lawyers and others who insisted that the ex post facto principle should have been respected, in which event, of course, Jackson's desired precedent would not have been established.

There is no likelihood that this particular clash of opinions will ever be reconciled. But for the future, the weight of the four big nations at London and Nuremberg had initially implanted the criminality of initiating aggressive war as an accepted rule of international law, further strengthened by the adherence of nineteen other nations. Additional authority was provided when, on December 11, 1946, the General Assembly of the United Nations "affirmed the principles of international law recognized by the Charter of the Nuremberg Tribunal and the judgment of the Tribunal."†

---

°A number of Japanese defendants were convicted of crimes against peace at the Tokyo War Crimes Trials and a few more in the last of the war crimes trials at Nuremberg in 1948–1949.

†United Nations Resolution 95-1, December 11, 1946. The wording of the resolution does

Certainly neither Jackson nor anyone else anticipated that declaring an international ban on waging aggressive wars would put an end to them, any more than the laws of war have ended war crimes. Furthermore, excepting World War II's gigantic war crimes in Eastern Europe, most war crimes are individual or group actions that can be handled locally. But waging aggressive war is a huge undertaking which, if seriously pressed, can only be stopped by sufficient countervailing threats or military actions. Since this may require a concert of nations, such situations are best put before the United Nations.

During the four or five years after the end of World War II there was an effort made at the United Nations to create a permanent International Criminal Court, but Republican presidents have shown no interest in such a project. Application of international rules of warfare thus remains generally determined by the nations concerned, except in the comparatively rare occasions when the United Nations takes action.

Since the United Nations rarely acts as referee, there are often situations in which the nature of a war, as aggressive or not, is arguable and remains so. Our own war in Vietnam is a good example. Secretary of State Dean Rusk told the American Society of International Law: "Surely we must have learned over the three decades that the acceptance of aggression leads only to a sure catastrophe. Surely we have learned that the aggressor must face the consequences of his actions."

Dean Rusk's aggressor was, of course, North Vietnam. But simultaneously the National Lawyers Guild, voicing the views of many thousands of youths facing the draft and others denouncing America's war in Vietnam, was proclaiming the aggressive nature of that war. Eric Norden declared: "Our actions in Vietnam fall within the prohibited classifications of warfare laid down at Nuremberg . . . the United States is clearly guilty of 'War Crimes,' 'Crimes Against Peace,' and 'Crimes against Humanity.' "

For us, however, the greater interest attaches to those war actions which are plainly aggressive, and the question is whether anyone will try to stop it. When the Soviet Union invaded and occupied Afghanistan, the aggression was indisputable. The United States gave some help to the resisters, but did not take up arms against the Soviet Union the way it had attacked North Vietnam and later Iraq. Why? Short of dropping the bomb there was little we could do, and it was quite clear that a war between the United States and the Soviet Union would be much more dangerous to the world than the Soviet Union's occupation of Afghanistan.

In sharp contrast was the Korean War. In 1950 North Korea suddenly

---

not explicitly affirm the ex post facto punishments, but since the Tribunal's "judgment" is affirmed, it is arguable that the punishments were included in the affirmation.

attacked South Korea. It was a clear case of aggression, and the United Nations soon approved America's joining in South Korea's military action to repel the invader. Although the United States provided the bulk of the defense, under the authority of the United Nations, some other nations sent military support to South Korea, and eventually the North Koreans and their Chinese allies were driven back to the original border between the two Koreas and a truce was declared.

A few years later an aggressive act was summarily blocked without the participation of the United Nations. Angered by Egyptian efforts to obtain full control of the Suez Canal, Britain and Israel sent forces into the Suez area to maintain British interests. But both the United States and the Soviet Union emphatically denounced the British-Israel military incursion, Prime Minister Anthony Eden backed off, and the foray was abandoned.

Very recently the attention of the world was focused on the crisis in the Persian Gulf caused by Iraq's aggressive seizure and annexation of Kuwait. Iraq, though not a large country, was armed to the teeth, and President Bush immediately started sending large bodies of American troops to Saudi Arabia to prevent any further advances by the Iraqis and ultimately to force Iraq to return Kuwait to its own government. No doubt other factors were involved, but President Bush, successfully seeking popular support for his actions, relied principally on the argument that international law forbids aggressive wars and that such gross and dangerous violations cannot be tolerated. The United Nations has adopted this view and supported the successful efforts to force Iraq to comply.

In 1863, Francis Lieber described war as "the means to obtain great ends of state, or to consist in defense against wrong." In 1938, Alfred Jodl wrote that "preservation of the State and Folk and the assurance of its historical future . . . give war its total character and ethical justification."

By the end of World War II, it was high time that such antediluvian and essentially murderous paeans to the morality of war be buried. The Nuremberg ban on aggressive war was so intended and, as the episodes described above show, the legal and moral validity of the ban has been repeatedly invoked in the interests of peace. To that extent, the International Military Tribunal was a success.

But it has also become clear that what might be called "the Bernays additions" did more harm than good. In the upshot they did little or no damage to Nuremberg defendants, but they left a black mark on the prosecution's judgment. This was the consequence, even though Bernays had important and valid purposes in proposing the inclusion in the case of "conspiracy" and the Organizations.

The Tribunal crushed Bernays's intended use of "conspiracy" by interpreting the Charter so as to confine its use to "crimes against peace." The Tribunal convicted eight of the defendants of conspiracy to commit "crimes against peace" under Count One, but it is unlikely that the conspiracy convictions had much independent effect on the punishments. It is true that only by a conspiracy charge could Schacht's conviction have been possible, but in the clutch the Tribunal found the evidence against Schacht insufficient.

As for the organizations, in their originally intended provisions they could have led to thousands of penalties imposed without granting the normal rights of defendants. But the treatment of "mass Nazism" was usurped by the substitution of the Denazification Program and by the Tribunal's modification of the organizational requirements of proof so that most of Bernays's original edifice came tumbling down.

Thus 99 percent of what the defendants had feared from conspiracy and Organizations was eliminated. Unfortunately for those who made the amends, they did not wipe the International Military Tribunal clean in the pages of German history.

Conspiracy had required days, and the organizations months, of study, argumentation, procurement of witnesses, and speeches. Throughout these tiring and ominous activities, the defendants and their counsel could not know how these matters, to them so baffling and fearful, might ultimately affect them. During the arguments in open court both Jackson and Fyfe had taken legal positions that today appear extreme, and that certainly added to defense counsels' worries.

It was, of course, too much to hope that even under the best of circumstances, the defendants and their lawyers would admire the actions and statements of the prosecution. But the Bernays proposals had brought into the trial these features, previously unknown to war crimes lore, and they were menacing to the defendants.

It was also too much to expect that Stimson, Jackson, and the other lawyers who put together the American prosecution's ideas should have foreseen the consequences of Bernays's proposals. In his opening speech to the Tribunal, Jackson had eloquently stressed the need for fairness toward the defendants, but Jackson was thinking of fairness as he saw it. Neither conspiracy (a familiar legal device to him) nor the organizations (which he thought necessary) appeared unfair to him.

But the very idea of an International Military Tribunal was unfamiliar to the German lawyers, who naturally regarded their erstwhile victors with fear and suspicion, sentiments which would deepen when this strange tribunal demanded that they confront new and dangerous obstacles called "conspiracies," "groups," and "organizations." Furthermore, the prosecution was also bringing into the arena new crimes against "peace" and "humanity," the unaware past violations of which could send the defendants to the gallows.

This is the way that the Charter, the Indictment, and the behavior of the judges and prosecutors must have struck the defendants and their counsel. Toward the end of the trial a few rays of hope emanated from the Tribunal's remarks and from its handling of the Organizations in its opinion. But nothing basically changed the German counsels initial impressions. No wonder, then, that so far as Germans thought about Nuremberg—an occupation which increased as economic conditions improved—their opinions of the International Military Tribunal were generally negative. To them, Nuremberg was not a success.

7

I will close with a few words about what I call "political warts" on Nuremberg and the IMT. The biggest wart was the presence, necessary as it was, of the Soviet judges on the bench. Despite Russia's major share in the destruction of Nazism, hatred and fear of communism and the Soviet Union was felt and voiced throughout the United States through much of this century and particularly from the 1930s to the 1970s.

The fortunes of war drew Britain, the Soviet Union, and the United States together as the Big Three, and Stalin participated with the other two in the discussion of war crimes trials for the Nazis. Military defeat and the collapse of the German government led to the quadripartite government in Berlin. Given the history of the relations between Russia and the other three, it would have been the height of political folly to proceed with an international trial of war criminals without the participation of the Soviet Union.

But the Russians came in with problems, as the British and Americans well knew. The Moscow trials of alleged traitors to Stalin had a very bad name. Jackson was intent on including crimes against peace, and the Soviet Union had participated in Germany's seizure of Poland and shared with Hitler the spoils of war. Shortly thereafter Russia attacked Finland and forced the annexation of parts of that nation. These power plays sat uneasily beside the punishment of German crimes against peace, and the naughty Seidl did all he could to embarrass the Tribunal, which was doing its best to protect Nikitchenko and Rudenko from embarrassment.

Rudenko made matters worse when he insisted, over Jackson's strong opposition, in including the Katyn massacre in the Indictment's catalogues of German war crimes. At that time there was no clear proof that the Russians rather than the Germans were to blame, but many thought so, and the Tribunal was handed another hot potato. Wisely, the Tribunal allowed both Russians and Germans to testify, but made no mention of the Katyn massacres in the opinion.

There was less open embarrassment but lamentable concealment of evidence in the Raeder case, when Siemers asked for the British Admiralty's documents on British plans to send troops into Norway to cut off the flow of iron ore from Sweden to Germany. Full disclosure was not made until after the Nuremberg trials had ended.

This is a notable list of political warts, and over the years opponents of Nuremberg have made the most of this material, sometimes combining the political with the legal sore spots. It has also been charged that British and American air attacks over Germany were so devastating that they should be regarded as war crimes just as much as the Nazi outrages.°

These last arguments, which I have discussed elsewhere, lie beyond the scope of this work, and here I will only remind the reader that there were no recognized laws of war pertaining to aerial bombardments during World War II and that none were formally proposed by the nations until 1977.


8


During the three years following the end of the International Military Tribunal, war crimes trials continued at the Palace of Justice and in many other countries and places. The relations among the Western powers and the Soviet Union steadily worsened, and Czechoslovakia, Poland, and Hungary became Soviet satellites. Steps were taken to revive German military power, John McCloy replaced General Clay, and a West German government under Konrad Adenauer was established.

The result of these and related developments was a rapid decrease of political interest in war crimes matters and eventually a desire to put an end to trials and liberate war criminals still in captivity. But war crimes trials did not disappear for long. In the early 1960s, West German courts began a long series of such trials, based not directly on the international laws of war but on German national law.

Major war crimes trials in more recent years, all based on national rather than international law, include Israel's trials of Adolf Eichmann and John Demjanuk, France's trial of Klaus Barbie, and the United States's trials of Lieutenant William Calley, Captain Ernest Medina, and others in connection with the massacre of civilians at My Lai in South Vietnam.

During the last twenty-five years, public interest in the laws of war has increased. In 1977 in Geneva, there were proposals to augment the existing Conventions with provisions applicable to aerial bombardment and to the

---

°Among the less temperate criticisms, consider the following excerpt: "Surely much of Allied war crimes policy as well as large portions of the basic American plan appear to be mistakes piled on folly. The actions of the negotiators and the prosecutors are also replete with blindness, miscalculation and a suicidal passion for complexity. Perhaps, more basically, the whole notion of Allied action to bring justice to a war-torn world ran headlong against the main thrust of the war itself." Bradley F. Smith, *Reaching Judgment at Nuremberg* (Basic Books, 1977) p. 301.

prisoner rights of irregular troops. These new protocols were signed by virtually all the participating countries, and some of them (not including the United States or Great Britain) have ratified the protocols.

That same year, and also in 1981, two United Nations Conventions proposed prohibitions against military action seriously destructive of the environment and against the use of unnecessarily injurious and painful weapons. In the United Nations General Assembly, there is increasing support for the establishment of a permanent tribunal for the trial of international crimes.

Reflecting on the jurisdiction of such a court, I recalled that the Nuremberg Tribunal had jurisdiction only over "the major war criminals of the European Axis countries." Considering the times and circumstances of its creation, it is hardly surprising that the Tribunal was given jurisdiction over the vanquished but not the victors. Many times I have heard Germans (and others) complain that "only the losers get tried."

Early in the Korean War, when General Douglas MacArthur's forces landed at Inchon, the American and South Korean armies drove the North Koreans all the way north to the border between North Korea and China, at the Yalu River. About a week later the Chinese attacked in force and their opponents were driven deep into South Korea.

During the brief period when our final victory appeared in hand, I received several telephone calls from members of the press asking whether the United States would try suspect North Koreans as war criminals. I was quite unable to predict whether or not such trials would be undertaken, but I replied that if they were to take place, the tribunal should be established on a neutral base, preferably by the United Nations, and given jurisdiction to hear charges not only against North Koreans but South Koreans and Americans (or any other participants) as well.

I am still of that opinion. The laws of war do not apply only to the suspected criminals of vanquished nations. There is no moral or legal basis for immunizing victorious nations from scrutiny. The laws of war are not a one-way street.

# APPENDICES

# *Appendix A*

## CHARTER OF THE INTERNATIONAL MILITARY TRIBUNAL

AGREEMENT by the Government of the UNITED STATES OF AMERICA, the Provisional Government of the FRENCH REPUBLIC, the Government of the UNITED KINGDOM OF GREAT BRITAIN AND NORTHERN IRELAND and the Government of the UNION OF SOVIET SOCIALIST REPUBLICS for the Prosecution and Punishment of the MAJOR WAR CRIMINALS of the EUROPEAN AXIS

WHEREAS the United Nations have from time to time made declarations of their intention that War Criminals shall be brought to justice;

AND WHEREAS the Moscow Declaration of the 30th October 1943 on German atrocities in Occupied Europe stated that those German Officers and men and members of the Nazi Party who have been responsible for or have taken a consenting part in atrocities and crimes will be sent back to the countries in which their abominable deeds were done in order that they may be judged and punished according to the laws of these liberated countries and of the free Governments that will be created therein;

AND WHEREAS this Declaration was stated to be without prejudice to the case of major criminals whose offenses have no particular geographical location and who will be punished by the joint decision of the Governments of the Allies;

NOW THEREFORE the Government of the United States of America, the Provisional Government of the French Republic, the Government of the United Kingdom of Great Britain and Northern Ireland and the Government of the Union of Soviet Socialist Republics (hereinafter called "the Signatories") acting in the interests of all the United Nations and by their representatives duly authorized thereto have concluded this Agreement.

Article 1. There shall be established after consultation with the Control Council for Germany an International Military Tribunal for the trial of war criminals whose offenses have no particular geographical location whether they be accused individually or in their capacity as members of the organizations or groups or in both capacities.

Article 2. The constitution, jurisdiction and functions of the International Military Tribunal shall be those set in the Charter annexed to this Agreement, which Charter shall form an integral part of this Agreement.

Article 3. Each of the Signatories shall take the necessary steps to make available for the investigation of the charges and trial the major war criminals detained by them who are to be tried by the International Military Tribunal. The Signatories shall also use their best endeavors to make available for investigation of the charges against and the trial before the International Military Tribunal such of the major war criminals as are not in the territories of any of the Signatories.

Article 4. Nothing in this Agreement shall prejudice the provisions established by the Moscow Declaration concerning the return of war criminals to the countries where they committed their crimes.

Article 5. Any Government of the United Nations may adhere to this Agreement by notice given through the diplomatic channel to the Government of the United Kingdom, who shall inform the other signatory and adhering Governments of each such adherence.

Article 6. Nothing in this Agreement shall prejudice the jurisdiction or the powers of any national or occupation court established or to be established in any allied territory or in Germany for the trial of war criminals.

Article 7. This Agreement shall come into force on the day of signature and shall remain in force for the period of one year and shall continue thereafter, subject to the right of any Signatory to give, through the diplomatic channel, one month's notice of intention to terminate it. Such termination shall not prejudice any proceedings already taken or any findings already made in pursuance of this Agreement.

IN WITNESS WHEREOF the Undersigned have signed the present Agreement.

DONE in quadruplicate in London this 8th day of August 1945 each in English, French and Russian, and each text to have equal authenticity.

For the Government of the United States of America

Robert H. Jackson

For the Provisional Government of the French Republic

Robert Falco

For the Government of the United Kingdom of Great Britain and Northern Ireland

Jowitt C.

For the Government of the Union of Soviet Socialist Republics

I. Nikitchenko
A. Trainin

## I. CONSTITUTION OF THE INTERNATIONAL MILITARY TRIBUNAL

Article 1. In pursuance of the Agreement signed on the 8th day of August 1945 by the Government of the United States of America, the Provisional Government of the French Republic, the Government of the United Kingdom of Great Britain and Northern Ireland and the Government of the Union of Soviet Socialist Republics, there shall be established an International Military Tribunal (hereinafter called "the Tribunal") for the just and prompt trial and punishment of the major war criminals of the European Axis.

Article 2. The Tribunal shall consist of four members, each with an alternate. One member and one alternate shall be appointed by each of the Signatories. The alternates shall, so far as they are able, be present at all sessions of the Tribunal. In case of illness of any member of the Tribunal or his incapacity for some other reason to fulfill his functions, his alternate shall take his place.

Article 3. Neither the Tribunal, its members nor their alternates can be challenged by the prosecution, or by the Defendants or their Counsel. Each Signatory may replace its members of the Tribunal or his alternate for reasons of health or for other good reasons, except that no replacement may take place during a Trial, other than by an alternate.

Article 4
  (a) The presence of all four members of the Tribunal or the alternate for any absent member shall be necessary to constitute the quorum.

  (b) The members of the Tribunal shall, before any trial begins, agree among themselves upon the selection from their number of a President, and the President shall hold office during the trial, or as may otherwise be agreed by a vote of not less than three members. The principle of rotation of presidency for successive trials is agreed. If, however, a session of the Tribunal takes place on the territory of one of the four Signatories, the representative of that Signatory on the Tribunal shall preside.

  (c) Save as aforesaid the Tribunal shall take decisions by a majority vote and in case the votes are evenly divided, the vote of the President shall be decisive: provided always that convictions and sentences shall only be imposed by affirmative votes of at least three members of the Tribunal.

Article 5. In case of need and depending on the number of the matters to be tried, other Tribunals may be set up; and the establishment, functions, and procedure of each Tribunal shall be identical, and shall be governed by this Charter.

## II. JURISDICTION AND
## GENERAL PRINCIPLES

Article 6. The Tribunal established by the Agreement referred to in Article 1 hereof for the trial and punishment of the major war criminals of the European

Axis countries shall have the power to try and punish persons who, acting in the interests of the European Axis countries, whether as individuals or as members of organizations, committed any of the following crimes.

The following acts, or any of them, are crimes coming within the jurisdiction of the Tribunal for which there shall be individual responsibility:

(a) CRIMES AGAINST PEACE: namely, planning, preparation, initiation or waging of a war of aggression, or a war in violation of international treaties, agreements or assurances, or participation in a common plan or conspiracy for the accomplishment of any of the foregoing;

(b) WAR CRIMES: namely, violations of the laws or customs of war. Such violations shall include, but not be limited to, murder, ill-treatment or deportation to slave labor or for any other purpose of civilian population of or in occupied territory, murder or ill-treatment of prisoners of war or persons on the seas, killing of hostages, plunder of public or private property, wanton destruction of cities, towns or villages, or devastation not justified by military necessity;

(c) CRIMES AGAINST HUMANITY: namely, murder, extermination, enslavement, deportation, and other inhumane acts committed against any civilian population, before or during the war;° or persecutions on political, racial or religious grounds in execution of or in connection with any crime within the jurisdiction of the Tribunal, whether or not in violation of the domestic law of the country where perpetrated.

Leaders, organizers, instigators and accomplices participating in the formulation or execution of a common plan or conspiracy to commit any of the foregoing crimes are responsible for all acts performed by any persons in execution of such plan.

Article 7. The official position of defendants, whether as Heads of State or responsible officials in Government Departments, shall not be considered as freeing them from responsibility or mitigating punishment.

Article 8. The fact that the Defendant acted pursuant to order of his Government or of a superior shall not free him from responsibility, but may be considered in mitigation of punishment if the Tribunal determines that justice so requires.

Article 9. At the trial of any individual member of any group or organization the Tribunal may declare (in connection with any act of which the individual may be

---

°In the Russian text, this punctuation is a comma, instead of the semicolon in the English and French texts. When the discrepancy was noted by the signatories, it was agreed that the Russian text was correct and that the English and French texts should be amended by the substitution of a comma in the English text and a comma and a suitable change of wording in the French text. This was accomplished by a protocol signed by the four chief prosecutors (Jackson, de Menthon, Shawcross, and Rudenko) on October 6, 1945 (Jackson, *Internat. Conf.* 429). The point of the change was to make the limiting phrase "in execution of or in connection with any crime within the jurisdiction of the Tribunal" clearly applicable to the first clause of paragraph (c).

convicted) that the group or organization of which the individual was a member was a criminal organization.

After the receipt of the Indictment the Tribunal shall give such notice as it thinks fit that the prosecution intends to ask the Tribunal to make such declaration and any member of the organization will be entitled to apply to the Tribunal for leave to be heard by the Tribunal upon the question of the criminal character of the organization. The Tribunal shall have power to allow or reject the application. If the application is allowed, the Tribunal may direct in what manner the applicants shall be represented and heard.

Article 10. In cases where a group or organization is declared criminal by the Tribunal, the competent national authority of any Signatory shall have the right to bring individual to trial for membership therein before national, military or occupation courts. In any such case the criminal nature of the group or organization is considered proved and shall not be questioned.

Article 11. Any person convicted by the Tribunal may be charged before a national, military or occupation court, referred to in Article 10 of this Charter, with a crime other than of membership in a criminal group or organization and such court may, after convicting him, impose upon him punishment independent of and additional to the punishment imposed by the Tribunal for participation in the criminal activities of such group or organization.

Article 12. The Tribunal shall have the right to take proceedings against a person charged with crimes set out in Article 6 of this Charter in his absence, if he has not been found or if the Tribunal, for any reason, finds it necessary, in the interests of justice, to conduct the hearing in his absence.

Article 13. The Tribunal shall draw up rules for its procedure. These rules shall not be inconsistent with the provisions of this Charter.

### III. COMMITTEE FOR THE INVESTIGATION AND PROSECUTION OF MAJOR WAR CRIMINALS

Article 14. Each Signatory shall appoint a Chief Prosecutor for the investigation of the charges against and the prosecution of major war criminals.

The Chief Prosecutors shall act as a committee for the following purposes:

(a) to agree upon a plan of the individual work of each of the Chief Prosecutors and his staff,

(b) to settle the final designation of major war criminals to be tried by the Tribunal,

(c) to approve the Indictment and the documents to be submitted therewith,

(d) to lodge the Indictment and the accompany documents with the Tribunal,

(e)   to draw up and recommend to the Tribunal for its approval draft rules of procedure, contemplated by Article 13 of this Charter. The Tribunal shall have the power to accept, with or without amendments, or to reject, the rules so recommended.

The Committee shall act in all the above matters by a majority vote and shall appoint a Chairman as may be convenient and in accordance with the principle of rotation: provided that if there is an equal division of vote concerning the designation of a Defendant to be tried by the Tribunal, or the crimes with which he shall be charged, that proposal will be adopted which was made by the party which proposed that the particular Defendant be tried, or the particular charges be preferred against him.

Article 15. The Chief Prosecutors shall individually, and acting in collaboration with one another, also undertake the following duties:

(a)   investigation, collection and production before or at the Trial of all necessary evidence,
(b)   the preparation of the Indictment for approval by the Committee in accordance with paragraph (c) of Article 14 hereof,
(c)   the preliminary examination of all necessary witnesses and of the Defendants,
(d)   to act as prosecutor at the Trial,
(e)   to appoint representatives to carry out such duties as may be assigned them,
(f)   to undertake such other matters as may appear necessary to them for the purposes of the preparation for and conduct of the Trial.

It is understood that no witness or Defendant detained by the Signatory shall be taken out of the possession of that Signatory without its assent.


### IV. FAIR TRIAL FOR DEFENDANTS

Article 16. In order to ensure fair trial for the Defendants, the following procedure shall be followed:

(a)   The Indictment shall include full particulars specifying in detail the charges against the Defendants. A copy of the Indictment and of all the documents lodged with the Indictment, translated into a language which he understands, shall be furnished to the Defendant at a reasonable time before the Trial.
(b)   During any preliminary examination or trial of a Defendant he shall have the right to give any explanation relevant to the charges made against him.
(c)   A preliminary examination of a Defendant and his Trial shall be con-

ducted in, or translated into, a language which the Defendant understands.

(d) A Defendant shall have the right to conduct his own defense before the Tribunal or to have the assistance of Counsel.

(e) A Defendant shall have the right through himself or through his Counsel to present evidence at the Trial in support of his defense, and to cross-examine any witness called by the Prosecution.

### V. POWERS OF THE TRIBUNAL AND CONDUCT OF THE TRIAL

Article 17. The Tribunal shall have the power

(a) to summon witnesses to the Trial and to require their attendance and testimony and to put questions to them,

(b) to interrogate any Defendant,

(c) to require the production of documents and other evidentiary material,

(d) to administer oaths to witnesses,

(e) to appoint officers for the carrying out of any task designated by the Tribunal including the power to have evidence taken on commission.

Article 18. The Tribunal shall

(a) confine the Trial strictly to an expeditious hearing of the issues raised by the charges,

(b) take strict measures to prevent any action which will cause unreasonable delay, and rule out irrelevant issues and statements of any kind whatsoever,

(c) deal summarily with any contumacy, imposing appropriate punishment, including exclusion of any Defendant or his Counsel from some or all further proceedings, but without prejudice to the determination of the charges.

Article 19. The Tribunal shall not be bound by technical rules of evidence. It shall adopt and apply to the greatest possible extent expeditious and nontechnical procedure, and shall admit any evidence which it deems to have probative value.

Article 20. The Tribunal may require to be informed of the nature of any evidence before it is offered so that it may rule upon the relevance thereof.

Article 21. The Tribunal shall not require proof of facts of common knowledge but shall take judicial notice thereof. It shall also take judicial notice of official governmental documents and reports of the United Nations, including the acts and documents of the committees set up in the various allied countries for the investigation of war crimes, and the records and findings of military or other Tribunals of any of the United Nations.

Article 22. The permanent seat of the Tribunal shall be in Berlin. The first meetings of the members of the Tribunal and of the Chief Prosecutors shall be held at Berlin in a place to be designated by the Control Council for Germany. The first trial shall be held at Nuremberg, and any subsequent trials shall be held at such places as the Tribunal may decide.

Article 23. One or more of the Chief Prosecutors may take part in the prosecution at each Trial. The function of any Chief Prosecutor may be discharged by him personally, or by any person or persons authorized by him.

The function of Counsel for a Defendant may be discharged at the Defendant's request by any Counsel professionally qualified to conduct cases before the Courts of his own country, or by any other person who may be specially authorized thereto by the Tribunal.

Article 24. The proceedings at the Trial shall take the following course:

(a)  The Indictment shall be read in court.
(b)  The Tribunal shall ask each Defendant whether he pleads "guilty" or "not guilty."
(c)  The prosecution shall make an opening statement.
(d)  The Tribunal shall ask the prosecution and the defense what evidence (if any) they wish to submit to the Tribunal, and the Tribunal shall rule upon the admissibility of any such evidence.
(e)  The witnesses for the Prosecution shall be examined and after that the witnesses for the Defense. Thereafter such rebutting evidence as may be held by the Tribunal to be admissible shall be called by either the Prosecution or the Defense.
(f)  The Tribunal may put any question to any witness and to any Defendant, at any time.
(g)  The Prosecution and the Defense shall interrogate and may cross-examine any witnesses and any Defendant who gives testimony.
(h)  The Defense shall address the court.
(i)  The Prosecution shall address the court.
(j)  Each Defendant may make a statement to the Tribunal.
(k)  The Tribunal shall deliver judgment and pronounce sentence.

Article 25. All official documents shall be produced, and all court proceedings conducted, in English, French and Russian, and in the language of the Defendant. So much of the record and of the proceedings may also be translated into the language of any country in which the Tribunal is sitting, as the Tribunal considers desirable in the interests of the justice and public opinion.

## VI. JUDGMENT AND SENTENCE

Article 26. The judgment of the Tribunal as to the guilt or the innocence of any Defendant shall give the reasons on which it is based, and shall be final and not subject to review.

Article 27. The Tribunal shall have the right to impose upon a Defendant, on conviction, death or such other punishment as shall be determined by it to be just.

Article 28. In addition to any punishment imposed by it, the Tribunal shall have the right to deprive the convicted person of any stolen property and order its delivery to the Control Council for Germany.

Article 29. In case of guilt, sentences shall be carried out in accordance with the orders of the Control Council for Germany, which may at any time reduce or otherwise alter the sentences, but may not increase the severity thereof. If the Control Council for Germany, after any Defendant has been convicted and sentenced, discovers fresh evidence which, in its opinion, would found a fresh charge against him, the Council shall report accordingly to the Committee established under Article 14 hereof, for such action as they may consider proper, having regard to the interests of justice.

## VII. EXPENSES

Article 30. The expenses of the Tribunal and of the Trials, shall be charged by the Signatories against the funds allotted for maintenance of the Control Council of Germany.

# Appendix B

## NOTE ON THE INDICTMENT

The Indictment, signed in Berlin on October 6, 1945, by Robert H. Jackson (U.S.), Francois de Menthon (France), Hartley Shawcross (G.B.), and R. Rudenko (U.S.S.R.), was lodged with the International Military Tribunal in Berlin on October 17, 1945.

The Indictment contained four counts against twenty-four named defendants. Count One was entitled "The Common Plan or Conspiracy"; Count Two "Crimes Against Peace"; Count Three "War Crimes"; and Count Four "Crimes Against Humanity."

The counts so titled were, respectively, legally dependent on:

Count One, on the third clause of Article 6(a) of the Charter;
Count Two, on the first two clauses of Article 6(a) of the Charter;
Count Three, on Article 6(b) of the Charter; and
Count Four, on Article 6(c) of the Charter.

Since during the trial the judges, prosecutors, defendants, and witnesses made frequent reference to the counts, it may help the reader to remember that:

Counts One and Two have to do with "Crimes Against Peace";
Count Three has to do with "War Crimes"; and
Count Four has to do with "Crimes against Humanity."

# SOURCE NOTES

The bracketed numbers preceding each paragraph of the notes correspond to the numbered sections of the chapters. The numbers in parentheses are those of the pages of the book to which the notes refer.

When the source is an authored book, the notes give the author's name, and the alphabetical bibliography gives the title of the work. If the author has more than one work listed there, a short title is also given in the notes. If the author is not listed in the bibliography, the title is given in full in the notes or in the text.

The following abbreviations are used for the major documentary sources utilized:

| | |
|---|---|
| BID | Papers of Francis Biddle, Bird Library, University of Syracuse, New York |
| BWCE | British War Crimes Executive |
| FO | British Foreign Office |
| FRUS | Foreign Relations of the United States (USGPO) |
| HAG | Minutes of Executive Meetings of the International Military Tribunal, Peace Palace, The Hague |
| LR | Law Reports of Trials of War Criminals, United War Crimes Commission, HMSO |
| NA | National Archives of the U.S. Government |
| NCA | Nazi Conspiracy and Aggression (USGPO) |
| ND | Nuremberg Documents |
| OH | Oral History, Butler Library, Columbia University, New York |
| PRO | Public Records Office, Kew, England |
| RHJ | Jackson files, Library of Congress, Manuscript Division |
| TMWC | Trial of the Major War Criminals |
| TMC | Trials of War Criminals, Nuremberg Military Tribunals (USGPO) |
| UNWCC | History of the United Nations War Crimes Commission (HMSO) |

CHAPTER 1

For more detail on the period covered by Chapter 1, see Friedman vol. I xiii–xxi and 3–524; Roberts and Guelf 1–151; Taylor, *Nuremberg and Vietnam* 19–71; UNWCC 24–86; Corvisier, *Armées et Sociétés en Europe de 1494 à 1789.*

[1] (6°) General Gage: *Encyclopædia Britannica* (1953 ed.) vol. 23 331. See also Peter Wetzler, *War and Subsistence: The Sambre and Meuse Army in 1794* (Peter Lang Publishing 1985), showing many death sentences imposed by French military tribunals on French soldiers for pillaging. (6–7) Rousseau, *Du Contrat Social* (Paris 1896) Livre I Chap. IV 24; *The Social Contract and Discourses* (Everyman's 1950) Book I Chap. IV 10; *L'Etat de Guerre and Projet de Paix Perpetuelle* (Putnam's 1920) xlii–xliv, 80. Talleyrand: Woolsey, *Introduction to the Study of International Law* (1860) 306. (8) Napoleon: Sloane, *The Life of Napoleon Bonaparte* (Century 1915) vol. 2 69–70; Hazlitt, *Life of Napoleon* (London 1892) vol. 2 45. (8) Subsequent capture of spy: Article XXXI, Hague Convention 1907; 1973 Protocol I. Art. 46(4) Additional to Geneva Convention.

[2] (8–9) Lieber and Halleck: Friedman xv–xvii, 158–86.

[3] (11) Legitimacy of war: Lieber Code Arts. XXX, LXVII.

[4] [5] [6] (12–20) The prime source of information on war crimes during and in the wake of World War I is Willis, *Prologue to Nuremberg: The Politics and Diplomacy of Punishing War Criminals of the First World War* (Greenwood Press 1982). See also Geo. G. Battle, "The Trials before the Leipsig Supreme Court of Germans Accused of War Crimes," 8 *Va. L. Rev.* 1 (1921). (13–20) The treaties discussed in this section are all to be found in Friedman vol. I 435–524.


CHAPTER 2

There is an account of the period covered by this chapter in Smith, *The Road to Nuremberg,* and some of the relevant documents are reproduced in Smith, *The American Road to Nuremberg.*

[1] (21–23) Hitler on Poland: ND 864–PS. (23) Stieff: Taylor, *The March of Conquest* 73–74. Blaskowitz: Id. 69–70. Hlond: Gunther Lewy, *The Catholic Church of Nazi Germany* (1964) 227, 246.

[2] (23–28) For a full account of the matters discussed in these pages, see *History of the United States War Crimes Commission* (HSMO 1948). (26°) Churchill and Byron: Churchill, *The Grand Alliance* (1950) 682–83. (26) Declaration of December 17, 1942: UNWCC 106. (26) Hurst: PRO LCO 2/2476. (27) Moscow Declaration: UNWCC 107–8; II *The Memoirs of Cordell Hull* (Macmillan 1948) 1278, 1289–91; Bohlen 129. (28) Pell: UNWCC 175; PRO FO 371/ 38993; Smith, *The Road* 19; NA Dip. Br. 740.00116, March 24, 1944.

[3] (28–29) Maisky: Tusa 63; Dilks, ed., *The Diaries of Sir Alexander Cadogan* 484–85; PRO LCO 2/2974. (29) British and summary execution: Tusa 61–63. (29–30) Teheran: Churchill, *Closing the Ring* 373–74; FRUS, *The Conferences at Cairo and Teheran* (1961) 553–54; Bohlen 146–47; Elliott Roosevelt, *As He Saw It* (Duell, Sloan & Pearce 1946) 188–91; Harriman and Abel, *Special*

*Envoy to Churchill and Stalin* (Random House 1975) 273–74; Leahy, *I Was There* (McGraw-Hill 1950) 205–6. Roosevelt: *Complete Presidential Press Conferences of Franklin Delano Roosevelt* vol. 24 32–34, July 29, 1944. British lists: Tusa 62–63; PRO FO 371/38994. (30–30) Quebec: FRUS, *The Conferences at Quebec* (1944) 91–93, 489–90, 466–67; Stimson and Bundy 568–78. (31) Churchill in Moscow: FRUS, *The Conference at Malta and Yalta* (1966) 400. (31–32) Yalta: Id. 849–57, 938, 975, 979; Edward R. Stettinius, Jr., *Roosevelt and the Russians—The Yalta Conference* (Doubleday 1949) 245; Leahy 314–15. (32–33) Rosenman in London: PRO LCO 2/2980. War Cabinet April 12: PRO LCO 2/2981. (47) War Cabinet May 3: PRO FO 371/51019.

[4] (34) Morgenthau Plan: Smith, *The American Road* Doc. 12 27–29. Stimson: Id. Doc. 14 30–31. President expressed: Stimson and Bundy 578–82. (35) Marshall and Cramer: Id. 33. JAG August directive: Taylor, *Final Report* 1–2. (35–37) Bernays plan: Smith, *The Road* 50–53; Smith, *The American Road* Doc. 16 33–37. (37) Bernays and Stimson: Stimson and Bundy 585–86; Smith, *The American Road* Doc. 18 38–41. (37–38) Chanler memorandum and Stimson: Smith, *The American Road* Docs. 23–24, 67–74. (38) FDR memorandum January 3: Smith, *The American Road* Doc. 29 92; FRUS, *Malta-Yalta Conf.* 401. (39) State War-Justice Jan. 22: Smith, *The American Road* Doc. 35 117–22. (39–40) Appointment of Jackson: Jackson Report 24. Backers of Jackson: Letters to me in early 1950s from Rosenman and Chanler and from McCloy in 1984. Jackson memorandum criticizing drafts: Smith, *The American Road* Doc. 52 180–81. (40) Big Three May 3: FRUS-I-1945 1 et seq. vol. III 1161–64.

[5] (41–42) American lawyers: Stimson and Bundy 183–86; Stimson, "The Nuremberg Trial—Landmark in Law," *Foreign Affairs*, January 1947. William E. Jackson: Jackson, "Putting the Nuremberg Law to Work," *Foreign Affairs*, July 1947.

CHAPTER 3

For a biography of Jackson, see Gerhart. There are four biographical essays in the *Columbia Law Review* under the title *Robert H. Jackson: 1892–1954*, 55 *Colum. L. Rev.* (1955) 435. These include my essay on Jackson and the Nuremberg Trials, 55 *Colum. L. Rev.* 488–525, hereinafter cited as Taylor, *Jackson*.

[1] (43–45) Jackson, aggressive war and neutrality: Taylor, *Jackson* 448–91. Jackson, April 13, 1945: Id. 493–94. (45–46) Jackson and penal labor: Id. 496–97; letters and notes furnished by Mrs. Elsie Douglas; Morgenthau, 1483–1513; Jackson OH 1184–1201.

[2] (46) Alderman: Alderman OH 796–99. (46–47) Donovan: NA Box 1 File 000.51, Donovan to McCloy October 5, 1944, transmitting OSS R & A No. 2577, September 28, 1944, "Problems Concerning the Treatment of War Criminals," OSS Micro. A24. War criminals: Jackson OH 1204–18. (48) Hitler Commando Order: Alderman OH 826.

[3] (49) Planning Memorandum and Memorandum on Trial Preparation: The former is printed in Jackson, *International Conference* 64–68; both docu-

ments are in NA RG 238, NA Assist. Sec. Box 16, and the Bernays files in the library of the University of Wyoming. Jackson and the evidence: Jackson OH 1212–17. (50–52) My memorandum is reproduced in part in Smith, *The American Road* Doc. 58 209–12, and the copies are in RG 165, G-1 Personnel 000.5, War Crimes, Box 314, Federal Records Center, Suitland, Md., and in both the Bernays files and the Shea files in my possession.

[4] (52–53) Jackson's trip: Jackson OH 1230–47. May 29 meeting: PRO LCO 2/2980 63267. (53–55) Jackson's report is reprinted in Jackson, *Nürnberg Case* 3–18.

CHAPTER 4

A stenographic rendering of the colloquy and decisions reached at the London Conference is set forth in Jackson, *Internat. Conf. on Military Trials*. There are also detailed renditions of many of the meetings in Alderman OH and the Shea diary, copy in my possession.

[1] (56–57) For Jackson's decision on and execution of his move to London: Shea Diary June 18–20; Alderman OH 907–14. (57) Ben Kaplan report is quoted in Bernays to Cutter, July 9, 1945, NA ASW 000.51 War Crimes. (57) Jackson, "great value": Jackson to Taylor July 19, 1945, NA RG 153-JAG, 103-1A-BK 1.

[2] (58) BWCE members: PRO CAB 65/53 69097 May 30, 1945. BWCE early June meetings: PRO FO 371/51025 and LCO 2/2980. Britain-U.S. meetings June 21, 22, 24, 1945: Jackson, *Internat. Conf.* 69–70; Alderman OH 917–61; very full account of these meetings in Shea Diary. (58) Novikoval proposal: Bernays file "Trial and Punishment."

[3] (59–60) Conference meetings June 26–July 4, 1945: These and all the other conference proceedings are set forth in Jackson, *Internat. Conf.* Most of the conferences up to July 25 are also described in Alderman OH and the Shea Diary. Therefore only items of special interest are separately cited in these notes. (60) Jackson-Nikitchenko debate: Jackson, *Internat. Conf.* 104–5, 115. Alderman and subcommittee draft: Id. 185–201. (60) Dean memorandum and Foreign Office comments: PRO FO 371/51024 62758. (61) Jackson trip: Jackson OH 1290–95; Storey 86–89. (61–64) "Bad luck Friday": Alderman OH 1059–66 and 1070; Shea Diary July 13–15, 1945. Nikitchenko: Jackson, *Internat. Conf.* 403. Falco: Id. 319. Jackson: Ibid. (64–65) Trip to Nuremberg and Soviet withdrawal: Jackson OH 1298–1306; Alderman OH 1084–1100; Shea Diary July 18–23, 1945. (65) Soviet draft: Jackson, *Internat. Conf.* 327. (65–66) French position: Jackson, *Internat. Conf.* 295, 335. Soviet position: Id. 298. (66–67) Jackson position: Id. 299–300. (67) Impasse: Id. 377, 381–82, 384–85.

[4] (67–68) Halifax June 29: FRUS, *Potsdam Conf.* vol. I 198. Jackson to Byrnes July 4: Id. 221. (68) Jackson's "absent treatment": Alderman OH 1181. (68–69) Jackson at Potsdam: NA ASW message July 25; FRUS, *Potsdam Conf.* vol. II 421–24. Jackson and redrafts: Jackson, *Internat. Conf.* 390–97. (68–69) Potsdam meetings July 26–27: FRUS, *Potsdam Conf.* vol. II 494, 525–27, 984–85, 1477, 1500. (71–72) Jackson-Rosenman telephone: Id. 987. (72–73) Attlee-Jowitt corre-

spondence: FO 271/51031 69097. (72–73) Potsdam August 1: FRUS, *Potsdam Conf.* vol. II 572 et seq. (73–74) Jackson-Jowitt meeting: Jackson, *Internat. Conf.* 398. (74) Final London conference: Id. 399–419.

[5] (75–76) Barnes and Jackson drafts: Id. 392–93. (77) Jackson to Taylor, July 12 and 19: NA RG 165 File grp. 000.5 and RG 153-JAG, 103-1A-Bk. 1. Jackson to McCloy July 18: NA State Dept. file.

### CHAPTER 5

[1] (78) Early staff dissatisfaction: Alderman OH 962–63, 975–91. Bernays letter: NA ASW 000.51 July 9, 1945. (78–79) James Donovan indiscretion: Shea Diary July 19, 1945. Staff troubles, August 5, 1945: Alderman OH 1185.

[2] (79–80) The four committees: Alderman OH 1221; Staff Memorandum "Assignment of Personnel," September 7, 1945, Shea files. (80) Committee 1: Shea Diary. (79–80) "Economic case": Shea Diary July 12 and 23, August 17 and 18, 1945. (81–82) Storey-Amen hostility to Shea: Alderman OH 1114–17, 1181. (82) Committee 4 meeting: Minutes from RHJ, August 16, 1945. (82–83) Delay in drafting conspiracy count: Shea Diary September 6, 1945. Shawcross to Bevin: PRO FO 371/50988 69097.

[3] (83–89) Meeting of Committees 2 and 3: Minutes of these eight meetings. Jackson files.

[4] (85–86) British list June 21: Alderman OH 925. (86) Alderman-Bernays-Donovan: Dennett and Johnson 82–83. Meeting June 23: Id.; Bernays files. (82) Foreign Office alarm: PRO FO/371 50983 69097. (87–88) Passant memoranda: PRO LCO/2 2980 63267. (89) Jackson memorandum for August 23 meeting: RHJ. (89) Difficulties with list of defendants and August 28 meeting: Alderman OH 1272–76; RHJ.

[5] (90–92) General information on Krupp: Manchester passim; IX TWC 60–98. (92) Passant: PRO LCO/2 2980 63267. (92) Shea on Krupp: Shea Diary July 23, 1945. British record of August 23 meeting: PRO FO 1019/96 80840. (92–93) Communications during snafu: RHJ. August 28 meeting: Ibid. Shea in the air: Shea Diary. (93–94) Neave and Phillimore letter: Neave 30.

[6] (94–95) Staff meeting August 31: RHJ. Prosecutors' meeting: Ibid. (95) Selection of judges: Jackson OH 1321–28; Biddle 369–74.

[7] (96) "We are worried": RHJ. (96–97) Calvocoressi group: Taylor to Jackson September 11, 1945, RHJ; FO 371/51036 62877. (97–98) Jackson plans: Alderman OH 1314–17. (97) Joint memorandum: Shea files. (98) Meeting September 13: RHJ. Staff meeting September 13: Alderman OH 1317–18. (99) Jackson to Storey: Copy supplied to me by Drexel Sprecher.

[8] (100–101) British draft: Alderman OH 1320–24; Dennett and Johnson 84–85, 88. (100–101) Meetings September 17 and 18: Id. 88–90; RHJ; Alderman OH 1325–30. (102) Fyfe-Jackson negotiations: PRO FO 1019/82 62877; FO 1019/86 62758; FO 311/50988 69097; Alderman OH 1333–38; Dennett and John-

son 90–92. Chief prosecutors' and committee meetings: RHJ. (102–103) Dubost: Jackson OH 1350–53; Alderman OH 1348; Dennett and Johnson 92–93. (104) Passant: PRO FO 371/90989.

[9] (105–107) There are many treatises on the German General Staff; see, e.g., Walter Goerlitz, *History of the German General Staff 1657–1945* (Praeger 1953); Taylor, *Sword and Swastika* (Simon & Schuster 1952). (107–108) Eisenhower-Halifax: Harry C. Butcher, *My Three Years with Eisenhower* 609–10 (Simon & Schuster 1952). (109) Eisenhower-Morgenthau: *The Papers of Dwight David Eisenhower* vol. IX 1877–78 (1978); Eisenhower, *Crusade in Europe* (Doubleday 1948) 287. (110) Fowler-McCloy: *Morgenthau Diaries* (Germany) 1505. (160–162) Stalin-Hopkins: FRUS, *The Conference of Berlin (The Potsdam Conference) 1945* vol. I (USGPO 1969) 47–48. Eisenhower-Chanler-Hildring-McCloy: NA ASW 000.51 War Crimes. (110) Eisenhower press conference: *Transcript* of Press Conference of General of the Army Dwight D. Eisenhower, June 18, 1945, War Dept. Bureau of Public Relations, Press Branch. (111) Bernays: RHJ. (111) Clay-Barker documents: NA RG OMGUS 388.3 and .4. (112) Calvocoressi-Taylor: Alderman OH September 8, 1945 1299. Jackson letter: PRO FO 1019/80 62877. (113) Passant: PRO FO 371/90989. BWCE decision: PRO FO 1019/86 62758. Jackson telephone call: Alderman OH 1350; Dennett and Johnson 93–94.

[10] (114–115) Minutes of meetings October 3 and 4: RHJ files; Alderman OH 1350–56.

CHAPTER 6

[1] Minutes of the private meetings of the International Military Tribunal, beginning with its first meeting on October 9, 1945, and recording all matters agreed upon and actions taken, are available for public use at the Peace Palace in The Hague, Netherlands. Stenographic records of the colloquy at these meetings prior to November 18, 1945, are included in the Biddle Papers deposited in the Bird Library of the University of Syracuse. The foregoing are the source references to and quotations from the IMT meetings in this and succeeding chapters. Such references to and quotations from the chief prosecutors' meetings are from the records of those meetings in the Jackson files, RHJ, in the Library of Congress, Manuscript Division.

[2] (118–119) Jackson to Truman: NA State Dept. 740.00116/10–1645. (119) Biddle party trip: BID letter diary. (120) Birkett: Hyde 494–95. "Two funny little men": BID letter diary. (121) Jackson-Biddle colloquy: My attitude corroborated by Wechsler. (123) Rudenko arrival October 11: Id. (123–124) Biddle and presidency: BID letter diary; Tribunal minutes. (125) RHJ-Shea telephone talk: Jackson OH. (125–126) Nikitchenko "might bolt": BID letter diary.

[3] (127°) Nazis and women: J. C. Fest, *The Face of the Third Reich* (Pantheon 1970) 263–75, esp. 269–70.

CHAPTER 7

The first paragraph of notes to Chapter 6 is equally applicable to this chapter. Minutes of chief prosecutors' and American prosecution staff meetings were obtained by me from the Jackson files then in Chicago (RHJ), later sent to the Library of Congress, Manuscript Division.

[1] (129) Hess: Alderman OH.

[2] (131–133) Service of the indictment: Neave, Part Two, passim. (132) Jim Rowe: BID Box 1; I TMWC 118. (132) Ley: Gilbert 13–14. (133) Meeting October 21: BID Box 1.

[3] (135–143) Documents in this subsection are from the Shea files and RHJ. Quotations are from Shea Diary and RHJ.

[4] (143–145) Jackson and the generals: RHJ and Jackson OH 1364–69.

[5] (145–146) Jackson and Storey administrative directives: (146) Shea files and Alderman OH. (146–147) Joint meetings: Alderman OH. (147–149) Donovan-Jackson correspondence: NA State Dept. 740.00116E Prosecution 12–1045. Jackson on witnesses: Jackson OH 1384. (149) Biddle on Donovan: BID Box 19.

[6] (150) Streicher: I TMWC 148–54; II TMWC 22–25; HAG November 19, 1945; Gilbert 33–35. (150–151) Hess: Alderman OH 1408; I TMWC 155–56, 159–65; HAG November 6, 1945. (152) Shea and Jackson memos: Shea files. Dubost-Phillimore: PRO FO 1019/19 63207. (152–153) Medical commission appointment: HAG October 30, 1945. Klefisch petition: I TMWC 124–25. Report: Id. 127–33. (153–154) Jackson-Alderman: Alderman OH 1408 et seq. (154–155) Prosecution responses: I TMWC 134–42. (155–157) Tribunal session: II TMWC 1–17. (157–158) Tribunal afternoon meeting: BID Box 2, November 14, 1945. Gustav Krupp announcement: I TMWC 143. (157) Tripartite motion: Id. 145. (158) Alfried Krupp rejection: Id. 146. Jackson memorandum: Id. 144. (158–161) Pokrovsky announcements: Jackson OH. (161) Dubost manifesto: I TMWC 147.

[7] (162) Birkett: Birkett 499. Dean report: PRO FO 1019/97.

CHAPTER 8

The first paragraphs of notes to Chapters 6 and 7 are equally applicable to this chapter.

[1] (165–166) Lawrence: II TMWC 29–30. Indictment: II TMWC 30–94. (166) Defense petition: II TMWC 95. (166) Defendants' pleas: II TMWC 95–98. (166°) Goering statement: Tusa 150°.

[2] (167–72) Jackson opening statement: II TMWC 98–155. (172) Acclaim: Gerhart 364; Birkett 500; BWCE FO 1019/97 62877. Jackson's retrospect: Jackson OH.

[3] (172–173) Jackson OH. (173) Storey: II TMWC 156–62. Albrecht: II TMWC 162–77. (173) Wallis: II TMWC 178–216. Dodd: II TMWC 216–41. (174) Jackson boast: Chief prosecutors' meeting December 5, 1945. BWCE: FO 1019/97 62877. (175) Stahmer-Storey: II TMWC 291–93. (175–177) Alderman's first pre-

sentation: II TMWC 241–431. Judges speak to Alderman: Alderman OH November 17, 1945. (176) Dix-Alderman: II TMWC 250. (176–177) New rules: II TMWC 255–56.

[4] (177–178) Hess doctors' reports: I TMWC 157–67. (178–180) Hess hearing and decision: II TMWC 478–496 and III TMWC 1.

[5] (180–182) Donovan, Calvocoressi, and Meltzer: Personal letters to me. Brauchitsch et al. memo: ND 3798 PS. (181–182) Lippe: Lippe 36–37. (182–183) Leverkuehn: Brown 127–29, 207, 387. (185) Biddle: BID Box 19. RHJ to President and Donovan documents: NA 740.00116 EW.

[6] (186–187) Concentration camp film: II TMWC 431–34; Lippe 48; Gilbert 46–50. (187–191) Lahousen: II TMWC 440–78; III TMWC 1–34. Lahousen cross-examination: III TMWC 2–33. (190) Defendants' cross-examinations: Gilbert 50–55. (190–192) Shawcross opening: III TMWC 91–145. (192–193) Shawcross reference to Munich: Id. 115. (193) Soviet objections: Jackson OH 1496. (193) Shawcross on Norway: Id. 138–31.

[7] (193–194) Alderman on Czechoslovakia: III TMWC 152–73. British prosecution presentation: III TMWC 173–324. (194–195) Elwyn Jones on Norway: Id. 264. (196) Birkett assessment: Birkett 501–2. (196–197) Alderman final presentation: III TMWC 324–99. (196–197) Alderman-Storey: Alderman OH 1523–27. (197) Biddle on Alderman: BID Box 19. (198–199) Tusa comparison: Tusa 181–82. (198°) Hossbach memorandum: ND 356-PS. (199) Alderman-Donovan: Alderman OH 1667.

[8] (200) *The Nazi Plan*: III TMWC 400–402; Lippe 61; Gilbert, 64–67. (201–203) Dodd on slave labor and concentration camps: III TMWC 402–518. Walsh on Nazi persecution of Jews: III TMWC 519–73; Lippe 65. Harris on Germanization: III TMWC 574–97; IV TMWC 3–17. (203) Tribunal revised ruling on receiving documents: IV TMWC 1–3. (203–204) Storey on Nazi Party Leadership Corps: IV TMWC 17–93. Storey on Reich Cabinet: IV TMWC 93–123. (204–205) Colloquies with Lawrence and Biddle: Id. 102, 105–6. (205) Storey on SA: IV TMWC 123–160. (205) Statement that defendants "roared with laughter": Tusa 170; Lippe 73. (205–206) Farr on SS: IV TMWC 161–230. Farr's colloquies with Tribunal: 170, 194–95. (205–206) Storey on Gestapo: IV TMWC 230–52. (206) Christmas recess: December 5 Chief prosecutors' meeting, U.S. minutes 5–6. Announcement of Christmas recess: III TMWC 209. (206–207) Jackson's holiday: Jackson OH 1471 et seq.

CHAPTER 9

Locations and addresses in this and other chapters are based partly on personal recollection and partly on entries in the telephone directories for the International Military Tribunal exchange, denominated "Justice," in my possession.

[4] (213–214) Fyfe administration: Kilmuir 104. (214) Fyfe and Elwyn Jones: Id. 101. (214) Jones-Shawcross: Information from Elwyn Jones.

[6] (219) Press statistics: U.S. State Department RG 59 Box 3698 File 740.0016; Charles W. Alexander and Anne Keeshan, *Justice at Nuremberg*, pic-

tures and text; Jackson file, list (partial) of correspondents at Nuremberg trials. (219–220) Shirer dispatch: New York *Herald-Tribune*, December 9, 1945.

[7] (221–223) For much of the information in this section, see Davis, *Come as a Conqueror: The United States Army's Occupation of Germany 1945–1949*, passim. (223) General Harmon and Lady Lawrence: As told to me by General Watson. (223–224) Brusque American guards: Cooper 151.

[8] (224–225) Judge Parker and the chairs: BID, Notes of Conferences, November 14, 1945. (226–227) Birkett letters: Birkett 503–4. (226) Biddle on colleagues: BID Box 19. (230) Kalnoky guests: Kalnoky, passim.

[9] (233) Jackson-Dean: RHJ Box 213. (233–234) Development of German press and reporters: *The German Press in the U.S. Occupied Area 1945–1948*, Special Report of the Military Governor, November 1946. (234–235) Bergold-Kempner letter: RHJ Box 231. (235) Jackson "neglected opportunity": Jackson OH 1631–36.

CHAPTER 10

[1] (236) Control Council disagreement and Jackson office:NA RG 163 File 000.5, Message October 17, 1945, Nr. S 28295. (236–238) Taylor-Kaplan memo: NA RG 238, Box 193. (238) Calvocoressi memo: RHJ. (239) Yamashita: II Friedman 1596–1623; Taylor, *Nuremberg and Vietnam* 91–92, 181–82. (239–240) Brown diagnosis: Brown 744.

[2] (241) Messersmith: II TMWC 349–352. (241) Schuschnigg: Id. 384–85. (241) Chief prosecutors December 5: Jackson, T.T. (242) Taylor memo December 7: NA RG 238, Box 193. Dodd affidavit: III TMWC 512–16. (242) Kauffmann challenge to affidavits and Tribunal decision: Id. 542–51, 571–72.

[3] (244–245) Graebe affidavit: I TMWC 236; IV Id. 253–57, XIX Id. 507–9. (246) Harris: Id. 288–311. (246–248) Ohlendorf direct testimony: Id. 311–30. (248) Biddle on Jekyll and Hyde: Conot 235. (248) Ice cold: Von der Lippe 83. Babel cross-examination: IV TMWC 353–54. (248) Wisliceny: Id. 355–73. (248) Schellenberg: Id. 374–86. (249) Hoellriegel: Id. 386–90.

[4] (249–250) General Staff as "group": Id. 393–408. (250–251) Blomberg and Blaskowitz affidavits: IV TMWC 413–15. Military liability for "crimes against peace": Id. 436–39. (253–255) "Commando Order": Id. 441–42. Supplemental orders: Id. 442–44. Documents distribution: Id. 444–48. (254–255) Norway: Id. 447–49. (255) Falkenhorst: XI LR 18–30. (255) Pescara: IV TMWC 449. Dostler: Id. 449–51; I LR 22–34. (255–256) Barbarossa order: Id. 455–59. (256–257) Reichenau: Id. 459–61. (257–258) Rottinger and other affidavits: Id. 468–74. (258–259) Bach-Zelewski testimony: (259) Funk and Goering: Gilbert 113. (260) T–BZ dialogue: IV TMWC 477–80. Goering, Funk, and Jodl: Gilbert 113. (260) Thoma: IV TMWC 493–95. (260–261) Taylor conclusion: Id. 496–98. (261) *New York Times*: January 8, 1946. (261) Washington *Post*: January 9, 1946.

# CHAPTER 11

[1] (262–263) Fyfe: IV TMWC 527. (263) Albrecht on Goering: Id. 529–57. Poke fun: Id. 532. (263) Fyfe on Ribbentrop: Id. 557–72; V TMWC 1–19. Roberts on Keitel and Jodl: Id. 26–41. (263–264) Brudno and Baldwin on Rosenberg and Frank: Id. 41–66, 66–91. (264) Griffith-Jones on Streicher: Id. 91–119. Legal issues: Id. 118–19. (264–265) Bryson and Meltzer on Schacht and Funk: Id. 119–51, 152–67. (265–266) Phillimore on Doenitz: Id. 201–55. (266) Witnesses Heisig and Moehle cross-examined by Kranzbuehler: Id. 222–45. (266) Elwyn Jones on Raeder: Id. 256–82. (267) Sprecher on Schirach: Id.. 282–304. (267) Lambert, Atherton, and Kempner on Bormann, Seyss-Inquart, and Frick: Id. 304–34, 334–52, 352–67. (267–268) Sprecher on Fritzsche: VI TMWC 53–73. (268) Barrington on Papen: Id. 73–98. Fyfe on Neurath: Id. 98–117. (268–269) Griffith-Jones on Hess: VII TMWC 120–45.

[2] (269–270) J.C.S. 1023/3: Taylor, *Final Report to the Secretary of the Army* 1–4. December 1944 War Department instructions: Id. 435–36. (270) U.S. war crimes trials in Germany, spring 1945: Ziemke 390–94. (270) Creation and growth of "War Crimes Group" under Straight: Straight Report for June 1944– July 1948, passim. (270–271) Bergen-Belsen trial: Bower 179–84.

[3] (272) J.C.S. 1023/10: Taylor, *Final Report* 4–6; Ziemke 394. (272–273) Fairman memo and Betts to Jackson: Shea files. (273) Conferences October 19–22, 1945: Shea and Jackson, RHJ; Fahy Diary, Columbia OH 248.

[4] (274–275) Fahy-Taylor: Fahy OH 248–49. (275) Letters, December 1 to 5, 1945: Taylor, *Final Report* 258–66. (275–276) Control Council Law No. 10: Id. 250–53.

[5] (276–278) Tribunal and chief prosecutors' meetings: HAG, December 8, January 5, and January 12; V TMWC 228–29; Chief prosecutors' meetings December 11, January 16, and February 5; BID Box 3, Vol. I, December 12, 1945.

[6] (278) Fahy to Taylor, January 10, 1946: RHJ. (278–279) Denazification: Clay 40, 67–70, 250–59; Backer 57–64, 99, 116–19, 141–42; Denazification, Report of the Military Governor No. 34 1–114 (April 1948). (279) Taylor to Jackson: RHJ. (280) "Law for Liberation": Denazification, Report 52–97.

[7] (281) Taylor to Jackson, January 18, 1946: RHJ. (281) Petersen letter: RHJ. Jackson to Horsky: RHJ. (281–282) Jackson before IMT: VIII TMWC 353–77. (283) Fyfe and Champetier de Ribes: Id. 377–87. Rudenko: Id. 387–90. (283–284) Defense lawyers: Id. 390–438. (283) Loeffler: Id. 429–30. Servatius: Id. 405. (283–284) Jackson response: Id. 441, 444, 449. (283) Fyfe response: Id. 458, 464. (284–285) Biddle-Rudenko: Id. 471. Defense counsel impression: Lippe 158.

[8] (286) Taylor memo January 30: RHJ. (287) RHJ memo February 5: RHJ. (288–289) Taylor memo February 6: NA.

[9] (290) RHJ to Patterson: NA. Fahy cable February 18: NA 000.5-1. Jackson cable March 2: RHJ. Jackson cable March 14: RHJ. (290–291) Public announcement March 29: Taylor files. (291–292) "Shipment" of "dependents" to American-occupied Germany and Austria: Davis 189–95; *New York Times* Index, April 17 and 26, 1946. (291) Marcus to OMGUS March 3: NA 000.5-1.

CHAPTER 12

[1] (293–298) De Menthon's address: V TMWC 368–426. Lippe: Lippe 99–100. De Menthon and law: Id. 370. (294–295) "Crime against the spirit": Id. 371–75. (295) Kellogg-Briand Pact: Id. 387. Four major categories: Id. 391–414. Hostages: Id. 399–400. (296) Auschwitz: Id. 403–4. (296) Germanization and Jews: Id. 412. (297) Nazi organizations: Id. 421. (297) De Menthon peroration: Id. 423–26. (298) "Very good": Jackson OH 1499. (298) Frank approval: Gilbert 124.

[2] (298) Faure announcement: V TMWC 427–38. (299) Herzog on forced labor: Id. 438–513. (299) Gerthoffer on pillage: Id. 513–573; VI TMWC 1–52. Gerthoffer conclusion: Id. 48–52. (299–300) Dubost's presentation: Id. 118–427. Hostages and other reprisals: Id. 120–183. Concentration camp witnesses: Id. 183–321. (301) Mme. Vaillant-Couturier. (302) Oradour-sur-Glane: Id. 411–17. (302–303) Dubost "incompetence": Tusa 91–92. (303) Dubost's presentation: VI TMWC 418–27. (303–305) Faure presentation: Id. 427–567; VII TMWC 1–50. Stahmer objection: Id. 430–31. (303) Biddle on Faure: BID Box 19. (303–304) Germanization of Alsace and Lorraine: VI TMWC 433–567; VII TMWC 1–22. Biddle's complaint: BID Box 19. (303–304) Faure on berets: VI TMWC 440–41. (304) Assassinations of Danes: VII TMWC 44–48. (304–305) Louvain: VI TMWC 531–40. Mounier: VII TMWC 94. (305–306) Defendants' reaction to Goering art plunder: Gilbert 132–33. (306) "Toneless" voice: Birkett 505–6.

[3] (307–308) Rudenko opening: VII TMWC 146–94. Goering impression: Gilbert 135, 136. Jewish population: VII TMWC 192. (308) Rudenko conclusion: Id. 193.

[4] (308–309) Zorya-Warlimont: VII TMWC 248–49. (309) Appearance of Paulus: Id. 250–52. (310–311) Paulus: There is no single authoritative source; the text is based on several reliable writings on the Nazi-Soviet war. Anticipation of Paulus's arrival: Lippe 126. Paulus testimony: VII TMWC 253–61, 279–304. Sting in the tail: TMWC VII 261. (311) Defendants' reaction: Gilbert 147. (311–312) Paulus's cross–examination: VII TMWC 279–304. Goering-Hess: Gilbert 148–49. Von der Lippe: Lippe 130. (312°) Buschenhagen: VII TMWC 309–15. (312–313) Pokrovsky, crimes against prisoners: Id. 345–437. (313) Katyn massacre: Id. 425–28. (313–317) Smirnov on indoctrination: Id. 443. (314) Backe document: Id. 443. (314) Lidice: Id. 530–31. (315) Birkett on credibility: Birkett 507. Hope of exaggeration: Lippe 139–40. Goering and "5 per cent": Gilbert 152. (316) Force of Soviet film: Gilbert 161–62. Defendants' reaction: Gilbert 162–64. (316–317) Churchill speech: Gilbert 182–84; Lippe 164. (317) Smirnov on "extermination": VIII TMWC 294–331. English translation: Id. 294. (317–318) Schmaglenskaya: Id. 319. Kranzbuehler, Doenitz, and Jodl: Gilbert 174–75.

CHAPTER 13

[1] (319) Prosecution case concluded: VIII TMWC 495. Expediting defense case: Chief prosecutors' meeting, January 16, 1946. (320) Defense proposals: Lippe 115. Prosecution proposals and defense counsel meeting: Id. 131, 133. Tribunal February 16: HAG No. 56. (320) Defense plea: VIII TMWC 516–24.

(321) Prosecution's motion denied: Id. 562. Defense protest: Lippe 140. Tribunal rulings: HAG Nos. 58A and 59. (321) Pronouncement February 23 and defense reaction: VIII TMWC 159–65.

[2] (322) Stahmer opening of Goering case: IX TMWC 2–7. Bodenschatz direct testimony: Id. 7–16. (322–323) Distribution of cross-examination: Chief prosecutors' meeting March 4, 1946. (323) Bodenschatz c-ex: IX TMWC 16–44. (323) Defense reaction to Jackson c-ex: Gilbert 185–86. (323–324) Erhard Milch: See Irving, *The Rise and Fall of the Luftwaffe: The Life of Field Marshal Erhard Milch* (Little, Brown 1973). Milch testimony and c-ex: IX TMWC 44–134. (324) Tribunal and slow pace: HAG No. 62. (324) Brauchitsch testimony and c-ex: IX TMWC 135–48. Koerner testimony and c-ex: Id. 148–73. (325) Albert Kesselring: Kesselring, *A Soldier's Record* (William Morrow 1954). (325–328) Kesselring testimony and c-ex: IX TMWC 172–235. (325–327) Bombing of Rotterdam: Taylor, *The March of Conquest* (Simon and Schuster 1958) 190–95. (327–328) Initial purpose of British heavy bombers and Trenchard-Weir doctrine: Taylor, *Munich: The Price of Peace* (Doubleday 1979) 236, 608, 645. (328°) Wehrmacht's strength and weakness: Taylor, *The March of Conquest* 35. (327–328) Jackson-Kesselring: IX TMWC 200. Stahmer difficulties: Lippe 171.

[3] (329) Goering's tension: Gilbert 185, 193–94. Siemers consultation: Lippe 174. (329–335) Goering direct testimony: IX TMWC 235–366. (329) Goering's reply to Stahmer: IX TMWC 254. (330) Praise for Goering: Gilbert 197. (330) Birkett's comments: Birkett 508–9. (331–333) Dahlerus's testimony: Id. 457–99. (332) Cadogan and Dahlerus: Dilks, ed., *The Diaries of Sir Alexander Cadogan* 220. (332) Siemers and Dahlerus: Lippe 164, 166, 174, 177–80, 183–85. (332–333) Fyfe c-ex: IX TMWC 476–89. Furtwaengler: Dahlerus 18–19. (333) Goering reply to Fyfe c-ex of Dahlerus: Id. 492–99. (333–334) Stalag Luft III: Id. 356–58. Foreign laborers: Id. 354–56. (334) Hague and Geneva conventions: Id. 361–64. (334–335) Goering's replies to other defendants' questions: Id. 366–417. "Conspiracy": Id. 401.

[4] (335) Jackson opening: IX TMWC 417. (335–336) Jackson plan: Jackson OH 1429 et seq. (336°) Gerhart: Gerhart 392. Concentration camp question: IX TMWC 420–21. (336–337) Lawrence interjection: Id. 421. (336) Jackson anger: Jackson OH 1432–33. (337) Dean: BWCE FO 1019/97. Von der Lippe: Lippe 181. (337–338) Rhineland question: IX TMWC 505–7. (338) Jackson explosion: Id. 507–8. (338–339) Jackson-Lawrence colloquy: Id. 509–11. (339) Stahmer interjection: Id. 511–12. (340) Dean: BWCE FO 5019/97. (340–341) Birkett: 509–12. (342) Fyfe 113. (342–343) Speer: Gilbert 210–11. (342°) Check of "legal details": Gilbert, page following dedication. (344) Jackson in "terrific state": BID Box 3 Vol. III 99. (344) Fyfe accusation: IX TMWC 593–94. (344–345) Lippe: Lippe 187. (345–346) Rudenko-Goering colloquy: IX TMWC 623–28. (346) Dean: BWCE FO 1019/97. (346) Goering forced labor: IX TMWC 430–31. Champetier de Ribes: Id. 653. Stahmer c-ex: Id. 653–57.

[5] (347) Tribunal: IX TMWC 673. (347–348) Hess decision not to testify: Gilbert 217; X TMWC 90. Seidl on Hess position: IX TMWC 692–93. Hess mental condition: Gilbert 190, 195–96, 217. (348–349) Bohle and Stroelin: X TMWC 12–74; Gilbert 217–19; Lippe 195. (349) Hess–Lord Simon: X TMWC 3–7. (349–

350) Seidl and Versailles: Id. 79–90. (350) Gaus affidavit: Id. 7–11, 78–79, 90, 311–14.

CHAPTER 14

(352) *Ribbentrop.* X TMWC 90–468. (352) Gilbert 221–22, 225, 230. (352) Ribbentrop and Jews: X TMWC 397–98, 400–42. (352–353) Paul Otto Schmidt: Id. 207. (353) Ribbentrop "washed up": Gilbert 235.

(353) *Keitel.* X TMWC 468–648; XI 1–202; see also Walter Ansel, *Hitler Confronts England* (Duke University Press 1960), 92. (353–354) Nelte-Keitel: X TMWC 470–71; 499–500. (355) Keitel affidavit: Id. 536. (355) Canaris-Keitel: Id. 558, 622–23. Keitel and Rudenko: Id. 603. (356) Keitel, Fyfe, and Stalag Luft III: XI TMWC 1–11. (356–357) Nelte-Keitel: Id. 26–27. (357) Lawrence: Id. 27–28. Gilbert reports: Gilbert 247. Lippe 212. (357) Lammers: XI TMWC 28–155. (357) Westhoff: Id. 155–89. (357–358) Pokrovsky: Id. 187. Jodl: Gilbert, 252–53. (358) April 4: HAG No. 67. (358) April 5: Chief prosecutors' meeting. (358) Jackson April 9: XI TMWC 73–88. (359) Birkett: Birkett 513. (359) Biddle-Jackson-Parker: BID Box 3 Vol. III 226. (359) Birkett: Birkett 515.

(360) *Kaltenbrunner.* Direct examination: XI TMWC 232–307. (360) Kaltenbrunner-Mueller: Id. 238–42. Eichmann: Id. 226. (360) Mauthausen and American soldiers: Id. 249–50. (361) Ohlendorf: Id. 245. Mauthausen: Id. 325–27. (361) Blaschke: 344–49. (362) Lippe: Lippe 219–20. Birkett: Birkett 514. Gilbert: Gilbert, 255–64. (362–364) Hoess: XI TMWC 396–422. (363) Gilbert: Gilbert, 259–60. (364) Lippe: Lippe 225.

(364) *Rosenberg.* XI TMWC 444–599. Doenitz on Rosenberg: Gilbert, 274. (364–365) Rosenberg on Norway: XI TMWC 455–58. (365) Einsatzstab: Id. 467–76. Reichsminister: Id. 476–517. (365–366) Policy conference July 17, 1941: Id. 480–82. (366) Feeding the German people: Id. 538–40. (367) Rosenberg's planned speech: Id. 553–62.

(367–369) *Frank.* (367–368) Malaparte: Curzio Malaparte, *Kaputt* (E. P. Dutton 1946), 64–86. (368) Frank and guilt: Gilbert 275; XII TMWC 7–8. Annihilation of Jews: Id. 13. (369) Frank's diary: Id. 7. Lippe on confession: Lippe 230–31. (369) Dodd on Polish professors and Frank on diary: Id. 20, 41.

(370–376) *Frick.* (370) Documents: Id. 157–66. Taciturn: Gilbert Diary 101, 284. (371–376) Gisevius testimony: XII TMWC 167–305. (371) Frick on Gisevius: Gilbert, 292. (371–372) Gisevius on Frick: Id. 167–76, 180–86. (372) Gisevius on Goering: Id. 168–75. (372–374) "Blomberg-Fritsch affair": Id. 176–80, 196–204. (372–374) Jackson cross-examination of Gisevius: Id. 246–79. (374) Schacht and 1937: XII TMWC 247. (374–375) Jackson on Frick: Id. 253–58. On Kaltenbrunner: Id. 58. On Neurath: Id. (375) On Keitel: Id. 265–67. (376) Defendants' attitude toward Gisevius: Gilbert 293–300.

(376–380) *Streicher.* XII TMWC 305–416. (377) Wegener impression: H. A. Turner, ed., *Hitler: Memoirs of a Confidant* (Yale University Press 1978) 92–94. (377) Hitler to Goebbels: Louis Lochner, ed., *The Goebbels Diaries* (Doubleday 1948) 47. (378) Rebecca West: West 5. (378) Streicher opening: XII TMWC

305–13. (379) His denials: Id. 331–42. (379–380) Griffith-Jones cross-examination: Id. 344–78. (380) Hiemer testimony: Id. 404–12. (380) Lawrence checks pornography: Id. 410.

CHAPTER 15

(382–391) *Schacht*. (382–384) Background: XII TMWC 416–24. (385) Annexation of Austria: Id. 435. (385–386) Gisevius final tribute: Id. 236. (386) Biddle on Gisevius: Biddle 439. (387) Elwyn Jones: British prosecution staff minutes, April 13, 1946. Birkett: Birkett 516. (388) Jackson intervention: XII TMWC 446. (387–388) Jackson c-ex on criminals and photographs: Id. 562–67. Papen: Id. 568. (388) Schacht letter November 12: Id. 569. Swastika decoration and contributions to Nazi Party: Id. 584–85. (389) Schacht on advantages of decoration: Id. 597. (389) Schacht and Jews: Id. 583, 588–93. (390) Schacht's salaries: XIII TMWC 26–28. Vocke testimony: Id. 56. Jackson c-ex of Vocke: Id. 66–70. (390) "Weak cross-examination": BID Box 3 May 2, 1946. Birkett: Birkett 516–17. (391) Gilbert: Gilbert, 316. Lippe: Lippe 255.

(391–398) *Funk*. (392) Wegener 267. Hindenburg, Hitler, and Reich Press Chief: XIII TMWC 92–96. (393) Lippe: Lippe 255, 256. (393) Funk's "threshold": XIV TMWC 101. (393) Funk's efforts in attack on Poland: Id. 106. (393) Funk and attack against Soviet Union: Id. 114–17. (393–394) Attitude toward Jews: Id. 117–20. (394) Central Planning Board: Id. 130–38. (394) Dodd c-ex on Kristallnacht: Id. 145–48. "War economic preparation": Id. 157. Black market: Id. 180. (394–398) SS deposits: Id. 162 et seq. Puhl affidavit: Id. 170–71. (396) Hysterical explosion: Id. 172. (396–397) Raginsky: 186, 189. (397) Puhl on film: Id. 562–63. Puhl information from interrogators: Id. 569–70. Dodd c-ex: Id. 585. Thoms affidavit: Id. 580–81. Thoms and gold teeth: Id. 612.

(399–409) *Doenitz*. (399) Personal background and status: XIII TMWC 247–48. (399–401) Argument on Kranzbuehler's application for Nimitz interrogatory: VIII TMWC 547–52. Biddle and Tribunal discussion: Biddle 451–53. (401) Doenitz on Counts One and Two: XIII TMWC 249–52. (401–403) Submarine warfare against the crews of merchant ships: Id. 254–95. (403) Relations with Hitler and Nazis: Id. 296–301. (403) Commando Order: Id. 301–3. High marks from fellow defendants: Gilbert 327–28. Questions from Laternser, Nelte, Dix: XIII TMWC 310–20. (404–406) Fyfe cross-examination on Doenitz-Hitler conferences: Id. 321–27. (405) Naval use of concentration camp labor: Id. 341–46. (405) Doenitz and Jewry: Id. 392. (406) Eck trial: Reported as *The Peleus* trial in Vol. I *Law Reports of Trials of War Criminals* 1–21 (HMSO 1942). (406) Wagner's testimony: TMWC 444–83. (407) Wagner cross-examination: TMWC 483–522. (407) Hessler on Kuppisch: Id. 554. (408) Wagner on Commando Order: Id. 471–73, and 502–20. (408°) Falkenhorst's trial: Reported in Vol. XI *Law Reports of Trials of War Criminals* 18–30. (408–409) Nimitz interrogatory answer: XVII TMWC 377–81.

(409–416) *Raeder*. (410) Versailles: XIII TMWC 597–99, 617–31; XIV TMWC 1–11. (410) Birkett: Birkett 518. (411) Raeder's minimizing of Hitler's statements: Id. 34–48. (412–413) Occupation of Norway: Id. 85–102. (413) Siemers's request for Foreign Office documents and refusal: VIII TMWC 568–69, XII 506–7; HAG No. 69 par. 2; see also Taylor, *The March of Conquest*, Chaps. 3 and 4. Foreign Office relief on Norway: Tusa 363. (414) Fyfe's "half-truth": XIV TMWC 193. (414) Raeder thought Commando Order "justified": Id. 214. (414) Severing and Weizsaecker on Nazi aggressive wars: Id. 271, 295. (415) Other defendants' lack of enthusiasm for Raeder's presentation and his Moscow statement: Gilbert 338, 342–44. (416) Schacht on Raeder: Gilbert 336.

CHAPTER 16

(418) Birkett: Birkett 518, 520. (419) Pearson and Fleeson on Jackson and Black: Gerhart 235–88. (420–421) Comments on Jackson's blast: Biddle, BID Box 19; Parker, Conot 443; *Stars and Stripes*, Lippe 318.

(421–427) *Schirach*. (423) Gilbert's discussions with Schirach: Gilbert 22–24, 70–71, 139–40, 200, 295, 302–3, 318–20. (424) Distancing the Hitler Jugend from military: XIV TMWC 377–400. Lawrence's sarcasm: Id. 388. Removal of Jews from Vienna: Id. 410. (424) Schirach approval of sending Jews to Poland: Id. 423–25. (424–425) Schirach speech September 1942: Id. 426. (425) Colin Ross information: Id. 431. (425) Schirach confession: Id. 432–33. Defendants' reactions: Gilbert 349–50. Schirach's satisfaction: Ibid. (426) *HJ Year Book:* Id. 463. (426) Einsatzgruppen: Id. 487–90. (426) Hitler conference October 1940: Id. 508–13. Schirach's explanation: Id. 516.

(427–431) *Sauckel*. (427–428) Goebbels: Lochner 150. (428) Sauckel's vile German: Lippe 296. (428) Who chose Sauckel: XIV TMWC 618–19; Speer, 218–19. (428) "Dullest of the dull": Lochner 325. (429) Central Planning Board meeting: NCA Vol. VIII, item R. 124 160–61. "Utterly improbable proportion": XV TMWC 202. (429–430) Dodd's proof on forced labor: Supra 336–37. Effect on Sauckel: Gilbert 75. (430) Sauckel's January 1943 speech: XV TMWC 16–17. (430–431) Alexandrov's pejoratives: Id. 139, 143–44. (431) Biddle's cross-examination: Id. 186–207. (431) Jaeger testimony: Id. 264–79. Last question and answer: Id. 55.

(431–439) *Alfred Jodl*. (432) Attitude toward Hitler: XV TMWC 285, 293–98. (433) Jodl "defense team": Lippe 304. (433) Commissar Decree: XV TMWC 308–14. Commando Order: Id. 314–29. (433–434) Jews: Id. 333. (434) International law: Id. 341–42. (434) Rhineland and Austria; Id. 347–56. (434–435) Czechoslovakia: Id. 707–9; Taylor, *Munich: The Price of Peace* 681–731. (434) "Monstrous incident": Id. 357. (435) "Unalterable decision": Ibid. "Occasion" after October 1: Ibid. Jodl and "nothing happened": Ibid. Jodl's diary: Ibid. Events May 30 to September 24: Taylor, supra. (436) Birkett: Birkett 518. (436) Jodl on war: Taylor, supra 387. Jodl on Norway: Id. 379. (436–437) Jodl on reasons for invading Holland and Belgium: Id. 381–83. (437) Jodl on Greece, Italy, and Yugoslavia: Id. 383–88. Jodl on attack against Soviet Union: Id. 388–95. (437–438) "Purely preventive war": Id. 394. Threat of Soviet attack: Id. 395. (438) Jodl's 1943 speech on Norway: Id. 465–66. Jodl on Danish Jews: Id. 492–93. Jodl and forced labor: Id. 494–95. (438) Gilbert: Gilbert 289. (439) "It is not the task of a soldier": Id. 509.

(439–444) *Arthur Seyss-Inquart.* (439) Reason for preceding Papen: Papen 552. (439–440) Fritzsche on Seyss: 30. (440) Gilbert: Gilbert 286–87. Papen: Papen 551–52. Speer: Speer 511. Fritzsche: Fritzsche 264. (440–441) Seyss and Jews: XV TMWC 633–34. (441) Seyss inspection trip to Poland: 4 NCA 2278 PS. (441–443) Seyss's mission in Netherlands: XV TMWC 642. (442) Seyss and Mussert: XVI TMWC 35, 186. Hitler on Seyss: *Hitler's Secret Conversations* 279. (442) Goebbels: Lochner 475. Attitude toward Jews: XV TMWC 666. Evacuation of Dutch Jews: XVI TMWC 3. (442–443) Seyss motive on Jews: XVI TMWC 2. (443) 250,000 Dutch workers: Id. 46. Confiscation of raw materials: Id. 6. (443) Hague Convention obsolete? Ibid. Reduction in hostage shootings: XV TMWC 655–56. (443–444) Preventing flooding: XVI TMWC 21–22. Trip to Kiel and Doenitz: Id. 17. (444) Hirshfeld testimony: Id. 210–27.

(444–447) *Papen.* (444) First statement: XVI TMWC 236. In the U.S. as attaché: Papen 51–52. (445) Probable reasons for Papen's selection as Chancellor: Id. 243–44. (446) Papen acknowledges that his (and Hitler's) policy was eventual "union" of Austria and Germany: Id. 309. Barrington on Papen: VI TMWC 73–98. (446) Praise of Fyfe cross-examination: Tusa 391; Conot 488–50. Papen's letters to Hitler: XVI TMWC 360–66. Fyfe's "why": Id. 416.

(448–451) *Speer.* (448) General background: *Speer* passim. (449) Widening of Speer's authority: XVI TMWC 437. Galbraith: George Ball, *The Past Has Another Pattern* (1982) 50–68. (450) Splitting the defendants: Gilbert 103, 121, 158. Ploy with Kubuschok: IV TMWC 342–43; Gilbert 102. (451) Speer and foreign workers: XVI TMWC 457. Speer efforts to prevent Hitler's destruction: Id. 483–93. Schacht and Rosenberg: Gilbert 396. (451–452) Attempt to assassinate Hitler: Id. 493–95. (452) "Limit his responsibilities": XVI TMWC 483. (452) Speer's disregard of Hague Convention: XVI TMWC 535. (453) Jackson and Speer on "responsibility": Id. 563. Flächsner and Speer on "responsibility": Id. 586. (454) Speer's impression on judges: Biddle 443; Fyfe 129. Steel switches: Fyfe 129.

(454–459) *Neurath.* Birkett: Birkett 520. (454–455) Personal background: XVI TMWC 593. (455) Lawrence to Lüdingshausen: Id. 620, 637. Jews: Id. 596. (455–456) Rhineland: Id. 625, 635–36. (456) Hossbach: 639–40. Response to British: Id. 643. Neurath and Czechs: Id. 645. (457) Neurath believed Czechs wanted occupation: Id. 654. Closing of Czech schools: XVII TMWC 6. (458) Neurath, admonished by Hitler, resigns: Id. 16. Goebbels on Neurath's appointment: Speer 147. Neurath "diddled" by Czech nobility: *Hitler's Secret Conversations* 192. On anti-Semitism: XVII TMWC 25. (459) Judges' questions to Neurath: Id. 99–107. Lippe: Lippe 344. (459) Neurath's visit to Goebbels: Goebbels 171.

(459–463) *Fritzsche.* (460) Tears: Gilbert 46. Career: XVII TMWC 135–42. Goebbels comment: Goebbels 91. (460–461) Fritzsche testimony: XVII TMWC 143–45. (461) Organization of the Nazi press: Id. 151. *Athenia:* Id. 156. (461) Charges Russian "physical terror": Id. 160–62. (461–462) Fritzsche in Russia, attitude toward Jews: Id. 165–78. Fritz questions to Paulus: VII TMWC 297. (463) Fritzsche vs. Rudenko: XVII 204, 218.

(463–466) *Bormann.* Opinions of Bormann: Speer 87; Keitel 214; Guderian, *Panzer leader* 449; Fritzsche: Fritzsche 301–2. (465) Bergold's documents: XVII

TMWC 261–70. Lawrence and Bergold dispute: Id. 246–48. (466) Kempka: Id. 447–54.

[2] (466–472) Goebbels: Goebbels 318. (466–467) Radio Moscow and Anders: *Crime of Katyn* 102–3. (467) Red Cross: Id. 106–10. Churchill: *Hinge of Fate* 757–60. German commission: *Crime of Katyn* 126 et seq. British reaction: *The Diaries of Sir Alexander Cadogan* 537. (467–468) Pokrovsky February 14: VII TMWC 425–28. Soviet Special Commission: Ibid. (468) March 12, 1946: HAG No. 63. (469) Rudenko petition: Biddle 415. Conference April 6: HAG No. 68; Biddle 415–16. May 11 and June 2: XIII TMWC 436; XV TMWC 289–90. (469–470) Nikitchenko suggestion: HAG No. 88 par. 13. (470) Stahmer's witnesses: XVII TMWC 274–321. (471) Smirnov's witnesses: Id. 321–71. Lawrence closes testimony: Id. 371. (472) Guilt for Katyn: *Crime of Katyn*, passim.

CHAPTER 17

[1] (473–474) Tribunal order: XVII TMWC 1–2. (474–475) Jahrreiss: Id. 458–94. (703) Ex post facto: Id. 494.

[2] (475–476) Stahmer: Id. 497–550. Lawrence admonition: Id. 498. (476) Chivalry: Id. 516. Appeal to League of Nations: Id. 520. Goering and art: Id. 526. Katyn massacres: Id. 539–44. (476) Seidl disaster: Id. 550–55. Dr. Horn: Id. 555–603. Hitler domination and "Common Plan": Id. 599. (476–478) Nelte: Id. 603–61; XVIII TMWC 1–40. Nelte-Lawrence arguments: XVII TMWC 603–4, 609–11. (477) "Carrying out the Führer's orders": Id. 640. (477–478) Nelte's peroration: XVIII TMWC 39–40. (478) Kauffmann: Id. 40–68. Kauffmann (for Kaltenbrunner) vs. Lawrence: Id. 43–45, 47. Kaltenbrunner's guilt: Id. 68. (478–479) Thoma (for Rosenberg): Id. 69–128. (479) Forced labor and the Geneva Convention: Id. 90–91. Anti-Semitism and Rudenko: Id. 92–93. Thoma on Rosenberg: Gilbert 347–48. (479–480) Seidl (for Hans Frank): Id. 129–63. (480) Pannenbecker (for Frick): Id. 164–89.

[3] (481) Marx for Streicher: Id. 190–220. Extent of Streicher's influence through *Der Stuermer*: Id. 198–204. Marx's conclusion: Id. 220. (481–482) Sauter (for Funk): Id. 220–63. (482–483) Dix's introduction: Id. 270–72. Dr. Dix (for Schacht): Id. 270–312. Dix reaction to Nelte: Id. 285–86. (482–483) Dix conclusion: Id. 312. (483–484) Kranzbuehler: Id. 312–72. "Two main groups": Id. 313. Kranzbuehler avoids mention of Hitler: Id. 369. (483–484) Expulsion of Jews: Ibid. (484) Siemers (for Raeder): Id. 372–430. (485) Sauter (for Schirach): Id. 430–66. (485–486) Dr. Servatius (for Sauckel): Id. 466–506. (485) Russian text of the Charter: Id. 467–69. Meaning of "deportation" and "slave labor": Id. 469–72. Inapplicability of Hague rules to forced labor: Id. 470–78. (486) Exner (for Jodl): Id. 506–10; XIX TMWC 1–46. Lawrence and Belgian loss of neutrality: XIX TMWC 10–12. Exner conclusion: Id. 46. (486–487) Steinbauer (for Seyss-Inquart): Id. 46–83, 98–111. (487) Hague Conventions: Id. 72–74. Testimonial evidence: Id. 106–9. (487) Bergold (for Bormann): Id. 111–24. (487) Kubuschok (for Papen): Id. 124–77. Conclusion on Papen: Id. 177. (487–488) Flächsner: Id. 177–216. (488) Speer not responsible: Id. 197. Lawrence inquiry on "Hague Rules": Id. 183-84. Lawrence inquiry on "waging of a war of aggression": Id. 178–79, 210. Conclusion

plea on Speer: Id. 216. (488) Lüdinghausen (for Neurath): Id. 216–55, 268–312. (488–489) Fritz (for Fritzsche): Id. 312–52. (489) Fritz on waging aggressive wars: Id. 327–30. (489) Sprecher: VI TMWC 69. German law on "accomplice": XIX TMWC 345. (489) Fritz conclusion: Id. 51–52. Lawrence: Id. 331. (489–490) Seidl on Hess: Id. 353–96. (489) "Article 6 does not exist": Id. 381. Article 9: Id. 386–88. (490) Passages deleted from Seidl's speech: Lippe 402–3. Seidl request, Lawrence refusal: Id. 381. Press reaction to Seidl: Lippe 403–4.

[4] (490–494) Jackson address: Id. 397–432. (491–492) Conspiracy groups: Id. 400–406. (493) Proof of Goering and others as conspirators: Id. 407–13. Jackson's refutation of defense arguments on "conspiracy": Id. 419–26. (493) "Nobody knew": Id. 426–28. Nature and crimes of individual defendants: Id. 415–17. (493–494) Last paragraph: Id. 432.

[5] (494) Defendants' reactions to Jackson: Gilbert 417–18. (494–497) Shawcross's address: Id. 433–529. (495) "Common murderers" charges enough for "supreme penalty": Id. 448. (495) Attacks without warning: Id. 458. Rebuttal to Jahrreiss: Id. 459–66. (496) "We need not concern ourselves": Id. 469. "Even if it were true": Id. 455. "Of Streicher, one need say nothing": Id. 518. (496–497) Goethe and German people: Id. 528.

[6] (497) Defendants' reactions to Shawcross: Gilbert 421–24. (497–499) French prosecution's address: Id. 530–69. (498–499) Dubost's delivery: Birkett 521. (498) Dubost on no necessity of "conspiracy": Id. 535, 543, 544, 548, 549. (498) Dubost on Schacht: 558–61. (499) Conclusion: Id. 568–69.

[7] (499–500) Rudenko's address: Id. 570–618; XX TMWC 1–18. (499) Rudenko on Hess and Bormann: XIX TMWC 583–87. Rudenko cross-examination: Id. 595. (500) "Noble-minded simpletons": Id. 591. Rudenko's last advice: XX TMWC 14.

CHAPTER 18

[1] (501–514) IMT No. 63. Neave: Neave 274–95.

[2] (505) Fyfe cross-examination of Kaufmann: XX TMWC 37–58, esp. 41. (505–507) Wegscheider: Id. 89–93. Griffith-Jones cross-examination of Wegscheider: Id. 93–95. (507–508) Servatius final argument: XXI TMWC 450–93. (507) Legal argument against criminality of prewar actions: Id. 450–70. Servatius's arguments in mitigation: Id. 479–93.

[3] (508) Gestapo, Werner Best testimony: XX TMWC 123–56. (509) Merkel final argument: XXI TMWC 495–545. (509) SD: XX TMWC 185–263. (509) Schellenberg affidavit: IV TMWC 242, Doc. 3033–PS. (509) SD and Einsatzgruppen: XX TMWC 196–201. (510) Stahlecker report: XXII TMWC 21, Doc. L-130. (510–511) Lawrence-Gawlik colloquy: Id. 21–24. (511) Gawlik's closing speech: XXI TMWC 618–32; XXII TMWC 3–44. (512) SS five full days in court: XX TMWC 278–515. (512) Eberstein testimony and Jones cross-examination: Id. 281–327. (513) Brill on drafting of Waffen-SS: Id. 337–56. Paul Hausser, atrocities by SS but not Waffen-SS: Id. 356–414. (513–514) Witnesses Reinecke and Morgen, Waffen-SS vs. "nominal SS": Id. 415–515. (514–516) Jones and Sievers: Id. 516–61. (516) Pelckmann's closing argument: XXI TMWC 563–618.

[4] (518) Brauchitsch's affidavits on General Staff and High Command: XX TMWC 583–86. (518–519) Cross-examination of Brauchitsch: Id. 587–94. (519–520) Direct and cross-examination of Manstein: Id. 594–646; XXI TMWC 4–18. (520) Manstein manifesto of November 20, 1941: XX TMWC 641–43. (521) Direct and cross-examination of Rundstedt: XXI TMWC 20–50. (521–522) Laternser closing argument: XXI TMWC 44–90. Laternser on Czechoslovakian occupation: Id. 67. "Three Field Marshals": Id. 74.

[5] (522–523) Reich Cabinet: XX TMWC 263–78; XXII TMWC 92–127. (523–524) Gruss testimony: XXI TMWC 106–23. (523–524) Juettner contradiction of Gruss: Id. 125–28. (524) Fyfe cross-examination of Juettner: Id. 146–200. (524–525) Early in Boehm final argument: XXII TMWC 128–70. Lawrence criticism of Boehm: Id. 132, 148. Boehm follows Gruss testimony: Id. 156–57. Boehm quotes Pope: Id. 169–70.

[6] (525–527) Fyfe final argument: Id. 170–239. (525) Defendants' lies: Id. 176–78. (526) Fyfe relies on Juettner testimony, not Gruss's: Id. 201–4. (526) Fyfe on "crimes of the SA": Id. 219. (527) Dodd swan song: Id. 239–70.

[7] (528–532) Taylor final argument: Id. 271–97. (528) Hitler discussion with generals: Id. 282. (529–530) Argument on Commando Order: Id. 285–86. (530) Decision of German military judge: Id. 290. (530) German Army lieutenant: Id. 290. (531) Taylor conclusion: Id. 296–97. (531–532) Champetier de Ribes final argument: Id. 297–308. (532) Champetier de Ribes conclusion: Id. 308. (532–533) Rudenko final argument: Id. 308–65. (533) Rudenko slap at Boehm: Id. 333–34. (533) Extermination of the Jews: Id. 341–46. (533) Rudenko conclusion: Id. 365.

CHAPTER 19

[1] (534) Lawrence: XXI TMWC 175–76. (535) Fritzsche: Fritzsche 316. (535–545) Defendants' last apologias: XXII TMWC 366–410. (535–536) Papen on Goering: Gilbert 429. (544–545) Fritzsche's and Birkett's assessment of the speeches: Fritzsche 317–18; Birkett 522. (545) Lawrence: XXII TMWC 410.

CHAPTER 20

[2] (549) Biddle notes on judges' discussions of convictions and penalties: Biddle Box 4.

[3] (549–570) Biddle notes as in [2]. (553–554) Fisher memo on conspiracy: Biddle Box 5.

[4] (555–558) Biddle notes on organizations.

[5] through [8] (559–570) Biddle notes on individual defendants.

CHAPTER 21

[1] (571–574) Jackson correspondence with son and Dodd: RHJ files.

[2] through [7] (574–600) Reading of the Tribunal's opinion and judgment: I TMWC 171–366; XXII TMWC 411–569. (575–580) On "Conspiracy and Aggres-

sive War": XXII TMWC 427–58. (580–583) Discussion of legal issues: Id. 459–70. (583–587) Discussion of organizations: Id. 498–523. (587–597) Convictions and acquittals: Id. 524–87. (598–599) Sentences: Id. 588–89.

[8] (600–603) Reaction of convicted defendants, the three acquitted, and petitions to the Control Council: Gilbert 429–36; Fritzsche 325–27; Papen 570, 575–77; Speer, *Spandau* 3–5; Schacht, *Confessions of "The Old Wizard"* 446.

[9] (603–607) Control Council and decision to affirm all Tribunal's decisions: Lord Douglas of Kirtleside, with Robert Wright, *Combat and Command* (Simon & Schuster 1963) 736–55.

[10] (607–611) Speer and the death cells: Speer, *Spandau* 9–10. (608) Papen and Frank: Gilbert 434.

CHAPTER 22

[1] (612–618) Fritzsche post-Nuremberg: Fritzsche 327–31; Davidson 550–51. (613–614) Schacht post-Nuremberg: Schacht, *Confessions* 446–71. (614) Papen post-Nuremberg: Papen 575–80. (614) Seven surviving convicts: Speer, *Spandau* passim, esp. 25, 74, 217, 245, 295–98, 309–10, 326–27. (618) Hess: Speer, *Spandau* 445–50.

[2] (618–624) Douglas: Douglas 754. (623–624) Swearingen with Wheelis's widow and on the baggage room: Swearingen 116.

[4] (626–629) Kranzbuehler: *De Paul Law Review* 347 (1965).

[6] (634–639) Dean Rusk and Eric Norden: Taylor, *Nuremberg and Vietnam* 96.

# BIBLIOGRAPHY

## I. OFFICIAL AND INSTITUTIONAL

Documents on German Foreign Policy 1918–1945, Series C (1933–37) and D (1937–1945), U.S. Department of State, Washington, D.C.: Government Printing Office.

Foreign Relations of the United States, U.S. Department of State, Annual, Washington, D.C.: Government Printing Office.

History of the United Nations War Crimes Commission (UNWCC), published by HMSO, London.

Law Reports of Trials of War Criminals, United Nations War Crimes Commission, published by HMSO, London.

Minutes of Executive Meetings of the International Military Tribunal, Peace Palace, The Hague, the Netherlands.

National Archives of the U.S. Government, Washington, D.C.

Nazi Conspiracy and Aggression, Vols. I–VIII, Supps. A and B. Office of United States Chief of Counsel for Prosecution of Axis Criminality, Government Printing Office, Washington, D.C.

Oral History, Butler Library, Columbia University, New York.

Jackson files, Library of Congress, Manuscript Division.

Trial of the Major War Criminals before the International Military Tribunal. 42 vols., published at Nuremberg, Germany (1947–1949).

Trial of War Criminals before the Nuremberg Military Tribunals Under Control Council Law No. 10. 15 vols. U.S. Department of the Army, Government Printing Office, Washington, D.C.

## II. INDIVIDUALLY AUTHORED

Alderman, Sidney S. *Negotiating the Nuremberg Trial Agreements*. See Dennet and Johnson, eds.

Andrus, Burton C. *The Infamous of Nuremberg*. London: Leslie Frewin, 1969.

Backer, John H. *Winds of History: The German Years of Lucius DuBignon Clay*. New York: Van Nostrand Reinhold Company, 1983.

Biddle, Francis. *In Brief Authority*. New York: Doubleday, 1962.

Bohlen, Charles E. *Witness to History: 1929–1969*. W. W. Norton, 1973.

Bower, Tom. *The Pledge Betrayed: America and Britain and the Denazification of Postwar Germany*. New York: Doubleday, 1982.

Brown, Anthony Cave. *The Last Hero: Wild Bill Donovan*. New York: Times Books, 1982.

Churchill, Winston. *The Gathering Storm*. Boston: Houghton Mifflin, 1948.

Clay, General Lucius D. *Decision in Germany*. New York: Doubleday, 1950.

Conot, Robert E. *Justice at Nuremberg*. New York: Harper & Row, 1983.

Cooper, Robert W. *The Nuremberg Trial*. Penguin Books, 1947.

*The Crime of Katyn: Facts and Documents*. London: Polish Cultural Foundation, 1965.

Dahlerus, Birger. *The Last Attempt*. Introduction by Sir Norman Birkett, P.C. Hutchinson & Co., 1947. Trans. Alexander Dick from the Swedish: Sista for Suket-London, Berlin, Sommers 1939, paperback by Norstedts.

Davidson, Eugene. *The Trial of the Germans*. New York: Macmillan, 1966.

Davis, Franklin M., Jr. *Come as a Conqueror: The United States Army's Occupation of Germany 1945–1949*. New York: Macmillan, 1967.

Dennet, R., and Johnson, J. E., eds. *Negotiating with the Russians*. World Peace Foundation, 1951.

Doenitz, Karl. *Ten Years and Twenty Days*. Trans. R. H. Stevens. Cleveland: World, 1959.

Flanner, Janet. *Janet Flanner's World: Uncollected Writings, 1932–1975*. New York: Harcourt Brace Jovanovich, 1979.

Friedman, Leon, ed. *The Laws of War*. Foreword by Telford Taylor. 2 vols. New York: Random House, 1972.

Fritzsche, Hans. *The Sword in the Scales*, as told to Hildegard Springer. Trans. Diana Pike and Heinrich Fraeker. London: Alan Wingate, 1953.

Gerhart, Eugene C. *America's Advocate: Robert H. Jackson*. Indianapolis: Bobbs-Merrill, 1958.

Gilbert, G. M. *Nuremberg Diary*. New York: New American Library, 1947.

———. *The Psychology of Dictatorship*. New York: The Ronald Press, 1950.

Gisevius, Hans Bernd. *To the Bitter End*. Trans. Richard and Clara Winston. Boston: Houghton Mifflin, 1947.

Goebbels, Joseph. *The Goebbels Diaries 1942–1943*. Ed. Louis Lochner. New York: Doubleday, 1948.

Harris, Whitney R. *Tyranny on Trial: The Evidence at Nuremberg*. Dallas: Southern Methodist University Press, 1954.

*Hitler's Secret Conversations 1941–44*. Trans. Norman Cameron and R. H. Stevens. New York: Farrar, Straus and Young, 1953.

Hyde, H. Montgomery. *Norman Birkett*. London: Hamish Hamilton, 1964.

Jackson, Robert H. *International Conference on Military Trials*. Washington, D.C.: Government Printing Office, 1947.

———. *The Nürnberg Case*. New York: Alfred A. Knopf, 1947.

Jones, Elwyn. *In My Time: Autobiography of Lord Elwyn-Jones*. London: Weidenfeld & Nicolson, 1983.

Kalnoky, Countess Ingeborg. *The Guest House*. New York: Bobbs-Merrill, 1974.

*The Memoirs of Field-Marshal Keitel*. London: William Kimber, 1965.

Kelley, Douglas M., M.D. *22 Cells in Nuremberg*. New York: Greenberg, 1947.

Kilmuir [David Maxwell-Fyfe]. *Political Adventure: The Memoirs of Lord Kilmuir*. London: Weidenfeld & Nicolson, 1964.

Knieriem, August von. *The Nuremberg Trials*. Preface by Max Rheirstein. Chicago: Henry Regnery, 1959.

Lippe, Victor Frh. von der. *Nürnberger Tagebuchnotizen: November 1945 bis Oktober 1946*. Frankfurt-am-Main: Verlag Fritz Knapp, 1951.

Manchester, William. *The Arms of Krupp*. Boston: Little, Brown, 1964.

Maser, Werner. *Nuremberg: A Nation on Trial*. New York: Charles Scribner's Sons, 1977.

Morgenthau Diary. Senate Committee to Investigate the Administration of the Internal Security Act and other International Security Laws of the Committee on the Judiciary, United States Senate. November 20, 1967. Government Printing Office, Washington, D.C., 1967.

Neave, Airey. *On Trial at Nuremberg*. Boston: Little, Brown, 1978.

Padfield, Peter. *Dönitz: The Last Führer*. London: Gollancz, 1984.

Papen, Franz von. *Memoirs*. Trans. Brian Connell. New York: E. P. Dutton, 1955.

Poltorak, Arkady. *The Nuremberg Epilogue*. Moscow: Progress Publishers, 1971. Trans. David Skwirsky.

Raeder, Erich. *My Life*. Trans. Henry W. Drexel. Annapolis: U.S. Naval Institute, 1960.

Ribbentrop, Joachim von. *The Ribbentrop Memoirs*. Trans. Oliver Watson. London: Weidenfeld & Nicolson, 1954.

Schacht, Hjalmar H. G. *Account Settled*. Trans. Edward Fitzgerald. London: Weidenfeld & Nicolson, 1949.

———. *Confessions of "The Old Wizard": The Autobiography of Hjalmar Horace Greeley Schacht*. Trans. Diana Pyke. Boston: Houghton Mifflin, 1956.

Smith, Bradley F. *The American Road to Nuremberg: The Documentary Record 1944–1945*. Stanford: Hoover Institution Press, 1982.

———. *Reaching Judgment at Nuremberg*. New York: Basic Books, 1977.

———. *The Road to Nuremberg*. New York: Basic Books, 1981.

Speer, Albert. *Inside the Third Reich: Memoirs by Albert Speer*. Trans. Richard and Clara Winston. New York: Macmillan, 1970.

———. *Spandau: The Secret Diaries*. Macmillan, 1976.

Stimson, Henry L., and Bundy, McGeorge. *On Active Service in Peace and War*. New York: Harper & Brothers, 1947.

Storey, Robert G. *The Final Judgment: Pearl Harbor to Nuremberg*. San Antonio: Naylor, 1968.

Swearingen, Ben E. *The Mystery of Hermann Goering's Suicide*. New York: Harcourt Brace Jovanovich, 1985.

Taylor, Telford. *Final Report to the Secretary of the Army*. Washington, D.C., 1949. USGPO

———. *Guilt, Responsibility and the Third Reich*. Cambridge: Heffer, 1970.

———. *Nuremberg and Vietnam: An American Tragedy*. Chicago: Quadrangle Books, 1970.

———. *Nuremberg Trials: War Crimes and International Law*. New York: Carnegie Endowment for International Peace, 1949.

Thompson, H. K., Jr., and Strutz, Henry, eds. *Doenitz at Nuremberg: A Reappraisal*. New York: Amber Publishing Co., 1976.

Tusa, Ann and John. *The Nuremberg Trial*. New York: Atheneum, 1983.

Wechsler, Herbert. "The Issues of the Nuremberg Trial," in *Principles, Politics, and Fundamental Law*. Cambridge, Mass.: Harvard University Press, 1961.

Wegener, Otto. *Hitler—Memoirs of a Confidant*. Ed. Henry Ashby Turner. Trans. Ruth Hain. New Haven: Yale University Press, 1985.

West, Rebecca. *A Train of Powder*. New York: Viking Press, 1955, copyright 1946.

Zawodny, J. K. *Death in the Forest: The Story of the Katyn Forest Massacre*. Notre Dame, Ind.: University of Notre Dame Press, 1962.

Ziemke, Earl F. *The U.S. Army in the Occupation of Germany 1944–46*. Washington, D.C.: Center of Military History, United States Army, 1975.

# Index

Abwehr, 182, 187, 190–1
Academy of German Law, 367
*Account Settled* (Schacht), 612
Adenauer, Konrad, 640
adversarial system, 63, 64
Afghanistan, Soviet invasion of, 636
aggressive war charges, 37–9, 41, 44, 45,
54, 93, 171, 294, 307, 320, 341, 474–5,
488–9, 491–2, 494–5, 518, 521, 542,
628–9, 635–7; and Charter, 65–7, 69,
75–6; deliberations on, 550, 552–4;
economic case and, 81; evidence of,
49–51, 57, 85, 170; in Indictment, 79,
80, 83, 100, 102, 116; against individual
defendants, 262–9, 352, 354–5, 365,
384–6, 391, 393, 397, 401, 410–16, 432,
436–8, 440, 446, 456–9, 480; under
J.C.S. 1023/10, 272; judgment of
Tribunal on, 575–81; organizations and,
241, 251–2, 507, 512, 524, 528–9;
presentation of case on, 145, 173,
175–6, 186, 191–200, 295, 309–12
Ahnenerbe (Ancestral Heritage Society),
514
Ahrens, Lt. Col. Friedrich, 468, 470, 471
air warfare, 19, 325–8, 640; in World
War I, 12, 13
Albany Law School, 43
Albrecht, Ralph, 138, 146, 173, 177–9,
182, 197, 263, 504, 574, 625
Alderman, Sidney, 40, 46–8, 50, 80, 83,
85, 129, 130, 146, 147, 148n, 216, 231,
276, 381, 398, 625; affidavits submitted
by, 241, 242; and Charter negotiations,
56, 58, 60, 63, 68, 69n, 70, 76; and
defendant selection process, 86, 89, 90,

92, 93, 152; and economic case, 81–2,
142; and Indictment, 97–104, 113–16,
118, 165; and Krupp incident, 153,
157; presentation of evidence by,
175–7, 186, 187, 191–4, 196–7, 199,
200, 221, 250, 307, 308, 332, 434, 518;
and staff dissatisfaction, 79, 137–9,
141–3
Alexander, Gen. G. A., 210, 430–1
Algeria, 23
Allgemeine SS, 511
Allied Control Council, 111, 112, 118,
120, 236, 239, 272, 280, 285, 287, 351,
507, 559, 573, 601–8, 615, 616, 618–21;
Allied Control Council, Law No. 10 of,
275–6, 283, 284, 558, 584
Almers, Col., 255
Amann, Reichsleiter Max, 461
Amen, Col. John Harlan, 47, 48, 139, 146,
216, 243, 478, 574, 625;
cross-examinations by, 353, 361–3;
documents gathered by, 52, 57, 61, 85;
Donovan and, 182–4; and economic
case, 81, 82, 142, 274, 387;
interrogations by, 129, 136, 137, 148n,
150, 349; witnesses called by, 185–8,
246–9
American Jewish Conference, 35
American Society for International Law,
44, 636
Anday, Rosette, 548
Anders, Gen. Wladyslaw, 218, 466,
471
Andersonville prison camp, 271
Andrus, Col. Burton C., 230, 547, 574,
601, 609–11, 614, 619–23

Anglo-German Naval Treaty (1935), 192, 496
Anschluss, 241, 336, 360, 440, 445, 446, 461, 542, 577, 595
Anti-Comintern Pact (1936), 196
Armenian massacres, 13, 18
art works, pillage of, 305–6, 316, 340, 476
Asquith, Herbert, 14
*Athenia* (ship), 405, 414, 461
Atherton, Lt. Henry, 267
Atlantic Wall, 448
*Atrocities by the German Fascist Invaders in the U.S.S.R., The* (film), 316
Attlee, Clement, 30, 67n, 70–3, 191, 603
Auschwitz, 24, 169n, 248, 296, 301, 316, 317, 362–4, 425, 442, 628
Auslandsorganisation, 348–9
Australia, 26
Austria, 16, 18; annexation of, 61, 177, 182, 186, 187, 268, 330, 385, 422, 434, 438–40, 446, 456, 459, 461, 486, 505, 521, 554; deportation of Jews from, 267, 352

Babel, Ludwig, 248, 301
Babi Yar massacre, 169, 462n
Bach-Zelewski, Erich von dem, 243, 258–61, 364, 621n
Backe, Herbert, 314
Badoglio, Marshal Pietro, 37n
Balachowsky, Alfred, 301
Baldwin, Lt. Col. William, 264
Ball, George, 26n, 449
Barbanova, Leba, 382
Barbarossa Plan, 255–6, 258, 355
Barbie, Klaus, 640
Barker, Maj. Gen. Ray W., 111, 112, 236, 239
Barnes, Harry Elmer, 51
Barnes, Sir Thomas, 58, 60, 61, 67, 69, 75, 80, 82, 86, 97, 101, 103, 116, 200
Barrington, Maj. J. Harcourt, 214, 268, 446
Barzilewsky, Boris, 471
Baukhage, H. R., 219
Beck, Gen. Ludwig, 374
Becker, Maj. Loftus, 101, 146, 240
Belgian Commission for War Crimes, 304
Belgium, 19; invasion and occupation of, 23, 24, 145, 192, 195, 204–5, 326, 328, 352, 436–8, 442, 448, 486, 579; retreat of Wehrmacht from, 33; slave labor from, 201, 295, 298–9, 430; in World War I, 12, 13, 17
Belsec, 316
Belsen, *see* Bergen-Belsen

Beneš, Eduard, 24, 435
Ben Gurion, David, 613n
Bentham, Jeremy, 6
Bergen-Belsen, 38, 169, 186, 270–1
Bergold, Friedrich, 234–5, 465–6, 487
Bergson, Henri, 531
Berlin Document Center, 514, 619
*Berliner Borsenzeitung*, 392
Berlin Philharmonic, 332
Bernays, Murray, 4, 37, 46, 48, 49, 82, 111, 270, 278; and Charter negotiations, 56, 68, 75, 76; in defendant selection process, 86; organizational guilt concept of, 35–6, 41, 42, 45, 75, 104, 108, 280, 297, 501, 512, 527, 556, 628, 637–8; resignation of, 79, 101
Best, Werner, 442, 508–9, 525
Bethmann-Hollweg, Theobald von, 12
Betts, Gen. Edward C., 52, 53, 68, 77, 270, 272–5, 286n, 290
Betts, Gen. T. J., 112
Bevin, Ernest, 70, 71, 73, 82, 604
Bidault, Georges, 40, 52, 212
Biddle, Francis, 131, 144, 149, 155, 175, 178, 185, 211, 212, 216, 225–7, 359, 381, 418, 420, 421, 546–8, 571, 572, 628, 631; appointment of, 95, 97; as Attorney General, 39, 40; at Berlin meeting, 118–25; and closing argument, 474, 477; and defense testimony, 320–1, 330, 336, 342, 344, 386, 390, 391, 400, 424, 431, 453–4, 459, 468, 469; during deliberations, 549–58, 560–70, 591n, 631–2; during holiday adjournment, 206; and judgment of Tribunal, 574, 582, 589, 591–4; and opening statements, 172; and organization of Tribunal, 133–5; during pretrial proceedings, 15, 157, 158, 160n, 161; and prosecution case, 196–8, 202, 204–5, 248, 258, 263, 277–8, 282–5, 303, 306, 312; and sentencing, 598; sixtieth birthday party for, 398; subsequent career of, 625
Biddle, Katherine, 359, 398
Birkenau, 317
Birkett, Sir Norman, 120, 121, 125, 155, 162, 212, 214, 215, 225–6, 611, 631; and closing arguments, 497; on defendants' final statements, 545; and defense testimony, 330, 340–2, 344, 359, 362, 387–8, 391, 418, 436, 445, 451, 453, 454, 487, 632; during deliberations, 549–55, 558, 564, 568–70; during holiday adjournment, 206; and opening statements, 172;

during pretrial proceedings, 157; and prosecution case, 196, 202, 306, 315

*Bis zum bittern Ende* (Gisevius), 371

Bitter, Maj. John, 127

Black, Hugo, 419–21

Blaschke, SS Brigadefuehrer, 361

Blaskowitz, Gen. Johannes, 23, 241, 251, 528

Blobel, Paul, 462n

Blomberg, Field Marshal Werner von, 106, 136–7, 241, 250–1, 353, 372–4, 383, 385, 423, 432, 446

Blücher, Field Marshal von, 8

Blum (Gestapo member), 314

Bodenschatz, Gen. Karl, 322, 323

Boehm, George, 523–4, 526, 533

Boettinger, Anna Roosevelt, 38n

Boettinger, Col. John, 38

Bohle, Ernst, 348, 349

Bohlen, Charles "Chip," 30, 108

Boix, François, 300

Bolshevism, 189, 256

Bonaparte, Napoleon, 7–8 and n, 15, 26n, 31, 75, 447n

Bonnet, Georges, 52

Bormann, Martin, 87, 89, 90, 203, 204, 345, 365, 384, 388, 394, 426, 428, 630; case against, 267, 269, 499; conviction of, 597; defense of, 144, 234, 417, 463–6, 474, 487; deliberations on, 569; indictment of, 132; petition for clemency for, 602; sentencing of, 382, 599

Bose, Herbert von, 446

Bowie, Robert, 279

Bradley, Gen. Omar, 222

Brandeis, Louis, 119

Brandt, Rudolf, 515

Brauchitsch, Col. Bernd von, 137, 324

Brauchitsch, Field Marshal Walter von, 106, 137, 180, 241, 243, 250, 254n, 257, 324, 373, 518–19, 528, 530, 603

Breyer, Col., 189

Briand, Aristide, 19

Brill, Robert, 513, 525, 527

Britain, 19, 331–2; Battle of, 325; and Geneva Conventions, 19, 640; governments-in-exile in, 24, 25; Labour Party victory in, 58, 69, 73; and Munich Agreement, 192, 434, 522, 554; and Soviet annexation of Baltic states, 118; and Suez crisis, 637; in World War I, 12–14, 16–18, 29; in World War II, 23, 26, 39, 44, 193, 195, 197, 254–5, 322, 326, 327, 401–3, 411–15, 436–8, 486, 496, 519, 554, 577–80, 639–40

British Conservative Party, 73, 214, 567, 624

British Foreign Office, 58, 60, 67, 69, 73n, 83, 86, 87, 93, 102, 115, 120, 122, 160n, 162, 214, 286, 337, 346, 413, 456, 555, 567, 603–6

British House of Commons, 14

British Labour Party, 58, 62, 73, 101, 191, 214, 624

British Military Courts, 270, 271

British War Crimes Executive (BWCE), 53, 58, 84, 93, 104, 113, 131n, 172, 174, 214

British War Office, 270

Brookhart, Lt. Col. Smith W., 248

Brooklyn Law School, 289n

Brown, Anthony Cave, 239, 240

Browning, Robert, 217

Brownshirts (*see* SA)

Bruce, David, 617

Brudno, Walter, 264, 398

Bruening, Heinrich, 383

Brunner, Anton, 424

Bryson, Brady, 264–5

Buchenwald, 38, 169, 186, 235, 242, 272, 301, 514

Buerckel, Josef, 303, 440

Bulgaria, 16, 18, 24, 196; deportation of Jews from, 248

Bulge, Battle of the, 39, 110n

Buschenhagen, Gen. Erich, 312n

Bush, George, 637

Butcher, Capt. Harry C., 107–8

Butz, Dr., 470

Byrnes, James F., 68–71, 73n, 74n, 95, 215

Byron, Lord, 26n

Cadogan, Sir Alexander, 60, 61, 332, 467n

Calley, Lt. William, 640

Calvocoressi, Peter, 96–7, 127, 216, 218, 276, 504, 548; closing argument prepared by, 528; cross-examination by, 519; and Indictment, 101, 112–15, 117, 147, 180, 238, 240; in preparation of General Staff–High Command case, 138, 146, 243, 244, 251; subsequent career of, 625

Canaris, Adm. Wilhelm, 182, 187–90, 355, 375, 385

Cardwell, Douglas, 619n

Case Green, 435

*Catch-22* (Heller), 179

Catholics, 23, 168; atrocities against, 28; *see also* Roman Catholic Church

Catling, Cecil, 611

Cato the Elder, 532

Cavell, Edith, 13

Center Party, 444

Central Intelligence Agency (CIA), 371n
Central Planning Board, 324, 394, 428, 429
Chalufour, Aline, 213
Chamberlain, Neville, 194, 332, 522
Champetier de Ribes, Auguste, 283, 298, 346, 497, 531–3, 624, 633
Chanler, Col. William C., 4, 37, 38, 41, 42, 75, 110, 270, 295n, 629
Charlotte, Grand Duchess of Luxembourg, 24
Charter, *see* London Charter
Chekhov, Anton, 316
Chelmno, 316, 533
Chicago, University of, 119
China, 26, 641
Christiansen, Gen. Friedrich, 442, 443
Churchill, Winston, 25–7, 29–32, 34, 58, 67n, 70, 73, 85, 107, 109, 151, 191, 224, 316–17, 413n, 461, 467, 567, 603
Ciano, Galeazzo, 52
civilians, attacks and atrocities against, 7, 12, 65; *see also* Gypsies; Jews; Poles; Slavs
Civil War, 8–9, 271
Clark, Gen. Mark, 291
Clark, Mary, 291
Clay, Gen. Lucius, 48, 61, 68, 77, 111, 112, 123, 236, 239, 272, 273, 275, 279, 280, 287, 291, 490n, 501, 517, 609n, 628, 640
Clay, Mrs. Lucius, 291
Clemenceau, Georges, 15, 16
Clyde, R. S., 69–70, 80
Colditz prison, 132n
Coleman, Maj. Lawrence, 56, 61
Collins, Gen. Joseph "Lightning Joe," 382
Columbia Law School, 8, 101, 119, 398, 549, 619n
Combined Chiefs of Staff, 269, 270
*Command of the Air* (Douhet), 19
Commando Order, 253–5, 266, 403, 408, 414, 433, 484, 521, 529, 569, 593, 594
Commissar Order, 433, 462, 521, 529, 530
Communists, 16, 162, 189, 202, 463, 613; extermination of, 247; German, 310, 379, 523; Polish, 467
concentration camps, 5, 21, 42, 168, 169, 201, 202, 296, 330, 334, 336, 360, 361, 432n, 438, 507, 511, 514, 526, 575; affidavits on, 242; film of, 186–7, 190; forced labor and (*see* forced labor program); liberation of, 39; medical experiments in, 171, 301, 323; testimony of inmates of, 300–1, 317; trials of staff of, 270–2; valuables confiscated in, 397, 540; *see also specific camps*

*Confessions of "The Old Wizard"* (Schacht), 614
conspiracy charges, 35–9, 41, 85, 93, 331, 334, 341, 491–2, 494, 497, 540, 629–30, 637–8; and Charter, 75–6; deliberations on, 550–4, 560; economic case and, 81; in Indictment, 80, 82–3, 100, 102, 116; against individual defendants, 262–9, 384, 393, 410–16, 424, 426, 432, 434–6, 440, 445, 460–1, 476, 480, 482, 488; judgment of Tribunal on, 575–6, 581–2; and organizational guilt, 284; presentation of case on, 145, 169, 173, 175, 186, 193–200
Continental Oil Company, 396
Cooper, Robert, 219, 601, 607
Council of Ministers for the Defense of the Reich, 204
Cour de Cassation, 59, 120, 212
Cracow, University of, 369
Cramer, Gen. Myron C., 35
Cravath law firm, 291
Crimean War, 9, 10
Cronkite, Walter, 219–21, 418
Cruscius, Maj., 17
Cutter, Col. Ammi, 36, 41, 68, 75, 78
Czechoslovakia, 640; annexation of, 24, 145, 192, 268, 269, 298, 307, 313, 324, 333, 352, 386, 411, 414, 434–5, 456–8, 521, 554, 555, 575–7; deportation of Jews from, 248

Dachau, 38, 169, 171, 186, 270, 272, 323, 324, 363, 379, 384, 433, 512, 611n
Dahlerus, Birger, 331–3, 337
Daniell, Ray, 219
Dartmouth College, 59
Dean, Maj. Ernest, 220
Dean, Gordon, 47, 56, 65, 92, 122, 141, 160, 172, 206, 216, 220, 231, 233
Dean, Patrick, 58, 60, 61, 67, 68, 102, 162, 212, 286, 337, 340, 346
Debenet (French prosecutor), 443
de Gaulle, Charles, 24, 32, 212
Deinard, Benjamin, 81, 138, 139, 387
Dellbrugge, Dr., 427
Demjanuk, John, 640
democratization, 279–80
denazification, 279–80, 510, 517, 556, 558, 584, 638
Denazification Policy Review Board, 278–80
Denmark, invasion and occupation of, 23, 145, 192, 194–5, 298, 304, 328, 405, 438, 442, 484, 508, 577n, 578
*De Profundis* (Wilde), 418

Devers, Gen., 222
Dickman, Maj. Otto, 302
Diels, Rudolf, 231
Dietrich, Otto, 268, 378, 460–2, 631
Dittman, Walter, 414
Dittmar, Gen. Kurt, 461
Dix, Rudolf, 133, 166, 173, 176, 228, 350, 372, 373, 384n, 385, 386, 388, 390, 404, 475, 482, 484, 601, 613, 625, 632
Dmitrieva (interpreter), 100–2, 209, 210
Dodd, Thomas, 138, 146, 215, 216, 243, 276, 286, 381, 571, 574, 625; cross-examinations by, 5, 366, 369, 394–7, 425–7, 481; interrogations by, 137; presentation of evidence by, 173–5, 197, 200, 201, 204, 242, 420, 527, 532
Doenitz, Adm. Karl, 30, 86, 87, 89, 90, 96, 187, 228, 318, 330, 362, 364, 383, 391, 415–16, 425, 439, 444, 449, 460, 628; case against, 199, 254, 265–6, 269, 494, 498, 500; conviction of, 592–4; defense of, 132, 227, 323, 382, 398–410, 483, 484; deliberations on, 566–8, 570, 631; final statement of, 540–1; petition for clemency for, 602; sentencing of, 599, 600; Seyss-Inquart and, 487; in Spandau, 615–17; Speer and, 448, 449, 454
Donnedieu de Vabres, Henri, 120, 122–4, 155, 157, 158, 161, 163, 212, 225, 424, 468, 631, 632; during deliberations, 550–3, 555–7, 559–66, 568, 569, 581–2, 591n, 595; reading of judgment by, 590, 592, 595; subsequent career of, 625
Donovan, Com. James, 47, 49, 56, 79, 86, 98, 138, 186, 200
Donovan, Gen. William J., 46–8, 53, 56, 60, 61, 68, 78–9, 80n, 123, 138, 139, 146–9, 180–6, 199, 211, 231, 238–40, 273–4, 387
Dorpmueller, Julius, 430
Dostert, Col., 344
Dostler, Gen. Anton, 255, 270, 521, 529
Douglas, Elsie, 56, 160, 172, 216, 227
Douglas, Air Chief Marshal Sir Sholto, 602–7, 618–19
Douglas, William O., 419
Douhet, Giulio, 19
Dresdner Bank, 383
Dubost, Charles, 102–3, 118, 121, 124–5, 140–2, 152–5, 157–63, 211–13, 298–303, 477n, 497–9, 532, 559, 633
Dulles, Allen W., 52, 61, 371n
Dunant, Henri, 10
Dunn, Lt. Col., 547

Dupont, Victor, 301
Dutch Army, 326

Earle, George, 182
Eberstein, Friedrich Karl Freiherr von, 512
Eck, Lt. Heinz, 266n, 406–8
economic case, 80–2, 86, 92, 142, 265
economic looting, 295, 298–9, 393, 394, 443
Eden, Anthony, 28–9, 32, 34n, 39, 40, 70, 73, 85, 191, 637
Egypt, 637
Ehrenburg, Ilya, 219
Eichhorn, Lt. Reinhard von, 470
Eichmann, Adolf, 166n, 202, 242, 248, 360, 362, 424, 428n, 533, 628, 640
Einsatzgruppen, 169, 202, 206, 242, 246–7, 249, 257, 317, 361, 367, 370, 427, 428, 462n, 470, 510–11, 519, 522, 529, 532, 533, 589
Einsatzstab Rosenberg, 104, 365
Eisenhower, Dwight D., 5, 52, 107–11, 119n, 131, 135, 144, 169n, 215, 222, 235, 238–9, 270, 272, 381–2, 513n, 603
*Emden* (cruiser), 399
Enlightenment, Age of, 5, 6
*Enola Gay* (bomber), 74
Estonia, 118
ETOUSA, 270
European Advisory Council, 108n
European Air Transport Service, 118
Exner, Franz, 259, 304–5, 311, 433–4, 436, 486, 625

Faber, Kaspar, 218
Faber-Castell, Baron, 218
Fahy, Charles, 68, 112, 121, 134, 273–5, 278, 279, 287, 288, 290, 628
Fairman, Col. Charles, 272–3
Falco, Robert, 59, 64, 66, 74, 100, 120–2, 125, 126, 155, 161, 163, 212, 224–7, 295, 550, 555, 561, 564, 566–9, 632
Falkenhorst, Gen. Nikolaus von, 255, 270, 312n, 408, 529
Farr, Maj. Warren, 205–6, 511
Faure, Edgar, 212, 242, 298, 303–5, 353, 624, 633
Fay, Sidney B., 51
Federal Bar Association, 572
Federal Communications Commission, 289
Fichte, Johann Gottlieb, 295
Finland, 24n, 490, 579
Fischer, Dr., 426
Fisher, Adrian S. "Butch," 119, 216, 549, 553–4, 562–5, 567n, 572, 625
Fite, Katherine, 127, 215

Flächsner, Hans, 324, 418, 450–3, 487–9
Flanner, Janet, 343
Fleeson, Doris, 419, 420
Flossenburg, 272, 384
forced labor program, 201, 267, 295,
298–9, 325, 334, 340, 346, 361, 366,
369, 405, 427–31, 449, 451–4, 479, 481,
485–8, 526
Ford, Henry, 422, 423
Four-Year Plan, 334, 336, 346, 366, 383,
392, 522
Fowler, Henry, 108
France, 19, 640; deportation of Jews
from, 352, 476, 537; invasion of, 189,
195, 269, 326, 328, 413, 436, 577, 578;
and Munich Agreement, 192, 434, 435,
522, 554; occupation of, 23, 24, 44, 293,
299, 302, 353, 394, 438, 448, 513;
retreat of Wehrmacht from, 33; slave
labor from, 201, 295, 298–9, 429, 430;
in World War I, 12–14, 16–18
Franco-Austrian War, 9, 10
Franco-German Armistice Convention
(1940), 299, 303
Franco-Prussian War, 7, 105
Frank, Hans, 22n, 25, 85, 89, 187, 228,
248, 298, 316, 322, 362, 365n, 391, 404,
441, 548, 596; case against, 201, 264,
493, 497; conviction of, 598; defense
of, 132, 268, 351, 367–70, 423, 480;
deliberations on, 561; execution of,
607, 608, 610; final statement of,
538–9; petition for clemency for, 601;
sentencing of, 598, 600
Frank, Karl Hermann, 457, 459
Frank, Wolfe, 229, 598
Frankfurter, Felix, 119, 419
Frederick the Great, 105, 107
Free French, 24
Free Germany Committee, 310
Freemasons, 364
French Army, 435
French Resistance, 132n, 189, 293, 301
Frick, Wilhelm, 85, 90, 323, 388, 394,
404, 577; case against, 199, 267, 296;
conviction of, 590, 629; defense of, 132,
351, 370–6, 385, 480; deliberations on,
561, 570; execution of, 610; family
visitors to, 547; final statement of, 539;
petition for clemency for, 602;
sentencing of, 598, 600
Fritsch, Gen. Werner von, 372–4, 385,
423, 446
Fritz, Heinz, 460, 462n, 488–9, 612
Fritzsche, Hans, 62, 89, 187, 204, 305,
311, 316, 352, 362, 369, 370, 375, 378,
391, 481, 535, 536, 542, 548, 613;

acquittal of, 597–601; on Bormann,
464–5; case against, 199, 268, 269;
defense of, 323, 417, 459–63, 488;
deliberations on, 551, 565, 566;
Denazification Court conviction of, 612;
final statement of, 544–5; indictment
of, 132, 631; Schirach and, 421–3, 425;
Seyss-Inquart and, 439–40, 444
Fromm, Gen. Fritz, 511n
Funk, Walter, 5, 81, 86, 90, 187, 228, 248,
258, 259, 323, 352, 374, 384, 423, 429,
460; case against, 199, 264, 265, 387;
conviction of, 590–1, 596; defense of,
132, 382, 391–8, 481–2, 484;
deliberations on, 560, 562; final
statement of, 540; judgment of
Tribunal on, 575; petition for clemency
for, 602; sentencing of, 599, 600; in
Spandau, 615–17; Speer and, 449, 615
Furtwaengler, Wilhelm, 332

Gage, Gen. Thomas, 6n
Galbraith, John Kenneth, 449
Gallagher, Wes, 219
*Gathering Storm, The* (Churchill), 413n
Gaus, Friedrich, 350
Gawlik, Hans, 510–11
Gebauer, Gen. Arthur, 316
General Orders No. 100, 9–11, 271n
Geneva Conventions, 10, 19, 20, 22, 84,
190, 191, 296n, 334, 357, 505, 593,
640–1
Geneva Disarmament Conference, 22
genocide, 103
George II, King, of Greece, 24
Gerecke, Pastor, 609, 619, 620
Gerhart, Eugene, 336n
German General Staff-High Command,
23, 104–15, 117, 146, 171, 180, 184,
203, 207, 236–40, 274–8, 291, 326, 334,
400, 404, 433, 444, 527; charges
against, 147–8; closing arguments on,
528–33; defense of, 517–22; defense
counsel for, 144, 311, 324; deliberations
on, 556, 557; Einsatzgruppen and, 510;
interrogation of, 137; judgment of
Tribunal on, 585–6, 599; preparation of
case against, 240–4, 249–62, 266
Germanization, 296, 303–4, 457
German Labor Front, 85, 104, 132
German Navy, 86, 88, 89, 106, 195, 265,
266, 328n, 399–415, 496, 541, 567, 578
German Supreme Court, 17
Germany: aggressive war waged by, *see*
aggressive war charges, *and specific
countries*; countries occupied by, *see
specific countries*; defeat of, 32, 39;

Japan and, 196–7; Morgenthau plan for, 31; nonaggression treaty with Soviet Union, *see* Nazi-Soviet Pact; rearmament of, 250–1, 330, 349, 383–6, 389, 455, 554, 574; reparations paid by, 19; slave labor in, *see* forced labor program; Weimar, *see* Weimar Republic; in World War I, 12–18, 21, 29, 105–6, 256

Gerthoffer, Charles, 299, 305, 624, 633

Gestapo, 45, 85–7, 108, 109, 112, 113, 168, 189, 231, 237, 297, 322, 360, 414, 503, 540, 589; closing arguments on, 525, 527, 532, 533; defense of, 508–10; deliberations on, 556–7; evidence against, 206, 244, 246, 304, 314, 493; Frick and, 371, 375; in Indictment, 104, 115; judgment of Tribunal on, 584; Schacht and, 385

Gilbert, G. M., 132, 187, 311, 317, 352, 353, 362, 391, 415, 479, 548; and death sentences, 600, 608; Doenitz and, 404, 416; Frank and, 298, 368; Frick and, 370, 371; Fritzsche and, 598; Goering and, 190, 200, 258, 305–7, 316, 323, 342, 376, 403, 621; Hess and, 177, 179, 207, 237, 238, 589n; Hoess and, 363; intelligence tests administered by, 150, 228, 360, 376, 383, 427, 432, 439, 449; Kaltenbrunner and, 478; Sauckel and, 429–30; Schacht and, 497; Schirach and, 422–3, 425; Seyss-Inquart and, 440; Speer and, 450, 497

Gill, Gen. Robert, 57, 61, 95, 129, 143–5, 215, 216, 231, 417, 574

Giraud, Gen. Henri, 189, 191

Gisevius, Hans Bernd, 371–6, 385–6, 390, 391, 404, 423, 480, 482

*Glowworm* (destroyer), 413

Gobineau, Joseph Arthur, Comte de, 298

Godchaux, Charlotte, 118

Godt, Adm. Eberhard, 406, 508

Goebbels, Joseph, 3, 25, 30, 87, 388, 427–8, 442, 464, 505, 628; Fritzsche and, 62, 89, 268, 460–3, 631; Funk and, 392–4; and Katyn Forest massacre, 466, 467; Neurath and, 458, 459; Streicher and, 377, 378; suicide of, 32, 33, 186, 231

Goerdeler, Carl, 386

Goering, Edda, 547

Goering, Emmy, 547, 619, 623, 624

Goering, Hermann, 3, 25, 30, 62, 71, 96, 137, 175, 237n, 251, 254n, 354, 365, 370, 394, 415, 425, 445, 448; behavior during trial of, 166, 178, 187, 190, 200, 205, 228, 248, 250, 258–60, 306, 307,

312, 315–17, 353, 357, 362, 403–4, 439, 450, 479, 494, 497, 531; Bormann and, 464; case against, 199, 201, 252, 263, 295, 296, 299, 305–6, 310–11, 391, 438, 480, 492; conviction of, 588, 589, 591, 595; cross-examination of, 335–46, 356, 358–9, 387, 388, 421, 491, 633; defense of, 133, 166, 304, 320–35, 346–7, 475–6, 627; deliberations on, 560; Donovan and, 182–6; family visitors to, 547; final statement of, 534–6, 542; and Four-Year Plan, 366; Funk and, 265, 392, 393; Gisevius and, 371–6; Hess and, 129, 151, 312; as Hitler's successor-designate, 177–8; indictment of, 85, 89; interrogation of, 136, 181; judgment of Tribunal on, 575–7; and Katyn Forest massacre, 468; Luftwaffe commanded by, 106n; Neurath and, 456; not guilty plea of, 167; petition for clemency for, 601, 606, 607; in prison, 230; Sauckel and, 428; Schacht and, 383–4, 389, 392; Schirach and, 422–3, 614; sentencing of, 598, 600; Speer and, 449; Streicher and, 377; suicide of, 609, 611, 618–24

Goerlitz, Walter, 608

Goethe, Johann Wolfgang von, 496–7

Gorman, Col. Robert O., 37

Gorshenin, Gen. K. P., 211, 212

Goulding, Ossian, 219

Graebe, Hermann Friedrich, 244–6

Grawitz, Ernst, 514

Greece: deportation of Jews from, 248; invasion and occupation of, 23, 61, 145, 192, 195–6, 437, 554–5, 579

Griffith-Jones, Mervyn, 194–6, 198, 199, 214, 264, 268, 349, 379, 380, 454, 503, 506, 624

Gros, André, 66, 67, 79, 83–5, 87, 92, 100

Grotius, Dr., 357–8

Gruss, Theodor, 523, 524, 526

Guderian, Gen. Heinz, 464

guilt by membership, *see* organizational guilt

Gurfein, Lt. Col. Murray, 82, 137, 146, 185n, 265, 387

Gusev, Fedor, 53

Gypsies, extermination of, 103, 169, 259

Haakon, King, of Norway, 24, 442n

Hácha, Emil, 356, 577

Hackworth, Green, 35

Hagelin, Viljam, 365

Hague Conventions, 10, 11, 13, 18, 20, 22, 48, 54n, 75, 84, 190, 251, 253, 296, 299, 302, 305, 325, 334, 357, 405, 429,

Hague Conventions (*continued*)
433, 441, 443, 452, 479, 485, 487, 488,
495n, 513, 580, 581
Halder, Gen. Franz, 180, 240–1, 243, 250,
254n, 309, 528
Hale, Nathan, 8
Halifax, Lord, 67, 107, 109, 332
Halleck, Gen. Henry W., 9
Handloser, Siegfried, 301
Hardy, Alexander, 514
Harlan, John, 4
Harmon, Gen. Ernest N., 223
Harriman, Averell, 46, 108
Harris, Capt. Samuel, 202–4, 387, 398
Harris, Tom, 289
Harris, Lt. Com. Whitney, 172, 216, 246,
508, 574, 608, 609n, 610, 611, 625
Harvard Law School, 119
Haushofer, Karl, 231
Hausser, Gen. Paul, 513, 525
Hayler, Franz, 397
Hazard, John, 101, 102
Hegel, Georg Wilhelm Friedrich, 295
Heime (Gestapo member), 314
Heisig, Lt. Peter, 266, 406–7
Heller, Joseph, 179
Henderson, Nevile, 490
Henlein, Konrad, 434
Herisson, Janine, 398
Herzog, Jacques, 299, 430
Hess, Rudolf, 25, 28–9, 31, 32n, 62, 73,
85, 87, 89, 96, 200, 231, 323, 382, 445n,
464, 468, 587, 609; case against, 203,
268–9, 492, 499; competency to stand
trial of, 150–1, 177–80, 228; conviction
of, 588–9, 629, 635; defense of, 133,
144, 320, 347–50, 370, 476, 489–90;
deliberations on, 559, 560; final
statement of, 536; Goering and, 312;
indictment of, 116–17; interrogation of,
129, 136; not guilty plea of, 167;
petition for clemency for, 602;
sentencing of, 598–600; in Spandau,
615–18
Hessler, Com. Guenter, 406, 408
Heusinger, Gen. Adolf, 258
Heydrich, Reinhard, 246, 355, 360, 364,
375, 388, 393, 395n, 424, 428, 443, 458,
462, 508, 511, 569, 589
Hiemer, Ernst, 380
Higgins, Marguerite, 219
Hill & Sons, 100
Hilldring, Gen. John R., 110, 289
Himmler, Heinrich, 3, 25, 29, 30, 87, 104,
257, 304, 316, 331, 344, 355, 366, 424,
428, 464, 465, 481, 505, 515–16, 590,
628; Bach-Zelewski and, 258; and

Commando Order, 403; and
concentration camps, 334, 363, 364,
507, 514; and Einsatzgruppen, 510–11,
520, 532; Frank and, 369, 480; Frick
and, 370–5; Funk and, 395, 396, 540;
Kaltenbrunner and, 478, 538, 589; and
Katyn Forest massacre, 472; and
Kristallnacht, 322; Mueller and, 360,
363; Neurath and, 457, 459; Ohlendorf
and, 246; Schacht and, 384, 388;
Seyss-Inquart and, 442, 443, 563, 595;
speeches of, 202–3, 314; Speer and,
450, 618; suicide of, 85, 186, 231; and
Warsaw Ghetto, 170
Hindenburg, Paul von, 105, 169, 383, 388,
392, 436, 445
Hipper, Adm. Franz von, 409
*Hipper* (cruiser), 413
Hirshfeld, Heinz, 444, 487
Hirt, August, 515
Hitler, Adolf, 3, 12, 23, 30, 38, 86, 89,
145, 180–2, 190, 231, 232, 256, 310,
316, 324, 483, 495, 500, 511n, 551, 614,
626, 628; attack on Poland ordered by,
170, 490, 639; attempted assassination
of, 190n, 249n, 322, 384, 511n; and
Blomberg-Fritsch affair, 136–7, 373–4;
Bormann and, 87, 464, 487;
Commando Order of, 48, 253–5, 403;
Doenitz and, 90, 399, 401–5, 593; and
economic defendants, 81; evidence
against, 176, 192–9, 202, 203, 304, 491,
493, 554; and extermination of Jews,
26; films of, 200; foreign policy of, 22;
Frank and, 367–70, 539; Frick and,
370, 371; Fritzsche and, 460, 461, 488,
597; Funk and, 392–4; and General
Staff, 106–8, 113, 114, 148, 241, 250,
251, 254n, 257, 259, 520–2, 528, 529,
532; Goering and, 25, 330–5, 344–6;
headquarters of, 187, 246n, 322; Hess
and, 117, 151, 269, 348, 349, 536, 537,
588, 602, 618; in Indictment, 103n;
Jodl and, 89, 417, 432–9, 595;
judgment of Tribunal on, 576, 577, 579,
580, 585, 586; and Katyn Forest
massacre, 472; Keitel and, 188, 252–8,
375, 477; and Nazi Party structure,
504; Neurath and, 455–9, 597; in pact
with Stalin, *see* Nazi-Soviet Pact;
Papen and, 268, 445–7; progenitors of,
295; Raeder and, 266, 409–12, 415,
416, 484, 496, 569, 594; Ribbentrop
and, 85, 351, 352, 476; rise to power
of, 21, 80, 91, 154, 169, 265, 329, 445,
574, 595; and Roehm purge, 523;
Rosenberg and, 364–7, 478–9, 538, 589;

Sauckel and, 427, 428; Schacht and, 88, 264, 383–6, 388–92, 482, 540, 564, 592, 602, 631–2; Schirach and, 422–6, 485, 618; Seyss-Inquart and, 267, 439–44, 486, 543, 563, 595–6; Speer and, 448–52, 454, 487, 488, 544, 563, 603, 616; Streicher and, 376–9, 562; suicide of, 32, 87, 186, 463, 466, 538; will of, 86

Hitler Jugend (Hitler Youth), 86, 110n, 206, 267, 422–6, 484–5, 498, 541, 594

Hitler-Stalin Pact (*see* Nazi-Soviet Pact)

Hlond, Cardinal, 23

Hodges, Tom, 382

Hodgson, Col. J. V., 28

Hoegner, Wilhelm, 601, 609

Hoellriegel, Alois, 249, 300

Hoess, Rudolf Franz Ferdinand, 362–4, 368, 425, 514

Hoettl, Wilhelm, 202, 242–3

Hoffman, Lt. August, 407

Hoffmann, Heinrich, 231, 422

Hoffmann, Henriette, 422

Holmes, Oliver Wendell, 175, 343

Holocaust, 24, 26n, 169n, 296, 307, 397, 481, 584; *see also* Jews: extermination of

Holy Roman Empire, 5

Hoover, Herbert, 95n

Hopkins, Harry, 47, 108–9, 239

Hore-Belisha, Leslie, 215

Horn, Martin, 321, 350, 352, 353, 476

Horsky, Charles, 281, 289

Horthy, Adm. Miklós, 352

Hossbach, Friedrich, 198

Hossbach conference, 456–7, 554, 597

hostages, killing of, 84, 295–6, 300

Hott, Lt., 468

Howe, Mark DeWolfe, 42n

Hughes, Charles Evans, 418

Hull, Cordell, 34, 35

humanity, crimes against, 294, 346, 491; deliberations on, 552, 553; Fritzsche and, 460; of Funk, 393; by General Staff, 241; in Indictment, 79, 84, 100, 103, 116; under J.C.S. 1023/10, 272; of Jodl, 432; judgment of Tribunal on, 582–3; presentation of case on, 201–3, 296–7, 303–4, 317–18; of Schirach, 424–7; of Seyss-Inquart, 440; of Streicher, 376–80

Hungary, 16, 18, 24, 580, 640; deportation of Jews from, 248, 452

Hurst, Sir Cecil, 26–8

I. G. Farben, 81, 152

India, 26

Indictment, 116, 143, 203, 322, 325, 351, 357, 368, 370, 378, 380, 388, 393, 423, 432, 440, 445, 446, 451, 456, 474, 477, 480, 489, 535, 549, 574, 580, 634; appendices of, 103–4, 115; Charter and, 64; Count One, 100, 101, 145, 197, 198, 200, 251, 252, 262–6, 327, 331, 353, 354, 384, 399, 401, 409, 427, 449, 458, 460, 475, 488, 489, 491, 495, 550–1, 560–2, 564–9, 575, 576, 582, 588, 590–7, 630; Count Two, 100, 101, 145, 191, 198, 200, 251, 252, 262–6, 327, 331, 353, 354, 384, 399, 401, 409, 427, 449, 458, 475, 483, 489, 491, 492, 495, 551, 552, 555, 560–4, 567–9, 575, 576, 588–97, 599, 629, 630; Count Three, 100, 117, 118, 124, 126, 253, 263, 265, 346, 384, 399, 409, 449, 460, 495, 560–4, 566–9, 589–94, 596, 597, 599, 629, 630; Count Four, 100, 124, 253, 263, 346, 376, 384, 424, 426, 449, 460, 495, 560–4, 566, 567, 569, 589–91, 594, 596; and defendant selection, 85, 90; defendants served with, 131–2, 150, 151; drafting of, 78–80, 82–5, 97–103, 112–13, 115, 135; organizations named in, 236–8, 240, 243, 249, 501, 508, 509, 517, 518, 586; proposed amendment of, 152, 157–8, 161; reading of, 165, 166; and self-proving trial briefs, 145; signing of, 117–18; submission to Tribunal of, 120, 122n, 123–6, 147

Industrial Revolution, 5

*Infiltration* (Speer), 395n

Informal Policy Committee on Germany, 45

inquisitorial system, 63

Inter-Allied Commission on the Punishment of War Crimes, 25, 626

Inter-Allied Reparations Commission, 45

Inter-American Bar Association, 44

International Business Machine (IBM), 94, 143

International Conference on Military Trials, 59, 71n

*International Jew, The* (Ford), 422

International Red Cross, 10, 467

International Treaty for the Renunciation of War as an Instrument of National Policy, *see* Kellogg-Briand Pact

Iraq, 636, 637

Irish Republican Army, 132n, 624

Israel, 637, 640

*Israelitisches Wochenblatt*, 380

Italy, 16, 19, 24, 26, 197, 402, 437, 522, 579; Allied Military Government in,

Italy *(continued)*
37; Commando Order enforcement in, 255, 521; deportation of Jews from, 352, 476
Ivanov (Counselor at Soviet Embassy in London), 97, 98, 100

J.C.S. 1023/10, 272–5
Jackson, Robert H., 4, 83, 85, 96, 178, 199, 216, 231, 303, 319–20, 346, 349, 358–9, 372, 382, 384n, 387, 419–21, 542, 634–6, 638; and acquittals, 592, 607; appointment of, 39–40, 45–6; and appointment of Tribunal, 94–5, 97; background of, 43–4; in Berlin, 118–19, 121–5, 127, 129; closing argument of, 490–4, 497; cross-examinations by, 323–5, 327, 328, 335–44, 374–5, 381, 386, 388–91, 418, 452–3, 633; death of, 625; and defendant selection process, 85–7, 89–95; and Denazification Policy Review Board, 279–80; Donovan and, 180–6; and economic case, 80–2; and establishment of Tribunal, 52–3, 57–74, 76, 77; evidence gathering by, 47–51; and executions, 608n, 609n; farewell dinner party of, 547–8; final report of, 611; and future trials, 273, 286–90; generals and, 144–5, 223, 272–5; and German General Staff prosecution, 236, 238–43, 261, 517; and German journalists, 233–4; Gilbert and, 187; during holiday adjournment, 206; and Indictment, 97, 98, 100–4, 111–15, 117, 509, 630, 631, 639; and judgment of Tribunal, 571–3; June 7, 1945, report of, 53–6, 62, 66, 91, 110, 233, 272, 276; moves operations to Nuremberg, 96–9; opening statement of, 167–72, 192, 202, 227, 233, 282, 293, 294, 298, 474, 477, 627; and organization of Tribunal, 133–4; on petitions to Control Council, 603, 604; and presentation of prosecution case, 174, 197, 203, 262, 264–5, 277–8, 281–5, 504; and pretrial proceedings, 146–9, 151–64; reorganization of staff by, 131, 135, 137–43, 274; and Soviet prosecutors, 193, 201, 211, 214, 215, 463n; staff assembled by, 46–8; and staff dissatisfaction, 78–9, 244
Jackson, William E., 42, 47, 56, 61, 68, 78, 79, 103, 129, 160, 172, 210, 216, 219, 231, 240, 420, 572, 573, 587
Jaeger, Wilhelm, 431
Jahrreiss, Hermann, 324, 433, 474–5, 491, 494, 495

Japan, 16, 26, 43, 196–7, 399, 408–9, 580
Jaworski, Col. Leon, 271n
*Jewell Ridge Coal Corp. v. United Mine Workers* (1945), 419n
Jews, 21, 22, 76, 88, 168, 268, 296, 355, 359, 364, 388, 405–6, 455, 458, 460, 463, 480, 484, 505, 526; atrocities against, 28, 54n, 75, 264, 526, 583, 584, 589; confiscation of property of, 365, 397, 476; deportation of, 267, 352, 424–6, 438, 442–3, 465, 487, 537, 589, 594; expulsion from Austria of, 602; expulsion from Germany of, 406, 483; extermination of, 24, 26, 27, 36n, 42, 103, 169–70, 188, 202, 244–8, 257–9, 267, 307–8, 317, 361, 363, 367, 368, 370, 379, 380, 414, 425, 433, 461–2, 470, 511–12, 519–20, 522, 525, 530, 532, 533, 539, 560, 590, 626–8 (*see also* Holocaust); in ghettos, 23, 369; prewar persecution of, 201, 203, 323, 328, 330, 340, 375–9, 389, 393–4, 424, 440–1, 481, 507, 508, 522, 523, 575, 582 (*see also* Kristallnacht); "scientific research" on, 515–16; Streicher on, 150, 264; valuables taken from, 5, 202
Jodl, Alfred, 89, 90, 96, 114, 148, 191, 228, 259, 318, 323, 358, 369, 391, 417, 445, 510, 531, 577, 593, 637; case against, 194, 199, 250–2, 263, 305, 309, 310, 492, 500, 528, 531; conviction of, 595; defense of, 304, 324, 431–40, 486; deliberations on, 559, 563, 569–70; Donovan and, 148, 180; execution of, 609, 610, 621; final statement of, 541–2; not guilty plea of, 167; petition for clemency for, 602, 603, 606, 607; sentencing of, 599, 600
Jodl, Felix, 431–2
Jodl, Luise, 603
Joint Chiefs of Staff, 269, 272
Jones, Maj. Elwyn, 101, 126, 194–6, 199, 214–15, 266, 286, 357, 387, 415, 512–16, 624
Jowitt, Sir William, 72–4, 78, 87, 118, 120, 215, 567
Juettner, Max, 523–4, 526
Juin, Field Marshal, 603
Jung, Edgar, 446

Kaiser, Bernard, 619n
Kalnoky, Ingeborg, 231
Kaltenbrunner, Ernst, 85, 89–90, 115, 165, 187, 228, 248, 323, 395n, 439, 482; case against, 246, 249, 263, 304, 375, 492, 508–10; conviction of, 589; defense of, 242, 324, 351, 359–64, 430,

478; deliberations on, 561; execution of, 610; final statement of, 538; indictment of, 132; interrogation of, 136; sentencing of, 598, 600, 601
Kaplan, Col. Benjamin, 48, 57, 82, 98, 103, 112, 129, 137, 138, 146, 236, 244
Kaplan, Com. Sidney, 57, 80, 82, 98, 103, 126, 127, 129, 138, 139, 143, 145, 176, 244
*Kaputt* (Malaparte), 367–8
Katyn forest massacre, 117, 124, 218, 312–13, 466–72, 476, 639
Kauffman, Kurt, 242, 324, 360–3, 478
Kaufmann, Gauleiter, 505
Kehrl, Hans, 429, 453
Keitel, Field Marshal Wilhelm, 30, 85, 87, 90, 96, 106, 114, 228, 310, 311, 322, 345, 362, 391, 415, 432, 445, 464, 510, 547; case against, 170, 187–91, 194, 199, 201, 251, 252, 255, 263, 296, 304, 305, 351, 375, 385, 438, 480, 492, 499, 500; conviction of, 589; defense of, 190, 309, 320, 353–8, 394, 404, 437, 476–8, 482, 488; deliberations on, 561, 564, 570; Donovan and, 148, 180; execution of, 607–8, 610, 621; final statement of, 537–8, 541, 542, 545; Goering and, 334; petition on behalf of, 602, 606, 607; sentencing of, 598, 600
Kelley, Douglas M., 179, 422–3
Kellogg, Frank B., 20
Kellogg-Briand Pact (1928), 20–2, 37n, 38, 44, 54, 166, 191, 295, 580
Kempka, Erich, 466
Kempner, Robert, 218, 234, 267, 325, 503, 520, 574, 619, 623
Kentish, Miss, 214
Keppler, Wilhelm, 439
Kesselring, Field Marshal Albert, 325–8
Ketteler, Baron Wilhelm von, 447
Kiendl, Theodore, 40
Kleffel, Gen. Philipp, 487
Klefisch, Theodor, 144, 152–7, 525
Klopfer, Dr., 465–6
Koch, Ilse, 242
Koch, Karl, 514
Koeltz, Gen. Louis, 275
Koenig, Gen. Joseph Pierre, 275, 603, 604, 606
Koenigstein prison, 189
Koerner, Paul, 325
Koestring, Gen. Ernest, 231
Korean War, 636–7, 641
Kramer, Josef, 270
Kranzbuehler, Otto, 132, 227–8, 266, 317–18, 320, 322, 398–403, 405–10, 413,

475, 483–4, 489, 567, 568, 602, 616, 625–30, 632, 635
Kraus, Herbert, 385
Kripo, 509–10, 514
Kristallnacht, 22, 322, 323, 330, 379, 393, 394, 397, 424, 505, 507, 508, 512
Krupp, Alfried, 81, 87–94, 151–64, 180, 227, 285, 630
Krupp, Bertha, 91, 152
Krupp, Friedrich Alfred, 91
Krupp, Gustav, 89–94, 105, 117, 123, 131n, 132, 144, 150–9, 164, 216, 227, 237n, 285, 387, 575, 630
Krupp firm, 431, 452, 545
Kubochok, Egon, 190, 418, 445, 450, 487, 522–3
Kuppisch, Herbert, 407
Kuwait, 637

*Laconia* (ship), 402
*Lady Chatterley's Lover* (Lawrence), 214
LaGuardia, Fiorello, 289n
Lahousen, General Erwin, 182–4, 186–91, 193, 221, 231
Lambert, Lt. Thomas, 267, 465
Lammers, Hans Heinrich, 357, 365
Lampe, Maurice, 300–1
Länderrat, 280
Langer, William L., 49n
Lansing, Robert, 15, 16, 66
Laternser, Hans, 144, 311, 324, 404, 503, 517–20, 522, 528–30
Latvia, 118
Lausanne, Treaty of (1923), 18
Laval, Pierre, 293, 352
"Law for Liberation from National Socialism and Militarism," 280
"Law of Land Warfare, The" (U.S. Army), 10
Lawrence, D. H., 214
Lawrence, Sir Geoffrey, 120–5, 131, 155, 161, 214, 215, 223, 225–7, 545, 546n, 572, 631, 632; appointment of, 120; chosen as presiding judge, 124; and closing arguments, 475–9, 482, 486–90, 516; and cross-examinations, 336, 338, 339, 343n, 362, 390, 397, 431, 438; and defendants' final statements, 534, 536; and defense testimony, 321, 347, 357–9, 364, 373, 378, 380, 400, 410, 418, 424, 428, 445, 451, 455, 459, 460, 465–6, 468, 469, 471, 504, 506, 508, 518, 522–4; during deliberations, 549–52, 556, 557, 560–9, 591n; and family visits, 547; and Hess's competency to stand trial, 178–9; and Krupp incident, 156, 157; and pleas of

Lawrence (*continued*)
  defendants, 166–7; and prosecution
  case, 173–5, 195, 203–6, 242, 243, 258,
  260, 263, 264, 268, 277, 284, 302–3,
  305, 306, 309, 503, 510–11, 517*n*; and
  reading of Indictment, 165; reading of
  judgment by, 574, 585–8, 590;
  sentencing by, 598, 599
Lawrence, Lady, 223
laws of war, 4–20, 44, 49, 54, 253, 343,
  352, 353, 434, 451, 485, 486, 583, 628;
  Charter and, 65, 66; history of, 5–9;
  during World War I, 10–16; *see also*
  Geneva Conventions; Hague
  Conventions
Leadership Principle, 336, 341
League of Nations, 15, 16, 19, 22, 191,
  455, 476, 488
Lehman, Herbert, 43
Lemkin, Raphael, 49*n*, 103
Lend-Lease Act (1941), 44
Leonard, Elizabeth, 56
Leventhal, Lt. Com. Harold, 57, 244
Leverkuehn, Paul, 182, 184, 231
Ley, Robert, 85, 89, 104, 132, 149, 204,
  229, 237*n*, 388, 622
*Liandovery Castle* case, 407*n*
Lidice massacre, 302, 314
Lieber, Francis, 8–9, 11, 75, 637
Lieber Code, 9, 10, 271*n*, 334*n*
Lincoln, Abraham, 9
Lippe, Victor von der, 181, 190, 248, 266,
  285, 293, 317, 320, 325, 349, 375, 397,
  399, 433, 444, 477, 520, 547, 573, 574,
  587, 589, 625; on closing arguments,
  481, 484, 488, 490; on defendants' final
  statements, 540, 541; on defendants'
  testimony, 362, 363, 369, 391, 393, 428,
  459; on Donovan, 181–2; on Goering,
  205, 328–30, 333, 337, 344; on Paulus's
  testimony, 310, 321; on prosecution
  evidence, 187, 200, 202, 246, 265, 305,
  316, 511
Lippmann, Walter, 55
Lithuania, 118, 250, 524
Lloyd George, David, 14–17, 29
Locarno Arbitration Treaty (1925), 191,
  456
Lochner, Louis, 219, 427
Loeffler, Martin, 283, 533
Loew Brothers, 505
London Charter, 79, 83, 99, 100, 117,
  119, 135, 143, 147, 159, 166, 168, 192,
  201*n*, 233, 238, 262, 269, 272, 275–7,
  281, 294, 295, 343, 348, 352, 353, 385,
  409, 441, 446, 453, 459, 481, 486, 491,
  495, 507, 518, 549, 550, 553, 567, 574,

581, 590, 593, 602, 603, 629, 634, 635,
  637, 638; Article 3, 475; Article 4, 559;
  Article 6, 65–7, 70, 75, 76, 84, 116, 200,
  252, 282, 384, 441*n*, 485, 488, 489, 492,
  502–3, 523, 526, 551, 552, 558, 560,
  575–7, 582–4, 594, 596; Article 8, 288*n*,
  630; Article 9, 86, 249–50, 282, 489,
  501, 502, 504, 513, 517, 522, 525,
  527–9, 555, 556, 585, 586; Article 10,
  508; Article 12, 155–6, 630; Article 14,
  157, 161; Article 16, 190; Article 17,
  283; Article 18, 338; Article 19, 242;
  Article 20, 319; Article 21, 313*n*, 468,
  469; Article 22, 98; Article 24, 74, 165,
  473, 500, 534; Article 29, 559, 602,
  606; negotiation of, 59–77
London *Star*, 611
London Submarine Agreement (1936), 19,
  266, 399–401, 409, 483
London Treaty (1930), 19, 568
Lord, Gen. Robert B., 119
Lorentz, Pare, 235
Louvain (Belgium), 12
Louvain, University of, 304–5
Low, David, 219
Lubin, Isador, 46
Ludendorff, Gen. Erich, 105, 436
Lüdinghausen, Otto Freiherr von, 349,
  454–6, 488
Luftwaffe, 44, 106*n*, 114, 322, 323, 325–8,
  333, 435, 483, 486*n*, 492, 569, 577
*Lusitania* (ship), 12
Luxembourg: invasion and occupation of,
  23, 24, 145, 192, 195, 352, 436, 448;
  slave labor from, 201, 295, 298

MacArthur, Gen. Douglas, 239, 641
Mackey transmission agency, 220
Magna Carta, 532
Maidanek, 33, 312, 315, 316
Maisky, Ivan, 28–9
Malaparte, Curzio, 367–8
Malcolmson, Charles T., 291, 417–18
Malmédy massacre, 39, 42, 48, 271, 490,
  513
Mamelukes, 9, 190
Mann, Thomas, 8, 496*n*
Manstein, General Fritz Erich von, 180,
  247, 518–22, 530, 531
Maquis, 302
Marcus, Col. David "Mickey," 289–91
Margolis, Daniel, 217*n*
Markov, Antonov, 471
Marshall, Gen. George C., 35, 223
Marwell, David G., 619
Marx, Hanns, 133, 150, 301, 378–80, 481
Maser, Werner, 619

Mason, Frank E., 238
Mastny, Vojtech, 456
Maugham, Lord Chancellor, 215
Mauthausen, 249, 272, 300–1, 360, 361
Maxwell-Fyfe, Sir David, 53, 58, 69, 73,
    84, 118, 178, 195, 211–14, 221, 268,
    319, 320, 342, 349–50, 359, 400, 413,
    418, 421, 454, 500, 567, 582, 595, 631,
    638; affidavits introduced by, 414; at
    Berlin meeting, 120–5; and cases
    against individual defendants, 262, 263;
    in Charter negotiations, 61–3, 67, 72;
    closing argument of, 525–7, 532;
    cross-examinations by, 326, 332–3, 344,
    345, 352, 353, 356, 357, 391, 404–6,
    408, 446–7, 458–9, 463, 471, 505, 524,
    633; and Indictment, 80, 85, 97–102,
    112, 165; journalists and, 220; and
    Krupp incident, 152–4; and
    organization cases, 283–5; presentation
    of documentary evidence by, 194, 196,
    199, 307, 308; subsequent career of,
    624; and translation of documents, 141,
    142
Mayes, Col. Charles W., 229
McCarthy, Joseph, 490n
McCloy, John Jay, 4, 36, 40, 41, 43, 48, 68,
    75, 77, 108, 110, 164, 216, 281, 617, 640
McCormack, Alfred, 291
McLean, Donald S., 279
McNarney, Gen. Joseph T., 144, 223,
    275, 291, 603, 604, 606
Medina, Capt. Ernest, 640
*Mein Kampf* (Hitler), 364, 377, 389, 491,
    576
Meistner, Jakob, 609
Meltzer, Bernard, 180, 264, 265, 398
Mendelsohn, Peter, 219
Mengele, Josef, 301
Menthon, François de, 97, 98, 100–4, 116,
    118, 152, 157, 162, 212, 283, 293–8,
    300, 307, 320, 489, 497, 624, 633
Merkel, Rudolf, 508–9
Messersmith, George S., 241
Mickelwaite, Col. Charles, 52
Milch, Field Marshal Erhard, 201, 323–5,
    327, 428
Mitchell, Gen. William L., 135, 144, 145
Model, Gen. Walter, 312
Moehle, Korvettenkapitän Karl Heinz,
    266, 403, 406, 407
Molkov, Gen., 608
Molotov, Vyacheslav, 39, 40, 70, 71, 108
Moltke, Helmuth von, 105
Monneray, Henri, 213
Montgomery, Field Marshal Bernard,
    275, 603

Moran, Lord, 151
Morel, Gen., 608
Morgan, Capt. Ralph, 56
Morgen, George Konrad, 514, 515
Morgenthau, Henry, Jr., 34, 42, 43, 46,
    108, 109, 216
Morgenthau Plan, 31, 34
Morocco, 23
Moscow Declaration, 27, 29, 31, 60, 70,
    269
Mounier, Pierre, 305
Mueller, Heinrich "Gestapo," 189, 360,
    363, 364, 478, 508, 509, 514, 538
Müller (Gestapo member), 314
Munich Agreement (1938), 22, 192, 194,
    298, 322, 331, 333, 434–5, 457, 554, 597
Murphy, Robert, 61, 123
Mussert, Anton, 442
Mussolini, Benito, 22, 32, 37, 52, 195–6,
    352, 579
Mutsuoka (Japanese Foreign Minister),
    580
My Lai massacre, 640
*Myth of the Twentieth Century, The*
    (Rosenberg), 364

Napoleon Bonaparte, 7–8 and n, 15, 26n,
    31, 75, 447n
Nasjonal Samling, 365
National Lawyers Guild, 636
Nazi Party, 21, 25, 45, 86, 87, 108, 278,
    445n, 497, 498, 574; Austrian, 360, 439,
    440; Bormann in, 267, 464, 465;
    creation of, 582; defense of, 283,
    504–8; defense counsel in, 133, 144,
    627; deliberations on, 556, 557;
    evidence against, 173, 203–5; film
    about, 200; final arguments on, 525,
    526; Frank in, 367; Fritzsche in, 460;
    Funk in, 392; in future trials, 280;
    Goering in, 335; Hess in, 117, 348; and
    Hitler Jugend, 424; Hoess in, 363; in
    Indictment, 104, 112, 277, 630;
    judgment on, 584; Krupp and, 92;
    Nuremberg rallies of, 61, 448; Office of
    Foreign Affairs of, 364; Ohlendorf in,
    246; press of, 461; Protection Squad of
    (*see* SS); Ribbentrop in, 351; rise to
    power of, 329; Rosenberg in, 364, 365;
    Sauckel in, 427; Schacht and, 388–9,
    391; Speer in, 448; Streicher in, 481;
    Sturmabteilung of (*see* SA); Supreme
    Court of, 377, 505
*Nazi Plan, The* (film), 200, 201
Nazi-Soviet Pact, 192, 307, 331, 350, 411,
    490, 555
Nazi Students League, 422

Neave, Lt. Col. Airey, 93, 131–4, 143–4, 473, 502–3, 624, 632
Nehring, Gen. Walter, 312
Nelte, Otto, 190, 309, 311, 320, 353–7, 404, 476–8, 482, 488, 625
Netherlands: deportation of Jews from, 443, 486; invasion and occupation of, 23, 24, 145, 192, 195, 267, 295, 300, 326, 328, 352, 436–8, 440–4, 448, 487, 543, 579; Kaiser in exile in, 14, 16; slave labor from, 201, 295, 298, 443
Neuland, Maj. Paul, 240
Neumann, Franz, 49n, 90, 117
Neurath, Constatin von, 62, 89, 90, 323, 351, 352, 373–5, 409, 411, 425, 481, 485, 615–16; case against, 199, 268, 269; conviction of, 597; defense of, 133, 349, 417, 454–9, 488; deliberations on, 563; final statement of, 544; judgment of Tribunal on, 575; sentencing of, 599, 600; in Spandau, 615, 616
New York City Department of Corrections, 289n
*New Yorker, The*, 343, 548
New York *Herald Tribune*, 219–20
*New York Times, The*, 238, 261, 421
Nicolson, Harold, 215
Niemoeller, Martin, 305
Nietzsche, Friedrich, 295
Nightingale, Florence, 10
Nikitchenko, I. T., 79, 82–4, 98, 100, 134, 155, 157, 212, 225, 227, 398, 607, 625, 631, 633, 639; at Berlin meeting, 121–6; in Charter negotiations, 59, 60, 62–7, 74; and closing arguments, 474; in defendant selection process, 86, 87, 89, 92; and defense testimony, 321, 459, 506; during deliberations, 549, 551, 552, 554–66, 568, 569, 591n, 595; and judgment of Tribunal, 584, 585, 589, 590, 597; and Katyn Forest massacre, 468–70; and Krupp incident, 158, 160, 161, 163; and prosecution case, 312
Nimitz, Adm. Chester W., 400, 401, 408–9, 483, 496, 567, 568, 592, 600
Nitze, Paul, 449
Noiret, Gen., 604
Norden, Eric, 636
North American Newspaper Alliance, 238
Norway: invasion and occupation of, 23, 24, 145, 192–5, 254–5, 266, 328, 352, 365, 401–3, 408, 412–14, 438, 442, 479, 484, 541, 554, 577n, 578, 640; slave labor from, 295, 298–9
Norwich University, 223

*Nuremberg: A Nation on Trial* (Maser), 619
Nuremberg Laws, 21, 340, 457, 560
Nuremberg rallies, 61, 448

Oberhauser, Gen. Eugen, 470
October Revolution, 210
Oesterreich, Gen. Curt von, 312
Office of Military Government, U.S. (OMGUS), 111, 112, 272, 279, 280, 286, 289, 291
Office of Strategic Services (OSS), 33, 34, 46, 47, 49, 52, 68, 138, 147, 148n, 182, 240, 371n
Ohlendorf, Otto, 5, 221, 246–9, 258, 282, 361, 364, 370, 394, 450, 511, 519
OKH, 246, 529
OKW, 187–90, 246, 256, 355–7, 404, 411, 438, 529, 533
O'Malley, Sir Owen, 467n
Oppenheimer, Lt. Col. Fritz, 279
Oradour-sur-Glane massacre, 84, 302, 513
Oranienburg, 369, 433, 526
organizational guilt, 36–9, 41–2, 45, 53, 75, 111, 171, 204, 238–9, 276–8, 280–5, 297, 628, 637–9; Charter on, 75, 119; deliberations on, 555–9; denazification and, 278–80, 287; and Indictment, 104, 112–13; under J.C.S. 1023/10, 272–3, 275; judgment of Tribunal on, 574, 583–7; Soviet opposition to charges of, 58, 59; *see also specific organizations*
Organization Todt, 435, 448
*Orzel* (submarine), 413
Oster, Gen. Hans, 386
Ottoman Empire, 12–13, 18
Oxford University, 84

Pannebecker, Otto, 370, 372, 373, 480
Papen, Franz von, 30, 89, 90, 323, 349, 352, 362, 388, 391, 425, 440, 458–60, 468, 481, 522, 547, 608; acquittal of, 595, 599, 601; case against, 199, 268, 269, 494, 498; defense of, 133, 190, 417, 444–7, 454, 487; deliberations on, 564–6; denazification court conviction of, 614; final statement of, 542; Goering and, 330, 375, 535–6; Hess and, 129; interrogation of, 137; judgment of Tribunal on, 575; in prison, 230
Papen, Friedrich von, 445
Paris, Treaty of (1928), 19, 295, 581
Paris Peace Conference, 15, 66
Parker, John J., 133, 155, 206, 211, 212, 216, 225, 226, 420, 421, 571, 572, 632; appointment of, 95, 97; at Berlin

meeting, 118–20; and
cross-examinations, 342, 359; and
defense testimony, 321, 424; during
deliberations, 549, 553, 554, 556–8,
560, 562, 564, 566, 568; and
prosecution case, 277
Passant, E. J., 87–8, 91–2, 104, 117, 387,
567
Pasteur Institute, 301
Patterson, Robert, 40, 48, 216, 281, 289,
290
Patton, Gen. George, 144, 223, 279
Patzig, Lt., 17
Pauley, Edwin W., 45, 46
Paulus, Field Marshal Friedrich, 309–12,
462
peace, crimes against, *see* aggressive war
charges
Pearl Harbor, 43
Pearson, Drew, 46, 419
Pelckmann, Horst, 512–14, 516
*Peleus* (ship), 406
Pell, Herbert C., 26, 28, 38
Pepper, Claude, 216
Persian Gulf War, 636, 637
Pétain, Marshal Henri Philippe, 293
Peter, King of Yugoslavia, 24
Petersen, Howard C., 216, 281, 284,
289–91, 603
Pfaffenberger, Andreas, 242, 243
Pfluecker, Dr., 609, 622
Philadelphia *Inquirer*, 172
Philippines, 239
Phillimore, Col. Harry, 93–4, 102, 131n,
152, 195–6, 199, 214, 265–6, 402,
406–8, 414
Pinion, Barbara, 127, 218
Pius XII, Pope, 83, 94, 524–5
Pohl, Oswald, 360, 363, 364, 396, 512,
514, 540
Pokrovsky, Col. Yuri, 100, 102, 150,
156–9, 161, 163, 209–12, 308–9, 312–13,
320, 327, 415, 426, 467–9, 503, 624, 633
Poland, 31, 640; death camps in, 24, 27,
169, 296, 316, 317, 425, 443; invasion
of, 22–3, 145, 170, 188, 192, 194, 241,
250, 269, 307, 328, 331, 333, 367, 374,
386, 393, 411, 414, 415, 457, 463, 476,
490, 500, 519, 554, 575–8; occupation
of, 23, 24, 190, 202, 204, 313, 314, 340,
367–70, 441, 481, 486, 513, 524, 526,
627, 639; prisoners of war in, 312–13
Poles: extermination of, 103, 188, 426,
476, 466–72 (*see also* Katyn Forest
massacre); as slave labor, 201, 506
Polish Corps, 218
Poltorak, Maj. Arkady, 210

Porter, Roy, 219
Potsdam Conference, 67–8, 70–3, 74n, 77,
85, 89, 90, 108, 111, 289n
Pradeau, Jenny, 398
Press Wireless, 220
prisoners of war, 7–8; atrocities against,
35, 39, 42, 84, 117, 170–1, 189–90, 267,
300–2, 312–13, 320, 324, 333–4, 344,
356–8, 360, 363, 462, 466–72, 490, 513,
521, 524, 526, 606–7; Charter on, 65;
commandos and, 253–4; German, 310,
334, 403; Italian, 402; as slave labor,
201, 299
Proserovski, Victor I., 471
Prussian Army, 447n
Prussian Secret Police, 371
Prussian State Parliament, 444
Puhl, Emil, 395–7
Pushkin, Alexander, 316

Quatre, Constant, 305
*Queen Mary* (ship), 119
Quisling, Vidkun, 195, 264–5, 412, 442

Radio Berlin, 466
Radio Moscow, 466
Raeder, Adm. Erich, 30, 89, 90, 96, 106n,
187, 254, 265, 311, 323, 362, 365, 391,
398, 399, 401, 403, 456, 460, 461; case
against, 194–5, 199, 252, 266, 492, 496,
500; conviction of, 592, 594;
cross-examination of, 413–14, 463;
defense of, 181, 324, 409–16, 484,
639–40; deliberations on, 567–9; family
visitors to, 547; final statement of, 541;
indictment of, 132; judgment of
Tribunal on, 575, 578; petition on
behalf of, 602, 606; sentencing of, 599;
in Spandau, 615–17
Raginsky, M. Y., 308, 316, 396–7
Rapp, Capt. Walter H., 240, 260, 291,
292, 520
Rascher, Sigmund, 514
Rasumov, I. V., 210, 212, 398
Rathenau, Walther, 543
Rauter, Gen. Hans, 442
Ravensbrück, 301, 384
RCA, 220
Red Army, 189
Red Cross, 10, 20n, 467
Reich Air Ministry, 323
Reich Cabinet, 104, 204, 278, 315, 517,
522–3; closing arguments on, 527;
deliberations on, 556, 557; judgment of
Tribunal on, 585, 599
Reich Chancellery, 357
Reich Defense Council, 337, 340

Reich Defense Law, 383
Reichenau, Field Marshal Walter von, 256–7, 312, 481, 520
Reich Ministry for Peoples Enlightenment and Propaganda, 460
Reichsbank, 5, 86, 88, 265, 382–4, 390, 393, 395–8, 481, 493, 540, 591, 592, 613
Reich Security Main Office (RSHA), 360, 361, 363, 478, 482, 508–11, 589
Reichsregierung (*see* Reich Cabinet)
Reichstag, 364, 378, 445
Reichstag fire, 169, 336, 492
Reinecke, Gunther, 513–14
Reinecke, Gen. Hermann, 189
Rex, Lt., 468
Ribbentrop, Joachim von, 3, 25, 30, 85, 89, 96, 323, 364, 373, 388, 411n, 415, 421, 423, 444, 455, 456, 497; case against, 188, 199, 218, 268, 438, 492, 500; conviction of, 589; defense of, 132, 190, 320, 321, 334, 350–3, 476; deliberations on, 561; execution of, 609–10; family visitors to, 547; final statement of, 537, 538; indictment of, 132; judgment of Tribunal on, 575, 577, 580; not guilty plea of, 167; petition for clemency for, 602; sentencing of, 598, 600
Rickard, Gen. Roy V., 608
Riefenstahl, Leni, 200
Rimsky-Korsakoff, Nikolai, 316
Robbins, Jack, 291
Roberts, Geoffrey Dorling "Khaki," 58, 84–6, 100, 103, 195, 199, 214, 221, 242, 263, 324, 438, 439, 624
Roberts, Owen, 40, 94
Robey, E. G., 214
Rode, Gen. Ernst, 257–8
Roechling, Hermann, 18
Roechling, Robert, 18
Roehm, Erich, 205
Roehm purge, 330, 336, 372, 375, 376, 423, 445–6, 455, 512, 522, 523, 526, 557, 575
Rohrscheidt, Gunther von, 151, 178, 268
Roman Catholic Church, 5, 506, 526, 539; *see also* Catholics
Romania, 24, 196, 579
Roosevelt, Franklin Delano, 25–34, 37, 38, 40, 43–5, 47, 95, 119, 418–19, 629
Roosevelt, Theodore, 554
Rosenberg, Alfred, 85, 89, 104, 323, 345, 371, 422, 430, 451; case against, 170, 194–5, 199, 201, 264, 305, 393, 394, 493; conviction of, 589; defense of, 166, 351, 358–9, 364–7, 478–9; deliberations on, 561; execution of,

610; final statement of, 538; judgment of Tribunal on, 596; not guilty plea of, 167; petition for clemency for, 602; sentencing of, 598, 600
Rosenman, Samuel, 4, 32, 38, 40, 41, 43, 45, 46, 71, 73n, 75, 77, 216
Ross, Colin, 425
Röttiger, Gen. Hans, 257
Rousseau, Jean-Jacques, 6–7
Rowahlt (publisher), 612
Rowe, James H., 119, 132, 143, 151, 175, 216, 549, 557, 566–7, 572, 588, 594n, 595, 625
Royal Air Force (RAF), 115, 152, 276, 327, 333, 437
Royal Navy, 401
Rudenko, Gen. Roman A., 100–1, 141, 150, 165, 178, 193, 209–12, 242, 262, 320, 350, 417, 479, 491, 535, 547, 633, 639; and Berlin meeting, 116–18, 121–6; closing argument of, 499–500, 503–4, 559; cross-examinations by, 324, 344–6, 353, 355–6, 463; and Katyn Forest massacre, 312, 469; and Krupp incident, 152, 155, 156, 158–63; and organizations case, 283–5, 532–3, 555; presentation of evidence by, 307–11; subsequent career of, 624
Rundstedt, Field Marshal Gerd von, 325, 518, 519, 521, 530
Rusk, Dean, 4, 636

SA, 45, 104, 112, 205, 283, 284, 297, 372, 447, 492, 512; closing arguments on, 525, 526, 533; defense of, 522–4; indictment of, 117
Sachsenhausen, 312, 363
Sagan case, 357
St. Germain, Treaty of, 439
St. James's Declaration (1942), 25–6, 28, 29, 293
St. John's University (Shanghai), 208
St. Louis *Post Dispatch*, 55
Salzburger Festispiele, 548
San Francisco Conference, 49, 191
Sapieha, Col. Paul, 218
Sauckel, Fritz, 25, 81, 89, 90, 187, 322, 334, 370, 422, 448, 459, 488; case against, 201, 204, 263, 295, 305, 325, 366, 387, 451, 453, 465, 493, 544; conviction of, 594; defense of, 132, 283, 324, 417, 427–31, 485–7; deliberations on, 562–3; execution of, 609, 610; final statement of, 541; indictment of, 132, 449n; not guilty plea of, 167; petition for clemency for, 602; sentencing of, 599, 600

Sauter, Fritz, 132, 133, 190, 249, 393–5, 397, 423–5, 428, 481–2, 484–5, 625
Scales, Junius Irving, 558n
Scanzoni (lawyer), 132
Schacht, Hjalmar Horace Greeley, 25, 30, 81, 86–90, 187, 316, 323, 349, 352, 362, 374, 375, 398, 425, 439, 445n, 448, 451, 468, 480, 481, 602; acquittal of, 591–2, 595, 599, 601, 638; arrested by German police, 608, 612–13; case against, 198, 264–5, 269, 386–7, 484, 494, 496–8; cross-examination of, 381, 387–91; defense of, 133, 173, 228, 350, 372, 373, 382–6, 404, 482; deliberations on, 552, 562, 564–6; Donovan and, 182–4, 186; family visitors to, 547; final statement of, 540; Goering and, 330, 336, 392; interrogation of, 136, 137, 181; judgment of Tribunal on, 575; not guilty plea of, 167; in prison, 230; subsequent career of, 613–14
Schaefer, Werner, 526
Schellenberg, Walter, 241, 248–9, 509
Schenckendorff, Gen. Max von, 258
Schickedanz, Villa, 398
Schirach, Baldur von, 86, 90, 231, 323, 391, 460, 548, 614–15; case against, 199, 204, 249, 267, 269; conviction of, 594; defense of, 132, 417, 421–7, 484–5; deliberations on, 569; final statement of, 541; Goering and, 376, 422–3, 450, 614; judgment of Tribunal on, 575; not guilty plea of, 167; petition for clemency for, 602, 606; sentencing of, 599; in Spandau, 615, 617, 618
Schirach, Henriette Hoffman von, 231
Schlegelberger, Franz, 522
Schleicher, Gen. Kurt von, 445, 447
Schlieffen, Graf Alfred von, 105
Schmaglenskaya, Severina, 317
Schmidt, Paul Otto, 352–3
Schmidt, Gen. Rudolf, 326
Schmitz, Herman, 152
Schmundt, Lt. Col. Rudolf, 194, 198
Schobert, Gen. Eugen Ritter von, 247
Schoerner, Field Marshal Ferdinand, 89
Schorske, Carl, 49n
Schrader, Adm. Otto von, 408
Schulberg, Budd, 200
Schulte-Monting, Erich, 415
Schuschnigg, Kurt von, 241–3, 439, 576n
Schutzstaffel, see SS
Schwarzkopf, Elisabeth, 548
Schwerin von Korsigk, Lutz, 396
Schwetz, von, 471
Scots Guards, 211

Scott, James Brown, 66
Scott-Fox, R. D. J., 69–70, 102, 122, 214
SD, 45, 109, 189, 206, 246, 257, 259, 297, 360, 403, 404, 408, 470, 472, 597; closing arguments on, 527, 532; defense of, 508–11; deliberations on, 556–7; judgment on, 584
Secret Cabinet Council, 204
Seefried, Irmgard, 548
Seidl, Alfred, 132, 133, 264, 268, 347–50, 368, 476, 479–80, 488–9, 536, 555, 588–9, 602, 625, 627, 639
Seldte, Franz, 523
Servatius, Robert, 283–4, 324, 428, 430, 431, 485–6, 504–8, 524, 625
Severing, Karl, 414, 415
Seydlitz–Kurzbach, Gen. Walter von, 310
Seyss-Inquart, Arthur, 86, 322, 360, 362, 383, 445, 460, 591; case against, 199, 201, 267, 296, 305; conviction of, 595–9, 629; defense of, 323, 417, 439–44, 453, 486–7; deliberations on, 563–4, 570; execution of, 607, 610; final statement of, 536, 542–3, 545; judgment of Tribunal on, 576; petition for clemency for, 602; sentencing of, 599, 600
SHAEF, 111, 222
Shawcross, Sir Hartley, 69, 82–3, 87, 96, 120, 213–14, 387, 617n, 629, 633; appointment of, 73; closing argument of, 245n, 491, 494–7, 500, 542, 618n; in defendant selection process, 79, 86, 567, 631; and Indictment, 97, 102, 114, 115, 117, 118; and Krupp incident, 92, 93, 154, 156, 157, 159, 160, 163, 285; opening statement of, 191–6, 198, 293, 294, 412; subsequent career of, 624, 625
Shea, Francis M., 46–8, 56, 78–82, 98, 129, 146, 164, 180, 231, 236, 265, 273–4, 387, 574; in Berlin, 122–5, 130; during Charter negotiations, 58, 61–3, 68; and defendant selection process, 92; and Indictment, 97, 103, 112; and staff reorganization, 137–40, 142–3; and translation of documents, 140–1
Shea, Hilda, 273
Shenin, L. R., 308, 316
Shirer, William L., 219–20
Sicherheitsdienst, see SD
Siemers, Walter, 181, 324, 329, 332, 410–15, 484, 547, 578, 616, 625, 639–40
Sievers, Wolfram, 514–16, 525
Sikorski, Gen. Vladislav, 24, 467
Simon, Lord, 26, 29–32, 34, 78, 349
SIPO, 188, 246, 508, 510

Skoda, 91n
Skorzeny, Otto, 37n
slave labor, *see* forced labor program
Slavs, 21, 203, 355, 429, 441;
　extermination of, 258, 260, 313, 317,
　627
Smirnov, L. N., 308, 313–17, 470–1, 624
Smith, Bradley F., 640n
Smith, Gen. Walter Bedell, 52, 145, 147,
　275
Smith Act (1940), 41, 282, 558
Sobibor, 316
*Social Contract, The* (Rousseau), 6n
Social Democrats, 379, 414
Sokolovsky, Gen. Vassily, 603–7
Sondercommandos, 462
Sonnenfeldt, Richard, 182–3, 231
Soskice, Sir Frank, 101, 102, 115
South Carolina College, 8
Southern Railway, 398
Soviet Extraordinary State Commission
　for War Crimes, 101, 313
Soviet Supreme Court, 59, 624
Soviet Union, 20, 26; in Afghanistan,
　636; and Baltic nations, 118;
　Churchill's denunciation of, 316–17;
　Constitution of, 532; invasion of, 23,
　24n, 145, 189, 192, 196, 199, 250, 255,
　307, 309–12, 322, 323, 336, 345, 352,
　354, 355, 365, 386, 411, 414, 437–9,
　448, 459, 461, 476, 479, 495, 519,
　579–80; and Katyn Forest massacre,
　466–72; Nazi atrocities in, 169–70, 188,
　244–7, 249, 255–8, 313–16, 366–7, 380,
　394, 427, 433, 462, 513; nonaggression
　treaty with Germany, *see* Nazi-Soviet
　Pact; satellites of, 640; slave labor
　from, 201; and Suez crisis, 637
Spandau Prison, 601, 614–18
Speer, Albert, 25, 81, 86, 323, 362, 369,
　387, 391, 394, 395n, 404, 415, 425, 428,
　440, 460, 464, 500, 591, 603; case
　against, 201, 263, 295, 325, 497; and
　condemned men, 608, 609; conviction
　of, 596; defense of, 324, 417, 418,
　448–54, 487–8; deliberations on, 563;
　final statement of, 544, 613n; Goering
　and, 305–6, 330, 342–3, 375, 422, 423;
　on responsibility, 452, 614–15;
　sentencing of, 599–601; in Spandau,
　615–18
Sprecher, Capt. Drexel, 267, 461, 489,
　574
Spruchkammer (Denazification Court),
　612
SS, 25, 37n, 85–7, 90, 152, 204, 243, 258,
　278, 283, 297, 369, 371, 452, 457, 498,
523, 540; affidavits of members of, 502;
　and Bernay's concept of organizational
　guilt, 35, 41–2, 75, 501; case against,
　205–6, 282; closing arguments on, 525,
　532; and compulsory labor service, 45;
　as concentration camp guards, 271;
　Dachau trial of, 490–1; defense of, 301,
　503, 508–16; deliberations on, 556,
　557; Economic and Administrative
　Main Office (WVHA) of, 360, 511, 514;
　Eisenhower's views on, 108–10;
　evidence against, 244–9, 302, 304, 316;
　extermination of Jews by, 5, 424, 427,
　462, 530 (*see also* Einsatzgruppen);
　Funk and, 394–5, 397, 398; Goering
　and, 324; Hoess in, 363; in Indictment,
　104, 112, 113, 237; judgment of
　Tribunal on, 584–6; and Katyn Forest
　massacre, 470; Keitel and, 188, 355; in
　Netherlands, 442; recruited from Hitler
　Jugend, 267; 2nd Panzer Division Das
　Reich of, 302; 12th Panzer Division
　Hitler Jugend of, 110, 206
Stahlecker, Brigade Fuehrer Franz, 510
Stahlhelm, 523, 524, 526
Stahmer, Otto, 133, 166, 175, 181, 190,
　259, 303, 304, 320–6, 328, 329, 332,
　336, 339, 341, 343, 344, 346, 347, 372,
　373, 468–71, 475–7, 482, 601, 625
Stalag Luft III murders, 333–4, 344, 345,
　356, 606–7
Stalin, Joseph, 26, 27, 29–34, 67n, 71, 73,
　107–9, 180, 193, 239, 350, 533, 602,
　603, 633, 639
Stark, Betty, 101, 128, 129, 225, 240, 623
*Stars and Stripes*, 220, 233, 317, 421, 573
Stauffenberg, Klaus von, 322
Steengracht von Moyland, Baron Gustav,
　352
Steinbauer, Gustav, 323, 440–4, 486–7
Stenger, Gen. Karl, 12, 17
Stettinius, Edward R., 35, 38, 39
Stewart, Maj. Robert, 119, 212, 216, 560,
　562
Stieff, Helmut, 23
Stimson, Henry L., 4–5, 34, 36–42, 46, 73,
　75, 76, 216, 270, 272, 295n, 626, 638
Stokes, Richard L., 219, 418
Stone, Harlan F., 419, 421
Storey, Col. Robert, 56, 99, 145–6, 172,
　174, 186, 215, 216, 220, 381, 574, 625,
　627, 634; Donovan, 147–9; and
　economic case, 81–2, 142, 274, 387;
　evidence gathering by, 57, 85, 143;
　presentation of evidence by, 200,
　203–6, 244, 245n, 504, 509–10;
　resignation of, 276; and Russians, 61,

77; and staff reorganization, 131,
135–6, 138, 139; and translation of
documents, 140, 173, 175, 176
Storm Troopers (*see* SA)
Straight, Lt. Col. Clio E., 270, 286n
Strasbourg, Reich University of, 515
Strasser, Gregor, 392
Streicher, Adele, 547
Streicher, Julius, 25, 85, 90, 150, 228, 301,
323, 360, 371, 388, 404, 422, 423, 425,
468, 500; case against, 204, 264, 268,
269, 385, 493, 496, 498; conviction of,
590; defense of, 133, 144, 351, 376–82,
481; deliberations on, 561–2, 631;
execution of, 609, 610; final statement
of, 539–40, 545; petition for clemency
for, 601; sentencing of, 598–9; visit of
wife to, 547
Stresemann, Gustav, 19
Strock, Gen. Karl, 316
Stroelin, Karl, 348–9
Stroop, Gen. Juergen, 170, 202
Student, Gen. Kurt, 326
*Stuermer, Der*, 25, 85, 264, 268, 363,
377–80, 481, 539, 590
Sturmabteilung (*see* SA)
submarine warfare, 19, 399–403, 405–10,
496, 540; illegal, 265–6; in World War
I, 12
Suez crisis, 637
Swearingen, Ben, 623
*Sword in the Scales, The* (Fritzsche), 612

Taft, Robert, 634
Talleyrand, Prince de, 7
Tass, 220
Taylor, Mary, 208, 290–2, 548
Teheran Conference, 107, 543n
Teich, Maj. F. C., 614
*Ten Years and Twenty Days* (Doenitz),
617
Terboven, Joseph, 442, 596
Tetjens, M., 548
Thatcher, Margaret, 624
Thirty Years War, 6
Thoma, Alfred, 166, 358–9, 364, 478–9
Thomas, Albert, 397
*Times* of London, 446, 601
Todt, Fritz, 394, 448, 449
Tokyo War Crimes Trials, 635n
Tolstoy, Leo, 316
Tomlinson, Col. Clarence, 291
*To the Bitter End* (Gisevius), 371n
Trainin, A. N., 59, 74, 79, 120
Treblinka, 24, 316, 317
Trenchard-Weir theory, 327
Tripartite Pact (1940), 26, 196–7, 579, 580

*Triumph of the Will* (film), 150, 200
Troyanovsky, Oleg A., 59, 84, 89, 209, 210
Truman, Harry S., 32, 46, 99, 108, 118,
129, 145, 183n, 185, 215, 216, 275, 381,
611, 625; Final Report to, 611; Jackson
appointed by, 39, 40, 45; judicial
appointees of, 94–5, 134; June 7, 1945,
report to, 53–6, 62, 66, 110, 233, 272,
276; OSS abolished by, 148n, 240; at
Potsdam Conference, 67n, 68, 71, 73,
91; Supreme Court appointments of,
419, 420
Truppenamt, 106
Truscott, Gen. Lucian K., 145
Turrell, Col., 214
*Tyranny on Trial* (Harris), 625

U-boats, *see* submarine warfare
United Nations, 4, 26, 50, 60, 211, 253,
468n, 629, 636, 637; Charter of, 6, 39,
42, 532; Conference on International
Organizations, 32; General Assembly,
635, 641; War Crimes Commission
(UNWCC), 26–8, 38, 47, 71, 84, 215,
475
United States, 19; and Geneva
conventions, 19, 641; in Persian Gulf
War, 637; and Soviet annexation of
Baltic states, 118; and Suez crisis, 637;
in Vietnam War, 637, 640; in World
War I, 14, 16; in World War II, 23, 26,
39, 43–4, 197, 326, 399–400, 402,
408–9, 580, 640
U.S. Army, 9, 110, 132, 133, 144, 146,
219, 221–4, 230, 239, 240, 251, 255,
270, 619; Air Corps, 44n
U.S. Congress, 39, 41, 44, 558n
U.S. Defense Department, 43
United States Forces European Theatre
(USFET), 222–3, 233
U.S. House of Representatives, Judiciary
Committee of, 420
U.S. Justice Department, 33, 34, 46–8, 57,
119, 270, 289n, 291, 417–18
U.S. National Archives, 619
U.S. Navy, 399–400, 408–9
U.S. Navy Department, 33, 34, 37
U.S. Office of Judge Advocate General
(JAG), 35, 41, 47–9, 52, 57, 269, 271,
272
U.S. Senate, 95n, 290, 292, 490n;
Interstate Commerce Commission, 57;
Judiciary Committee, 420
U.S. State Department, 33–5, 37, 38, 43,
57, 60, 67, 99, 127, 148n, 185, 215, 270
United States Strategic Bombing Survey,
449

U.S. Supreme Court, 39, 40, 43, 46, 94, 95, 124, 273, 418–20, 571, 611, 625, 632
U.S. Treasury Department, 33, 42, 45, 108
U.S. War Department, 33–7, 39, 40, 43, 45, 47, 109, 110, 148n, 270, 501, 625, 626; Civil Affairs Division, 289
U.S. Women's Auxiliary Air Force (WAAF), 127, 218

Vaillant-Couturier, Marie Claude, 301
Vandenberg, Gen. Hoyt, 291
Van der Essen, Prof., 304
Vassilitchikoff, Georgi, 229
Versailles Treaty (1919), 15–16, 18, 22, 51, 66, 81, 105, 106, 192, 241, 304–5, 322, 328, 330, 336, 349, 383–5, 399, 410, 414, 476, 480, 494, 496, 580
Vichy France, 293
Vieth, Jean-Frederick, 300
Vietnam War, 4, 636
Villa Schickedanz, 398
Vinson, Fred M., 420
Vishinsky, Andrei I., 211–12
Vlaer, Anton, 615
Vocke, William, 390
*Voelkischer Beobachter*, 364, 458
Volchkov, Lt. Col. A. F., 120, 122, 125, 155–8, 163, 212, 225, 560, 562, 564
Voltaire, 6

Waffen–SS, 202, 206, 243, 257–9, 508, 510–14, 584–5
Wagener, Otto, 377, 392
Wagner, Gen. Eduard, 249, 258
Wagner, Adm. Gerhard, 406–8, 414
Wagner, Robert, 303
Wallis, Maj. Frank, 146, 173, 174
Walsh, Gen. Walter, 608
Walsh, Maj. William F., 201–2, 204, 242–3
war crimes, 170–1, 265–9, 294, 346, 491; deliberations on, 552, 553; of Frank, 368–70; of Frick, 370–1; Fritzsche and, 460–3; of Funk, 393, 397; of Goering, 334; in Indictment, 79, 84, 100, 103, 116; of Jodl, 432–3, 438; judgment of Tribunal on, 582–3; of Kaltenbrunner, 360–4; of Keitel, 354, 356; military court trials for, 271–2; organizational responsibility for, 203–4, 243, 253–61; presentation of case on, 295–6, 298–302, 312–17; of Raeder, 414, 484; of Ribbentrop, 352, 476; of Rosenberg, 366–7; of Sauckel, 427–31; of Seyss-Inquart, 440; of Speer, 449; subsequent trials for, 272–6, 286–92

War Crimes Group, 270, 273
Warlimont, Gen. Walter, 309
War Refugee Board, 35
Warsaw Ghetto, 170, 202, 257
Washington Conference, 18
Washington *Post*, 261
Watson, Gen. Leroy H., 144–5, 208, 223–4, 381–2
Wechsler, Herbert, 41, 75, 119, 121, 216, 226, 381, 398, 469, 549–53, 557, 567n, 572, 625
Wegscheider, Hans, 505–6
Wehrmacht, 23, 86, 114, 136, 268, 324, 325, 328, 372, 373, 401, 408, 427, 515, 518, 528–30, 593, 594, 630; and Anschluss, 446; antipartisan operations of, 259; and Commando Order, 254; and extermination of Jews, 532; and Hitler Jugend, 424, 484–5; Jodl and, 90, 435, 438, 440, 541; and Katyn Forest massacre, 468; Keitel and, 90, 106, 187, 296n, 375, 394, 432, 477; Krupp and arming of, 91; Medical Services of, 301; and Munich Agreement, 22, 194, 435; organizational structure of, 240, 250; Poland invaded by, 188, 415, 425; retreat from France and Belgium of, 33; SA and SS men in, 523; Soviet Union invaded by, 231, 355; transports to Auschwitz by, 363; *see also* German General Staff-High Command
Weimar Republic, 16, 106, 169, 335, 410
Weir, Gen. John, 48
Weizsaecker, Ernst von, 414, 415
West, Rebecca, 228, 343, 360, 378, 546–8, 574, 587
Westerborg, 443
West Germany, 640
Westhoff, Gen. Adolf, 357
West Point, 289n
Weygand, Marshal Maxime, 188–9
Wheeler, Col. Leonard, 82, 131, 136, 138, 262
Wheeler-Bennett, John, 215
Wheelis, Lt. Jack George "Tex," 623–4
Whitney, William D., 53, 62, 68
Wilde, Oscar, 418
Wilhaus, Com., 314
Wilhelm II, Kaiser, 12, 14–16, 29, 91, 106
Wilhelmina, Queen of the Netherlands, 24, 442n
Willey, Harold B., 124, 133, 135
Wilson, Woodrow, 14–16
Winkelmann, Gen. H. G., 326
Wirz, Capt. Henry, 271n
Wisliceny, Dieter, 248

Witzleben, Field Marshal Erwin von, 386
Wolfe, Robert, 619
Woods, Sgt. John C., 609–11
World War I, 19, 21, 24, 51, 66, 114, 304, 436, 442, 461, 523; Bach-Zelewski in, 243; Doenitz in, 399; Donovan in, 46; Fritzsche in, 460; Goering in, 260, 322, 601; Krupp firm and, 91, 152; Lawrence in, 120; laws of war during, 10–14, 581; Papen in, 444; Raeder in, 409; Roberts in, 84; Sauckel in, 427
Wright, Lord, 28, 215
Wright, Quincy, 119
Wright brothers, 10

Yalta Conference, 31, 32, 38, 277
Yamashita, Gen. Tomoyuki, 239, 251
Yanov Camp, 314, 315
Yorck von Wartenburg, Gen. Peter, 447
Yugoslavia, 18, 145; deportation of Jews from, 248; invasion and occupation of, 23, 24, 192, 195–6, 258, 307, 313, 314, 328, 352, 412, 437, 513, 579

Zeitzler, Gen. Kurt, 254n
Zetterberg, Harriet, 217n
Zhukov, Marshal Georgi, 274
Zorya, Gen. N. D., 308–10, 213n, 417

Telford Taylor graduated from Williams College and Harvard Law School, and filled various federal legal posts during the Roosevelt and Truman administrations. During World War II he served in Europe as a U.S. Army intelligence officer, and was awarded the Distinguished Service Medal. After the war he joined the American prosecution staff at the first Nuremberg trial, and in 1946 was promoted to brigadier general and made Chief Prosecutor for the ensuing Nuremberg trials. Since then he has practiced law in New York City, taught law at Columbia Law School and the Benjamin Cardozo School of Law, and published a number of books, including *Munich: The Price of Peace*, which won the Book Critics Circle Award for the best nonfiction work of 1979.

A NOTE ON THE TYPE

This book was set in Caledonia, a type face designed by W(illiam) A(ddison) Dwiggins (1880-1956) for the Mergenthaler Linotype Company in 1939. Dwiggins chose to call his new type face Caledonia, the Roman name for Scotland, because it was inspired by the Scottish types cast about 1833 by Alexander Wilson & Son, Glasgow type founders. However, there is a calligraphic quality about Caledonia that is totally lacking in the Wilson types.

Dwiggins referred to an even earlier type face for this "liveliness of action"—one cut around 1790 by William Martin for the printer William Bulmer. Caledonia has more weight than the Martin letters, and the bottom finishing strokes (serifs) of the letters are cut straight across, without brackets, to make sharp angles with the upright stems, thus giving a modern-face appearance.

W. A. Dwiggins began an association with the Mergenthaler Linotype Company in 1929 and over the next twenty-seven years designed a number of book types, the most interesting of which are Metro, Electra, Caledonia, Eldorado, and Falcon.

Composed by the Haddon Craftsmen, Inc.,
Scranton, Pennsylvania

Designed by Cassandra J. Pappas